FUNDAMENTAL FINANCIAL **accounting** CONCEPTS

ACt - 4-7
p5 →7B
PC -7B

THIRD EDITION

FUNDAMENTAL FINANCIAL **accounting** CONCEPTS

Thomas P. Edmonds
University of Alabama–Birmingham

Frances M. McNair
Mississippi State University

Edward E. Milam
Mississippi State University

Philip R. Olds
Virginia Commonwealth University

Cindy D. Edmonds
Contributing Author
University of Alabama-Birmingham

Irwin McGraw-Hill

Boston   Burr Ridge, IL   Dubuque, IA   Madison, WI   New York   San Francisco   St. Louis
Bangkok   Bogotá   Caracas   Lisbon   London   Madrid   Mexico City   Milan
New Delhi   Seoul   Singapore   Sydney   Taipei   Toronto

McGraw-Hill Higher Education

A Division of The **McGraw-Hill** *Companies*

FUNDAMENTAL FINANCIAL ACCOUNTING CONCEPTS

Copyright © 2000, 1998, 1996 by The McGraw-Hill Companies, Inc. All rights reserved. Printed in the United States of America. Except as permitted under the United States Copyright Act of 1976, no part of this publication may be reproduced or distributed in any form or by any means, or stored in a data base or retrieval system, without the prior written permission of the publisher.

This book is printed on acid-free paper.

domestic   3 4 5 6 7 8 9 0 VNH/VNH 9 0 9 8 7 6 5 4 3 2 1 0
international   1 2 3 4 5 6 7 8 9 0 VNH/VNH 9 0 9 8 7 6 5 4 3 2 1 0 9

ISBN 0-07-229903-7 (student's edition)
         0-07-232804-5 (annotated instructor's edition)

Vice president/Editor-in-chief: *Michael W. Junior*
Publisher: *Jeffrey J. Shelstad*
Developmental editor: *Marc Chernoff*
Editorial assistant: *Melissa Larmon*
Senior marketing manager: *Rhonda Seelinger*
Marketing manager: *Richard Kolsa*
Project manager: *Kimberly D. Hooker*
Production supervisor: *Rose Hepburn*
Designer: *Chris Reese/Michael Warrell*
Cover illustrator: *Guy Crittenden*
Photo research coordinator: *Sharon Miller*
Photo researcher: *Mary Reeg*
Supplement coordinator: *Mark Sienicki*
Compositor: *GAC Indianapolis*
Typeface: *10/12 Trump Medieval*
Printer: *Von Hoffmann Press, Inc.*

Library of Congress Cataloging-in-Publication Data

Fundamental financial accounting concepts / Thomas P. Edmonds . . . [et al.]. — 3rd ed.
        p.   cm.
    Various supplementary teaching aids available, including SPATS software (instructor and student versions), and a web page with self-study quizzes, links to homepages of companies in the book, etc.
    Includes index.
    ISBN 0-07-229903-7
    1. Accounting.   I. Edmonds, Thomas P.
HF5635.F95 2000
657—dc21   99-21003

INTERNATIONAL EDITION   ISBN 0-07-116945-8

Copyright © 2000. Exclusive rights by The McGraw-Hill Companies, Inc., for manufacture and export.
This book cannot be re-exported from the country to which it is consigned by McGraw-Hill.
The International Edition is not available in North America.

http://www.mhhe.com

This book is dedicated to our students whose questions have so frequently caused us to reevaluate our method of presentation that they have, in fact, become major contributors to the development of this text.

Thomas P. Edmonds, Ph.D.

Dr. Edmonds holds the Friends and Alumni Professorship in the Department of Accounting at the University of Alabama at Birmingham (UAB). He has been actively involved in teaching accounting principles throughout his academic career. Dr. Edmonds has **coordinated the accounting principles courses at the University of Houston and UAB.** He currently teaches introductory accounting in mass sections that frequently include more than 180 students. Dr. Edmonds has received five prestigious teaching awards including the UAB President's Excellence in Teaching Award and the distinguished Ellen Gregg Ingalls Award for excellence in classroom teaching. He has written a number of articles for many publications including *Issues in Accounting;* the *Journal of Accounting Education; Advances in Accounting Education; Accounting Education: A Journal of Theory, Practice and Research;* the *Accounting Review; Advances in Accounting;* the *Journal of Accountancy; Management Accounting;* the *Journal of Commercial Bank Lending;* the *Banker's Magazine;* and the *Journal of Accounting, Auditing, and Finance.* He has published four textbooks, five practice problems (including two computerized problems), and a variety of supplemental materials including study guides, working papers, and solutions manuals. Dr. Edmonds's writing is influenced by a wide range of business experience. He was a successful entrepreneur, worked as a management accountant for Refrigerated Transport, a trucking company, and worked in the not-for-profit sector as a commercial lending officer for the Federal Home Loan Bank. In addition, he has acted as a consultant to major corporations including First City Bank of Houston, AmSouth Bank in Birmingham, Texaco, and Cortland Chemicals. Dr. Edmonds began his academic training at Young Harris Community College in Young Harris, Georgia. He received a B.B.A. degree with a major in finance from Georgia State University in Atlanta, Georgia. He obtained an M.B.A. degree with a concentration in finance from St. Mary's University in San Antonio, Texas. His Ph.D. degree with a major in accounting was awarded by Georgia State University. Dr. Edmonds's work experience and academic training have enabled him to bring a unique user perspective to this textbook.

Frances M. McNair, Ph.D., CPA

Dr. McNair holds the KPMG Peat Marwick Professorship in Accounting at Mississippi State University (MSU). She has been involved in teaching principles of accounting for the past 12 years and currently serves as the **coordinator for the principles of accounting courses at MSU.** She joined the MSU faculty in 1987 after receiving her Ph.D. from the University of Mississippi. The author of various articles that have appeared in the *Journal of Accountancy, Management Accounting, Business and Professional Ethics Journal, The Practical Accountant, Taxes,* and other publications, she also coauthored the book *The Tax Practitioner* with Dr. Denzil Causey. Dr. McNair is currently serving on committees of the

American Taxation Association, the American Accounting Association, and the Institute of Management Accountants as well as numerous School of Accountancy and MSU committees.

Edward E. Milam, Ph.D., CPA

Dr. Milam is Professor of Accounting at Mississippi State University (MSU). In 1995, the Federation of Schools of Accountancy selected him for its *Outstanding Educator Award,* and he was named Mississippi's *1994 Educator of the Year* by the Mississippi Society of CPAs. In 1993, he was named the Outstanding Graduate Teacher of the Year in the College of Business and Industry at MSU. Prior to joining the MSU faculty, Dr. Milam served on the accounting faculty at the University of Mississippi from 1971 to 1990. He was chair of the accounting department when the School of Accountancy was established. He became the first dean of the School of Accountancy and during his tenure, the School of Accountancy became 1 of the first 20 schools in the nation to receive separate accounting accreditation. In 1989, he was selected as the Outstanding Teacher in the School of Accountancy at the University of Mississippi. In the fall of 1990, Dr. Milam joined the accounting faculty at MSU and assisted MSU in obtaining separate accounting accreditation. Also at MSU, he has been instrumental in designing, developing, and implementing a graduate program in taxation. Dr. Milam has served as president of the Federation of Schools of Accountancy (FSA), on the Standards Committee of the American Academy of Collegiate Schools of Business (Business and Accounting Accrediting Association), as treasurer/secretary of the American Taxation Association (ATA), on the Mississippi Tax Institute Board of Directors, and on various committees of the ATA, FSA, American Institute of Certified Public Accountants, American Accounting Association, and the Mississippi Society of Certified Public Accountants. He authored numerous articles that appeared in publications including *Journal of Accountancy, Taxes, Management Accounting, Financial Executive, Estate Planning, Trusts and Estates*, the *CPA Journal,* and others. He also coauthored seven books.

Philip R. Olds, Ph.D., CPA

Professor Olds is Associate Professor of Accounting at Virginia Commonwealth University (VCU) where he has taught since 1981. He serves as the **coordinator of the introduction to accounting courses at VCU.** Professor Olds received his A.S. degree from Brunswick Junior College in Brunswick, Georgia (now Brunswick College). He received a B.B.A. in Accounting, at Georgia Southern College (now Georgia Southern University), and his M.P.A. and Ph.D. degrees are from Georgia State University. After graduating from Georgia Southern, he worked as an auditor with the U.S. Department of Labor in Atlanta, Georgia. A CPA in Virginia, Professor Olds has published articles in various professional journals and presented papers at national and regional conferences. He also served as the faculty adviser to the VCU chapter of Beta Alpha Psi for 5 years. In 1989, he was recognized with an Outstanding Faculty Vice-President Award by the national Beta Alpha Psi organization.

This is a conceptually based/user-oriented book that stresses meaningful learning over rote memorization. More specifically, the text focuses on the relationships between business events and financial statements. **The primary objective is to develop students who can explain how any given business event will affect the income statement, balance sheet, and the statement of cash flows.** Did the event cause assets to increase, decrease, or stay the same? Similarly, what was the effect on liabilities, equity, revenue, expense, gains, losses, net income, and distributions? Furthermore, how did the event affect cash flows? These are the *big picture* relationships that both accounting majors and general business students need to understand to function effectively in the business world. The text contains numerous innovative features that are designed to facilitate the students' comprehension of the *events affect statements* paradigm.

Innovative Features

A Horizontal Financial Statements Model Is the Teaching Platform

A horizontal financial statements model replaces the accounting equation as the predominant teaching platform. The model enables students to visualize the simultaneous effects of a single business event on the income statement, balance sheet, and statement of cash flows by arranging the statements horizontally across a single line of text in the following manner:

Assets = Liabilities + Equity	Revenue − Expense = Net Income	Cash Flow

One of the more powerful explanatory features of the horizontal statements model stems from the fact that individual events are recorded directly in financial statements that are visually adjacent to their discussions. Traditionally, a series of events is recorded in accounts and summative information is presented in the statements. Accordingly, students do not observe the **effects of individual events on financial statements.** The horizontal statements model remedies this condition by requiring students to record statement effects transaction by transaction. For example, Event No. 1 in Exhibit 1 demonstrates that the recognition of revenue on account affects the balance sheet and income statement but not the statement of cash flows. These effects are *visibly* isolated from the effects of other events. Accordingly, students can see how a particular event affects the financial statements. The horizontal statements model also provides an effective means for comparing the effects of one transaction with the effects of another transaction. By comparing Event No. 1 with Event No. 2 in Exhibit 1, students can see how the recognition of cash revenue differs from the recognition of

EXHIBIT 1
Financial Statements Model

Event No.	Balance Sheet										Income Statement					Cash Statement
	Assets		=	Liabilities			+	Equity			Rev.	− Exp.	=	Net Inc.		Cash Flow
	Cash	+ Acct. Rec.	=	Acct. Pay.	+ Con. Cap.	+	Ret. Ear.									
1.	n/a	+ 500	=	n/a	+ n/a	+	500			500	− n/a	=	500			n/a
2.	500	+ n/a	=	n/a	+ n/a	+	500			500	− n/a	=	500			500 OA
3.	(800)	+ n/a	=	n/a	+ n/a	+	(800)			n/a	− n/a	=	n/a			(800) FA
4.	n/a	+ n/a	=	n/a	+ 800	+	(800)			n/a	− n/a	=	n/a			n/a

EXHIBIT 2
Horizontal Statements Models

Type	Balance Sheet							Income Statement				Cash Statement
	Asset			Equity								
	Investment Securities	=	Liab.	+	Retained Earnings	+	Unreal. Gain	Rev./ Gain	− Exp./ Loss	=	Net Inc.	Cash Flow
Held	n/a		n/a	=	n/a	+	n/a	n/a	− n/a	=	n/a	n/a
Trading	700		n/a	=	700	+	n/a	700	− n/a	=	700	n/a
Available	700		n/a	=	n/a	+	700	n/a	− n/a	=	n/a	n/a

revenue on account. Similarly, a comparison of Events No. 3 and 4 highlights differences between the effects of cash dividends versus stock dividends. Also, note that students are required to identify cash flows as being financing activities (FA), investing activities (IA), or operating activities (OA) by placing the appropriate letters in the cash statement column.

The horizontal model also can be used to demonstrate how alternative accounting procedures affect financial statements. For example, the recognition of unrealized gains on investment securities affects financial statements differently, depending on whether the securities are classified as (1) held to maturity, (2) trading, or (3) available for sale. Exhibit 2 demonstrates how the recognition of a $700 unrealized gain affects financial statements under each of the three alternative accounting treatments.

When reviewing the text, you will notice that the statements model is introduced gradually with increasing emphasis after Chapter 3. One of the more destructive forces in the learning process is the temptation to move too far too fast. When you overload the students' ability to understand, they retreat to the safe confines of memorization. The statements model cannot serve as an effective instructional tool until the students have fully grasped the rudiments of the accounting cycle. A student who does not recognize the difference between an expense and a liability is not likely to find the statements model insightful.

Accordingly, the model should be used sparingly until the student gains a thorough understanding of the elements of financial statements and the cyclical nature of the accounting discipline. Thereafter, it constitutes an extremely effective teaching tool with abundant applications.

A Separate Section of Innovative End-of-Chapter Materials Encourages Students to Analyze, Communicate, Think

An innovative **act**ivities section entitled *Analyze, Communicate, Think (ACT)* has been added to the end of chapter materials. This section is composed of business applications cases, group exercises, writing assignments, ethics cases, Excel spreadsheet applications, and Internet assignments. These *activities* let you decide the appropriate level of emphasis between a user- versus a preparer-oriented approach to accounting education. Furthermore, the material in this section permits you to stress computer applications to the extent you deem appropriate. Although the text is not designed to teach spreadsheet technicalities, Excel problems and exercises do include instructional tips that facilitate the students' ability to use spreadsheets. Spreadsheet problems were created by Linda Bell of William Jewell College.

By focusing on the materials in the ACT section, you can place heavy emphasis on a user orientation or on computer technology. Indeed, you can even teach the course without debits and credits if you are inclined to do so. However, the text includes a healthy supply of problems that require the use of debits and credits, journal entries, T-accounts, and other technical recording procedures. Accordingly, you can emphasize the preparer approach by selectively choosing the end-of-chapter materials that contain traditional requirements. The ACT section of the end-of-chapter materials permits you to emphasize those areas that you consider to be most important for your particular academic environment. An example of an ACT case from Chapter 2 is shown below; and an example of an ACT Excel assignment from Chapter 5 is shown on the following page.

ACT 2-3

REAL-WORLD CASE   **Unusual Types of Liabilities**

In the liabilities section of its 1997 balance sheet, First Union Corporation reported "non-interest-bearing deposits" of almost $22 billion. First Union is a very large banking company. In the liabilities section of its 1997 balance sheet, Newmont Mining Corporation reported "reclamation and remediation liabilities" of almost $89 million. Newmont Mining is involved in gold mining and refining activities. In the accrued liabilities reported on its 1997 balance sheet, Phillips Petroleum Company included $83 million for "environmental accruals."

Required

a. For each of the preceding liabilities, write a brief explanation of what you believe the nature of the liability to be and how the company will pay off the liability. To develop your answers, think about the nature of the industry in which each of the companies operates.

b. Of the three liabilities described, which do you think poses the most risk for the company? In other words, which liability is likely to have actual cost that exceed the reported cost shown on the balance sheet? Uncertainty creates risk.

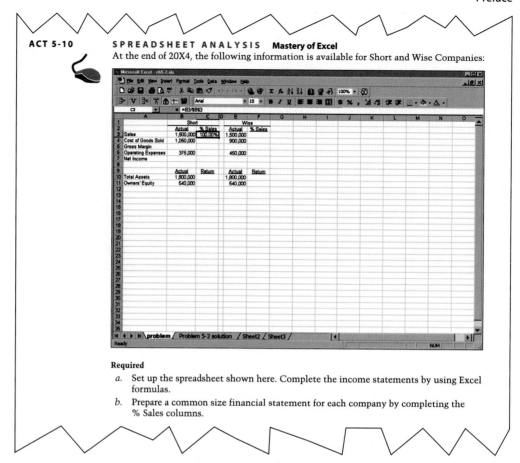

ACT 5-10

SPREADSHEET ANALYSIS **Mastery of Excel**

At the end of 20X4, the following information is available for Short and Wise Companies:

Required

a. Set up the spreadsheet shown here. Complete the income statements by using Excel formulas.

b. Prepare a common size financial statement for each company by completing the % Sales columns.

A variety of writing, group, technology, and ethics assignments are included. These problems are marked appropriately for easy identification.

| Writing | Group | Technology | Ethics |

Financial Statement Effects Are Demonstrated over Multiple Accounting Cycles

The text also employs the use of a **vertical statements model,** which presents the statements in an upright pattern from the top to the bottom of the page. The income statement is presented first, the balance sheet directly below the income statement; and the statement of cash flows directly below the balance sheet. Financial data for a sequence of accounting cycles are displayed in adjacent columns. An example of a vertical statements model from Chapter 9 is shown on the following page.

EXHIBIT 9–5

Financial Statements under Double-Declining Balance Depreciation

DRYDEN ENTERPRISES
Financial Statements

Income Statements

	20X1	20X2	20X3	20X4	20X5
Rent Revenue	$15,000	$ 9,000	$ 5,000	$ 3,000	$ 0
Depreciation Expense	(12,000)	(6,000)	(2,000)	0	0
Operating Income	3,000	3,000	3,000	3,000	0
Gain	0	0	0	0	500
Net Income	$ 3,000	$ 3,000	$ 3,000	$ 3,000	$ 500

Balance Sheets

	20X1	20X2	20X3	20X4	20X5
Assets					
Cash	$16,000	$25,000	$30,000	$33,000	$37,500
Van	24,000	24,000	24,000	24,000	0
Accumulated Depreciation	(12,000)	(18,000)	(20,000)	(20,000)	0
Total Assets	$28,000	$31,000	$34,000	$37,000	$37,500
Equity					
Contributed Capital	$25,000	$25,000	$25,000	$25,000	$25,000
Retained Earnings	3,000	6,000	9,000	12,000	12,500
Total Equity	$28,000	$31,000	$34,000	$37,000	$37,500

Statements of Cash Flows

	20X1	20X2	20X3	20X4	20X5
Operating Activities					
Inflow from Customers	$15,000	$ 9,000	$ 5,000	$ 3,000	$ 0
Investing Activities					
Outflow to Purchase Van	(24,000)				
Inflow from Sale of Van					4,500
Financing Activities					
Inflow from Capital Acquisition	25,000				
Net Change in Cash	16,000	9,000	5,000	3,000	4,500
Beginning Cash Balance	0	16,000	25,000	30,000	33,000
Ending Cash Balance	$16,000	$25,000	$30,000	$33,000	$37,500

The vertical statements model enables the instructor to link related events **over multiple accounting cycles.** A student can see how expense recognition is spread over an asset's useful life. Furthermore, since a full set of statements is presented on a single page, the student can visually contrast expense recognition with cash flow. Similarly, the vertical statements model enables a student to observe the multicycle effects of accumulating depreciation or amortizing a bond discount. An important difference between a vertical statements model and the traditional comparative financial statements is that the vertical statements model is presented in a simplified form on a single page of paper. Students cannot comprehend the linkage between financial statements as easily when the statements and/or accounting periods are shown on separate pages.

The statements models are presented for instructional purposes. They are very helpful in understanding how accounting events affect financial statements.

Accordingly, statements models are used extensively in this text. Notice, however, that the models are not intended to represent the formal presentation formats that appear in annual reports. For example, although a full set of four financial statements is normally presented in published financial statements, the horizontal model shows only a partial set of statements. Similarly, the vertical instructional model may vary in form and content, depending on the learning task. Since the statements are presented in aggregate, the description of dates (i.e., "as of" versus "for the period ended") cannot be used to distinguish periodic from cumulative data. When using this text, keep in mind that statement models are intended to facilitate learning tasks. They do not conform to the detailed requirements of formal reporting practices.

Effects of Cash Flows Are Shown throughout the Entire Text

Coverage of the statement of cash flows begins in the first chapter and continues throughout the text. Students can be taught to prepare a statement of cash flows in the first chapter of an introductory accounting text by having them analyze the Cash account. When the Cash account is used as the data source, preparing a statement of cash flows is simply a matter of learning how to classify events as operating, investing, or financing activities. The easy to use classification scheme is summarized in Exhibit 1–4 which is shown below. This approach provides a logical learning environment that facilitates an understanding of the essential differences between cash flow and accrual-based income. More complicated topics such as the indirect method and a T-account approach for the conversion of accruals to cash are covered in a separate chapter at the end of the text.

EXHIBIT 1–4			
Classification Scheme for Cash Inflows and Outflows			
	Type of Activity		
	Financing	Investing	Operating
Cash Inflows from	(1) Creditors (2) Owners	(1) Sale of Long-Term Assets* (2) Collections of Loans	(1) Collections of Revenue
Cash Outflows for	(1) Repayment of Debt (2) Distributions to Owners	(1) Purchase of Long-Term Assets* (2) Loans to Debtors	(1) Payments for Expenses

*Long-term assets include productive assets and long-term investments in the equity of other companies.

Accounting Concepts Are Introduced in a Logical Stepwise Fashion

Students are confused when too many new concepts are introduced simultaneously. Most books overwhelm students by introducing cash, accrual, and deferral events in the first chapter. This text introduces these components in a logical stepwise manner. Cash transactions are discussed in Chapter 1. Accruals are introduced in Chapter 2, and deferrals are covered in Chapter 3. Nontechnical terminology (i.e., increase/decrease) is used to discuss the effects of events on the elements of financial statements in the first three chapters of the text. Recording procedures including debits and credits are demonstrated in Chapter 4. Accordingly, technical details are delayed until students have grasped the *big picture* relationships associated with articulating financial statements.

An Appropriate Balance between Theory and Practice Is Maintained

A conceptual foundation enables students to think instead of memorize. Students who understand concepts are better able to communicate ideas and are more effective at solving unstructured problems. Accordingly, **this text addresses the issues raised by the Accounting Education Change Commission.** It is important to note, however, that the call for change in accounting education is not a call for the abandonment of technical competence. Instead, the enhancement of communication and thinking skills must accompany technical proficiency. Practicing accountants continue to book transactions, and real-world communication requires nonaccountants to possess an adequate technical vocabulary. Although the coverage of recording procedures has been significantly curtailed, it has not been eliminated. We continue to cover the basic components of double-entry bookkeeping including debits and credits, journal entries, T-accounts, and trial balances. Accordingly, **it is not necessary to change your intermediate accounting course if you adopt this book.** Indeed, users of previous editions have consistently reported that their students are better prepared for intermediate accounting than they were under the traditional approach. This edition of the text continues to maintain the delicate balance between enhanced relevance and technical competence.

Business Transactions Are Classified into Four Logical Categories

Instead of attempting to memorize transactions, students learn to identify events as belonging to one of four conceptual categories. More specifically, students learn to classify transactions as being (1) asset sources, (2) asset uses, (3) asset exchanges, or (4) claims exchanges. This classification approach encourages students to think about the effects of events rather than to memorize recording procedures.

A Consistent Point of Reference Is Provided

Do you ever wonder why good students sometimes have so much trouble grasping the simplest concepts? For example, why do so many students have difficulty distinguishing the effects of an owner investment from those of a business investment? A participant in a recent introductory accounting workshop provided the answer that enabled us to avoid a common pitfall that needlessly confuses so many students. Normally, accounting events are described from the perspective of the business entity. For example, we say that the business borrowed money, purchased assets, earned revenue, or incurred expenses. For some unknown reason, however, we usually shift the point of reference when we speak of equity transactions. We say that the owners contributed capital, provided cash, or invested assets in the business. From the perspective of the business, these are capital acquisitions, not owner investments. To understand how this *reference shift* affects the entry-level accounting student, try it on a different type of transaction. Suppose that we say, "A customer purchased services from the business." What kind of transaction is this? It is a revenue transaction, of course. How about "a supplier provides services to the business?" This is just a more confusing way of saying the business incurred an expense. Likewise, an owner investment is just a more confusing way of saying the business acquired assets from the owner. Your students will certainly appreciate the fact that this text uses the business entity as a consistent point of reference in the description of all accounting events. We steadfastly use the term *capital acquisition* rather than *owner investment* when describing equity events.

Content That Is Manageable and Relevant Has Been Maintained

Accounting is a dynamic discipline. It changes to reflect new and emerging business practices. As academicians, we are certainly obligated to keep current and to introduce our students to the latest developments. As teachers, however, we must also recognize the limited ability of our students to meaningfully process an ever increasing supply of information. **Remember that information overload equals memorization.** Although we have found it necessary to add new material, we determined that eliminating the older, less relevant subject matter is equally important. The first editions of our text made real progress toward the elimination of alternative recording procedures, meaningless details, and subject matter that is too advanced for introductory accounting students. Like its predecessors, the new edition contains only 12 chapters.

Stimulating Student Interest

A good textbook must be more than pedagogically sound. It must be designed in a manner that motivates student interest. Toward this end, we have added several features that highlight real-world applications. Each chapter of the revised text opens with a sidebar entitled **The Curious Accountant.** The sidebar poses a question regarding a real-world accounting issue. The question is answered in a separate sidebar located a few pages after the question. Pictures that stimulate interest are attached to each sidebar. An example of the Curious Accountant feature is shown on the following two pages. The new edition contains other real-world features such as actual financial statements, footnote quotations, and management analyses drawn from the **annual reports of well-known companies.** Most chapters now contain a sidebar that discusses interesting **international accounting issues.** In addition, most chapters include colorful graphs that provide summary facts about financial reporting. The data source for these graphs is the AICPA's source book *Accounting Trends and Techniques.* Finally, the end-of-chapter material includes real-world cases requiring the use of the **World Wide Web.**

the **curious** accountant

In 1997 CUC and HFS merged to form Cendant Corporation. Cendant operates numerous businesses in different industries, including Avis rental cars, Century 21 Real Estate, and Days Inn. Its businesses also include discount shopping and travel clubs.

On April 15, 1998, the company announced that earnings of the then combined companies had been overstated during the prior three years. At that time, it estimated that 1997 net income would need to be restated downward by $100 to $115 million. In July, the company reported that nonexistent revenues had been recorded from 1995 to 1997 for an estimated $300 million; by September, this estimate had increased to $500 million. After a thorough review of its accounting records, Cendant revised its 1997 earnings downward by approximately $272.6 million; what had originally been reported as $55.4 million of net income became $217.2 million of net loss. Within six months of the initial disclosure of accounting irregularities, the price of Cendant's stock had declined by approximately 75% of its previous value. How could the accounting system at such a large and sophisticated company allow such large misstatements of revenues and earnings?

©Tom Pantages

The successful operation of a business enterprise requires control. How can upper management of a major retailer such as Wal-Mart know that all its stores will open at a certain time? How can the president of General Motors rest assured that the numbers in the company's financial reports accurately reflect the company's operating activities? How can the owner of a small restaurant be confident that the wait staff is not giving food to friends and relatives? The answer to each of these questions is "by exercising effective control over the enterprise." The policies and procedures used to provide *reasonable assurance* that the objectives of an enterprise will be accomplished are called **internal controls.**[1]

Internal controls can be divided into two categories: accounting controls and administrative controls. **Accounting controls** are composed of procedures designed to safeguard the assets and ensure that the accounting records contain reliable information. **Administrative controls** concern the evaluation of performance and the assessment of the degree of compliance with company policies and public laws.

[1]*AICPA Professional Standards*, vol. 1, sec. 320, par. 6 (June 1, 1989).

an answer for the curious accountant

Based on the company's public disclosures, many inappropriate accounting practices were used at the CUC portion of Cendant Corporation. On October 15, 1998, Henry R. Silverman, CEO of Cedant, was interviewed on CNN. When he was asked how the fraudulent activities were not detected before the merger of the two companies was finalized, he responded, "Our financial system is based on trust. . . . We have to rely upon, really, the honor system. . . . Our system is very vulnerable to fraud because it is based on trust. . . . We can't do . . . polygraphs of every management that you happen to do business with. . . ."

Perhaps some or all of the irregularities at CUC and Cendant should have been detected earlier by the companies' internal controls and/or independent auditors; the courts will answer those questions ultimately. Nevertheless, Mr. Silverman's answer has a certain degree of truth. No system of internal controls can prevent all fraud from occurring if several members of management decide to work together to circumvent those controls.

If you wish to read a detailed report by Cendant's audit committee regarding these matters, using EDGAR, download Cendant's 8-K report that was filed with the SEC on August 28, 1998. Instructions for using EDGAR are contained in Appendix A of this book.

Financial ratios introduced throughout the book are logically related to the chapter material. For example, accounts receivable turnover is introduced in the chapter that covers bad debts, and the times-interest-earned ratio is discussed in the bonds chapter. Industry data are shown to provide students with a basis for establishing a sense of normalcy regarding business practice. The 1997 annual report for Gateway 2000 is included in Appendix B, and the "Analyze, Comunicate, Think" section that relates directly to the annual report are in the end-of-chapter material.

Supplemental Materials

The text is supported by a complete package of supplements. **Rather than farming the supplements out, we have prepared these materials ourselves.** Accordingly, you can rest assured that the supplements match the text. The package includes the following items.

Instructors' Guide: Prepared by Thomas P. Edmonds (ISBN 0-07-229907-X)

The text is suitable to new teaching approaches such as group dynamics and active pedagogy. The Instructors' Guide provides step-by-step, explicit instructions as to how the text can be used to implement these alternative teaching methodologies. Guidance is also provided for instructors who choose to use the traditional lecture method. The guide includes lesson plans and demonstration problems with student work papers, and solutions for them.

Solutions Manual: Prepared by Edmonds, McNair, Milam, and Olds (ISBN 0-07-229908-8)

The Solutions Manual has been prepared by the authors and contains complete answers to all questions, exercises, problems, and cases. The manual has been tested using a variety of quality control procedures to ensure accuracy. After the initial preparation of the *solutions*, the problems and exercises were reworked "blind." An independent reviewer then compared the second set of answers with the previous solutions. Any differences were reconciled. After this process, the solutions manual was again proofed and checked for accuracy by two independent error checkers including Barbara Schnathorst of the Write Solution, Inc., and Bruce Duckworth of the University of Wisconsin–Baraboo. Although the author team retains the responsibility for any errors that may occur, we express our appreciation for the individuals who have exhibited a zero tolerance attitude that is required to maintain the highest standards of excellence.

Check Figures (ISBN 0-07-234389-3)

Check figures are available for selected exercises and problems.

Annotated Instructor's Edition (ISBN 0-07-232804-5)

New marginal annotations provide additional support for instructors, including Teaching Strategies, Real-World References, Key Concepts, and suggestions for additional group and communications activities. Annotations were created by Philip R. Olds, Eric Carlsen (Kean University), and Kathleen Sevigny (Bridgewater State College).

Working Papers: Prepared by Frances M. McNair and Edward E. Milam (ISBN 0-07-229904-5)

The working papers provide forms that are useful in the completion of both exercises and problems. Working papers for the exercises provide headings and prerecorded example transactions that enable students to get started quickly and to work in an efficient manner. The forms provided for the problems can be used with either series A or B problems.

Solutions Transparencies: Prepared by Frances M. McNair and Edward E. Milam (ISBN 0-07-229909-6)

Transparencies are prepared in easy-to-read 14-point bold type. They are mirror images of the answers provided in the solutions manual and are consistent with the forms contained in the working papers. This ensures congruence between your in-class presentations and the follow-up exposure that students attain when they view the solutions manual or use the working papers.

Test Bank: Prepared by Thomas P. Edmonds, Cindy D. Edmonds, Bor-Yi Tsay, Alan Falcon (Loyola Marymount University), John Marts (North Carolina at Wilmington), and David L. Davis (Tallahassee Community College) (ISBN 0-07-229910-X)

The Test Bank has been significantly revised and expanded. It includes true/false, multiple-choice, and short discussion questions as well as open-ended problems. The testing material is coded by learning objective and level of difficulty.

Computest (ISBN 0-07-234390-7)

A computerized version of the test bank for more efficient use is available in a Windows platform.

Teletest

By calling a toll-free number, users can specify the content of exams and have a laser-printed copy of the exams mailed to them.

Study Guide: Prepared by Philip R. Olds (ISBN 0-07-229906-1)

Each chapter of the Study Guide includes a review and an explanation of the chapter's learning objectives, as well as multiple-choice problems and short exercises. Unique to this Study Guide is a series of articulation problems that require students to indicate how accounting events affect (i.e., increase, decrease, no effect) the elements of financial statements. They not only reinforce the student's understanding of how events affect statements but also help them to understand how the income statement, balance sheet, and statement of cash flows interrelate. The guide contains approximately 200 pages and includes appropriate working papers and a complete set of solutions.

Computerized Practice Problem: *Broadway Babies, Inc.*: Prepared by Thomas P. Edmonds and Bor-Yi Tsay (ISBN 0-07-844325-3)

Broadway Babies, Inc., is a computerized practice problem. Beginning account balances are presented in a trial balance. Students record accounting events including appropriate *adjusting* entries in general journal format. The software program automatically updates the beginning balances and provides students with an adjusted trial balance. Students use the adjusted trial balance to manually prepare a complete set of financial statements. The software is a DOS-based program designed to operate on IBM-compatible systems using DOS versions of 3.0 or higher.

Manual Practice Problem: *Mark's Racquets, Inc.*: Prepared by Cindy D. Edmonds (ISBN 0-07-021399-2)

Mark's Racquets, Inc., is a manual practice problem that can be introduced approximately two-thirds of the way through the course. Students record accounting events in general journal format and post transaction data to running balance general ledger accounts. They prepare unadjusted, adjusted, and post-closing trial balances. They use the *information* contained in the adjusted trial balance to prepare an income statement, a balance sheet, a statement of changes in equity, and a statement of cash flows. The problem minimizes procedural detail. It does not use special journals, a worksheet, posting references, and so on. Most students are able to complete the problem in less than 8 hours.

Ready Shows (ISBN 0-07-231622-5), Ready Slides (ISBN 0-07-237829-8), and Ready Notes (ISBN 0-07-229905-3): Prepared by J. Lawrence Bergin, (Winona State University)

Ready Shows is a package of multimedia lecture-enhancement aids that use PowerPoint software to illustrate chapter concepts. *Ready Slides* are selected four-color transparencies printed from the PowerPoint Ready Shows. *Ready Notes* is a booklet of Ready Shows screen printouts that enable students to take notes during Ready Shows or Ready Slides presentations.

SPATS (Instructor Version ISBN 0-07-234452-0, Student Version ISBN 0-07-234453-9)

This software includes Excel templates for selected problems and exercises from the text. The templates gradually become more complex, requiring students to build a variety of formulas. "What-if" questions are added to show the power of spreadsheets, and a simple tutorial is included. Instructors may request a free master template for students to use or copy, or shrinkwrapped versions are available for a nominal fee.

Web Page (www.mhhe.com/edmonds_financial)

Our Web page was created for both students and instructors. It includes self-study quizzes, links to home pages of companies in the book, and much more.

Presentation Manager (ISBN 0-07-235971-4)

This integrated CD-ROM allows you to maneuver from PowerPoint slides to solutions to test bank questions and much more. Ideal for using in class.

Tutorial Software (ISBN 0-07-234388-5)

Prepared by Leland Mansuetti and Keith Weidkamp (both of Sierra College). This Windows-based tutorial provides multiple-choice, true/false, and glossary review questions that can be randomly accessed by students. Explanations of correct answers are provided and scores are tallied.

Acknowledgments

We are indebted to many individuals who have contributed to the development of this textbook. Many of the users of previous editions have shared their experiences and suggestions. Participants in workshops and focus groups have provided useful feedback. We are also appreciative of our colleagues and friends who have provided encouragement and support. Among these individuals our sincere appreciation is extended to

Charles Richard Aldridge
Western Kentucky University

Debra Barbeau
Southern Illinois University–Carbondale

Beryl Barkman
University of Massachusetts–Dartmouth

Jim Bates
Mountain Empire Community College

Linda Bell
William Jewell College

Wilbur Berry
Jacksonville State University

Nancy Bledsoe
Millsaps College

Cendy and David Boyd

Arthur Boyett
Francis Marion University

Cassie Bradley
Troy State University

James Cahsell
Miami University

Frederic J. Carlson
LeTourneau University

Alan Cherry
Loyola Marymount University

Ron Colley
State University of West Georgia

William Cress
University of Wisconsin–La Cross

Walter Doehring
Genesee Community College

George Dow
Valencia Community College

Melanie Earls
Mississippi State University

Cindy Edmonds
University of Alabama–Birmingham

M. J. Edwards
Adirondack Community College

David Ganz
University of Missouri–Saint Louis

William T. Geary
College of William and Mary

Frank Gersich
Gustavus Adolphus College

Lorraine Glasscock
University of North Alabama

Larry Hagler
East Carolina University

Phillip Harsha
Southwest Missouri State University

Charles Hart
Copiah–Lincoln Community College

Inez Heal
Youngstown State University

Karen Hull
Kansas Wesleyn University

Pamela Jones
Mississippi State University

Khondkar Karim
Monmouth University

Nathan Kranowski
Radford University

Helen LaFrancois
University of Massachusetts–Dartmouth

William Lathen
Boise State University

David Law
Youngstown State University

William Link
University of Missouri–Saint Louis

Catherine Lumbattis
Southern Illinois University–Carbondale

Joseph Marcheggiani
Butler University

Herb Martin
Hope College

Nancy Meade
Radford University

George Minmier
University of Memphis

Lu Montondon
Southwest Texas State University

Tim Nygaard
Madisonville Community College

Brian O'Doherty
East Carolina University

Lawrence Ozzello
University of Wisconsin–Eau Claire

Eileen Peacock
Oakland University

Thomas Phillips, Jr.
Louisiana Tech University

Mary Raven
Mount Mary College

Jane Reimers
Florida State University

Ken Ruby
Idaho State University

Nancy Schneider
Lynchburg College

Jeffrey Schwartz
Montgomery College

Suzanne Sevalstad
University of Nevada, Las Vegas

Jill Smith
Idaho State University

Paul E. Solomon

John Sperry
Virginia Commonwealth University

Paul Steinbart
Saint Louis University–Saint Louis

Mary Stevens
University of Texas at El Paso

James Swayze
University of Nevada, Las Vegas

Maurice Tassin
Louisiana Tech University

Kim Temme
Maryville University

Beth Vogel
Mount Mary College

J. D. Weinhold
Concordia College

Judith Welch
University of Central Florida

Thomas Whitacre
University of South Carolina

Macil C. Wilkie, Jr.
Grambling State University

Marie Winks
Lynchburg College

Kenneth Winter
University of Wisconsin–La Cross

The text underwent an extensive review process by a diverse group of instructors located at schools across the country. The comments and suggestions of the reviewers have significantly influenced the writing of the text. Our efforts to establish a meaningful but manageable level of content was greatly influenced not only by their suggestions regarding what to include but also by their opinions regarding what to leave out. Our grateful appreciation is extended to those who reviewed this edition and previous editions: Charles Richard Aldridge, Western Kentucky University; Linda Bell, William Jewell College; Cendy Boyd, Northeast Louisiana State; Gregory Bushong, Wright State University; Judith Cadle, Tarleton State University; Scott Cairns, Shippensburg College; Eric Carlsen, Kean University; Joan Carroll, SUNY–College at Oswego; Alan Cherry, Loyola Marymount University; Ron Colley, State University of West Georgia; George Dow, Valencia Community College; Cindy Edmonds, University of Alabama at Birmingham; Ralph Fritzsch, Midwestern State University; Lou Fowler, Missouri Western State College; Mary Anne Gaffney, Temple University; Michael Garner, Salisbury State University; Claudia Gilbertson, North Hennepin Community College; Penny Hanes, Virginia Tech University; Leon Hanouille, Syracuse University; Kenneth M. Hiltebeitel, Villanova University;

Nitham Hindi, Shippensburg College; Richard Hulme, California State Poly-technic University–Pomona; Robert Landry, Massasoit Community College; Larry Logan, University of Massachusetts–Dartmouth; Cheryl Mitchem, Virginia State University; Joseph Onyeocha, South Carolina State University; Cathy Pitts, Highline Community College; Jane Reimers, Florida State University; Jill Smith, Idaho State University; Suzanne Sevalstad, University of Nevada, Las Vegas; Leonard Stokes, Siena College; Janice Swanson, Southern Oregon University; Maurice Tassin, Louisiana Tech University; Bor-Yi Tsay, University of Alabama at Birmingham; Suneel Udpa, St. Mary's College of California; Sterling Wetzel, Oklahoma State University; Thomas Whitacre, University of South Carolina; Stephen Willits, Bucknell University.

We would like to offer a special thanks to Linda Bell of William Jewell College for her work on the end-of-chapter spreadsheet problems, and to Eric Carlsen of Kean University and Kathleen Sevigny of Bridgewater State College for their work on the Annotated Instructor's Edition.

We are deeply indebted to our publisher, Jeff Shelsted. His direction and guidance have added clarity and quality to the text. We especially appreciate the efforts of our developmental editor, Marc Chernoff. Marc has coordinated the exchange of ideas among our class testers, reviewers, copy editor, and error checkers; he has done far more than simply pass along ideas. He has contributed numerous original suggestions that have enhanced the quality of the text. Our editors have certainly facilitated our efforts to prepare a book that will facilitate a meaningful understanding of accounting. Even so, their contributions are to no avail unless the text reaches its intended audience. We are most grateful to Rhonda Seelinger, Melissa Caughlin, and the sales staff for providing the informative advertising that has so accurately communicated the unique features of the concepts approach to accounting educators. Many others at Irwin/McGraw-Hill at a moment's notice redirected their attention to focus their efforts on the development of this text. We extend our sincere appreciation to Kimberly Hooker, Madelyn Underwood, Rose Hepburn, Michael Warrell, Sharon Miller, and Mark Sienicki. We deeply appreciate the long hours that you committed to the formation of a high-quality text.

Thomas P. Edmonds

Frances M. McNair

Edward E. Milam

Philip R. Olds

BRIEF CONTENTS

CONTENTS

Contents xxvii

Third Accounting Cycle 113
   Effect of 20X6 Transactions on the Accounting Equation and
   the Financial Statements 114

**Analysis of Financial Statements to Assess Managerial
Performance 118**
   Assessment of the Effective Use of Assets 118
   Assessment of the Risk of Debt 118
   Real-World Data 120
   Scope of Coverage 121

A Look Back 122

A Look Forward 123

Key Terms 123

Questions 123

Exercises 124

Problems 129

Analyze, Communicate, Think 139

CHAPTER 4

The Recording Process

Debit/Credit Terminology 146

Collins Consultants Case 147
   Asset Source Transactions 147
   Asset Exchange Transactions 150
   Asset Use Transactions 153
   Claims Exchange Transactions 154
   Adjustments for Accruals 155
   Adjustments for Deferrals 157

Overview of Debit/Credit Relationships 160

Summary of T-Accounts 160

The Ledger 160

The General Journal 161

Financial Statements 165

Closing Entries 165

Trial Balance 166

Components of an Annual Report 167
   Footnotes to Financial Statements 169
   Management's Discussion and Analysis 170
   Role of the Independent Auditor Revisited 170
   The Securities and Exchange Commission 172

A Look Back 172

A Look Forward 173

Key Terms 174

Questions 174

Exercises 175

Problems 183

Analyze, Communicate, Think 200

CHAPTER 5

Accounting for Merchandising Business

**Product Costs versus Selling and Administrative
Costs 210**

**Allocation Inventory Cost between Asset and
Expense Accounts 210**

Inventory Cost Recorded 213

Perpetual Inventory Method 214
   Effect of Events on Financial Statements 214
   Journal Entries and Ledger T-Accounts 215

**Other Events Affecting Purchases and Sales of
Inventory 216**
   Effect of Events on Financial Statements 216
   Journal Entries and Ledger Accounts 223
   Financial Statements 223

Periodic Inventory Method 225
   Schedule of Cost of Goods Sold 227

Lost, Damaged, or Stolen Merchandise 227
   Adjustment for Lost, Damaged, or Stolen Inventory 228

Financial Analysis for Merchandising Companies 228
   Common Size Financial Statements 229
   Gross Margin Percentage 230
   Real-World Data 230
   Return on Sales 231
   Use of Common Size Financial Statements 231
   Merchandise Inventory Financed 232

A Look Back 233

A Look Forward 234

Key Terms 234

Questions 235

Exercises 236

Problems 243

Analyze, Communicate, Think 251

CHAPTER 6

Internal Control and Accounting for Cash

Key Features of Internal Control Systems 260
   Separation of Duties 260
   Quality of Employees 260
   Bonded Employees 261
   Periods of Absence 261
   Procedures Manual 261
   Authority and Responsibility 262
   Prenumbered Documents 262

CHAPTER 7

Accounting for Accruals—Advanced
Topics: Receivables and Payables

CHAPTER 8

Asset Valuation: Accounting for
Investments and Inventories

CHAPTER 9

Long-Term Operational Assets

CHAPTER 10

Accounting for Long-Term Debt

CHAPTER 11

Accounting for Equity Transactions

CHAPTER   12

Statement of Cash Flows

1 Elements of Financial Statements

LEARNING OBJECTIVES

AFTER COMPLETING THIS CHAPTER, YOU SHOULD BE ABLE TO:

1 Understand the role of accounting in society.

2 Understand the role of accounting in business.

3 Comprehend the need for generally accepted accounting principles (GAAP).

4 Identify, describe, and prepare the four basic financial statements.

5 Identify the major elements of financial statements.

6 Grasp the relationships expressed in the accounting equation.

7 Record business events under an accounting equation.

8 Classify business events as being asset source, use, or exchange transactions.

9 Record business events in financial statements models.

10 Identify the major components of real-world annual reports and some of the technical terms used in them.

Who owns Coca-Cola Corporation? Who owns the American Cancer Society (ACS)? In addition to the owners, many other people and organizations have an interest in the operations of Coke and the ACS. The parties that are interested in operations of an organization are called *stakeholders*. Among others, they include lenders, employees, suppliers, customers, benefactors, researcher institutions, hospitals, doctors, patients, lawyers, bankers, financial analysts, and government agencies such as the Internal Revenue Service and the Securities and Exchange Commission. Organizations communicate information to stakeholders through documents called *financial reports*. How do you think the financial reports of Coke might differ from those of the ACS?

James Randklev © Tony Stone Images

People around the world use some form of accounting every day. Consumers account for the money they spend; students have to plan for their educational expenses; and companies use accounting to track the performance of their managers. **Accounting** is a diverse and dynamic industry. Much like the fields of medicine or law, *accounting is a service-based discipline.* The accountant's responsibility is to provide reliable and relevant *information* that is useful in making decisions. Do not underestimate the importance of information. Think of the money you could make if you had reliable information regarding the winner of next year's Superbowl football game. Likewise, reliable information regarding next year's earnings of major companies such as IBM, Sears, and Wendy's could make you a wealthy Wall Street investor.

Users of accounting information hold either a direct or an indirect interest in the companies that issue the accounting reports. Direct users of financial information include investors, managers, creditors, suppliers, and employees. Indirect users advise and influence the direct users of financial information and include financial analysts, brokers, bankers, government regulators, and news reporters. The role of accounting in commerce is so important that accounting is frequently called the *language of business.*

Role of Accounting in Society

How much emphasis should society place on the production of food versus the development of a cure for cancer? Should we devote more time and energy to making computers or cars? Should a city build a new football stadium or a museum? Accounting provides information that is useful in answering resource allocation questions such as these.

Market-Based Allocations

The U.S. economy uses markets to allocate resources. A **market** is a gathering of people or organizations for the purpose of buying and selling resources. The allotment of resources is determined by competition among the market participants. For example, a parcel of land could be used as a building site for a bank, a medical building, or a fast-food restaurant. In a market economy, the land will be assigned to the business that is willing to pay the most money to obtain it. The business's ability to pay for the land will depend on consumer preferences. In other words, the amount of money consumers are willing to pay for bank services versus medical treatment versus fast food will determine the amount of money each business has available for the purchase of land and other resources. Accordingly, consumer desires dictate the allocation of resources through competitive markets.

Usually, nature does not provide goods and services in the form consumers want. For example, nature provides trees but consumers want furniture. Businesses exist for the purpose of transforming resources to more desirable states. The transformation process is affected by three market participants: *resource owners*, *conversion agents*, and *consumers*.

The **demand** for transformation is established by consumer preferences. *Consumers* express their preferences by offering more money for more desirable goods or services. For example, your willingness to pay more for a car than for a horse expresses your preference for fast, comfortable transportation over a slower mode of navigation that exposes your body to the harsh elements of nature.

The resource owners and conversion agents provide the **supply** of goods and services that respond to consumer preferences. The *resource owners* furnish the inputs the *conversion agents* use to produce the outputs that consumers demand. These owners expect to be rewarded for the resources they provide. Businesses and other conversion agents are able to provide the rewards that resource owners demand by *adding value* to products and services. The outputs created from the transformation of the inputs are *more valuable* because they are more useful after conversion. A house is more valuable than the materials and labor used in its construction. Labor or materials alone will not provide shelter. The total is more valuable than the sum of the parts. Exhibit 1–1 describes the market trilogy that accomplishes the allocation of resources.

Competition for Resources

The added value created in the transformation process is commonly called **profit** or **income.** It is defined as the difference between the cost of a product or service and the selling price of that product or service. Conversion agents who successfully anticipate consumer preferences and who are able to provide services or make products efficiently (i.e., at a low cost) are rewarded with high profits. *Since these profits are shared with resource owners, conversion agents who exhibit a high potential for adding value are more likely to obtain resources.*

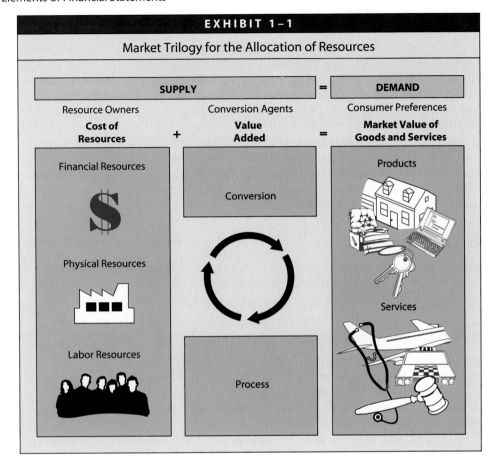

EXHIBIT 1–1

Market Trilogy for the Allocation of Resources

Financial Resources

It takes money to make money. Conversion agents need **financial resources** (i.e., money) to establish and operate their businesses. There are two primary types of financial resource providers: *investors* and *creditors*. **Investors** accept an ownership interest in the business. As such, they share in the distribution of profits. If the business prospers, they are rewarded handsomely. If it fails, they risk losing the resources they invested in the business. Investors allocate their resources to businesses according to the investors' assessments of the likelihood of profitability versus the risk of failure.

Creditors lend financial resources to businesses. In the event of a business failure, financial resources are returned to creditors before they are returned to the owners. Suppose a business acquired $100 in cash from investors and $200 in cash from creditors. Now assume the business loses $75 and returns the remaining financial resources to the providers. The creditors receive $200, whereas only $25 is returned to the owners. If the business lost $120, only $180 (that is, $300 − $120) would be available to return to the creditors. Accordingly, creditors as well as investors can lose resources when businesses fail. Even so, creditors are in a more secure position than owners are. As a result of their more secure position, creditors normally do not share in profitability. Instead, they are paid a fixed fee, known as *interest.* Creditors allocate financial resources to businesses on the basis of the amount of the interest payment relative to the level of risk of losing resources due to collection failure (i.e., the greater the risk, the higher the interest charge).

Physical Resources

In their most primitive form, **physical resources** are natural resources. However, the conversion process may include several stages that involve numerous independent businesses. One conversion agent's output becomes another agent's input. For example, most furniture makers do not own timberlands. Instead, they buy the wood to make their products. The resource furniture makers use is lumber rather than trees. Accordingly, physical resources are composed of natural resources that may be in different levels of refined condition. Owners of physical resources want to transfer their resources to businesses that are able to add benefit because profitable businesses are more likely to be able to pay for the resources entrusted to them. Accordingly, physical as well as financial resources are allocated on the basis of a business's ability to add value in the conversion process.

Labor Resources

Labor resources include intellectual as well as physical labor. Like other resource providers, workers seek relationships with businesses with high profit potential because these businesses are in a position to pay the highest wages.

Accounting Is Information

As indicated, owners of financial, physical, and labor resources want to give their resources to conversion agents with the highest profit potential relative to specified levels of risk. How do the resource owners identify the conversion agents with high profits and low risk? This is where accounting enters the picture. Accounting provides information that is useful in evaluating a conversion agent's profit potential and relative risk. Accounting information that is designed to satisfy the needs of resource owners is called **financial accounting.** Since resource providers are viewed as entities that are separate from the business, they are frequently called *external users* of accounting information.

Another branch of accounting, known as **managerial accounting,** provides information that is useful in operating an organization. Since managers are a part of the accounting entity, they are commonly called *internal users* of accounting information. The information needs of both user groups frequently overlap. For example, both external and internal users are interested in the amount of income that a business earns. However, managerial accounting information is usually more detailed than financial information. Whereas an investor is interested in knowing whether Wendy's or Burger King produces more income relative to risk, a regional manager of Wendy's is interested in knowing which of the restaurants under her or his control produce the highest amount of revenue relative to the expenses incurred. Indeed, a manager is interested in many nonfinancial measures, such as the number of employees needed to operate a restaurant, the number of parking spaces needed, the times at which customer demand is high versus low, and measures of cleanliness and customer satisfaction. The role of accounting in society is to provide information needed to operate and evaluate business organizations. In doing so, accounting has a vital function in the allocation of resources.

Nonbusiness Resource Allocations

The United States is not a *pure* market-based economy. The allocation of resources is affected by many factors other than profitability. For example, governments make allocations for the purpose of national defense, the redistribution of wealth, or the protection of the environment. Foundations, religious groups, the Peace Corps, and other benevolent organizations allocate resources on the basis of humanitarian concerns. Similarly, groups are formed for the support of the arts, music, dance, and theater. These organizations also add value through a transformation process. For example, like a profit-oriented restaurant, a nonprofit soup kitchen adds value by transforming raw meats and vegetables into a more desirable form for human consumption. It is not the *existence* but the *treatment* of added value that differs between profit and not-for-profit organizations. The consumers of the soup kitchen are unable to pay for the costs, much less a charge for the added value of the products they receive. Accordingly, the motive for delivering the resources and added value is humanitarian rather than profit based. Organizations that are not motivated by profit are referred to by several different names, including **not-for-profit entities** (also called *nonprofit* and *nonbusiness entities*).

The absence of a profit motive by no means negates the need for accounting. Accounting information can be useful in the measurement of the goods and services provided by a not-for-profit organization, its efficiency and effectiveness in producing goods and providing services, and its ability to continue to produce goods and provide services. This information is useful to a host of stakeholders, including taxpayers, contributors, lenders, suppliers, employees, managers, financial analysts, attorneys, and beneficiaries. As depicted in Exhibit 1–2, accounting serves the information needs of a variety of business and nonbusiness

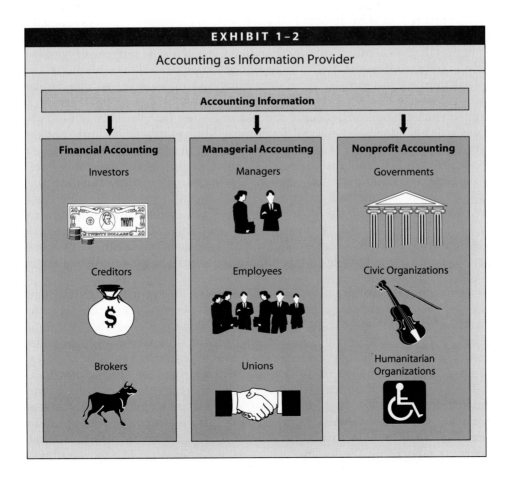

EXHIBIT 1–2

Accounting as Information Provider

Accounting Information

Financial Accounting	Managerial Accounting	Nonprofit Accounting
Investors	Managers	Governments
Creditors	Employees	Civic Organizations
Brokers	Unions	Humanitarian Organizations

user groups. The exhibit shows three distinct areas of accounting; in practice, these areas frequently overlap. Certainly, managers of not-for-profit organizations as well as those of business entities use managerial accounting information.

Role of Accounting in Business

L.O. 2

Understand the role of account- ing in business.

Early in life, you learned how long a yard is. Now when you hear that a quarter- back threw a 60-yard pass, you know what that means. In business, you need to know the meanings of financial measurements so that you can respond appropri- ately to statements such as "the company's earnings are down 10 percent while cash flows from operations are about the same." As this discussion implies, ac- counting is a *measurement discipline.* Many people and organizations in our so- ciety make decisions based on financial information that accountants prepare. It is important for these people and organizations to understand how that informa- tion was measured. To facilitate your understanding of financial measurement, consider some of the issues related to other types of measurement with which you are more familiar.

How long is 1 *yard*? One yard is 0.944 meter. So, how long is 1 meter? Ac- cording to the International System of Units, 1 meter is the distance traveled by light in a vacuum during 1/299,792,458 second. Now, that is helpful! Is it impor- tant to know the precise definition of 1 meter? No. However, if you wish to com- municate the length of a particular object to another person, it is important that you both agree on a definition of the unit of measure. Imagine the problems that would result if you were to build a house with a carpenter who considered the length of 1 foot as 10 inches. Think of your disappointment when you walked into rooms that were much smaller than you expected. The length of 1 foot is not nearly as important as the ability to reach agreement on its measurement.

Accounting has similar problems. Financial measurements can be inter- preted differently by different people. To facilitate communication, accountants establish rules that businesspeople can use to ensure that they are talking about the same thing. Suppose a store sells a compact disk player in December to a cus- tomer who agrees to pay for it in January. Should the store owner state that the sale occurred in December or in January? A rule requiring recognition when the sale occurred in December is called *accrual accounting.* A rule requiring recogni- tion when cash is collected in January is called *cash accounting.* Whether the store owner uses the accrual or the cash rule is not important as long as a third rule is established that requires the owner to disclose which method is being used in the reporting process. Accordingly, rule making does not preclude diversity in financial reporting. Effective communication can still be accomplished through full and fair disclosure.

L.O. 3

Comprehend the need for gener- ally accepted accounting principles (GAAP).

Certainly, communication would be easier if only one measurement method were used to report each type of business activity. Unfortunately, world economies have not yet evolved to the point at which it is possible to attain uni- formity in financial reporting. Indeed, significant diversity continues to exist even in highly sophisticated countries such as the United States. A well-educated businessperson must be able to understand and interpret accounting information that has been prepared under a variety of measurement rules. The rules of meas- urement for accounting used in the United States are called **generally accepted accounting principles (GAAP).** This textbook introduces you to these principles so that you will be able to understand business activity as it is presented in accounting reports.

Financial Statements

Businesses communicate information to the public through a process known as *financial reporting.* The central feature of external financial reporting is a set of **financial statements.** Accordingly, financial statements constitute the principal means of communicating economic information to individuals and institutions residing outside the reporting enterprise. The four general-purpose financial statements that business enterprises use are the (1) income statement, (2) statement of changes in equity, (3) balance sheet, and (4) statement of cash flows. These statements may be assigned other names. For example, the income statement is frequently called a *statement of operations* or an *earnings statement.* The frequency of use of these terms is shown in Exhibit 1–3.

Similarly, alternative names exist for the other statements. The balance sheet is also known as a *statement of financial position.* The statement of changes in equity may be called a *capital statement* or *statement of stockholders' equity.* Since the **Financial Accounting Standards Board (FASB)** has specifically called for the use of the title *statement of cash flows,* title diversity is virtually nonexistent for this statement. To promote understanding, this text consistently uses the four titles numbered here. However, do not expect all real-world annual reports to bear the same titles.

The items reported in financial statements are organized into classes or categories known as **elements.** The FASB[1] identified 10 elements of financial statements. Eight of these elements are discussed in this chapter: *assets, liabilities, equity, contributed capital, revenue, expenses, distributions,* and *net income.*[2] The other two elements, *gains* and *losses,* are discussed in a later chapter. The elements represent broad classifications as opposed to specific items. In other words, cash, equipment, buildings, and land are particular economic resources and should not be identified as elements. Rather, they represent specific items or subclassifications of the element known as *assets.* The information regarding specific items is frequently collected and summarized in **accounts.** The accounts appear in the financial statements under the broader classifications that have been identified as elements. Accordingly, the balance sheet contains the element assets, which includes subclassifications known as *accounts* that describe specific items such as cash, inventory, equipment, and land.

L.O. 4

Identify, describe, and prepare the four basic financial statements.

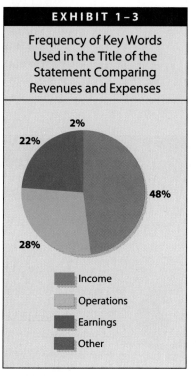

EXHIBIT 1–3

Frequency of Key Words Used in the Title of the Statement Comparing Revenues and Expenses

- Income
- Operations
- Earnings
- Other

Data Source: AICPA, *Accounting Trends and Techniques,* 1998.

---

[1]The Financial Accounting Standards Board is a privately funded organization with the primary authority for the establishment of accounting standards in the United States. The Board consists of seven full-time members appointed by the supporting organization, the Financial Accounting Foundation (FAF). The membership of the FAF is intended to represent the broad spectrum of individuals and institutions that have an interest in accounting and financial reporting. FAF members include representatives of the accounting profession, industry, financial institutions, the government, and the investing public.

[2]Net income is not specifically identified as an element of financial statements by the FASB. *Concepts Statement No. 6* uses a broader-based term, *comprehensive income.* However, the measurements associated with this term are not commonly found in accounting practice. In keeping with contemporary practice, this book uses the more common term, *net income.* Further, the book displays the traditional measurement techniques associated with the derivation of net income.

Elements of Financial Statements

As previously indicated, the ultimate objective of a business **enterprise** is to increase the wealth of its owners (i.e., to generate income). The economic resources a business employs to accomplish this objective are called **assets.** To increase the wealth of its owners, an enterprise must transform its existing assets into larger amounts of other assets. The existing resources (i.e., assets) are exchanged, used, or otherwise exhausted by an enterprise in its efforts to provide goods and services to consumers. Consumers reward a business by transferring cash or other assets to it in exchange for the goods and services that the enterprise provides. A business is profitable to the extent that it receives more assets from consumers than it uses to produce the goods and services it provides. Profitability permits the business to compensate the resource providers (i.e., owners and creditors).

Some common examples of business assets include equipment, buildings, land, patents, and mineral rights. Since the existing assets stand ready for transformation to larger amounts of other assets, they are said to represent *probable future economic benefits.* To be formally recognized in financial statements

focus on
international issues

Is There Global GAAP?

his chapter introduces the fact that financial reporting is a measurement and communication discipline based on a set of rules referred to as *generally accepted accounting principles.* Business students must be aware that the accounting rules that are the primary focus of this course are based on the GAAP of the United States. Not all economies throughout the world use the same accounting rules. Although there are many similarities among the GAAP used in different countries, there are major differences. There have been attempts to create international accounting standards, but individual countries have retained the authority to establish their own GAAP. Simply put, each country has its own GAAP; there is no single "global GAAP." Throughout this book, text examples of how financial reporting in other countries differ from those in the United States are presented.

Accounting rules differ among countries due to a variety of factors, including the economic and legal environments that exist in each country and how the GAAP in that country is established. Generally accepted accounting principles in the United States are primarily established by the Financial Accounting Standards Board (FASB). The FASB is a non-government rule-making body that was established by the accounting profession. In some countries, Germany and Japan, for example, the GAAP is established by government bodies. Thus, the establishment of GAAP in these countries is more like the way federal laws and regulations are established in the United States.

Furthermore, in the United States there is very little connection between GAAP established by the FASB and tax accounting regulations established by Congress and the Internal Revenue Service (IRS). As discussed in Chapter 8, in some countries there is a close connection between tax accounting rules and GAAP.

as an asset, (1) the potential economic benefit must be assignable to a particular **entity,**[3] and (2) the event giving rise to the assignment must have already occurred. For example, if a business owns a truck that was purchased in the past, the truck is an asset of the enterprise. However, a truck that a business *plans* to purchase in the future is not considered an asset of that business, no matter how certain the future purchase may be.

The assets of a business belong to the resource providers who are said to have **claims** on the assets. An expression of the relationship between the assets and the claims on those assets is known as the **accounting equation:**

L.O. 6

Grasp the relationships expressed in the accounting equation.

Assets = Claims

Since the creditors have first claim on the assets, the *owners* are said to have a **residual interest.** This means that in the case of a business liquidation, assets are distributed first to the creditors. If there are assets remaining after the creditors' claims have been settled, those residual assets are the property of the owners of the business. The following expression of the accounting equation recognizes the relationship among the assets, creditors' claims (called **liabilities**), and owners' claims (called **equity**).

Claims
$\overline{\hspace{4cm}}$
Assets = Liabilities + Equity

Since the liabilities represent claims on the assets, liabilities can also be viewed as *obligations of the enterprise.* When the obligations are settled in the future, the business probably will have to relinquish some of its assets (e.g., pay off its debts with cash), provide services to its creditors (e.g., work off its debts), or accept other obligations.

Algebraically, the amount of total assets minus total liabilities is equal to the *equity.* Since equity is equal to the net difference between the assets and the liabilities, it is also called **net assets.** Accordingly, *equity, net assets,* and *residual interest* are synonymous terms that represent the ownership interest in the business. The owners ultimately bear the risk of—and reap the rewards associated with—operating the business.

To illustrate, assume that Hagan Company has assets of $500, liabilities of $200, and equity of $300. These amounts appear in the accounting equation as follows:

Claims
$\overline{\hspace{5cm}}$
Assets = Liabilities + Equity

$500 = $200 + $300

Given the equality expressed in the accounting equation, the equity (i.e., net assets or residual interest) can be computed as follows:

Assets − Liabilities = Equity

$500 − $200 = $300

---

[3]An entity is a specific unit (i.e., individual, business, or institution) for which the accountant records and reports economic information; the boundaries of the accounting entity are distinct and separate from those of its owners, creditors, managers, and employees.

Accounting Events and Transactions

L.O. 7

Record business
events under
an accounting
equation.

An **accounting event** is an economic occurrence that causes changes in an enterprise's assets, liabilities, and/or equity. Events may be internal actions, such as using raw material or equipment for the production of goods or services. Events also may relate to external actions, such as an exchange of goods or services with another company. A **transaction** is a particular kind of event that involves the transfer of something of value between two entities. Examples of transactions include acquiring assets from owners, borrowing funds from creditors, and purchasing or selling goods and services. The following illustration explains how a company's assets, liabilities, and equity can be affected by several different types of accounting events and transactions.

The New Company Illustration— Events for 20X1

Event 1
Assets Acquired from
Owners

The illustration begins with the assumption that on January 1, 20X1,[4] a group of individuals pools its resources to form a business named *The New Company*. The business is formed when it acquires $10,000 cash (i.e., assets) from the owners. The effect of the acquisition on the accounting equation follows:

		Claims
	Assets	= Liabilities + Equity
Effect of Contribution	+$10,000 =	+ $10,000

L.O. 8

Classify business
events as being
asset source, use,
or exchange
transactions.

Notice that this single transaction is recorded twice, once as an asset and a second time as the source of that asset (i.e., equity). Every transaction is recorded at least twice. It is from this practice that the **double-entry bookkeeping** system derives its name. Since this transaction provided assets to the enterprise, it will be called an *asset source transaction*. Asset source transactions result in an increase in an asset account and an increase in one of the claims accounts.

Next, suppose that the enterprise acquires an additional $4,000 of assets by borrowing them from creditors. This transaction would also be classified as an asset source transaction. Its effect on the accounting equation is indicated. Note that the beginning balances are derived from the ending balances produced in the prior transaction. This practice will be followed throughout the illustration.

Event 2
Assets Acquired from
Creditors

		Claims	
	Assets =	Liabilities +	Equity
Beginning Balances	$10,000 =	$ 0	+ $10,000
Effect of Borrowing	+4,000	+4,000	
Ending Balances	$14,000 =	$4,000	+ $10,000

The claims on assets are frequently affected by the way that the business acquires its assets. For example, when a bank loans assets (e.g., money) to a business, it establishes a claim for the return of those assets at some future date.

---

[4]The X in the year 20X1 represents whatever decade the reader chooses to insert. The practice of substituting X for the decade in dates is followed throughout this text.

Accordingly, the right side of the accounting equation can be viewed as a list of the sources of assets as well as claims on those assets. In other words, the bank has a claim on the assets because it provided them to the business. As a result, in some circumstances, liabilities can be viewed as a source of assets.

When equity is viewed as a source of assets, it becomes necessary to subdivide the owner's interest into two separate components. First, an owner's claim is established when a business acquires assets from the owners. Since these claims result from the contributions of capital resources (i.e., assets) by the owners, they are frequently called **contributed capital.** The second source of assets that is associated with equity occurs when the business obtains assets through its earnings activities (i.e., the business acquires assets by working for them). Assets that have been earned by the business can be either distributed to the owners or retained in the business. Accordingly, **retained earnings** is a separate source of assets. This accounting equation describes the three sources of assets:

	Equity	
	Contributed	Retained
Assets = Liabilities +	Capital	+ Earnings

The *increase in assets* obtained from the process of providing customers with goods and services is called **revenue.** Accordingly, a revenue transaction can also be an asset source transaction. In this case, an asset account would increase, which would be balanced by an increase in the retained earnings section of equity. To illustrate the effects of revenue on the accounting equation, assume that the enterprise received $7,000 in exchange for services that it provided to its customers. The increase in assets is balanced by an increase in equity (i.e., retained earnings), as shown in the following equation:

Event 3
Assets Acquired through Operations

			Equity	
			Contributed	Retained
	Assets = Liabilities +		Capital	+ Earnings
Beginning Balances	$14,000 = $4,000	+	$10,000	+ $ 0
Effect of Revenue	+ 7,000			+ 7,000
Ending Balances	$21,000 = $4,000	+	$10,000	+ $7,000

Normally, a business consumes some of its assets in the process of trying to obtain more amounts of other assets. The assets acquired by operating activities are called *revenues;* the assets used in the process of generating the revenues are called **expenses.** Since the owners bear the ultimate risk and reap the rewards of operating the business, revenues act to increase equity (i.e., retained earnings), and expenses act to decrease retained earnings. To illustrate the effects of expense transactions on the accounting equation, assume that The New Company had been required to use $4,500 of its assets to earn the $7,000 of revenue shown in the prior transaction. The effect of this *asset use* transaction on the accounting equation is as follows:

Event 4
Assets Used to Produce Revenue (Expense)

L.O. 8

Classify business events as being asset source, use, or exchange transactions.

			Equity	
			Contributed	Retained
	Assets = Liabilities +		Capital	+ Earnings
Beginning Balances	$21,000 = $4,000	+	$10,000	+ $7,000
Effect of Expense	(4,500)			(4,500)
Ending Balances	$16,500 = $4,000	+	$10,000	+ $2,500

Notice that the enterprise's *net assets* have increased by $2,500 (that is, $7,000 revenue − $4,500 expense) as a result of its operating activities. Since the risks and rewards of operating a business rest with its owners, the owners are entitled to claim ownership of these additional assets. The enterprise can choose to leave the additional assets in the business or transfer them to the owners. If the business chooses to transfer some or all of the additional assets to the owners, the transfer is called a **distribution.** To illustrate the effects of a distribution, assume that The New Company distributes $1,500 of assets to its owners. The effect on the accounting equation is as follows:

				Equity	
	Assets	= Liabilities +		Contributed Capital	Retained + Earnings
Beginning Balances	$16,500 =	$4,000	+	$10,000	+ $2,500
Effect of Distribution	(1,500)				(1,500)
Ending Balances	$15,000 =	$4,000	+	$10,000	+ $1,000

Note that a distribution and an expense have the same effect on the accounting equation. Both reflect a decrease in assets that triggers a corresponding decrease in equity (i.e., retained earnings). The difference between expenses and distributions results from the cause of the decline in assets. An expense is recognized when assets decline because of a firm's efforts to earn revenue. A distribution occurs when asset declines are caused by transfers of wealth to the owners. In summary, *expenses* are incurred to produce revenue, and *distributions* are made for the satisfaction of the owners.

Summary of Transactions

The following table is a summary of the effects of the three asset source transactions (i.e., Event Nos. 1 through 3) and the two asset use transactions (Event Nos. 4 and 5) on the accounting equation. As indicated earlier, accounting information is normally presented to external users in four general-purpose financial statements. The data in the table are color coded to facilitate your understanding of the source of information used to prepare financial statements. The numbers in *green* are used in the *statement of cash flows* to define the net change in cash that occurs during an accounting period. The numbers in *red* are used to prepare the *balance sheet.* Finally, the numbers in *blue* are used to prepare the *income statement.* The numbers appearing in the statement of changes in equity have not been color coded because they appear in more than one statement. The next section explains how the information in the table is used to prepare financial statements.

Event No.		Assets	= Liabilities +	Equity	
				Contributed Capital	Retained + Earnings
	Beginning Balances	$ 0	$ 0	$ 0	$ 0
1	Effect of Contribution	+10,000		+10,000	
2	Effect of Borrowing	+ 4,000	+4,000		
3	Effect of Revenue	+ 7,000			+7,000
4	Effect of Expense	(4,500)			(4,500)
5	Effect of Distribution	(1,500)			(1,500)
	Ending Balances	$15,000 =	$ 4,000 +	$ 10,000	+ $ 1,000

Elements Presented in Financial Statements

L.O. 4

Identify, describe, and prepare the four basic financial statements.

The *income statement, statement of changes in equity,* and *statement of cash flows* provide unique perspectives on the performance of the enterprise *during some designated period.* The fourth statement, the *balance sheet,* provides information regarding the financial condition of the enterprise *at some designated time.*

Income Statement

The **income statement** measures the difference between the asset increases and the asset decreases associated with running the business.[5] The asset increase resulting from the operating activities was labeled *revenue.* The asset decrease was called an *expense.* If revenues are greater than expenses, the difference between these two elements is called **net income.** If the expenses exceed the revenues, the difference is referred to as a **net loss.** Accordingly, net income indicates that the company's net assets increased as a result of operating activities; a net loss shows that net assets declined. The income statement for The New Company appears as follows:

Observe the use of the terminology *for the period ended 20X1* in the income statement. Income is measured over some period. The customary length of the **accounting period** is 1 year. While 1 year is normal, it is not required. Indeed, income can be measured weekly, monthly, quarterly, semiannually, or over any other time period that the users deem appropriate in relation to their needs for information.

The New Company Income Statement For the Period Ended 20X1	
Revenue (i.e., *asset increase*)	$7,000
Expense (i.e., *asset decrease*)	(4,500)
Net Income (i.e., *change in net assets*)	$2,500

Statement of Changes in Equity

The **statement of changes in equity** is used to explain the effects of transactions on equity during the accounting period. It includes the beginning and ending balances for the amount of contributed capital and reflects any new capital acquisitions made during the accounting period. It also shows the portion of the net earnings retained in the business. Note that the amounts of distributions are reflected on this statement. Recall that distributions are different from expenses. *Distributions are wealth transfers.* They are made for the satisfaction of the owners. *In contrast, expenses are economic sacrifices incurred for the production of revenue.* They are therefore matched with revenue on the income statement to determine the amount of net

The New Company Statement of Changes in Equity For the Period Ended 20X1		
Beginning Contributed Capital	$ 0	
Plus: Capital Acquisition	10,000	
Ending Contributed Capital		$10,000
Beginning Retained Earnings	0	
Plus: Net Income	2,500	
Less: Distributions	(1,500)	
Ending Retained Earnings		1,000
Total Equity		$11,000

---

[5]This explanation of the income statement is expanded in subsequent chapters as additional relationships among the elements of the financial statements are introduced.

income. Once net income has been determined, the company must decide whether to retain it or distribute it to the owners. The equity is increased by the amount of net income and is decreased by the amount of distributions. In other words, equity is increased by the amount of income that is retained in the business. Accordingly, net income and distributions appear on the statement of changes in equity. The statement of changes in equity for The New Company is on page 15.

Balance Sheet

The New Company Balance Sheet As of the End of the Period, 20X1		
Assets		$15,000
Liabilities		$ 4,000
Equity		
Contributed Capital	$10,000	
Retained Earnings	1,000	
Total Equity		11,000
Total Liabilities and Equity		$15,000

The statement that lists the assets and the corresponding claims on those assets is called the **balance sheet.** Logically, the assets are owned by some party. Accordingly, the assets must balance with (i.e., be equal to) the claims on them. The balance sheet for The New Company appears on the left. Note that the total claims (i.e., liabilities plus equity) are equal to the total assets. Also note that the terminology *as of the end of the period* used to date the balance sheet differs from the phrase *for the period ended* that was used to date the income statement and the statement of changes in equity. At any given time, a company has a specific amount of assets and claims on those assets. The balance sheet describes the financial condition of the company at a specific point in time (i.e., normally the end of the accounting period).

Statement of Cash Flows

The **statement of cash flows** explains how a company obtained and used cash during the accounting period (i.e., usually one year). The sources of cash are called *cash inflows*, and the uses are known as *cash outflows.* The statement classifies cash receipts (inflows) and payments (outflows) into three categories: financing activities, investing activities, and operating activities. The **financing activities** describe the cash transactions associated with the resource providers (i.e., owners and creditors). In other words, the financing activities section of the statement of cash flows explains where a business gets its money (i.e., cash inflows) and to what extent it returns cash to the resource providers (i.e., cash outflows). Once cash has been obtained through financing activities, a business turns its attention to investing the cash in assets that will be used in the process of providing goods and services to consumers. More specifically, **investing activities** include cash received or spent by the business on productive assets[6] and investments in the debt or equity of other companies.[7] In general, the **operating activities** section of the statement of cash flows explains the cash generated through revenue and the cash

---

[6]Productive assets are those assets an enterprise holds for use in the production of goods and services. They are sometimes called *long-term assets* because they are used in operating activities that span several accounting periods. For example, cash outflows for the purchase of land or cash inflows from the sale of a building would go into the investing activities section of the cash flow statement because they are cash flows associated with long-term productive assets. In contrast, cash spent for the purchase of supplies would go in the operating section because the supplies represent short-term assets that would generally be used within a single accounting period.

[7]Investments in the debt or equity of other companies include cash that is loaned to another company or cash that is given in exchange for an ownership interest in another company.

spent for expenses. *Note that the classification of a cash flow depends on the activity of the business rather than on the type of element being considered.* For example, money loaned is included in investing activities, but cash borrowed goes in the financing activities section. The primary cash inflows and outflows associated with each type of business activity are shown in Exhibit 1–4.

The New Company Statement of Cash Flows For the Period Ended 20X1		
Cash Flows from Operating Activities		
Cash Receipts from Revenue	$ 7,000	
Cash Payments for Expenses	(4,500)	
Net Cash Flow from Operating Activities		$2,500
Cash Flows from Investing Activities		0
Cash Flow from Financing Activities		
Cash Receipts from Borrowed Funds	4,000	
Cash Receipts from Capital Acquisitions	10,000	
Cash Payments for Distributions	(1,500)	
Net Cash Flow from Financing Activities		12,500
Net Increase in Cash		15,000
Plus: Beginning Cash Balance		0
Ending Cash Balance		$15,000

The statement of cash flows for The New Company appears at right.

The statement of cash flows explains the change between the beginning and ending cash balances during the accounting period. In this case, the amount of cash increased by $15,000 during the period. The beginning balance in the Cash account was zero; adding the $15,000 increase results in a $15,000 ending balance. Notice that this amount is consistent with the amount of cash shown on the December 31 year-end balance sheet.

Completing the Cycle

Accounting is a cyclical activity. This means that once all the activities are completed for a given period, a new period starts and the accounting activities are repeated during that period. The process continues for as long as the accounting entity exists. The information for balance sheet items (i.e., assets, liabilities, contributed capital, and retained earnings) is cumulative. Accordingly, last period's ending balances become next period's beginning balances. Since The New Company had $15,000 of assets at the end of the first accounting period, it will begin the second accounting cycle with $15,000 of assets. Because of their continuing nature, the balance sheet accounts are sometimes called **permanent accounts.**

In contrast, revenue, expense, and distribution accounts are **temporary accounts** that are used to collect information about a single accounting period. Data are not permitted to accumulate in these accounts. Because of their temporary nature, these accounts are referred to as **nominal accounts.** At the end of the

EXHIBIT 1–4			
Classification Scheme for Cash Inflows and Outflows			
	Type of Activity		
	Financing	**Investing**	**Operating**
Cash Inflows from	(1) Creditors (2) Owners	(1) Sale of Long-Term Assets* (2) Collections of Loans	(1) Collections of Revenue
Cash Outflows for	(1) Repayment of Debt (2) Distributions to Owners	(1) Purchase of Long-Term Assets* (2) Loans to Debtors	(1) Payments for Expenses

*Long-term assets include productive assets and long-term investments in the equity of other companies.

accounting period, amounts in the revenue, expense, and distributions accounts are transferred to Retained Earnings, which is a summary account that contains all cumulative data regarding the nominal accounts from the company's inception. Accordingly, the revenue, expense, and distribution accounts have zero balances at the beginning of each accounting period. The process of transferring the balances from the nominal accounts to the permanent account, Retained Earnings, is called **closing the accounts.**

<table>
<tr><td>

L.O. 7

Record business events under an accounting equation.

</td><td>

The New Company Illustration— Events for 20X2

To demonstrate the cyclical nature of the accounting process, assume that The New Company experienced the following events during the company's second accounting period (i.e., second cycle). Assume that all transactions involve the payment or receipt of cash.

</td></tr>
</table>

Event 1–6

1. The business purchased a plot of land costing $14,000.
2. The business acquired an additional $5,000 from the owners.
3. The business borrowed an additional $2,000 from creditors.
4. The business provided services to customers and received $8,200.
5. The business paid $4,900 for operating expenses.
6. The business distributed $1,100 of cash to the owners.

<table>
<tr><td>

L.O. 8

Classify business events as being asset source, use, or exchange transactions.

</td><td>

Before we review the effect of these transactions on the accounting equation, note that the first transaction is a new type of transaction. It is neither an asset source transaction nor an asset use transaction. It is instead an *asset exchange* transaction. One asset, *cash*, decreased and another asset, *land*, increased. The amount of total assets remains unchanged. This transaction also demonstrates the need for specific subclassifications called *accounts*. The balance sheet now shows two accounts (cash and land) under the classification known as *assets*. The effects of the six transactions on the accounting equation are shown below. Again, the items have been color coded, with green amounts appearing in the cash statement, red amounts appearing on the balance sheet, and blue items appearing on the income statement.

</td></tr>
</table>

	Assets			=	Liabilities	+	Equity		
	Cash	+	Land	=	Liabilities	+	Contributed Capital	+	Retained Earnings
Beginning Balances	$15,000			=	$4,000	+	$10,000	+	$1,000
Effect of Asset Exchange	(14,000)		$14,000						
Effect of Capital Acquisition	5,000						5,000		
Effect of Borrowing	2,000				2,000				
Effect of Revenue	8,200								8,200
Effect of Expense	(4,900)								(4,900)
Effect of Distribution	(1,100)								(1,100)
Ending Balances	$10,200	+	$14,000	=	$6,000	+	$15,000	+	$3,200

an **answer** for the curious accountant

Anyone who owns "stock" in Coca-Cola owns a part of the company. Coke has many owners. In contrast, nobody actually owns the American Cancer Society (ACS). The ACS has a board of directors that is responsible for overseeing its operations, but the board is not the owner.

Ultimately, the purpose of a business entity is to increase the wealth of its owners. To this end, it "spends money to make money." The expense that Coke incurs for cola beans is a cost incurred in the hope that it will generate revenues when its beverages are sold. The financial statements of a business show, among other things, if and how the company made a profit during the current year.

The ACS is a "not-for-profit" entity. It operates to provide services to society at large, not to make a profit. It cannot increase the wealth of its owners because it has no owners. When the ACS spends money on research to find the cause of cancer, it does not spend this money in the expectation that it will generate "revenues." The revenues of the ACS come from contributors who wish to support efforts related to reducing cancer. Because the ACS does not spend money to make money, there is no reason for it to prepare an *income statement* like that of Coke.

Not-for-profit entities do prepare financial statements that are similar in appearance to those of commercial enterprises. The financial statements of not-for-profit entities are called the *statement of financial position*, the *statement of activities*, and a *cash flow statement*.

Financial Statements for 20X2

The financial statements for 20X2 follow. Notice that the amounts of revenue and expense shown on the income statement were earned only in 20X2. Revenue and expense items that pertain to 20X1 have been transferred to Retained Earnings through the closing process. Accordingly, the beginning balances in these accounts were zero. In contrast, the amounts in the balance sheet accounts contain cumulative information. For example, the ending cash balance was determined by adding the current period data (that is, 20X2) to the beginning cash balance.

L.O. 4

Identify, describe, and prepare the four basic financial statements.

The New Company Income Statement For the Period Ended 20X2	
Revenue (i.e., *asset increase*)	$8,200
Expense (i.e., *asset decrease*)	(4,900)
Net Income (i.e., *change in net assets*)	$3,300

The New Company Statement of Changes in Equity For the Period Ended 20X2		
Beginning Contributed Capital	$10,000	
Plus: Capital Acquisition	5,000	
Ending Contributed Capital		$15,000
Beginning Retained Earnings	1,000	
Plus: Net Income	3,300	
Less: Distributions	(1,100)	
Ending Retained Earnings		3,200
Total Equity		$18,200

The New Company Balance Sheet As of the End of the Period, 20X2		
Assets		
Cash	$10,200	
Land	14,000	
Total Assets		$24,200
Liabilities		$6,000
Equity		
Contributed Capital	$15,000	
Retained Earnings	3,200	
Total Equity		18,200
Total Liabilities and Equity		$24,200

Note the order of the assets in the balance sheet. Cash appears first, followed by the land account. Assets are displayed in the balance sheet in accordance with their level of **liquidity.** This means that assets are listed in order of how rapidly they will be converted to cash.

As previously indicated, the financing activities section describes transactions with the resource providers. Cash inflow was received from creditors (that is, $2,000) and owners (that is, $5,000). Also, a $1,100 cash distribution was paid to the owners. A new item is in the investing activities section of the cash flows statement. This section shows that the company used some of its cash ($14,000) to invest in the purchase of land. Finally, the operating activities section shows that more cash was received ($8,200) than was spent ($4,900) in the process of operating the business. The net result was a $3,300 cash inflow from operating activities. The beginning cash balance of $15,000 minus the 20X2 net decrease of $4,800 explains the ending cash balance of $10,200.

The New Company Statement of Cash Flows For the Period Ended 20X2		
Cash Flows from Operating Activities		
Cash Receipts from Revenue	$8,200	
Cash Payments for Expenses	(4,900)	
Net Cash Flow from Operating Activities		$ 3,300
Cash Flows from Investing Activities		
Cash Payment for Land		(14,000)
Cash Flows from Financing Activities		
Cash Receipts from Creditors	2,000	
Cash Receipts from Capital Acquisitions	5,000	
Cash Payments for Distributions	(1,100)	
Net Cash Flow from Financing Activities		5,900
Net Decrease in Cash		(4,800)
Plus: Beginning Cash Balance		15,000
Ending Cash Balance		$10,200

Use of the Financial Statements Model

Financial statements are the scorecard of business activity. If you want to succeed in business, you must know how your actions affect your company's financial statements. The most efficient way to learn how events affect financial statements is to create a model that enables you to visualize all the statements simultaneously on a single sheet of paper. The simultaneous display of a set of financial statements is henceforth called a **statements model.** Statements models can be presented in two different formats: a *vertical model* and a *horizontal model.*

L.O. 9

Record business events in financial statements models.

Vertical Statements Model

As its name implies, the **vertical statements model** arranges a full set of financial statements on a single page, with account titles arranged in a vertical pattern from the top to the bottom of the page. The income statement is presented first. The statement of changes in equity is shown below the income statement. The balance sheet is presented directly below the statement of changes in equity. Finally, the statement of cash flows is shown directly below the balance sheet. The 20X1 and 20X2 financial statements for The New Company are illustrated in the vertical statements model in Exhibit 1–5.

The vertical model enables you to visualize several important interrelationships among the financial statements over the two accounting cycles. Notice how the amount of net income is transferred to the statement of changes in equity, where it becomes part of the computation of the amount of ending retained earnings. The ending retained earnings is then shown on the balance sheet. By

EXHIBIT 1-5

Vertical Statements Model

The New Company
Financial Statements

	For the Years	
	20X1	**20X2**
Income Statements		
Revenue (Cash)	$ 7,000	$ 8,200
Expense (Cash)	(4,500)	(4,900)
Net Income (Loss)	$ 2,500	$ 3,300
Statements of Changes in Equity		
Beginning Contributed Capital	$ 0	$10,000
Plus: Contributions	10,000	5,000
Ending Contributed Capital	10,000	15,000
Beginning Retained Earnings	0	1,000
Plus: Net Income (Loss)	2,500	3,300
Less: Distributions	(1,500)	(1,100)
Ending Retained Earnings	1,000	3,200
Total Equity	$11,000	$18,200
Balance Sheets		
Assets		
Cash	$15,000	$10,200
Land	0	14,000
Total Assets	$15,000	$24,200
Liabilities	$ 4,000	$ 6,000
Equity		
Contributed Capital	10,000	15,000
Retained Earnings	1,000	3,200
Total Equity	11,000	18,200
Total Liabilities and Equity	$15,000	$24,200
Statements of Cash Flows		
Cash Flows from Operating Activities		
Cash Receipts from Revenue	$ 7,000	$ 8,200
Cash Payments for Expenses	(4,500)	(4,900)
Net Cash Flows from Operating Activities	2,500	3,300
Cash Flows from Investing Activities		
Cash Payments for Land	0	(14,000)
Cash Flows from Financing Activities		
Cash Receipts from Borrowed Funds	4,000	2,000
Cash Receipts from Capital Acquisition	10,000	5,000
Cash Payments for Distributions	(1,500)	(1,100)
Net Cash Flows from Financing Activities	12,500	5,900
Net Change in Cash	15,000	(4,800)
Plus: Beginning Cash Balance	0	15,000
Ending Cash Balance	$15,000	$10,200

tracing these relationships, you can see how net income acts to increase retained earnings. Also observe how last year's ending balances become this year's beginning balances. For example, the 20X1 ending balance in the retained earnings account ($1,000) becomes the beginning balance for 20X2. Finally, notice how the ending cash balance on the balance sheet is validated by the computations shown in the statement of cash flows. Specifically, the net change in cash is added to the beginning cash balance to produce the ending cash balance.

Horizontal Statements Model

The **horizontal statements model** is so named because it arranges a set of financial statements horizontally across a single page of paper. This model is extremely useful in analyzing the effects of a single event on the financial statements. The balance sheet is presented first, followed by the income statement, and then the statement of cash flows. Because of limited space and the fact that the effects of equity transactions can be analyzed by referring to the balance sheet, the statement of changes in equity is not included in the horizontal statements model. The statement of cash flows uses abbreviations. For example, activity classifications are identified with a simple two-letter designation. Cash flow from operating activities is identified with the capital letters OA. The letters IA designate investing activities, and FA identifies financing activities. Finally, NC designates the net change in cash flow. The model used in this chapter follows.

Balance Sheet	Income Statement	Statement of Cash Flows
Assets = Liabilities + Equity	Revenue − Expense = Net Income	

The background of the *balance sheet* is in red, that of the *income statement* is in blue, and that of the *statement of cash flows* is in green. To demonstrate the usefulness of the horizontal statements model, we will apply it to four accounting events discussed extensively in this chapter. To maximize your understanding, draw a statements model on a piece of paper and try to record the effects of each event before you look at the explanation provided. Assume that during a single accounting period, a business (1) borrows $6,000 cash, (2) pays $5,000 cash to purchase land, (3) leases the land for $1,000 cash, and (4) pays $600 cash for expenses. The effects of these transactions on the financial statements follow. The letters n/a indicate that the element is not affected by the event.

Event No.	Balance Sheet											Income Statement								Statement of Cash Flows	
	Cash	+	Land	=	L. Pay	+	Ret. Earn.					Rev.	−	Exp.	=	Net Inc.					
1	6,000	+	n/a	=	6,000	+	n/a					n/a	−	n/a	=	n/a				6,000	FA
2	(5,000)	+	5,000	=	n/a	+	n/a					n/a	−	n/a	=	n/a				(5,000)	IA
3	1,000	+	n/a	=	n/a	+	1,000					1,000	−	n/a	=	1,000				1,000	OA
4	(600)	+	n/a	=	n/a	+	(600)					n/a	−	600	=	(600)				(600)	OA
Totals	1,400	+	5,000	=	6,000	+	400					1,000	−	600	=	400				1,400	NC

With respect to Event No. 1, it is clear that borrowing cash affects the balance sheet and statement of cash flows but does not affect the income

Not-for-Profit
©Doug Armand/
Tony Stone World-
wide, Ltd.

statement. Furthermore, you can see that assets and liabilities increase and that the cash inflow is defined as a financing activity. Event No. 2 affects the same statements as Event No. 1, but Event No. 2 affects different elements on those statements. Event No. 2 is an asset exchange transaction. As such, it does not affect liabilities or equity on the balance sheet. Notice that Event No. 3 affects all three financial statements. On the balance sheet, assets and equity increase. The recognition of revenue causes net income to increase, and the cash inflow is shown as an operating activity on the statement of cash flows. Finally, Event No. 4 is an asset use transaction. The event acts to reduce assets and equity. Likewise, the recognition of the cash expense acts to decrease net income and cash flow from operating activities. Do not be discouraged if these relationships are somewhat difficult to grasp. The statements are new to you, but you will gain proficiency with practice.

The statements models are presented for instructional purposes. They are very helpful in understanding how accounting events affect financial statements. Accordingly, statements models are used extensively in this book. However, note that the models do not represent presentation formats that appear in accounting practice. For example, although a full set of four financial statements is normally presented in published financial statements, the horizontal model shows only a partial set of statements. Similarly, the vertical instructional model may vary in form and content, depending on the learning task. Also, since the statements are presented in aggregate, the description of dates (i.e., *as of* versus *for the period ended*) cannot be used to distinguish periodic from cumulative data.

Merchandising/ Service
©Amy C. Etra/Photo
Edit

Real-World Financial Reports

Real-World Complications

Organizations exist in many different forms. As previously indicated, two major classifications include *business* and *not-for-profit* entities. Business entities can be further subdivided into three categories: service organizations, merchandising businesses, and manufacturing companies. As the name implies, **service organizations** provide services to consumers. Examples of service businesses include doctors, attorneys, accountants, dry cleaners, and maids. **Merchandising businesses** are sometimes called retail or wholesale companies. They sell goods other entities make. **Manufacturing companies** make the goods that they sell to their customers. Some businesses include combinations of these three categories. For example, an automotive repair shop may change oil (service function), sell parts such as oil filters (retail function), and rebuild engines or other parts (manufacturing function).

The nature of the reporting entity affects the form and content of the information contained in an organization's financial statements. For example, not-for-profit entities prepare statements of revenues, expenditures, and changes in fund equity; business entities produce income statements. Similarly, income statements of retail companies show an expense item called *cost of goods sold,* but service companies that do not sell goods have no such item in their income statements. Organizations normally provide information, including financial statements, to *stakeholders* yearly in a document known as an **annual report. Stakeholders** are parties that are interested in the operations of an organization. Examples of stakeholders include owners, creditors, employees, suppliers, customers, and governmental agencies.

Manufacturing
©Jim Pickerall/Tony
Stone Worldwide, Lt.d

Annual Report for Gateway 2000

Appendix B is the 1997 *annual report* for Gateway 2000, Inc. The report contains the company's financial statements (see pages 23–26 of the report). Immediately following the statements are footnotes that provide more detailed information about the items described in the statements (see pages 27–32). In addition to financial statements, the annual report contains the *auditor's report*, discussed in Chapter 2. A company's annual report also includes written commentary that describes management's assessment of significant events that affected the company during the reporting period. This section of the report, called *management discussion and analysis* (MD&A), is explained in Chapter 4.

Gateway Computers
AP SIOUX CITY
JOURNAL

Special Terms for Corporations

When looking at the equity section of the Gateway 2000 balance sheet (see page 24 of the annual report), you will encounter new terminology. Specifically, the equity section is called *stockholders' equity* and the terms *common stock* and *preferred stock* are used to identify the amount of contributed capital. There are several forms of business organization, discussed in detail in a later chapter. Each form of business uses different terminology in the equity section of its balance sheet. At this point, simply be aware that Gateway 2000 is a corporation. Corporations may be owned by many individuals. When individuals contribute assets to the business, they are given a special receipt known as a *stock certificate.* Stock certificates describe the rights of ownership. Accordingly, owners of corporations are frequently called *stockholders* and the investments that they make in the business are labeled as *stock* on the books of the corporation. Depending on the nature of the owner's investment, the stock may be labeled as preferred or common. These terms are discussed more fully in Chapter 11.

Unusual Items on the Income Statement

When you are making business decisions, it helps to know whether a company's future earnings (i.e., net income) will increase, decrease, or remain constant. Suppose that a company owns a manufacturing plant that was destroyed in an earthquake. Should the loss from earthquake damage be treated the same as a continuing expense, such as salaries? Most accountants agree that unusual items should be shown separately on the financial statements to alert users to the fact that such items are not useful in predicting future earnings since they are not likely to recur. As a result, financial statements show a separate "income" figure that excludes the effects of special items. The income amount that excludes effects of unusual items is called *income from continuing operations* or *operating income.* Unusual items are then added or subtracted from the amount of income from continuing operations to arrive at the *net income* figure.

A company may have to show three types of unusual items separately from the income from continuing operations. The first relates to **discontinued operations,** which occur when a company is discontinuing a major part of its business. Usually, the company sells the part of the business that is discontinued to another company. The second type of unusual item is called an *extraordinary item.* These are events that occurred during the year that are both *unusual in nature and infrequent.* Because they are not likely to happen again anytime soon to a particular company, their effects are shown separately from those of continuing operations. The last type of unusual item results from a **change in accounting principle.** As later chapters of this textbook discuss, companies often have the

EXHIBIT 1–6

Waste Management, Inc. and Subsidiaries
Consolidated Statement of Income
For the Year Ended December 31, 1997
(000s omitted except per share amounts)

Revenue	$ 9,188,582
Operating Expenses	7,195,376
Special Charges	145,990
Asset Impairment Loss	1,480,262
Selling and Administrative Expenses	1,129,237
Interest Expense	446,888
Interest Income	(37,580)
Minority Interest	45,442
Income (loss) from Continuing Operations Held for Sale, Net of Minority Interest	9,930
Sundry Income, Net	(173,290)
Income (loss) from Continuing Operations before Income Taxes	(1,053,673)
Provision for Income Taxes	215,667
Income (loss) from Continuing Operations	(1,269,340)
Discontinued Operations	
Income (loss) On Disposal or from Reserve Adjustment, Net of Applicable Income Taxes and Minority Interest of $100,842	95,688
Income (loss) before Extraordinary Item and Cumulative Effect of Changes in Accounting Principles	(1,173,652)
Tax Benefit and Minority Interest of $767	(516)
Cumulative Effect of Changes in Accounting Principles, Net of Tax Benefit of $1,100	(1,936)
Net Income (loss)	$(1,176,104)
Earnings (loss) per Share	
Continuing Operations	$ (2.72)
Discontinued Operations	0.20
Extraordinary Item	—
Cumulative Effect of Changes in Accounting Principles	—
Net Income (loss)	$ (2.52)

The accompanying notes are an integral part of these statements.

option of measuring an accounting event in more than one way. When a company changes from one method of measurement to another, special disclosure of a change in accounting principle on the income statement is usually required. Exhibit 1–6 contains the income statements that were included in the 1997 annual report of Waste Management, Inc. These statements demonstrate the diversity of unusual items that may appear in real-world reports.

As the previous discussion suggests, the financial statements of real-world companies contain numerous items relating to advanced topics that are not covered in introductory accounting textbooks, especially the first chapter of an introductory accounting textbook. Do not let this discourage you from browsing through real-world annual reports. Indeed, your learning will significantly improve if you look at many annual reports and attempt to identify all the items that your current knowledge permits. As your academic knowledge grows, most likely you will experience a corresponding increase in interest in real-world financial reports and the business practices that they describe. We encourage you to look up annual reports in your local library or ask your employer for a copy of your company's financial statements. Truly, the best way to learn accounting is to become involved. Look at accounting information, and ask questions about things that you do not understand. Accounting is the language of business. Learning the language will serve you well in almost any area of business that you pursue.

A LOOK
BACK

This chapter discussed the role of accounting in society and business. Accounting's role is to provide information that facilitates the ability to operate and evaluate organizational performance. Accounting is a measurement discipline. To facilitate communication, it is necessary to attain agreement on the rules of measurement. **Generally accepted accounting principles (GAAP)** constitute the set of rules used by the accounting profession to promote consistency in financial reporting. GAAP is a work in progress that will continue to evolve.

The chapter has described and discussed eight elements of financial statements including *assets, liabilities, equity, contributed capital, revenue, expenses, distributions,* and *net income.* The elements represent broad classifications of information that appear on financial statements. Four basic financial statements appear in public reports: the *balance sheet,* the *income statement,* the *statement of changes in equity,* and the *statement of cash flows.* The chapter discussed the form and content of each statement as well as the interrelationships among the statements.

This chapter introduced a *horizontal financial statements model* as a tool to facilitate your understanding of how business events affect a set of articulated financial statements. This model will be used throughout the text. Accordingly, you should carefully study this model before proceeding to Chapter 2.

A LOOK
FORWARD

To keep matters simple and to focus attention on the interrelationships among financial statements, this chapter considered only cash events. Obviously, many events in the real world do not involve an immediate cash exchange. An example of a noncash event is a customer's use of telephone service throughout the month without paying for it until the end of the month. As mentioned briefly in this chapter, events such as this are called *accruals.* Understanding the effects that accrual events have on the financial statements is the subject of Chapter 2.

KEY TERMS

Account   A record used for the classification and summary of transaction data.   *(p. 9)*

Accounting   A service-based profession that provides reliable and relevant financial information useful in making decisions.   *(p. 6)*

Accounting Equation   An expression of the relationship between the assets and the claims on those assets.   *(p. 11)*

Accounting Event   An economic occurrence that causes changes in an enterprise's assets, liabilities, and/or equity.   *(p. 12)*

Accounting Period   The span of time covered by the financial statements, normally 1 year. However, statements are also prepared semiannually, quarterly, and monthly, each of which could constitute an accounting period.   *(p. 15)*

Annual Report   The document in which an organization provides information to stockholders, usually on an annual basis.   *(p. 24)*

Asset   An economic resource used by a business for the production of revenue.   *(p. 10)*

Balance Sheet   The statement that lists the assets of a business and the corresponding claims (i.e., liabilities and equity) on those assets.   *(p. 16)*

Change in Accounting Principle   A change in the option an organization uses for measurement.   *(p. 25)*

Claims   The owners' and creditors' interests in a business's assets.   *(p. 11)*

Closing the Accounts   The process of transferring balances from nominal accounts to the permanent account, Retained Earnings.   *(p. 18)*

Contributed Capital   The balance sheet term used to designate the portion of assets contributed to a business by its owners.   *(p. 13)*

Creditor   An individual or institution that has loaned goods or services to a business.   *(p. 5)*

Demand   Consumer preferences expressed by offering money for goods or services.   *(p. 4)*

Discontinued Operations   Operations of a company that are discontinued.   *(p. 25)*

Distribution   A transfer of wealth from a business to its owners.   *(p. 14)*

Double-Entry Bookkeeping   A method of keeping records that provides a system of checks and balances by recording transactions in a dual format.   *(p. 12)*

Elements   The primary components of financial statements, including assets, liabilities, equity, contributions, revenue, expenses, distributions, and net income.   *(p. 9)*

Enterprise   A business organization designed to undertake activity directed toward the generation of profit.   *(p. 10)*

Entity   A specific unit (individual, business, or institution) for which the accountant records and reports economic information; its boundaries are distinct and separate from those of the owners, creditors, managers, and employees.   *(p. 11)*

Equity   The portion of the assets remaining after the creditors' claims have been satisfied (i.e., Assets − Liabilities = Equity); also called *residual interest* or *net assets*.   *(p. 11)*

Expenses   Assets used in the process of generating revenues.   *(p. 13)*

Financial Accounting   Accounting information designed to satisfy the needs of an organization's external users, including business owners, creditors, and government agencies.   *(p. 6)*

Financial Accounting Standards Board (FASB)   A privately funded organization with the primary authority for the establishment of accounting standards in the United States.   *(p. 9)*

Financial Resources   Money or credit arrangements supplied to a business by investors (owners) and creditors.   *(p. 5)*

Financial Statements   The primary means of communicating the financial information of an organization to the external users. The four general-purpose financial statements are the (1) income statement, (2) statement of changes in equity, (3) balance sheet, and (4) statement of cash flows.   *(p. 9)*

Financing Activities   One of the three categories of cash inflows and outflows shown on the statement of cash flows. Financing activities are cash transactions associated with owners and creditors. This category of cash activities shows the amount of cash provided by these resource providers and the amount of cash that is returned to them.   *(p. 16)*

Generally Accepted Accounting Principles (GAAP)   The rules and regulations that accountants agree to follow when preparing financial reports for public distribution.   *(p. 8)*

Horizontal Statements Model   The arrangement of a set of financial statements horizontally across a sheet of paper.   *(p. 23)*

Income   The added value created in transforming resources into more desirable states.   *(p. 4)*

Income Statement   A statement that measures the difference between the asset increases and the asset decreases associated with running a business. This definition is expanded in subsequent chapters as additional relationships among the elements of the financial statements are introduced.   *(p. 15)*

Investing Activities   One of the three categories of cash inflows and outflows shown on the statement of cash flows. Investing activities include cash received and spent by the business on productive assets and investments in the debt and equity of other companies.   *(p. 16)*

Labor Resources   Both intellectual and physical labor used in the process of converting goods and services to products of greater value.   *(p. 6)*

Liabilities   Obligations of a business to relinquish assets, provide services, or accept other obligations.   *(p. 11)*

Liquidity   The ability to convert assets to cash.   *(p. 20)*

Managerial Accounting   The branch of accounting that provides information useful in operating an organization. This information is useful to internal decision makers and managers.   *(p. 6)*

Manufacturing Companies   Makers of goods that are sold to customers.   *(p. 24)*

Market   A gathering of people or organizations for the purpose of buying and selling resources.   *(p. 4)*

Merchandising Businesses   Sellers of goods that other entities make.   *(p. 24)*

Net Assets   The portion of the assets remaining after the creditors' claims have been satisfied (i.e., Assets − Liabilities = Net Assets). This element is also called *equity* or *residual interest*.   *(p. 11)*

Net Income   An increase in net assets resulting from operating activities.   *(p. 15)*

Net Loss   A decrease in net assets resulting from operating activities.   *(p. 15)*

Nominal Accounts   Accounts that contain information applicable to a single accounting period. These accounts are sometimes called *temporary accounts*.   *(p. 18)*

Not-for-Profit Entities   Organizations (also called *nonprofit* or *nonbusiness entities*) whose primary motive is something other than making a profit. These motives may be to provide goods and services for the social good. Examples of not-for-profit entities include state-supported universities and colleges, hospitals, public libraries, and public charities.   *(p. 7)*

Operating Activities   One of the three categories of cash inflows and outflows that is shown on the statement of cash flows. Operating activities show the amount of cash generated by revenue and the amount of cash spent for expenses.   *(p. 16)*

Permanent Accounts   Accounts that contain information transferred from one accounting period to the next.   *(p. 17)*

Physical Resources   Natural resources that are used in the transformation process to create resources of more value.   *(p. 6)*

Profit   The value created by transforming goods and services to more desirable states.   *(p. 4)*

Residual Interest   The portion of the assets remaining after the creditors' claims have been satisfied (i.e., Assets − Liabilities = Residual Interest). This element is also called *equity* or *net assets*.   *(p. 11)*

Retained Earnings   The increase in equity that results from the retention of assets obtained through the operation of the business.   *(p. 13)*

Revenue   An increase in assets resulting from the normal operating activities of an enterprise. This definition is expanded in subsequent chapters.   *(p. 13)*

Service Organizations   Organizations that provide services to consumers. Examples include accountants, lawyers, and dry cleaners.   *(p. 24)*

Stakeholders   Parties interested in the operations of a business. Included in this group are owners, lenders, employees, suppliers, customers, and government agencies.   *(p. 24)*

Statement of Cash Flows   Statement that explains how a business obtained and used cash during an accounting period.   *(p. 16)*

Statement of Changes in Equity   Statement that summarizes the transactions occurring during the accounting period that affected the owners' equity.   *(p. 15)*

Statements Model   The simultaneous display of a set of financial statements.   *(p. 21)*

Temporary Accounts   Accounts used to collect information for a single accounting period (i.e., usually revenue, expense, and distribution accounts).   *(p. 17)*

Transaction   A particular event that involves the transfer of something of value between two entities.   *(p. 12)*

Users   Individuals or organizations that use financial information for decision making.   *(p. 3)*

Vertical Statements Model   The arrangement of a full set of financial statements on a single page with account titles arranged from the top to the bottom of the page.   *(p. 21)*

QUESTIONS

1. What are several groups of direct users of financial information? List several groups of indirect users of financial information. Give an example of financial information that you use directly.
2. Why is accounting called the *language of business*?
3. What is the primary mechanism that the United States uses to allocate resources?
4. What does the term *market* mean as it is used in the business sense?
5. What are the components of the market trilogy that are involved in the process of transforming resources to more desirable states?
6. What is an example of a financial resource, a physical resource, and a labor resource?
7. What type of income or profit does an investor expect from the investment of a financial resource in a business? What type of income does a creditor expect from the investment of financial resources in an organization or business?
8. How do financial and managerial accounting differ?
9. Describe a not-for-profit or nonprofit enterprise. What is the motivation for these types of entities?
10. What are the U.S. rules of accounting information measurement called?
11. How is the establishment of the GAAP of the United States different from that of Japan and Germany?
12. What body has the primary responsibility for establishing GAAP in the United States?
13. What are the 10 elements of financial statements identified by the FASB?
14. What is the most basic form of the accounting equation?
15. What is the role of assets in terms of the profitability of a business?
16. To whom do the assets of a business belong?
17. What is the nature of the creditors' claims on assets?
18. What is meant by *residual interest*? Name two other terms that are used to label the residual interest.
19. What term is used to describe creditors' claims on the assets of a business?
20. What is the accounting equation? Describe each of its three components.
21. Who ultimately bears the risk of and collects the rewards associated with operating a business?
22. What does a double-entry bookkeeping system mean?
23. Describe an asset source transaction, an asset use transaction, and an asset exchange transaction. What is an example of each?
24. How does an acquisition of capital from owners affect the accounting equation?
25. What is the difference between assets that are acquired by contributed capital and those that are retained earnings?
26. How do revenues affect the accounting equation?
27. How do expenses affect the accounting equation?
28. What are the three primary sources of assets?
29. What causes a business to have retained earnings?
30. How does a distribution of assets to an owner affect the accounting equation?
31. What are the similarities and differences between distributions and expenses?
32. What are the four general-purpose financial statements used by business enterprises?
33. Which of the general-purpose financial statements provides information about the enterprise at a designated time?
34. How does net income affect equity?
35. What causes a net loss?
36. What are the three categories of cash receipts and cash payments shown on the statement of cash flows? Describe each.
37. How are asset accounts arranged in the balance sheet?
38. What is the difference between a permanent account and a nominal account?
39. What type of information is contained in the annual report of a business?

EXERCISES

Effect of Transactions on the Accounting Equation

The accounting equation for A&M Service Co. follows.

Event	Assets		=	Liabilities	+	Equity	
						A&M Service Co. **Accounting Equation** **January 1, 20X2**	
	Cash	Land				Contributed Capital	Retained Earnings
Balance 1/1/X2	25,000	10,000		4,000		18,000	13,000

A&M Service Co. experienced the following events during the 20X2 accounting period.

1. Purchased land for $12,000 cash.
2. Acquired an additional $5,000 cash from the owners.
3. Provided services to customers and received $75,000 cash.
4. Paid operating expense of $64,000.
5. Paid $2,000 to creditors.
6. Distributed $1,000 cash to the owners.

Required

Show the effects of these events on the accounting equation.

Components of the Accounting Equation

Required

Fill in the missing information in each of the three following independent situations.

    a. If Jim's Auto Parts has assets of $6,200, what is the amount of claims?

    b. Bill's Pet Store has liabilities of $2,200 and equity of $1,400. What is the amount of assets? What is the amount of net assets?

    c. Mary's Sports has assets of $56,700 and liabilities of $32,300. What is the amount of equity? What is the amount of net assets?

Effect of Capital Acquisition on the Accounting Equation and Financial Statements

Phillips Company was started in 20X9 by acquiring $6,000 cash from Randy Phillips. The cash acquired was the only event that affected the business in 20X9.

Required

    a. Draw an accounting equation and record the effects of the capital acquisition on the books of Phillips Company under the appropriate headings.

    b. Prepare an income statement, statement of changes in equity, balance sheet, and statement of cash flows for the 20X9 accounting period.

Effect of Borrowing Activity on the Accounting Equation and Financial Statements

Black Company was started in 20X7 when it borrowed $8,000 in cash from a foundation for the establishment of small businesses. The borrowing activity was the only event that affected the business in 20X7.

Required

    a. Draw an accounting equation and record the effects of the borrowing event under the appropriate headings.

    b. Prepare an income statement, statement of changes in equity, balance sheet, and statement of cash flows for the 20X7 accounting period.

    c. Explain how the equity of the company is affected by the accounting event.

EXERCISE 1-5
L.O. 4, 7

Effect of Revenue, Expense, and Distribution on the Accounting Equation and Financial Statements

Steve Wong started Wong Company in 20X9. During 20X9, the company was affected by three accounting events: (1) earned cash revenues of $9,500, (2) incurred cash expenses of $5,800, and (3) paid a $700 cash distribution to Mr. Wong. These were the only events that affected the company during 20X9.

Required

    a. Draw an accounting equation and record the effects of each accounting event under the appropriate headings.

    b. Prepare an income statement, statement of changes in equity, balance sheet, and statement of cash flows for the 20X9 accounting period.

    c. Discuss the information about Wong Company that is presented in the 20X9 balance sheet.

EXERCISE 1-6
L.O. 4, 7

Effect of Events on the Accounting Equation

Mike McKee started McKee Printing in 20X1. During 20X1, the company was affected by the following four events: (1) acquired $8,000 cash from Mr. McKee; (2) earned cash revenue of $15,000; (3) paid cash expense of $8,800; (4) made a cash distribution to McKee of $500.

Required

    a. Draw an accounting equation and record the effects of each accounting event under the appropriate headings.

    b. Prepare an income statement, statement of changes in equity, balance sheet, and statement of cash flows for the 20X1 accounting period.

    c. What does the income statement tell you about the profitability of this business?

EXERCISE 1-7
L.O. 1, 2

Common Uses of Accounting Information

Required

Describe three situations in which you use accounting information on a regular basis. Include in your description the importance of the financial information to you.

EXERCISE 1-8
L.O. 5, 9

Classified and Identified Cash Flow Events and Their Effect on Financial Statements— Horizontal Statements Model

Ace Tutoring Services experienced the following events during the first month of 20X6.

1. Started the business by depositing into a business checking account cash that was acquired from the owners.
2. Provided tutoring services to clients and collected cash.
3. Paid cash for operating expenses.
4. Borrowed cash on an interest-free loan from a local government small business foundation.
5. Purchased land for cash.
6. Made a cash distribution to the owners.

Required

    a. Indicate whether each event constitutes a financing, investing, or operating activity.

    b. Use a horizontal statements model to show how each event affects the balance sheet, income statement, and statement of cash flows. Indicate whether the event acts to increase (I) or to decrease (D) or not affected (n/a) each element of the financial statements. Also, in the cash flow column, indicate whether the cash flow is associated with operating activities (OA), investing activities (IA), or financing activities (FA). The first transaction has been recorded as an example.

Event No.	Balance Sheet													Income Statement						Statement of Cash Flows	
					Loan		Cont.		Ret.												
	Cash	+	Land	=	Pay.	+	Cap.	+	Earn.			Rev.	−	Exp.	=	Net Inc.					
1	I	+	n/a	=	n/a	+	I	+	n/a			n/a	−	n/a	=	n/a			I		FA

Classification of Events as to Asset Source, Use, or Exchange

EXERCISE 1-9
L.O. 8

Jay's Pet Hotel experienced the following events during its first year of operations.

1. Acquired $5,000 cash from the owner to begin business operations.
2. Borrowed $8,000 cash from First Bank.
3. Paid $3,000 cash to purchase land.
4. Provided boarding services and received $4,500 cash.
5. Acquired an aditional $2,000 from the owner.
6. Purchased additional land for $3,500 cash.
7. Paid $3,200 cash for expenses.
8. Provided additional services and received $2,500 cash.
9. Made a $1,000 cash distribution to the owner.

Required

    a. Classify each event as an asset source, use, or exchange transaction.

    b. Determine the amount in the cash account at the end of the accounting period.

    c. Determine the amount of total assets at the end of the accounting period.

Effect of Events on the Accounting Equation

EXERCISE 1-10
L.O. 7

Solar Enterprises experienced the following events during 20X6.

1. Acquired cash from the owners to begin operations.
2. Borrowed cash.
3. Purchased land with cash.
4. Provided services to clients and collected cash.
5. Paid operating expenses with cash.
6. Made a cash distribution to the owners.

Required

Explain how each of the events would affect the accounting equation by writing a + for increase, − for decrease, and n/a for not affected under each of the components of the accounting equation. The first event has been recorded as an example.

Event No.	Assets	=	Liabilities	+	Contributed Capital	+	Retained Earnings
					Equity		
1	+		n/a		+		n/a

EXERCISE 1-11   **Effect of Events on the Accounting Equation and Financial Statements**
   L.O. 4, 7   Mars Company experienced the following events during 20X2.

1. Acquired $20,000 cash from the owners.
2. Paid $9,000 cash to purchase land.
3. Borrowed $5,000 cash.
4. Provided services for $12,000 cash.
5. Paid $7,500 cash for operating expenses.
6. Made a $2,000 cash distribution to the owners.

Required

a. Explain how each of the events would affect the accounting equation by writing a + for increase, − for decrease, and n/a for not affected under each of the components of the accounting equation. Also record the dollar amount of the effect of each event on the accounting equation. The first event has been recorded as an example.

					Equity		
Event No.	Assets	=	Liabilities	+	Contributed Capital	+	Retained Earnings
1	+ 20,000		n/a		+ 20,000		n/a

b. Prepare an income statement, statement of changes in equity, balance sheet, and statement of cash flows for the 20X2 accounting period.

EXERCISE 1-12   **Effect of Events on the Accounting Equations and Financial Statements**
   L.O. 4, 7   Jeff King started Tax Time on January 1, 20X4. The company experienced the following events during its first year of operation.

1. Acquired $20,000 cash from the owner to begin operations.
2. Paid $8,000 cash to purchase land.
3. Provided tax services to customers and received $18,000 cash.
4. Paid $9,500 cash for expenses.
5. Acquired an additional $2,000 cash from the owner.
6. Borrowed $10,000 cash from the bank.
7. Purchased additional land for $5,000 cash.
8. Paid an additional $4,000 cash for expenses.
9. Made a $1,800 cash distribution to the owner.

Required

a. Explain how each of the events would affect the accounting equation by writing a + for increase, − for decrease, and n/a for not affected under each of the components of the accounting equation. Also record the dollar amount of the effect of each event on the accounting equation. The first event has been recorded as an example.

	Assets			=	Liabilities	+	Equity		
Event No.	Cash	+	Land	=	Notes Pay.	+	Contributed Capital	+	Retained Earnings
1	+ 20,000		n/a		n/a		+ 20,000		n/a

(*Hint:* It may be helpful to prepare a set of financial statements before you attempt to answer the following questions.)

    b. What is the amount of net income earned in 20X4?

    c. What is the amount of total assets at the end of 20X4?

    d. What is the amount of cash flow from operating activities for 20X4?

    e. What is the amount of net cash flow from financing activities for 20X4?

    f. What is the amount of net cash flow from investing activities for 20X4?

    g. What is the cash balance at the end of 20X4?

    h. What is the net change in cash on the 20X4 cash flow statement?

Identification of Transaction Types and Their Effects on Financial Statements—Horizontal Statements Model

EXERCISE 1-13
L.O. 8, 9

Club Sports experienced the following events during its first year of operations, 20X8.

1. Acquired cash from the owner to begin operations.
2. Borrowed cash on a noninterest-bearing note from a small business development foundation.
3. Provided services and collected cash.
4. Paid cash for operating expenses.
5. Purchased land with cash.
6. Made a cash distribution to the owner.

Required

    a. Indicate whether each event constitutes an asset source, asset use, or asset exchange transaction.

    b. Use a horizontal statements model to show how each event affects the balance sheet, income statement, and statement of cash flows. Indicate whether the event acts to increase (I) or to decrease (D) or not affect (n/a) each element of the financial statements. Also indicate in the cash column whether the cash flow is associated with operating activities (OA), investing activities (IA), or financing activities (FA). The first transaction has been recorded as an example.

Event No.	Balance Sheet									Income Statement					Statement of Cash Flows	
				Note		Cont.		Ret.								
	Cash	+	Land	=	Pay.	+	Cap.	+	Earn.	Rev.	−	Exp.	=	Net Inc.		
1	I	+	n/a	=	n/a	+	I	+	n/a	n/a	−	n/a	=	n/a	I	FA

Missing Information in the Accounting Equation

EXERCISE 1-14
L.O. 6

Required

Calculate the missing amounts for each of the following:

Company	Assets	=	Liabilities	+	Equity Contributed Capital	+	Equity Retained Earnings
A	$?		$55,000		$20,000		$15,000
B	62,000		?		25,000		20,000
C	57,750		12,500		16,000		?
D	41,300		19,400		?		18,100

EXERCISE 1-15
L.O. 6

Missing Information in the Accounting Equation

As of December 31, 20X2, Donns Company had total assets amounting to $144,000, liabilities amounting to $72,600, and contributed capital amounting to $48,400. During 20X3 Donns earned $15,000 of cash revenue, paid $9,500 for cash expenses, and made a $900 cash distribution to the owners.

Required

    a. Determine the amount of retained earnings as of December 31, 20X2.

    b. Determine the amount of net income earned in 20X3.

    c. Determine the amount of retained earnings as of December 31, 20X3.

EXERCISE 1-16
L.O. 6

Missing Information for Determining Net Income

The December 31, 20X6, balance sheet for Parker Company showed a total equity of $51,500. Total equity increased by $46,400 between December 31, 20X6 and December 31, 20X7. During 20X7 Parker Company acquired $8,000 cash from the owners. Parker Company made a $4,000 cash distribution to the owners during 20X7.

Required

Determine the amount of net income or loss reported on the 20X7 income statement. (*Hint:* Remember that total equity is changed by capital acquisition, net income, and distributions.)

EXERCISE 1-17
L.O. 10

Unusual Items Identified on the Income Statement

The following are three situations that exist at three different companies.

  1. A grocery store chain sold several old trucks that previously had been used to deliver goods from the company's warehouses to its stores. The old trucks, which are being replaced, were sold at a loss.

  2. A company that manufactures textiles had a net loss (negative earnings) in the most recent year due to a strike by its workers.

  3. A company that produces a food additive had to destroy a significant amount of its goods because the government banned the continued use of the additive.

Required

Indicate whether each item should be included in *operating income* or should receive special disclosure on the company's income statement. This requires that you use your judgment in deciding whether someone analyzing the financial statements would want special disclosure of the information for making business decisions. Provide a brief explanation to support your decision in each situation.

PROBLEMS—SERIES A

PROBLEM 1-1A
L.O. 4, 7

Effect of Events on Financial Statements

Azure Co. was started January 1, 20X4, when it acquired $20,000 cash from the owner, Mrs. Azure. The company borrowed an additional $10,000 so that a total of $30,000 cash was available to operate the business. During 20X4, Azure Co. earned cash revenues of $15,500, paid cash expenses of $8,500, and paid cash distributions amounting to $2,100. During 20X5, an additional $4,200 cash was acquired from the owner. Cash revenues amounted to $13,750, cash expenses were $8,220, and cash distributions to the owner were $2,100 during the 20X5 accounting period. Finally, $1,075 of liabilities was repaid during 20X5.

Required

Based on this information, calculate the following. (*Hint:* It may be helpful to identify the accounting events and to record them under the appropriate headings of an accounting equation before you attempt to make the required computations.)

    a. The amount of total assets that would appear on the 20X4 balance sheet.

    b. The amount of net cash flow from operating activities that would appear on the 20X4 statement of cash flows.

c. The amount of net income on the 20X4 income statement.

d. The amount of total liabilities on the 20X4 balance sheet.

e. The amount of the cash flow from financing activities that would appear on the 20X4 statement of cash flows.

f. The amount of ending contributed capital that would appear on the 20X5 statement of changes in equity.

g. The amount of retained earnings that would appear on the 20X5 balance sheet.

h. The amount of net income that would appear on the 20X5 income statement.

i. The amount of cash flow from investing activities on the 20X5 statement of cash flows.

j. The amount of total liabilities that would appear on the 20X5 balance sheet.

k. The amount of total equity that would appear on the 20X5 statement of changes in equity.

Events for Two Complete Accounting Cycles

PROBLEM 1-2A
L.O. 4, 7, 9

Bradley's Professional Services experienced the following transactions for 20X1 and 20X2. *Assume all transactions involve the receipt or payment of cash.*

Transactions for 20X1:

1. Acquired $60,000 cash from the owner to begin operations.
2. Provided services to customers and received $100,000 cash in payment of these services.
3. Borrowed $25,000 cash from creditors.
4. Paid expenses amounting to $70,000.
5. Purchased land for $40,000 cash.

Transactions for 20X2:

1. Acquired an additional $20,000 from the owner.
2. Performed services in 20X2 and received $120,000 cash.
3. Paid $10,000 cash to creditors.
4. Paid expenses amounting to $80,000 in 20X2.
5. Made a $15,000 cash distribution to the owner.

Required

a. Draw an accounting equation and record the effects of each accounting event under the appropriate headings for each year.

b. Prepare an income statement, statement of changes in equity, balance sheet, and statement of cash flows for each year. Use the vertical format when you prepare the financial statements.

c. Compare the information provided by the income statement with the information provided by the statement of cash flows. Note any similarities and differences.

Events for Three Complete Accounting Cycles

PROBLEM 1-3A
L.O. 4, 7, 9

The following transactions apply to the Baldwell Company. *Assume that all transactions involve the receipt or payment of cash.*

Transactions for 20X2:

1. Acquired $8,000 cash from the owners to begin operations.
2. Borrowed $4,800 cash from creditors.
3. Provided services to its customers and received $3,500.
4. Paid expenses amounting to $1,900.
5. Made a $750 distribution to its owners.

Transactions for 20X3:

1. Purchased a plot of land for $1,375.
2. Acquired an additional $2,100 from the owners.
3. Borrowed an additional $2,000 cash from creditors.
4. Provided services to its customers and received $2,700 cash.
5. Paid expenses amounting to $1,650.
6. Made a $1,075 distribution to its owners.

Transactions for 20X4:

1. Acquired $1,000 from the owners.
2. Made a $4,350 payment to creditors. *Finance activity*
3. Provided services to its customers and received $1,900.
4. Paid expenses amounting to $1,975.
5. Made a $500 cash distribution to its owners.

Required

a. Draw an accounting equation and record the effects of each accounting event under the appropriate headings for each year.
b. Prepare an income statement, statement of changes in equity, balance sheet, and statement of cash flows for each year. Use the vertical format when you prepare the financial statements.
c. Explain what information the balance sheet provides. What does this information tell the reader about the company for the 3-year period?
d. What does the income statement indicate about the company for the 3-year period?

PROBLEM 1-4A
L.O. 4, 6

Interrelationships among Financial Statements

Western Electronics started the accounting period with $10,000 of assets, $2,200 of liabilities, and $4,550 of retained earnings. During the period, Western earned cash revenues of $9,200, incurred cash expenses of $5,010, and paid a cash distribution to owners that amounted to $625. Also Western paid $1,000 cash to reduce the liability owed to a bank, and the business acquired an additional $2,000 cash contribution of capital from the owners.

Required

Prepare an income statement, statement of changes in equity, balance sheet, and statement of cash flows as of the end of the accounting period. (*Hint:* It may be helpful to determine the amount of beginning contributed capital before you consider the effects of the events of the current period. It may also help to record all events under an accounting equation before you attempt to prepare the statements.)

PROBLEM 1-5A
L.O. 4, 5, 9

Missing Information in Financial Statements

Required

Fill in the blanks (indicated by the alphabetic letters in parentheses) in the following financial statements. Assume the company started operations January 1, 20X1.

	For the Years		
	20X1	**20X2**	**20X3**
Income Statements			
Revenue (cash)	$ 400	$ 500	$ 800
Expense (cash)	(250)	(l)	(425)
Net Income (loss)	$ (a)	$ 100	$ 375
Statement of Changes in Equity			
Beginning Contributed Capital	$ 0	$ (m)	$ 9,100
Plus: Capital Acquisitions	(b)	1,100	310
Ending Contributed Capital	8,000	9,100	(s)
Beginning Retained Earnings	0	25	75
Plus: Net Income (loss)	(c)	100	375
Less: Distributions	(d)	(50)	(150)
Ending Retained Earnings	25	(n)	300
Total Equity	$ (e)	$ 9,175	$ (t)
Balance Sheets			
Assets			
Cash	$ (f)	$ (o)	$ (u)
Land	0	(p)	2,500
Total Assets	$11,000	$11,650	$10,550
Liabilities	$ (g)	$ (q)	$ 840
Equity			
Contributed Capital	(h)	(r)	9,410
Retained Earnings	(i)	75	300
Total Equity	8,025	9,175	9,710
Total Liabilities and Equity	$11,000	$11,650	$10,550
Statements of Cash Flows			
Cash Flows from Operating Activities			
Cash Receipts from Revenue	$ (j)	$ 500	$ (v)
Cash Payments for Expenses	(k)	(400)	(w)
Net Cash Flows from Operating Activities	150	100	375
Cash Flows from Investing Activities			
Cash Payments for Land	0	(5,000)	0
Cash Receipt from Sale of Land	0	0	2,500
Net Cash Flows from Investing Activities	0	(5,000)	2,500
Cash Flows from Financing Activities			
Cash Receipts from Borrowed Funds	2,975	0	0
Cash Payments to Reduce Debt	0	(500)	(x)
Cash Receipts from Capital Acquisitions	8,000	1,100	(y)
Cash Payments for Distributions	(125)	(50)	(z)
Net Cash Flows from Financing Activities	10,850	550	(1,475)
Net Change in Cash	11,000	(4,350)	1,400
Plus: Beginning Cash Balance	0	11,000	6,650
Ending Cash Balance	$11,000	$ 6,650	$ 8,050

PROBLEM 1-6A
L.O. 8

Classification of Events as to Asset Source, Use, or Exchange

Required

Identify each of the following unrelated events as an asset source, asset use, or asset exchange transaction. Some events may not be recordable under current accounting practice. In this case, classify the event as not applicable. Also for each event, indicate whether total assets will increase, decrease, or remain unchanged. Organize your answer according to the following table. The first event has been recorded in the table as an example.

Event No.	Type of Event	Effect on Total Assets
a	Asset Source	Increase

- a. Started a CPA firm when it acquired a cash contribution from owners.
- b. Borrowed cash from the local bank.
- c. Purchased supplies with cash.
- d. Made plans to purchase office equipment.
- e. Traded a used car for a computer. Both assets had identical values.
- f. Used supplies in the process of rendering services to customers.
- g. Agreed to represent a client in an IRS audit. The owner, an accountant, will be paid when the audit is complete.
- h. Received cash from customers who had received services.
- i. Paid employees' salaries with cash.
- j. Repaid a bank loan with cash.
- k. Paid interest to the bank with cash.
- l. Transferred cash from its checking account to a money market account.
- m. Sold land for $6,000 cash. The land originally cost $6,000.
- n. Distributed cash to the owner.
- o. Learned that a financial analyst determined the company's debt-to-equity ratio to be 40%.

PROBLEM 1-7A
L.O. 9

Effect of Events on Financial Statements—Horizontal Statements Model

Barham Services experienced the following transactions during 20X3.

1. Started the company when it acquired $4,500 from the owners.
2. Borrowed $10,000 from the local bank.
3. Performed services and received $15,675 cash during 20X3.
4. Paid $8,200 of cash expenses.
5. Purchased land for $3,000 cash.
6. Repaid the $10,000 bank loan.
7. Made a cash distribution of $2,500 to the owners.

Required

- a. Use a horizontal statements model to show how each event affects the balance sheet, income statement, and statement of cash flows. Indicate whether the event acts to increase (I) or to decrease (D) or not affect (n/a) each element of the financial statements. Also indicate in the cash flow column whether the cash flow is associated with operating activities (OA), investing activities (IA), or financing activities (FA). The first transaction has been recorded as an example.

Event No.	Balance Sheet					Income Statement				Statement of Cash Flows	
				Loan	**Cont.**	**Ret.**					
	Cash	**+**	**Land**	**=** **Pay.**	**+** **Cap.**	**+** **Earn.**	**Rev.**	**–** **Exp.**	**=** **Net Inc.**		
1	I	+	n/a	= n/a	+ I	+ n/a	n/a	– n/a	= n/a	I	FA

b. What kind of activities affected the statement of cash flows but not the income statement?

Real-World Terminology

The following information was drawn from the accounts of Hartford Company:

PROBLEM 1-8A
L.O. 10

Assets	$720,000
Revenue	320,000
Retained Earnings	?
Income from Discontinued Operations	35,000
Liabilities	330,000
Operating Expenses	240,000
Common Stock	260,000

Required

Use the preceding information to prepare an income statement and balance sheet.

PROBLEMS   SERIES B

Effect of Events on Financial Statements

PROBLEM 1-1B
L.O. 4, 7

Marx Company was started January 1, 20X3, when it acquired $24,000 cash from the owner, Rich Marx. The company borrowed an additional $16,000 so that a total of $40,000 was available to operate the business. During 20X3, Marx Company earned cash revenues of $36,000, paid cash expenses of $25,000, and paid cash distributions to the owner amounting to $10,000. During 20X4, the owner contributed an additional $20,000 cash to the business. Cash revenues amounted to $50,000, cash expenses were $36,000, and cash distributions were $12,000 during the 20X4 accounting period. Finally, $14,000 of liabilities was repaid during 20X4.

Required

Based on the preceding information, calculate the following. (*Hint:* It may be helpful to identify the accounting events and to record them under the appropriate headings of an accounting equation before you attempt to make the required computations.)

a. The amount of total assets that would appear on the 20X3 balance sheet.

b. The amount of net cash flow from operating activities that would appear on the 20X3 statement of cash flows.

c. The amount of net income on the 20X3 income statement.

d. The amount of total liabilities on the 20X3 balance sheet.

    e. The amount of the cash flow from financing activities that would appear on the 20X3 statement of cash flows.

    f. The amount of ending contributed capital that would appear on the 20X4 statement of changes in equity.

    g. The amount of retained earnings that would appear on the 20X4 balance sheet.

    h. The amount of net income that would appear on the 20X4 income statement.

    i. The amount of cash flow from investing activities on the 20X4 statement of cash flows.

    j. The amount of total liabilities that would appear on the 20X4 balance sheet.

    k. The amount of total equity that would appear on the 20X4 statement of changes in equity.

PROBLEM 1-2B
L.O. 4, 7, 9

Events for Two Complete Accounting Cycles

Reynolds Consulting experienced the following transactions for 20X6 and 20X7. *Assume that all transactions involve the receipt or payment of cash.*

Transactions for 20X6:

1. Started the company when it acquired $25,000 cash from the owner.
2. Provided services to customers and received $72,000 cash in payment of these services.
3. Borrowed $16,000 cash from creditors.
4. Paid expenses amounting to $28,000.
5. Purchased land for $44,000 cash.

Transactions for 20X7:

1. Acquired an additional $24,000 from the owner.
2. Performed services in 20X7 and received $94,000 cash.
3. Paid $10,000 cash to creditors.
4. Paid expenses amounting to $56,000.
5. Made a $6,000 distribution to the owner.

Required

    a. Draw an accounting equation and record the effects of each accounting event under the appropriate headings for each year.

    b. Prepare an income statement, statement of changes in equity, balance sheet, and statement of cash flows for each year. Use the vertical format when you prepare the financial statements.

    c. Examine the balance sheet for the 2 years. How did assets change from 20X6 to 20X7?

PROBLEM 1-3B
L.O. 4, 7, 9

Events for Three Complete Accounting Cycles

The following transactions apply to Carolina Company. Assume that all transactions involve the receipt or payment of cash.

Transactions for 20X6:

1. Acquired $3,500 of capital from the owners.
2. Borrowed $2,000 from creditors.
3. Provided services to its customers and received $1,850.
4. Paid expenses amounting to $800.
5. Made a $350 distribution to its owners.

Transactions for 20X7:

1. Purchased a plot of land costing $3,500.
2. Acquired $2,000 of capital from the owners.
3. Borrowed an additional $5,000 from creditors.
4. Provided services to its customers and received $3,200.
5. Paid expenses amounting to $1,900.
6. Made a $700 distribution to its owners.

Transactions for 20X8:

1. Acquired $1,000 of capital from the owners.
2. Made $4,500 payment to creditors.
3. Provided services to its customers and received $4,100.
4. Paid expenses amounting to $2,600.
5. Made a $500 distribution to its owners.

Required

    a. Draw an accounting equation and record the effects of each accounting event under the appropriate headings.

    b. Prepare an income statement, statement of changes in equity, balance sheet, and statement of cash flows for each year.

    c. Explain how the equity of the company changed over the 3 years by examining the statement of changes in equity.

    d. Examine the cash outflows on the statement of cash flows for the 3 years. How has the business been spending its money?

Interrelationships among Financial Statements

Chase Manufacturing started the accounting period with $30,000 of assets consisting solely of cash, $18,000 of liabilities, and $4,000 of contributed capital. During the period, Chase earned cash revenues of $36,000, paid cash expenses of $23,000, and paid a cash distribution to owners that amounted to $2,000. Chase acquired an additional $10,000 cash from the owners and paid $6,000 cash to reduce the liability owed to a bank.

Required

Prepare an income statement, statement of changes in equity, balance sheet, and statement of cash flows as of the end of the accounting period. (*Hint:* It may be helpful to determine the amount of beginning Retained Earnings before you consider the effects of the events of the current period. It may also help to record all events under an accounting equation before attempting to prepare the statements.)

Information Missing in Financial Statements

Fill in the blanks (indicated by alphabetic letters in parentheses) in the following financial statements. Assume that the company started operations January 1, 20X1.

PROBLEM 1-4B
L.O. 4, 6

PROBLEM 1-5B
L.O. 4, 5, 9

	For the Years		
	20X1	20X2	20X3
Income Statements			
Revenue (assume cash)	$ 700	$1,300	$ 2,000
Expense (assume cash)	(a)	(700)	(1,300)
Net Income (Loss)	$ 200	$ (m)	$ 700
Statement of Changes in Equity			
Beginning Contributed Capital	$ 0	$ (n)	$ 6,000
Plus: Capital Acquisition	5,000	1,000	2,000
Ending Contributed Capital	5,000	6,000	(t)
Beginning Retained Earnings	0	100	200
Plus: Net Income (loss)	(b)	(o)	700
Less: Distributions	(c)	(500)	(300)
Ending Retained Earnings	100	(p)	600
Total Equity	$ (d)	$6,200	$ 8,600
Balance Sheets			
Assets			
Cash	$ (e)	$ (q)	$ (u)
Land	0	(r)	8,000
Total Assets	$ (f)	$11,200	$10,600
Liabilities	$ (g)	$ 5,000	$ 2,000
Equity			
Contributed Capital	(h)	(s)	8,000
Retained Earnings	(i)	200	600
Total Equity	(j)	6,200	8,600
Total Liabilities and Equity	$8,100	$11,200	$10,600
Statements of Cash Flows			
Cash Flows from Operating Activities			
Cash Receipts from Revenue	$ (k)	$ 1,300	$ (v)
Cash Payments for Expenses	(l)	(700)	(w)
Net Cash Flows from Operating Activities	200	600	700
Cash Flows from Investing Activities			
Cash Payments for Land	0	(8,000)	0
Cash Flows from Financing Activities			
Cash Receipts from Loan	3,000	3,000	0
Cash Payments to Reduce Debt	0	(1,000)	(x)
Cash Receipts from Capital Acquisitions	5,000	1,000	(y)
Cash Payments for Distributions	(100)	(500)	(z)
Net Cash Flows from Financing Activities	7,900	2,500	(1,300)
Net Change in Cash	8,100	(4,900)	(600)
Plus: Beginning Cash Balance	0	8,100	3,200
Ending Cash Balance	$8,100	$ 3,200	$ 2,600

Event Classification as to Asset Source, Use, or Exchange

Required

Identify each of the following unrelated events as an asset source, asset use, or asset exchange transaction. Some events may not be recordable under current accounting practice. In this case, classify the event as *not applicable* (n/a). Also indicate whether total assets for each event will increase, decrease, or remain unchanged. Organize your answer according to the following table. The first event has been recorded in the table as an example.

Event No.	Type of Event	Effect on Total Assets
a	Asset Source	Increase

 a. Acquired a cash contribution of capital from owners.
 b. Paid monthly rent on the office building.
 c. Purchased land with cash.
 d. Borrowed cash from the bank.
 e. Purchased equipment with cash.
 f. Hired a new office manager.
 g. Provided services for cash.
 h. Bought land by accepting a liability (i.e., agreed to pay cash in the future).
 i. Distributed cash to the owners.
 j. Paid cash for operating expenses.
 k. Paid the office manager's salary with cash.
 l. Received cash for services that have been performed.
 m. Discussed plans for a new office building with the architect.
 n. Repaid part of the bank loan.
 o. Paid cash to purchase the new office building.

Effect of Events on Financial Statements—Horizontal Statements Model

Lighthouse Services experienced the following transactions during 20X6:
 1. Started the company when it acquired $1,000 from the owners.
 2. Borrowed $17,000 from the local bank.
 3. Performed services and received $32,000 cash during 20X6.
 4. Paid $21,000 of cash expenses.
 5. Purchased land for $2,000 cash.
 6. Repaid $2,500 of the bank loan.
 7. Made a cash distribution of $2,500 to the owners.

Required

 a. Use a horizontal statements model to show how each event affects the balance sheet, income statement, and statement of cash flows. Indicate whether the event acts to increase (I) or to decrease (D) or not affect (n/a) each element of the financial statements. Also indicate in the cash flow column whether the cash flow is associated with operating activities (OA), investing activities (IA), or financing activities (FA). The first transaction has been recorded as an example.

Event No.	Balance Sheet					Income Statement			Statement of Cash Flows
	Cash	+ Land	= Loan Pay.	+ Cont. Cap.	+ Ret. Earn.	Rev.	− Exp.	= Net Inc.	
1	I	+ n/a	= n/a	+ I	+ n/a	n/a	− n/a	= n/a	I FA

b. What types of activities affect the statement of cash flows but not the income statement?

PROBLEM 1-8B   **Real-World Terminology**
L.O. 10   The following information was drawn from the accounts of Altman Company:

Common Stock	$110,000
Retained Earnings	?
Operating Expenses	140,000
Assets	420,000
Revenue	190,000
Extraordinary Item—Storm Damage	(40,000)
Liabilities	290,000

Required
Use the preceding information to prepare an income statement and a balance sheet.

analyze, communicate, think

ACT 1-1

BUSINESS APPLICATIONS CASE   **Gateway 2000 Annual Report**
Use the Gateway 2000 financial statements in Appendix B to answer the following questions.
  a. What was Gateway's net income for 1997?
  b. How does net income for 1997 compare to net income for 1996?
  c. What was Gateway's accounting equation for 1997?
  d. Identify one or more reasons that Gateway's net income decreased from 1996 to 1997.

ACT 1-2

GROUP ASSIGNMENT   **Missing Information**
The following selected financial information is available for H&R Block for the past four years. Amounts are in millions of dollars.

Income Statements	1998	1997	1996	1995
Revenue	$1,307	$ (a)	$ 894	$1,239
Cost and Expenses	(a)	(1,859)	(769)	(a)
Income from Continuing Operations	174	71	(a)	(b)
Unusual Items	218	(b)	(b)	0
Net Income	$ (b)	$ 47	$ 177	$ 107
Balance Sheets				
Assets				
Cash and Marketable Securities	$1,247	$ (c)	$ 419	$ 353
Other Assets	(c)	1,226	(c)	725
Total Assets	$2,904	$ (d)	$1,418	$1,078
Liabilities	$ (d)	$ 907	$ (d)	$ (c)
Equity				
Contributed Capital	356	(e)	313	(14)
Retained Earnings	(e)	684	(e)	(d)
Total Equity	1,342	(f)	1,040	686
Total Liabilities and Equity	$ (f)	$ 1,906	$1,418	$1,078

Required

a. Divide the class into groups of four or five students each. Organize the groups into four sections. Assign Task 1 to the first section of groups, Task 2 to the second section, Task 3 to the third section, and Task 4 to the fourth section.

Group Tasks

1. Fill in the missing information for 1995.
2. Fill in the missing information for 1996.
3. Fill in the missing information for 1997.
4. Fill in the missing information for 1998.

b. Each section should select two representatives. One representative is to put the financial statements assigned to that section on the board, underlining the missing amounts. The second representative is to explain to the class how the missing amounts were determined.

c. Each section should list events that may have caused the unusual item category on the income statement.

REAL WORLD CASE   Unusual Events   ACT 1-3

During 1997, the Philip Morris Company reached agreements with the states of Mississippi, Florida, and Texas to make current and future payments related to health care costs these states had incurred to treat certain illnesses of smokers. As a result, on its 1997 income statement, Philip Morris recognized an expense called "settlement charges" for $1.457 billion. This type of expense had not been recognized in 1995 or 1996. The settlement charges were included in operating income; they were *not* classified as extraordinary. Philip Morris's operating incomes, before subtracting income taxes, for 1995, 1996, and 1997 were as follows:

1995	1996	1997
$9.347 billion	$10.683 billion	$10.611 billion

Required

a. Compute the percentage growth in Philip Morris's *operating income—before taxes* from 1995 to 1996 and from 1996 to 1997.

b. Determine what Philip Morris's *operating income—before taxes* would have been in 1997 if there had been no settlement charges expense. Using this revised number, compute the percentage growth in *operating income—before taxes* from 1996 to 1997.

c. Assuming that Philip Morris experiences the same average growth rate in earnings from 1997 to 1998 as it averaged from 1995 to 1997, develop a rough estimate of its 1998 *operating income—before taxes* under two separate assumptions:

1. No settlement charges were made in 1997 or 1998.
2. The settlement charges in 1998 are the same amount as in 1997.

Think carefully before answering!

BUSINESS APPLICATIONS CASE   Future Predicted by Using Continuing   ACT 1-4
Operations versus Discontinued Operations

During 20X7, three companies in the same industry each discontinued operation of part of their businesses. The income earned (or lost) on these discontinued operations was disclosed separately on the companies' income statements, portions of which follow:

	Cruise Co.	Precision Co.	Newark Co.
Income from Continuing Operations	$ 20,000	$120,000	$ 99,000
Income (loss) from Discontinued Operations	80,000	(20,000)	1,000
Net Income	$100,000	$100,000	$100,000

Required

Based only on the information provided here, predict how each company will perform in 20X8. Prepare a memorandum to your supervisor supporting each of your predictions.

ACT 1-5

BUSINESS APPLICATIONS CASE   **Use of Real-World Numbers for Forecasting**

The following information was drawn from the annual report of Machine Import Company (MIC):

	For the Years	
	20X1	**20X2**
Income Statements		
Revenue	$600,000	$690,000
Operating Expenses	480,000	552,000
Income from Continuing Operations	120,000	138,000
Extraordinary Item—Lottery Win		62,000
Net Income	$120,000	$200,000
Balance Sheets		
Assets	$880,000	$880,000
Liabilities	$200,000	$ 0
Common Stock	380,000	380,000
Retained Earnings	300,000	500,000
Total Liabilities and Equity	$880,000	$880,000

Required

a.   Compute the percentage of growth in net income from 20X1 to 20X2. Can stockholders expect a similar increase between 20X2 and 20X3?

b.   Assuming that MIC collected $200,000 cash from earnings (i.e., net income), explain how this money was spent in 20X2.

c.   Assuming that MIC experiences the same percentage of growth from 20X2 to 20X3 as it did from 20X1 to 20X2, determine the amount of income from continuing operations that the owners can expect to see on the 20X3 income statement.

d.   During 20X3, MIC experienced a $40,000 loss due to storm damage (note that this would be shown as an extraordinary loss on the income statement). Liabilities and common stock were unchanged from 20X2 to 20X3. Use the information that you computed in part c plus the additional information provided in the previous two sentences to prepare an income statement and balance sheet as of December 31, 20X3.

ACT 1-6

WRITING ASSIGNMENT   **Elements of Financial Statements Defined**

Bob and his sister, Marsha, both attend the state university. As a reward for their successful completion of the past year (Bob had a 3.2 GPA in business, and Marsha had a 3.7 GPA in art), their father gave each of them 100 shares of The Walt Disney Company stock. They have just received their first annual report. Marsha does not understand what the information means and has asked Bob to explain it to her. Bob is currently taking an accounting course, and she knows he will understand the financial statements.

Required

Assume you are Bob. Write Marsha a memo explaining the following financial statement items to her. In your explanation, describe each of the two financial statements and explain the financial information each contains. Also define each of the elements listed for each financial statement and explain what it means.

Balance Sheet
Assets
Liabilities
Equity
Income Statement
Revenue
Expense
Net Income

ETHICAL DILEMMA   **Loyalty versus the Bottom Line**   **ACT 1-7**

Assume that Jones has been working for you for 5 years. He has had an excellent work history and has received generous pay raises in response. The raises have been so generous that Jones is quite overpaid for the job he is required to perform. Unfortunately, he is not qualified to take on other, more responsible jobs available within the company. A recent job applicant is willing to accept a salary $5,000 per year less than the amount currently being paid to Jones. The applicant is well qualified to take over Jones's duties and has a very positive attitude. The financial statements shown below were reported by your company at the close of its most recent accounting period.

Required

a. Reconstruct the financial statements, assuming that Jones was replaced at the beginning of the most recent accounting period. Both Jones and his replacement are paid in cash. No other changes are to be considered.

b. Discuss the short- and long-term ramifications of replacing Jones. There are no right answers. However, assume that you are required to make a decision. Use your judgment and common sense to support your choice.

Financial Statements		
Income Statement		
Revenue		$57,000
Expense		(45,000)
Net Income		$12,000
Statement of Changes in Equity		
Beginning Contributed Capital	$20,000	
Plus: Capital Acquisition	5,000	
Ending Contributed Capital		$25,000
Beginning Retained Earnings	50,000	
Net Income	12,000	
Distribution	(2,000)	
Ending Retained Earnings		60,000
Total Equity		$85,000
Balance Sheet		
Assets		
Cash		$85,000
Equity		
Contributed Capital		$25,000
Retained Earnings		60,000
Total Equity		$85,000

Statement of Cash Flows	
Operating Activities	
Inflow from Customers	$57,000
Outflow for Expenses	(45,000)
Net Inflow from Operations	12,000
Investing Activities	0
Financing Activities	
Inflow from Capital Acquisition	5,000
Outflow for Distributions	(2,000)
Net Change in Cash	15,000
Plus: Beginning Cash Balance	70,000
Ending Cash Balance	$85,000

ACT 1-8

SPREADSHEET ASSIGNMENT   Using Excel

The financial statements for Simple Company are reported here using an Excel spreadsheet.

Required

Recreate the financial statements using your own Excel spreadsheet.

    a. For each number with an arrow by it, enter a formula in that particular cell address to solve for the number shown. The formula for net income (cell B6) is shown as an example.

    b. When complete, print the spreadsheet with formulas rather than absolute numbers.

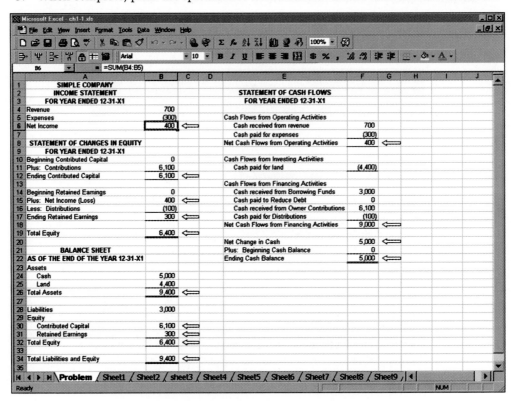

Spreadsheet Tips

1. Widen a column by positioning the mouse on the vertical line between two column headings until a crosshair appears. Either double click to automatically widen or click and drag the crosshair to the desired width.

2. Negative numbers can be parenthesized by choosing Format and then Cells. Under Category, choose Custom and under Type, choose the first option containing parentheses.

3. The SUM function is one way to add a series of numbers. For example, the formula for net income in cell B6 is =SUM(B4:B5).

4. Single and double lines can be drawn using the Borders icon.

5. Print a spreadsheet on one page by choosing File, Page Setup, and Fit to 1.

6. Print without gridlines by choosing File, Page Setup, and Sheet and uncheck Gridlines. Another option is to choose Tools and Options and uncheck Gridlines.

7. Print formulas by choosing Tools, Options, and Formulas.

SPREADSHEET ASSIGNMENT   **Mastering Excel**   ACT 1-9

Required

a. Enter the following headings for the horizontal statements model onto a blank spreadsheet.

	Balance Sheet						Income Statement			Statement of Cash Flows	
	Assets			Liabilities	Equity						
Event				Loan	Contributed	Retained			Net		
Number	Cash	Land	=	Payable	Capital	Earnings	Revenue	- Expense	= Income	Amount	Activity
1	$6,100				$6,100					$6,100	Financing
2											
3											
4											
5											
6											
Totals	$6,100	$0		$0	$6,100	$0	$0	$0	$0	$6,100	
		$6,100		$6,100							
		Total		Total							
		Assets		Claims							

b. Under the appropriate headings, record the effects of each of the following accounting events for the first month of operations. Notice that the first event has already been recorded.

1. Acquired $6,100 from the owner.
2. Paid $4,400 to purchase land.
3. Borrowed $3,000 cash.
4. Provided services to customers and received $700 in cash.
5. Paid $300 for expenses.
6. Made a $100 distribution to the owner.

Note: The statement of cash flows amounts can be referenced to the Cash account on the balance sheet. In other words, recording the cash amounts twice is not necessary. Instead enter formulas in the Statement of cash flows column equating those cell addresses to the respective cell in the cash column. Notice the formula in cell O6 (statement of cash flows) is set equal to cell B6 (cash on the balance sheet). Once the formula is completed for cell O6, it can be easily copied to cells O7 through O11.

c. Using formulas, sum each of the quantitative columns to arrive at the end-of-month amounts reported on the financial statements.

Spreadsheet Tips

1. Center the heading *Balance Sheet* across columns by entering the entire heading in cell B1. Position the mouse on B1 until a fat cross appears. Click and drag the mouse across B1 through G1. Click on the Merge and Center icon (it's highlighted in the screen in the computer display).

2. Enter arithmetic signs as headings by placing an apostrophe in front of the sign. For example, to enter the equals sign in cell D4, enter '=.

3. Copy cells by positioning the mouse in the bottom right corner of the cell to copy from (such as cell O6) until a thin cross appears. Click and drag the mouse down through the desired locations to copy to (through cell O11).

4. To enter the dollar sign, choose Format, Cells, and Currency.

2 Accounting for Accruals

LEARNING OBJECTIVES   AFTER COMPLETING THIS CHAPTER, YOU SHOULD BE ABLE TO:

1 Explain the concept of accrual versus cash accounting.

2 Identify business events that involve accruals.

3 Demonstrate a better understanding of how events are recorded under an accounting equation.

4 Prepare simple financial statements for a business that engages in cash and accrual transactions.

5 Explain how accrual transactions (as well as cash transactions introduced in Chapter 1) affect the financial statements of a business.

6 Define *revenue* and *expense* in terms of their relationships to assets and liabilities.

7 Explain the effects of end-of-period adjustments related to accruals.

8 Understand the auditor's role in financial reporting.

9 Develop an appreciation of the importance of a code of ethics.

10 Classify accounting events into one of four categories, including
  a. asset source transactions.
  b. asset use transactions.
  c. asset exchange transactions.
  d. claims exchange transactions.

Suppose a company located in St. Louis, Missouri, needs to ship goods to a customer located 868 miles away in Philadelphia, Pennsylvania. The company agrees to pay the CSX Corporation $1,500 to deliver the goods by rail. When should CSX report that it has earned revenue? More specifically, should the revenue be recognized before, during, or after the delivery of the goods?

Courtesy CSX Corporation

All the transactions presented in Chapter 1 have direct cash consequences. For example, cash is received in the same period that revenue is earned, and cash is paid in the same period that expenses are incurred. Such exact consistency seldom occurs in business practice. Indeed, most revenue transactions are initiated under credit terms. A "buy now, pay later" philosophy is predominant in all the major industrialized economies. Customers frequently purchase services in one accounting period and pay for them in a different pe-

riod. **Accrual accounting** recognizes the effects of accounting events in the period in which events occur, regardless of when cash is exchanged. Suppose a business provides services in 20X1 but collects cash for those services in 20X2. Under accrual accounting, the revenue is recognized in 20X1. Similarly, if a business consumes resources in 20X1 that are paid for in 20X2, an expense is recognized in 20X1 even though the cash payment is made in 20X2.

Comprehension of accrual accounting requires a clear dis-

tinction between the recognition of accounting events and the realization of the cash consequences associated with those events. **Recognition** is the act of *recording an event* in the financial records. Events may be recorded (i.e., recognized) before or after cash is paid or collected. The term **accrual** applies to events that are recognized *before* the associated cash is paid or collected. The following illustration highlights the critical distinction between recognition and collection or payment of cash.

Accrual Accounting Illustrated

Mary Haynes started a consulting practice called Haynes Consultants. The business began operation on January 1, 20X1, when it acquired a $5,000 cash contribution of capital from the owner. Haynes' clients provide office space and secretarial support, so the business is able to avoid many operating expenses. However, Haynes does incur salary expenses for one part-time employee. During 20X1, Haynes performed consulting services for which clients were billed $84,000. By December 31, 20X1, she had collected $60,000 cash from the clients, leaving a $24,000 balance due at the year's end. Also during 20X1, Haynes incurred $18,000 of liabilities for salaries for the part-time employee. The company had paid $12,000 of this amount during 20X1, leaving a year-end balance due of $6,000. As of December 31, 20X1, Haynes had outstanding contracts for consulting services to be performed in 20X2 that amounted to $42,000.

The preceding narrative contains five accounting events that are discussed in the next section:

1. The business acquired a $5,000 cash contribution of capital from the owner.
2. Assets generated from the performance of consulting services amounted to $84,000 in the 20X1 accounting period, and contracts for services to be performed in 20X2 amounted to $42,000.
3. Cash collected from customers amounted to $60,000.
4. Salary expense for the part-time employee amounted to $18,000.
5. Cash paid to the part-time employee amounted to $12,000.

Effect of Events on the Accounting Equation

Event 1
Owner Provides Assets

The $5,000 capital acquisition is an **asset source transaction.** It acts to increase the business's assets and its equity (i.e., contributed capital). The effect of the acquisition on the accounting equation follows. The equation includes all accounts that apply to the discussion of the Haynes case. You should ignore account titles that are unfamiliar at this time. Each title is explained when it is introduced.

	Assets			=	Liabilities	+	Equity		
	Cash	+	Accounts Receivable	=	Salaries Payable	+	Contributed Capital	+	Retained Earnings
Beginning Balances	$ 0		$ 0		$ 0		$ 0		$ 0
Capital Acquisition	+5,000						+5,000		
Ending Balances	$ 5,000	+	$ 0	=	$ 0	+	$ 5,000	+	$ 0

Event 2
Operating Activity Provides Assets (Recognition of Consulting Revenue)

The application of accrual accounting requires the recognition of $84,000 of assets and corresponding revenue for the 20X1 accounting period. The fact that only $60,000 of the revenue was *collected* in the form of cash receipts does not affect the amount of assets and revenue to be *recognized*. In this case, the productive activity of Haynes caused the assets of her company to increase by $84,000. The specific asset that increases is called an **account receivable.** As its name implies, the receivables account contains amounts of future cash receipts that are due from customers (i.e., amounts that are expected to be collected in the future). The revenue recognition transaction is an *asset source* transaction. Its effect on the accounting equation is shown as follows:

	Assets		=	Liabilities	+	Equity		
	Cash	+	**Accounts Receivable**	=	**Salaries Payable**	+	**Contributed Capital**	+	**Retained Earnings**
Beginning Balances	$ 5,000		$ 0		$ 0		$5,000		$ 0
Recognized Asset/Revenue			+84,000						+84,000
Ending Balance	$ 5,000	+	$84,000	=	$ 0	+	$5,000	+	$84,000

Note that the contracts for $42,000 of consulting services to be performed in 20X2 are not recognized in the financial statements. Revenues are earned by adding value to the company's assets through the performance of its productive activities. Since no productive activity (i.e., no work) has been performed with respect to these contracts, assets have not increased and revenue is not recognized. In other words, revenue is not recognized before the work is accomplished no matter how certain the likelihood of the future performance may be.

Although accounts receivable increased by $84,000, only $60,000 of this amount was collected by the end of 20X2. The conversion of $60,000 of accounts receivable to cash is an **asset exchange transaction.** The amount in the Cash account increases, and the amount in the Accounts Receivable account decreases. Also, the amount of total assets is unchanged. The effect of the $60,000 collection of receivables on the accounting equation is:

Event 3
Exchange Accounts Receivable for Cash

	Assets		=	Liabilities	+	Equity		
	Cash	+	**Accounts Receivable**	=	**Salaries Payable**	+	**Contributed Capital**	+	**Retained Earnings**
Beginning Balances	$ 5,000		$84,000		$ 0		$5,000		$84,000
Cash Collection	+60,000		(60,000)						
Ending Balances	$ 65,000	+	$24,000	=	$ 0	+	$5,000	+	$84,000

Observe carefully that the collection of the cash did not trigger the recognition of revenue. The full $84,000 of revenue was recognized at the time that the account receivable was generated. Revenue would be double counted if it were recognized again when the cash was collected.

Liabilities and corresponding expenses also may be recognized before the cash consequences are realized. In the case of Haynes Consultants, $18,000 of salary obligations and expenses would be recognized in 20X1. As its name implies, the **Salaries Payable** account represents amounts of future cash payments owed to the employee. The effect of the expense recognition on the accounting equation is as follows:

Event 4
Operating Activities Cause Increase in Liabilities (Expense Recognition)

	Assets		=	Liabilities	+	Equity		
	Cash	+	**Accounts Receivable**	=	**Salaries Payable**	+	**Contributed Capital**	+	**Retained Earnings**
Beginning Balances	$65,000		$24,000		$ 0		$5,000		$84,000
Recognized Liability/ Expense					+18,000				(18,000)
Ending Balances	$65,000	+	$24,000	=	$18,000	+	$5,000	+	$66,000

The expense recognition is a **claims exchange transaction.** Note that the claims of the creditors (i.e., liabilities) increase, and the claims of the owners (i.e., retained earnings) decrease by $18,000. Total claims remain the same, at $89,000. Also, assets are not affected by the transaction.

Cash payments to creditors are **asset use transactions.** When Haynes pays the part-time employee, amounts in the asset account, Cash, and the Liabilities account, Salaries Payable, decrease by $12,000. The effect of this transaction on the accounting equation is shown here:

	Assets			=	Liabilities	+	Equity		
	Cash	+	Accounts Receivable	=	Salaries Payable	+	Contributed Capital	+	Retained Earnings
Beginning Balances	$65,000		$24,000		$18,000		$5,000		$66,000
Made Cash Payment	(12,000)				(12,000)				
Ending Balances	$53,000	+	$24,000	=	$ 6,000	+	$5,000	+	$66,000

Note that the actual cash payment did not trigger the recognition of an expense. The expense was recognized in full at the time the liability was incurred. Double counting would occur if it were recognized again when the payment was made.

L.O. 3

Demonstrate a better understanding of how events are recorded under an accounting equation.

Summary of Transactions

Remember that amounts in green appear in the statement of cash flows. Those in red appear on the balance sheet. Items in blue are shown on the income statement.

	Assets			=	Liabilities	+	Equity		
	Cash	+	Accounts Receivable	=	Salaries Payable	+	Contributed Capital	+	Retained Earnings
Beginning Balances	$ 0		$ 0		$ 0		$ 0		$ 0
(1) Capital Acquisition	5,000						5,000		
(2) Recognized Asset/Revenue			84,000						84,000
(3) Cash Collection	60,000		(60,000)						
(4) Recognized Liability/ Expense					18,000				(18,000)
(5) Made Cash Payment	(12,000)				(12,000)				
Ending Balances	$53,000	+	$24,000	=	$ 6,000	+	$5,000	+	$66,000

L.O. 4

Prepare simple financial statements for a business that engages in cash and accrual transactions.

The 20X1 Financial Statements

The financial statements for Haynes Consultants for the 20X1 accounting period are shown in Exhibit 2–1 on pages 60–61.

Effects of Accrual Accounting

L.O. 5

Explain how accrual transactions affect the financial statements of a business.

Observe and note that the amount of *net income* ($66,000) reported on the income statement is different from the amount of *net cash flow from operations* ($48,000) shown in the statement of cash flows. This difference results from the application of accrual accounting. Recall that although $84,000 of revenue was recognized, only $60,000 was collected. Similarly, $18,000 of expenses was recognized, but only $12,000 of cash was paid. Since the revenue and expense items are not cash-equivalent figures, the amount of net income is not a cash-equivalent figure.

It is also important to note that the amount in the Cash account shown on the balance sheet ($53,000) is different from the amount of net income ($66,000) and the amount of cash flow from operations ($48,000). This condition occurs because the amount of cash is affected by more than revenue and expense events. In this case, the business acquired $5,000 of capital from the owner. This acquisition

The accrual concept requires a company to recognize revenue when it is "earned" rather than when it collects cash. In some business operations, it is not always easy to know precisely when the revenue is earned. CSX Corporation, a very large transportation company, recognizes revenue "proportionately as shipments move from origin to destination."

This means that if CSX agrees to ship goods 868 miles for $1,500, it recognizes approximately $1.73 of revenue for every mile the goods are moved. If you are thinking that this must require a very sophisticated computer system, you are correct!

Notice that the "recognize-as-you-go" practice does not violate the rule that revenue cannot be recognized before it is earned. CSX cannot recognize the entire $1,500 until the point of destination has been reached. However, the company can recognize the revenue in proportion to the amount of the trip that is completed. If one-half of the trip is completed, one-half of the revenue can be recognized.

does not affect revenue or expense but does affect the Cash account. Other events, such as borrowing funds, repaying debt, and purchasing assets, affect the amount of cash without affecting the net income or the cash flow from operations. Students who are new to accounting often confuse cash flow and net income. To avoid this pitfall, note that the economic benefits and sacrifices of operating the business appear on the income statement as they occur, regardless of their immediate cash consequences. In contrast, cash consequences appear on the statement of cash flows regardless of their effect on net income.

The Income Statement

The income statement explains the changes in equity from all sources other than transactions with the owners of an enterprise. As such, it represents the change in net assets associated with operating the business. In the case of Haynes Consultants, assets—specifically, accounts receivable—increased by $84,000; and liabilities—specifically, salaries payable—increased by $18,000. Since the term *net assets* is defined as assets minus liabilities, net assets increased by $66,000 (or $84,000 − $18,000).[1] Accordingly, the amount of net income ($66,000) represents the net economic benefit associated with owning the business. In other words, the wealth of the business increased as a result of the performance of its consulting activities. The net income increases the owner's claims on the business's assets and thereby enhances the wealth of the owners.

[1]Note that subsequent cash realizations associated with revenue and expense recognitions do not affect net assets. The receipt of $60,000 cash from the collection of accounts receivable was an asset exchange that left total assets and therefore net assets unchanged. The $12,000 cash payment made to reduce the Salaries Payable account was an asset use transaction that reduced assets and liabilities by a like amount, thereby leaving net assets unchanged.

L.O. 6

Define *revenue* and *expense* in terms of their relationships to assets and liabilities.

An alert reader may have observed that the recognition of the salaries expense in the Haynes illustration represents an expansion of the definition of expense given in Chapter 1. Previously, *expenses* were defined as economic sacrifices resulting in a decrease in assets. In this illustration, the recognition of salaries expense occurred in response to an increase in liabilities (i.e., salaries payable). Accordingly, **expenses** can be defined *as a decrease in assets or an increase in liabilities* that results from operating activities undertaken for the purpose of generating revenue. Similarly, revenue recognition can be triggered by decreases in liabilities. For example, a person could work off a debt rather than pay cash to the creditor. In this case, the liability decreases and revenue increases. As a result, the definition of **revenue** can be expanded as follows: *an increase in assets or a decrease in liabilities* resulting from the *operating activities* of a business enterprise.

The Statement of Changes in Equity

The statement of changes in equity displays the effects of capital acquisitions from and distributions to owners. It identifies the ways in which an entity's equity increases and decreases as a result of transactions with its owners. In the Haynes case, the statement reveals that the business acquired a $5,000 cash contribution of capital from the owner. The statement also indicates that none of the

EXHIBIT 2–1		
Vertical Statements Model		
Haynes Consultants **Financial Statements** **for the 20X1 Accounting Period***		
Income Statement		
Consulting Revenue		$84,000
Salary Expense		(18,000)
Net Income		$66,000
Statement of Changes in Equity		
Beginning Contributed Capital	$ 0	
Plus: Capital Acquisition	5,000	
Ending Contributed Capital		$ 5,000
Beginning Retained Earnings	0	
Plus: Net Income	66,000	
Less: Distributions	0	
Ending Retained Earnings		66,000
Total Equity		$71,000

(cont'd)

*As previously indicated, the vertical model format does not distinguish individual statement characteristics through the description of dates (i.e., *as of* versus *for the period ended*). This practice continues through the text whenever the four financial statements are presented simultaneously. In real-world annual reports, financial statements are normally presented separately, with appropriate descriptions of the date to indicate whether the statement applies to the entire accounting period or to a specific time.

Balance Sheet		
Assets		
Cash	$53,000	
Accounts Receivable	24,000	
Total Assets		$77,000
Liabilities		$ 6,000
Equity		
Contributed Capital	5,000	
Retained Earnings	66,000	
Total Equity		71,000
Total Liabilities and Equity		$77,000
Statement of Cash Flows		
Cash Flows from Operating Activities		
Cash Receipts from Revenue	$60,000	
Cash Payments for Expenses	(12,000)	
Net Cash Flow from Operating Activities		$48,000
Net Cash Flow from Investing Activities		0
Net Cash Flow from Financing Activities		
Cash Receipts from Capital Acquisition		5,000
Net Change in Cash		53,000
Plus: Beginning Cash Balance		0
Ending Cash Balance		$53,000

$66,000 of net earnings was distributed. Accordingly, the amount of ending equity is $71,000.

The Balance Sheet

The balance sheet provides information about an entity's assets, liabilities, and equity and their relationships to one another at a particular time. It provides a list of the economic resources (i.e., assets) that the enterprise has available for its operating activities. In addition, it displays the claims on those resources. Haynes Consultants had two assets at the end of the 20X1 accounting period: cash amounting to $53,000 and accounts receivable of $24,000. These assets are listed on the balance sheet in accordance with their respective levels of liquidity. Of the total $77,000 of assets, the creditors have a $6,000 claim, leaving a $71,000 claim that represents the owner's interest.

The Statement of Cash Flows

The statement of cash flows explains the change in cash from one accounting period to the next. Accordingly, it can be prepared by analyzing the cash account. Since Haynes Consultants was established in the 20X1 accounting period, it had a beginning cash balance of zero. By the end of the accounting period, the balance increased to $53,000. The statement of cash flows explains how this occurred. Specifically, the Cash account balance increased by $60,000 due to the consulting activities (i.e., operations). Furthermore, $12,000 was spent in the process of operating the business. As a result, there was a net cash inflow from operations of $48,000. Also, the business acquired a $5,000 cash contribution of capital from Haynes. The combination of these two factors explains the $53,000 (or $48,000 + $5,000) increase in cash during the 20X1 accounting period.

Second Accounting Cycle

Assume that the following accounting events apply to the operations of Haynes Consultants during 20X2:

L.O. 2

Identify business events that involve accruals.

1. Haynes Consultants acquired an additional $25,000 cash contribution of capital from the owner.
2. During the period, $96,000 of revenue was recognized on account.
3. There was $102,000 of cash collected from accounts receivable.
4. Accrued salary expenses amounted to $22,000.
5. Cash paid toward the settlement of salaries payable amounted to $20,000.
6. A $10,000 distribution was made to the owner.
7. On March 1, 20X2, Haynes invested $60,000 in a certificate of deposit (CD). The certificate carried a 6% annual rate of interest and a 1-year term to maturity.
8. On December 31, 20X2, Haynes adjusted the books to recognize interest revenue earned on the certificate of deposit.

L.O. 3

Demonstrate a better understanding of how events are recorded under an accounting equation.

Effect of Events on the Accounting Equation

Exhibit 2–2 summarizes the effects of the transactions on the accounting equation. Green signifies cash flow; red, the balance sheet; and blue, the income statement.

EXHIBIT 2–2							
Effect of 20X2 Events on the Accounting Equation							
	Assets				= **Liabilities** +	**Equity**	
	Cash +	**Accounts Receivable** +	**Interest Receivable** +	**Certificate of Deposit** =	**Salaries Payable** +	**Contributed Capital** +	**Retained Earnings**
Beginning Balances	$ 53,000	$ 24,000	$ 0	$ 0	$ 6,000	$ 5,000	$ 66,000
(1) Capital Acquisition	+25,000					+25,000	
(2) Recognized Revenue		+96,000					+96,000
(3) Collected Accounts Receivable	+102,000	(102,000)					
(4) Recognized Expense					+22,000		(22,000)
(5) Paid Liability for Salaries	(20,000)				(20,000)		
(6) Distributed Cash to Owners	(10,000)						(10,000)
(7) Invested in CD	(60,000)			+60,000			
(8) Recognized Accrued Interest			+3,000				+3,000
Ending Balances	$ 90,000 +	$ 18,000 +	$ 3,000 +	$ 60,000 =	$ 8,000 +	$ 30,000 +	$ 133,000
		Total Assets $171,000			Total Liabilities = $8,000 +	Total Equity $163,000	

The first five transactions in the 20X2 accounting cycle are a repeat of the transactions that appeared in the 20X1 period. If you are having difficulty understanding the effects of these transactions on the accounting equation, review the previous material.

Events 1–5

The distribution of cash to the owner of the business constitutes an *asset use* transaction. It represents a transfer of wealth from the business to its owner. The transaction acts to reduce total assets (i.e., cash) and equity (i.e., retained earnings).

Event 6
Assets Transferred to Owners

The purchase of the certificate of deposit represents an **investment** *by the business enterprise.* The event acts to decrease the asset account, Cash, and to increase the asset account, Certificate of Deposit. Total assets remain unchanged.

Event 7
Exchange of Cash for Certificate of Deposit

When Haynes Consultants (i.e., the business) invested in (purchased) the certificate of deposit, the company, in fact, loaned the bank money. In exchange for the privilege of using Haynes' money, the bank agreed to return the money (principal) and an additional 6% of the principal amount (interest) to Haynes 1 year from the date that the funds were borrowed. In other words, in exchange for receiving $60,000 on March 1, 20X2, the bank agreed to pay Haynes $63,000 (or $60,000 + [0.06 × $60,000]) on February 28, 20X3. This means that Haynes will be paid $3,600 per year as compensation for letting the bank use its cash.

Event 8
(Adjusting Entry) Recognition of Interest Revenue

It is important to recognize the fact that interest is earned on a continuous basis even though the payment is made at the maturity date. In other words, the amount of interest due increases proportionally with the passage of time. Specifically, Haynes' asset account, Interest Receivable (i.e., amount due from bank), and its equity account, Interest Revenue, increase continuously with the passage of time. Without the use of sophisticated computer equipment, recording (recognizing) interest as it occurs is impossible.

L.O. 7

Explain the effects of end-of-period adjustments related to accruals.

As a practical matter, many businesses let the interest accrue without being recognized until it is time to prepare financial statements. The accounts are then adjusted to reflect the amount of interest due as of the date of the financial statements. For example, when Haynes purchased the certificate of deposit on March 1, 20X2, the asset exchange was recorded immediately, showing the decrease in cash and the increase in the Certificate of Deposit account. However, the interest associated with the certificate was not recognized until the date of the financial statements on December 31, 20X2. At this time, a single entry could be made to recognize the accrual of 10 months of interest. This entry is called an **adjusting entry** because it corrects (i.e., updates) the account balances prior to the preparation of financial statements. The adjusting entry for the accrual of interest for Haynes Consultants is shown as the last entry in Exhibit 2–2. The amount is computed by multiplying the face value by the rate by the length of time for which the loan was outstanding [$60,000 × 0.06 × ($\frac{10}{12}$) = $3,000].

L.O. 4

Prepare simple financial statements for a business that engages in cash and accrual transactions.

The 20X2 Financial Statements

Exhibit 2–3 contains the financial statements for the 20X2 accounting period. The relationships among the statements are now discussed.

Effects of Accrual Accounting

The Income Statement

Note that the amount of net income ($77,000) is not a cash-equivalent figure. The cash flow from operating activities is $82,000, as shown in the statement of cash

L.O. 5

Explain how accrual transactions affect the financial statements of a business.

flows. Although $96,000 of consulting revenue was recognized, $102,000 of cash was collected. This result occurs because some of the revenue recognized in 20X1 was actually collected in 20X2. Also, the income statement displays the recognition of $3,000 of interest revenue. None of this revenue was collected during 20X2. Accordingly, the total amount of cash collected from revenue transactions was $102,000. Finally, although the amount of salary expense recognized was $22,000, the amount paid was only $20,000. Accordingly, the net cash inflow from operations was $82,000 ($102,000 − $20,000). In contrast, the income state-

EXHIBIT 2–3		
Vertical Statements Model		
Haynes Consultants **Financial Statements** **for the 20X2 Accounting Period**		
Income Statements		
Consulting Revenue	$ 96,000	
Interest Revenue	3,000	
Total Revenue		$ 99,000
Salary Expense		(22,000)
Net Income		$ 77,000
Statement of Changes in Equity		
Beginning Contributed Capital	$ 5,000	
Plus: Capital Acquisition	25,000	
Ending Contributed Capital		$ 30,000
Beginning Retained Earnings	66,000	
Plus: Net Income	77,000	
Less: Distributions	(10,000)	
Ending Retained Earnings		133,000
Total Equity		$163,000
Balance Sheet		
Assets		
Cash	$ 90,000	
Accounts Receivable	18,000	
Interest Receivable	3,000	
Certificate of Deposit	60,000	
Total Assets		$171,000
Liabilities		$ 8,000
Equity		
Contributed Capital	$ 30,000	
Retained Earnings	133,000	
Total Equity		163,000
Total Liabilities and Equity		$171,000

(cont'd)

Statement of Cash Flows		
Cash Flows from Operating Activities		
Cash Receipts from Revenue	$102,000	
Cash Payments for Expenses	(20,000)	
Net Cash Flow from Operating Activities		$82,000
Cash Flows from Investing Activities		
Cash Payment to Purchase CD		(60,000)
Cash Flows from Financing Activities		
Cash Receipt from Capital Acquisition	25,000	
Cash Payment for Distribution	(10,000)	
Net Cash Inflow from Financing Activities		15,000
Net Change in Cash		37,000
Plus: Beginning Cash Balance		53,000
Ending Cash Balance		$90,000

ment displays the amount of net income recognized ($96,000 + $3,000 − $22,000 = $77,000).

The Statement of Changes in Equity

The beginning balances for the Contributed Capital and Retained Earnings are accounts drawn from last year's ending balances. The $25,000 capital acquisition is added to the $5,000 beginning capital balance to arrive at the $30,000 ending balance. Of the $77,000 of net income, $10,000 is distributed to the owner of the business. Accordingly, Retained Earnings increases by $67,000 from a beginning balance of $66,000 to an ending balance of $133,000. The ending balance in total equity amounts to $163,000 ($30,000 + $133,000).

The Balance Sheet

Although two additional asset accounts are in the 20X2 balance sheet, all assets continue to be listed in accordance with their respective levels of liquidity. Total assets amount to $171,000, which is equal to the claims of $171,000. The claims are divided into the claim associated with salaries payable of $8,000 and the owner's claim of $163,000.

The Statement of Cash Flows

The $82,000 of net cash inflow from operations is discussed in the section pertaining to the income statement. In addition to this amount, an analysis of the Cash account reveals that a $60,000 cash outflow occurred as a result of the purchase of the certificate of deposit. Furthermore, an additional $25,000 cash inflow resulted from capital acquisitions, and, finally, a $10,000 cash outflow occurred in the form of a distribution to the owner. Accordingly, the net change in cash amounted to a $37,000 increase ($82,000 − $60,000 + $15,000). This amount can be verified by comparing the cash balance at the beginning of the period ($53,000) with the cash balance at the end of the period ($90,000). The difference is a $37,000 increase.

Third Accounting Cycle

L.O. 2

Identify business events that involve accruals.

Assume that the following events apply to Haynes Consultants' 20X3 accounting period.

1. The business acquired an additional $15,000 cash contribution of capital from Haynes.
2. During the period, $116,000 of revenue was recognized on account.
3. There was $110,000 of cash collected from accounts receivable.
4. Accrued salary expenses amounted to $28,000.
5. Cash paid toward the settlement of salaries payable amounted to $30,000.
6. A $5,000 distribution was made to the owner.
7. On February 28, 20X3, Haynes received the return of principal and collected the cash for interest when the certificate of deposit matured.
8. On September 1, 20X3, Haynes borrowed $90,000 from a local bank. The note carried a 9% annual rate of interest and a 1-year term.
9. On October 1, 20X3, Haynes purchased a plot of land that cost $300,000. Due to the approval of commercial zoning, the value of the land had risen to $350,000 by December 31, 20X3.

L.O. 3

Demonstrate a better understanding of how events are recorded under an accounting equation.

Events 1–6

Event 7
Maturity of
Certificate of Deposit

Effect of Events on the Accounting Equation

Exhibit 2–4 on the following page is a summary of the effects of the 20X3 transactions on the accounting equation. Green is for cash flow, red for the balance sheet, and blue for the income statement.

Again, the first five transactions for the 20X3 accounting period mirror those shown in the exhibit for the 20X1 period. The sixth transaction was shown in the exhibit for the 20X2 accounting period. For explanations of these transactions, refer to the appropriate earlier sections of this chapter.

Event 7 pertains to the maturity of the certificate of deposit. The effects of this event on the accounting equation are shown in three separate entries. The first consideration applies to the accrual of 2 months of interest. Recall that 10 months' interest was recognized in the 20X2 accounting period. Accordingly, only 2 additional months (i.e., January and February) remained to be accounted for during 20X3. The amount of accrued interest to be recognized in 20X3 was $600 (that is, $60,000 \times 0.06 \times \frac{2}{12}$). The entry to record the accrued interest revenue is an *asset source* transaction. Specifically, the asset account Interest Receivable increases, and the equity account, Retained Earnings, increases. (Refer to entry 7[a] in Exhibit 2–4).

The second entry records the collection of the interest receivable. This transaction is an *asset exchange* transaction. The asset, Cash, increases by $3,600, and the asset, Interest Receivable, decreases by the same amount. Note that the payment is for the entire $3,600. Even though $3,000 of the interest was recognized as revenue in 20X2, no cash was collected at that time. Accordingly, the cash collection in 20X3 covers the entire year's amount of interest. (Refer to entry 7[b] in Exhibit 2–4.)

The final entry associated with the maturity of the certificate of deposit involves the collection of the principal. This entry represents an *asset exchange* transaction. The asset, Cash, increases by $60,000, and the asset, Certificate of Deposit, decreases by the same amount. (Refer to entry 7[c] in Exhibit 2–4.)

EXHIBIT 2-4

Effect of 20X3 Events on the Accounting Equation

	Assets					=	Liabilities			+	Equity	
	Cash	Accts. Rec.	Int. Rec.	CD	Land	=	Sal. Pay.	Int. Pay.	Note Pay.	+	Cont. Cap.	Ret. Ear.
Beginning Balances	$ 90,000	$ 18,000	$3,000	$60,000	$ 0	=	$ 8,000	$ 0	$ 0	+	$30,000	$133,000
(1) Capital Acquisition	+15,000										+15,000	
(2) Recognized Revenue		+116,000										+116,000
(3) Collected Cash from Rec.	+110,000	(110,000)										
(4) Recognized Expense							+28,000					(28,000)
(5) Paid Liability for Salaries	(30,000)						(30,000)					
(6) Distributed Cash to Owners	(5,000)											(5,000)
(7a) Recognized Accrued Interest			+600									+600
(7b) Collected Cash for Interest	+3,600		(3,600)									
(7c) Redeemed Principal of CD	+60,000			(60,000)								
(8) Borrowed Funds from Bank	+90,000								+90,000			
(9) Purchased Land	(300,000)				+300,000							
(10) Recognized Interest on Note								2,700				(2,700)
Ending Balances	$ 33,600	$ 24,000	$ 0	$ 0	$300,000	=	$ 6,000	$ 2,700	$90,000	+	$45,000	$213,950

Total Assets $357,600

Total Liabilities $98,700 + Total Equity $258,900

The accounting Event No. 8 describes the borrowing of funds from a bank. This is an *asset source* transaction. The asset account, Cash, increases by $90,000, and the liability account, Note Payable, increases by a like amount. The account title **Note Payable** is used because the bank normally requires the borrower to sign a note that describes the terms of the loan. Typical items included in the note are the rate of interest, the term to maturity, and collateral that is pledged to secure the loan. The borrower gives the note to the bank and receives money from the bank. The borrower is known as the **issuer of a note,** and the bank is called the *creditor* or *lender*.

Event No. 9 describes the purchase of a $300,000 plot of land. This is an *asset exchange* transaction. The asset account, Cash, decreases; and the Land account increases. The amount of total assets is unchanged. The land is reported on the balance sheet at its **historical cost** ($300,000), even though its market value rose to $350,000 by the close of the accounting cycle. The information in financial statements reflects events that have already happened. Users of financial statements are expected to assess the possible impact of factors that may change the historical cost amounts and to form their own expectations about the future and its relation to the past.

An *adjusting entry* is necessary to recognize the accrual of interest on the bank loan from the date the note was issued to the date of the financial statements. In the Haynes case, $90,000 was borrowed on September 1, 20X3. Accordingly, 4 months of interest accrued by the financial closing date, December 31, 20X3. The amount of accrued interest is $2,700 (that is, $90,000 × 0.09 × 4/12). The entry to record the accrued interest involves a *claims exchange*. The liability account, Interest Payable, increases, and the equity account, Retained Earnings, decreases.

L.O. 7

Explain the effects of end-of-period adjustments related to accruals.

The 20X3 Financial Statements

Exhibit 2–5 contains the financial statements for the 20X3 accounting period. The beginning balances in these statements were taken from the ending balances appearing on the 20X2 statements. Review the statements thoroughly; explanations of the preparation and analysis of financial statements are in the earlier sections of

EXHIBIT 2–5		
Vertical Statements Model		
Haynes Consultants **Financial Statements** **For the 20X3 Accounting Period**		
Income Statement		
Consulting Revenue	$116,000	
Interest Revenue	600	
Total Revenue		$116,600
Salary Expense	28,000	
Interest Expense	2,700	
Total Expense		(30,700)
Net Income		$ 85,900

(cont'd)

Statement of Changes in Equity

Beginning Contributed Capital	$ 30,000	
Plus: Capital Acquisition	15,000	
Ending Contributed Capital		$ 45,000
Beginning Retained Earnings	133,000	
Plus: Net Income	85,900	
Less: Distributions	(5,000)	
Ending Retained Earnings		213,900
Total Equity		$258,900

Balance Sheet

Assets		
Cash	$ 33,600	
Accounts Receivable	24,000	
Land	300,000	
Total Assets		$357,600
Liabilities		
Salaries Payable	$ 6,000	
Interest Payable	2,700	
Note Payable	90,000	
Total Liabilities		$ 98,700
Equity		
Contributed Capital	45,000	
Retained Earnings	213,900	
Total Equity		258,900
Total Liabilities and Equity		$357,600

Statement of Cash Flows

Cash Flows from Operating Activities		
Cash Receipts from Consulting Revenue	$110,000	
Cash Receipts from Interest Revenue	3,600	
Cash Payments for Salaries	(30,000)	
Net Cash Inflow from Operating Activities		$ 83,600
Cash Flows from Investing Activities		
Cash Receipt from CD Maturity	60,000	
Cash Payment to Purchase Land	(300,000)	
Net Cash Outflow from Investing Activities		(240,000)
Cash Flows from Financing Activities		
Cash Receipt from Bank Loan	90,000	
Cash Receipt from Capital Acquisition	15,000	
Cash Payment for Distribution	(5,000)	
Net Cash Inflow from Financing Activities		100,000
Net Change in Cash		(56,400)
Plus: Beginning Cash Balance		90,000
Ending Cash Balance		$ 33,600

reality bytes

© Alex Bartel/Science Photo Researchers, Inc.

Under the accrual system, accountants recognize revenue after the work has been done but before the cash is collected. Investors are more aggressive than accountants with respect to income recognition. They recognize income even before the work is done. This explains why stock (ownership) of some companies sells for more than stock of other companies. Investors buy stock because they want to participate in the profit (net income) that the company earns. Accordingly, investors are willing to pay more for a company whose future earnings potential is significantly greater than average. For example, since Microsoft operates in an industry with significant growth potential, its stock may sell for 40 times earnings while Exxon's is selling for only 10 times earnings. This means if Microsoft and Exxon were earning $1 per share of stock, Microsoft's stock would be selling for $40 while Exxon's stock would be selling for $10. In other words, investors are basing their purchases on the companies' potential to earn future profits rather than their past earnings history as depicted in the companies' financial statements. Does this mean that financial statements are not useful in making investment decisions? This answer is no. Past earnings provide insight into the future. In other words, a company that has a history of earnings that grow at a rate of 30% per year is more likely to continue to experience rapid growth than a company with a 10% historical growth rate. Accordingly, financial statements that are based on accrual accounting can provide insight into the future even though they are historically based.

this chapter, the 20X1 Financial Statements and the 20X2 Financial Statements. Refer to these sections if you have trouble interpreting the financial statements or understanding the derivation of the numbers presented in the statements.

Role of the Independent Auditor

L.O. 8

Understand the auditor's role in financial reporting.

The four basic financial statements presented in annual reports are the income statement, statement of changes in equity, balance sheet, and statement of cash flows. As previously indicated, these statements are prepared in accordance with certain rules, called *generally accepted accounting principles,* or simply *GAAP.* Thus, when General Electric publishes its financial statements, it is saying not only "here are our financial statements," but more specifically, "here are our financial statements prepared according to GAAP." As discussed throughout this course, the application of GAAP requires considerable judgment and calls for some interpretation, estimation, and assumption making. How can users of financial statements be sure a company really did follow GAAP and whether it exercised reasonable judgment and good faith in the application of GAAP to its financial reporting practices? Users rely on **audits** conducted by certified public accountants (CPAs).

Although the information in this chapter focuses on the audit function, CPAs provide many services across a wide spectrum of jobs. Exhibit 2–6 on the following page is from the January 1996 Special Student Edition of the Alabama

EXHIBIT 2–6

No Rubber Stamp for Accountants

An accounting degree is, indeed, "the one degree with 360 degrees of possibilities." And personalities within the profession are as diverse as the range of job opportunities available to the accounting graduate. There is no rubber stamp for today's accountants. Consider the experiences of the following individuals.

Jerry Gibbons is a partner in the accounting firm Gibbons & Dees. Jerry teaches a course in the fundamentals of sports accounting in several Asian countries. As an adjunct professor for the United States Sports Academy, Jerry had the opportunity to meet with the Olympic committees when he taught in Hong Kong, Singapore, Kuala Lumpur, and Bangkok. Although it was his second Asian assignment, Gibbons says he was again overwhelmed with the friendliness and generosity of the Asian people.

Danny Martin was recently promoted to manager at Wilson, Price, Barranco & Billingsley, a regional firm of certified public accountants. Danny worked his way through college as a paramedic and has just never gotten over the thrill of flying down the highway in an ambulance. "That's my stress management," says the father of two, who still works two weekends a month as a paramedic for Haynes Ambulance. His adventures with CPR, heart defibrillation, and drug therapy take him a world away from his job in the Business Services Department of his firm.

Sister Rose Marie of Divine Love left public accounting to enter the cloistered life at Our Lady of the Angels Monastery. She now helps the bookkeepers at Eternal Word Television Network (EWTN), a 24-hour-a-day network that has more than 160 employees and broadcasts into Europe, Moscow, the Middle East, Africa, and all the Americas. Sister Rose Marie took a vow of poverty when she entered the Order of Poor Clares of Perpetual Adoration (P.C.P.A.), which may be why one auditor at EWTN, she says, asked her if the initials after her name stood for "poor CPA."

Society of Certified Public Accountants. Reading the information in the exhibit will give you a better understanding of the diversity of job opportunities that await graduates with degrees in accounting. The following sections will discuss in detail the overall roles and responsibilities the independent auditor assumes. Briefly, the independent auditor performs several functions:

1. Conducts a financial audit, which is a detailed review of a company's financial statements and documents.
2. Assumes both legal and professional responsibilities to the public, not to the company paying the auditor.
3. Guarantees that financial statements are materially correct rather than absolutely correct.
4. Presents conclusions in an audit report, which includes an opinion resulting from the audit. When necessary, the auditor issues a disclaimer.
5. Maintains professional confidentiality with clients. However, if necessary to testify in court, this does not exempt the auditor from legal obligations.

The Financial Audit

What is an audit? First, you must realize that there are several different types of audits. The type most relevant to this course is called a **financial audit,** which is a detailed examination of a company's financial statements and the documents that support the information presented in those statements. The audit includes a verification process that tests the reliability of the underlying accounting system used to produce the financial reports. A financial audit is conducted by a CPA who is known as the **independent auditor.**

Understanding the role of an independent auditor is almost as important as understanding what a financial audit is. Normally, the term *independent auditor* designates a *firm of* **certified public accountants.** CPAs are licensed by state governments to provide accounting services to the public. CPAs who perform financial audits are paid by the companies that they audit. However, CPAs are not employees of those companies. In fact, neither the CPAs nor their immediate family members may own stock or have any other type of investment in the companies they audit. Furthermore, the payment of CPAs is not to be based on the outcome of the audit. The CPAs are to be as independent of the companies they audit as is reasonably possible.

Although the independent auditors are chosen by, paid by, and can be fired by the company that they are auditing, the auditors have a primary responsibility to *the public.* In fact, auditors have a legal responsibility to those members of the public who have a financial interest in the company being audited. If investors in a company lose money, they sometimes sue the independent auditors in an attempt to recover their losses. This is more likely to occur if the loss was due to something dramatic, such as the company's filing for bankruptcy. The lawsuit will be successful only if it can be shown that the auditors failed in their professional responsibilities when conducting the audit. The fact that a company declares bankruptcy does not imply that the auditors can be sued successfully. In reality, auditors are not sued very often, given the number of audits they perform.

Auditors' professional responsibility is to ensure that the company properly reports its financial situation, whether good or bad. Auditors get into trouble when a company has a problem that is not properly reported and the auditors do not detect the improper reporting practice. For example, a company might overstate the amount of its net income. If the auditors allow the incorrect amount to be reported and the size of the error is material, the auditors create a problem for which they may suffer legal consequences.

Materiality and Financial Audits

Now things get a bit fuzzy. What is a **material error?** An error, or other reporting problem, is considered material if knowing about the problem would affect the decisions of an *average prudent investor.* Thus, the concept of materiality is very subjective. However, it means that the auditors are not guaranteeing that the financial statements are absolutely correct—only that they are *materially* correct. If General Motors inadvertently overstated its sales by $1 million, would this be material? In 1997, GM had approximately $178 billion of sales! A $1 million error in computing sales at GM is like a $1 error in computing the pay of a person who makes $178,000 per year—not material at all!

A financial audit is not concerned with absolute precision, and it is not primarily looking for fraud on the part of the company's employees. Even so, auditors are responsible for providing *reasonable assurance* that their audits will detect

focus on international issues

Is Historical Cost Used in Other Countries?

ccounting rules in the United States require the use of the historical cost to record most accounting transactions. Thus, if Coca-Cola Company purchased land in Atlanta for $10,000 in 1920, that land, if still owned, will be on the company's 2020 balance sheet at $10,000 even if it is worth $5,000,000 by then. Not everyone in the United States thinks this is the best way to report accounting numbers, but U.S. GAAP requires the use of historical costs.

The accounting rules of most countries around the world also use the historical cost as the primary means of measuring and reporting costs; however, there are exceptions. The major exceptions occur in economies that have experienced high inflation. In the hypothetical Coca-Cola example, a time frame of 100 years was used to make the change in the value of the land look dramatic. In short time spans, land prices in the United States do not change so radically, so most accountants are comfortable with using historical costs. In some South American countries, prices have risen much faster than those in the United States. For example, while the annual rate of inflation in the United States typically ranges from 2 to 6%, in Brazil it has seldom been below 20% and in some years has exceeded 1,000%. Not surprisingly, the GAAP in Brazil does not use historical costs as the primary way of reporting financial information.

In some countries, such as the Netherlands, companies use historical costs as their primary way of measuring costs but may report the value of some assets, such as land and buildings, at the amount it would cost to replace them "today" rather than at their historical costs. Accounting is a discipline created to serve the needs of financial statement users. It is logical that accounting rules reflect the unique needs of users in different countries.

material misstatements (i.e., fraud). Also, auditors are responsible for ensuring that internal control procedures (explained in Chapter 6) are in place to help prevent fraud. If fraud is widespread in a company, normal audit procedures should detect it.

Accounting majors take at least one and often two or more courses in auditing to understand how to conduct an audit to detect material accounting problems. Obviously, there is not enough time in this course to explain auditing techniques, but at least be aware that auditors do not review how the company accounted for every transaction. Along with other methods, auditors use statistical sampling to systematically review company records.

Types Of Audit Opinions

Once an audit is complete, the auditors present their conclusions in an audit report, which includes an audit opinion. There are three basic types of audit opinions, with variations.

An **unqualified opinion,** despite its negative-sounding name, is the best that auditors can give. It means that the auditor believes the financial statements are in compliance with GAAP without qualification, reservation, or exception.

The most negative report that an auditor can issue is an **adverse opinion.** This means that something(s) in the financial statements is (are) not in compliance with GAAP and the auditors think these things would be material to the average prudent investor. The auditor's report explains the unacceptable accounting practice(s) that resulted in the adverse opinion's being issued. Adverse opinions are very rare. To avoid receiving an adverse opinion, a company usually corrects the accounting issue that concerns the auditors.

A **qualified opinion** falls between an unqualified and an adverse opinion. A qualified opinion means that for the most part, the company's financial statements are in compliance with GAAP, but the auditors have reservations about something in the statements or have some other reason not to give a fully unqualified opinion. At least an entire chapter could be written about reasons to issue qualified opinions, but typically they result from the auditors' need to bring special attention to some accounting attribute in the financial statements. A qualified opinion usually does not imply a serious accounting problem, but users should read the auditors' report and draw their own conclusions about the relevance of the issues involved. The auditors' report explains why a qualified opinion is being issued.

If an auditor is unable to perform the audit procedures necessary to determine whether the statements are prepared in accordance with GAAP, the auditor cannot issue an opinion on the financial statements. Instead, the auditor issues a **disclaimer of audit opinion.** A disclaimer is neither negative nor positive; it simply means that the auditor is unable to obtain enough information to confirm compliance or noncompliance with GAAP.

It is very important to understand that the ultimate responsibility for the financial statements rests with the executives of the reporting company. Just like auditors, managers can be sued by investors who believe that they lost money due to improper financial reporting. This is one reason nonaccounting business-people should understand accounting fundamentals.

Confidentiality

The code of ethics for CPAs forbids auditors from **voluntarily disclosing** information that they have acquired as a result of their accountant-client relationships. However, accountants may be required to testify in a court of law. In general, federal law does not recognize an accountant-client privilege as it does with attorneys and clergy. Even so federal courts have taken exception to this position, especially as it applies to tax cases. State law varies with respect to its treatment of accountant-client privilege. Furthermore, if auditors terminate a client relationship because of ethical or legal disagreements and they are subsequently contacted by a successor accountant, they may be required to inform the successor of the reasons that led to the termination. In addition, the particular circumstances surrounding the case must be taken into consideration when assessing the appropriateness of making such a disclosure. Given the legal diversity, with respect to the issue of accountant-client confidentiality, it is wise to seek legal counsel prior to making any disclosures of information obtained in an accountant-client relationship.

To illustrate, assume that Joe Smith, CPA, discovers that his client Jane Doe is misrepresenting information shown in her financial statements. Smith tries to convince Doe to reform her practices, but she refuses to cease and desist. Smith is required by the code of ethics to terminate his relationship with Doe. However, Smith is not permitted to disclose Doe's dishonest reporting practices unless he is called on to provide testimony in a legal hearing or is responding to an inquiry by Doe's successor accountant.

With respect to the discovery of significant fraud, the auditor is required to inform management at one level above the position of the employee who is engaged in the fraud and to notify the board of directors of the company. Suppose that Joe Smith, CPA, discovers that Jane Doe, employee of Western Company, is embezzling money from Western. Smith is required to inform Doe's supervisor and to notify Western's board of directors. However, Smith is restricted from speaking publicly about the fraud.

Importance of Ethics

L.O. 9

Develop an appreciation of the importance of a code of ethics.

The accountant's role in society cannot be performed without the establishment of trust and credibility. An audit opinion is worthless if the auditor is not trustworthy. Similarly, tax and consulting advice is useless if it emanates from a source that lacks credible competence. In view of the high ethical standards required by the profession, "a certified public accountant assumes an obligation of self-discipline above and beyond requirements of laws and regulations."[2] Indeed, the **American Institute of Certified Public Accountants** requires its members to conduct themselves in accordance with its provisions, the **Code of Professional Conduct.** Section I of the code includes six articles that are summarized in Exhibit 2–7. The importance of ethical conduct is universally recognized across a broad spectrum of accounting organizations. The Institute of Management Accountants requires its members to follow a set of Standards of Ethical Conduct. Likewise, the membership of the Institute of Internal Auditors is required to subscribe to the organization's Code of Ethics.

Common Features of Ethical Misconduct

People who become involved in unethical or criminal behavior usually do so unexpectedly. They start with small indiscretions that evolve gradually into more serious violations of trust. Accordingly, awareness constitutes a key ingredient for the avoidance of unethical or illegal conduct. In an effort to increase

---

[2]American Institute of Certified Public Accountants, Inc. (AICPA), *Code of Professional Conduct* (New York: AICPA, 1992).

EXHIBIT 2–7

Articles of AICPA Code of Professional Conduct

Article I   Responsibilities
In carrying out their responsibilities as professionals, members should exercise sensitive professional and moral judgments in all their activities.

Article II   The Public Interest
Members should accept the obligation to act in a way that will serve the public interest, honor the public trust, and demonstrate commitment to professionalism.

Article III   Integrity
To maintain and broaden public confidence, members should perform all professional responsibilities with the highest sense of integrity.

Article IV   Objectivity and Independence
A member should maintain objectivity and be free of conflicts of interest in discharging professional responsibilities. A member in public practice should be independent in fact and appearance when providing auditing and other attestation services.

Article V   Due Care
A member should observe the profession's technical and ethical standards, strive continually to improve competence and the quality of services, and discharge professional responsibility to the best of the member's ability.

Article VI   Scope and Nature of Services
A member in public practice should observe the principles of the Code of Professional Conduct in determining the scope and nature of services to be provided.

---

awareness, Donald Cressey studied hundreds of criminal cases to identify the primary factors that lead to trust violations.[3] Cressey found that three factors were common to all cases:

> The existence of a nonsharable problem;
> The presence of an opportunity;
> The capacity for rationalization.

As the term implies, a *nonsharable problem* is one that must be kept secret. However, note that individuals have different ideas about what they think must be kept to themselves. Consider two responses to the problem of an imminent business failure. One person may feel so ashamed that he or she cannot discuss the problem with anyone. Another person in the same situation may want to talk to anyone, even a stranger, in the hope of getting help. Cressey's findings suggest that the person who is inclined toward secrecy is more likely to accept an unethical or illegal solution. In other words, secrecy increases vulnerability.

Accountants establish policies and procedures that are designed to reduce the opportunities for fraud. These policies and procedures are commonly called **internal controls.** Specific internal control procedures are tailored to meet the individual needs of particular businesses. For example, a bank may use vaults, but a university has little use for this type of equipment. Chapter 6 has a more detailed discussion of internal control procedures. At this point, simply recognize the fact that accountants are very aware of the need to reduce the opportunity for unethical and criminal activities.

Few individuals like to think of themselves as evil, so they develop rationalizations that enable the justification of their misconduct. Cressey found a significant number of embezzlers who contended that they were only "borrowing

---

[3]D. R. Cressey, *Other People's Money* (Montclair, NJ: Paterson Smith, 1973).

the money," even after being convicted and sentenced to jail. Some of the more common rationalizations include peer pressure, loyalty to unscrupulous superiors, family needs, revenge, and personal vices such as drug addiction, gambling, and promiscuity. To avoid involvement in ethical misconduct, accountants must develop a strong sense of personal responsibility. They cannot allow themselves to blame other people or unfair circumstances for their problems. They must learn to hold themselves personally accountable for their actions.

Ethical misconduct is a serious offense in the accounting profession. Accountants must realize that in this arena, their careers are vulnerable to a single mistake. If you are caught in white-collar crime, you normally lose the opportunity to hold a white-collar job. Second chances are rarely granted; it is extremely important that you learn how to recognize and avoid the common features of ethical misconduct. To help you prepare for the real-world situations you are likely to encounter, we include an ethical dilemma in the end-of-chapter materials. When working with these dilemmas, try to identify the (1) secret, (2) opportunity, and (3) rationalization associated with the particular ethical situation under consideration.

A LOOK BACK

Chapters 1 and 2 introduced four types of transactions. It is helpful to identify transactions by type. Although businesses engage in an infinite number of different transactions, all transactions can be classified into one of four types. By learning to identify transactions by type, you can learn how to incorporate unfamiliar events within the bounds of a conceptual framework. The four types of transaction follow:

L.O. 10
Classify accounting events into one of four categories.

1. **Asset source transactions:** An asset account increases, and a corresponding claims account increases.
2. **Asset use transactions:** An asset account decreases, and a corresponding claims account decreases.
3. **Asset exchange transactions:** One asset account increases, and another asset account decreases.
4. **Claims exchange transactions:** One claims account increases, and another claims account decreases.

Also, the definitions of revenue and expense have been expanded. The complete definitions of these two elements are as follows:

L.O. 6
Define *revenue* and *expense* in terms of their relationships to assets and liabilities.

1. **Revenue:** Revenue is the *economic benefit* associated with operating the business. Its recognition is triggered by an increase in assets or a decrease in liabilities that results from the normal operating activities of the business.
2. **Expense:** An expense is an *economic sacrifice* that is incurred in the process of generating revenue. Its recognition is triggered by a decrease in assets or an increase in liabilities that results from an effort to produce revenue.

Finally, this chapter introduced the *accrual accounting* concept. The application of this concept causes significant differences in the amount of revenues and expenses reported on the income statement and the amount of cash flow from operating activities on the statement of cash flows. These differences become readily apparent when relevant events are recorded in a horizontal financial statements model. To illustrate, review the following transactions and the corresponding statements model. To facilitate your understanding, draw a statements model on a piece of paper and try to record the effects of each event before you look at the explanation provided.

List of Events

1. Provided $600 of services on account.
2. Collected $400 cash from accounts receivable.
3. Accrued $350 of salary expense.
4. Paid $225 cash in partial settlement of salaries payable.

Event No.	Balance Sheet									Income Statement						Statement of Cash Flows	
	Cash	+	Acct. Rec.	=	S. Pay.	+	Ret. Earn.		Rev.	−	Exp.	=	Net Inc.			
1	n/a	+	600	=	n/a	+	600		600	−	n/a	=	600		n/a	
2	400	+	(400)	=	n/a	+	n/a		n/a	−	n/a	=	n/a		400	OA
3	n/a	+	n/a	=	350	+	(350)		n/a	−	350	=	(350)		n/a	
4	(225)	+	0	=	(225)	+	n/a		n/a	−	n/a	=	n/a		(225)	OA
Totals	175	+	200	=	125	+	250		600	−	350	=	250		175	NC

Notice that the amount of net income ($250) is different from the amount of cash flow from operating activities ($175). A review of the entries in the statements model should make the reasons for this difference clear. Although $600 of revenue is recognized, only $400 of cash was collected. The remaining $200 is expected to be collected in the future and is currently shown on the balance sheet as accounts receivable. Also, although $350 of salary expense is recognized, only $225 was paid in cash. The remaining $125 is expected to be paid in the future. This obligation is shown as salaries payable on the balance sheet. You should study these relationships carefully to develop a clear understanding of how accrual accounting affects financial reporting.

A LOOK

FORWARD

Chapter 3 continues the examination of the accrual accounting system. In addition to accruals, the accrual system also involves deferrals. *Deferrals* result when a company receives or pays cash before it recognizes the related revenue or expense. A magazine subscription is an example of a deferral event because magazine companies receive the cash before they provide magazines to their customers. The cash is collected in advance, but the revenue is not recognized until the magazines are delivered. Chapter 3 also reinforces what you have learned about asset source, use, and exchange transactions and claims exchange transactions. Also, you will be given the opportunity to broaden your understanding of how business events affect financial statements.

KEY TERMS

Accounts Receivable Amounts of future cash receipts that are due from customers; that is, revenue from customers has been recognized, but the cash has not been collected. *(p. 56)*

Accrual The recognition of events before the cash consequences are realized. *(p. 55)*

Accrual Accounting A method of accounting that records the effects of accounting events in the period in which such events occur regardless of when cash is exchanged. *(p. 55)*

Adjusting Entry An entry that updates account balances prior to preparation of the financial statements. *(p. 63)*

Adverse Opinion An audit opinion for a set of financial statements issued by a certified public accountant that means that part of or all of the financial statements are not in compliance with GAAP and the auditors believe this noncompliance would be material to the average prudent investor. *(p. 74)*

American Institute of Certified Public Accountants' Code of Professional Conduct A set of ethical rules and guidelines above and beyond the requirements of laws and regulations that certified public accountants must follow. *(p. 75)*

Asset Exchange Transaction A transaction that decreases one asset account while increasing another asset account so that total assets do not change. For example, the purchase of land with cash is an asset exchange transaction. *(p. 57)*

Asset Source Transaction A transaction that increases an asset account and a claims account. There are three types of asset source transactions. Assets can be acquired from owners (equity), borrowed from creditors (liabilities), or earned through operations (revenues). *(p. 56)*

Asset Use Transaction A transaction that decreases an asset account and a claims account. There are three types of asset use transactions. Assets can be transferred to owners (distributions), used to pay creditors (liabilities), or used to operate the business (expenses). *(p. 58)*

Audit A detailed examination of a company's financial statements and the documents that support the information presented in those statements. *(p. 70)*

Certified Public Accountant (CPA) Accountant who is licensed by the state government to provide accounting services to the public. To be licensed, the accountant must meet certain educational and experiential requirements. *(p. 72)*

Claims Exchange Transaction A transaction that decreases one claims account and increases another so that total claims do not change. For example, the accrual of interest expense is a claims exchange transaction. Liabilities increase, and the recognition of the expense causes retained earnings to decrease. *(p. 57)*

Disclaimer of Audit Opinion A position that an auditor can take with respect to financial statements when there is not enough information to confirm compliance or noncompliance with GAAP. A disclaimer is neither positive nor negative. *(p. 74)*

Expense (expanded definition) A decrease in assets or an increase in liabilities that occurs in the process of generating revenue. *(p. 60)*

Financial Audit A detailed examination of a company's financial statements and the documents that support the information presented in those statements. It includes a verification process that tests the reliability of the underlying accounting system used to produce the financial reports. *(p. 72)*

Historical Cost The actual price paid for an asset when it was purchased. *(p. 68)*

Independent Auditor A certified public accountant who is licensed to perform audits and who is independent of the company being audited. *(p. 72)*

Internal Controls The policies and procedures of a company that are designed to reduce the opportunity for fraud. *(p. 76)*

Investment The commitment of assets (i.e., usually cash) by a business to acquire other assets that will be used for the production of revenue. *(p. 63)*

Issuer of a Note The individual or business that is borrowing funds (i.e., the party receiving the cash when a note is issued). *(p. 68)*

Material Error An error or other reporting problem that, if known, would have affected the decision of an average prudent investor. *(p. 73)*

Note Payable A liability that results from the execution of a legal document called a *note*. The note describes technical terms, including interest charges, maturity date, collateral, and so on. *(p. 68)*

Qualified Opinion   An opinion issued by a CPA that falls between an unqualified opinion (see later definition) and an adverse opinion. It means that for the most part, the company's financial statements are in compliance with GAAP, but the auditors have reservations about something in the statements or have other reasons not to give a fully unqualified opinion. The auditor's report explains the reasons that a qualified opinion is being issued.   *(p. 74)*

Recognition   The act of recording an accounting event in the financial statements.   *(p. 55)*

Revenue (expanded definition)   An increase in assets or a decrease in liabilities that results from the operating activities of the business.   *(p. 60)*

Salaries Payable   Amounts of future cash payments owed to employees for services that have already been performed.   *(p. 57)*

Unqualified Opinion   An opinion on financial statements audited by a CPA that means the auditor thinks the financial statements are in compliance with GAAP.   *(p. 74)*

Voluntarily Disclosing   The professional responsibility to clients that forbids CPAs from voluntarily disclosing information that has been obtained as a result of their client–accountant relationships.   *(p. 74)*

QUESTIONS

1. What does accrual accounting attempt to accomplish?
2. Define recognition. How does it differ from the collection or payment of cash?
3. What does the term *asset source transaction* mean?
4. What effect does a capital acquisition have on the accounting equation?
5. How does the recognition of revenue on account (i.e., accounts receivable) affect the income statement in comparison to its effect on the statement of cash flows?
6. Give an example of an asset source transaction. What is the effect of this transaction on the accounting equation?
7. When is revenue recognized under accrual accounting?
8. Give an example of an asset exchange transaction. What is the effect of this transaction on the accounting equation?
9. What effect does expense recognition have on the accounting equation?
10. What does the term *claims exchange transaction* mean?
11. What type of transaction is a cash payment to creditors? How does this type of transaction affect the accounting equation?
12. When are expenses recognized under accrual accounting?
13. Why may net cash flows from operations on the cash flow statement be different from the amount of net income reported on the income statement?
14. What are the contents of the income statement in terms of changes in assets and liabilities?
15. What does the term *net assets* mean?
16. How does net income affect the owners' claims on the business's assets?
17. What does the term *expense* mean?
18. What does the term *revenue* mean?
19. What is the purpose of the statement of changes in equity?
20. What is the main purpose of the balance sheet?
21. Why is the balance sheet dated *as of* a specific date when the income statement, statement of changes in equity, and statement of cash flows are dated with the phrase *for the period ended?*
22. In what order are assets listed on the balance sheet?
23. What does the statement of cash flows explain?
24. When is interest earned on an investment recognized?
25. What does the term *adjusting entry* mean? Give an example.
26. What type of transaction is the entry to record the accrued interest revenue? How does it affect the accounting equation?
27. What type of transaction is the entry to record accrued interest expense? How does it affect the accounting equation?
28. Is land purchased in 1920 listed on a current balance sheet at its current value? If not, at what value is it shown?
29. What is the historical cost concept of accounting measurement?
30. Do all countries use the historical cost for accounting measurement? Why or why not?
31. What is a financial audit? Who is qualified to perform it?

32. What is an independent auditor? Why is independence necessary in the audit process?

33. What is considered a material error in the financial statements?

34. What are the three basic types of auditors' opinions that can be issued for financial statements in the audit process? Describe each.

35. What are the implications of an unqualified opinion?

36. When might an auditor issue a disclaimer on financial statements?

37. In what circumstances can an auditor disclose confidential information about a client without the client's permission?

38. What are the six articles of ethical conduct set out under section I of the AICPA's Code of Professional Conduct?

39. What is the purpose of internal controls in an organization?

EXERCISES

Where applicable in all exercises, round computations to the nearest dollar.

Effect of Accounts Receivable on the Accounting Equation and Financial Statements

EXERCISE 2-1
L.O. 1, 4, 5

K. Dalme started a dance studio in 20X7. The only event in that year was the recognition of $9,000 of revenue earned on account (i.e., Dalme provided dance lessons for a client but was not paid cash during the 20X7 accounting period).

Required

a. Draw an accounting equation and record the effect of recognizing revenue on account under the appropriate headings.

b. Prepare an income statement, statement of changes in equity, balance sheet, and statement of cash flows for the 20X7 accounting period.

c. Explain why cash flow from operating activities is different from net income.

Effect of Accounts Receivable Collection on the Accounting Equation and Financial Statements

EXERCISE 2-2
L.O. 1, 3, 5

Callaway Company earned $10,500 of revenue on account during 20X8. The company collected $5,000 cash from accounts receivable during 20X8. Based on this information alone, determine the following. (*Hint:* It may be helpful to record the events under an accounting equation before you satisfy the requirements.)

Required

a. The amount of the balance in the accounts receivable account that would appear on the 20X8 balance sheet.

b. The amount of net income that would appear on the 20X8 income statement.

c. The amount of cash flow from operating activities that would appear on the 20X8 statement of cash flows.

d. The amount of retained earnings that would appear on the 20X8 balance sheet.

e. What causes the answers to parts b and c to be different?

Examining Cash Flows

EXERCISE 2-3
L.O. 5

PepsiCo, formed in 1965, is a combination of Pepsi-Cola and Frito-Lay. The company is growing in both distribution of products and profits. One of the new strategies of PepsiCo for 1997 was to better manage cash on the theory that more cash fuels success. The following selected information is available for 1996 and 1997 (given in millions):

	December 31	
	1996	**1997**
Cash	$ 307	$ 1,928
Accounts Receivable	2,276	2,150
Sales	20,337	20,917
Costs and Operating Expenses	18,297	18,255
Accounts Payable	3,378	3,617

Required

  a. Which is higher for 1997, credit sales or collection of accounts receivable? By what amount?

  b. Did PepsiCo charge more on accounts payable or pay more accounts payable during 1997? By what amount?

  c. Based on the limited information given, does it appear that PepsiCo is meeting its goal of better cash management? Explain.

EXERCISE 2-4
L.O. 1, 5, 7

Effect of Accruals on Accounting Equation

Jeanette Rogers started a part-time cleaning service to help pay part of her college costs. She contracted with several businesses to clean offices at night or on the weekend for a monthly fee. She billed the client at the end of the month and received payment a few days later. Rogers started the business by borrowing $300 from her father to purchase cleaning supplies and equipment. She plans to pay him back by the end of the year and will pay interest at the rate of 8%. She purchased $140 of cleaning supplies to use during September. She had no other expenses. During September 20X2, she billed the following amounts:

Clay Law Firm	$200
Jim's Pottery Shop	150
Sewon Oh, Medical Doctor	100

Required

Draw an accounting equation and record these events in it. Be sure to include the accrued interest on the note for the month of September.

EXERCISE 2-5
L.O. 1, 5, 7

Effects of Recognition of Accrued Interest on Financial Statements

Mike Dees started Dees Company on January 1, 20X7. The company experienced the following events during its first year of operation.

  1. Earned $900 of cash revenue.

  2. Borrowed $2,400 cash from the bank.

  3. Adjusted the accounting records to recognize accrued interest expense on the bank note. The note was issued on September 1, 20X7. It carried a 1-year term and a 10% annual interest rate.

Required

  a. What is the amount of interest payable at December 31, 20X7?

  b. What amount of cash was paid for interest in 20X7?

  c. Use a horizontal statements model to show how each event affects the balance sheet, income statement, and statement of cash flows. Indicate whether the event acts to increase (I) or decrease (D) or not affect (n/a) each element of the financial statements. Also, in the cash flows column, indicate whether the cash flow is associated with operating activities (OA), investing activities (IA), or financing activities (FA). The first transaction has been recorded as an example.

Event No.	Balance Sheet									Income Statement						Statement of Cash Flows	
	Cash	=	Note Pay.	+	Int. Pay.	+	Cont. Cap.	+	Ret. Earn.	Rev.	−	Exp.	=	Net Inc.			
1	I	=	n/a	+	n/a	+	n/a	+	I	I	−	n/a	=	I		I	OA

EXERCISE 2-6
L.O. 2, 3, 5

Net Income versus Changes in Cash

In the period 20X4, Weir Inc. performed services for $90,000 and billed its customers. The company subsequently collected $73,000 of the amount billed. Weir incurred $61,000 of operating expenses but paid cash for only $54,000 of that amount. Weir acquired a $27,000 cash capital contribution from the owners. The company invested $21,000 cash in the purchase of land.

Required

Use the preceding information to answer the following questions. (*Hint:* It may be helpful to identify the six events described in the paragraph and to record them under an accounting equation before you attempt to answer the questions.)

a. What is the amount of revenue that will be recognized on the income statement for the period?

b. What is the amount of cash flow from revenue that will appear on the statement of cash flows?

c. What is the amount of net income for the period?

d. What is the net cash flow from operating activities for the period?

e. Why is the amount of net income different from the net cash flow from operating activities for the period?

f. What is the amount of cash flow from investing activities?

g. What is the amount of cash flow from financing activities?

h. What is the amount of total assets, liabilities, and equity that will appear on the year-end balance sheet?

Effect of Accounts Receivable and Accounts Payable on Financial Statements

EXERCISE 2-7
L.O. 1, 5, 7

The following events apply to Wilson and Wilson, a firm that practiced as public accountants for the 20X6 accounting period.

1. Performed $110,000 of services for clients on account.
2. Performed $20,000 of services and collected cash.
3. Incurred $47,000 of operating expenses on account.
4. Paid $18,000 cash to an employee for salary.
5. Collected $91,000 cash from accounts receivable.
6. Paid $36,000 cash on accounts payable.
7. Paid an $8,000 cash distribution to the owners.
8. Had accrued salaries of $2,500 at the end of 20X6.

Required

a. Show the effects of the events on the financial statements using a horizontal statements model like the following one. In the cash flow column, use the initials OA to designate operating activity, IA for investment activity, FA for financing activity, and NC for net change in cash flow. The notation n/a indicates that the element is not affected by the event. The first event is recorded as an example.

Event No.	Assets		=	Liabilities			+	Equity	Rev.	−	Exp.	=	Net Inc.	Cash Flow
	Cash +	Acct. Rec.	=	Acct. Pay. +		Sal. Pay. +		Ret. Earn.						
1	n/a +	110,000	=	n/a	+	n/a	+	110,000	110,000 −		n/a	=	110,000	n/a

b. What is the amount of total assets at the end of 20X6?

c. What is the balance of accounts receivable at the end of 20X6?

d. What is the balance of accounts payable at the end of 20X6?

e. What is the difference in accounts receivable and accounts payable?

f. What is net income for 20X6?

g. What is the amount of net cash flow from operating activities for 20X6?

Recognition of Accrued Interest Revenue

EXERCISE 2-8
L.O. 1, 5, 7

Tapia Company invested $120,000 in a certificate of deposit on April 1, 20X6. The certificate carried a 6% annual rate of interest and a 1-year term to maturity.

Required

a. What amount of income will be recognized for the year ending December 31, 20X6?

b. Show how the December 31, 20X6, adjusting entry to recognize the accrued interest revenue would affect the accounting equation.

c. What amount of cash will be collected for interest revenue in 20X6?

d. What is the amount of interest receivable as of December 31, 20X6?

e. What amount of cash will be collected for interest revenue in 20X7?

f. What amount of interest revenue will be recognized in 20X7?

g. What is the amount of interest receivable as of December 31, 20X7?

EXERCISE 2-9
L.O. 1, 5, 7

Recognition of Accrued Interest Expense

Hewitt Corporation borrowed $60,000 from the bank on September 1, 20X3. The note carried an 8% annual rate of interest and was set to mature on February 28, 20X4. Interest and principal were paid in cash on the maturity date.

Required

a. What was the amount of interest expense paid in cash in 20X3?

b. What was the amount of interest expense recognized on the 20X3 income statement?

c. What was the amount of total liabilities shown on the 20X3 balance sheet?

d. What was the total amount of cash that was paid to the bank on February 28, 20X4, for principal and interest?

e. What was the amount of interest expense shown on the 20X4 income statement?

EXERCISE 2-10
L.O. 10

Identification of Source, Use, and Exchange Transactions

Required

Indicate whether each of the following transactions is an asset source (AS), asset use (AU), asset exchange (AE), or claims exchange (CE) transaction.

a. Acquired a cash contribution of capital from the owners.

b. Paid cash on accounts payable.

c. Collected cash from accounts receivable.

d. Made a cash distribution to the owners.

e. Paid cash for rent expense.

f. Invested cash in a certificate of deposit.

g. Purchased land with cash.

h. Performed services for clients on account.

i. Incurred operating expenses on account.

j. Performed services for cash.

EXERCISE 2-11
L.O. 10

Identification of Asset Source, Use, and Exchange Transactions

Required

a. Name an asset source transaction that will *not* affect the cash statement.

b. Name an asset source transaction that will affect the income statement.

c. Name an asset use transaction that will *not* affect the income statement.

d. Name an asset exchange transaction that will affect the cash statement.

e. Name an asset exchange transaction that will *not* affect the cash statement.

f. Name an asset source transaction that will *not* affect the income statement.

Effect of Transactions on the Balance Sheet

Davis Corp. was formed on January 1, 20X1. The business acquired an $85,000 cash contribution of capital from the owners. The business performed $300,000 of services on account and collected $225,000 of the amount due. Operating expenses recognized on account amounted to $235,000. By the end of 20X1, $180,000 of that amount had been paid with cash. The business paid $30,000 cash to purchase land. The business borrowed cash from the bank in the amount of $30,000. On December 31, 20X1, there was $750 of accrued interest expense.

Required

Using the preceding information, answer the following questions. (*Hint:* It may be helpful to identify the eight events described in the preceding paragraph and to record them under an accounting equation before you attempt to answer the questions.)

  a. What is the cash balance at the end of 20X1?
  b. What is the balance of accounts receivable at the end of 20X1?
  c. What is the amount of total assets at the end of 20X1?
  d. What is the amount of total liabilities at the end of 20X1?
  e. What is the amount of contributed capital at the end of 20X1?
  f. What is the amount of retained earnings at the end of 20X1?

Effects of Revenue and Expense Recognition on the Income Statement and Statement of Cash Flows

The following transactions pertain to the operations of Lawson & Co., CPAs.

  1. Acquired a $125,000 cash contribution of capital from the owners.
  2. Performed accounting services and billed the clients $90,000.
  3. Made a $15,000 cash distribution to the owners.
  4. Collected $80,000 cash from accounts receivable.
  5. Paid $58,000 cash for operating expense.
  6. Performed accounting services for $7,500 cash.

Required

  a. For each of these transactions, identify the ones that cause revenue and expense recognition for Lawson & Co., CPA.
  b. Based on your response to part *a*, determine the amount of net income that will appear on Lawson & Co.'s income statement.
  c. For each of the preceding transactions, identify the ones that affect cash flow from operating activities.
  d. Based on your response to part *c*, determine the amount of net cash flow from operating activities that will appear on the statement of cash flows.

Complete Accounting Cycle

The following information is available for Boyler Co. for the year 20X4. The business had the following transactions:

  1. Acquired a $50,000 cash contribution of capital from the owners.
  2. Performed $145,000 of services on account.
  3. Incurred operating expenses on account in the amount of $80,000.
  4. Purchased land for $10,000 cash.
  5. Collected $105,000 cash from accounts receivable.
  6. Paid $60,000 cash on accounts payable.
  7. Performed services for $18,500 cash.
  8. Paid additional operating expenses of $7,500 cash for salaries.

9. Made a $15,000 cash distribution to the owners.
10. Borrowed $20,000 cash from the state bank.

Event That Applies to Adjusting Entry:

11. Accrued interest expense at the end of the accounting period amounting to $1,200.

Required

a. Explain how each of the transactions affects the accounting equation by placing a + for *increase*, − for *decrease*, and n/a for *not affected* under each of the components. Also record the dollar amount of the effect of each event on the accounting equation. The first event is recorded as an example.

Event No.	Assets	=	Liabilities	+	Contributed Capital	+	Retained Earnings
1	+ 50,000		n/a		+ 50,000		n/a

(The "Equity" label spans the Contributed Capital and Retained Earnings columns.)

b. What is the amount of net income for 20X4?
c. What is the amount of total assets at the end of 20X4?
d. What is the amount of total liabilities at the end of 20X4?

EXERCISE 2-15
L.O. 4, 5

Classification of Events on Statement of Cash Flows

The following transactions pertain to the operations of Maddox Company. The company had the following transactions:

1. Acquired an $18,000 cash contribution of capital from the owners.
2. Provided $40,000 services on account.
3. Incurred $22,000 of operating expenses on account.
4. Collected $32,000 cash from accounts receivable.
5. Made a $3,000 cash distribution to the owners of the business.
6. Paid $16,000 cash on accounts payable.
7. Performed services for $3,000 cash.
8. Paid $1,200 cash for expenses.

Required

a. Classify each of these transactions as a cash flow from operating activities (OA), investing activities (IA), or financing activities (FA). Transactions that do not affect the statement of cash flows should be identified as n/a.
b. Prepare a statement of cash flows.

EXERCISE 2-16
L.O. 4

Relation of Elements to Financial Statements

Required

Tell whether each of the following items would appear on the income statement (IS), statement of changes in equity (CE), balance sheet (BS), or statement of cash flows (CF). Some items may appear on more than one statement; if so, identify all applicable statements. If an item will not appear on any financial statement, label it n/a.

a. Notes Receivable
b. Note Payable
c. Interest Receivable
d. Utilities Payable
e. Accounts Receivable
f. Retained Earnings

g. Land
h. Auditor's Opinion
i. Net Income
j. Salaries Expense
k. Distributions
l. Interest Revenue
m. Cash Flow from Investing Activities
n. Interest Payable
o. Ending Cash Balance

PROBLEMS—SERIES A

Where applicable in all problems, round computations to the nearest dollar.

Effect of Events on the Accounting Equation and Financial Statements

PROBLEM 2-1A
L.O. 3, 4, 5

Fix It Auto Service experienced the following transactions during 20X3.

1. Provided services to customers and received $4,000 cash.
2. Paid $1,000 cash for operating expenses.
3. Borrowed $12,000 from the bank on October 1, 20X3. The note carried an 8% annual interest rate and a 1-year term to maturity.
4. Provided service to customers and billed them $18,000.
5. Incurred $6,000 of operating expenses on account.
6. Collected $13,500 of accounts receivable.
7. Paid $3,100 of the amount due on accounts payable.
8. Recognized the accrued interest on the note payable.

Required

a. Show the effects of each event on the accounting equation. The first event is recorded as an example.

	Assets			=	Liabilities							+	Equity		
Event No.	Cash	+	Acct. Rec.	=	Acct. Pay.	+	Note Pay.	+	Int. Pay.	+	Cont. Cap.	+	Ret. Earn.
1	4,000	+	n/a	=	n/a	+	n/a	+	n/a	+	n/a	+	4,000

b. Prepare the income statement, statement of changes in equity, balance sheet, and statement of cash flows for the 20X3 accounting period.

c. What is the amount of ending retained earnings? What is the amount of net income? Why are these amounts the same in this example? Give an example of a transaction that would cause these amounts to be different.

Effect of Events on the Accounting Equation

PROBLEM 2-2A
L.O. 3

Required

Explain how each of the following independent accounting events would affect the accounting equation by placing a plus + or minus − under the appropriate columns. The effects of the first event are shown for your convenience:

Letter of Event	Assets	=	Liabilities	+	Contributed Capital	+	Retained Earnings
a	+				+		

     a. Received assets from owner contributions.

     b. Purchased land with cash.

     c. Paid cash for interest expense accrued in a previous period.

     d. Recognized revenue on account.

     e. Received utility bill; cash payment will be made in the future.

     f. Borrowed cash from creditors.

     g. Made cash distribution to owners.

     h. Accrued interest expense on note payable.

     i. Paid cash for salaries.

     j. Collected cash from accounts receivable.

     k. Repaid borrowed funds with cash.

PROBLEM 2-3A
L.O. 3, 5

Effect of Accrued Interest on Financial Statements

Mink Enterprises borrowed $36,000 from a local bank on July 1, 20X6, when the company was started. The note carried an 8% annual interest rate and a 1-year term to maturity. Mink Enterprises recognized $2,500 of revenue on account in 20X6 and $9,000 of revenue on account in 20X7. Cash collections of accounts receivable were $1,200 in 20X6 and $7,000 in 20X7. (*Hint:* It may be helpful to record the events under an accounting equation before you answer the following questions.)

Required

Based on this information, answer the following questions.

     a. What is the amount of interest expense that would appear on the December 31, 20X6, income statement?

     b. What is the amount of net cash flow from operating activities that would appear on the 20X6 statement of cash flows?

     c. What is the amount of total liabilities that would appear on the December 31, 20X6, balance sheet?

     d. What is the amount of retained earnings that would appear on the December 31, 20X6, balance sheet?

     e. What is the amount of cash flow from financing activities that would appear on the 20X6 statement of cash flows?

     f. What is the amount of interest expense that would appear on the 20X7 income statement?

     g. What is the amount of net cash flow from operating activities that would appear on the 20X7 statement of cash flows?

     h. What is the amount of total assets that would appear on the December 31, 20X7, balance sheet?

     i. What is the amount of cash flow from investing activities that would appear on the 20X7 statement of cash flows?

     j. If Mink Enterprises made a $300 distribution during 20X7, what would be the balance of retained earnings on the December 31, 20X7, balance sheet?

PROBLEM 2-4A
L.O. 3, 4

Two Complete Accounting Cycles

The following accounting events apply to Fox Company.

Accounting Events for 20X7

    1. Started business when it acquired a $40,000 cash contribution of capital from the owner.

    2. Recognized $95,000 of revenue on account.

    3. Collected $83,000 cash from accounts receivable.

    4. Paid the owner a $5,000 cash distribution.

5. Paid $46,000 cash for salaries expense.
6. Invested $24,000 cash in a 12-month certificate of deposit.

Events Relating to December 31 End-of-Year Adjusting Entries

7. Accrued salary expense amounting to $3,000.
8. Recorded accrued interest on the certificate of deposit. The CD was purchased on July 1, 20X7, and carried a 10% annual rate of interest.

Accounting Events for 20X8

1. Paid cash for salaries payable of $3,000.
2. Received an additional $30,000 cash contribution of capital from the owner.
3. Earned revenue on account of $105,000 for the year.
4. Received cash collections from accounts receivable of $112,000.
5. Made a $15,000 cash distribution.
6. Paid $35,000 cash for salaries expense.
7. Purchased a plot of land on May 31, 20X8, that cost $140,000 cash. The value of the land rose to $160,000 by December 31.
8. Borrowed on June 1, 20X8, $42,000 cash on a 2-year, 8% note issued by Star Bank.
9. Received cash for the principal and interest due on the certificate of deposit of $24,000 when it matured on June 30, 20X8.

Events Relating to Adjusting Entries

10. Accrued salary expenses of $5,000 for the period.
11. Recorded accrued interest expense for the bank note (see Event No. 8 in 20X8).

Required

a. Record the effect of each of the events on the accounting equation for the 20X7 and 20X8 fiscal years.

b. Prepare an income statement, statement of changes in equity, balance sheet, and statement of cash flows for the 20X7 and 20X8 fiscal years.

Identification of Elements on Financial Statements

PROBLEM 2-5A
L.O. 4

The following accounts were drawn from the records of Mura & Associates:

Land	$195,000	Capital Acquisition	$ 20,000
Salaries Payable	34,000	Salary Expense	45,000
Interest Expense	2,750	Beginning Contributed	
Accounts Receivable	41,200	Capital	24,000
Notes Payable	70,000	Ending Retained Earnings	121,000
Cash Flow from Oper.		Cash Flow from Inv.	
Activities	30,800	Activities	(15,400)
Cash	33,400	Interest Payable	600
Revenue	102,000	Interest Revenue	750
Cash Flow from Fin.		Distributions	4,000
Activities	14,000		

Required

Use the preceding information to construct an income statement, statement of changes in equity, balance sheet, and statement of cash flows.

PROBLEM 2-6A
L.O. 4, 5, 10

Classification of Events as to Source, Use, or Exchange and Effect of Events on Financial Statements—Horizontal Statements Model

The following events pertain to Larrs Financial Services for 20X2.

1. Started business when it acquired a $20,000 cash contribution of capital from the owners.
2. Paid $2,400 cash for rent expense.
3. Performed services for clients and billed them $16,000. Cash was expected to be collected at a later date (i.e., the revenue was earned on account).
4. Incurred $3,500 of other operating expenses on account (i.e., cash payment was expected to be made at a later date).
5. Paid $2,800 cash on the account payable created in Event No. 4.
6. Acquired an additional $3,000 cash contribution of capital from the owners.
7. Paid $700 cash on the balance of the account payable created in Event No. 4.
8. Performed additional services for $7,000 cash.
9. Distributed $1,000 cash to the owner Mr. Larrs.
10. Collected $14,500 cash from accounts receivable.

Required

a. Classify each of the preceding transactions of Larrs Financial Services as asset source (AS), asset use (AU), asset exchange (AE), or claims exchange (CE).

b. Show the effects of the events on the financial statements using a horizontal statements model like the following one. In the cash flow column, use the initials OA to designate operating activity, IA for investing activity, FA for financing activity, and NC for net change in cash flow.

The notation n/a indicates that the element is not affected by the event. The first event has been recorded as an example.

Event No.	Assets		= Liab.	+	Equity		Rev.	−	Exp.	=	Net Inc.	Cash Flow	
	Cash +	Acc. Rec.	= Pay.	+ Cont. Cap.	+	Ret. Earn.							
1	20,000 +	n/a	= n/a	+ 20,000	+	n/a	n/a	−	n/a	=	n/a	20,000	FA

c. What is the amount of net income for 20X2?

d. What is the amount of net cash flow from operating activities for 20X2?

PROBLEM 2-7A
L.O. 3, 4, 5

Missing Information in Financial Statements

Thompson Properties had the following assets at the beginning of the accounting period (January 1, 20X7): Cash—$800, Accounts Receivable—$1,200, Certificate of Deposit—$2,500, and Land—$10,000. The beginning balances in the liability accounts were Accounts Payable—$500 and Notes Payable—$4,000. A $2,700 balance was in the Contributed Capital account at the beginning of the accounting period. During the accounting period, $1,800 of service revenue was earned on account. The ending balance in the Accounts Receivable account was $1,900. Operating expenses on account amounted to $1,050. There was $1,300 paid on accounts payable. In addition, there was $200 of accrued interest revenue and $350 of accrued interest expense as of the end of the accounting period (December 31, 20X7). Finally, a $400 cash distribution was made to the owners. (*Hint:* It may be helpful to record the events under an accounting equation before you attempt to satisfy the requirements.)

Required

a. Determine the amount of cash collected from accounts receivable.

b. Prepare a balance sheet as of January 1, 20X7.

c. Prepare an income statement, statement of changes in equity, balance sheet, and statement of cash flows as of December 31, 20X7.

d. Determine the interest rate earned on the certificate of deposit.

e. Determine the interest rate paid on the note payable.

PROBLEMS—SERIES B

Effect of Events on the Accounting Equation and Financial Statements

PROBLEM 2-1B
L.O. 3, 4, 5

A&A Auto experienced the following transactions during 20X4.

1. Provided service to customers and billed them $8,600.

2. Borrowed $4,000 from the bank on September 1, 20X4. The note carried a 6% annual interest rate and a 1-year term to maturity.

3. Paid $1,700 of operating expenses.

4. Provided service to customers and collected $2,300 cash.

5. Incurred $3,900 of operating expenses on account.

6. Collected $7,500 of the accounts receivable.

7. Paid $3,400 of the accounts payable.

8. Recognized the accrued interest on the note payable.

Required

a. Show the effects of each event on the accounting equation. The first event is recorded as an example.

Event No.	Assets			=	Liabilities						+	Equity		
	Cash	+	Acct. Rec.	=	Acct. Pay.	+	Note Pay.	+	Int. Pay.	+		Cont. Cap.	+	Ret. Earn.
1	n/a	+	8,600	=	n/a	+	n/a	+	n/a	+		n/a	+	8,600

b. Prepare the income statement, statement of changes in equity, balance sheet, and statement of cash flows for the 20X4 accounting period.

c. What is the amount of ending retained earnings? What is the amount of net income? Why are these amounts the same in this example? Is the balance in retained earnings and the amount of net income likely to be the same at the end of 20X5? Explain your answer.

Effect of Events on the Accounting Equation

PROBLEM 2-2B
L.O. 3

Required

Explain how each of the following independent accounting events would affect the accounting equation by placing a plus + or minus − under the appropriate columns. The effects of the first event are shown for your convenience:

Letter of Event	Assets	=	Liabilities	+	Contributed Capital	+	Retained Earnings
a	+				+		

a. Acquired a cash contribution of capital from the owner.

b. Paid cash for rent expense.

c. Incurred operating expenses on account.

d. Performed services for clients on account.

e. Distributed cash to the owners.

f. Collected cash from accounts receivable.

g. Performed services for cash.

h. Paid cash to creditors on account.

i. Bought equipment by issuing a note payable.

j. Purchased office supplies with cash.

k. Accrued interest expense on note payable.

l. Repaid note payable with cash.

PROBLEM 2-3B **Effect of Accrued Interest on Financial Statements**

L.O. 3, 5 Wilmington Enterprises borrowed $12,000 from the local bank on May 1, 20X8, when the company was started. The note carried a 10% annual interest rate and a 1-year term to maturity. Wilmington Enterprises recognized $28,000 of revenue on account in 20X8 and $34,000 of revenue on account in 20X9. Cash collections on account were $22,000 in 20X8 and $32,000 in 20X9. (*Hint:* It may be helpful to record the events under an accounting equation before you answer the following questions.)

Required

Based on the preceding information, answer the following questions:

a. What is the amount of net cash flow from operating activities that would appear on the 20X8 cash flow statement?

b. What amount of interest expense would appear on the December 31, 20X8, income statement?

c. What is the amount of total liabilities that would appear on the December 31, 20X8, balance sheet?

d. What is the amount of retained earnings that would appear on the December 31, 20X8, balance sheet?

e. What is the amount of cash flow from financing activities that would appear on the 20X8 statement of cash flows?

f. What is the amount of interest expense that would appear on the December 31, 20X9, income statement?

g. What is the amount of cash flows from operating activities that would appear on the 20X9 cash flow statement?

h. What is the amount of total assets that would appear on the December 31, 20X9, balance sheet?

i. What is the amount of cash flow from investing activities that would appear on the December 31, 20X9, cash flow statement?

j. If Wilmington Enterprises made a $700 distribution during 20X9, what would be the balance of retained earnings on the December 31, 20X9, balance sheet?

PROBLEM 2-4B **Two Complete Accounting Cycles**

L.O. 3, 4 The following accounting events apply to Coleman Company.

Accounting Events for 20X3

1. Started the company when it acquired a $30,000 cash contribution of capital from the owner, Pam.

2. Recognized $87,000 of revenue on account during the period.

3. Collected $73,000 cash from accounts receivable.

4. Paid an $8,000 cash distribution.

5. Paid $32,000 cash for salaries expense.

6. Paid $21,000 cash for other operating expenses.

7. Invested $18,000 in a certificate of deposit with an 18-month term.

Events Relating to Adjusting Entries (Books are closed on December 31)

8. Accrued salaries expense of $3,000.
9. Recorded accrued interest on the certificate of deposit. The certificate was purchased on July 1, 20X3, and carried a 5% annual rate of interest.

Accounting Events for 20X4

1. Made cash payment of $3,000 for salaries payable.
2. Borrowed $20,000 from a local bank.
3. Received an additional $6,000 from the owner.
4. Recognized $120,000 of revenue on account during 20X4.
5. Collected $112,000 of cash on accounts receivable during the period.
6. Purchased land for the company that cost $55,000 cash. A few months later, the land was appraised at $60,000.
7. Made a $12,000 cash distribution to the owner of the company.
8. Received the principal amount plus the interest earned on the certificate of deposit. (See Event No. 7 in year 20X3 for details regarding the original investment.)
9. Paid cash of $40,000 for salaries expense.
10. Paid $33,000 cash for other operating expenses.

Events That Relate to Adjusting Entries

11. Accrued salaries expense for the period of $7,000.
12. Recorded accrued interest expense for the bank note (see Event No. 2 in 20X4). The note was issued to the bank on June 1, 20X4. It carried a 12% annual rate of interest and a 2-year term to maturity.

Required

a. Record the effect of each of the events on the accounting equation for the 20X3 and 20X4 fiscal years.

b. Prepare an income statement, statement of changes in equity, balance sheet, and statement of cash flows for the 20X3 and 20X4 fiscal years.

Identification of Elements on Financial Statements

PROBLEM 2-5B
L.O. 4

The following items were drawn from the records of Simmons & Associates:

Consulting Revenue	$58,000	Notes Payable	$24,000
Land	52,000	Salaries Payable	6,500
Distributions	8,000	Salary Expense	36,000
Cash Flow from Fin.		Capital Acquisition	17,000
Activities	50,000	Beginning Contributed	
Interest Revenue	3,000	Capital	19,000
Ending Retained Earnings	43,500	Accounts Receivable	29,000
Cash	31,000	Cash Flow from Inv.	
Interest Payable	2,000	Activities	(75,000)
Interest Expense	6,000	Cash Flow from Oper.	
		Activities	40,000

Required

Use the preceding information to construct an income statement, statement of changes in equity, balance sheet, and statement of cash flows.

PROBLEM 2-6B **Classification of Events as to Source, Use, or Exchange and Effect of Events on Financial**
L.O. 4, 5, 10 **Statements—Horizontal Statements Model**

The following events pertain to Wayne Advisory Services for 20X2:

1. Started business when the company acquired a $42,000 cash contribution of capital from the owners.
2. Paid $22,000 cash to purchase land.
3. Paid $3,600 cash for rent expense.
4. Performed services for clients and billed them $13,800. Cash was expected to be collected at a later date (i.e., the revenue was earned on account).
5. Incurred $8,400 of other operating expenses on account (i.e., cash payment was expected to be made at a later date).
6. Received an $800 bill for utilities. The amount due was payable within 30 days.
7. Paid $4,400 cash on the account payable created in Event No. 5.
8. Acquired an additional $7,000 cash contribution of capital from Ms. Wayne.
9. Paid $4,000 cash on the balance of the account payable created in Event No. 5.
10. Performed additional services for $4,500 cash.
11. Distributed $1,800 cash to the owner, Ms. Wayne.
12. Collected $7,600 cash from accounts receivable.

Required

a. Classify each of these transactions of Wayne Advisory Services as asset source (AS), asset use (AU), asset exchange (AE), or claims exchange (CE).

b. Show the effects of the events on the financial statements, using a horizontal statements model like the following one. In the cash flow column, use the initials OA to designate operating activity, IA for investing activity, FA for financing activity, and NC for net change in cash flow. The notation n/a indicates that the element is not affected by the event. The first event is recorded as an example.

Event No.	Assets			=	Liab.	+	Equity		Rev.	–	Exp.	=	Net Inc.	Cash Flow	
	Cash	+ Acct. Rec.	+ Land	=	Acct. Pay.	+	Con. Cap.	+ Ret. Earn.							
1	42,000	+ n/a	+ n/a	=	n/a	+	42,000	+ n/a	n/a	–	n/a	=	n/a	42,000	FA

c. What is the amount of net income for 20X2?
d. What is the amount of net cash flow from operating activities for 20X2?

PROBLEM 2-7B **Missing Information in Financial Statements**
L.O. 3, 4, 5 Lake Properties had the following assets at the beginning of the accounting period (January 1, 20X6): Cash—$21,000, Accounts Receivable—$33,000, Certificate of Deposit—$16,000, and Land—$62,000. The beginning balances in the liability accounts were Accounts Payable—$27,000 and Notes Payable—$20,000. A $51,000 balance was in Contributed Capital at the beginning of the accounting period. During the accounting period, service revenue on account was $44,000. The ending balance in the Accounts Receivable account was $31,000. Operating expenses on account amounted to $29,000. There was $33,000 paid on accounts payable. In addition, there was $1,200 of accrued interest revenue and $1,700 of accrued interest expense as of the end of the accounting period (December 31, 20X6). Finally, a $2,500 cash distribution was made to the owners. (*Hint:* It may be helpful to record the events under an accounting equation before you attempt to satisfy the requirements.)

Required

a. Determine the amount of cash collected from accounts receivable.

b. Prepare a balance sheet as of January 1, 20X6.

c. Prepare an income statement, statement of changes in equity, balance sheet, and statement of cash flows as of December 31, 20X6.

d. Determine the interest rate earned on the certificate of deposit.

e. Determine the interest rate paid on the note payable.

analyze, communicate, think

BUSINESS APPLICATIONS CASE   **Gateway 2000 Annual Report**   **ACT 2-1**

L.O. 7,8

Required

Using the Gateway 2000 financial statements in Appendix B, answer the following questions:

a. Who are the independent auditors for Gateway?

b. What type of opinion did the independent auditors issue on Gateway's financial statements?

c. On what date does it appear the independent auditors completed the audit work related to Gateway's 1997 financial statements?

d. Does the auditors' report give any information about how the audit was conducted? If so, what does it suggest was done?

e. Does the auditors' report tell the reader that the audit was concerned with materiality rather than absolute accuracy in the financial statements?

GROUP ASSIGNMENT   **Missing Information**   **ACT 2-2**

Tricom, Inc., is a company composed of KFC, Pizza Hut, and Taco Bell. The following information, taken from the annual report, is available for the years 1998 (estimated), 1997, and 1996. Information is given in millions.

	1998	1997	1996
Revenue	$9,681	$10,232	$10,250
Operating Costs	9,266	9,614	9,998
Unusual Charges	174	246	—
Interest Expense	317	276	300

Required

a. Divide the class into groups of four or five students. Organize the groups into three sections. Assign each section of groups the financial data for one of the preceding accounting periods.

Group Tasks

1. Determine the amount of net income for the year assigned.

2. How does the result in task *a* affect the retained earnings of the company?

3. If the average interest rate is 7%, what is the average amount of debt for the year?

4. Have a representative of each section put the income statement for their respective year on the board.

Class Discussion

b. Have the class discuss the trend in revenue and net income. The company has new leadership teams and new management processes that will make Tricom a company "that stands for growth." If this is true, what actual results would you expect to see from the company in 1998?

ACT 2-3

REAL-WORLD CASE   **Unusual Types of Liabilities**

In the liabilities section of its 1997 balance sheet, First Union Corporation reported "non-interest-bearing deposits" of almost $22 billion. First Union is a very large banking company. In the liabilities section of its 1997 balance sheet, Newmont Mining Corporation reported "reclamation and remediation liabilities" of almost $89 million. Newmont Mining is involved in gold mining and refining activities. In the accrued liabilities reported on its 1997 balance sheet, Phillips Petroleum Company included $83 million for "environmental accruals."

Required

   a. For each of the preceding liabilities, write a brief explanation of what you believe the nature of the liability to be and how the company will pay off the liability. To develop your answers, think about the nature of the industry in which each of the companies operates.

   b. Of the three liabilities described, which do you think poses the most risk for the company? In other words, which liability is likely to have actual cost that exceed the reported cost shown on the balance sheet? Uncertainty creates risk.

ACT 2-4

BUSINESS APPLICATIONS CASE   **Decisions about Materiality**

The accounting firm of Espey & Davis, CPAs, has recently completed the audits of three separate companies. During these audits, the following events were discovered, and Espey & Davis is trying to decide if each event is material. If an item is material, the CPA firm will insist that the company correct the problem.

   1. In 20X3, Foxx Company reported service revenues of $1,000,000 and net earnings of $80,000. Because of an accounting error, the company recorded $6,000 as revenue in 20X3 for services that will not be performed until early 20X4.

   2. Guzza Company plans to report a cash balance of $70,000. Because of an accounting error, this amount is $5,000 too high. Guzza also plans to report total assets of $4,000,000 and net earnings of $415,000.

   3. Jeter Company's 20X3 balance sheet shows a cash balance of $200,000 and total assets of $9,000,000. For 20X3, the company had a net income of $750,000. These balances are all correct, but they would have been $5,000 higher if the president of the company had not claimed business travel expenses that were, in fact, the cost of personal vacations for him and his family. He charged the costs of these trips on the company's credit card. The president of Jeter Company owns 25% of the business.

Required

Write a memorandum to the partners of Espey & Davis, explaining your decision as to the materiality of each of these events.

ACT 2-5

BUSINESS APPLICATIONS CASE   **Limitations of Audit Opinion**

The statement of financial position (balance sheet) of Trident Company shows assets of $4,500,000. Jan Lewis advises you that a major accounting firm has reviewed the statements and attested that they were prepared in accordance with generally accepted accounting principles. She tells you that she can buy the total owner's interest in the business for only $2,750,000 and is seriously considering the offer. She says that the auditor's unqualified opinion validates the $4,500,000 value of the assets. Lewis believes she would be foolish to pass up the opportunity to purchase the assets at a price of only $2,750,000.

Required

   a. What piece of the accounting equation is Lewis failing to consider?

   b. Comment on Lewis's misconceptions regarding the auditor's role in providing information that is useful in making investment decisions.

WRITING ASSIGNMENT   **Definition of Elements of Financial Statements**

Putting "yum" on people's faces around the world is the mission of Tricom, Inc., a new company that resulted from a spin-off from PepsiCo. The company is composed of KFC, Pizza Hut, and Taco Bell. A spin-off occurs when a company separates its operations into two or more distinct companies. In this case, the Tricom restaurants were operated as part of PepsiCo prior to the spin-off, which was financed by having Tricom borrow $4.55 billion. These funds were used to pay PepsiCo for the value of the fast-food restaurants. Tricom's net income for 1997 was $308 million.

Required

a. If Tricom's debt remains constant at $4.55 billion for 1998, how much interest will Tricom incur in 1998, assuming that the average interest rate is 7%?

b. Does this amount of debt seem excessive compared with the amount of net income? Explain.

c. Assume that you are the president of the company. Write a memo to the shareholders explaining how Tricom, Inc., could have negative equity. You will need to make your own assumptions. Also offer some explanation of how Tricom may be able to meet its interest payments.

ETHICAL DILEMMA   **Now It Is Your Turn to Cover for Me**

Johnny Travera and Tim Sanders were unusual friends. Travera came from a background of poverty while Sanders had an extremely affluent family. Indeed, the two would have never known each other except for an unusual set of events. Sanders' parents bought him a new car for his 16th birthday. Not being used to the new vehicle, Sanders misjudged a curve and wrecked the car. Travera happened to see the accident and helped Sanders get out of the vehicle. Sanders was unhurt but extremely distraught. He told Travera that his own parents would never trust him again. When the police arrived, Travera told them that he had seen a child run in front of Sanders' car and that Sanders had swerved off the road to save the child's life. Upon hearing the story, Sanders' parents considered him a hero. The insurance company bought a new car, and Sanders made a friend for life.

Sanders went to college and became a CPA in his father's accounting firm. Travera worked for several restaurants and finally managed to start one of his own. The restaurant became successful, and Travera turned the accounting work over to Sanders. Having no formal education, Travera had little knowledge of technical business practices.

At the beginning of 20X6, Travera's balance sheet contained a Cash account with a $10,000 balance, other assets with balances amounting to $380,000, liabilities of $80,000, and contributed capital of $25,000. Sanders provided Travera with accounting services for several years and was reasonably certain as to the accuracy of these figures. Since Sanders always advised Travera on financial matters, Sanders was aware that during 20X6 Travera had paid cash to purchase $50,000 of restaurant equipment. Also, Travera had been able to repay $15,000 cash on a note payable that evidenced the restaurant's liability to a bank. Finally, Travera had received a $20,000 cash distribution from the restaurant. Travera made no contributions to the business during 20X6. Even so, the records that Travera provided Sanders for 20X6 indicated that the restaurant earned $200,000 in cash revenues and incurred $175,000 in cash expenses. The ending balance in the Cash account was $12,000.

After analyzing the data, Sanders became convinced that Travera was not reporting accurate information to him for the determination of net income. He confronted Travera with the issue and Travera admitted that he was not reporting all the sales information. He said he did not report some of the cash sales because he did not feel the income tax system was fair and he did not want to pay any more taxes than he had to pay. He defended himself by saying, "I'm only doing what everybody else does. Your dad's biggest client, Billy Abbott, has been skimming a million a year off his chain of restaurants. He's been doing it for the last 5 years. I know; I used to work for him. Even so, you and your dad give him an unqualified audit opinion every year. So why won't you do the same thing for me? I'm supposed to be your friend, and you keep telling me you think this Abbott guy is a real jerk." Indeed, Travera became so indignant that he told Sanders, "Either you sign my tax return, or I find a new accountant and a new friend to boot. I've always stood up for you, and this is the thanks I get."

Required

a. Based on the information provided in the case, determine the amount of Travera's unreported income. (*Hint:* The beginning balances were correct, but the entries for the current year's transactions were recorded incorrectly. It may be helpful to open an accounting equation with the beginning balances provided in the case and to record the current period's transactions under the equation. Assume that the ending cash balance is an accurate measure of cash on hand at the end of the accounting period. The amount of unrecorded cash is equal to the amount of unrecorded income.)

b. Explain how Travera's failure to report cash revenue will affect the elements of financial statements by indicating whether each element will be overstated, understated, or not affected by the reporting omission. The elements to be considered are Assets, Liabilities, Contributed Capital, Retained Earnings, Revenue, Expenses, Net Income, and Distributions.

c. Explain how Sanders' audit firm could be honest and still have provided an unqualified opinion on Abbott's financial statements. What is the auditor's responsibility for the detection and reporting of fraud?

d. If you were Sanders, would you sign Travera's tax return as it was presented to you by Travera?

e. Assume that you are Sanders, that you refuse to sign Travera's tax return, and that some other CPA without knowledge of Travera's deceitful reporting practice signs his tax return. Would you report Travera to the Internal Revenue Service?

f. Suppose that you are Sanders and that you investigate Travera's charges regarding Abbott. You find that Abbott is in fact underreporting income to the extent that Travera accused him of so doing. Would you report Abbott to the Internal Revenue Service?

ACT 2-8

SPREADSHEET ASSIGNMENT   **Use of Excel**

Required

a. Refer to Problem 2-5A. Use an Excel spreadsheet to construct the financial statements as indicated. To complete part *b*, be sure to use formulas where normal arithmetic calculations are made within the financial statements (in particular the statement of changes in equity).

b. It is interesting to speculate what would happen if certain operating results change for better or worse. After completing part *a*, change certain account balances for each of the following independent operating adjustments. After each adjustment, notice how the financial statements would differ if the change in operations were to occur. After the effect of each adjustment is noted, return the data to the original amounts in Problem 2-5A and then go to the next operating adjustment.

In the following table, note the new amounts on the financial statements for the various operating changes listed.

	Original	1	2	3	4	5
Net Income						
Total Assets						
Total Liabilities						
Total Equity						
Total Liabilities & Equity						

Independent Operating Adjustments

1. Revenue and the related Accounts Receivable increased $10,000.
2. Revenue and the related Accounts Receivable decreased $10,000.
3. Salary Expense and the related Salaries Payable decreased $4,000.
4. Salary Expense and the related Salaries Payable increased $4,000.
5. Distributions paid decreased $500 and the related Cash changed accordingly.

SPREADSHEET ASSIGNMENT   **Mastery of Excel**   **ACT 2-9**

Refer to Problem 2-6A. Complete parts *b, c,* and *d* using an Excel spreadsheet. Refer to Chapter 1 problem ACT 1–9 for ideas on how to structure it.

3 Accounting for Deferrals

If a person wishes to subscribe to *Reader's Digest* for 1 year
(12 issues), the subscriber must pay for the magazines before they
are actually published. Suppose Paige Long sends $12 to the
Reader's Digest Association in September 20X1 for a 1-year subscription; she will receive her first issue in October. How should
Reader's Digest account for the receipt of this cash? How would
this event be reported on *Reader's Digest*'s December 31, 20X1,
financial statements?

Summer Production

In Chapter 2, we defined *accruals*
as the recognition of revenue and
expense *before* the receipt or payment of cash. In this chapter, you
will learn that accrual accounting
is, in fact, a much broader concept
that includes not only accruals but
also deferrals and allocations. A
deferral involves the recognition
of revenue or expense at some
time *after* cash has been collected
or paid. For example, a business
may collect cash in 20X1 for services performed in 20X2. In this case,
revenue is recognized in 20X2 even
though the cash was collected in
20X1. *In summary, when recognition
comes before cash flow, it is called
an accrual. When recognition comes
after cash flow, it is called a deferral.*

When deferred amounts are
spread over several accounting periods, the process of assigning a
portion of the total amount to each
accounting period is called an **allocation.** To illustrate, assume that an
attorney received a retainer fee of
$30,000 from a client at the begin-
ning of 20X1. In exchange for the
cash receipt, the attorney agreed to
act as a trustee for the client's children for the years 20X1, 20X2, and
20X3. From the perspective of accrual accounting, the cash receipt
obligates the attorney to work for
the 3-year period. Because of this
future obligation, a liability is established in 20X1 when the cash is collected. The recognition of revenue
is deferred until the attorney's obligation (i.e., liability) to work is satisfied. If the work were spread evenly
over the 3-year period, it would be
reasonable *to allocate* the $30,000
evenly so that $10,000 of revenue
was recognized during each of the
three accounting periods.

L.O. 1

Provide a more complete explanation of the accrual accounting system.

L.O. 2

Identify business events that involve deferrals.

Accounting for Deferrals Illustrated

Stephen Peck was a brilliant young advertising executive employed by the Westberry Corporation. Peck's ad campaigns were credited with a virtual doubling of Westberry's sales over a 3-year period. Peck always wanted to start an advertising agency in which he could be his own boss. He believed that his recent success with Westberry gave him the level of credibility necessary to attract a respectable client base. He informed his employer of his plans and tendered his resignation. Westberry was stunned. The company's executives encouraged Peck to reconsider his decision and offered a generous raise. Peck was grateful but refused the offer. In desperation, Westberry negotiated the following deal.

Peck was free to start his own company. Indeed, Westberry agreed to become Peck's first client, paying him $72,000 in advance to develop ad campaigns for the company. Peck was required to provide services for 1 year, beginning March 1, 20X4. The cash payment for the contract would be made on January 1, 20X4. Peck worked at his clients' offices and utilized their secretarial support services. Peck's only operating expense involved the acquisition of a $12,000 computer system purchased on January 1, 20X4. The system was expected to have a useful life of 4 years and a **salvage value** (i.e., expected selling price at the end of its useful life) of $2,000. Peck named his company Marketing Magic. Marketing Magic began operations on January 1, 20X4, when the company acquired a $1,000 cash contribution of capital from Peck. Although Peck was able to sign $58,000 of contracts for advertising services to be performed by Marketing Magic in 20X5, the only work performed by the company in 20X4 dealt with the fulfillment of the Westberry contract. Marketing Magic distributed $50,000 cash to Peck during the 20X4 accounting period. This scenario contains six accounting events discussed in the next section:

1. There is a $1,000 cash capital acquisition.
2. There is $72,000 cash collected in advance for services to be performed between March 1, 20X4, and February 28, 20X5.
3. A computer system is purchased at a cost of $12,000 cash. The system has an expected useful life of 4 years and a $2,000 salvage value.
4. An adjusting entry is required to recognize the revenue earned in 20X4.
5. An adjusting entry is required to recognize the expense for the 20X4 accounting period associated with the computer system.
6. There is $50,000 of cash distributed to the owner.

Event 1
Business Acquires Assets from Owners

The capital acquisition is an *asset source* transaction. Its impact on the financial statements was discussed in previous chapters. If you have difficulty understanding the effects of this event, see Chapters 1 and 2. The impact of the capital acquisition on the accounting equation follows:

	Assets	=	Liabilities	+	Equity
	Cash	=			Contributed Capital
Beginning Balances	$ 0				$ 0
Capital Acquisitions	1,000				1,000
Ending Balances	$1,000				$1,000

On January 1, 20X4, Marketing Magic received $72,000 cash. In exchange, Marketing Magic agreed to provide advertising development services for a 1-year period between March 1, 20X4, and February 28, 20X5. Revenue could not be recognized on January 1, 20X4, because services had not been performed (i.e., no work had been done). Even though the cash had been realized, the revenue recognition had to be *deferred* until the performance of services had been accomplished. The amount of the deferred revenue represents a liability to Marketing Magic because the company is *obligated* to perform services in the future. The descriptive title **unearned revenue** is used as the name of the liability reported in Marketing Magic's accounting records. The cash receipt is an *asset source* transaction. The asset, Cash, increases; and the liability account, Unearned Revenue, increases by the same amount, $72,000. The effects of this transaction on the accounting equation are shown here:

Event 2
Cash Collected in Advance of Services

	Assets	=	Liabilities	+	Equity
	Cash	=	Unearned Revenue	+	Contributed Capital
Beginning Balances	$ 1,000		$ 0		$1,000
Realized Cash Collection	72,000		72,000		
Ending Balances	$73,000	=	$72,000	+	$1,000

Notice that even though $58,000 of contracts was signed for services to be performed in 20X5, no cash was exchanged with regard to these contracts. Accordingly, there is no historical activity to record in the financial statements. The contracts will be reported later when cash is received or when service is performed. Since no service has been performed and no cash has been exchanged, there is no realization or recognition to report in the accounting records.

The purchase of the computer is an *asset exchange* transaction. The asset, Cash, decreases; and the asset, Office Equipment, increases. Total assets are unchanged. The effects of this transaction on the accounting equation are shown here:

Event 3
Exchange of Cash for Computer

	Assets			=	Liabilities	+	Equity
	Cash	+	Office Equipment	=	Unearned Revenue	+	Contributed Capital
Beginning Balances	$73,000		$ 0		$72,000		$1,000
Purchased Equipment	(12,000)		12,000				
Ending Balances	$61,000	+	$12,000	=	$72,000	+	$1,000

Marketing Magic must recognize the amount of revenue earned on the Westberry contract during the 20X4 accounting period. Marketing Magic began earning revenue on the Westberry contract on March 1, 20X4. Assuming that the work is distributed evenly throughout the contract period, the earnings process is continuous. Recording revenue as it is earned (i.e., continuously) is impractical, if not impossible. A more reasonable approach is simply to adjust the accounting records at the end of the accounting period by the amount of revenue

Event 4
Recognition of Revenue (adjusting entry)

L.O. 6

Explain effects of end-of-period adjustments related to deferrals.

earned for the entire accounting period. For example, the $72,000 of unearned revenue can be divided by 12 to determine the amount of revenue to recognize on a monthly basis ($72,000 ÷ 12 = $6,000). Since 10 months of service were performed in 20X4, $60,000 (or 10 × $6,000) of revenue could be recognized in a single year-end adjustment. This adjustment is made by removing $60,000 from the Unearned Revenue account and placing it into the Revenue account. This entry represents a *claims exchange* with the liability account, Unearned Revenue, decreasing and the equity increasing (i.e., recognizing the revenue will cause net income to increase and ultimately a corresponding increase in retained earnings). Total claims remain unchanged. It is the decrease in the liability account that triggers the recognition of the revenue. As the company satisfies its obligation to perform services, the creditor's claim on the firm's assets decreases and the owner's claim increases. Recall that *revenue* is defined as an increase in assets or a *decrease* in liabilities. The effect of the revenue recognition on the accounting equation follows:

	Assets			=	Liabilities	+	Equity		
	Cash	+	Office Equipment	=	Unearned Revenue	+	Contributed Capital	+	Retained Earnings
Beginning Balances	$61,000		$12,000		$72,000		$1,000		$ 0
									Revenue
Recognized Revenue Earned					(60,000)				60,000
Ending Balances	$61,000	+	$12,000	=	$12,000	+	$1,000	+	$60,000

Event 5
Recognition of Expense for Use of Computer (adjusting entry)

L.O. 6

Explain effects of end-of-period adjustments related to deferrals.

Marketing Magic must recognize an expense for an amount that represents the portion of the computer equipment used during the 20X4 accounting period. To assess the net economic benefit associated with running the business, it is necessary to determine how much of the computer equipment was sacrificed (i.e., used) in the process of earning the revenue. Assuming that the equipment is used evenly over its 4-year life, it is logical to allocate an equal amount as expense for each year that the equipment is operated. Recall that the computer cost $12,000 and has an estimated salvage value of $2,000. Since the $2,000 salvage value represents the portion of the cost that is expected to be recovered at the end of its useful life, only $10,000 worth of the equipment is ultimately expected to be used. Accordingly, the amount of expense to be recognized in the 20X4 accounting period is $2,500 (that is, [$12,000 − $2,000] ÷ 4). This allocation plan is commonly referred to as the **straight-line method.** As this discussion implies, the formula for determining a straight-line allocation is *cost minus salvage, divided by the number of years of useful life.* The recognition of the use of a long-term, tangible asset is commonly called **depreciation expense.** *Long term* is usually defined as a period longer than the typical accounting cycle (i.e., longer than 1 year). The recognition of depreciation expense constitutes an *asset use* transaction. The use of the asset (i.e., decrease) triggers the expense recognition. Recall that an *expense* is defined as a *decrease* in assets or an increase in liabilities. The effects of the expense recognition on the accounting equation are as follows:

	Assets		=	Liabilities	+	Equity		
	Cash	+	**Office Equipment**	=	**Unearned Revenue**	+	**Contributed Capital**	+	**Retained Earnings**
Beginning Balances	$61,000		$12,000		$12,000		$1,000		$60,000
			Accumulated Depreciation						**Depreciation Expense**
Recognized Depreciation Expense			(2,500)						(2,500)
Ending Balances	$61,000	+	$9,500	=	$12,000	+	$1,000	+	$57,500

Note that the asset account, Office Equipment, was not directly decreased. Rather, a **contra asset account** called **Accumulated Depreciation** was used to reflect the reduction. This is the generally accepted approach for reporting the effects of depreciation. The Accumulated Depreciation account is subtracted from the original cost of the asset to determine the **book value** (i.e., carrying value) of the asset. Both the historical cost of the asset and the Accumulated Depreciation account are shown in the financial statements. This treatment is shown in the financial statements in Exhibit 3–1 on page 107.

The astute reader may have noticed that the depreciation expense covered the period from January 1, 20X4, to the end of that year. Conversely, the revenue was recognized from a starting point on March 1, 20X4. Accordingly, it could be argued that the computer was used for purposes other than the generation of the revenue recognized from the Westberry contract. In other words, revenues and expenses do not perfectly match. Many expenses are not directly related to particular revenues, or the revenues to which they relate are indeterminable, or the identification process is not worth the effort it requires. Accordingly, many expenses are matched with the period in which they are incurred without reference to any particular revenue item.

Also be aware that accounting is not an exact science. Slight imperfections are to be expected. Indeed, the **concept of materiality** recognizes practical limitations in financial reporting matters. Proper treatment is required for material items only. As previously indicated, an omission or misstatement of accounting information is considered material if the decisions of a reasonable person would have been influenced by the omission or misstatement.

The treatment of depreciation also highlights the fact that financial reports contain information from approximate, rather than exact, measures. Notice that both the amount of the salvage value and the expected useful life of the asset are estimated amounts. Accordingly, the amounts of depreciation expense, net income, and retained earnings constitute estimated, rather than exact, amounts.

As discussed in Chapters 1 and 2, the distribution to owners represents an *asset use* transaction. Its effect on the accounting equation is shown here:

Event 6
Assets Transferred to Owners (Distribution)

	Assets		=	Liabilities	+	Equity		
	Cash	+	**Office Equipment**	=	**Unearned Revenue**	+	**Contributed Capital**	+	**Retained Earnings**
Beginning Balances	$61,000		$9,500		$12,000		$1,000		$57,500
Distributed Cash to Owners	(50,000)								(50,000)
Ending Balances	$11,000	+	$9,500	=	$12,000	+	$1,000	+	$ 7,500

Summary of Transactions for 20X4

	Assets		=	Liabilities	+	Equity		
	Cash	+	Office Equipment	=	Unearned Revenue	+	Contributed Capital	+	Retained Earnings
Beginning Balances	$ 0		$ 0		$ 0		$ 0		$ 0
Capital Acquisitions	1,000						1,000		
Realized Cash Collection	72,000				72,000				
Purchased Equipment	(12,000)		12,000						
									Revenue
Recognized Revenue Earned					(60,000)				60,000
			Accumulated Depreciation						Depreciation Expense
Recognized Depreciation Expense			(2,500)						(2,500)
									Distribution
Distributed Cash to Owners	(50,000)								(50,000)
Ending Balances	$11,000	+	$ 9,500	=	$12,000	+	$1,000	+	$ 7,500

L.O. 3

Demonstrate an understanding of how events are recorded under an accounting equation.

The 20X4 Financial Statements

Exhibit 3–1 contains the financial statements for Marketing Magic for the 20X4 accounting period. You should be familiar with most of the components of the financial statements by this point. However, it is important to trace the effects of all the transactions to the financial statements. Pay particular attention to the fact that deferrals as well as accruals cause differences between the amount of reported net income and the amount of cash flow from operations.

The income statement displays the allocations for revenue recognition ($60,000) and depreciation expense ($2,500), thereby showing a reported net income of $57,500. In contrast, the operating activities section of the statement of cash flows shows the $72,000 of cash received from the Westberry contract. Note that the $12,000 cash paid for office equipment is shown in the investing activities section rather than the operating activities section. This treatment applies to the purchase or sale of any long-term asset.

L.O. 4

Prepare financial statements that include cash, accrual, and deferral events.

L.O. 5

Explain how deferral events affect financial statements.

Another item that should be scrutinized is the treatment of the Accumulated Depreciation account. Note that the full amount of the original cost is shown in the Office Equipment account. The amount of the accumulated depreciation is subtracted from this amount to arrive at the carrying value (i.e., book value) of the asset (that is, $12,000 − $2,500 = $9,500). It is the carrying value ($9,500) that is added to the other assets to arrive at the amount of total assets appearing on the balance sheet.

Second Accounting Cycle

L.O. 2

Identify business events that involve deferrals.

Stephen Peck moved the offices of Marketing Magic to a new location on January 1, 20X5. Westberry continued to be a client but decided to pay for services as rendered, rather than in advance. Marketing Magic consummated the following transactions during the 20X5 accounting period.

EXHIBIT 3–1

Vertical Statements Model

Marketing Magic
Financial Statements
for the 20X4 Accounting Period

Income Statement

Service Revenue	$60,000
Depreciation Expense	(2,500)
Net Income	$57,500

Statement of Changes in Equity

Beginning Contributed Capital	$ 0	
Plus: Capital Acquisitions	1,000	
Ending Contributed Capital		$ 1,000
Beginning Retained Earnings	0	
Plus: Net Income	57,500	
Less: Distributions	(50,000)	
Ending Retained Earnings		7,500
Total Equity		$ 8,500

Balance Sheet

Assets		
Cash		$11,000
Office Equipment	$12,000	
Less: Accumulated Depreciation	(2,500)	9,500
Total Assets		$20,500
Liabilities		
Unearned Revenue		$12,000
Equity		
Contributed Capital	$ 1,000	
Retained Earnings	7,500	
Total Equity		8,500
Total Liabilities and Equity		$20,500

Statement of Cash Flows

Cash Flows from Operating Activities		
Cash Receipt from Revenue		$72,000
Cash Flow from Investing Activities		
Cash Payment for Computer Equipment		(12,000)
Cash Flows from Financing Activities		
Cash Receipt from Capital Acquisitions	$ 1,000	
Cash Payment for Distributions	(50,000)	
Net Cash Outflow from Financing Activities		(49,000)
Net Change in Cash		11,000
Plus: Beginning Cash Balance		0
Ending Cash Balance		$11,000

an answer for the curious accountant

Because the Reader's Digest Association receives cash from customers before actually providing any magazines to them, the company has not earned any revenue at the time it receives the cash. Thus, Reader's Digest has a liability, which is called *unearned revenue*. If Reader's Digest closed its books on December 31, then $3 of Paige Long's subscription would be recognized as revenue in 20X1. The remaining $9 would appear on Reader's Digest's balance sheet as a liability.

Reader's Digest actually ends its accounting year on June 30 each year. Exhibit 3–2 is a copy of the June 30, 1998, balance sheet for Reader's Digest. Notice the liability for unearned revenue amounting to $355.4 million—this liability represented about 27% of Reader's Digest's total liabilities!

Will Reader's Digest need cash to pay off these subscription liabilities? Not exactly. The liabilities will not be paid off with cash. Instead, they will be satisfied by providing magazines to the sub-scribers. However, Reader's Digest will need cash to pay for the production and distribution of the magazines supplied to the customers. Even so, the amount of cash required to provide magazines will probably differ significantly from the amount of unearned revenues. In most cases, subscription fees do not cover the cost of producing and dis-tributing magazines. Publishers collect significant advertising revenues that enable them to provide magazines to customers at prices well below the cost of publication. Accordingly, the amount of unearned revenue is not likely to represent the amount of cash needed to cover the cost of satis-fying the company's obligation to produce and distribute magazines. Although the association between unearned revenues and the cost of pro-viding magazines to customers is not direct, a knowledgeable financial analyst can use the infor-mation to make estimates regarding future cash flows and revenue recognition.

1. Acquired an additional $5,000 cash contribution of capital from the owner.
2. Paid $400 cash for supplies.
3. Paid $1,200 cash for an insurance policy that covered the company for 1 year, beginning February 1, 20X5.
4. Recognized revenue for services provided on account in the amount of $108,000.
5. Collected $89,000 of the receivables due from customers.
6. Recognized accrued operating expenses, other than supplies and insur-ance, charged on account in the amount of $32,000.
7. Paid suppliers $28,000 of the amount due on the accounts payable.
8. Distributed $70,000 cash to the owner.
9. Purchased land that cost $3,000 cash.

EXHIBIT 3-2

Excerpt from the Reader's Digest 1998 Annual Report

The Reader's Digest Association, Inc., and Subsidiaries

Consolidated Balance Sheets (in millions)

	June 30	
	1998	**1997**
Assets		
Current Assets		
Cash and Cash Equivalents	$ 122.8	$ 69.1
Receivables, Net	376.4	398.3
Inventories	162.2	167.8
Prepaid Expenses and Other Current Assets	311.2	290.6
Total Current Assets	972.6	925.8
Property, Plant and Equipment, Net	285.4	314.8
Intangible Assets, Net	41.8	59.1
Other Noncurrent Assets	264.2	344.1
Total Assets	$1,564.0	$1,643.8
Liabilities and Stockholders' Equity		
Current Liabilities		
Accounts Payable	$ 172.1	$ 193.0
Accrued Expenses	377.4	373.6
Income Taxes Payable	21.0	22.1
Unearned Revenue	355.4	356.5
Other Current Liabilities	90.0	67.9
Total Current Liabilities	1,015.9	1,013.1
Postretirement and Postemployment Benefits Other than Pensions	157.6	153.3
Other Noncurrent Liabilities	131.9	131.4
Total Liabilities	1,305.4	1,297.8
Stockholders' Equity		
Capital Stock	16.6	29.0
Paid-In Capital	144.8	141.8
Retained Earnings	845.0	924.2
Foreign Currency Translation Adjustment	(49.8)	(33.4)
Net Unrealized Losses on Certain Investments	—	(0.3)
Treasury Stock, at Cost	(698.0)	(715.3)
Total Stockholders' Equity	258.6	346.0
Total Liabilities and Stockholders' Equity	$1,564.0	$1,643.8

Adjusting entries

10. Recognized the remainder of the unearned revenue. All services had been provided by February 28, 20X5, as per the original contract.

11. Recognized depreciation expense.

12. Recognized supplies expense; $150 of supplies was on hand at the close of business on December 31, 20X5.

13. Recognized 11 months of insurance expense.

L.O. 3

Demonstrate an understanding of how events are recorded under an accounting equation.

L.O. 7

Distinguish between a cost that is an asset and a cost that is an expense.

Effect of 20X5 Transactions on the Accounting Equation and the Financial Statements

Exhibit 3–3 is a summary of the effects of the transactions on the accounting equation. The effects are referenced by the transaction number in parentheses to the left of the transaction amount. The beginning balances were carried forward from the last period's ending balances. Many of the transactions were introduced in previous sections of this book. Those transactions that are new are discussed here.

Transaction 2 is a deferral. The cost of the supplies is first placed in an asset account (i.e., *asset exchange* transaction). The conversion of the asset to an expense is deferred until the supplies are used in the process of earning revenue. It is helpful at this point to draw a clear distinction between *cost* and *expense*. A *cost* can be either an asset or an expense. If the item acquired has already been used in the process of earning revenue, its cost represents an *expense*. If the item will be used in the future to generate revenue, its cost represents an *asset*. The cost is held in the asset account (i.e., the expense recognition is deferred) until the item is used to pro-

EXHIBIT 3–3

Effect of 20X5 Transactions on the Accounting Equation

Assets					=	Liabilities		+	Equity			
Cash		**Prepaid Insurance**				**Unearned Revenue**			**Contributed Capital**		**Retained Earnings**	
Bal.	$ 11,000	Bal.	$ 0		Bal.	$ 12,000		Bal.	$1,000	Bal.	$ 7,500	
(1)	5,000	(3)	1,200		(10)	(12,000)		(1)	5,000			
(2)	(400)	(13)	(1,100)		Bal.	$ 0		Bal.	$6,000	**Revenue**		
(3)	(1,200)	Bal.	$ 100							(4)	$108,000	
(5)	89,000				**Accounts Payable**					(10)	12,000	
(7)	(28,000)	**Office Equipment**								Bal.	$120,000	
(8)	(70,000)				Bal.	$ 0						
(9)	(3,000)	Bal.	$12,000		(6)	32,000				**Operating Expenses**		
Bal.	$ 2,400				(7)	(28,000)						
		Accumulated Depreciation			Bal.	$ 4,000				(6)	$(32,000)	
Accounts Receivable												
		Bal.	$(2,500)							**Depreciation Expense**		
Bal.	$ 0	(11)	(2,500)									
(4)	108,000									(11)	$ (2,500)	
(5)	(89,000)	Bal.	$(5,000)									
Bal.	$ 19,000									**Supplies Expense**		
										(12)	$ (250)	
Supplies												
Bal.	$ 0									**Insurance Expense**		
(2)	400											
(12)	(250)									(13)	$ (1,100)	
Bal.	$ 150											
										Distribution		
Land												
Bal.	$ 0									(8)	$(70,000)	
(9)	3,000											
Bal.	$ 3,000											

duce revenue. When the revenue is generated, the asset is converted to an expense to match revenues with their related expenses. Exhibit 3–4, below, demonstrates the relationship between a cost and an expense.

L.O. 5

Explain how deferral events affect financial statements.

It is impractical to recognize supplies expense as the supplies are being used. For example, it is too tedious to record an expense every time a pencil, a piece of paper, or an envelope is used. Instead, normal practice is to recognize the total amount of supplies used during the entire accounting period in a single adjusting entry at the end of the accounting period. The amount of supplies used is determined by subtracting the amount of supplies on hand at the end of the period from the amount of supplies that were available for use. Since Marketing Magic had no supplies at the beginning of the period, the only supplies available for use were the $400 of supplies purchased during 20X5. Transaction 12 states that $150 of supplies was on hand at the end of the accounting period. In practice, this amount is determined by counting the supplies on hand at the end of the period. Based on the information provided in the case, $250 of supplies must have been used during the period (that is, $400 − $150). This explains the year-end adjusting entry (i.e., transaction 12) that removes the amount of the used supplies from the asset account and inserts it into the Supplies Expense account. Recall that an expense is defined as a decrease in assets or an increase in liabilities. In this case, the decrease in the asset, Supplies, triggers the expense recognition. The $150 of supplies on hand at the end of the accounting period is shown as an asset on the balance sheet. The parentheses surrounding the amounts in the expense and dividend accounts indicate that the business events acted to decrease the Retained Earnings equity account. Although events 6, 8, 11, 12, and 13 increase the amount of an expense or distribution account, they acted to decrease equity.

L.O. 6

Explain effects of end-of-period adjustments related to deferrals.

Note that the deferral causes a difference between the amount of expense recognized and the amount of cash flow. Although $400 of cash is paid for supplies, only $250 of this is recognized as an expense. The remaining $150 is deferred as an asset. The $400 appears as an outflow under the operating activities section of the statement of cash flows, the $250 is reported as supplies expense on the income statement, and the $150 is displayed as an asset (i.e., supplies) on the balance sheet. Verify these effects by reviewing the financial statements shown in Exhibit 3–5.

Transaction 3 is also a deferral. The $1,200 cost of the insurance must be allocated between an asset account and an expense account. Since the insurance policy provided coverage for 1 year, the cost of coverage per month is $100 (i.e., $1,200 ÷ 12). By the end of the accounting period, 11 months of the coverage have been used and 1 month of coverage is available for use in 20X6. Accordingly, $1,100 (i.e., $100 × 11) should be charged to expense, and the remaining $100 represents an asset. Since the insurance is paid for in advance of its use, the title *Prepaid Insurance* is an appropriate descriptor of the asset account.

As a practical matter, the full cost of the insurance is placed in the Prepaid Insurance account at the time of the purchase (see transaction 3 in Exhibit 3–3). An adjusting entry is made at the end of the accounting period to recognize the

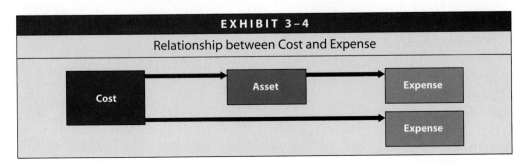

EXHIBIT 3–4

Relationship between Cost and Expense

amount of the insurance that has been used. The adjustment (transaction 13) moves the amount of used insurance from the asset account to the expense account. Be aware that other recording schemes are possible. For example, some sophisticated computer programs can allocate costs between asset and expense

EXHIBIT 3–5
Vertical Statements Model

Marketing Magic
Financial Statements
For the 20X5 Accounting Period

Income Statement

Service Revenue		$120,000
Operating Expense	$32,000	
Depreciation Expense	2,500	
Supplies Expense	250	
Insurance Expense	1,100	
Total Expenses		(35,850)
Net Income		$ 84,150

Statement of Changes in Equity

Beginning Contributed Capital	$ 1,000	
Plus: Capital Acquisitions	5,000	
Ending Contributed Capital		$ 6,000
Beginning Retained Earnings	7,500	
Plus: Net Income	84,150	
Less: Distributions	(70,000)	
Ending Retained Earnings		21,650
Total Equity		$ 27,650

Balance Sheet

Assets		
Cash		$ 2,400
Accounts Receivable		19,000
Supplies		150
Prepaid Insurance		100
Office Equipment	$12,000	
Less: Accumulated Depreciation	(5,000)	7,000
Land		3,000
Total Assets		$ 31,650
Liabilities		
Accounts Payable		$ 4,000
Equity		
Contributed Capital	$ 6,000	
Retained Earnings	21,650	
Total Equity		27,650
Total Liabilities and Equity		$ 31,650

(cont'd)

Statement of Cash Flows		
Cash Flows from Operating Activities		
Cash Receipt from Revenue		$ 89,000
Cash Payment for Supplies	$ 400	
Cash Payment for Insurance	1,200	
Cash Payment for Operating Expenses	28,000	
Total Cash Outflows from Operations		(29,600)
Net Cash Flow from Operating Activities		59,400
Cash Flow from Investing Activities		
Cash Outflow to Purchase Land		(3,000)
Cash Flows from Financing Activities		
Cash Receipt from Capital Acquisitions	5,000	
Cash Payment for Distributions	(70,000)	
Net Cash Outflow from Financing Activities		(65,000)
Net Change in Cash		(8,600)
Plus Beginning Cash Balance		11,000
Ending Cash Balance		$ 2,400

accounts on a continuous basis. Regardless of the recording method, the ultimate impact on the financial statement is the same.

The deferral for the insurance cost causes a difference between the amount of insurance expense and the cash flow. The $1,200 cash cost is shown in the cash flow from operating activities section of the statement of cash flows. The used portion of the cost is shown as an $1,100 expense on the income statement; and the remaining $100 is deferred as an asset, Prepaid Insurance, on the balance sheet. Verify this allocation and the effects of the remaining transactions by reviewing the financial statements in Exhibit 3–5.

Third Accounting Cycle

Marketing Magic consummated the following transactions during the 20X6 accounting period.

L.O. 2

Identify business events that involve deferrals.

1. Acquired an additional $1,000 cash contribution of capital from one of Peck's friends.
2. Sold the land that it owned for $2,500 cash.
3. Purchased $400 of supplies with cash.
4. Borrowed $20,000 from a local bank on February 1, 20X6. The bank note carried a 9% annual rate of interest and a 1-year term.
5. Paid $1,200 cash to renew the insurance policy for a 1-year term beginning February 1, 20X6.
6. Recognized revenue for services provided on account in the amount of $167,000.
7. Collected $129,000 of the receivables due from customers.
8. Recognized accrued operating expenses, other than supplies and insurance. These operating expenses were charged on account in the amount of $62,000.

9. Paid suppliers $65,000 of the amount due on the accounts payable.

10. Received advance payment of $18,000 cash from a customer. Marketing Magic agreed to provide marketing services to the customer for a 1-year period beginning December 1, 20X6.

11. Distributed $80,000 cash to the owners of the business.

Adjusting entries

12. Recognized 1 month of the unearned revenue.

13. Recognized depreciation expense.

14. Recognized supplies expense; $200 of supplies was on hand at the close of business on December 31, 20X6.

15. Recognized 12 months of insurance expense.

16. Recognized the accrued interest on the bank note.

Effect of 20X6 Transactions on the Accounting Equation and the Financial Statements

L.O. 3

Demonstrate an understanding of how events are recorded under an accounting equation.

L.O. 8

Distinguish gains and losses from revenues and expenses.

The effects of the 20X6 accounting events are shown in Exhibit 3–6 on the following page. Transaction 1 demonstrates the fact that ownership interest may be shared by two or more individuals. Indeed, literally millions of individuals and institutions hold ownership interests in major corporations, such as General Motors, Sears, and International Business Machines (IBM). The treatment of the $1,000 capital acquisition from Peck's friend is no different from the effects of other acquisitions shown previously. The acquisition is an *asset source* transaction that is recorded by an increase in the asset account, Cash, and a corresponding increase in the equity account, Contributed Capital.

The sale of the land resulted in the recognition of a $500 loss. Since the asset was carried on the books at $3,000 and was sold for $2,500, total assets decreased by $500. This decrease in assets is called a loss. **Losses** are similar to expenses in that they are defined as decreases in assets or increases in liabilities. Losses differ from expenses in that losses result from **peripheral (incidental) transactions,** rather than ordinary operating activities. In this case, Marketing Magic is not in the business of selling land. The sale is incidental to its normal operating activities. Accordingly, the decrease in assets is labeled a *loss* rather than an *expense*. **Gains** are similar to revenues in that they are defined as increases in assets or decreases in liabilities. However, gains differ from revenues in that gains result from peripheral rather than ordinary operating activities.

The sale of the land results in an increase in the Cash account. Furthermore, it is necessary to remove the amount in the Land account from the records and to recognize the loss as a reduction in equity. Recording the effects requires a $2,500 increase to the Cash account, a $3,000 decrease to the Land account, and a $500 reduction in Retained Earnings. These effects are shown in Exhibit 3–6, labeled as transaction 2. The $500 loss is shown on the income statement as a separate line item after **income from operations,** which is determined by subtracting expenses from revenues. However, the loss does not measure the cash flow consequences of the sale. Recall that the land was sold for $2,500 cash. This amount is shown as a source (i.e., cash inflow) of funds under the investing activities section of the statement of cash flows. Cash flow from operations is not affected by the sale. Remember, the loss was associated with a *peripheral activity* rather than an ordinary operating activity. Verify these effects by reviewing the financial statements in Exhibit 3–7 on pages 116–117.

EXHIBIT 3–6

Effect of 20X6 Transactions on the Accounting Equation

| Assets | = | Liabilities | + | Equity |

Cash

Bal.	$ 2,400
(1)	1,000
(2)	2,500
(3)	(400)
(4)	20,000
(5)	(1,200)
(7)	129,000
(9)	(65,000)
(10)	18,000
(11)	(80,000)
Bal.	$ 26,300

Accounts Receivable

Bal.	$ 19,000
(6)	167,000
(7)	(129,000)
Bal.	$ 57,000

Supplies

Bal.	$ 150
(3)	400
(14)	(350)
Bal.	$ 200

Land

Bal.	$ 3,000
(2)	(3,000)
Bal.	$ 0

Prepaid Insurance

Bal.	$ 100
(5)	1,200
(15)	(1,200)
Bal.	$ 100

Office Equipment

Bal.	$12,000

Accumulated Depreciation

Bal.	$(5,000)
(13)	(2,500)
Bal.	$(7,500)

Unearned Revenue

Bal.	$ 0
(10)	18,000
(12)	(1,500)
Bal.	$16,500

Accounts Payable

Bal.	$ 4,000
(8)	62,000
(9)	(65,000)
Bal.	$1,000

Interest Payable

(16)	$ 1,650

Notes Payable

(4)	$20,000

Contributed Capital

Bal.	$6,000
(1)	1,000
Bal.	$7,000

Retained Earnings

Bal.	$ 21,650

Revenue

(6)	$167,000
(12)	1,500
Bal.	$168,500

Operating Expense

(8)	$ (62,000)

Depreciation Expense

(13)	$ (2,500)

Supplies Expense

(14)	$ (350)

Insurance Expense

(15)	$ (1,200)

Interest Expense

(16)	$ (1,650)

Loss

(2)	$ (500)

Distribution

(11)	$ (80,000)

The amount of supplies expense is determined by the same approach that was used in 20X5 except that there is a beginning balance in the Supplies account in this case. Since the Supplies account has a beginning balance of $150 and $400 of supplies is purchased during the period, $550 of supplies is available to be used. Given that $200 of supplies was on hand at December 31, 20X6, then $350 of supplies must have been used during the accounting period. Accordingly, the year-end adjusting entry (transaction 14) removes $350 from the asset account, Supplies, and places it in the Supplies Expense account. Note that the amount of supplies expense does not correspond to the amount of cash spent. The operating activities section of the statement of cash flows displays the $400 cash outflow made to purchase supplies. Note that the beginning balances in the expense and

L.O. 6

Explain effects of end-of-period adjustments related to deferrals.

EXHIBIT 3-7

Vertical Statements Model

Marketing Magic
Financial Statements
For the 20X6 Accounting Period

Income Statement

Service Revenue		$168,500
Operating Expense	$ 62,000	
Depreciation Expense	2,500	
Supplies Expense	350	
Insurance Expense	1,200	
Interest Expense	1,650	
Total Expenses		(67,700)
Net Operating Income		100,800
Less: Loss on Sale of Land		(500)
Net Income		$100,300

Statement of Changes in Equity

Beginning Contributed Capital	$ 6,000	
Plus: Capital Acquisitions	1,000	
Ending Contributed Capital		$ 7,000
Beginning Retained Earnings	21,650	
Plus: Net Income	100,300	
Less: Distributions	(80,000)	
Ending Retained Earnings		41,950
Total Equity		$ 48,950

Balance Sheet

Assets		
Cash		$ 26,300
Accounts Receivable		57,000
Supplies		200
Prepaid Insurance		100
Office Equipment	$ 12,000	
Less Accumulated Depreciation	(7,500)	4,500
Total Assets		$ 88,100
Liabilities		
Accounts Payable	$ 1,000	
Unearned Revenue	16,500	
Interest Payable	1,650	
Notes Payable	20,000	
Total Liabilities		$ 39,150
Equity		
Contributed Capital	7,000	
Retained Earnings	41,950	
Total Equity		48,950
Total Liabilities and Equity		$ 88,100

(cont'd)

Statement of Cash Flows		
Cash Flows from Operating Activities		
Cash Receipt from Receivables	$129,000	
Cash Receipt from Advance Collections	18,000	
Cash Payment for Supplies	(400)	
Cash Payment for Insurance	(1,200)	
Cash Payment for Operating Expenses	(65,000)	
Net Cash Flow from Operating Activities		$ 80,400
Cash Flows from Investing Activities		
Cash Receipt from Sale of Land		2,500
Cash Flows from Financing Activities		
Cash Receipt from Bank Loan	20,000	
Cash Receipt from Capital Acquisitions	1,000	
Cash Payment for Distributions	(80,000)	
Net Cash Outflow from Financing Activities		(59,000)
Net Increase in Cash		23,900
Plus Beginning Cash Balance		2,400
Ending Cash Balance		$ 26,300

distribution accounts are assumed to be zero because the prior year's balances were closed (i.e., transferred) to the Retained Earnings account.

The Prepaid Insurance account increased as a result of $1,200 of insurance purchased on February 1, 20X6 (transaction 5). Given the $100 beginning balance in the Prepaid Insurance account, $1,300 of insurance is available to use over a 13-month period. Since 12 months of insurance were used in 20X6, the year-end adjusting entry removes $1,200 from the Prepaid Insurance account and places it in the Insurance Expense account (transaction 15).

The borrowed funds from the bank loan (transaction 4) require the accrual of interest expense. The amount of interest is determined by multiplying the principal by the rate by the time ($20,000 \times .09 \times [11 \div 12] = $1,650$). The accrued interest represents a liability to Marketing Magic as of December 31, 20X6. The increase in liabilities requires the recognition of interest expense as depicted in transaction 16 in Exhibit 3–6.

The advance payment described in transaction 10 is a deferral. The cash receipt is first recorded as a liability, called *unearned revenue.* Assuming that the work associated with the contract is spread evenly over the 1-year period, the monthly allocation for revenue recognition is $1,500 ($18,000 \div 12$). Since 1 month of service has been provided by the close of business on December 31, 20X6, the year-end adjusting entry (transaction 12) removes $1,500 from the liability account and places it in the revenue account. Note that this treatment is consistent with the definition of revenue as being a decrease in liabilities. The deferral causes a difference between the amount of revenue recognized on the income statement (that is, $1,500 is included in the $168,500 of revenue reported on the income statement) and the amount of cash receipt shown in the operating activities section of the statement of cash flows ($18,000). Trace the effect of these transactions to the financial statements.

The other transactions for 20X6 should be familiar to you. However, a positive reinforcement experience can be gained by tracing the results of each transaction to the related financial statements. Accordingly, you are encouraged to fully review all the effects of the transactions in Exhibit 3–6 and the financial statements in Exhibit 3–7.

Analysis of Financial Statements to Assess Managerial Performance

Assessment of the Effective Use of Assets

Suppose you are told that a company earned net income of $1,000,000. Does this mean that the company's performance has been good or bad? If the company is General Motors, the answer is probably poor performance. If it is Al Bundy's shoe store, $1,000,000 indicates outstanding performance. Clearly, the evaluation of performance requires reference to the size of the investment required to produce the income. The relationship between the level of income and the size of the investment can be expressed in a single figure known as the **return-on-assets ratio,** which is defined as follows:

$$\frac{\text{Net Income}[1]}{\text{Total Assets}}$$

This ratio provides a common unit of measure that enables comparisons between different-size companies. To illustrate the importance of comparing ratios rather than absolute dollar values, consider the following comparison between Ford Motor Company and Chrysler Corporation. Both Ford and Chrysler had positive net incomes in 1997. Ford's earnings for that year were $6.9 billion, and Chrysler's were $2.8 billion, making Ford's earnings more than double those of Chrysler. However, the return-on-asset ratios for the two companies reveal that Chrysler produced higher earnings relative to the amount of assets invested. Ford's ratio was 2.5% while Chrysler's was 4.6%. This analysis suggests that even though Chrysler generated a lower amount of income expressed in total dollars, the company did a better job of managing its assets. Accordingly, different companies cannot be compared fairly on the basis of absolute dollar values.

Although the preceding example demonstrates the usefulness of a particular relationship (i.e., income relative to assets), other ratios could be computed that also enhance the capacity to analyze financial statements. Two of these ratios are discussed in the following paragraphs.

Assessment of the Risk of Debt

Borrowing money can be a risky business. To illustrate, assume that two companies have the following financial structures:

	Assets	=	Liabilities	+	Equity
Eastern Company	100	=	20	+	80
Western Company	100	=	80	+	20

Which company has the greater financial risk? To answer, look at the financial structures that will exist if each company incurs a $30 loss.

	Assets	=	Liabilities	+	Equity
Eastern Company	70	=	20	+	50
Western Company	70	=	80	+	(10)

---

[1]The use of net income in this ratio does not consider the effects of debt financing and income taxation. The application of these topics to the return on assets is discussed in Chapter 10.

Clearly, Western Company is at greater risk. Notice that Eastern Company could survive a $30 loss that reduced assets and equity. After such a loss, Eastern Company would still have a $50 balance in equity and would still have more than enough assets ($70) to cover the creditor's $20 claim. In contrast, a $30 loss would throw Western Company into bankruptcy. The company would have a $10 deficit (i.e., negative) balance in equity. Furthermore, the remaining balance in assets ($70) would be insufficient to cover the creditor's $80 claim on assets.

focus on
international issues

Why Not Have One Global GAAP?

Although no two countries have exactly the same accounting rules, there are many similarities in the various accounting systems used around the world. Furthermore, geographic, political, and social forces tend to promote similar views within selected sets of countries. For example, the GAAP of the United Kingdom is more likely to match the GAAP of New Zealand than the GAAP of Brazil. This has led some to try to group countries based on the similarity of their respective accounting rules.

One accounting research study* concluded that the accounting systems of the world can be divided into four groups: (1) British Commonwealth model, (2) Latin American model, (3) Continental European model, (4) U.S. model.

According to this study, countries with accounting rules similar to (but not exactly the same as) GAAP in the United States include Canada, Japan, Mexico, Panama, and the Philippines.

If there already exist similarities among the GAAP of different countries, why not have only one set of accounting rules for all countries? There are many reasons that one set of rules, and one rule-making body, does not exist for the entire world, but consider two easy examples. First, different countries have different political structures (e.g., democracy versus communism). What are the chances that a country with strong government controls would allow its accounting rules to be established by a nongovernment body such as the Financial Accounting Standards Board? Second, different countries have different economic structures. In the United States, most industries, even those related to national defense, are privately owned. In some countries, major industries are owned by the government, while smaller industries are privately owned. In a few countries, almost all resources are owned by the government. It is impossible to have one set of rules that would work well in such diverse settings.

Even though each country establishes its own GAAP, there is an international "rule-suggesting" body for accounting. The International Accounting Standards Committee (IASC) has more than 100 member countries participating in its activities. The IASC tries to improve the uniformity of accounting practices around the world by recommending the appropriate accounting treatment for various business events. However, the IASC has no enforcement power, so its pronouncements are simply recommendations, not requirements.

*R. D. Nair and W. G. Frank, "The Impact of Disclosure and Measurement Practices on International Accounting Classifications," *The Accounting Review,* July 1980.

The level of risk can be measured in part through the computation of a **debt-to-assets ratio.** The ratio is as follows:

Total Debt
Total Assets

For example, Eastern Company has a 20% debt-to-assets ratio ($20 ÷ $100) while Western Company has an 80% debt-to-assets ratio ($80 ÷ $100). Why would the owners of Western Company be willing to accept greater risk? To answer this question, assume that both companies produce $12 of revenue and that they are required to pay 10% interest on the money they have borrowed. Income statements for the two companies appear as follows:[2]

	Eastern Company	**Western Company**
Revenue	$12	$12
Interest Expense	2	8
Net Income	$10	$ 4

At first glance, it appears that the owners of Eastern Company are still better off because that company produced higher net income. However, a closer look discloses that, in fact, the owners of Western Company are better off. Remember that the owners of Eastern Company had to put $80 of their own money into the business in order to get the $10 of income. Accordingly, the return on their invested funds is 12.5% ($10 ÷ $80). In contrast, the owners of Western Company were required to invest only $20 to obtain $4 of net income. Their return on invested funds amounts to 20% ($4 ÷ $20). In different terms, an $80 investment would buy four companies like Western Company or one like Eastern Company. Four companies like Western Company would produce $16 of net income ($4 income per company × 4 companies). This compares favorably to $10 of net income produced by Eastern Company. Clearly, Western Company is the more profitable investment. The relationship between the amount of net income and the owner's equity is called the **return-on-equity ratio.** As suggested, the return-on-equity ratio is:

Net Income
Owner's Equity

In business, the practice of using borrowed money to increase the return on owner's investment is called **financial leverage.** Financial leverage explains why companies are willing to accept the risk of debt. Companies borrow money to make money. If a company can borrow money at 10% and invest it at 12%, the owners will be better off by 2% of the amount borrowed. A business that does not use borrowed funds may be missing an opportunity to increase its return on equity.

Real-World Data

Exhibit 3–8 shows the debt-to-assets, return-on-assets, and return on equity ratios for six real-world companies in two different industries. These ratios are for 1997.

Notice that Cigna's 1997 return-on-assets ratio was 1.0% and Allstate's was 3.8%. Taken in isolation, neither ratio seems very good; banks often pay more than

Associated Press AP

---

[2]This illustration does not consider the effect of income taxes on debt financing. This subject is covered in Chapter 10.

EXHIBIT 3–8				
Three Ratios (in Percentages) for Six Real-World Companies				
Industry	**Company**	**Debt-to-Assets**	**Return-on-Assets**	**Return-on-Equity**
Insurance	Aetna	88	1.0	8.0
	Allstate	80	3.8	19.9
	Cigna	93	1.0	13.7
Oil	Exxon	52	8.8	19.4
	Mobil	54	7.5	16.8
	Texaco	55	9.0	20.9

3.8% interest on deposits in savings accounts. However, the *return-on-equity* ratios for Cigna and Allstate show a different picture; Cigna's was 13.7% and Allstate's was 19.9%—much better than banks pay depositors. Also note in Exhibit 3–8 that Cigna's return-on-assets ratio was the same as Aetna's (1.0%), but Cigna's return-on-equity ratio was much higher than Aetna's (13.7% versus 8.0%). How did this happen? Compare their debt-to-assets ratios. Cigna financed 93% of its assets with debt compared to 88% for Aetna. Because it is more highly leveraged, Cigna's return-on-assets ratio translated into a higher return-on-equity ratio than Aetna's.

Given that leveraged companies produce higher returns, why does every company not leverage itself to the maximum? Remember the downside. These data are drawn for economic periods in which prosperity and growth prevailed. In hard economic times, highly leveraged companies are likely to produce lower rather than higher returns. Increased risk usually accompanies increased returns.

Finally, in Exhibit 3–8, compare the debt-to-assets ratios for companies in the oil industry to the same ratios for companies in the insurance industry. There are distinct differences *between* industries, but there are considerable similarities *within* each industry. The debt-to-assets ratio is significantly higher for the insurance industry than for the oil industry. However, within each industry, the ratios tend to be clustered fairly close together. Distinct differences between industries accompanied by similarities within industries are common features of business practice. Thus, when you compare accounting information for different companies, you must consider the industries in which those companies operate.

©Bob Thomason/Tony Stone Worldwide, Ltd.

Scope of Coverage

Throughout this text, new ratios directly related to the topics being covered in each chapter are introduced. Even so, only a few of the many ratios available to users of financial statements are introduced. A more extensive examination of ratios and other topics related to financial statement analysis are part of most introductory finance courses. Many business programs include an entire course that focuses solely on financial statement analysis. These courses develop your capacity to make judgments regarding the ratio results that signal "good" or "bad" performance. However, the development of such judgment requires an understanding of how accounting policies and procedures can affect financial ratios.

The ratios introduced in this text are designed to enhance your understanding of accounting and thereby give you the foundation that you will need to further your comprehension of business practice, as you are introduced to more advanced topics in subsequent courses.

A LOOK

BACK

L.O. 10

Record deferral events in a financial statements model.

This chapter introduced the practice of deferring revenue and expense recognition. More specifically, *deferrals* involve the recognition of revenue or expense at some time *after* cash has been collected or paid. Deferrals cause significant differences in the amount of revenue and expenses reported on the income statement and the amount of cash flow from operating activities. These differences become readily apparent when relevant events are recorded in a horizontal financial statements model. To illustrate, review the following transactions and the corresponding statements model that follows them. To facilitate your understanding, draw a statements model on a piece of paper and try to record the effects of each event before you look at the explanation provided in the text.

List of Events

1. Received an advanced payment of $1,200 cash for services to be performed in the future.
2. Provided $800 of the services agreed on in Event No. 1.
3. Paid $900 in advance for a 1-year contract to rent office space.
4. Used 8 months (that is, $600) of the office space leased in Event No. 3.

Event No.	Balance Sheet					Income Statement					Statement of Cash Flows	
	Assets		=	Liab.	+	Equity	Rev.	−	Exp.	=	Net Inc.		
	Cash	+	P. Rent	=	U. Rev.	+	Ret. Earn.						
1	1,200	+	n/a	=	1,200	+	n/a	n/a	−	n/a	=	n/a	1,200	OA
2	n/a	+	n/a	=	(800)	+	800	800	−	n/a	=	800	n/a	
3	(900)	+	900	=	n/a	+	n/a	n/a	−	n/a	=	n/a	(900)	OA
4	n/a	+	(600)	=	n/a	+	(600)	n/a	−	600	=	(600)	n/a	
Totals	300	+	300	=	400	+	200	800	−	600	=	200	300	NC

Note that the amount of net income ($200) is different from the amount of cash flow from operating activities ($300). A review of the entries in the statements model should make the reasons for this difference clear. Although $1,200 of cash was collected, only $800 of revenue was recognized. The remaining $400 will be recognized in the future when the work is done. The $400 obligation to perform the work in the future is currently shown on the balance sheet as unearned revenue. Also, although $900 cash was paid for rent, only $600 of rent expense was recognized. The remaining $300 is shown on the balance sheet as an asset called *prepaid rent*. In general, costs are **capitalized** (i.e., recorded) in asset accounts when cash is paid. Expense recognition is deferred until the time that the assets (i.e., capitalized costs) are used to produce revenue. This practice is applied to many costs, including those incurred for supplies, insurance, equipment, and buildings. Study these relationships carefully to develop a clear understanding of how deferrals affect financial reporting.

A LOOK FORWARD

To this point, we have used plus and minus signs to record the effects of business events on financial statements. In the real world, so many transactions occur that recording them with simple mathematical notations is impractical. In practice, accountants frequently maintain records under a system of rules known as a *double-entry bookkeeping.* Chapter 4 introduces you to the basic components of this bookkeeping system. You will learn how to record business events using a debit/credit format. You will be introduced to ledgers, journals, and trial balances. When you finish Chapter 4, you will have a clear understanding of how accountants maintain records of business activity.

KEY TERMS

Accumulated Depreciation The contra asset account used to record the total depreciation reported on an asset. *(p. 105)*

Allocation Distribution according to a plan such as the process of expense recognition by systematically assigning the cost of an asset to periods of use. *(p. 101)*

Book Value The historical cost of an asset minus the accumulated depreciation. *(p. 105)*

Capitalized The process of accumulating cost in an asset account until the item is used to produce revenue. *(p. 122)*

Concept of Materiality Recognizes practical limits in financial reporting by allowing flexible handling of matters that are not considered material. An omission or misstatement of accounting information is considered material if the decisions of a reasonable person would be influenced by the omission or misstatement. *(p. 105)*

Contra Asset Account An account that has the effect of reducing the account with which it is associated. *(p. 105)*

Debt-to-Assets Ratio A financial ratio that is a measure of the level of risk of a company. *(p. 120)*

Deferral The recognition of revenue or expense in a period after the cash consequences are realized. *(p. 101)*

Depreciation Expense The recognition of the used portion of a long-term tangible asset by allocating its cost to an expense account over its useful life. *(p. 104)*

Financial Leverage Investment of money at a higher rate than that required to borrow the money. *(p. 120)*

Gains Increases in assets or decreases in liabilities that result from peripheral or incidental transactions. *(p. 114)*

Income from Operations Determined by subtracting operating expenses from operating revenues. Gains and losses and other peripheral activities are added to or subtracted from income from operations to determine net income or loss. *(p. 114)*

Losses Decreases in assets or increases in liabilities that result from peripheral or incidental transactions. *(p. 114)*

Peripheral (Incidental) Transactions Transactions that do not arise from ordinary business operations. *(p. 114)*

Return-on-Assets Ratio The ratio that measures the relationship between the level of net income and the size of the investment in assets. *(p. 118)*

Return-on Equity Ratio The ratio that measures the relationship between the amount of net income and the owner's equity of a company. *(p. 120)*

Salvage Value The expected selling price of an asset at the end of its useful life. *(p. 102)*

Straight-Line Method Method of allocation that is computed by taking the cost minus the salvage value, divided by the number of years of useful life. *(p. 104)*

Unearned Revenue Revenue that has been collected but for which the service has not yet been performed. *(p. 103)*

QUESTIONS

1. What is the role of assets in terms of the profitability of a business?
2. What does the term *deferral* mean?
3. If cash is collected in advance for services, when is the associated revenue recognized?
4. What does the term *salvage value* mean?
5. If cash is collected in advance for services, how is the accounting equation affected on the claims side?
6. What does the term *unearned revenue* mean?

7. How is straight-line depreciation computed?

8. Define the term *depreciation expense.* What type of asset is depreciated?

9. Define the term *contra asset account.* What is an example?

10. How is the book value of an asset determined?

11. If a piece of equipment originally cost $12,000, had an estimated salvage value of $1,000, and has accumulated depreciation of $10,000, what is the book value of the equipment?

12. What does the term *financial leverage* mean?

13. In which section of the statement of cash flows is cash paid for office equipment shown?

14. What is the difference between cost and expense?

15. When does a cost become an expense? Do all costs become expenses?

16. How and when are the *supplies used* recognized in an accounting period?

17. Define *losses.* How do they differ from expenses?

18. Define *gains.* How do they differ from revenues?

19. How is income from operations computed?

20. What does the term *peripheral activity* mean?

21. Assume that company A has revenues of $45,000, operating expenses of $36,000, and a gain from the sale of land of $12,500. What is the amount of income from operations? What is the amount of net income?

22. What are several factors that prevent the establishment of a global GAAP?

23. How is the return-on-assets ratio computed? How is this measure useful in comparing two companies?

24. How is the debt-to-assets ratio computed? What does this ratio measure?

25. How can financial leverage be used to increase the return-on-equity ratio?

EXERCISES

EXERCISE 3-1
L.O. 1

Transactions That Affect the Elements of Financial Statements

Required

Give an example of a transaction that will

   a. Decrease an asset and decrease equity (asset use event).

   b. Increase a liability and decrease equity (claims exchange event).

   c. Increase an asset and increase equity (asset source event).

   d. Decrease a liability and increase equity (claims exchange event).

   e. Increase an asset and decrease another asset (asset exchange event).

   f. Increase an asset and increase a liability (asset source event).

   g. Decrease an asset and decrease a liability (asset use event).

EXERCISE 3-2
L.O. 2

Identification of Deferral and Accrual Events

Required

Identify each of the following events as accruals, deferrals, or neither.

   a. Incurred operating expenses on account.

   b. Paid cash for utilities expense.

   c. Collected $1,200 in advance for services to be performed over the next 6 months.

   d. Paid cash to purchase supplies that are to be used over the next several months.

   e. Recorded expense for salaries owed to employees at the end of the accounting period.

   f. Made a cash distribution to the owner.

   g. Provided services on account.

   h. Recognized interest on a note payable before cash is paid.

   i. Paid 1 year's rent in advance.

   j. Purchased a computer with a 3-year life.

Effect of Deferrals on the Accounting Equation

Required

For each of the following independent cases, show the effect of the deferred transaction and the related December 31, 20X1, adjustment on the accounting equation.

a. Kang Shipping paid $18,000 for a 12-month lease on warehouse space on September 1, 20X1.

b. Judy Holdman, owner of JH Business Services, purchased a new computer system for $5,200 on January 1, 20X1. The computer system has an estimated useful life of four years and a $400 salvage value.

c. Marshall Vernon, J.D., accepted $10,000 advance from his client on November 1, 20X1. The services are to be performed over the next six months.

Identification of the Type of Transaction and Its Effect on the Accounting Equation

Required

For each of the following transactions, identify the type of event as asset source (AS), asset use (AU), asset exchange (AE), or claims exchange (CE). Also explain how the occurrence of each event would affect the accounting equation by placing a + for *increase*, − for *decrease*, or n/a for *not affected* under each of the elements of the accounting equation. The first two events are recorded as examples.

Event No.	Type of Event	Assets	=	Liabilities	+	Equity Contributed Capital	+	Retained Earnings
a	AU	−		−		n/a		n/a
b	AS	+		+		n/a		n/a

a. Paid cash on accounts payable.
b. Received cash advance for services to be provided in the future.
c. Incurred operating expenses on account.
d. Acquired a cash contribution from the owners.
e. Purchased land for cash.
f. Paid cash to purchase office equipment.
g. Performed services on account.
h. Paid cash advance for rental of office space.
i. Adjusted books to reflect the amount of prepaid rent expired during the period.
j. Performed services for cash.
k. Paid cash for operating expenses.
l. Recorded accrued salaries.
m. Made a cash distribution to the owners.
n. Collected cash from accounts receivable.
o. Recorded depreciation expense on office equipment.
p. Purchased a building with cash *and* issued a note payable.
q. Paid cash for salaries accrued in a prior period.

Effect of Prepaid Rent on the Accounting Equation and Financial Statements

The following events apply to the first year of operations of Help-U Consulting Services:

1. Acquired $30,000 cash from the owners.
2. Paid $24,000 cash in advance for 1-year rental contract for office space.
3. Provided services for $36,000 cash.
4. Adjusted the records to recognize the use of the office space. The one-year contract started on February 1, 20X7. The adjustment is made as of December 31, 20X7.

Required

a. Draw an accounting equation and record the effects of each accounting event under the appropriate headings.

b. Prepare an income statement, statement of changes in equity, balance sheet, and statement of cash flows for the 20X7 accounting period.

c. Explain the difference between the amount of net income and amount of net cash flow from operating activities.

EXERCISE 3-6
L.O. 3, 4, 7

Effect of Supplies on the Accounting Equation and Financial Statements

Kopy King, Inc., started the 20X3 accounting period with $1,000 cash, $400 of contributed capital, and $600 of retained earnings. Kopy King was affected by the following accounting events during 20X3:

1. Purchased $3,600 of paper and other supplies on account.
2. Earned and collected $10,000 of cash revenue.
3. Paid $2,500 cash on accounts payable.
4. Adjusted the records to reflect the use of supplies. A physical count indicated that $400 of supplies was still on hand on December 31, 20X3.

Required

a. Draw an accounting equation and record the effects of each accounting event under the appropriate headings.

b. Prepare an income statement, statement of changes in equity, balance sheet, and statement of cash flows for the 20X3 accounting period.

c. Explain the difference between the amount of net income and amount of net cash flow from operating activities.

EXERCISE 3-7
L.O. 3, 4, 7

Effect of Depreciation on the Accounting Equation and Financial Statements

The following events apply to Tasty Bar B Q for the 20X6 fiscal year:

1. Started the company when it acquired $24,000 cash from the owners.
2. Purchased a new pit that cost $22,000 cash.
3. Earned $16,000 in cash revenue.
4. Paid $4,000 of cash operating expenses.
5. Adjusted the records to reflect the use of the barbecue pit. The pit was purchased on January 1, 20X6. It has an expected useful life of 4 years and an estimated salvage value of $2,000. Assume straight-line depreciation. The adjusting entry is made as of December 31, 20X6.

Required

a. Draw an accounting equation and record the effects of each accounting event under the appropriate headings.

b. Prepare an income statement, statement of changes in equity, balance sheet, and statement of cash flows for the 20X6 accounting period.

c. What is the amount of depreciation expense that would appear on the December 31, 20X7, income statement?

d. What is the amount of accumulated depreciation that would appear on the December 31, 20X7, balance sheet?

e. Would the cash flow from operating activities be affected by depreciation in 20X7?

EXERCISE 3-8
L.O. 3, 4

Effect of Unearned Revenue on Financial Statements

Chris Dew started a personal financial planning business when she accepted $36,000 cash as advance payment for managing the financial assets of a large estate. Dew agreed to manage the estate for a 1-year period, beginning March 1, 20X3.

Required

a. Draw an accounting equation and record the effects of each accounting event under the appropriate headings.

b. Prepare an income statement, statement of changes in equity, balance sheet, and statement of cash flows for the 20X3 accounting period.

c. How much revenue would be recognized on the 20X4 income statement?

d. What is the amount of cash flow from operating activities in 20X4?

Effect of Gains and Losses on the Accounting Equation and Financial Statements

On January 1, 20X2, Vega Enterprises purchased a parcel of land for $12,000 cash. At the time of purchase, the company planned to use the land for future expansion. In 20X4, Vega Enterprises determined it no longer needed the land. The land was sold immediately.

EXERCISE 3-9
L.O. 8

Required

a. Assume that the land was sold for $11,000 in 20X4.

   (1) Show the effect of the sale on the accounting equation.

   (2) What amount would be shown on the income statement from the sale of the land?

   (3) What amount would be shown on the statement of cash flows from the sale of the land?

b. Assume the land was sold for $14,000 in 20X4.

   (1) Show the effect of the sale on the accounting equation.

   (2) What amount would be shown on the income statement from the sale of the land?

   (3) What amount would be shown on the statement of cash flows from the sale of the land?

Effect of Accounting Events on the Income Statement and Statement of Cash Flows

Required

EXERCISE 3-10
L.O 5, 6

Explain how the combined effect of each of the following events and the associated adjusting entry will affect the amount of *net income* and the amount of *cash flow from operating activities* reported on the year-end financial statements. Identify the direction of change (i.e., increase, decrease, or no effect) and the amount of the change. Organize your answers according to the following table. The first event is recorded as an example. If an event does not have an adjusting entry, record the effects of the event alone.

	Net Income		Cash Flow from Operating Activities	
Event No.	Direction of Change	Amount of Change	Direction of Change	Amount of Change
a	Decrease	$1,200	Decrease	$7,200

a. Paid $7,200 cash on November 1 to purchase a 1-year insurance policy.

b. Paid $40,000 cash to purchase equipment. The equipment was purchased on January 1. It had an estimated salvage value of $8,000 and an expected useful life of 4 years.

c. Purchased $800 of supplies on account. Paid $600 cash on accounts payable. The ending balance in the Supplies account, after adjustment, is $100.

d. Accrued salaries amounting to $3,000.

e. Earned $6,000 of revenue on account. Collected $5,000 cash from accounts receivable.

f. Collected $1,200 in advance for services to be performed in the future. The contract called for services to start on April 1 and to continue for 1 year.

g. Acquired $12,000 cash from the owners.

h. Sold land that cost $3,500 for $4,500 cash.

i. Paid cash operating expenses of $1,000.

j. Provided services for $3,000 cash.

EXERCISE 3-11   **Effect of Accruals and Deferrals on Financial Statements—the Horizontal Statements Model**
L.O. 10   Dowes Attorney at Law experienced the following transactions in 20X2, the first year of
operations:

1. Accepted $18,000 on May 1, 20X2, as a retainer for services to be performed evenly
over the next 12 months.
2. Purchased $1,600 of office supplies on account.
3. Performed legal services for cash of $25,600.
4. Paid cash for operating expenses of $13,400.
5. Made a cash distribution to the owners of $8,000.
6. Paid $1,400 of the amount due on accounts payable.
7. At the end of the accounting period, only $150 of office supplies remained on
hand.
8. On December 31, 20X2, recognized the revenue that had been earned for services
performed in accordance with transaction 1.

Required
Show the effects of the events on the financial statements using a horizontal statements
model like the following one. In the Cash Flow column, use the initials OA to designate
operating activity, IA for investing activity, FA for financing activity, and NC for net
change in cash flow. The notation n/a indicates that the element is not affected by the
event. The first event has been recorded as an example.

Event No.	Assets		=	Liabilities		+	Equity	Rev.	−	Exp.	=	Net Inc.	Cash Flow	
	Cash	+ Supp. =		Acct. Pay.	+		Unearn. Rev.	Ret. Earn.						
1	18,000	+ n/a =		n/a	+		18,000	+	n/a	−	n/a	= n/a	18,000	OA

EXERCISE 3-12   **Identification of the Difference between an Expense and a Cost**
L.O. 7   Steve Stuart tells you that the accountants where he works are real hair splitters. For example, they make a big issue over the difference between a cost and an expense. He says
the two terms mean the same thing to him.

Required
a. Explain to Steve the difference between a cost and an expense from an accountant's
perspective.
b. Explain whether each of the following events produces an asset or an expense.
(1) Purchased supplies for cash.
(2) Purchased land for cash.
(3) Used supplies to produce revenue.
(4) Purchased equipment on account.
(5) Recognized accrued salaries.

EXERCISE 3-13   **Effect of an Error on Financial Statements**
L.O. 5, 6   On May 1, 20X7, Stack Corporation paid $8,100 to purchase an 18-month insurance pol-
icy. Assume that Stack records the purchase as an asset and that the books are closed on
December 31.

Required
a. Provide the adjusting entry to record the 20X7 insurance expense.
b. Assume that Stack Corporation failed to record the required entry to reflect the use
of insurance. How would the error affect the company's 20X7 income statement and
balance sheet?

Revenue and Expense Recognition

Required

a. Describe a revenue recognition event that results in an increase in assets.

b. Describe a revenue recognition event that results in a decrease in liabilities.

c. Describe an expense recognition event that results in a decrease in assets.

d. Describe an expense recognition event that results in an increase in liabilities.

Unearned Revenue Defined as a Liability

Suzie Gaves received $400 in advance for tutoring fees when she agreed to help Mike Jagger with his introductory accounting course. Upon receiving the cash, she mentioned that she would have to record the transaction as a liability on her books. Jagger asked, "Why a liability? You don't owe me any money, do you?"

Required

Respond to Jagger's question regarding Gaves's liability.

PROBLEMS—SERIES A

Events Recorded in a Horizontal Statements Model

The following events pertain to Golf Land:

1. Acquired a $6,000 cash contribution of capital from the owners.
2. Provided services for $2,000 cash.
3. Provided $8,000 of services on account.
4. Collected $2,000 cash from the account receivable created in Event No. 3.
5. Received $2,400 cash in advance for services to be performed in the future.
6. Performed $1,200 of the services agreed to in Event No. 5.
7. Paid $950 for cash expenses.
8. Incurred $2,200 of expenses on account.
9. Paid $1,400 cash on the account payable created in Event No. 8.
10. Paid $2,100 cash in advance for 1-year contract to rent office space.
11. Recognized rent expense for 9-month use of office space acquired in Event No. 10.
12. Paid a $1,000 cash distribution to the owners.

Required

Show the effects of the events on the financial statements, using a horizontal statements model like the following one. In the Cash Flow column, use the letters OA to designate operating activity, IA for investing activity, FA for financing activity, and NC for net change in cash flow. The notation n/a indicates that the element is not affected by the event. The first event is recorded as an example.

Event No.	Assets			=	Liabilities		+	Equity		Rev.	−	Exp.	=	Net Inc.	Cash Flows
	Cash	+ Acct. Rec.	+ Pre Rent	=	Acct. Pay.	+ Unearn. Rev.	+	Con. Cap.	+ Ret. Earn.						
1	6,000	+ n/a	+ n/a	=	n/a	+ n/a	+	6,000	+ n/a	n/a	− n/a	=	n/a	6,000 FA	

Effect of Deferrals on Financial Statements—Three Separate Single-Cycle Examples

Required

a. On February 1, 20X6, Boston Company was formed when it acquired $6,000 cash from the owners. On March 1, 20X6, the company paid $3,600 cash in advance to rent office space for the coming year. The office space was used as a place to consult with clients. The consulting activity generated $4,800 of cash revenue during 20X6.

Based on this information alone, prepare an income statement, statement of changes in equity, balance sheet, and statement of cash flows for 20X6.

b. On January 1, 20X5, the law firm called Webber & Associates was formed. On February 1, 20X5, the company received an $18,000 retainer (i.e., was paid in advance) for monthly services to be performed over a 1-year period of time. Assuming that this was the only transaction completed in 20X5, prepare an income statement, statement of changes in equity, balance sheet, and statement of cash flows for 20X5.

c. The Bug Company was started when it acquired $9,000 cash from the owners on January 1, 20X4. The cash received by the company was immediately used to purchase a $9,000 asset that had a $1,000 salvage value and an expected useful life of 4 years. The asset was used to produce $4,800 of cash revenue during the accounting period. Prepare an income statement, statement of changes in equity, balance sheet, and statement of cash flows for 20X4.

PROBLEM 3-3A
L.O. 3, 6

Effect of Adjusting Entries on Accounting Equation

Required

Each of the following independent events requires a year-end adjusting entry. Show how each event and its associated adjusting entry affects the accounting equation. Assume a December 31 closing date. The first event is recorded as an example.

| Event/ Adjustment | Total Assets | | | | | | Equity | | |
	Asset 1	+	Asset 2	=	Liabilities	+	Contributed Capital	+	Retained Earnings
a	−2,400		+2,400		n/a		n/a		n/a
Adj.	n/a		−800		n/a		n/a		−800

a. Paid $2,400 cash in advance on September 1 for a 1-year insurance policy.

b. Borrowed $10,000 by issuing a 1-year note with 7% annual interest to National Bank on October 1.

c. Paid $16,000 cash to purchase a delivery van on January 1. The van was expected to have a 3-year life and a $1,000 salvage value. Depreciation is computed on a straight-line basis.

d. Received an $1,800 cash advance for a contract to provide services in the future. The contract required a 1-year commitment, starting April 1.

e. Purchased $640 of supplies on account. At year's end, $75 of supplies remained on hand.

f. Invested $9,000 cash in a certificate of deposit that paid 4% annual interest. The certificate was acquired on May 1 and carried a 1-year term to maturity.

g. Paid $7,800 cash in advance on September 1 for a 1-year lease on office space.

PROBLEM 3-4A
L.O. 1, 3, 4

Events for Two Complete Accounting Cycles

Classic Company was formed on January 1, 20X5.

Required

Events Affecting the 20X5 Accounting Period

1. Acquired $20,000 cash from the owners.
2. Purchased office equipment that cost $5,500 cash.
3. Purchased land that cost $4,000 cash.
4. Paid $300 cash for supplies.
5. Recognized revenue on account amounting to $7,000.
6. Paid $2,300 cash for other operating expenses.
7. Collected $4,500 cash from accounts receivable.

Events Applying to Adjusting Entries

8. Accrued salaries amounting to $2,700.
9. Had $50 of supplies on hand at the end of the accounting period.
10. Used the straight-line method to depreciate the equipment acquired in Event No. 2. The equipment was purchased on January 1. It had an expected useful life of 5 years and a $1,000 salvage value.

Events Affecting the 20X6 Accounting Period

1. Acquired $8,000 cash from the owners.
2. Paid $2,700 cash to settle the obligation for salaries payable. ⋉
3. Paid $4,800 cash in advance for a lease on office facilities.
4. Sold the land that cost $4,000 for $7,000.
5. Received $7,200 cash in advance for services to be performed in the future.
6. Purchased $1,500 of supplies on account during the year.
7. Provided services on account of $9,000.
8. Collected $4,000 cash from accounts receivable.
9. Paid a cash distribution of $3,000 to the owners.

Events Applying to Adjusting Entries

10. The advance payment for rental of the office facilities (see Event No. 3) was made on February 1. The term of the lease was 1 year.
11. The cash advance for services to be provided in the future was collected on September 1 (see Event No. 5). The 1-year contract started on September 1.
12. Had $200 of supplies remaining on hand at the end of the period.
13. Recorded depreciation on office equipment for 20X6.
14. Had accrued salaries of $5,000 at the end of the accounting period.

Required

a. For each event affecting the 20X5 and 20X6 accounting period, identify the type of event as asset source (AS), asset use (AU), asset exchange (AE), or claims exchange (CE). Record the effects of each event under the appropriate heading of the accounting equation.

b. Prepare an income statement, statement of changes in equity, balance sheet, and statement of cash flows as of December 31, 20X5 and 20X6.

Effect of Events on Financial Statements

The accounting records for Ming Company contained the following balances as of December 31, 20X3:

PROBLEM 3-5A
L.O. 3, 5

Assets		Claims	
Cash	$18,000	Accounts Payable	$ 3,400
Accounts Receivable	11,000	Contributed Capital	8,000
Land	9,000	Retained Earnings	26,600
Total	$38,000	Total	$38,000

The following accounting events apply to Ming Company's 20X4 fiscal year.

Jan. 1 Acquired $10,000 cash from the owners.

1 Purchased a delivery van that cost $8,000. The van had an $800 salvage value and a 3-year useful life.

Feb. 1 Borrowed $10,000 by issuing a note that carried a 9% annual interest rate and a 1-year term.

1 Paid $2,400 cash in advance for a 1-year lease for office space.

Mar. 1 Made a $3,000 cash distribution to the owners.

April 1 Purchased land that cost $7,000 cash.

May 1 Made a cash payment on accounts payable amounting to $1,500.

July 1 Received $4,200 cash in advance as a retainer for services to be performed monthly over the coming year.

Sept. 1 Sold land for $10,000 cash. The land originally cost $9,000.

Oct. 1 Purchased $2,000 of supplies on account.

Nov. 1 Purchased a 1-year $5,000 certificate of deposit that paid a 6% annual rate of interest.

Dec. 31 Earned service revenue on account during the year that amounted to $25,000.

31 Received cash collections from accounts receivable amounting to $20,000.

31 Incurred other operating expenses on account during the year that amounted to $8,000.

31 Had accrued salaries expense amounting to $3,200.

31 Had $100 of supplies on hand at the end of the period.

Required

Based on the preceding information, answer the following questions. All questions pertain to the 20X4 financial statements. (*Hint:* It may be helpful to enter items in the accounting equation before you attempt to answer the questions.)

a. Based on the transactions described above, there are five additional adjustments that you should be able to identify. Describe these adjustments.

b. What is the amount of interest expense that would appear on the income statement?

c. What is the amount of net cash flow from operating activities that would appear on the statement of cash flows?

d. What is the amount of rent expense that would appear on the income statement?

e. What is the amount of total liabilities that would appear on the balance sheet?

f. What is the amount of supplies expense that would appear on the income statement?

g. What is the amount of unearned revenue that would appear on the balance sheet?

h. What is the amount of net cash flow from investing activities that would appear on the statement of cash flows?

i. What is the amount of interest payable that would appear on the balance sheet?

j. What is the amount of total expenses that would appear on the income statement?

k. What is the amount of retained earnings that would appear on the balance sheet?

l. What is the total amount of all revenues appearing on the income statement?

m. What is the amount of cash flow from financing activities that would appear on the statement of cash flows?

n. What is the amount of the gain from the sale of land appearing on the income statement?

o. What is the amount of net income appearing on the income statement?

PROBLEM 3-6A
L.O. 4

Preparation of Financial Statements

The following accounts and balances were drawn from the records of Jefferson Company:

Supplies	$ 1,000	Beginning Retained Earnings	$10,000
Cash Flow from Investing Act.	(8,000)	Cash Flow from Financing Act.	3,500
Prepaid Insurance	3,500	Depreciation Expense	2,000
Service Revenue	80,000	Distributions	8,000
Operating Expense	65,000	Cash	5,000
Supplies Expense	500	Accounts Receivable	11,000
Insurance Expense	1,000	Office Equipment	16,000
Beginning Contributed Capital	2,000	Accumulated Depreciation	10,000
Cash Flow from Operating Act.	9,000	Land	15,000
Acquisitions from Owners	5,000	Accounts Payable	21,000

Required

Use the accounts and balances from Jefferson Company to construct an income statement, statement of changes in equity, balance sheet, and statement of cash flows.

Relationship of Accounts to Financial Statements

Required

Tell whether each of the following items would appear on the income statement (IS), statement of changes in equity (CE), balance sheet (BS), or statement of cash flows (CF). If some items appear on more than one statement, identify all applicable statements. If an item will not appear on any financial statement, label it not applicable (n/a).

a.	Depreciation Expense	t.	Cash
b.	Interest Receivable	u.	Supplies
c.	Certificate of Deposit	v.	Cash Flow from Financing Activities
d.	Unearned Revenue	w.	Interest Revenue
e.	Service Revenue	x.	Ending Retained Earnings
f.	Cash Flow from Investing Activities	y.	Net Income
g.	Consulting Revenue	z.	Distributions
h.	Interest Expense	aa.	Office Equipment
i.	Ending Contributed Capital	bb.	Debt-to-Equity Ratio
j.	Total Liabilities	cc.	Land
k.	Debt-to-Assets Ratio	dd.	Interest Payable
l.	Cash Flow from Operating Activities	ee.	Salaries Expense
m.	Operating Expenses	ff.	Notes Receivable
n.	Supplies Expense	gg.	Accounts Payable
o.	Beginning Retained Earnings	hh.	Total Assets
p.	Beginning Contributed Capital	ii.	Salaries Payable
q.	Prepaid Insurance	jj.	Insurance Expense
r.	Salary Expense	kk.	Notes Payable
s.	Accumulated Depreciation	ll.	Accounts Receivable

Missing Information in Financial Statements

Deluxe Printing started the accounting period with $4,000 cash, accounts receivable of $10,000, prepaid rent of $5,000, supplies of $200, computers that cost $40,000, accumulated depreciation on computers of $8,000, accounts payable of $10,000, and contributed capital of $15,000. During the period, Deluxe recognized $80,000 of revenue on account and collected $70,000 of cash from accounts receivable. There was $6,000 cash paid for rent in advance and $5,000 of rent expense shown on the income statement. Deluxe paid $900 cash for supplies, and the income statement showed supplies expense of $1,000. Depreciation expense shown on the income statement amounted to $4,000. There was $40,000 of operating expenses incurred on account and $32,000 cash paid toward the settlement of accounts payable. The company acquired capital of $5,000 cash from the owners, who were paid a $700 cash distribution. (*Hint:* It may be helpful to record the events under an accounting equation before you attempt to satisfy the requirements.)

Required

a. Determine the balance in the Retained Earnings account at the beginning of the accounting period.

b. Prepare an income statement, statement of changes in equity, balance sheet, and statement of cash flows as of the end of the accounting period.

PROBLEM 3-9A   **Use of Accounting Information**

L.O. 1   Brogan Fairchild told his friend that he was very angry with his father. He had asked his father
 for a sports car, and his father had replied that he did not have the cash. Fairchild said that he
knew his father was not telling the truth because he had seen a copy of his father's business
records. These records contained a balance sheet that showed a Retained Earnings account
with $650,000 in it. He said that anybody with $650,000 had enough cash to buy his son a car.

Required

Explain why Fairchild's assessment of his father's cash position may be invalid. What financial statements and which items on those statements would enable him to make a
more accurate assessment of his father's cash position?

PROBLEMS—SERIES B

PROBLEM 3-1B   **Events Recorded in a Horizontal Statements Model**

L.O. 10   The following events pertain to Ohio Company:

1. Acquired a $4,000 cash contribution of capital from the owners.
2. Provided services for $1,000 cash.
3. Provided $5,000 of services on account.
4. Collected $2,500 cash from the account receivable created in Event No. 3.
5. Paid $500 cash to purchase supplies.
6. Had $150 of supplies on hand at the end of the accounting period.
7. Received $2,000 cash in advance for services to be performed in the future.
8. Performed $200 of the services agreed to in Event No. 7.
9. Paid $1,500 for cash expenses.
10. Incurred $1,900 of expenses on account.
11. Paid $1,000 cash on the account payable created in Event No. 10.
12. Paid a $500 cash distribution to the owners.

Required

Show the effects of the events on the financial statements using a horizontal statements
model like the following one. In the Cash Flow column, use the letters OA to designate operating activity, IA for investing activity, FA for financing activity, and NC for net change
in cash flow. The notation n/a indicates that the element is not affected by the event. The
first event is recorded as an example.

Event No.	Assets			=	Liabilities			+	Equity			Rev.	–	Exp.	=	Net. Inc.	Cash Flow
	Cash	+	Acc. Rec.	+	Supp.	=	Acc. Pay	+	Unearn. Rev.	+	Con. Cap.	+	Ret. Earn.							
1	4,000	+	n/a	+	n/a	=	n/a	+	n/a	+	4,000	+	n/a	n/a	–	n/a	=	n/a	4,000 FA

PROBLEM 3-2B   **Effect of Deferrals on Financial Statements—Three Separate Single-Cycle Examples**

L.O. 4, 5, 6   **Required**

  a.   On March 1, 20X5, Candles Galore was formed when the owners invested $60,000
        cash in the business. On April 1, 20X5, the company paid $48,000 cash in advance to
        rent office space for the coming year. The office space was used as a place to consult
        with clients. The consulting activity generated $50,000 of cash revenue during 20X5.
        Based on this information alone, prepare an income statement, statement of changes
        in equity, balance sheet, and statement of cash flows as of December 31, 20X5.

  b.   On January 1, 20X1, the accounting firm of Brignac & Associates was formed. On Feb-
        ruary 1, 20X1, the company received a retainer fee (i.e., was paid in advance) of $21,000

for services to be performed monthly during the coming year. Assuming that this was the only transaction completed in 20X1, prepare an income statement, statement of changes in equity, balance sheet, and statement of cash flows as of December 31, 20X1.

c. Fashion Flair was started when its owners invested $35,000 in the business on January 1, 20X3. The cash received by the company was immediately used to purchase a $35,000 asset that had a $5,000 salvage value and an expected useful life of 5 years. The company earned $10,000 of cash revenue during 20X3. Based on this information alone, prepare an income statement, statement of changes in equity, balance sheet, and statement of cash flows as of December 31, 20X3.

Effect of Adjusting Entries on the Accounting Equation

PROBLEM 3-3B
L.O. 3, 6

Required

Each of the following independent events requires a year-end adjusting entry. Show how each event and its associated adjusting entry affects the accounting equation. Assume a December 31 closing date. The first event is recorded as an example.

Event/ Adjustment	Total Assets					Equity		
	Asset 1	+	Asset 2	=	Liabilities	+	Contributed Capital	+	Retained Earnings
a	−4,200		+4,200		n/a		n/a		n/a
Adj.	n/a		−1,050		n/a		n/a		−1,050

a. Paid $4,200 cash in advance on September 30 for a 1-year insurance policy.

b. Borrowed $10,000 by issuing a 1-year note with 12% annual interest to National Bank on April 1.

c. Paid $19,000 cash to purchase a delivery van on January 1. The van was expected to have a 3-year life and a $4,000 salvage value. Depreciation is computed on a straight-line basis.

d. Received a $6,000 cash advance for a contract to provide services in the future. The contract required a 1-year commitment starting August 1.

e. Purchased $2,000 of supplies on account. At year's end, $200 of supplies remained on hand.

f. Invested $20,000 cash in a certificate of deposit that paid 5% annual interest. The certificate was acquired on July 1 and carried a 1-year term to maturity.

g. Paid $9,000 cash in advance on March 1 for a 1-year lease on office space.

Events for Two Complete Accounting Cycles

PROBLEM 3-4B
L.O. 1, 3, 4

Texas Drilling Company was formed on January 1, 20X2.

Events Affecting the 20X2 Accounting Period

1. Acquired capital of $40,000 cash from the owners.
2. Purchased office equipment that cost $12,000 cash.
3. Purchased land that cost $8,000 cash.
4. Paid $600 cash for supplies.
5. Recognized revenue on account amounting to $14,000.
6. Paid $4,600 cash for other operating expenses.
7. Collected $10,000 cash from accounts receivable.

Events Applying to Adjusting Entries

8. Had accrued salaries amounting to $5,400.
9. Had $100 of supplies on hand at the end of the accounting period.
10. Used the straight-line method to depreciate the equipment acquired in Event No. 2. The equipment was purchased on January 1. It had an expected useful life of 5 years and a $1,000 salvage value,

Events Affecting the 20X3 Accounting Period

1. Acquired an additional $8,000 cash from the owners.
2. Paid $5,400 cash to settle an obligation for salaries payable.
3. Paid $2,100 cash in advance for lease on office facilities.
4. Sold the land that cost $8,000 for $7,500 cash.
5. Received $4,800 cash in advance for services to be performed in the future.
6. Purchased $1,000 of supplies on account during the year.
7. Provided services on account amounting to $12,000.
8. Collected $13,000 cash from accounts receivable.
9. Made a cash distribution of $1,000 to the owners.

Events Applying to Adjusting Entries

10. The advance payment for rental of the office facilities (see Event No. 3) was made on May 1. The term of the lease was 1 year.
11. The cash advance for services to be provided in the future was collected on August 1 (see Event No. 5). The 1-year contract started August 1.
12. Had $120 of supplies on hand at the end of the period.
13. Recorded depreciation on office equipment for 20X3.
14. Had accrued salaries amounting to $4,000 at the end of the accounting period.

Required

a. For each event affecting the 20X2 and 20X3 accounting period, identify the type of event as to asset source (AS), asset use (AU), asset exchange (AE), or claims exchange (CE). Record the effects of each event under the appropriate heading of the accounting equation.

b. Prepare an income statement, statement of changes in equity, balance sheet, and statement of cash flows as of December 31, 20X2 and 20X3.

PROBLEM 3-5B
L.O. 3, 5

Effect of Events on Financial Statements

The accounting records for Andrews Company contained the following balances as of December 31, 20X1:

Assets		Claims	
Cash	$35,000	Accounts Payable	$22,000
Accounts Receivable	20,500	Contributed Capital	40,000
Land	20,000	Retained Earnings	13,500
Totals	$75,500		$75,500

The following accounting events apply to Andrews's 20X2 fiscal year:

Jan. 1 Acquired an additional $20,000 cash from the owners.
     1 Purchased a delivery van that cost $12,000. The van had a $3,000 salvage value and a 3-year useful life.
Mar. 1 Borrowed $8,000 by issuing a note that carried a 12% annual interest rate and a 1-year term.
May 1 Paid $2,100 cash in advance for a 1-year lease for office space.

June 1 Made a $1,000 cash distribution to the owners.

July 1 Purchased land that cost $12,000 cash.

Aug. 1 Made a cash payment on account payable amounting to $7,000.

Sep. 1 Received $5,600 cash in advance as a retainer for services to be performed monthly during the next 8 months.

Sept. 30 Sold land for $17,000 cash. The land originally cost $20,000.

Oct. 1 Purchased $1,500 of supplies on account.

Nov. 1 Purchased a 1-year $10,000 certificate of deposit that paid a 6% annual rate of interest.

Dec. 31 Earned service revenue on account during the year that amounted to $45,000.

31 Received cash collections from accounts receivable amounting to $47,000.

31 Incurred other operating expenses on account during the year that amounted to $6,000.

31 Had accrued salaries expense amounting to $2,000.

31 Had $100 of supplies on hand at the end of the period.

Required

Based on the preceding information, answer the following questions. All questions pertain to the 20X2 financial statements. (*Hint:* It may be helpful to record the events under an accounting equation before you attempt to answer the questions.)

a. What five transactions need adjusting entries?

b. What is the amount of interest expense that would appear on the income statement?

c. What is the amount of net cash flow from operating activities that would appear on the statement of cash flows?

d. What is the amount of rent expense that would appear in the income statement?

e. What is the amount of total liabilities that would appear on the balance sheet?

f. What is the amount of supplies expense that would appear on the income statement?

g. What is the amount of unearned revenue that would appear on the balance sheet?

h. What is the amount of net cash flow from investing activities that would appear on the statement of cash flows?

i. What is the amount of interest payable that would appear on the balance sheet?

j. What is the amount of total expenses that would appear on the income statement?

k. What is the amount of retained earnings that would appear on the balance sheet?

l. What is the total amount of all revenues appearing on the income statement?

m. What is the amount of cash flow from financing activities that would appear on the statement of cash flows?

n. What is the amount of the loss from the sale of land appearing on the income statement?

o. What is the amount of net income appearing on the income statement?

Identification of Elements on Financial Statements

The following accounts and balances were drawn from the records of Jackson Company:

PROBLEM 3-6B

L.O. 4

Land	$12,000	Cash Flow from Operating Act.	$15,000
Insurance Expense	1,500	Beginning Retained Earnings	12,000
Distributions	2,500	Beginning Contributed Capital	6,500
Prepaid Insurance	6,000	Service Revenue	40,000
Cash	30,000	Cash Flow from Financing Act.	20,000
Accounts Payable	23,000	Acquisitions from Owners	8,000
Supplies	150	Accumulated Depreciation	1,500
Supplies Expense	850	Cash Flow from Investing Act.	(20,000)
Depreciation Expense	2,000	Operating Expense	10,000
Accounts Receivable	8,000	Office Equipment	18,000

Required

Use the accounts and balances from Jackson Company to construct an income statement, statement of changes in equity, balance sheet, and statement of cash flows.

PROBLEM 3-7B
L.O. 4

Relationship of Accounts to Financial Statements

Required

Tell whether each of the following items would appear on the income statement (IS), statement of changes in equity (CE), balance sheet (BS) or statement of cash flows (CF). Some items may appear on more than one statement; if so, identify all applicable statements. If an item will not appear on any financial statement, label it with the letters n/a.

a.	Interest Receivable	t.	Total Assets
b.	Salary Expense	u.	Consulting Revenue
c.	Notes Receivable	v.	Depreciation Expense
d.	Unearned Revenue	w.	Supplies Expense
e.	Cash Flow from Investing Activities	x.	Salaries Payable
f.	Insurance Expense	y.	Notes Payable
g.	Ending Retained Earnings	z.	Ending Contributed Capital
h.	Accumulated Depreciation	aa.	Interest Payable
i.	Supplies	bb.	Office Equipment
j.	Beginning Retained Earnings	cc.	Interest Revenue
k.	Certificate of Deposit	dd.	Land
l.	Cash Flow from Financing Activities	ee.	Operating Expenses
m.	Accounts Receivable	ff.	Total Liabilities
n.	Prepaid Insurance	gg.	Debt-to-Equity Ratio
o.	Cash	hh.	Salaries Expense
p.	Interest Expense	ii.	Net Income
q.	Accounts Payable	jj.	Service Revenue
r.	Beginning Contributed Capital	kk.	Cash Flow from Operating Activities
s.	Distributions	ll.	Return-on-Assets Ratio

PROBLEM 3-8B
L.O. 3, 4

Missing Information in Financial Statements

The following data apply to the revenue and expense accounts of Olinger Corporation during 20X4. The Accounts Receivable balance amounted to $45,000 on January 1, 20X4. Consulting services provided to customers on account during the year amounted to $128,000. The receivables balance on December 31, 20X4, amounted to $28,000. Olinger received $21,000 in advance payment for training services to be performed over a 24-month period beginning March 1, 20X4. Furthermore, Olinger purchased a $30,000 certificate of deposit on September 1, 20X4. The certificate carried a 15% interest rate, which was payable in cash on August 31 of each year. During 20X4, Olinger recorded depreciation expense that amounted to $18,000. Salaries earned by employees during 20X4 amounted to $25,000. The Salaries Payable account increased by $3,500 during the year. Other operating expenses paid in cash during 20X4 amounted to $70,000. No revenue or expense transactions other than those specifically referenced here were consummated during 20X4.

Required

a. Prepare an income statement, assuming that Olinger utilizes the accrual basis of accounting.

b. Determine the amount of cash inflow from operating the business during 20X4.

Use of Accounting Information

Mary Beth Stanley is trying to decide whether to start a small business or put her capital into a savings account. To help her make a decision, two of her friends shared their business experiences with her. Karen Richmond had started a small business approximately 3 years ago. As of the end of the most recent year of operations, Richmond's business had total assets of $185,000 and net income of $11,220. The second friend, Olivia Harrison, placed $20,000 in a bank savings account that paid $900 in interest during the last year.

Required

a. Assume that you are an investment counselor. Show Stanley how the return-on-assets ratio can be used to determine whether Richmond's or Harrison's investment is producing a higher return.

b. Using your own personal judgment, identify any other factors that Stanley should consider before she decides whether to start her own business or deposit her money in a savings account. Make a recommendation to Stanley as to which alternative you think she should accept.

analyze, communicate, think

BUSINESS APPLICATIONS CASE **Gateway 2000 Annual Report**

Required

Using the Gateway 2000 financial statements in Appendix B, answer the following questions:

a. What was Gateway's debt-to-assets ratio for 1997?

b. What was Gateway's return-on-assets ratio for 1997?

c. What was Gateway's return-on-equity ratio for 1997?

d. Why was Gateway's 1997 return-on-equity ratio approximately double its 1997 return-on-assets ratio?

GROUP ASSIGNMENT **Missing Information**

Crossroads Theater Company is a local performing arts group that sponsors various theater productions. The company sells season tickets for the regular performances. It also sells tickets to individual performances called *door sales*. The season tickets are sold in June, July, and August for the season that runs from September through April of each year. The season tickets package contains tickets to eight performances, one per month. The first year of operations was 20X6. All revenue not from season ticket sales is from door sales. The following selected information was taken from the financial records for December 31, 20X6, 20X7, and 20X8, the company's year end:

	20X6	20X7	20X8
Revenue (per income statement)	$450,000	$575,000	$625,000
Unearned Revenue (per balance sheet)	127,000	249,000	275,000
Operating Expense	231,000	326,000	428,000

Required

a. Divide the class into groups consisting of four or five students. Organize the groups into three sections. Assign the groups in each section the financial data for one of the preceding accounting periods.

Group tasks

(1) Determine the total of season ticket sales for the year assigned.

(2) Determine the total of season door sales for the year assigned.

(3) Compute the net income for the year assigned.

(4) Have a representative of each section put its income statement on the board.

Class Discussion

b. Compare the income statements for 20X6, 20X7, and 20X8. Discuss the revenue trend; that is, are door sales increasing more than season ticket sales? What is the company's growth pattern?

ACT 3-3

REAL-WORLD CASE **Different Numbers for Different Industries**

The following are the debt-to-assets, return-on-assets, and return-on-equity ratios for four companies from two different industries. The range of interest rates each company was paying on its long-term debt is provided. Each of these public companies is a leader in its particular industry, and the data are for the fiscal years ending in 1997. *All numbers are percentages.*

	Debt-to-Assets	Return-on-Assets	Return-on-Equity	Interest Rates
Banking Industry				
Wachovia Corporation	92	1.0	11.5	5.7–7.0
Wells Fargo & Co.	87	1.2	9.0	6.1–11.0
Home Construction Industry				
Pulte Corporation	62	2.5	6.5	7.0–10.1
Toll Brothers, Inc.	66	5.8	16.9	7.8–10.5

Required

a. Based only on the debt-to-assets ratios, the banking companies appear to have the most financial risk. Generally, lower interest rates are usually charged for companies that have lower financial risk. Given this, write a brief explanation as to why the banking companies can borrow money at lower interest rates than the construction companies.

b. Explain why Wachovia's return-on-equity is more than 10 times higher than its return-on-assets ratio while Pulte's return-on-equity ratio is less than 3 times higher than its return-on-assets ratio.

ACT 3-4

BUSINESS APPLICATIONS CASE **Ratio Analysis Used to Assess Financial Risk**

The following information was drawn from the balance sheets of two companies:

Company	Assets	=	Liabilities	+	Equity
New-Graphics	175,500		43,000		132,500
Quality Prints	735,000		308,500		426,500

Required

a. Use the debt-to-assets ratio to formulate a common unit of measure for the level of financial risk of both companies.

b. Compare the two ratios computed in part *a* to determine whether New-Graphics or Quality Prints has the higher level of financial risk.

ACT 3-5

BUSINESS APPLICATIONS CASE **Ratio Analysis Used to Make Comparisons between Companies**

At the end of 20X7, the following information is available for Thompson Builders and Custom Construction.

Statement Data	Thompson Builders	Custom Construction
Total Assets	$735,000	$185,000
Total Liabilities	477,500	77,000
Owners' Equity	257,500	108,000
Net Income	51,450	12,950

Required

a. For each company, compute the debt-to-assets ratio and the return-on-equity ratio.

b. Determine what percentage of each company's assets was financed by the owners.

c. Which company had a higher level of financial risk?

d. Based on profitability alone, which company performed better?

e. Do the preceding ratios support the concept of financial leverage? Support your answer with an appropriate explanation.

WRITING ASSIGNMENT   Definition of the Elements of Financial Statements   **ACT 3-6**

Star Company owns land that cost $800,000 that is being held for future use. However, company plans have changed and the company may not need the land in the foreseeable future. The president is concerned about the return on assets. Current net income is $325,000 and total assets are $3,200,000.

Required

a. Write a memo to the company president, explaining the effect of disposing of the land, assuming that it has a current value of $1,200,000.

b. Write a memo to the company president, explaining the effect of disposing of the land, assuming that it has a current value of $600,000.

ETHICAL DILEMMA   What Is a Little Deceit among Friends?   **ACT 3-7**

Glenn's Cleaning Services Company is experiencing cash flow problems and is in need of a loan. Glenn has a friend who is willing to lend her the money that she needs provided he can be convinced that she will be able to repay the debt. Glenn has assured her friend that her business is viable, but her friend has asked to see the company's financial statements. Glenn's accountant produced the following financial statements:

Income Statement		Balance Sheet	
Service Revenue	$ 38,000	Assets	$ 85,000
Operating Expenses	(70,000)		
Net Loss	$(32,000)	Liabilities	$ 35,000
		Equity	
		Contributed Capital	82,000
		Retained Earnings	(32,000)
		Total Liability and Equity	$ 85,000

Glenn made the following adjustments to these statements before showing them to her friend. She recorded $82,000 of revenue on account from Barrymore Manufacturing Company for a contract that she was negotiating to clean its headquarters office building for the next month. Barrymore had scheduled a meeting to sign a contract the following week, so she was sure that she would get the job. Barrymore was a reputable company, and Glenn was confident that she could ultimately collect the $82,000. Also, she subtracted $30,000 of accrued salaries expense and the corresponding liability. She reasoned that since she had not paid the employees, she had not incurred any expense.

Required

a. Reconstruct the income statement and balance sheet as they would appear after Glenn's adjustments. Comment on the accuracy of the adjusted financial statements.

b. Comment on the ethical implications of Glenn's actions. Before you formulate your answer, consider the following scenario. Suppose that you are Glenn and that the $30,000 you owe your employees is due next week. If you are unable to pay them, they will quit and the business will go bankrupt. You are sure that you will be able to repay your friend when your employees perform the $82,000 of services for Barrymore and you collect the cash. However, your friend is risk averse and will not be likely to make the loan on the basis of the financial statements your accountant prepared. Would you make the changes that Glenn made to get the loan and thereby save your company? Defend your position with a rational explanation.

ACT 3-8

SPREADSHEET ASSIGNMENT   **Using Excel**

Set up the following spreadsheet for Hubbard Company to calculate financial ratios based on given financial information.

	Total Assets	=	Total Liabilities	±	Owners' Equity		Net Income
1							
2							
3 Original Amounts	100,000		40,000		60,000		20,000
4 Transaction	10,000		0		10,000		0
5 Revised Amounts	110,000		40,000		70,000		20,000
6							
7 **Ratios**	Original		Revised				
8 Debt to Assets	40.00%		36.36%				
9 Debt to Equity	66.67%		57.14%				
10 Return on Assets	20.00%		18.18%				
11 Return on Equity	33.33%		28.57%				

Steps to Prepare Spreadsheet

1. Enter the information in column A.
2. Enter the headings in rows 1 and 2.
3. In row 3, enter the numbers for the Original Amounts.
4. In column B, beginning with row 8, formulate the ratios based on the Original Amounts. Format the ratios as percentages.
5. The following independent transactions apply to Hubbard Corporation.
   a. Acquired $10,000 cash from the owners.
   b. Borrowed $10,000 cash.
   c. Earned $5,000 revenue and received cash.
   d. Accrued $3,000 of expenses.
   e. Incurred and paid $3,000 of expenses.

Required

a. In row 4, enter the effect of transaction a on both the accounting equation and net income.

b. Formulate the revised amounts in row 5 for each heading after considering the effect of transaction a on the original amounts.

c. Design formulas for the ratios in column D based on the Revised Amounts.

d. Enter the ratios for the Original and Revised transaction *a* amounts in the following table.

Ratios	Original	Ratios for Various Scenarios				
		a	*b*	*c*	*d*	*e*
Debt-to-Assets						
Equity-to-Assets						
Return-on-Assets						
Return-on-Equity						

e. Delete the effect of transaction *a* in row 4. Enter the effect of transaction *b* in row 4. Notice that Excel automatically recalculates the Revised Amounts and Ratios on your spreadsheet as the result of the changed data.

f. Continue to delete transactions in row 4 as completed and enter the effect of each subsequent transaction *c* through *e* one at a time. Enter the ratios for each independent scenario in the preceding table.

Spreadsheet Tip

1. Format percentages by choosing Format, Cells, and Percentage.

ACT 3-9

SPREADSHEET ASSIGNMENT   **Mastering Excel**

a. Refer to Problem 3-6A. Using an Excel spreadsheet, prepare the financial statements as indicated. To complete part *b* below, be sure to use formulas where normal arithmetic calculations are made in the financial statements.

b. It is interesting to speculate what would happen if certain operating results change for better or worse. After completing part *a*, change certain account balances for each of the following independent operating adjustments. After each adjustment, note how the financial statements would differ if the change in operation were to occur. After the effect of each adjustment is noted, return the data to the original amounts in Problem 3-6A, and then go to the next operating adjustment.

In the following table, record the new amounts on the financial statements for the various operating changes listed.

	Original	1	2	3	4	5
Net Income						
Total Assets						
Total Liabilities						
Total Equity						
Total Liabilities & Equity						

Independent Operating Adjustments

1. Service Revenue increased $7,500. Assume that all services are provided on account.

2. Insurance Expense decreased $500. The related prepaid insurance account changed accordingly.

3. Supplies Expense decreased $100. The related supplies account changed accordingly.

4. Depreciation Expense increased $300. The related accumulated depreciation account changed accordingly.

5. Distributions paid decreased $1,000 and the related cash account changed accordingly.

4 The Recording Process

LEARNING OBJECTIVES

AFTER COMPLETING THIS CHAPTER, YOU SHOULD BE ABLE TO:

1 Understand the fundamental concepts associated with double-entry accounting systems.

2 Describe business events using debit/credit terminology.

3 Record transactions in T-accounts.

4 Understand the need for adjusting entries.

5 Understand the need for closing entries.

6 Prepare and interpret a trial balance.

7 Record transactions using the general journal format.

8 Describe the components of an annual report, including the management, discussion and analysis (MD&A) section and the footnotes to financial statements.

9 Understand the role of the Securities and Exchange Commission (SEC) in financial reporting.

the **curious** accountant

As previously indicated, most companies prepare financial statements at least once a year. The year for which accounting records are maintained is called the company's **fiscal year**. This book usually assumes that the fiscal year is the same as a calendar year; that is, it ends on December 31. In practice, many companies have fiscal years that do not end on December 31. For example, Tommy Hilfiger, a company that produces clothing, has a fiscal year that ends on March 31. The Limited, a company that also sells clothing, has a fiscal year that ends on January 31. Why do you think these companies choose these dates to end their fiscal years?

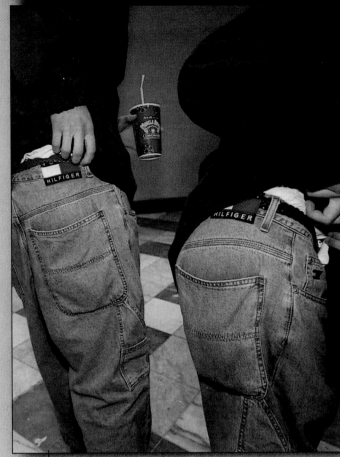

Associated Press AP

The task of accounting for business activity becomes more complex as the size of the business increases. Double-entry accounting systems provide the structure necessary to maintain the records for complex as well as simple business organizations. This chapter discusses the fundamental concepts associated with double-entry accounting systems.

A simplified accounting form known as a **T-account** is a good starting point for learning the recording procedures used in double-entry accounting systems. The account title is placed at the top of the horizontal bar of the T, and increases and decreases are placed on either side of the vertical bar. This account form omits the detailed information concerning a transaction and thereby permits observers to focus their attention on the accounting concepts. As a result, the T-account form is frequently used in the classroom, in textbooks, and in business discussions. However, it does not appear in the formal records of a business. It should be viewed simply as a convenient format that enhances communication.

Debit/Credit Terminology

The left side of the T-account is referred to as the **debit** side, and the right side is called the **credit** side. It is common practice to abbreviate the terms *debit* and *credit* with the initials Dr. and Cr., respectively. Furthermore, it is customary to say that an account has been *debited* when an amount is placed on the left side of the account and *credited* when an amount is entered on the right side. For any given account, the difference between the debit and credit amounts is known as the **account balance.** An account can have either a debit or a credit balance.

The **double-entry accounting** system is designed so that total debits always equal total credits. Accordingly, the recording of each transaction can be checked for accuracy by verifying that the debits and credits are equal. Furthermore, the entire list of accounts can be checked by verifying that the total of all debit balances is equal to the total of all credit balances. However, this system cannot ensure complete accuracy. For example, although it may have been appropriate to make a debit entry, the accountant may select the wrong account when recording the debit. As a result, the debits and credits will be equal, but the records will be inaccurate. Although the system is not perfect, it has proved very effective in eliminating or reducing incomplete entries, transposed or incorrect amounts, and inaccurate entries to accounts.

There are two fundamental equality requirements of the double-entry accounting system: (1) The equality of the basic accounting equation (i.e., Assets = Claims) must be maintained and (2) total debits must equal total credits. A recording scheme that maintains these two equalities simultaneously is discussed now.

Suppose that a company borrows $1,000 from a bank. In accordance with the first equality requirement, assets and liabilities increase, thereby maintaining the equality of the accounting equation. If the increase in assets is recorded as a debit, the second equality rule (i.e., Debits = Credits) requires that the corresponding increase in liabilities be recorded as a credit. Therefore, the financing activity is recorded as a debit to Cash and a credit to Notes Payable. Similarly, increases in all asset accounts are recorded as debits, and increases in liability and equity accounts are recorded as credits. Extending the logic requires that decreases in asset accounts be recorded as credits and decreases in liability and equity accounts be recorded as debits. Accordingly, the repayment of the $1,000 debt is recorded with a debit to Notes Payable and a credit to Cash.

Other recording schemes could be devised to satisfy the two equality requirements. Such schemes could function with equal effectiveness. Accordingly, the establishment of the recording scheme is somewhat arbitrary. However, once established, the scheme must be followed by everyone if there is to be effective communication. It is useful to draw a parallel between the requirements of the recording process and those of a simpler system, such as a traffic light. It makes no difference whether *red* is defined as *go* or *stop*; what is important is that the users of the system agree on the definition. Similarly, the users of the double-entry accounting system must agree on the recording rules. In summary, these rules are as follow:

1. Debits increase assets and decrease liabilities and equity.
2. Credits increase liabilities and equity and decrease assets.

The rules for debits and credits are shown in T-account form here.

		Claims			
Assets	**=**	**Liabilities**	**+**	**Equity**	

Debit	Credit	Debit	Credit	Debit	Credit
+	−	−	+	−	+

Collins Consultants Case

L.O. 3

Record transactions in T-accounts.

The rules for debits and credits will be demonstrated by recording the accounting events that affect a small business, known as Collins Consultants. Assume that Raymond Collins started his consulting practice on January 1, 20X3. The accounting equation reflects zero assets and zero claims at the inception of the practice. The case utilizes the following format: Business events are introduced. The impact of each event is described in debit/credit terminology and then is visually demonstrated in T-account format. The effects of each event on the balance sheet, income statement, and statement of cash flows are shown in a horizontal statements model. The events are numbered, and the event number is used as a recording reference. Recall that accounting events can be divided into four categories. The transactions used in the Collins Consultants case are organized according to the following categories:

1. Asset source transactions
2. Asset exchange transactions
3. Asset use transactions
4. Claims exchange transactions

Asset Source Transactions

A business may obtain assets from three primary sources: (1) acquired from the owners, (2) borrowed from creditors, or (3) produced through operating activities. The debit/credit recording scheme is identical for all three source transactions. They all result in an increase to an asset account, which is recorded with a debit entry, and a corresponding increase in a claims account, which is recorded with a credit entry.

Event 1
Owners Provide
Assets

Collins Consultants was established on January 1, 20X3, when it acquired $15,000 cash from Collins. This accounting event acts to increase assets and equity. The increase in assets (i.e., Cash) is recorded as a debit, and the increase in equity (i.e., Contributed Capital) as a credit. In T-account form, this transaction appears as follows:

Assets	**=**	**Liabilities**	**+**	**Equity**
Cash				**Contributed Capital**

Debit	Credit		Debit	Credit
+				+
(1) 15,000				15,000 (1)

The entry affects the elements of the financial statements as indicated:

Assets	=	Liab.	+	Equity	Rev.	−	Exp.	=	Net Inc.	Cash Flow	
15,000	=	n/a	+	15,000	n/a	−	n/a	=	n/a	15,000	FA

Event 2
Creditor Provides
Assets

On February 1, Collins Consultants borrowed $10,000 from National Bank. Collins issued a note to the bank that obligated the company to pay 12% annual interest. The note carried a 1-year term to maturity. Interst and principal were payable in cash at the maturity date. Since the party borrowing the money *issues* the note, that party is called the issuer of a note, as previously indicated. In this case, Collins Consultants is the issuer. From Collins's perspective, issuing the note in exchange for cash acts to increase assets and liabilities. The increase in assets (i.e., Cash) is recorded as a debit, and the increase in liabilities (i.e., Notes Payable) is recorded as a credit. After the transaction has been recorded, the T-account appear as follows:

Assets	=	**Liabilities**	+	**Equity**

Cash		**Notes Payable**	
Debit	Credit	Debit	Credit
+			+
(2) 10,000			10,000 (2)

Because of space limitations, only the accounts affected by the particular event being analyzed are shown. Since Event No. 2 affects Cash and Notes Payable, these are the only two accounts shown. Collins's records still contain the Contributed Capital account created in Event No. 1, even though that account is not shown here. Furthermore, only the effects of the particular event being discussed are shown in the accounts. For example, even though the first transaction affected the Cash account, only the effects of the second transaction are shown in the T-account for Cash. The effects of each event are labeled with the event number shown in parentheses, in this case (2). This practice is continued throughout the chapter. Cumulative data for all accounts are shown late in this chapter.

The entry affects the elements of the financial statements as indicated:

Assets	=	Liab.	+	Equity	Rev.	−	Exp.	=	Net Inc.	Cash Flow	
10,000	=	10,000	+	n/a	n/a	−	n/a	=	n/a	10,000	FA

Event 3
Creditor Provides
Assets

On February 17, Collins consultants purchased $850 of office supplies on account (i.e., agreed to pay for the supplies at a later date) from Morris Supply Company. Purchasing the supplies on account acts to increase assets and liabilities. The increase in assets (i.e., Supplies) is recorded as a debit, and the increase in liabilities (i.e., Accounts Payable) is recorded as a credit. After the transaction is recorded, the T-accounts appear as follows:

Assets	=	**Liabilities**	+	**Equity**

Supplies		**Accounts Payable**	
Debit	Credit	Debit	Credit
+			+
(3) 850			850 (3)

The entry affects the elements of the financial statements as indicated:

Assets	=	Liab.	+	Equity	Rev.	−	Exp.	=	Net Inc.	Cash Flow	
850	=	850	+	n/a	n/a	−	n/a	=	n/a	n/a	

On February 28, Collins Consultants agreed to review the internal control structure of Kendall Food Stores. Kendall paid Collins $5,000 in advance for the services to be performed. Although Collins Consultants is not required to pay Kendall Food Stores any cash, the firm is obligated to provide services to the food store. As a result, a liability will be converted to revenue. The liability is called *unearned revenue.* Recording the event acts to increase assets and liabilities. The increase in assets (i.e., Cash) is recorded as a debit, and the increase in liabilities (i.e., Unearned Revenue) is recorded as a credit. After the transaction is recorded, the T-accounts appear as follows:

Event 4
Creditor Provides Assets

Assets	=	Liabilities	+	Equity

Cash		Unearned Revenue	
Debit	Credit	Debit	Credit
+			+
(4) 5,000			5,000 (4)

The entry affects the elements of the financial statements as indicated:

Assets	=	Liab.	+	Equity	Rev.	−	Exp.	=	Net Inc.	Cash Flow	
5,000	=	5,000	+	n/a	n/a	−	n/a	=	n/a	5,000	OA

On March 1, Collins Consultants received $18,000 as a result of signing a contract that required Collins to provide advice to Harwood Corporation over the coming year. The event acts to increase assets and liabilities. The increase in assets (i.e., Cash) is recorded as a debit, and the increase in liabilities (i. e., Unearned Revenue) is recorded as a credit. After the transaction is recorded, the T-accounts appear as follows:

Event 5
Creditor Provides Assets

Assets	=	Liabilities	+	Equity

Cash		Unearned Revenue	
Debit	Credit	Debit	Credit
+			+
(5) 18,000			18,000 (5)

The entry affects the elements of the financial statements as indicated in the following statements model:

Assets	=	Liab.	+	Equity	Rev.	−	Exp.	=	Net Inc.	Cash Flow	
18,000	=	18,000	+	n/a	n/a	−	n/a	=	n/a	18,000	OA

On April 10, Collins Consultants provided services on account (i.e., agreed to receive payment at a future date) to Rex Company. Collins sent Rex a bill for the amount of $2,000. Recognition of the revenue acts to increase assets and equity.

Event 6
Operating Activity Provides Assets

The increase in assets (i.e., Accounts Receivable) is recorded as a debit, and the increase in equity (i.e., Consulting Revenue) is recorded as a credit. After the transaction is recorded, the T-accounts appear as follows:

Assets	=	Liabilities	+	Equity

Accounts Receivable				Consulting Revenue	
Debit	Credit			Debit	Credit
+					+
(6) 2,000					2,000 (6)

The entry affects the elements of the financial statements as indicated:

Assets	=	Liab.	+	Equity	Rev.	−	Exp.	=	Net Inc.	Cash Flow
2,000	=	n/a	+	2,000	2,000	−	n/a	=	2,000	n/a

Event 7
Operating Activity
Provides Assets

On April 29, Collins completed a 2-week training seminar for which his company was paid $8,400 in cash. Recognizing the revenue acts to increase assets and equity. The increase in assets (i.e., Cash) is recorded as a debit, and the increase in equity (i.e., Consulting Revenue) is recorded as a credit. After the transaction has been recorded, the T-accounts would appear as follows:

Assets	=	Liabilities	+	Equity

Cash				Consulting Revenue	
Debit	Credit			Debit	Credit
+					+
(7) 8,400					8,400 (7)

The entry affects the elements of the financial statements as indicated:

Assets	=	Liab.	+	Equity	Rev.	−	Exp.	=	Net Inc.	Cash Flow	
8,400	=	n/a	+	8,400	8,400	−	n/a	=	8,400	8,400	OA

Summary of Asset Source Transactions

To facilitate your understanding of the application of the rules of debits and credits, it is helpful to emphasize that each of the preceding transactions supplied assets to the business. In each case, an asset and a corresponding claims account increased. Since debits are used to increase assets and credits to increase equities, each transaction resulted in a debit to an asset account and an offsetting credit to a liability or equity account. Other transactions that provide assets to a business are recorded similarly.

Asset Exchange Transactions

Certain transactions involve an exchange of one asset for another asset. Because the decline in one asset account is offset by an increase in another asset account, the amount of total assets is unchanged by asset exchange transactions. Such transactions are recorded by crediting the account for the asset that decreased (i.e., the asset given) and debiting the account for the asset that increased (i.e., the asset obtained). In T-account form, the effects on the accounting equation appear as follows:

Assets			=	Claims

Asset 1		Asset 2	
Debit	Credit	Debit	Credit
+			−

Event 8
Exchange Cash for
Note Receivable

On May 1, Collins Consultants loaned Reston Company $6,000. Reston issued a 1-year note to Collins and agreed to pay a 9% annual rate of interest. From Collins's perspective, the loan represents an investment in Reston. Recognizing the loan (i.e., investment) acts to increase one asset account and decrease another. The increase in assets (i.e., Notes Receivable) is recorded as a debit, and the decrease in assets (i.e., Cash) is recorded as a credit. After the transaction is recorded, the T-accounts appear as follows:

Assets			=	Claims

Notes Receivable		Cash	
Debit	Credit	Debit	Credit
+			−
(8) 6,000			6,000 (8)

The entry would affect the elements of the financial statements as indicated:

Assets			=	Liab.	+	Equity	Rev.	−	Exp.	=	Net Inc.	Cash Flow	
Cash	+	Note Rec.											
(6,000)	+	6,000	=	n/a	+	n/a	n/a	−	n/a	=	n/a	(6,000)	IA

Event 9
Exchange Cash for
Office Equipment

On June 30, Collins paid cash to purchase $42,000 of office equipment for his business. The equipment was expected to have a 5-year useful life and a $2,000 salvage value. The purchase of equipment acts to increase one asset account and decrease another. The increase in assets (i.e., Office Equipment) is recorded as a debit, and the decrease in assets (i.e., Cash) is recorded as a credit. After the transaction is recorded, the T-accounts appear as follows:

Assets			=	Claims

Office Equipment		Cash	
Debit	Credit	Debit	Credit
+			−
(9) 42,000			42,000 (9)

The entry affects the elements of the financial statements as indicated:

Assets			=	Liab.	+	Equity	Rev.	−	Exp.	=	Net Inc.	Cash Flow	
Cash	+	Office Equip.											
(42,000)	+	42,000	=	n/a	+	n/a	n/a	−	n/a	=	n/a	(42,000)	IA

Event 10
Exchange Cash for
Prepaid Rent

On July 31, Collins entered into a contract with the owner of a building to rent office space. Collins paid $3,600 cash in advance for rent for the coming year. The advance payment for rent acts to increase one asset account and to decrease another. The increase in assets (i.e., Prepaid Rent) is recorded as a debit, and the decrease in assets (i.e., Cash) is recorded as a credit. After the transaction is recorded, the T-accounts appear as follows:

Assets				=	Claims
Prepaid Rent		**Cash**			
Debit	Credit	Debit	Credit		
+			−		
(10) 3,600			3,600 (10)		

The entry affects the elements of the financial statements as indicated:

Assets			= Liab.	+ Equity	Rev.	− Exp.	= Net Inc.	Cash Flow
Cash	+	**PrPd Rent**						
(3,600)	+	3,600	= n/a	+ n/a	n/a	− n/a	= n/a	(3,600) OA

Event 11
Exchange Receivable
for Cash

On August 8, Collins Consultants collected a $1,200 partial payment on the receivable from Rex Company (see Event No. 6). The collection acts to increase one asset account and to decrease another. The increase in assets (i.e., Cash) is recorded as a debit, and the decrease in assets (i.e., Accounts Receivable) is recorded as a credit. After the transaction is recorded, the T-accounts appear as follows:

Assets				=	Claims
Cash		**Accounts Receivable**			
Debit	Credit	Debit	Credit		
+			−		
(11) 1,200			1,200 (11)		

The entry affects the elements of the financial statements as indicated:

Assets			= Liab.	+ Equity	Rev.	− Exp.	= Net Inc.	Cash Flow
Cash	+	**Acct. Rec.**						
1,200	+	(1,200)	= n/a	+ n/a	n/a	− n/a	= n/a	1,200 OA

Summary of Asset Exchange Transactions

Event Nos. 8–11 represent exchanges of assets. In each case, one asset account is increased and another is decreased. The increase in the asset account is recorded with a debit entry, and the decrease in the other asset account is recorded with a credit entry. The amounts of total assets and total claims are unaffected by these transactions.

Asset Use Transactions

There are three primary purposes for the use of assets. First, a company may use assets in the process of producing revenue. Recall that assets used to produce revenue are called *expenses*. Second, assets may be used to pay off liabilities. Third, a business may want to transfer some of the assets generated by its operating activities to the owners. Assets used for this purpose are called *distributions*. The debit/credit recording scheme for all three asset use transactions results in a credit to an asset account and a debit to a claims account. Both assets and claims decrease.

On September 4, Collins Consultants paid $2,400 for salaries of employees who worked part-time for the company. Recognizing the expense acts to decrease assets and equity. The decrease in assets (i.e., Cash) is recorded as a credit, and the decrease in equity (i.e., Salaries Expense) is recorded as a debit. After the transaction is recorded, the T-accounts appear as follows:

Event 12
Assets Used to
Produce Revenue
(Expenses)

Assets	=	Liabilities	+	Equity
Cash				**Salaries Expense**

Debit	Credit		Debit	Credit
	−		+ Expense	
	2,400 (12)		− Equity	
			(12) 2,400	

Observe carefully that the debit entry has a dual effect on the equity elements. If Collins were to pay additional salaries, this amount would be added (debited) to the Salaries Expense account. Accordingly, debit entries act to increase expense accounts. However, expenses act to decrease equity. As a result, debits to expense accounts are considered additions to the ultimate reduction in equity. In summary, debits act to increase expenses, and expenses act to reduce equity.

The entry affects the elements of the financial statements as indicated:

Assets	=	Liab.	+	Equity	Rev.	−	Exp.	=	Net Inc.	Cash Flow
(2,400)	=	n/a	+	(2,400)	n/a	−	2,400	=	(2,400)	(2,400) OA

On September 20, Collins Consultants paid a $1,500 cash distribution to its owner. Recognizing the distribution acts to decrease assets and equity. The decrease in assets (i.e., Cash) is recorded as a credit, and the decrease in equity (i.e., Distribution) is recorded as a debit. After the transaction is recorded, the T-accounts appear as follows:

Event 13
Assets Transferred to
Owners
(Distributions)

Assets	=	Liabilities	+	Equity
Cash				**Distribution**

Debit	Credit		Debit	Credit
	−		+ Dist.	
	1,500 (13)		− Equity	
			(13) 1,500	

The debit entry can be viewed as an increase (+) in the Distribution account or a decrease (−) in equity. The traditional practice is to view the debit as an increase in the Distribution account. Accordingly, it is said that debit entries increase the Distribution account. The total balance in the Distribution account then acts to reduce equity.

The entry affects the elements of the financial statements as indicated:

Assets	=	Liab.	+	Equity	Rev.	−	Exp.	=	Net Inc.	Cash Flow	
(1,500)	=	n/a	+	(1,500)	n/a	−	n/a	=	n/a	(1,500)	FA

Event 14
Assets Used to Pay Liabilities

On October 10, Collins Consultants paid the $850 owed to Morris Supply Company (see Event No. 3). Recognizing the cash payments acts to decrease assets and liabilities. The decrease in assets (i.e., Cash) is recorded as a credit, and the decrease in liabilities (i.e., Accounts Payable) is recorded as a debit. After the transaction is recorded, the T-accounts appear as follows:

Assets	=	Liabilities	+	Equity

Cash			Accounts Payable		
Debit	Credit		Debit	Credit	
	−		−		
	850 (14)		(14) 850		

The entry affects the elements of the financial statements as indicated:

Assets	=	Liab.	+	Equity	Rev.	−	Exp.	=	Net Inc.	Cash Flow	
(850)	=	(850)	+	n/a	n/a	−	n/a	=	n/a	(850)	OA

Summary of Asset Use Transactions

Each of these transactions acted to reduce assets and either liabilities or equity. Debit entries increased expense and distribution accounts. The total balances in these accounts then acted to reduce equity. Each entry for asset use transactions required a debit to a liability or an equity account and a credit to an asset account.

Claims Exchange Transactions

Certain transactions involve an exchange of one claims account for another claims account. The amount of total claims is unaffected by these transactions because the decrease in one account is offset by an increase in another account. Such transactions are recorded by debiting one claims account and crediting the other.

Event 15
Recognition of Revenue (Unearned to Earned)

On November 15, Collins completed the work for the review of the internal control structure of Kendall Food Stores. Kendall accepted Collins's report and expressed satisfaction with the services performed. The original contract price was $5,000 (see Event No. 4). Recognition of the revenue acts to decrease liabilities and to increase equity. The decrease in liabilities (i.e., Unearned Revenue) is recorded as a debit, and the increase in equity (i.e., Revenue) is recorded as a credit. After the transaction is recorded, the T-accounts appear as follows:

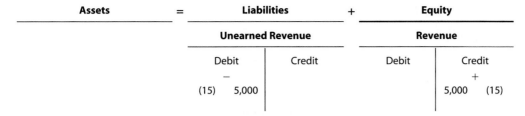

Assets	=	Liabilities	+	Equity
		Unearned Revenue		**Revenue**

Debit	Credit	Debit	Credit
–			+
(15) 5,000			5,000 (15)

The entry affects the elements of the financial statements as indicated:

Assets	=	Liab.	+	Equity	Rev.	–	Exp.	=	Net Inc.	Cash Flow
n/a	=	(5,000)	+	5,000	5,000	–	n/a	=	5,000	n/a

On December 18, Collins Consultants received a $900 bill from Creative Ads for advertisements placed in regional magazines. Collins plans to pay the bill later. The event acts to increase liabilities and to decrease equity. The increase in liabilities (i.e., Accounts Payable) is recorded as a credit, and the decrease in equity (i.e., Advertising Expense) is recorded as a debit. After the transaction is recorded, the T-accounts appear as follows:

Event 16
Recognition of Expense

Assets	=	Liabilities	+	Equity
		Accounts Payable		**Advertising Expense**

Debit	Credit	Debit	Credit
	+	+ Expense	
	900 (16)	– Equity	
		(16) 900	

The entry affects the elements of the financial statements as indicated:

Assets	=	Liab.	+	Equity	Rev.	–	Exp.	=	Net Inc.	Cash Flow
n/a	=	900	+	(900)	n/a	–	900	=	(900)	n/a

Summary of Claims Exchange Transactions

The two preceding transactions reflect exchanges on the claims side of the accounting equation. In each case, one claims account was debited, and another claims account was credited. Total claims and total assets were unaffected by the transactions.

Adjustments for Accruals

Assume that the preceding 16 items described represent all the accounting events that affected Collins Consultants during 20X3. As previously indicated, accrual accounting requires the recognition of revenues and expenses in the period in which they are earned or incurred, regardless of when cash changes hands. Collins's accounts were affected by three accruals during 20X3. Since Collins has both notes receivable and notes payable that require accruals for interest, it is necessary to recognize interest revenue and interest expense in the adjusting process. Also, there is an unrecorded transaction for accrued salaries that is discussed in this section of the text.

L.O. 4

Understand the need for adjusting entries.

Asset/Revenue Adjustments

When Collins Consultants loaned Reston Company $6,000, Reston agreed to pay Collins interest for the privilege of using the money. The interest is expressed as a percentage of the amount borrowed for a designated time. Accordingly, as time passes, the amount of interest due increases. The accrual acts to increase assets and revenue on Collins's books. Thus, the adjustment made to reflect the accrual of revenue is called **asset/revenue adjustment.**

Adjustment 1
Accrual of Interest Revenue

Collins Consultants loaned Reston the $6,000 on May 1 at an annual interest rate of 9%. As a result, Collins earned $360 (that is, [$6,000 × 0.09] × [$\frac{8}{12}$]) in interest revenue during 20X3. The required adjusting entry acts to increase assets and equity. The increase in assets (i.e., Interest Receivable) is recorded as a debit, and the increase in equity (i.e., Interest Revenue) is recorded as a credit. After the transaction has been recorded, the T-accounts would appear as follows:

Assets	=	Liabilities	+	Equity
Interest Receivable				**Interest Revenue**

Debit	Credit		Debit	Credit
+				+
(A1) 360				360 (A1)

Note that the transaction is labeled (A1). This notation is used to represent the first adjusting entry. The second adjusting entry is labeled (A2). Subsequent entries follow this referencing scheme.

The adjustment affects the elements of the financial statements as indicated:

Assets	=	Liab.	+	Equity	Rev.	−	Exp.	=	Net Inc.	Cash Flow
360	=	n/a	+	360	360	−	n/a	=	360	n/a

Liability/Expense Adjustments

When Collins Consultants borrowed funds from National Bank, Collins agreed to pay the bank interest. As with interest revenue, interst expense increases with the length of time for which the money is borrowed. The increase in interest expense is offset by a corresponding increase in liabilities. Accordingly, the adjustments made to reflect the accrual of expenses are called **liability/expense adjustments.**

Adjustment 2
Accrual of Interest Expense

On February 1, Collins Consultants borrowed $10,000 from National Bank at a 12% annual interest rate. Interest expenses on the note for the 20X3 accounting period amounts to $1,100 (that is [$10,000 × .12] × [$\frac{11}{12}$]). The required adjusting entry acts to increase liabilities and to decrease equity. The increase in liabilities (i.e., Interest Payable) is recorded as a credit, and the decrease in equity (i.e., Interest Expense) is recorded as a debit. After the transaction is recorded, the T-accounts appear as follows:

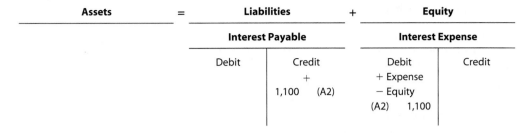

Assets	=	Liabilities	+	Equity

Interest Payable

Debit	Credit
	+
	1,100 (A2)

Interest Expense

Debit	Credit
+ Expense	
− Equity	
(A2) 1,100	

The adjustment affects the elements of the financial statements as indicated:

Assets	=	Liab.	+	Equity	Rev.	−	Exp.	=	Net Inc.	Cash Flow
n/a	=	1,100	+	(1,100)	n/a	−	1,100	=	(1,100)	n/a

Adjustment 3
Accrual of Salary
Expense

Another common liability/expense adjustment involves accrued but unpaid salaries. Note that the last time Collins Consultants paid salaries was on September 4. Assume that Collins owes $800 to part-time employees for work they performed during 20X3. Collins agreed to pay these salaries in 20X4 when the projects on which the employees worked will be completed. The required adjusting entry acts to increase liabilities and to decrease equity. The increase in liabilities (i.e., Salaries Payable) is recorded as a credit, and the decrease in equity (i.e., Salaries Expense) is recorded as a debit. After the transaction is recorded, the T-accounts appear as follows:

Assets	=	Liabilities	+	Equity

Salaries Payable

Debit	Credit
	+
	800 (A3)

Salaries Expense

Debit	Credit
+ Expense	
− Equity	
(A3) 800	

The adjustment affects the elements of the financial statements as indicated:

Assets	=	Liab.	+	Equity	Rev.	−	Exp.	=	Net Inc.	Cash Flow
n/a	=	800	+	(800)	n/a	−	800	=	(800)	n/a

Adjustments for Deferrals

As indicated in Chapter 3, deferrals involve revenue and expense recognition that succeeds (i.e., comes after) the cash realizations. During 20X3, Collins Consultants was affected by four deferrals. Cash was paid for office equipment, prepaid rent, and supplies, but no expenses were recognized to reflect the use of these resources during the accounting periods. Also, cash was collected for services provided, but revenue was not recognized. Each of these four deferrals requires adjustments on Collins's books to reflect the appropriate recognition of revenue and expenses for the 20X3 fiscal year.

Asset/Expense Adjustments

When the equipment, rent, and supplies were acquired, their costs were placed in asset accounts. At the end of the accounting period, the portion of the costs that represents used resources must be removed from the asset accounts and placed into expense accounts. Since the entry involves an asset account and an expense account, it is referred to as an **asset/expense adjustment.** Three asset/expense adjustments are shown next.

Adjustment 4
Equipment Used to
Produce Revenue
(Depreciation
Expense)

Since the office equipment was purchased on June 30, it was used for one-half of the year. Accordingly, the depreciation expense amounts to $4,000 ([$42,000 − $2,000] ÷ 5 = $8,000 ÷ 2 = $4,000). The adjusting entry necessary to record depreciation acts to decrease assets and equity. The decrease in assets (i.e., equipment) is recorded as a credit to the contra asset account Accumulated Depreciation; and the decrease in equity (i.e., Depreciation Expense) is recorded as a debit. After the transaction is recorded, the T-accounts appear as follows:

Assets	=	Liabilities	+	Equity
Accumulated Depreciation				**Depreciation Expense**

Debit	Credit			Debit	Credit
	+ Acc. Depr.			+ Expense	
	− Assets			− Equity	
	4,000 (A4)			(A4) 4,000	

The plus sign in the Accumulated Depreciation account indicates that the balance in this account increases when additional amounts of depreciation are credited to the account. Accordingly, credit entries act to increase accumulated depreciation. However, increases in the Accumulated Depreciation account act to reduce total assets. Since the Accumulated Depreciation account has a balance that is opposite to the normal asset balances, it is called a **contra account.**

The adjustment affects the elements of the financial statements as indicated:

Assets	=	Liab.	+	Equity	Rev.	−	Exp.	=	Net Inc.	Cash Flow
(4,000)	=	n/a	+	(4,000)	n/a	−	4,000	=	(4,000)	n/a

Adjustment 5
Office Space Used to
Produce Revenue
(Rent Expense)

On July 31, Collins paid $3,600 in advance for a 1-year lease of office space. The monthly rate of $300 ($3,600 ÷ 12 months) is multiplied by the 5 months for which the office was *used* during 20X3 to determine the amount of rent expense ($300 × 5 = $1,500). Recognition of the rent expense accounts to decrease assets and equity. The decrease in assets (i.e., Prepaid Rent) is recorded as a credit, and the decrease in equity (i.e., Rent Expense) is recorded as a debit. After the transaction is recorded, the T-accounts appear as follows:

Assets	=	Liabilities	+	Equity
Prepaid Rent				**Rent Expense**

Debit	Credit			Debit	Credit
	−			+ Expense	
	1,500 (A5)			− Equity	
				(A5) 1,500	

The adjustment affects the elements of the financial statements as indicated:

Assets	=	Liab.	+	Equity	Rev.	−	Exp.	=	Net Inc.	Cash Flow
(1,500)	=	n/a	+	(1,500)	n/a	−	1,500	=	(1,500)	n/a

Assume that a physical count indicates that $125 worth of supplies is on hand at the end of the accounting period. Accordingly, $725 ($850 − $125) of supplies must have been used during the period. The recognition of the supplies expense acts to decrease assets and equity. The decrease in assets (i.e., Supplies) is recorded as a credit and the decrease in equity (i.e., Supplies Expense) is recorded as a debit. After the transaction is recorded, the T-accounts appear as follows:

Adjustment 6
Supplies Used to Produce Revenue (Supplies Expense)

Assets	=	Liabilities	+	Equity

Supplies			**Supplies Expense**	
Debit	Credit		Debit	Credit
	−		+ Expense	
	725 (A6)		− Equity	
			(A6) 725	

The adjustment affects the elements of the financial statements as indicated:

Assets	=	Liab.	+	Equity	Rev.	−	Exp.	=	Net Inc.	Cash Flow
(725)	=	n/a	+	(725)	n/a	−	725	=	(725)	n/a

Liability/Revenue Adjustments

When the cash was received from Harwood Corporation in Event No. 5, Collins recorded the receipt as a liability to reflect the obligation to provide services over the 1-year contract period. By the end of the accounting period, Collins would have provided some of the services that it had obligated itself to perform. Accordingly, an amount of revenue representing the services provided must be recognized by transferring that amount from the liability to the revenue account. Since the entry involves a liability and a revenue account, it is referred to as a **liability/revenue adjustment.**

On March 1, Collins Consultants received $18,000 as a result of signing a contract that required Collins to provide services to Harwood Corporation for a 1-year period. By December 31, 20X3, Collins would have provided Harwood services for 10 months. Accordingly, $15,000 ($18,000 ÷ 12 = $1,500 × 10 = $15,000) of the obligation would have been satisfied during 20X3. This amount must be removed from the Unearned Revenue (i.e., liability) account and placed into the Consulting Revenue account. The recognition of the revenue acts to decrease liabilities and to increase equity. The decrease in liabilities (i.e., Unearned Revenue) is recorded as a debit; and the increase in equity (i.e., Consulting Revenue) is recorded as a credit. After the transaction is recorded, the T-accounts appear as follows:

Adjustment 7
Recognition of Revenue (Unearned to Earned)

Assets	=	Liabilities	+	Equity

		Unearned Revenue		**Consulting Revenue**	
	Debit	Credit		Debit	Credit
	−				+
(A7)	15,000				15,000 (A7)

The adjustment affects the elements of the financial statements as indicated in the following statements model:

Assets	=	Liab.	+	Equity	Rev.	–	Exp.	=	Net Inc.	Cash Flow
n/a	=	(15,000)	+	15,000	15,000	–	n/a	=	15,000	n/a

Overview of Debit/Credit Relationships

L.O. 2

Describe business events using debit/credit terminology.

A review of the transactions presented in this chapter reveals the relationships shown in Panel A, Exhibit 4–1. These relationships are also depicted in T-account form in Panel B. Debit/credit terminology is essential to the communication of accounting information. Practice using the terminology until it becomes a natural part of your vocabulary. It is very important for you to establish a solid foundation early so you can easily incorporate new concepts into your base of knowledge.

Summary of T-Accounts

L.O. 3

Record transactions in T-accounts .

Exhibit 4–2 on page 162 is a summary of the accounts affected by the preceding transactions. It is important to verify that the application of the recording scheme has resulted in the satisfaction of the two equality requirements. In recording each transaction, debits were always equal to credits. Furthermore, each transaction was recorded in accordance with the requirement that total assets equal total claims. As a result, the total of all asset balances amounted to $48,635, which is equal to the total amount of all balances in the liability and equity accounts. Note that the balance of an account is located on the plus (i.e., increase) side of that account. As a result, asset, distribution, and expense accounts are said to carry *debit balances*; and liability, equity, and revenue accounts are said to carry *credit balances*.

The Ledger

L.O. 1

Understand the fundamental concepts associated with double-entry accounting systems.

A collection of accounts as in Exhibit 4–2 is commonly referred to as a **ledger.** In manual systems, a ledger may be a book containing pages that represent accounts. Transaction information is recorded on the books by hand. In more sophisticated systems, a set of magnetic tapes may constitute the ledger. Input of transaction information to this type of ledger may be provided by electronic keyboards or scanners. Ledger accounts are generally assigned a name and a number that are descriptive of certain classifications of data. The accounts are frequently listed in the ledger according to the sequence of their numbers. A list of the various accounts and their corresponding account numbers, which are contained in the ledger, is called a **chart of accounts.** Since it contains all accounts, the ledger is the primary information source for the financial statements.

EXHIBIT 4–1
Debit/Credit Relationships

Panel A

Account	Debits	Credits
Assets	Increase	Decrease
Contra Assets	Decrease	Increase
Liabilities	Decrease	Increase
Equity	Decrease	Increase
Contributed Capital	Decrease	Increase
Revenue	Decrease	Increase
Expenses	Increase	Decrease
Distributions	Increase	Decrease

Panel B

Assets = **Liabilities** + **Equity**

Assets			Liabilities			Equity	
Debit	Credit		Debit	Credit		Debit	Credit
+	−		−	+		−	+

Contra Assets

Debit	Credit
+ Assets	− Assets
− Contra	+ Contra

Contributed Capital

Debit	Credit
−	+

Revenue

Debit	Credit
−	+

Expense

Debit	Credit
− Equity	+ Equity
+ Exp.	− Exp.

Distributions

Debit	Credit
− Equity	+ Equity
+ Dist.	− Dist.

The General Journal

As business activity expands, it becomes increasingly difficult to enter transaction data directly into ledger accounts. For example, think about the number of entries that would be required to record a single day's cash transactions for a large grocery store. If customers were required to wait for the cashier to make a formal entry to ledger accounts for every food item sold, lines would become so long that shopping would be discouraged and the store would lose business. To simplify the record-keeping process, transaction data are usually recorded by nonaccounting personnel on general-purpose business documents before the data are transferred to the accounting department. For example, a salesclerk may record data about a

L.O. 1

Understand the fundamental concepts associated with double-entry accounting systems.

EXHIBIT 4–2

Ledger Accounts

Assets	=	Liabilities	+	Equity

Cash

(1)	15,000	6,000	(8)
(2)	10,000	42,000	(9)
(4)	5,000	3,600	(10)
(5)	18,000	2,400	(12)
(7)	8,400	1,500	(13)
(11)	1,200	850	(14)
Bal.	1,250		

Accounts Receivable

(6)	2,000	1,200	(11)
Bal.	800		

Supplies

(3)	850	725	(A6)
Bal.	125		

Prepaid Rent

(10)	3,600	1,500	(A5)
Bal.	2,100		

Notes Receivable

(8)	6,000		
Bal.	6,000		

Interest Receivable

(A)	360		
Bal.	360		

Office Equipment

(9)	42,000		
Bal.	42,000		

Accumulated Depreciation

		4,000	(A4)
		4,000	Bal.

Accounts Payable

(14)	850	850	(3)
		900	(16)
		900	Bal.

Unearned Revenue

(15)	5,000	5,000	(4)
(A7)	15,000	18,000	(5)
		3,000	Bal.

Notes Payable

		10,000	(2)
		10,000	Bal.

Interest Payable

		1,100	(2)
		1,100	Bal.

Salaries Payable

		800	(A3)
		800	Bal.

Contributed Capital

		15,000	(1)
		15,000	Bal.

Consulting Revenue

		2,000	(6)
		8,400	(7)
		5,000	(15)
		15,000	(A7)
		30,400	Bal.

Interest Revenue

		360	(A1)
		360	Bal.

Salaries Expense

(12)	2,400		
(A3)	800		
Bal.	3,200		

Advertising Expense

(16)	900		
Bal.	900		

Interest Expense

(A2)	1,100		
Bal.	1,100		

Depreciation Expense

(A4)	4,000		
Bal.	4,000		

Rent Expense

(A5)	1,500		
Bal.	1,500		

Supplies Expense

(A6)	725		
Bal.	725		

Distributions

(13)	1,500		
Bal.	1,500		

Total Assets	=	Total Liabilities	+	Total Equity
		15,800		32,835

		Total Claims	
48,635		**48,635**	

sales transaction on a cash register tape. The tape then becomes a **source document** that the accountant uses to enter the transaction data into the accounting system. Other examples of source documents include invoices, time cards, check stubs, and cash receipts.

Ledger accounts contain information about a particular part of a transaction. For example, a debit in the ledger account for Cash indicates that cash increased. However, it does not identify the cause of the increase, nor does it explain when the increase occurred in relation to the timing of other transactions. To maintain a *complete chronological record* (i.e., a record arranged in order of time) of all business transactions, accountants initially record the data from source documents in a **journal.** In other words, *information is recorded in journals before it is entered in the ledger accounts.* Accordingly, journals are frequently referred to as the **books of original entry.**

A single company may use several different journals to maintain a chronological record of accounting events. Most transactions are recorded in a **general journal.** However, **special journals** could be used to record repetitive transactions that occur frequently. For example, a journal could be specially designed to record only transactions involving sales on account. A different journal could be used to record receipts of cash. Special journals are frequently named to be consistent with the types of transactions recorded in them. The journal used to record purchases on account may be called a *purchases journal.* Likewise, cash payments may be recorded in a *cash payments journal.*

After complete transaction data have been recorded in a journal, portions of the data are summarized and transferred to the ledger accounts. For example, the total amount of many cash transactions that were recorded individually in a cash receipts journal may be posted as a single debit to the Cash account in the general ledger. The process of transferring information from journals to ledgers is called **posting.** After the information has been posted to the ledger accounts, the respective debit and credit balances of the accounts are determined and tested for equality. Finally, the ledger account balances are used to prepare financial statements. Accordingly, the recording process is composed of five steps: (1) preparing and analyzing source documents, (2) journalizing the transaction data selected from the analysis of the source documents, (3) posting the transaction data from the journals to ledger accounts, (4) determining balances of the ledger accounts and testing the equality of debits and credits, and (5) using the ledger account balances to prepare financial statements.

An increasing number of companies are using computer technology to facilitate the process of recording transaction data and preparing financial statements. Although the computer can accomplish the required work at incredible speed with unparalleled accuracy, it follows the same basic five-step sequence that is used in manual systems. Accordingly, the analysis of a simple manual accounting system can provide significant insight into the more complex operation of computer-based systems. In recognition of this point, the following section demonstrates the recording procedures used in a simple manual accounting system.

The illustration uses a general journal. While *special journals* can facilitate the recording process their use is not required. As in the case described later, all transactions can be recorded in the *general journal.* At a minimum, the general journal provides space for the date, account titles, and amount of each transaction. Exhibit 4–3 shows the typical format used in a general journal; it contains entries for all the transactions discussed thus far for Collins Consultants. The date of the transaction is recorded in the first column. The account to be debited is written first at the extreme left edge of the column provided for the account titles. The account to be credited is indented and placed on the line directly below the

L.O. 7

Record transactions using the general journal format.

EXHIBIT 4–3

General Journal

Date	Account Titles	Debit	Credit
Jan. 1	Cash	15,000	
	Contributed Capital		15,000
Feb. 1	Cash	10,000	
	Notes Payable		10,000
17	Office Supplies	850	
	Accounts Payable		850
28	Cash	5,000	
	Unearned Revenue		5,000
Mar. 1	Cash	18,000	
	Unearned Revenue		18,000
Apr. 10	Accounts Receivable	2,000	
	Consulting Revenue		2,000
29	Cash	8,400	
	Consulting Revenue		8,400
May 1	Notes Receivable	6,000	
	Cash		6,000
June 30	Office Equipment	42,000	
	Cash		42,000
July 31	Prepaid Rent	3,600	
	Cash		3,600
Aug. 8	Cash	1,200	
	Accounts Receivable		1,200
Sept. 4	Salaries Expense	2,400	
	Cash		2,400
20	Distributions	1,500	
	Cash		1,500
Oct. 10	Accounts Payable	1,500	
	Cash		1,500
Nov. 15	Unearned Revenue	5,000	
	Consulting Revenue		5,000
Dec. 18	Advertising Expense	900	
	Accounts Payable		900
	Adjusting Entries		
Dec. 31	Interest Receivable	360	
	Interest Revenue		360
31	Interest Expense	1,100	
	Interest Payable		1,100
31	Salaries Expense	800	
	Salaries Payable		800
31	Depreciation Expense	4,000	
	Accumulated Depreciation		4,000
31	Rent Expense	1,500	
	Prepaid Rent		1,500
31	Supplies Expense	725	
	Supplies		725
31	Unearned Revenue	15,000	
	Consulting Revenue		15,000

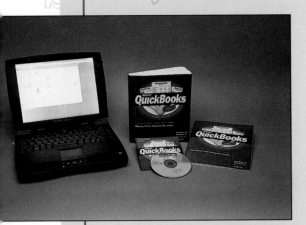

hn S. Reid

account to be debited. The money amount of the transaction is recorded in the Debit and Credit columns on the same lines with their respective account titles.

Financial Statements

The general ledger contains the information necessary to prepare the financial statements for Collins Consultants. The income statement, statement of changes in equity, balance sheet, and statement of cash flows are shown in Exhibits 4–4, 4–5, 4–6, and 4–7.

Closing Entries

Exhibit 4–8 shows the **closing entries** for Collins Consultants in general journal form. After the closing entries are posted to the ledger accounts, the revenue, expense, and distribution accounts have zero balances. The closing process clears the nominal accounts of all 20X3 information and therefore readies them for use during the 20X4 fiscal year.

Suppose that all companies close their books on December 31 of each year. Under these circumstances, the demand for financial reporting services would cluster

L. O. 5

Understand the need for closing entries.

EXHIBIT 4–4		
COLLINS CONSULTANTS **Income Statement** **For the Year Ended December 31, 20X3**		
Revenue		
Consulting Revenue	$30,400	
Interest Revenue	360	
Total Revenue		$30,760
Less Expenses:		
Salaries Expense	3,200	
Advertising Expense	900	
Interest Expense	1,100	
Depreciation Expense	4,000	
Rent Expense	1,500	
Supplies Expense	725	
Total Expenses		(11,425)
Net Income		$19,335

EXHIBIT 4–5		
COLLINS CONSULTANTS **Statement of Changes in Equity** **For the Year Ended December 31, 20X3**		
Beginning Contributed Capital	$ 0	
Plus: Capital Acquisitions	15,000	
Ending Contributed Capital		$15,000
Beginning Retained Earnings	0	
Plus: Net Income	19,335	
Less: Distributions	(1,500)	
Ending Retained Earnings		17,835
Total Equity		$32,835

around one specific time period. Accountants, printers, lawyers, government agencies, and other who work with the production and distribution of annual reports would be caught in a year-end bottleneck that would overburden their resources. Furthermore, after the year-end rush was over, there would be very little work to keep employees busy during the other parts of the year. In an effort to smooth the workload, companies have been encouraged to adopt a natural business year. A natural business year ends when the activities of an entity have reached the lowest point in an annual cycle. In many instances, the natural business year ends on December 31. However, as we indicated in the Curious Accountant, many companies have business cycles that end at times other than December 31. Indeed, Exhibit 4–9 shows that almost one-half of the companies sampled in the American Institute of Certified Public Accountants' (AICPA) *Accounting Trends and Techniques* survey closed their books in months other than December.

L.O. 6

Prepare and interpret a trial balance.

Trial Balance

As previously indicated, the double-entry system permits a check on the accuracy of the recording and posting practices through a test of the equality of debits and

EXHIBIT 4–6		
COLLINS CONSULTANTS **Balance Sheet** **As of December 31, 20X3**		
Assets		
Cash		$ 1,250
Accounts Receivable		800
Supplies		125
Prepaid Rent		2,100
Notes Receivable		6,000
Interest Receivable		360
Office Equipment	$42,000	
Less: Accumulated Depreciation	(4,000)	38,000
Total Assets		$48,635
Liabilities		
Accounts Payable		$ 900
Unearned Revenue		3,000
Notes Payable		10,000
Interest Payable		1,100
Salaries Payable		800
Total Liabilities		$15,800
Equity		
Contributed Capital		15,000
Retained Earnings		17,835
Total Equity		32,835
Total Claims		$48,635

credits. This test is commonly referred to as a **trial balance.** A trial balance is a list of ledger account titles and their respective balances. The debit and credit balances are arranged in separate columns. Each column is totaled, and the two totals are compared for the verification of equality. A failure to attain this equality signals an error in the recording process. Even if the debits balance with the credits, caution must still be taken regarding the level of assurance assigned to the "balance." For example, the trial balance does not reveal errors such as the failure to record an important transaction, misclassifications such as recording debits or credits to the wrong accounts, or counterbalancing errors such as overstating both debit and credit amounts of an entry. It follows then that the attainment of equal debits and credits in the trial balance should be viewed as evidence, as opposed to proof, of accuracy in journalizing and posting transactions.

A trial balance should be prepared whenever the accountant feels that it would be useful to test the equality of debits and credits. Some companies prepare a trial balance daily; others may prepare one monthly or quarterly. Again, the needs of the company should dictate the accounting policy, and a trial balance should be prepared whenever it is beneficial to do so. Exhibit 4–10 is a trial balance of the accounts of Collins Consultants after the closing entries have been posted to the ledger.

Components of an Annual Report

L.O. 8

Describe the components of an annual report.

Published annual reports, also called *financial reports,* usually are printed in color on high-quality paper and contain lots of photographs, which is why accountants sometimes refer to them as the company's "glossies." Although this book focuses

EXHIBIT 4–7

COLLINS CONSULTANTS
Statement of Cash Flows
For the Year Ended December 31, 20X3

Cash Flow from Operating Activities		
Inflow from Customers*	$32,600	
Outflow for Rent	(3,600)	
Outflow for Salaries	(2,400)	
Outflow for Supplies	(850)	
Net Cash Inflow from Operations		$25,750
Cash Flow from Investing Activities		
Outflow for Loan	(6,000)	
Outflow to Purchase Equipment	(42,000)	
Net Cash Outflow from Investing		(48,000)
Cash Flow from Financing Activities		
Inflow from Owner Contributions	15,000	
Inflow from Borrowing	10,000	
Outflow for Distributions	(1,500)	
Net Cash Inflow from Financing		23,500
Net Change in Cash		1,250
Plus: Beginning Cash Balance		0
Ending Cash Balance		$ 1,250

*The sum of cash inflows from Event Nos. 4, 5, 7, and 11.

EXHIBIT 4–8

Closing Entries

Date	Account Titles	Debit	Credit
	Closing Entries		
Dec. 31	Consulting Revenue	30,400	
	Interest Revenue	360	
	Retained Earnings		30,760
31	Retained Earnings	11,425	
	Salaries Expense		3,200
	Advertising Expense		900
	Interest Expense		1,100
	Depreciation Expense		4,000
	Rent Expense		1,500
	Supplies Expense		725
31	Retained Earnings	1,500	
	Distributions		1,500

on financial statements, you should understand that accounting information involves much more than just the financial statements. Annual reports are often 40 or more pages long. The financial statements themselves require only 4 to 6 of these pages, so what are all those other pages for?

For the purposes of this course, the annual report of a large company can be divided into the following four major sections: (1) financial statements, (2) footnotes to the financial statements, (3) management's discussion and analysis, and (4) audi-

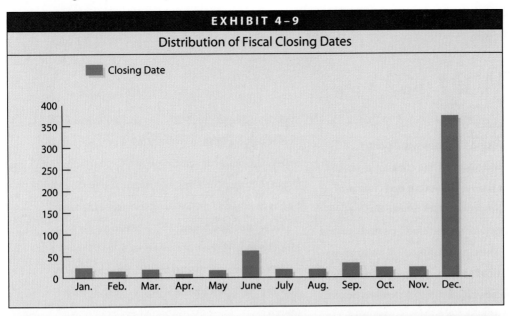

EXHIBIT 4–9

Distribution of Fiscal Closing Dates

EXHIBIT 4–10

Trial Balance

Account Titles	Debit	Credit
Cash	$ 1,250	
Accounts Receivable	800	
Supplies	125	
Prepaid Rent	2,100	
Notes Receivable	6,000	
Interst Receivable	360	
Office Equipment	42,000	
Accumulated Depreciation		$ 4,000
Accounts Payable		900
Unearned Revenue		3,000
Notes Payable		10,000
Interest Payable		1,100
Salaries Payable		800
Contributed Capital		15,000
Retained Earnings		17,835
Totals	$52,635	$52,635

tors' report. Previous chapters introduced the financial statements and the auditors' report, but the bulk of the annual report actually consists of footnotes and management's discussion and analysis.

Footnotes to Financial Statements

Footnotes to the financial statements help explain the information contained in the financial statements themselves. The need for this additional information will become clearer in future chapters, but for now keep in mind that companies have to make estimates when performing accounting calculations. They also often have the option of accounting for a given transaction in different ways.

an **answer** for the curious accountant

Part 1

The process of closing the books and going through a year-end audit is time consuming for a business. Also, it is time spent that does not produce revenue. Thus, companies whose business is highly seasonal often choose "slow" periods to end their fiscal year. The Limited does a lot of business during the Christmas season, so it might find December 31 an inconvenient time to close its books. Toward the end of January, business activity is slow, and inventory levels are at their low points. This is a good time to count the inventory and to assess the financial condition of the company. For these reasons, The Limited has chosen to close its books to end its fiscal year at the end of January.

Now that you know why a business like The Limited might choose to end its fiscal year at the end of January, can you think of a reason why Tommy Hilfiger closes its books at the end of March?

Generally accepted accounting principles (GAAP) allow considerable flexibility. Footnotes explain some of the estimates that were made as well as which of the options available under GAAP were used. It would be foolish, and even dangerous, for a user to try to understand a company's financial statements without reading the footnotes. To emphasize this point, financial statements often have a statement at the bottom of the pages, such as "the accompanying footnotes are an integral part of these financial statements."

Management's Discussion and Analysis

Management's discussion and analysis (MD&A) is usually located at the beginning of the annual report. MD&A is the section of the annual report that management uses to explain many different aspects of the company's past performance and future plans. For example, MD&A typically discusses this year's sales compared to those of the past year and explains reasons for the changes. If the company is planning significant acquisitions of assets or other businesses, this information should be included in MD&A. Likewise, plans to dispose of part of the existing business should be discussed. Some events included in MD&A might also be discussed in the footnotes.

Role of the Independent Auditor Revisited

The auditors' report is explained in Chapter 2. A well-educated businessperson should be aware that the auditor has a different role and responsibility for different parts of the annual report. Auditors have great responsibility for the financial statements and the footnotes to those statements. From an auditor's point of view, the footnotes are a part of the financial statements, which means that information in the footnotes is audited in the same manner as information in the balance sheet.

Auditors' responsibility for information in MD&A is less than that for the financial statements and footnotes, but they do have some responsibility for this section of the annual report. Auditors *review* the MD&A section to be sure

an **answer** for the curious accountant

Part 2

Tommy Hilfiger sells most of its clothes through retailers. Therefore, it must ship goods weeks before they will eventually be sold by stores such as The Limited. March 31 probably is a relatively slow time of year for Tommy Hilfiger. The Christ-mas season has passed and most of the spring clothing probably has been shipped to retailers by the end of March, so this is a good time of year for clothing manufacturers to close their books. Polo Ralph Lauren also closes its fiscal year at the end of March.

focus on
international issues

Is There a Global GAAP Leader?

Chapter 3 discussed some reasons that there is no single set of global GAAP. Nevertheless, one may wonder if there are certain countries that tend to take the lead in the establishment of GAAP. Although no single country has led in the overall development of accounting rule making, a few countries have led in some specific areas of accounting development.

For example, the double-entry bookkeeping system explained in this chapter began in Italy. This system was first formally publicized in the late 1400s by an Italian monk, Luca Pacioli. Pacioli did not actually develop the double-entry system; he published an explanation of the system as he had observed it in use by Italian merchants of his day. The use of the terms *debit* and *credit* results from the Italian origins of the bookkeeping system. Today, this system is used throughout the world.

As another example, consider that the public accounting profession as we know it in the United States and many other countries originated in the United Kingdom. The idea of an independent auditing professional (i.e., the CPA in the United States) came to the United States from the United Kingdom around the turn of the 20th century. Not all countries have the strong nongovernment accounting profession that exists in the United Kingdom and United States, but those that do can trace their roots back to the United Kingdom. No doubt, this is the reason why five of the "Big 6" accounting firms in the world originated, at least in part, in the United Kingdom. The remaining firm originated entirely in the United States.

it does not contain comments that conflict with information in the financial statements. For example, if the current year's net income is down from last year's, management cannot say in MD&A that "earnings continue to grow."

However, MD&A often contains expressions of opinion not found in the financial statements or footnotes. If current earnings are down relative to last year's earnings, management could say, "We *believe* the decline to be temporary and expect substantial growth in the coming year." Management's opinion cannot be verified, or audited, in the same way as the balance in the Cash account can be.

The Securities and Exchange Commission

L.O. 9

Understand the role of the Securities and Exchange Commission in financial reporting.

A final note about published financial reports is in order. Much of the preceding discussion relates more to large- and medium-size companies than to small companies, even though many small companies are audited. (*Small* is obviously a subjective term.) The annual reports of large companies are often different from those of small companies because large companies are more likely to be registered with the **Securities and Exchange Commission,** usually referred to as the **SEC.** SEC companies, as they are often called, have to follow the reporting rules of the SEC as well as GAAP. These rules require some additional disclosures not required by GAAP. For example, SEC rules require that annual reports include an MD&A section. GAAP rules do not, so non-SEC companies usually do not include MD&A, although they could if management wanted.

The SEC is a government organization whose responsibilities include overseeing the accounting rules to be followed by SEC companies. Although in theory the SEC could "overrule" GAAP that are established by the private accounting profession, this has very seldom occurred. More often, the SEC requires companies registered with it to give information in addition to GAAP. All companies whose stock trades on public stock exchanges, and some that do not, are required to register with the SEC. The SEC has no jurisdiction over non-SEC companies.

SEC companies must file a good deal of information directly with the SEC. There are many different reports, and each is referred to by a different form number, but the most common are 10-Ks and 10-Qs. The 10-K is a company's annual report, and it is very similar to the annual report of Gateway 2000 in Appendix B. The major differences between the 10-K filed with the SEC and the glossies are the absence of pictures in the 10-Ks and the fact that the 10-Ks often contain more detailed information than is included in the glossies. The 10-Qs are quarterly reports. They normally contain less detail than the 10-Ks.

Most of the reports filed with the SEC are available electronically through the SEC's EDGAR database. EDGAR is an acronym for Electronic Data Gathering, Analysis, and Retrieval system, and it is accessible through the World Wide Web on the Internet. Instructions for using EDGAR are in Appendix A.

A LOOK BACK

This chapter introduced the *double-entry accounting* system, which has been in existence since at least the 1400s, and is used by most companies that have formal bookkeeping systems. You should be familiar with the following components of the double-entry system.

1. Business events can be described succinctly using debit/credit terminology. *Debits* are used to record increases in asset accounts and decreases in liability and equity accounts. *Credits* are used to record

decreases in asset accounts and increases in liability and equity accounts.

2. *T-accounts* are frequently used to communicate information. The account title is placed at the top of the horizontal bar of the T, and increases and decreases are placed on either side of the vertical bar. Debits are recorded on the left side and credits are recorded on the right side of a T-account.

3. To maintain a complete chronological record of all business events, accountants initially record data into journals. The *general journal* recording format is used not only for data entry but also to communicate information in a succinct manner. Each journal entry contains at least one debit and one credit. The entry is recorded in at least two lines with the debit recorded on the top line and the credit on the bottom line. The credit is indented to distinguish it from the debit. The general journal format is illustrated here:

Debit	XXX	
Credit		XXX

4. Information is posted (i.e., transferred) from the journals to *ledger* accounts. The ledger accounts provide a means to summarize information for presentation in the financial statements.

5. *Trial balances* are used to check the accuracy of the recording process. Ledger accounts with their associated debit and credit balances are listed in the trial balance. The debit and credit amounts are totaled and compared. An equal amount of debits and credits provides evidence that transactions have been recorded correctly, although errors may still exist. A failure to attain a balance between debits and credits is proof that errors exist.

It is important to remember that the double-entry system is just another way to organize accounting data. No matter how we organize the data, the objective is to convert it into information that is useful for making decisions. Most decisions that are based on accounting data use information obtained from companies' financial statements. Therefore, whether data are organized using the horizontal model, a manual debit/credit system, or a computerized system, it is important that business managers understand how business events affect financial statements and the related ratios.

A LOOK FORWARD

If you think back on the types of businesses discussed in Chapters 1 through 4, you will realize that they are service enterprises. None of them sold a physical product. Obviously, in the real world, many businesses do sell products. The early chapters of this course used service businesses to keep matters relatively simple. Chapter 5 introduces some special accounting issues associated with companies that purchase and sell products. A word of caution is in order. If you do not understand Chapter 5, you cannot possibly understand Chapter 8, so give Chapter 5 careful attention.

KEY TERMS

Account Balance The difference between total debits and total credits in an account. *(p. 146)*

Asset/Expense Adjustment An adjusting entry that acts to decrease assets and increase expenses. *(p. 158)*

Asset/Revenue Adjustment An adjusting entry that acts to increase assets and revenues. *(p. 156)*

Books of Original Entry The journals in which a transaction is recorded first. *(p. 163)*

Chart of Accounts A list of various accounts and their corresponding account numbers that are contained in the ledger. *(p. 160)*

Closing Entries Entries used to transfer the balances in revenue, expense, and distribution accounts to the Retained Earnings account. *(p. 165)*

Contra Account An account that normally has a balance opposite to that of the other accounts in a particular category; i.e., Accumulated Depreciation is shown in the asset section of the accounting equation, but it normally has a credit balance. *(p. 158)*

Credit An increase in liability and equity accounts or a decrease in asset accounts. *(p. 146)*

Debit An increase in asset accounts or a decrease in liability and equity accounts. *(p. 146)*

Double-Entry Accounting A method of keeping records that provides a system of checks and balances by recording transactions in a dual format. *(p. 146)*

Fiscal Year The year for which a company's accounting records are kept. *(p. 145)*

Footnotes to the Financial Statements Explanations of the information in the financial statements such as estimates used and options allowable under GAAP that have been chosen. *(p. 169)*

General Journal A journal in which all types of accounting transactions can be entered. However, it is commonly used to record adjusting and closing entries and unusual types of transactions. *(p. 163)*

Journal The books of original entry in which accounting data are entered chronologically before being entered into the ledger accounts. *(p. 163)*

Ledger A collection of all accounts of a business that is the primary information source for the financial statements. *(p. 160)*

Liability/Expense Adjustment An adjusting entry that acts to increase liabilities and expenses. *(p. 156)*

Liability/Revenue Adjustment An adjusting entry that acts to decrease liabilities and increase revenue. *(p. 159)*

Management's Discussion and Analysis (MD&A) The section of the annual report that management uses to explain many different aspects of the company's past performance and future plans. *(p. 170)*

Posting The process of transferring information from journals to ledgers. *(p. 163)*

Securities and Exchange Commission (SEC) A government organization whose responsibilities include overseeing the accounting rules to be followed by companies required to be registered with the SEC. *(p. 172)*

Source Document A document such as a cash register tape, invoice, time card, or check stub where accounting information is collected before being recorded in the accounting journals and ledgers. *(p. 163)*

Special Journals Journals that are designed to improve the efficiency of recording specific types of repetitive transactions. *(p. 163)*

T-Account A simplified account form, named for its shape, with the account title placed at the top of a horizontal bar. Debit entries are listed on the left side, and credit entries are shown on the right side of the vertical bar. *(p. 145)*

Trial Balance A list of ledger accounts and their balances that is used as a check on the accuracy of the recording process. *(p. 167)*

QUESTIONS

1. What are the two fundamental equality requirements of the double-entry accounting system?

2. Define *debit* and *credit.* How are assets, liabilities, contributed capital, retained earnings, revenues, expenses, and distributions affected (i.e., increased or decreased) by debits and by credits?

3. How is the balance of an account determined?

4. What are the three primary sources of assets for a business?

5. What are the three primary ways the business may use assets?

6. Why is an adjusting entry necessary to record depreciation expense? What accounts are affected? How are the account balances affected?

7. What is an asset/revenue adjustment? Give an example.

8. What is a liability/expense adjustment? Give an example.

9. Explain and give two examples of an asset/expense adjustment. What accounts are affected by each adjustment? Are the accounts debited or credited? Do the account balances increase or decrease?

10. Explain and give an example of a liability/revenue adjustment. What accounts are debited or credited in your example? Do the account balances increase or decrease?

11. How does a debit to an expense account ultimately affect retained earnings? Equity?

12. What accounts normally have a debit balance? What accounts normally have a credit balance?

13. What constitutes the primary information source for preparation of the financial statements?

14. What is the purpose of a journal?

15. What is the difference between a *general journal* and special journals?

16. What is a ledger? What is its function in the accounting system?

17. What are the five steps of the recording process?

18. What is the purpose of closing entries?

19. At a minimum, what information is recorded in the general journal?

20. What is the purpose of a trial balance?

21. When should a trial balance be prepared?

22. What is meant by the term *posting*?

23. Where did the terms *debit* and *credit* originate?

24. What country is responsible for the accounting profession's having "independent accounting professionals"?

25. What type of information is found in the footnotes to the financial statements?

26. What type of information is found in the MD&A section of the annual report?

27. What is the Securities and Exchange Commission? What are its responsibilities concerning a company's financial statements? What types of companies are under the SEC's jurisdiction?

EXERCISES

Debit/Credit Terminology

Two introductory accounting students were arguing about the treatment of a transaction entailing an exchange involving cash and land. Monica stated that the transaction should include a debit to Land and a credit to Cash, while Mark argued that the reverse (i.e., debit to Cash and credit to Land) represented the appropriate treatment.

EXERCISE 4-1
L.O. 1, 2

Required

Which student was correct? Defend your position.

Debit and Credit Terminology Matched with Accounting Elements

EXERCISE 4-2
L.O. 2

Required

Complete the following table by indicating whether a debit or credit is used to increase or decrease the balance of accounts belonging to each elemental category. The appropriate debit/credit terminology has been identified for the first elemental category (that is, assets) as an example.

Elemental Category	Used to Increase This Element	Used to Decrease This Element
Assets	Debit	Credit
Contra Asset		
Liabilities		
Contributed Capital		
Retained Earnings		
Revenue		
Expense		
Distributions		

EXERCISE 4-3
L.O. 2

Debit and Credit Terminology Matched with Account Titles

Required

Indicate whether the following accounts would normally have a debit balance or a credit balance.

a. Salaries Expense

b. Accumulated Depreciation

c. Cash

d. Prepaid Insurance

e. Contributed Capital

f. Land

g. Distributions

h. Accounts Payable

i. Unearned Revenue

j. Revenue

EXERCISE 4-4
L.O. 2, 4

Identification of Increases and Decreases in T-Accounts

Required

For each of the following T-accounts, indicate the side of the account that should be used to record an increase or decrease in the accounting element.

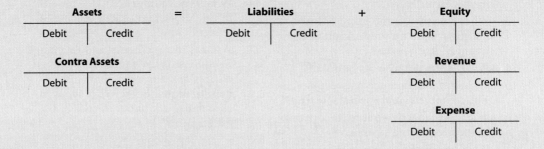

EXERCISE 4-5
L.O. 2

Application of Debit/Credit Terminology to Accounting Events

Required

In parallel columns, list the accounts that would be debited and credited for each of the following unrelated transactions:

a. Provided services on account.

b. Paid for operating expense.

c. Acquired additional cash from the owners.

d. Purchased supplies on account.

e. Purchased equipment for cash.

f. Made a cash distribution to the owners.

g. Provided services for cash.

h. Recognized accrued salaries at the end of the period.

EXERCISE 4-6
L.O. 2, 3

T-Accounts and the Accounting Equation

Required

Record each of the following events relating to Cabanna Co. in T-accounts, and then explain how the event affects the accounting equation.

a. Borrowed $10,000 cash by issuing a note to a bank.

b. Purchased supplies for $500 cash.

c. Purchased land for $20,000. The company paid $5,000 cash.

d. Performed services on account for $1,000.

Debit/Credit Terminology

Required

For each of the following independent events, identify the account that would be debited and the account that would be credited. The accounts for the first event are identified as an example.

Event No.	Account Debited	Account Credited
a	Cash	Notes Payable

a. Borrowed cash by issuing a note.

b. Received cash for services to be performed in the future.

c. Recognized depreciation expense.

d. Paid salaries payable.

e. Provided services on account.

f. Repaid principal balance on note payable.

g. Paid cash for operating expenses.

h. Purchased supplies on account.

i. Recognized accrued interest expense.

j. Recognized revenue for services completed. Cash had been collected in Event *b*.

k. Paid accounts payable.

l. Purchased office equipment with cash.

m. Received cash in payment of accounts receivable.

n. Recognized accrued interest revenue.

o. Distributed cash to the owners of the business.

Identification of the Type of Transaction, Its Effect on the Accounting Equation, and Whether the Effect Is Recorded with a Debit or Credit

Required

For each of the following transactions, identify the type of event as to asset source (AS), asset use (AU), asset exchange (AE), or claims exchange (CE). Also explain how the occurrence of each event affects the accounting equation by placing a + for *increase,* − for *decrease,* and n/a for *not affected* under each of the components of the accounting equation. Finally, indicate whether the effect is accomplished with a debit or credit entry. The first event is recorded as an example.

Event No.	Type of Event	Assets	=	Liabilities	+	Equity Contributed Capital	+	Equity Retained Earnings
a	AS	+ Debit		n/a		n/a		+ Credit

a. Provided services on account.

b. Purchased office equipment with cash.

c. Paid accounts payable.

d. Acquired a cash contribution of capital from the owners.

e. Received cash in payment of accounts receivable.

f. Repaid principal balance on note payable.

g. Purchased supplies on account.

    h. Received cash for services to be performed in the future.

    i. Recognized accrued interest expense.

    j. Paid cash in advance for 1 year's rent.

    k. Paid salaries payable.

    l. Recognized revenue for services completed. Cash had been collected previously.

    m. Recognized accrued interest revenue.

    n. Distributed cash to the business owners.

    o. Recognized depreciation expense on the equipment.

EXERCISE 4-9
L.O. 7

Events Recorded in the General Journal

Required

Record each of the following transactions in general journal form.

    a. Performed $26,000 of services on account.

    b. Purchased equipment that cost $48,000. Paid $8,000 cash and issued a $40,000 note for the balance.

    c. Purchased supplies for $1,060 cash.

    d. Received $6,000 cash for services to be performed at a later date.

    e. Collected $16,800 cash on accounts receivable.

    f. Had repairs made on equipment; the $3,400 of repairs were charged on account.

    g. Sold land that cost $20,000 for $26,800.

    h. Paid $4,600 cash in advance for an insurance policy on the equipment.

    i Paid $2,400 on accounts payable.

    j. Recorded the adjusting entry to recognize $1,600 of insurance expense.

    k. Recorded $12,400 depreciation expense on the equipment.

    l. Recorded accrued interest expense of $1,600.

EXERCISE 4-10
L.O. 6

Preparation of a Trial Balance

Required

On December 31 of 20X6, Harring Company had the following open accounts in its general ledger. Use this information to prepare a trial balance.

Land	$40,000
Unearned Revenue	26,000
Distributions	10,000
Depreciation Expense	3,000
Prepaid Rent	9,600
Cash	14,400
Salaries Expense	25,000
Accounts Payable	6,000
Contributed Capital	40,000
Operating Expense	25,000
Office Supplies	5,000
Advertising Expense	2,000
Retained Earnings, 1–1–X6	9,000
Revenue	92,000
Office Equipment	32,000
Accounts Receivable	13,000
Accumulated Depreciation	6,000

Preparation of Closing Entries

The following financial information was taken from the books of Better Form Health Club, a small spa and health club.

Partial list of Account Balances as of December 31, 20X8	
Accounts Receivable	$12,300
Accounts Payable	11,100
Accrued Salaries	4,300
Accumulated Depreciation	15,600
Cash	21,450
Certificate of Deposit	11,300
Depreciation Expense	6,300
Distributions	2,500
Equipment	25,000
Interest Expense	4,300
Interest Payable	500
Operating Expense	43,100
Prepaid Rent	1,200
Rent Expense	8,400
Retained Earnings	65,300
Salaries Expense	22,400
Service Revenue	96,800
Supplies	800
Supplies Expense	8,480

Required

a. Prepare the necessary closing entries at December 31, 20X8, for Better Form.

b. What is the balance in the Retained Earnings account after the closing entries are made?

Events Recorded in T-Accounts and Trial Balance Prepared

The following events apply to Telephone Accessories Inc.

1. Acquired a $40,000 cash contribution of capital from the owners.
2. Borrowed $32,000 from Salem Bank.
3. Earned $28,000 revenue on account.
4. Incurred $15,200 expense on account.
5. Collected $26,400 cash from accounts receivable.
6. Made a $13,600 payment on accounts payable.
7. Made a $2,000 cash distribution to owners.
8. Paid $8,000 cash to purchase office equipment.
9. Received a $9,600 cash advance for services to be provided in the future.
10. Purchased $1,600 of supplies on account.
11. Recorded accrued interest expense of $2,080.
12. Recognized $1,600 of depreciation expense.
13. Recognized $2,400 of revenue for services provided to the customer in Event No. 9.
14. Recognized $1,200 of supplies expense.

Required

a. Record the events in T-accounts.

b. Test the equality of the debit and credit balances of the T-accounts by preparing a trial balance.

EXERCISE 4-13   **Determination of Effect of Errors on Trial Balance**
L.O. 6
Required

Explain how each of the following posting errors affects a trial balance. State whether the trial balance will be out of balance because of the posting error, and indicate which side of the trial balance will have a higher amount after each independent entry is posted. If the posting error does not affect the equality of debits and credits shown in the trial balance, make a statement indicating that the error will not cause an inequality and tell why it does not affect the balance.

   a. A $600 debit to Rent Expense was debited twice.
   b. An $1,800 credit to Accounts Payable was not posted.
   c. A $900 credit to Notes Payable was credited to Revenue.
   d. A $400 debit to Cash was posted as a $2,000 debit.
   e. A $440 debit to Office Supplies was debited to Office Equipment.

EXERCISE 4-14   **Events Recorded in the General Journal, T-Accounts Posted, and Closing Entries Prepared**
L.O. 3, 5, 7   At the beginning of 20X6, Speedies Tacos had the following balances in its accounts:

Account	Balance
Cash	$12,500
Accounts Receivable	8,200
Accounts Payable	2,400
Contributed Capital	10,000
Retained Earnings	8,300

The following events apply to Speedies Tacos for 20X6.
   1. Provided $124,000 of services on account.
   2. Incurred $10,250 of operating expenses on account.
   3. Collected $130,400 of accounts receivable.
   4. Paid $61,000 cash for salaries expense.
   5. Paid $11,600 cash as a partial payment on accounts payable.
   6. Made a $10,000 cash distribution to owner.

Required
   a. Record these transactions in the general journal.
   b. Open the T-accounts, and post the beginning balances and the preceding transactions to the appropriate accounts.
   c. Record the beginning balances and the transactions in the horizontal statements model such as the following one:

Assets			= Liab. +	Equity		Rev. −	Exp. =	Net Inc.	Cash Flow
Cash	+	Accts. Rec.	= Accts. Pay. +	Cont. Cap. +	Ret. Earn.				

   d. Record the closing entries in the general journal and post them to the T-accounts. What is the amount of net income for the year?
   e. What is the amount of *change* in retained earnings for the year? Is the change in retained earnings different from the amount of net income? If so, what causes the difference?

EXERCISE 4-15
L.O. 3, 5

Receivables Recorded and Their Effect on Financial Statements Identified
Driskel Company performed services on account for $30,000 in 20X6. Driskel collected $18,000 cash from accounts receivable during 20X6. The remaining $12,000 was collected in cash during 20X7.

Required
  a. Record the 20X6 transactions in T-account format.
  b. Record the 20X6 transactions in a horizontal statements model like the following one:

Assets			= Liab. +	Equity	Rev.	− Exp.	= Net Inc.	Cash Flow
Cash	+	Accts. Rec.	= n/a +	Ret. Earn				

  c. Determine the amount of revenue that would appear on the 20X6 income statement.
  d. Determine the amount of cash flow from operating activities that would appear on the 20X6 statement of cash flows.
  e. Open a T-account for Retained Earnings, and close the 20X6 Revenue account to the Retained Earnings account.
  f. Record the 20X7 cash collection in the appropriate T-accounts.
  g. Record the 20X7 transactions in the horizontal statements model like the one shown in part b.
  h. Assuming no other transactions occur in 20X7, determine the amount of net income and the net cash flow from operating activities for 20X7.

EXERCISE 4-16
L.O. 3–6

Supplies Recorded and Their Effect on Financial Statements Identified
Juanita Anderson started and operated a small family consulting firm in 20X7. The firm was affected by two events: (1) Anderson provided $10,000 of services on account, and (2) she purchased $1,400 of supplies on account. There were $300 of supplies on hand as of December 31, 20X7.

Required
  a. Open T-accounts and record the two transactions in the accounts.
  b. Record the required year-end adjusting entry to reflect the use of supplies.
  c. Prepare an income statement, statement of changes in equity, balance sheet, and cash statement.
  d. Explain why the amount of net income and the cash flow from operations differ.
  e. Make the required closing entries, and prepare an after-closing trial balance.

EXERCISE 4-17
L.O. 4, 7

Prepaids Recorded and Their Effect on Financial Statements Identified
Nevada Company paid $36,000 cash in advance for a 1-year contract to lease delivery equipment for the business. The lease agreement was signed on March 1, 20X7, and was effective immediately. Nevada Company earned $40,000 cash revenue for 20X7.

Required
  a. Record the March 1 cash payment in general journal format.
  b. Record in general journal format the asset/expense adjustment required as of December 31, 20X7.
  c. Record each event in a horizontal statements model like the following one:

Assets			= Liab. +	Equity	Rev.	− Exp.	= Net Inc.	Cash Flow
Cash	+	PrPd. Lease		Rec. Earn.				

d. What is the amount of net income that would appear on the 20X7 income statement? What is the amount of net cash flow from operating activities for 20X7?

e. Determine the amount of Prepaid Rent that would appear on the 20X7 balance sheet.

EXERCISE 4-18   **Accrued Salaries Recorded and Their Effect on Financial Statements Identified**
L.O. 4, 7   On December 31, 20X8, HJ Company had accrued salaries of $7,200.

Required

a. Record in general journal format the expense/liability adjustment required as of December 31, 20X8.

b. Determine the amount of net income that would appear on the 20X8 income statement, assuming that HJ earns $9,000 of cash revenue. What is the amount of net cash flow from operating activities for 20X8?

c. Determine the amount of liability that would appear on the 20X8 balance sheet.

EXERCISE 4-19   **Depreciation Recorded and Its Effect on Financial Statements Identified**
L.O. 3, 4   On January 1, 20X7, Delco bought a computer for $30,000 cash. The computer had a useful life of 3 years and a salvage value of $6,000.

Required

a. Show in T-account format the result of Delco's purchase of the computer.

b. Show in T-account format the asset/expense adjustment required on December 31, 20X7.

c. Determine the book value of the computer that would appear on the December 31, 20X7, balance sheet.

d. Determine the amount of net income that would appear on the 20X7 income statement, assuming that Delco earned $12,000 of cash revenue in 20X7.

e. What is the amount of net cash flow from operating activities for 20X7?

f. What is the amount of depreciation expense that would appear on the 20X8 income statement?

g. Determine the book value of the computer that would appear on the December 31, 20X8, balance sheet.

EXERCISE 4-20   **Note Payable Recorded and Its Effect on Financial Statements Identified**
L.O. 3, 4   On April 1, 20X7, Queen Company borrowed $50,000 from First Mississippi Bank. The note carried a 9% annual interest rate and a 1-year term to maturity.

Required

a. Identify the transaction type (i.e., asset source, use, or exchange or claims exchange), and show in T-account format the entries for the financing event on April 1, 20X7.

b. Identify the transaction type, and show in T-account format the liability/expense adjustment as of December 31, 20X7.

c. Determine the amount of net income on the 20X7 income statement, assuming Queen Company earned $8,000 of cash revenue.

d. What is the amount of net cash flow from operating activities for 20X7?

e. Determine the total liabilities on the December 31, 20X7, balance sheet.

f. Record (1) the 20X8 accrual of interest and (2) the cash payment of principal and interest on April 1, 20X8.

g. Are the April 1, 20X8, transactions asset source, asset use, asset exchange, or claims exchange transactions?

Unearned Revenue Recorded and Its Effect on Financial Statements Identified

Allen received a $54,000 cash advance payment on June 1, 20X5, for legal services to be performed in the future. Services were to be provided for a 1-year term beginning June 1, 20X5.

Required

a. Record the June 1 cash receipt in the appropriate T-accounts.

b. Record in T-account format the liability/revenue adjustment required as of December 31, 20X5.

c. Record the preceding transaction and related adjustment in the horizontal statements model like the following example:

Assets	= Liab. + Equity	Rev. – Exp. = Net Inc.	Cash Flow

d. Determine the amount of net income on the 20X5 income statement. What is the amount of net cash flow from operating activities for 20X5?

e. Determine the amount of liability that would appear on the 20X5 balance sheet.

T-Account Used to Determine Cash Flow from Operating Activity

CTV began the accounting period with a $46,000 debit balance in its Accounts Receivable account. During the accounting period, CTV produced revenue on account amounting to $114,000. The ending accounts receivable balance amounted to $42,000.

Required

Based on this information alone, determine the amount of cash inflow from operating revenue during the accounting period. (*Hint:* It may be helpful to open a T-account for Accounts Receivable. Enter the debits and credits associated with the events discussed, and solve for the missing amount.)

T-Account Used to Determine Cash Flow from Operating Activities

Tin Cup Company began the accounting period with a $30,000 credit balance in its Accounts Payable account. During the accounting period, Tin Cup incurred expenses on account amounting to $90,000. The ending Accounts Payable balance was $24,000.

Required

Based on this information , determine the amount of cash outflow for expenses during the accounting period. (*Hint:* It may be helpful to open T-accounts for Accounts Payable and related accounts. Enter the debits and credits associated with the events discussed, and solve for the missing amount.)

PROBLEMS—SERIES A

Identification of Debit and Credit Balances

Required

Tell whether each of the following accounts has a debit or credit balance.

a. Contributed Capital
b. Retained Earnings
c. Certificate of Deposit
d. Interest Expense
e. Accounts Receivable
f. Interest Revenue
g. Insurance Expense
h. Interest Payable
i. Cash
j. Distributions

k. Unearned Revenues
l. Operating Expense
m. Accumulated Depreciation
n. Accounts Payable
o. Office Equipment
p. Depreciation Expense
q. Service Revenue
r. Notes Payable
s. Notes Receivable
t. Supplies

u. Utilities Payable
v. Consulting Revenue
w. Interest Receivable
x. Supplies Expense
y. Salaries Expense

z. Equipment
aa. Salaries Payable
bb. Land
cc. Prepaid Insurance

PROBLEM 4-2A
L.O. 1, 2

Transaction Type and Debit/Credit Terminology

The following events apply to Tarr Enterprises.

1. Acquired a $12,500 cash contribution of capital from the owner.
2. Paid salaries to employees, $875 cash.
3. Collected $4,050 cash for services to be performed in the future.
4. Paid cash for utilities, $201.
5. Recognized $11,250 of revenue on account.
6. Purchased equipment costing $7,500 by paying cash of $1,500 and borrowing the balance from Bay City National Bank by issuing a 4-year note.
7. Made a $625 cash distribution to the owner, Felecia Tarr.
8. Purchased $800 of supplies on account.
9. Received $3,125 cash for services rendered.
10. Paid cash to rent office space for the next 12 months, $3,000.
11. Made a $1,875 principal payment on the bank note.
12. Paid cash of $4,375 for other operating expenses.
13. Paid creditor on account payable, $438.
14. Paid cash to purchase office furniture, $2,500.
15. Recognized $1,875 of depreciation expense.
16. Recognized $750 of rent expense. Cash had been paid in a prior transaction (see Event No. 10).
17. Recognized $1,250 of revenue for services performed. Cash had been previously collected (see Event No. 3).
18. Recognized $188 of accrued interest expense.

Required

For each event, identify the type of event as to asset source (AS), asset use (AU), asset exchange (AE), or claims exchange (CE). Also identify the account that is to be debited and the account that is to be credited when the transaction is recorded.

Event No.	Type of Event	Account Debited	Account Credited
1	AS	Cash	Contributed Capital

PROBLEM 4-3A
L.O. 4, 7

Adjusting Entries Recorded in General Journal Format

Required

Each of the following independent events will require a year-end adjusting entry. Record each event and its associated adjusting entry in general journal format. The first event is recorded as an example. Assume a December 31 closing date.

Event No.	Date	Account Titles	Debit	Credit
a	Sept. 1	Prepaid Rent	13,950	
		Cash		13,950
a	Dec. 31	Rent Expense	4,650	
		Prepaid Rent		4,650

    a. Paid $13,950 cash in advance on September 1 for a 1-year lease on office space.

    b. Borrowed $45,000 cash by issuing a note to Bay City National Bank on October 1. The note carried a 1-year term and a 6% annual rate of interest.

    c. Paid $19,400 cash to purchase equipment on September 1. The equipment was expected to have a 5-year life and a $5,000 salvage value. Depreciation is computed on a straight-line basis.

    d. Invested $22,000 cash in a certificate of deposit that paid 6% interest annually. The certificate was acquired on June 1 and carried a 1-year term to maturity.

    e. Purchased $1,725 of supplies on account on April 15. At year-end, $250 of supplies remained on hand.

    f. Received a $7,200 cash advance on July 1 for a contract to provide services for 1 year.

    g. Paid $10,200 cash in advance on February 1 for a 1-year insurance policy.

One Complete Accounting Cycle

PROBLEM 4-4A
L.O. 3–7

The following events apply to Merlin Company's first year of operations:

1. Began operations when it acquired a $15,000 cash contribution of capital on January 1, 20X6.
2. Purchased $450 of supplies on account.
3. Paid $9,000 cash in advance for a 1-year lease on office space.
4. Earned $10,500 of revenue on account.
5. Incurred $6,750 of other operating expenses on account.
6. Collected $5,400 cash from accounts receivable.
7. Paid $6,000 cash on accounts payable.
8. Distributed $500 cash to the owners.

Events That Relate to Adjusting Entries

9. There was $75 of supplies on hand at the end of the accounting period.
10. The lease on the office space covered a 1-year period beginning September 1, 20X6.
11. There was $1,800 of accrued salaries at the end of the period.

Required

    a. Record these transactions in general journal form.

    b. Post the transaction data from the journal to ledger T-accounts.

    c. Prepare a trial balance.

    d. Prepare an income statement, statement of changes in equity, a balance sheet, and a statement of cash flows.

    e. Close the nominal accounts (i.e., Revenue, Expense, and Distribution) to Retained Earnings.

    f. Post the closing entries to the T-accounts, and prepare an after-closing trial balance.

Two Complete Accounting Cycles

PROBLEM 4-5A
L.O. 3–7

Chow Enterprises experienced the following events for 20X6, the first year of operation.

1. Began operations when it acquired $10,000 of cash from the owners.
2. Paid $2,000 cash for rent in advance. The payment was for the period April 1, 20X6 to March 31, 20X7.
3. Performed services for customers on account for $23,000.
4. Incurred operating expenses on account of $10,500.
5. Collected $21,250 cash from accounts receivable.
6. Paid $7,500 cash for salary expense.
7. Paid $8,000 cash as a partial payment on accounts payable.

Adjusting Entries

8. Made the adjusting entry for the expired rent.
9. Had $800 of accrued salaries at the end of 20X6.

Events for 20X7

1. Paid $800 cash for the salaries accrued in the prior accounting period.
2. Performed services for cash of $6,700.
3. Borrowed $3,000 from the local bank by issuing a note.
4. Paid $2,500 cash for rent in advance. The payment was for 1 year beginning April 1, 20X7.
5. Performed services for customers on account for $34,000.
6. Incurred operating expense on account of $18,500.
7. Collected $33,500 cash from accounts receivable.
8. Paid $19,250 cash as a partial payment on accounts payable.
9. Paid $12,500 cash for salary expense.
10. Made a $5,000 cash distribution to the owners.

Adjusting Entries

11. Made the adjusting entry for the expired rent.
12. The note was made on September 1, 20X7, for a 1-year term and carried an interest rate of 9%.

Required

a. Record the transactions and adjusting entries for 20X6 in general journal form.
b. Post the transactions to the T-accounts.
c. Prepare a trial balance.
d. Prepare an income statement, statement of changes in equity, balance sheet, and statement of cash flows for 20X6.
e. Record the entries to close the nominal accounts to Retained Earnings in the general journal and post to the T-accounts.
f. Prepare an after-closing trial balance for December 31, 20X6.
g. Repeat requirements a through f for 20X7.

PROBLEM 4-6A
L.O. 7

Use of Journal Entries to Identify Accounting Events

Required

The following information was drawn from the records of attorney Ray Fremont. Write a brief description of the accounting event that is represented in each of the general journal entries.

Date	Account Titles	Debit	Credit
Jan. 1	Cash	10,000	
	Contributed Capital		10,000
Feb. 10	Cash	2,000	
	Unearned Revenue		2,000
Mar. 5	Supplies	1,000	
	Cash		1,000
Apr. 10	Office Supplies	6,000	
	Cash		1,000
	Note Payable		5,000
Apr. 30	Prepaid Rent	4,000	
	Cash		4,000
May 1	Accounts Receivable	12,000	
	Commission Revenue		12,000

(cont'd)

Date	Account Titles	Debit	Credit
June 1	Salaries Expense	1,000	
	Cash		1,000
Aug. 5	Accounts Receivable	6,000	
	Commission Revenue		6,000
10	Distributions	500	
	Cash		500
Sept. 10	Cash	2,200	
	Accounts Receivable		2,200
Oct. 1	Property Tax Expense	1,500	
	Cash		1,500
Dec. 31	Depreciation Expense	500	
	Accumulated Depreciation		500
31	Supplies Expense	400	
	Supplies		400
31	Rent Expense	2,200	
	Prepaid Rent		2,200
31	Unearned Revenue	3,120	
	Commission Revenue		3,120

Events Recorded in Statements Model and T-Accounts and Trial Balance Prepared

The following accounting events apply to Kevin's Diner for the year 20X7.

PROBLEM 4-7A
L.O. 3-6

Asset Source Transactions

1. Began operations when it acquired $80,000 of cash from the owner.
2. Purchased $28,000 of equipment on account.
3. Performed services and collected cash of $4,000.
4. Collected $24,000 of cash in advance for services to be provided over the next 12 months.
5. Provided $48,000 of services on account.
6. Purchased supplies of $6,000 on account.

Asset Exchange Transactions

7. Purchased $16,000 of equipment for cash.
8. Collected $28,000 of cash from accounts receivable.
9. Loaned $9,600 to Lustag, who issued a 12-month, 7% note.
10. Purchased $2,520 of supplies and paid cash.
11. Purchased a $19,200 certificate of deposit. The CD carried a 6-month term and paid 4% annual interest.

Asset Use Transactions

12. Paid $16,000 cash for salaries of employees.
13. Paid cash distribution of $8,000 to the owners.
14. Paid for the equipment that had been charged on account (see Event No. 2).
15. Paid off $2,520 of the accounts payable with cash.

Claims Exchange Transactions

16. Placed an advertisement in the local newspaper for $3,200 to be billed.
17. Incurred utility expense of $2,400 on account.

Adjustments

18. Recognized $17,600 of revenue for the performance of services. The collection of cash for these services occurred in a prior transaction. (See Event No. 4.)
19. Recorded $400 of interest revenue that had accrued on the note receivable from Lustag. (See Event No. 9.)
20. Recorded $672 of interest revenue that had accrued on the certificate of deposit. (See Event No. 11.)

21. Had $6,000 of accrued salary expense at the end of 20X7.
22. Recognized $5,600 of depreciation on the equipment. (See Event Nos. 2 and 7.)
23. Had $2,400 of supplies on hand at the end of the accounting period.

Required

a. Use a horizontal statements model to show how each event affects the balance sheet, income statement, and statement of cash flows. Indicate whether the event acts to increase (+) or decrease (−) or does not affect (n/a) each element of the financial statements. Also, in the Cash Flow column, use the letters OA to designate operating activity, IA for investing activity, and FA for financing activity. The first event is recorded as an example.

Assets	=	Liab.	+	Equity	Rev.	−	Exp.	=	Net Inc.	Cash Flow	
+		n/a		+	n/a		n/a		n/a	+	FA

b. Record each of the preceding transactions in T-accounts.
c. Prepare a before-closing trial balance.

PROBLEM 4-8A
L.O. 7

Effect of Journal Entries on Financial Statements

Entry	Account Titles	Debit	Credit
1	Cash	xxx	
	Contributed Capital		xxx
2	Office Equipment	xxx	
	Cash		xxx
	Note Payable		xxx
3	Prepaid Rent	xxx	
	Cash		xxx
4	Distribution	xxx	
	Cash		xxx
5	Utility Expense	xxx	
	Cash		xxx
6	Accounts Receivable	xxx	
	Service Revenue		xxx
7	Salaries Expense	xxx	
	Cash		xxx
8	Cash	xxx	
	Service Revenue		xxx
9	Cash	xxx	
	Unearned Revenue		xxx
10	Supplies	xxx	
	Accounts Payable		xxx
11	Depreciation Expense	xxx	
	Accumulated Depreciation		xxx
12	Cash	xxx	
	Accounts Receivable		xxx
13	Rent Expense	xxx	
	Prepaid Rent		xxx
14	Supplies Expense	xxx	
	Supplies		xxx
15	Unearned Revenue	xxx	
	Commission Revenue		xxx

Required

The preceding 15 different accounting events are presented in general journal format. Use a horizontal statements model to show how each event affects the balance sheet, income statement, and statement of cash flows. Indicate whether the event acts to increase (+) or decrease (−) or does not affect (n/a) each element of the financial statements. Also, in the Cash Flow column, use the letters OA to designate operating activity, IA for investing activity, and FA for financing activity. The first event is recorded as an example.

Assets	=	Liab.	+	Equity	Rev.	−	Exp.	=	Net Inc.	Cash Flow	
+		n/a		+	n/a		n/a		n/a	+	FA

Effect of Errors on Trial Balance

PROBLEM 4-9A
L.O. 6

Required

Consider each of the following errors independently (i.e., assume that it is the only error that has occurred). Complete the following table. The first error is recorded as an example.

Error No.	Is the Trial Balance Out of Balance?	By What Amount?	Which Is Larger Debit or Credit?
a	no	n/a	n/a

a. A debit of $1,000 to Supplies Expense was recorded as a debit of $1,000 to Rent Expense.

b. A credit of $300 to Consulting Revenue was not recorded.

c. A credit of $580 to Accounts Payable was recorded as $850.

d. A debit of $1,000 to Cash was recorded as a credit of $1,000 to Cash.

e. An entry requiring a debit to Cash of $700 and a credit to Accounts Receivable of $700 was not posted to the T-accounts.

f. A debit of $3,300 to Prepaid Rent was recorded as a credit of $3,300 to Prepaid Rent.

Effect of Errors on Trial Balance

PROBLEM 4-10A
L.O. 6

The following trial balance was drawn from the ledger accounts of Kanala Company. When the trial balance failed to produce an equality of debits and credits, the accountant reviewed the records and discovered the following errors:

1. The company received $370 as payment for services rendered. The credit to Revenue was recorded correctly, but the debit to Cash was recorded as $730.

2. A $310 receipt of cash that was received as a payment on accounts receivable was not recorded.

3. An $800 purchase of supplies on account was properly recorded as a debit to the Supplies account. However, the credit to Accounts Payable was not recorded.

KANALA COMPANY
Trial Balance
As of April 30, 20X6

Account Title	Debit	Credit
Cash	$ 3,440	
Accounts Receivable	20,000	
Supplies	1,200	
Prepaid Insurance	1,600	
Equipment	38,400	

(cont'd)

Account Title	Debit	Credit
Accounts Payable		$ 4,700
Notes Payable		16,000
Contributed Capital		48,000
Retained Earnings		37,200
Service Revenue		20,000
Rent Expense	3,600	
Salaries Expense	13,200	
Operating Expense	32,620	
Distributions	3,000	
Totals	$117,060	$125,900

4. Equipment valued at $5,000 was contributed to the business by the owners. The entry to record the transaction was recorded as a $5,000 credit to both the Equipment account and the Contributed Capital account.

5. A $100 rent payment was properly recorded as a credit to Cash. However, the Salaries Expense account was incorrectly debited for $100.

Required

Based on this information, prepare a corrected trial balance for Kanala Company.

PROBLEM 4-11A
L.O. 3-7

Comprehensive Problem—Single Cycle

The following transactions pertain to Sun Dance Company for 20X8.

Jan.	30	Established the business when it acquired $60,000 cash from the owners.
Feb.	1	Paid rent for office space for 2 years, $14,400 cash.
Mar.	1	Borrowed $40,000 cash from Bay City National Bank. The note issued had a 9% annual rate of interest and a 1-year maturity date.
Apr.	10	Purchased $2,400 of supplies on account.
June	1	Paid $36,000 cash for a computer system which had a 3-year useful life and no salvage value.
July	1	Received $40,000 cash in advance for services to be provided over the next year.
	20	Paid $1,600 of the accounts payable created on April 10.
Aug.	15	Billed a customer $28,000 for services provided during July.
Sept.	15	Completed a job and received $16,000 cash for services rendered.
Oct.	1	Paid employee salaries of $18,000 cash.
	15	Received $20,000 cash from accounts receivable.
Nov.	16	Billed customers $34,000 for services rendered on account.
Dec.	1	Made a distribution of $4,000 cash to the owners of the business.
	31	Adjusted records to recognize the services provided on contract of July 1.
	31	Recorded the accrued interest on the note to Bay City National Bank. (See March 1.)
	31	Recorded depreciation on the computer system used in the business. (See June 1.)
	31	Recorded $3,600 of accrued salaries as of December 31.
	31	Recorded the rent expense for the year. (See February 1.)
	31	Physically counted supplies, indicating $320 was still on hand at the end of the period.

Required

a. Record the preceding transactions in the general journal.

b. Post the transactions to the appropriate T-accounts.

c. Calculate the account balances and prepare a trial balance.

d. Prepare the balance sheet, income statement, statement of changes in equity, and statement of cash flows.

e. Prepare the closing entries at December 31.

f. Prepare a trial balance after the closing entries are posted.

Comprehensive Problem—Two Cycles

This is a two-cycle problem. The second cycle is contained in Problem 4-12B. The first cycle *can* be completed without making reference to the second cycle.

Amy and Glenn organized a flower shop that began operations on April 1, 20X7. A & G Flowers consummated the following transactions during the first month of operation.

April 1 Established the company by acquiring $20,000 from the owners and issuing a $20,000 bank note. The note carried a 5-year term and a 9% annual interest rate. Interest was payable in cash on March 31 of each year.

1 Paid $3,600 in advance rent for office space. The disbursement represented payment for a 1-year lease.

1 Paid $30,000 to purchase wedding décor. The décor was expected to have a useful life of 5 years and a salvage value of $3,000.

6 Purchased supplies that cost $220 cash.

9 Received $500 cash as an advance payment from Malcom Heckler to reserve wedding décor to be used in May.

10 Recorded flower sales to customers. Cash receipts amounted to $850, and invoices for sales on account amounted to $1,200.

15 Paid $960 cash for employee salaries.

16 Collected $450 from accounts receivable.

23 Received monthly utility bills amounting to $233. The bills will be paid during the month of May.

25 Paid advertising expense for advertisements run during April, $240.

30 Recorded rental of wedding décor. Cash receipts amounted to $1,150 and invoices for rentals on account amounted to $1,600.

30 Paid $960 cash for employee salaries.

Additional Data as of April 30

1. Counted the supplies inventory, which contained $80 of supplies.

2. Be sure to make adjustments for interest expense, rent expense, and depreciation expense.

Required

a. Record the transactions for the month of April in general journal format.

b. Open a general ledger, using T-accounts, and post the general journal entries into the ledger.

c. Prepare an unadjusted trial balance.

d. Record and post the appropriate adjusting entries.

e. Prepare an adjusted trial balance.

f. Prepare an income statement, statement of changes in equity, balance sheet, and statement of cash flows.

g. Record and post the closing entries.

h. Prepare an after-closing trial balance.

PROBLEMS—SERIES B

Identification of Debit and Credit Balances

Required

Tell whether each of the following accounts has a debit or credit balance.

a. Service Revenue

b. Supplies

c. Accounts Payable

d. Depreciation Expense

e. Unearned Revenue

f. Supplies Expense

g. Prepaid Rent

h. Accumulated Depreciation

i. Equipment

j. Interest Payable

k. Accounts Receivable   u. Prepaid Insurance
l. Salaries Payable   v. Retained Earnings
m. Cash   w. Land
n. Contributed Capital   x. Interest Receivable
o. Rent Expense   y. Distributions
p. Interest Revenue   z. Operating Expense
q. Certificate of Deposit   aa. Truck
r. Salaries Expense   bb. Gain on Sale of Land
s. Notes Payable   cc. Loss on Sale of Equipment
t. Insurance Expense

PROBLEM 4-2B   **Transaction Type and Debit/Credit Terminology**
L.O. 2   The following events apply to Williams Enterprises.

1. Acquired a $20,000 cash contribution of capital from the owners.
2. Paid salaries to employees, $3,000 cash.
3. Collected $18,400 cash for services to be performed in the future.
4. Paid cash for utilities, $600.
5. Recognized $18,000 of revenue on account.
6. Purchased equipment costing $100,000 by paying cash of $20,000 and borrowing the balance from Third National Bank by issuing a 4-year note.
7. Made a $3,000 cash distribution to the owner, Randall Williams.
8. Purchased $1,500 of supplies on account.
9. Received $12,000 cash for services rendered.
10. Paid cash to rent office space for the next 12 months, $13,200.
11. Made a $10,000 principal payment on the bank note.
12. Paid cash of $10,000 for other operating expenses.
13. Paid creditor on account payable, $1,500.
14. Paid cash to purchase office furniture, $2,000.
15. Recognized $20,000 of depreciation expense.
16. Recognized $8,800 of rent expense. Cash had been paid in a prior transaction (see Event No. 10).
17. Recognized $12,200 of revenue for services performed. Cash had been previously collected (see Event No. 3).
18. Recognized $4,000 of accrued interest expense.

Required

For each event, identify the type of event as to asset source (AS), asset use (AU), asset exchange (AE), or claims exchange (CE). Also identify the account to be debited and the account to be credited when the transaction is recorded. The first event is recorded as an example.

Event No.	Type of Event	Account Debited	Account Credited
1	AS	Cash	Contributed Capital

PROBLEM 4-3B   **Adjusting Entries Recorded in General Journal Format**
L.O. 4, 7

Required

Each of the following independent events will require a year-end adjusting entry. Record each event and its associated adjusting entry in general journal format. The first event is recorded as an example. Assume a December 31 closing date.

Date	Account Titles	Debit	Credit
Oct. 1	Prepaid Rent	3,500	
	Cash		3,500
Dec. 31	Rent Expense	875	
	Prepaid Rent		875

   a. Paid $3,500 cash in advance on October 1 for a 1-year lease on office space.

   b. Borrowed $60,000 cash by issuing a note to Third National Bank on April 1. The note carried a 1-year term and a 7% annual rate of interest.

   c. Paid $31,000 cash to purchase equipment on October 1. The equipment was expected to have a 5-year life and a $5,000 salvage value. Depreciation is computed on a straight-line basis.

   d. Invested $12,500 cash in a certificate of deposit that paid 4% interest annually. The certificate was acquired on April 1 and carried a 1-year term to maturity.

   e. Purchased $2,400 of supplies on account on June 15. At year end, $250 of supplies remained on hand.

   f. Received an $8,100 cash advance on July 1 for a contract to provide services for 1 year.

   g. Paid $2,400 cash in advance on March 1 for a 1-year insurance policy.

One Complete Accounting Cycle

PROBLEM 4-4B
L.O. 1

The following events apply to Arnold Company's first year of operations:

1. Acquired a $12,500 cash contribution of capital from the owners on January 1, 20X5.
2. Purchased $500 of supplies on account.
3. Paid $3,400 cash in advance for a 1-year lease on office space.
4. Earned $16,000 of revenue on account.
5. Incurred $10,200 of other operating expenses on account.
6. Collected $14,500 cash from accounts receivable.
7. Paid $8,000 cash on accounts payable.
8. Distributed $1,200 cash to the owners.

Events Relating to Adjusting Entries

9. There was $110 of supplies on hand at the end of the accounting period.
10. The lease on the office space covered a 1-year period beginning October 1.
11. There was $1,400 of accrued salaries at the end of the period.

Required

   a. Record these transactions in general journal form.

   b. Post the transaction data from the journal to ledger T-accounts.

   c. Prepare a trial balance.

   d. Prepare an income statement, statement of changes in equity, a balance sheet, and a statement of cash flows.

   e. Close the nominal accounts (i.e., Revenue, Expense, and Distribution) to Retained Earnings.

   f. Post the closing entries to the T-accounts, and prepare an after-closing trial balance.

Two Complete Accounting Cycles

PROBLEM 4-5B
L.O. 3-7

Blue Hill Tree Care experienced the following events during 20X1.

1. Started operations when it acquired $20,000 of cash from the owners.
2. Paid $3,000 cash in advance for rent during the period from February 1, 20X1, to February 1, 20X2.

3. Received $2,400 cash in advance for services to be performed evenly over the period from September 1, 20X1, to September 1, 20X2.
4. Performed services for customers on account for $38,500.
5. Incurred operating expenses on account of $17,000.
6. Collected $32,500 cash from accounts receivable.
7. Paid $12,000 cash for salaries expense.
8. Paid $14,500 cash as a partial payment on accounts payable.

Adjusting Entries

9. Made the adjusting entry for the expired rent.
10. Recognized revenue for services performed in accordance with Event No. 3.
11. Had $1,600 of accrued salaries at the end of 20X1.

Events for 20X2

1. Paid $1,600 cash for the salaries accrued during the previous year.
2. Performed services for cash, $20,100.
3. Borrowed $15,000 cash from the local bank by issuing a note.
4. Paid $12,500 cash to purchase land.
5. Paid $3,600 cash in advance for rent during the period from February 1, 20X2, to February 1, 20X3.
6. Performed services for customers on account for $64,000.
7. Incurred operating expenses on account of $35,200.
8. Collected $42,500 cash from accounts receivable.
9. Paid $32,000 cash as a partial payment on accounts payable.
10. Paid $28,000 cash for salaries expense.
11. Made a $5,000 cash distribution to the owner.

Adjusting Entries

12. Recognized revenue for services performed in accordance with Event No. 3 in 20X1.
13. Made the adjusting entry for the expired rent. (*Hint:* Part of the rent was paid in 20X1.)
14. Issued a note on March 1, 20X2, for a 1-year term and carried an interest rate of 9% (see Event No. 3).

Required

a. Record the transactions and adjusting entries for 20X1 in general journal form.
b. Post the transactions to the T-accounts.
c. Prepare a trial balance.
d. Prepare an income statement, statement of changes in equity, balance sheet, and statement of cash flows for 20X1.
e. Record the entries to close the nominal accounts to Retained Earnings in the general journal and post to the T-accounts.
f. Prepare an after-closing trial balance for December 31, 20X1.
g. Repeat parts a through f for 20X2.

PROBLEM 4-6B   **Use of Journal Entries to Identify Accounting Events**
L.O. 7
Required

The following information was drawn from the records of Swafford Realty Company. Write a brief description of the accounting event that is represented in each of the general journal entries.

Date	Account Titles	Debit	Credit
Jan. 1	Cash	12,500	
	Contributed Capital		12,500
Feb. 15	Cash	13,000	
	Unearned Revenue		13,000
Mar. 10	Supplies	1,550	
	Accounts Payable		1,550
Apr. 1	Office Equipment	17,000	
	Cash		4,000
	Note Payable		13,000
May 1	Prepaid Rent	10,200	
	Cash		10,200
20	Accounts Receivable	18,400	
	Commission Revenue		18,400
June 15	Salaries Expense	6,100	
	Cash		6,100
Aug. 28	Cash	9,300	
	Commission Revenue		9,300
30	Distribution	3,000	
	Cash		3,000
Sept. 19	Cash	16,000	
	Accounts Receivable		16,000
Oct. 31	Property Tax Expense	3,000	
	Cash		3,000
Dec. 31	Depreciation Expense	2,700	
	Accumulated Depreciation		2,700
31	Supplies Expense	2,025	
	Supplies		2,025
31	Rent Expense	6,400	
	Prepaid Rent		6,400
31	Unearned Revenue	8,500	
	Commission Revenue		8,500

Events Recorded in Statements Model and T-Accounts and Trial Balance Prepared

The following accounting events apply to Sarah's Inventions for the year 20X2:

PROBLEM 4-7B
L.O. 3-6

Asset Source Transactions

1. Began operations when the business acquired $10,000 cash contribution of capital from the owner.
2. Purchased $3,250 of equipment on account.
3. Performed services and collected cash of $600.
4. Collected $3,000 of cash in advance for services to be provided over the next 12 months.
5. Provided $6,500 of services on account.
6. Purchased supplies of $650 on account.

Asset Exchange Transactions

7. Purchased $5,000 of equipment for cash.
8. Collected $5,500 of cash from accounts receivable.
9. Loaned $500 to Tedesco Capocci, who issued a 12-month, 9% note.
10. Purchased $400 of supplies and paid cash.
11. Purchased a $2,400 certificate of deposit. The CD carried a 6-month term and paid 5% annual interest.

Asset Use Transactions

12. Paid $2,500 cash for salaries of employees.
13. Made cash distribution of $1,500 to the owners.
14. Paid for the equipment that had been charged on account (see Event No. 2).
15. Paid $650 for supplies that had been purchased on account.

Claims Exchange Transactions

16. Placed an advertisement in the local newspaper for $125 and agreed to pay for the ad later.
17. Incurred utilities expense of $100 on account.

Adjustments

18. Recognized $2,100 of revenue for the performance of services. The collection of cash for these services occurred in a prior transaction. (See Event No. 4.)
19. Recorded $40 of interest revenue that had accrued on the note receivable from Capocci (see Event No. 9).
20. Recorded $45 of interest revenue that had accrued on the certificate of deposit (see Event No. 11).
21. Had $450 of accrued salary expense at the end of 20X2.
22. Recognized $750 of depreciation on the equipment (see Event Nos. 2 and 7).
23. Had $75 of supplies on hand at the end of the accounting period.

Required

a. Use a horizontal statements model to show how each event affects the balance sheet, income statement, and statement of cash flows. Indicate whether the event acts to increase (+) or decrease (−) or does not affect (n/a) each element of the financial statements. Also, in the Cash Flow column, use the letters OA to designate operating activity, IA for investing activity, and FA for financing activity. The first event is recorded as an example.

Assets	=	Liab.	+	Equity	Rev.	−	Exp.	=	Net Inc.	Cash Flow	
+		n/a		+	n/a		n/a		n/a	+	FA

b. Record each of the preceding transactions in T-accounts.
c. Prepare a before-closing trial balance.

PROBLEM 4-8B
L.O. 7

Effect of Journal Entries on Financial Statements

Entry No.	Account Titles	Debit	Credit
1	Cash	xxx	
	Contributed Capital		xxx
2	Accounts Receivable	xxx	
	Commission Revenue		xxx
3	Salaries Expense	xxx	
	Cash		xxx
4	Cash	xxx	
	Commission Revenue		xxx
5	Distribution	xxx	
	Cash		xxx
6	Cash	xxx	
	Unearned Revenue		xxx
7	Supplies	xxx	
	Accounts Payable		xxx

(cont'd)

Entry No.	Account Titles	Debit	Credit
8	Office Equipment	xxx	
	Cash		xxx
	Note Payable		xxx
9	Prepaid Rent	xxx	
	Cash		xxx
10	Cash	xxx	
	Accounts Receivable		xxx
11	Property Tax Expense	xxx	
	Cash		xxx
12	Depreciation Expense	xxx	
	Accumulated Depreciation		xxx
13	Supplies Expense	xxx	
	Supplies		xxx
14	Rent Expense	xxx	
	Prepaid Rent		xxx
15	Unearned Revenue	xxx	
	Commission Revenue		xxx

Required

The preceding 15 different accounting events are presented in general journal format. Use a horizontal statements model to show how each event affects the balance sheet, income statement, and statement of cash flows. Indicate whether the event acts to increase (+) or decrease (−) or does not affect (n/a) each element of the financial statements. Also, in the Cash Flow column, use the letters OA to designate operating activity, IA for investing activity, and FA for financing activity. The first event is recorded as an example.

Assets	=	Liab.	+	Equity	Rev.	−	Exp.	=	Net Inc.	Cash Flow	
+		n/a		+	n/a		n/a		n/a	+	FA

Effect of Errors on Trial Balance

PROBLEM 4-9B
L.O. 6

Required

Consider each of the following errors independently (i.e., assume that it is the only error that has occurred). Complete the following table. The first error is recorded as an example.

Error No.	Is the Trial Balance Out of Balance?	By What Amount?	Which Is Larger Debit or Credit?
a	yes	90	debit

a. A credit of $430 to Accounts Payable was recorded as $340.

b. A credit of $620 to Accounts Receivable was not recorded.

c. A debit of $700 to Rent Expense was recorded as a debit of $700 to Salaries Expense.

d. An entry requiring a debit of $325 to Cash and a credit of $325 to Accounts Receivable was not posted to the T-accounts.

e. A credit of $2,000 to Prepaid Insurance was recorded as a debit of $2,000 to Prepaid Insurance.

f. A debit of $200 to Cash was recorded as a credit of $200 to Cash.

PROBLEM 4-10B   **Effect of Errors on Trial Balance**

L.O. 6   The following trial balance was drawn from the ledger accounts of Shaw Company:

SHAW COMPANY Trial Balance As of May 30, 20X6		
Account Title	**Debit**	**Credit**
Cash	$ 1,100	
Accounts Receivable	1,770	
Supplies	420	
Prepaid Insurance	2,400	
Equipment	10,000	
Accounts Payable		$ 1,500
Notes Payable		1,000
Contributed Capital		1,800
Retained Earnings		4,000
Service Revenue		19,600
Rent Expense	3,600	
Salaries Expense	9.000	
Operating Expense	2,500	
Distributions	400	
Totals	$31,190	$27,900

The following errors were committed by the accountant of Shaw Company during the month of September 20X7.

1. The cash purchase of a $2,110 typewriter was recorded as a $2,200 debit to Office Equipment and a $2,110 credit to Cash.

2. An $800 purchase of supplies on account was properly recorded as a debit to the Supplies account but was incorrectly recorded as a credit to the Cash account.

3. The company provided services valued at $7,500 to a customer. The accountant recorded the transaction in the proper accounts but in the incorrect amount of $17,500.

4. A $500 cash receipt for a payment on an account receivable was not recorded.

5. A $300 cash payment of an account payable was not recorded.

6. The September utility bill, which amounted to $600, was not recorded.

Required

a. Identify the errors that would cause a difference in the total amounts of debits and credits that would appear in a trial balance. Indicate whether the Debit or Credit column would be larger as a result of the error.

b. Indicate whether each of the preceding errors would overstate, understate, or have no effect on the amount of total assets, liabilities, and equity. Your answer should take the following form:

Event No.	Assets	=	Liabilities	+	Equity
1	Overstate		No effect		No effect

PROBLEM 4-11B   **Comprehensive Problem—Single Cycle**

L.O. 3–7   The following transactions pertain to Fulton Corporation for 20X3.

Jan.   1   Began operations when the business acquired a $60,000 cash contribution of capital from the owners.

Mar.   1   Paid rent for office space for 2 years, $19,200 cash.

Apr.	1	Borrowed $40,000 cash from First National Bank. The note issued had a 10% annual rate of interest and a 1-year maturity date.
	14	Purchased $600 of supplies on account.
June	1	Paid $30,000 cash for a computer system. The computer system had a 5-year useful life and no salvage value.
	30	Received $36,000 cash in advance for services to be provided over the next year.
July	5	Paid $400 of the accounts payable created on April 14.
Aug.	1	Billed a customer $6,600 for services provided during June.
	8	Completed a job and received $4,000 cash for services rendered.
Sept.	1	Paid employee salaries of $24,000 cash.
	9	Received $5,000 cash from accounts receivable.
Oct.	5	Billed customers $18,400 for services rendered on account.
Nov.	2	Made a distribution of $800 cash to the owners of the business.
Dec.	31	Adjusted records to recognize the services provided on contract of June 30.
	31	Recorded the accrued interest on the note to First National Bank. (See April 1.)
	31	Recorded depreciation on the computer system used in the business. (See June 1.)
	31	Recorded $1,800 of accrued salaries as of December 31.
	31	Recorded the rent expense for the year. (See March 1.)
	31	Physically counted supplies, indicating $50 was still on hand at the end of the period.

Required

a. Record the preceding transactions in the general journal.

b. Post the transactions to the appropriate T-accounts.

c. Calculate the account balances and prepare a trial balance.

d. Prepare the balance sheet, income statement, statement of changes in equity, and statement of cash flows.

e. Prepare the closing entries at December 31.

f. Prepare a trial balance after the closing entries are posted.

Comprehensive Problem—Two Cycles

PROBLEM 4-12B
L.O. 3-7

This problem extends Problem 4-12A involving A & G Flowers and *should not* be attempted until that problem has been completed. The transactions consummated by A & G Flowers during May 20X7 (i.e., the company's second month of operation) consisted of the following:

May	1	Recorded rentals of wedding décor to customers. Cash receipts amounted to $420, and invoices for rentals on account amounted to $1,200.
	2	Purchased supplies on account that cost $300.
	7	Collected $2,500 cash from customer accounts receivable.
	8	Malcolm Heckler rented the wedding décor that had been paid for in advance (see April 9 in Problem 4-12A).
	10	Paid the utility company for the monthly utility bills that had been received in the previous month, $233.
	15	Paid $2,100 cash for employee salaries.
	15	Purchased a 1-year insurance policy that cost $1,200.
	16	Paid $300 on the account payable that was established when supplies were purchased on May 2.
	20	Paid a $300 cash distribution to the owners.
	27	Received monthly utility bills amounting to $310. The bills would be paid during the month of June.
	31	Recorded rentals of wedding décor to customers. Cash receipts amounted to $625, and invoices for rentals on account amounted to $1,100.
	31	Paid $2,100 cash for employee salaries.
	31	Counted the supplies inventory, which contained $40 of supplies.

Required

    a. Open a general ledger with T-accounts, using the ending account balances computed in Problem 4-12A.

    b. Record the preceding transactions directly into the T-accounts.

    c. Record the adjusting entries directly into the T-accounts. *Note:* Reference must be made to Problem 4-12A to obtain all the information needed to prepare the adjusting entries.

    d. Prepare an income statement, statement of changes in equity, balance sheet, and statement of cash flows.

    e. Record the closing entries directly into the T-accounts.

    f. Answer the following questions.

        (1) Why is the amount in the May 31, 20X7, Retained Earnings account not equal to the amount of net income or loss for the month of May?

        (2) Why is the amount in the Accumulated Depreciation account on the May 31, 20X7, statement of financial position not equal to the amount of depreciation expenses for the month of May?

analyze, communicate, think

ACT 4-1   **BUSINESS APPLICATIONS CASE**   **Gateway 2000 Annual Report**

Required

Using the Gateway 2000 financial statements in Appendix B, answer the following questions:

    a. On December 31, 1997, Gateway had a balance of $634.509 million in Retained Earnings. On December 31, 1996, the balance in Retained Earnings was $524.712 million. Explain the change in Retained Earnings during 1997.

    b. What is the nature of Gateway's business; that is, what does it produce and sell?

    c. Could part *b* be answered by examining only Gateway's income statement, balance sheet, and cash statement?

    d. Does the Other account in the Liabilities and Stockholders Equity section of the 1997 balance sheet have a debit or credit balance?

ACT 4-2   **GROUP ASSIGNMENT**   **Financial Statement Analysis**

The account balances for Collins Company were as follows:

	January 1		
	20X2	**20X3**	**20X4**
Cash	$12,000	$ 5,800	$29,400
Accounts Receivable	6,000	10,000	6,000
Equipment	25,000	25,000	25,000
Accumulated Depreciation	(12,000)	(13,200)	(14,400)
Prepaid Rent	0	1,000	1,400
Accounts Payable	4,000	3,000	7,000
Notes Payable	12,000*	0	0
Interest Payable	300	0	0
Salaries Payable	0	0	2,100
Contributed Capital	10,000	10,000	10,000
Retained Earnings	4,700	15,600	28,300

*Funds were originally borrowed on October 1, 20X1, with an interst rate of 10%.

Collins Company experienced the following events for the accounting periods 20X2, 20X3, and 20X4.

20X2

1. Performed services for $36,000 on account.
2. Paid rent of $6,000 for the period March 1, 20X2, to March 1, 20X3.
3. Incurred operating expense of $18,000 on account.
4. Collected $32,000 of accounts receivable.
5. Paid $19,000 of accounts payable.
6. Paid note and interest due on October 1.
7. Recorded expired rent.
8. Recorded depreciation expense of $1,200.

20X3

1. Performed services on account of $48,000.
2. Paid rent of $8,400 for the period March 1, 20X3, to March 1, 20X4, and recorded the expired rent for the period January 1, 20X3, to March 1, 20X3.
3. Incurred operating expenses of $24,000 on account.
4. Collected $52,000 of accounts receivable.
5. Paid $20,000 of accounts payable.
6. Recorded expired rent.
7. Recorded accrued salaries of $2,100.
8. Recorded depreciation expense of $1,200.

20X4

1. Paid accrued salaries.
2. Performed services on account of $56,000.
3. Paid rent of $9,000 for the period March 1, 20X4, to March 1, 20X5, and recorded the expired rent for the period January 1, 20X4, to March 1, 20X4.
4. Incurred operating expenses of $32,000 on account.
5. Collected $55,000 of accounts receivable.
6. Paid $33,000 of accounts payable.
7. Sold equipment for $2,000; the equipment had a cost of $5,000 and accumulated depreciation of $4,000.
8. Recorded expired rent.
9. Recorded depreciation expense of $1,000.

Required

> a. Divide the class into groups consisting of four or five students. Organize the groups into three sections. Assign each section of groups the financial data for one of the preceding accounting periods.

Group Task

> (1) Prepare an income statement, balance sheet, and statement of cash flows. It may be helpful to open T-accounts and post transactions to these accounts before attempting to prepare the statements.

Class Discussion

> b. Review the cash flows associated with the collection of receivables and the payment of payables. Comment on the company's collection and payment strategy.

> c. Explain why depreciation decreased in 20X4.

> d. Did net income increase or decrease between 20X2 and X3? What were the primary causes?
>
> e. Did net income increase or decrease between 20X3 and X4? What were the primary causes?

ACT 4-3   **R E A L - W O R L D   C A S E**   **Date Used to Prepare the Numbers**

Consider the following brief descriptions of four companies, listed alphabetically, from different industries. Dekalb Genetics Corporation is a North American company that develops new varieties of seeds, such as corn, and sells them to farmers. Kaufman & Broad Home Corporation builds residential homes in seven western states and in France and Mexico. It claims to be the largest homebuilder west of the Mississippi River. Toys R Us, Inc., is the well-known international retailer of toys. Vail Resorts, Inc., operates several ski resorts in Colorado, including Vail Mountain, the largest in the United States, and Breckenridge Mountain.

This chapter explained that companies often choose to close their books when business usually is slow. Each of these companies ends its fiscal year on a different date. The closing dates, listed chronologically, are as follows:

> January 31
> August 31
> September 30
> November 30

Required

> a. Try to determine which fiscal year end matches which company. Write a brief explanation to explain the reason for your decisions.
>
> b. Because many companies deliberately choose to prepare their financial statements at a slow time of year, try to identify problems this may present for someone trying to analyze the balance sheet for Toys R Us. Write a brief explanation of the issues you identify.

ACT 4-4   **B U S I N E S S   A P P L I C A T I O N S   C A S E**   **Components of Financial Statements**

A stockbroker handed Dr. Nguyen a set of financial statements for a company the broker described as a "sure bet" for a major increase in stock price. The broker assured Nguyen that the company was a legitimate business. As proof, she stated that the company was listed with the Securities and Exchange Commission. After looking over the financial statements, Nguyen wanted additional information. He has an Internet connection and can access SEC files. Assume that Nguyen obtains a 10-K annual report through the EDGAR database.

Required

Name three major sections of information that are likely to be contained in the 10-K annual report. Describe the content of each section, and explain the independent auditors' role as it relates to each section.

ACT 4-5   **B U S I N E S S   A P P L I C A T I O N S   C A S E**   **Components of Financial Statements**

Beth Hughes just finished reading the annual report of Muncy Company. Hughes is enthusiastic about the possibility of investing in the company. In the management's discussion and analysis section of the report, Muncy's new president, Bill Karn, stated that he was committed to an annual growth rate of 25% over the next 5 years. Hughes tells you that the company's financial statements received an unqualified audit opinion from a respected firm of CPAs. Based on the audit report, Hughes concluded that the auditors agree with Karn's forecast of a 5-year, 25% growth rate. She will tell you, "These accountants are usually very conservative. If they forecast 25% growth, actual growth is likely to be close to 35%. I'm not going to miss an opportunity like this. I am buying the stock."

Required

Comment on Hughes's understanding of the auditor's relationship with management's discussion and analysis section of a company's annual report.

WRITING ASSIGNMENT   Fiscal Closing Date

ACT 4-6

Assume that you are the auditor for Counce Boat and Marine Sales. Counce currently has a December 31 year end of which you perform the audit. You would like for Counce to change the year end to another time (almost any time except December 31).

Required

Write a memo to the owner of Counce Boat and Marine Sales and propose a new year end. In the memo explain why it would be reasonable or better to have a different year end and specify what the year end would be. Also give reasons that the change would be beneficial from your perspective.

ETHICAL DILEMMA   Choice of Brothers—Ethics, Risk, and Accounting
Numbers in a Medieval Setting

ACT 4-7

In the late 1400s, a wealthy land owner named Caster was trying to decide which of his twin sons, Rogan or Argon, to designate as the first heir to the family fortune. He decided to set up each son with a small farm consisting of 300 sheep and 20 acres of land. Each twin would be allowed to manage his property as he deemed appropriate. After a designated period, Caster would call his sons before him to account for their actions. The heir to the family fortune would be chosen on the basis of which son had produced a larger increase in wealth during the test period.

On the appointed day of reckoning, Argon boasted that he had 714 sheep under his control while Rogan had only 330. Furthermore, Argon stated that he had increased his land holdings to 27 acres. The 7-acre increase resulted from two transactions: First, on the day that the contest started, Argon used 20 sheep to buy 10 additional acres; and second, he sold 3 of these acres for a total of 9 sheep on the day of reckoning. Also, Argon's flock had produced 75 newborn sheep during the period of accounting. He had been able to give his friends 50 sheep in return for the help that they had given him in building a fence, thereby increasing not only his own wealth but the wealth of his neighbors as well. Argon boasted that the fence was strong and would keep his herd safe from predatory creatures for 5 years (assume the fence had been used for 1 year during the contest period). Rogan countered that Argon was holding 400 sheep that belonged to another herder. Argon had borrowed these sheep on the day that the contest had started. Furthermore, Argon had agreed to return 424 sheep to the herder. The 24 additional sheep represented consideration for the use of the herder's flock. Argon had agreed to return the sheep immediately after the day of reckoning.

During the test period, Rogan's flock had produced 37 newborn sheep, but 2 sheep had gotten sick and died during the accounting period. Rogan had also lost 5 sheep to predatory creatures. He had no fence, and some of his sheep strayed from the herd, thereby exposing themselves to danger. Knowing that he was falling behind, Rogan had taken a wife in order to boost his productivity. His wife owned 170 sheep on the day they were married; her sheep had produced 16 newborn sheep since the date of her marriage to Rogan. Argon had not included the wife's sheep in his count of Rogan's herd. If his wife's sheep had been counted, Rogan's herd would contain 516 instead of 330 sheep suggested by Argon's count.

Argon charged that 7 of Rogan's sheep were sick with symptoms similar to those exhibited by the 2 sheep that were now dead. Rogan interjected that he should not be held accountable for acts of nature such as illness. Furthermore, he contended that by isolating the sick sheep from the remainder of the herd, he had demonstrated prudent management practices that supported his case to be designated first heir.

Required

a. Prepare an income statement, balance sheet, statement of sheep flow (i.e., cash flow) for each twin, using contemporary (2000) accounting standards. Note that you have to decide whether to include the sheep owned by Rogan's wife when making his financial statements (i.e., what is the accounting entity?). (*Hint:* Use the number of sheep rather than the number of dollars as the common unit of measure.)

b. Refer to the statements you prepared in part *a* to answer the following questions:
   (1)   Which twin has more owner's equity at the end of the accounting period?
   (2)   Which twin produced the higher net income during the accounting period?
   (3)   Which son should be designated heir based on conventional accounting and reporting standards?

c. What is the difference in the value of the land of the twins if the land is valued at market value (that is, 3 sheep per acre) rather than historical cost (that is, 2 sheep per acre)?

d. Did Argon's decision to borrow sheep increase his profitability? Support your answer with appropriate financial data.

e. Was Argon's decision to build a fence financially prudent? Support your answer with appropriate financial data.

f. Assuming that the loan resulted in a financial benefit to Argon, think of some reasons why the shepherd who owned the sheep may have been willing to loan them to Argon.

g. Which twin is likely to take risks to improve profitability? What would be the financial condition of each twin if one-half of the sheep in both flocks died as a result of illness? How should such risk factors be reported in financial statements?

h. Should Rogan's decision to "marry for sheep" be considered from an ethical perspective, or should the decision be made solely on the basis of the bottom-line net income figure?

i. Prepare a report that recommends which twin should be designated heir to the family business. Include a set of financial statements that support your recommendation. Since this is a managerial report that will not be distributed to the public, you are not bound by generally accepted accounting principles.

ACT 4-8   **EDGAR DATABASE**   **Investigating Nike's 10-k report**

As explained in this chapter, many companies must file financial reports with the SEC. Many of these reports are available electronically through the EDGAR database. EDGAR is an acronym for Electronic Data Gathering, Analysis, and Retrieval system and it is accessible through the World Wide Web on the Internet. Instructions for using EDGAR are in Appendix A.

   Using the most current 10-K available on EDGAR, answer the following questions about Nike.

a. In what year did Nike begin operations?

b. Other than athletic shoes and clothing, what business does Nike operated.

c. How many employees does Nike have?

d. Describe, in dollar amounts, Nike's accounting equation at the end of the most recent year.

e. Has Nike's performance been improving or deteriorating over the past three years? Explain the rationale for your answer.

SPREADSHEET ASSIGNMENT   **Use of Excel**   ACT 4-9

Adams Company started operations on January 1, 20X0. Six months later on June 30, 20X0, the company decided to prepare financial statements. The Adams Company's accountant decided to problem solve for the adjusting journal entries and the final adjusted account balances by using an electronic spreadsheet. Once the spreadsheet is complete, she will record the adjusting entries in the general journal and post to the ledger. The accountant has started the following spreadsheet but wants you to finish it for her.

Required

a. On a blank spreadsheet, enter the following trial balance in columns A through C. Also enter the headings for columns E through I.

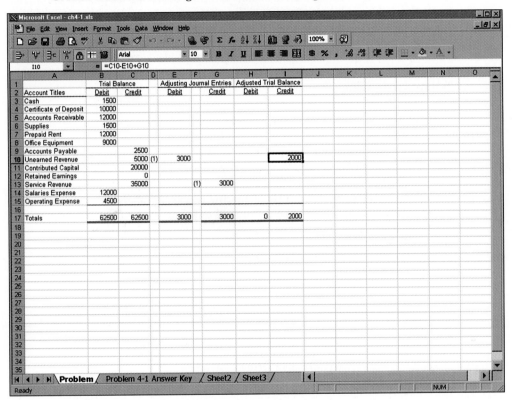

b. Each of the following events requires an adjusting journal entry. Instead of recording entries in general journal format, record the adjusting entries in the Debit and Credit columns under the heading Adjusting Journal Entries. Entry (1) has already been recorded as an example. Be sure to number your adjusting entries on the spreadsheet. It will be necessary to insert new accounts for the adjustments. Recall that the accounting period is for 6 months.

(1) Received a $5,000 cash advance on April 1 for a contract to provide 5 months of service.

(2) Had accrued salaries on June 30 amounting to $1,500.

(3) On January 1 invested in a 1-year, $10,000 certificate of deposit that carried a 5% interest rate.

(4) On January 1 paid $12,000 in advance for a 1-year lease on office space.

(5) Received in the mail a utility bill dated June 30 for $150.

(6) Purchased $1,500 of supplies on January 1. As of June 30, $700 of supplies remained on hand.

(7) Paid $9,000 for office equipment on January 1. The equipment was expected to have a 4-year expected life and a $1,000 salvage value. Depreciation is computed on a straight-line basis.

c. Develop formulas to sum both the Debit and Credit columns under the Adjusting Journal Entries heading.

d. Develop formulas to derive the adjusted balances for the Adjusted Trial Balance. For example, the formula for the ending balance of Unearned Revenue is =C10-E10+G10. In other words, a credit balance minus debit entries plus credit entries equals the ending balance. Once an ending balance is formulated for one credit account, that formula can be copied to all other credit accounts; the same is true for debit accounts. Once an ending balance is formulated for a debit account, that formula can be copied to all other debit accounts.

e. Develop formulas to sum both the Debit and Credit columns under the Adjusted Trial Balance heading.

Spreadsheet Tips

1. Rows and columns can be inserted by positioning the mouse on the immediate row or column after the desired position. Click on the *right* mouse button. With the *left* mouse button, choose Insert and then either Entire Column or Entire Row. Use the same method to delete columns or rows.

2. Enter the sequential numbering of the adjusting entries as labels rather than values by positioning an apostrophe in front of each entry. The first adjusting entry should be labeled '(1).

SPREADSHEET ASSIGNMENT   **Mastery of Excel**

At the end of the accounting period, Adams Company's general ledger contained the following adjusted balances.

Account Titles	Adjusted Trial Balance Debit	Credit	Closing Entries Debit	Credit	Ending Trial Balance Debit	Credit
Cash	1500					
Certificate of Deposit	10000					
Interest Receivable	250					
Accounts Receivable	12000					
Supplies	700					
Prepaid Rent	6000					
Office Equipment	9000					
Accumulated Depreciation		1000				
Accounts Payable		2650				
Salaries Payable		1500				
Unearned Revenue		2000				
Contributed Capital		20000				
Retained Earnings		0				
Service Revenue		36000				
Interest Revenue		250				
Salaries Expense	13500					
Rent Expense	6000					
Utilities Expense	150					
Supplies Expense	800					
Depreciation Expense	1000					
Operating Expense	4500					
Totals	65400	65400				

Required

a. Set up the preceding spreadsheet format. (The spreadsheet tips for ACT 4-8 also apply for this problem.)

b. Record the closing entries in the Closing Entries column of the spreadsheet.

c. Compute the Ending Trial Balance amounts.

5 Accounting for Merchandising Business

LEARNING OBJECTIVES
AFTER COMPLETING THIS CHAPTER, YOU SHOULD BE ABLE TO:

1 Distinguish between service and merchandising businesses.

2 Distinguish between product costs and selling and administrative costs.

3 Understand how product costs affect financial statements.

4 Compare and contrast the perpetual and periodic inventory methods.

5 Understand the primary features of the perpetual inventory system.

6 Explain the meaning of terms used to describe transportation costs, cash discounts, and returns or allowances.

7 Compare and contrast single- and multistep income statements.

8 Understand the primary features of the periodic inventory system.

9 Understand how lost, damaged, or stolen inventory affects financial statements.

10 Use common size financial statements to evaluate managerial performance.

11 Use ratio analysis to evaluate managerial performance.

12 Understand the cost of financing inventory.

Associated Press AP CULPERPER
STAR-EXPONENT

Previous illustrations and problems assumed that businesses generated revenue by providing services to their customers. Another large form of business activity generates revenue by selling goods to customers. Companies that sell goods normally accumulate a supply of those goods that is used for delivery when sales are made. This supply is called **inventory.**

Inventory includes goods that are in the process of being made (i.e., unfinished goods) as well as goods that are finished and ready for sale. For example, unprocessed lumber, partially assembled tables, and finished goods stored in a warehouse would all be included in the inventory of a furniture manufacturer. The term *inventory* also describes stockpiles of goods that are used indirectly in the process of selling merchandise or providing services, such as supplies, stamps, stationery, cleaning materials, and so on.

At this point, it is helpful to note that many businesses concentrate on the resale of finished goods. These businesses buy merchandise from a supplier and resell that merchandise to their customers. When the merchandise is resold, it is essentially in the same condition as it was when it was purchased from the supplier. Finished goods held for resale are commonly called **merchandise inventory.** Companies that buy and sell merchandise inventory are called **merchandising businesses.** Merchandising businesses include **retail companies** (companies that sell goods to the final consumer) and **wholesale companies** (companies that sell to other businesses.) Businesses that concentrate on the resale of goods include Sears Roebuck and Co., JC Penney, Sam's Clubs, and National Tire Wholesale (NTW).

L.O. 1

Distinguish between service and merchandising businesses.

L.O. 2

Distinguish between product costs and selling and administrative costs.

Product Costs Versus Selling and Administrative Costs

Inventory costs are capitalized in (i.e., accumulated in) the Merchandise Inventory account and shown as an asset on the balance sheet. Any cost incurred to acquire goods or to make them ready for sale should be accumulated in the Inventory account. Examples of inventory costs incurred by merchandising companies include the price of goods purchased, transportation or packaging costs associated with obtaining merchandise, storage costs, and transit insurance. Note that all these costs are associated with products. As a result, inventory costs are frequently referred to as **product costs.** Costs that cannot be directly traced to products are usually classified as **selling and administrative costs.** Typical examples of selling and administrative costs include advertising, administrative salaries, insurance, and interest. Since selling and administrative costs are usually recognized as expenses *in the period* in which they are incurred, they are sometimes called **period costs.** Product costs are expensed when the inventory is sold regardless of when it was purchased. In other words, you may buy products in one period and expense them in a different period.

Allocation of Inventory Cost between Asset and Expense Accounts

L.O. 3

Understand how product costs affect financial statements.

The total inventory cost for any given accounting period is determined by adding the cost of inventory on hand at the beginning of the period to the cost of inventory purchased during the period. The total cost (i.e., beginning inventory plus purchases) is called the **cost of goods available for sale.** The cost of goods available for sale is allocated between an asset account called *Merchandise Inventory* and an expense account called *Cost of Goods Sold.* The cost of the items that have not been sold (i.e., merchandise inventory) is shown as an asset on the balance sheet, and the cost of the items sold (i.e., **cost of goods sold**) is expensed on the income statement. The difference between the sales revenue and the cost of goods sold is called the **gross margin.** The selling and administrative expenses (i.e., period costs) are subtracted from the gross margin to obtain the net income.

Exhibit 5–1 contains income statements drawn from the annual reports of Nordstrom, Inc., and Estee Lauder, Inc. For each company, review the most current income statement and determine the amount of gross margin. The gross

EXHIBIT 5–1

NORDSTROM, INC., AND SUBSIDIARIES
Consolidated Statements of Earnings
Year Ended January 31,
(dollars in thousands)

	1998	1997	1996
Net Sales	$4,851,624	$4,453,063	$4,113,517
Costs and Expenses			
Cost of Sales and Related Buying and Occupancy	3,295,813	3,082,037	2,806,250
Selling, General, and Administrative	1,322,929	1,217,590	1,120,790
Interest, net	34,250	39,400	39,295
Service Charge Income and Other, net	(108,581)	(129,469)	(125,130)
Total Costs and Expenses	4,544,411	4,209,558	3,841,205
Earnings before Income Taxes	307,213	243,505	272,312
Income Taxes	121,000	96,000	107,200
Net Earnings	$186,213	$147,505	$165,112

THE ESTEE LAUDER COMPANIES INC.
Consolidated Statements of Earnings
(dollars in millions)

	Year Ended June 30		
	1997	1996	1995
Net Sales	$3,381.6	$3,194.5	$2,899.1
Cost of Sales	765.1	731.0	674.8
Gross Profit	2,616.5	2,463.5	2,224.3
Selling, General, and Administrative Expenses			
Selling, General, and Administrative	2,224.6	2,116.0	1,957.7
Related-Party Royalties (Note 1)	32.8	37.2	35.7
	2,257.4	2,153.2	1,993.4
Operating Income	359.1	310.3	230.9
Interest Income (expense), net			
Interest Income (expense), net	3.8	—	(2.8)
Interest Income from Stockholders, net	—	2.7	4.9
	3.8	2.7	2.1
Earnings before Income Taxes and Minority Interest	362.9	313.0	233.0
Provision for Income Taxes (Note 5)	152.4	138.3	108.0
Minority Interest (Note 3)	12.9	14.3	3.8
Net Earnings	$ 197.6	$ 160.4	$ 121.2

margin for Nordstrom must be computed. Using data from the 1998 income statement, we determine gross margin to be $1,555.8 million (that is, $4,851.6 in sales − $3,295.8 in cost of goods sold). No computation is necessary to determine the amount of the gross margin (gross profit) for Estee Lauder because its report includes the computation directly in its income statement. Estee Lauder's 1997 income statement shows a gross profit (i.e., a gross margin) of $2,616.5 million.

The following illustration demonstrates the accounting treatment of product costs in a merchandising business. June Gardener was appropriately named. She loved plants, and they grew for her as they did for no one else. At the encouragement of her friends, Gardener decided to start a small retail plant store. She started the business on January 1, 20X1, with $4,000 of her own plants. In addition, $11,000 in cash was contributed by several friends, who along with Gardener became owners of the company. The company was named June's Plant Shop (JPS). During the first year of operation, the company purchased additional plant inventory that cost $10,000. Plants costing $8,000 were sold for $12,000. Finally, the company incurred selling expenses of $1,000 during the period. All sales, purchases, and payments of expenses were made with cash.

Exhibit 5–2 outlines the effects of these transactions on the financial statements for JPS. Note that the $4,000 of beginning inventory plus the $10,000 of purchases results in a cost of goods available for sale of $14,000. This cost is allocated between the income statement and balance sheet. Specifically, $14,000 of total cost is allocated to (1) cost of goods sold ($8,000), which appears on the income statement, and (2) merchandise inventory ($6,000), which appears on the balance sheet. The $6,000 of product cost in ending inventory will be expensed in the period in which the remaining plants are sold. The beginning cash balance of $11,000 was spent for $10,000 of product cost and $1,000 of selling expenses. The $12,000 ending cash balance resulted from cash inflows from customers (i.e., revenue). Finally, equity increased by $3,000, which represented the increase in retained earnings resulting from the net earnings. The $15,000 of contributed capital was unchanged.

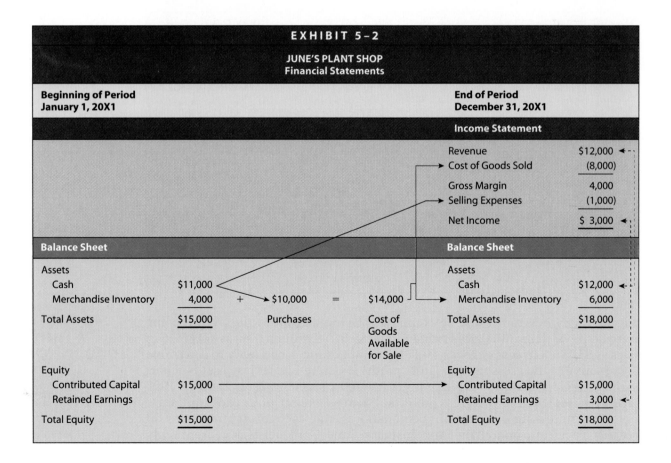

Inventory Cost Recorded

Inventories are accounted for under either the perpetual or the periodic method. The **perpetual inventory method** derives its name from the fact that the balance in the Inventory account is adjusted perpetually. Each time merchandise is purchased, the Inventory account is increased; each time it is sold, the Inventory account is decreased. In contrast, the **periodic inventory method** adjusts the Inventory balance only at the end of the accounting period. The Inventory account is unaffected by purchases or sales of inventory during the period. Note that the two methods represent alternative procedures for reporting the same information. The amount of cost of goods sold and ending inventory reported on the financial statements will be the same regardless of whether the perpetual or periodic procedures are applied.

> **L.O. 4**
> Compare and contrast the perpetual and the periodic inventory methods.

The chief advantage of the periodic method is recording efficiency. Recording inventory transactions occasionally (i.e., periodically) requires less work than recording them on a continuous basis (i.e., perpetually). Think of the number of transactions that a typical grocery store would have to record every business day under a perpetual system. The recording advantage of the periodic system must be weighed against the control advantage inherent in the perpetual system. Since the perpetual system increases and decreases the Inventory account balance when purchases and sales are made, the book balance of inventory should agree with the amount of inventory in stock at any given time. Accordingly, the amount of lost, damaged, destroyed, or stolen inventory can be determined by checking the book balance against a physical count of inventory. Also, reorder decisions and profitability assessments are facilitated by the availability of immediate feedback.

Fortunately, the advent of computer technology has removed most of the practical constraints associated with recording inventory transactions on a continual basis. Electronic scanners can capture accounting information rapidly and efficiently. Computer programs that access the data captured by the scanners can

©Paul Shambroom/ Photo Researchers

update the accounting records instantaneously. As a result, the use of the perpetual inventory system has increased rapidly in recent years. Continued growth in the application of the perpetual method can be expected as technology advances. Accordingly, this book concentrates on the perpetual inventory method.

Perpetual Inventory Method

L.O. 5

Understand the primary features of the perpetual inventory system.

The following section demonstrates the application of the perpetual inventory method by analyzing the accounting events for JPS's 20X1 fiscal year. The five distinct accounting events are as follows:

1. The business acquired $4,000 of plants from the primary owner.
2. The business acquired $11,000 cash from other owners.
3. A $10,000 cash purchase of inventory was made.
4. Inventory that cost $8,000 sold for $12,000 cash.
5. A $1,000 cash payment was made for selling expenses.

Effect of Events on Financial Statements

Exhibit 5–3 shows the effect of each event on the financial statements. Try to anticipate the effect of each event before you look at the exhibit. For example, the first event involves an owner's contribution of plants to the business. Ask yourself how this event will affect the balance sheet, income statement, and statement of cash flows. Then check your answer by looking at Exhibit 5–3. Continue this type of active inquiry throughout the chapter. The learning process is easier if you become actively involved with the material. To facilitate the tracing of events in the exhibits, the transaction data are referenced by the event numbers.

Acquired $4,000 of Plants from June Gardener

Event 1
Capital Acquisition

The acquisition of personal property (i.e., plants) from the owner is an asset source transaction. With respect to the balance sheet, the event acts to increase assets (i.e., Inventory) and equity (i.e. Contributed Capital). This event illustrates the fact that businesses can acquire different types of property from their owners. Indeed, a business can even acquire services from its owners. For example, ownership rights are frequently granted to attorneys who contribute services rather than cash toward the establishment of a business. Regardless of the type of asset or services acquired from owners, capital acquisitions do not affect the income statement. Since the business acquired plants instead of cash, the statement of cash flows is not affected by the capital acquisition.

Acquired $11,000 Cash from Other Owners

Event 2
Capital Acquisition

This event is also an asset source transaction. The $11,000 acquisition of cash acts to increase assets (i.e., Cash) and equity (i.e., Contributed Capital). The income statement is not affected. The statement of cash flows shows an $11,000 cash inflow from financing activities.

Paid $10,000 Cash to Purchase Inventory

Event 3
Inventory Purchase

The Merchandise Inventory account is increased when goods are purchased. Since cash is used to purchase the goods, the purchase constitutes an asset exchange. The asset account, *Cash*, decreases and the asset account, *Merchandise Inventory*,

EXHIBIT 5-3										
Effect of Events on Financial Statements										
Business Events		Balance Sheet					Income Statement			Cash Statement
Event No.	Description	Cash +	Inv. =	Cont. Cap. +	Ret. Earn.		Rev. –	Exp. =	Net Inc.	Cash Flow
1	Capital Acquisition	n/a +	4,000 =	4,000 +	n/a		n/a –	n/a =	n/a	n/a
2	Capital Acquisition	11,000 +	n/a =	11,000 +	n/a		n/a –	n/a =	n/a	11,000 FA
3	Inventory Purchase	(10,000) +	10,000 =	n/a +	n/a		n/a –	n/a =	n/a	(10,000) OA
4(a)	Sale of Inventory	12,000 +	n/a =	n/a +	12,000		12,000 –	n/a =	12,000	12,000 OA
4(b)	Cost of Goods Sold	n/a +	(8,000) =	n/a +	(8,000)		n/a –	8,000 =	(8,000)	n/a
5	Selling Expenses	(1,000) +	n/a =	n/a +	(1,000)		n/a –	1,000 =	(1,000)	(1,000) OA
	Totals	12,000 +	6,000 =	15,000 +	3,000		12,000 –	9,000 =	3,000	12,000 NC

increases; the total amount of assets is unchanged. The income statement is not affected by this event. Remember that product costs are expensed when the goods are sold, not when they are purchased. However, the $10,000 cash outflow is shown in the operating activities section of the statement of cash flows. Notice that spending cash does not constitute an expense. As you will see in the discussion of the following event, using (i.e., selling) the inventory will trigger the expense recognition.

Sold Inventory Costing $8,000 for $12,000 Cash

This event is composed of two transactions. The *first transaction* (4a in the exhibit) is an asset source transaction (i.e., cash is required by generating revenue). As with other revenue transactions, *sales transactions* act to increase assets (i.e., cash) and equity (i.e., retained earnings). The sales revenue acts to increase net income on the income statement. Also, the $12,000 cash inflow from the sale is shown in the operating activities section of the statement of cash flows.

Event 4
Sale of Inventory

The *second transaction* (4b in the exhibit) is an asset use transaction. An expense (cost of goods sold) is recognized because the asset, inventory, was used to produce the sales revenue. Accordingly, $8,000 of cost must be transferred from the asset account, *Merchandise Inventory,* to the expense account, *Cost of Goods Sold.* The effect on the balance sheet is to reduce assets (i.e., Inventory) and equity (i.e., Retained Earnings). On the income statement, the expense, cost of goods sold, will act to reduce net income. This event does not affect the statement of cash flows. The case outflow occurred when the goods were bought, not when they were sold.

Paid $1,000 Cash for Selling Expenses

This event is an asset use transaction. The payment acts to decrease assets (i.e., Cash) and equity (i.e., Retained Earnings). The increase in selling expenses decreases net income. The $1,000 cash outflow is shown in the operating activities section of the statement of cash flows.

Event 5
Paid Selling Expenses

Journal Entries and Ledger T-Accounts

Exhibit 5–4 shows the general journal entries for each of the events and the required closing entry. The closing entry, which is designated by the initials "CL," is necessary to transfer the balances in the revenue and expense accounts to the

	EXHIBIT 5-4		
	General Journal Entries		
Event No.	**Account Title**	**Debit**	**Credit**
1	Inventory	4,000	
	Contributed Capital		4,000
2	Cash	11,000	
	Contributed Capital		11,000
3	Inventory	10,000	
	Cash		10,000
4(a)	Cash	12,000	
	Sales Revenue		12,000
4(b)	Cost of Goods Sold	8,000	
	Inventory		8,000
5	Selling Expenses	1,000	
	Cash		1,000
CL	Sales Revenue	12,000	
	Cost of Goods Sold		8,000
	Selling Expenses		1,000
	Retained Earnings		3,000

Retained Earnings account. The closing entry is an equity exchange transaction, with some equity accounts decreasing while others increase. The amount of total equity is not affected by the closing entry.

Exhibit 5–5 is the ledger T-accounts. The accounting events have been posted from the general journal into these ledger accounts. The ledger account balances are used to prepare the financial statements shown in Exhibit 5–2. To confirm your understanding of the accounting process, trace the ledger account balances to the financial statements.

Other Events Affecting Purchases and Sales of Inventory

Three other accounting events frequently affect inventory transactions: (1) incurring transportation costs, (2) making or accepting returns or allowance, and (3) receiving or granting cash discounts. The effects of these events are demonstrated through an analysis of the operating activities of JPS during its second accounting cycle. The closing balances for the 20X1 fiscal year became the opening balances for the 20X2 fiscal year. Accordingly, the beginning balances are as follows: Cash of $12,000, Inventory of $6,000, Contributed Capital of $15,000, and Retained Earnings of $3,000. Fourteen events are introduced. Exhibit 5–6 shows the effect of each event on the financial statements. Read about each event, anticipate how it will appear in the exhibit, and then check yourself by looking at the exhibit.

Effect of Events on Financial Statements

Purchased $8,000 of Merchandise Inventory on Account

Event 1
Inventory Purchase
The effect of the purchase on the balance sheet is to increase assets (i.e., Inventory) and liabilities (i.e., Accounts Payable). The income statement is not affected

EXHIBIT 5–5					
General Ledger					

Assets	**=**	**Liabilities**	**+**	**Equity**

Cash			**Liabilities**		**Contributed Capital**	
(2)	11,000	10,000	(3)	0 Bal.	4,000	(1)
(4a)	12,000	1,000	(5)		11,000	(2)
Bal.	12,000				15,000	Bal.

Inventory				**Retained Earnings**	
(1)	4,000	8,000	(4b)	3,000	(cl.)
(3)	10,000			3,000	Bal.
Bal.	6,000				

Sales Revenue			
(cl.)	12,000	12,000	(4a)
		0	Bal.

Cost of Goods Sold			
(4b)	8,000	8,000	(cl.)
Bal.	0		

Selling Expense			
(5)	1,000	1,000	(cl.)
Bal.	0		

by this event. Revenue and expense recognition occurs at the point of sale rather than at the time of purchase. Since the goods were purchased on account, cash flow was not affected.

Paid $300 Cash for Freight Cost Required to Obtain Goods Purchased in Event No. 1

The party responsible for transportation costs is designated by the terms **FOB shipping point** and **FOB destination.** The term *FOB* means *free on board* at the shipping and destination points, respectively. An easy way to interpret the terms is to note that the seller's responsibility ends at the point designated in the term. If goods are shipped FOB shipping point, then the seller's responsibility ends at the point of shipment and the buyer must pay the freight costs. On the other hand, if goods are shipped FOB destination, the seller remains responsible for the transportation costs.

Event 2
Transportation-in

The cost of freight on goods purchased under terms FOB shipping point is called **transportation-in** or **freight-in.** Since transportation costs are a necessary part of obtaining inventory, they are added to (i.e., capitalized in) the Inventory account. Assuming that the goods purchased in Event No. 1 were delivered under terms FOB shipping point, the buyer (JPS) is responsible for the freight. Accordingly, the freight costs act to increase the balance in the Inventory account and decrease the balance of cash. The income statement is not affected by this transaction. Since the freight costs are included in the Inventory account, they will be expensed as part of *costs of goods sold* when the inventory is sold to customers,

EXHIBIT 5-6

Effect of Events on Financial Statements

Business Events			Balance Sheet							Income Statement			Statement of Cash Flows
		Assets			=	Liabilities	+	Equity					
Event No.	Description	Cash	Accts. Rec.	Inventory	=	Accts. Pay	Note Pay.	Cont. Capital	Ret. Earn.	Rev. −	Exp. =	Net Inc.	Cash Flows
	Beginning Balances	12,000	0	6,000	=	0	0	15,000	3,000	n/a	n/a	n/a	n/a
1	Inventory Purchase	n/a	n/a	8,000	=	8,000	n/a	n/a	n/a	n/a	n/a	n/a	n/a
2	Transportation-in	(300)	n/a	300	=	n/a	n/a	n/a	n/a	n/a	n/a	n/a	(300) OA
3	Purchase Return	n/a	n/a	(1,000)	=	(1,000)	n/a	n/a	n/a	n/a	n/a	n/a	n/a
4(a)	Purchase Discount	n/a	n/a	(140)	=	(140)	n/a	n/a	n/a	n/a	n/a	n/a	n/a
4(b)	Payment of Acct. Pay.	(6,860)	n/a	n/a	=	(6,860)	n/a	n/a	n/a	n/a	n/a	n/a	(6,860) OA
5	Issue Note Payable	5,000	n/a	n/a	=	n/a	5,000	n/a	n/a	n/a	n/a	n/a	5,000 FA
6(a)	Sale of Inventory	n/a	26,200	n/a	=	n/a	n/a	n/a	26,200	26,200	n/a	26,200	n/a
6(b)	Cost of Sale	n/a	n/a	(12,300)	=	n/a	n/a	n/a	(12,300)	n/a	12,300	(12,300)	n/a
7	Transportaton-out	(450)	n/a	n/a	=	n/a	n/a	n/a	(450)	n/a	450	(450)	(450) OA
8(a)	Sales Return	n/a	(1,200)	n/a	=	n/a	n/a	n/a	(1,200)	(1,200)	n/a	(1,200)	n/a
8(b)	Cost of Goods Sold	n/a	n/a	800	=	n/a	n/a	n/a	800	n/a	(800)	800	n/a
9(a)	Sales Discount	n/a	(250)	n/a	=	n/a	n/a	n/a	(250)	(250)	n/a	(250)	n/a
9(b)	Receivable Collection	24,750	(24,750)	n/a	=	n/a	n/a	n/a	n/a	n/a	n/a	n/a	24,750 OA
10	Inventory Purchase	n/a	n/a	14,000	=	14,000	n/a	n/a	n/a	n/a	n/a	n/a	n/a
11(a)	Interest Payment	(250)	n/a	n/a	=	n/a	n/a	n/a	(250)	n/a	250	(250)	(250) OA
11(b)	Principal Payment	(5,000)	n/a	n/a	=	n/a	(5,000)	n/a	n/a	n/a	n/a	n/a	(5,000) FA
12(a)	Sale of Inventory	n/a	16,800	n/a	=	n/a	n/a	n/a	16,800	16,800	n/a	16,800	n/a
12(b)	Cost of Goods Sold	n/a	n/a	(8,660)	=	n/a	n/a	n/a	(8,660)	n/a	8,660	(8,660)	n/a
13	Payment of Acct. Pay.	(7,000)	n/a	n/a	=	(7,000)	n/a	n/a	n/a	n/a	n/a	n/a	(7,000) OA
14	Selling and Admin. Exp.	(8,000)	n/a	n/a	=	n/a	n/a	n/a	(8,000)	n/a	8,000	(8,000)	(8,000) OA
	Totals	13,890 +	16,800 +	7,000	=	7,000 +	0 +	15,000 +	15,690	41,550 −	28,860 =	12,690	1,890 NC

not when it is delivered to JPS. However, the cash paid for freight at the time of delivery is shown as an outflow in the operating activities section of the statement of cash flows.

Returned $1,000 of Goods Purchased in Event No. 1

"Satisfaction or your money back" is a prevalent business promised in today's economy. Goods may be returned because the buyer becomes dissatisfied with the size, color, design, and so on, of the product. It is sometimes advantageous to appease the dissatisfactions of the buyer by negotiating a reduction in the selling price of certain goods instead of accepting a return of the goods. Such reductions are referred to as **allowances** and are frequently granted to buyers who receive defective goods or goods that are of a lower quality than the customer ordered. Recall that the Inventory account is increased when goods are purchased. The reverse applies when goods are returned. Similarly, reductions in price due to allowances provided by the supplier act to reduce the balance in the Inventory account. In the case of JPS, the $1,000 purchase return acts to decrease assets (i.e., Inventory) and liabilities (i.e., Accounts Payable). The income statement and the statement of cash flows are not affected.

Event 3
Purchase Returns and Allowances

Received Cash Discount on Goods Purchased in Event No. 1

Assume that the goods were purchased under terms 2/10, n/30. The terms **2/10, n/30** mean that the seller will give the purchaser a 2% discount on the gross invoice price if the purchaser pays cash for the merchandise within 10 days from the date of purchase. The amount not paid within the first 10 days is due at the end of 30 days from the date of purchase. **Cash discounts** are extended to encourage prompt payment. Assuming that JPS pays for the goods within the discount period, the company will receive a $140 purchase discount (i.e., original cost of $8,000 − purchase return of $1,000 = $7,000 balance due × 2% discount = $140). The discount acts to reduce the cost of the inventory and thereby lowers the amount due on the account payable. Accordingly, the **purchase discount** reduces the asset account, *Inventory,* and the liability account, *Accounts Payable.* Recall that product costs are expensed at the time inventory is sold. Since the purchase discount occurs prior to the point of sale, it does not affect the income statement. Although the purchase discount will affect future cash flows, there is no immediate impact. As a result, the discount event does not affect the statement of cash flows.

Event 4a
Purchase Discounts

Paid Remaining Balance of $6,860 Due on Account Payable

The effect of the payment on the balance sheet is to reduce assets (i.e., Cash) and liabilities (i.e., Accounts Payable). The event does not affect the income statement. However, the $6,860 ($7,000 − $140) cash outflow is shown in the operating activities section of the statement of cash flows.

Event 4b
Payment of Account Payable

Borrowed $5,000 from State Bank

JPS issued an interest-bearing note with a 6-month term and a 10% annual interest rate. The borrowing event increased assets (i.e., Cash) and liabilities (i.e., Notes Payable). The income statement is not affected. The $5,000 inflow is classified as a financing activity on the statement of cash flows.

Event 5
Issue Note Payable

Recognized $26,200 of Revenue on Sale of Merchandise That Cost $12,300

Event 6a
Sale of Inventory

The merchandise was sold on account. The sale acts to increase assets (i.e., Accounts Receivable) and equity (i.e., Retained Earnings). The revenue recognition causes the net income to increase. Since the sale was made on account, cash flow is not affected.

Recognized $12,300 of Cost of Goods Sold

Event 6b
Cost of Sale

Recall that at the time goods are sold, the product cost—*including a proportionate share of transportation-in and adjustments for purchases returns and allowances*—is taken out of the Merchandise Inventory account and placed into the Cost of Goods Sold expense account. Accordingly, the recognition of the cost of goods sold acts to decrease assets (i.e., Inventory) and equity (i.e., Retained Earnings). The expense recognition for cost of goods sold causes the net income to decrease. Cash flow is not affected.

Incurred $450 of Freight Costs on Goods Delivered to Customers

Event 7
Transportation-out

Assume that the merchandise sold in Event No. 6 was delivered under terms FOB destination. The freight cost of $450 was paid in cash. Recall that FOB destination means that the seller is responsible for the merchandise until it reaches its destination. Accordingly, JPS is responsible for the freight costs in this case. If the seller is responsible for the freight costs, then the cost is considered to be an operating expense that is shown after the computation of gross margin on the income statements. This treatment is logical because the cost of freight on goods delivered to customers is incurred *after* the goods are sold and, therefore, cannot be considered as part of the costs of obtaining goods or making them ready for sale. The freight cost for goods delivered to customers under terms of FOB destination is called **transportation-out** or **freight-out.** When paid in cash, transportation-out is an expense that reduces assets (i.e., Cash) and equity (i.e., Retained Earnings). The event acts to increase operating expenses and thereby reduces net income. The $450 cash outflow is shown in the operating activities section of the statement of cash flows.

Accepted Return of $1,200 of Goods Sold in Event No. 6. The Cost of These Goods to JPS Was $800

Event 8a
Sales Return

Occasionally, it is necessary to adjust the amount of sales because customers *return* merchandise that they have purchased. It may also be necessary to adjust the sales account when customers are given allowances (i.e., price reductions) for damaged or defective goods. Sales that have been reduced to reflect returns and/or allowances are called **net sales.** The amount of net sales is reported on the income statement.[1] The sales return has a twofold effect. The first is the reversal of the

---

[1]For the purpose of internal decision making, many companies record sales returns and allowances in separate contra accounts instead of making a direct adjustment to the Sales account. Maintaining separate accounts enables managers to compare the current levels of returns and allowances with those of prior periods or with industry norms. If the amount of returns and allowances is inconsistent with expectations, management can take corrective action by changing the company's refund policies.

revenue recognition that was made when the goods were sold. This event acts to reduce assets (i.e., Accounts Receivable) and equity (i.e., Retained Earnings). The reduction in sales revenue acts to decrease the amount of net income. Since credit was given on accounts receivable, cash flow is not affected.

Added the $800 of Returned Merchandise Back to Inventory

The second dimension of the sales return is the reversal of the recognition of the cost of goods sold expense for the $800 cost of merchandise that has been returned. In this case, assets increase when the returned goods are added back to the Inventory account. Also, the Retained Earnings account increases when the cost of merchandise is removed from the Cost of Goods Sold expense account, thereby increasing net income. Cash flow is not affected.

Event 8b
Add Back Cost of Return to Inventory

Provided Cash Discount on Goods Sold in Event No. 6

Assume the goods were sold under credit terms 1/10, n/30. Also assume JPS collected the receivable within the discount period. Since the purchaser paid within the discount period, JPS grants a $250 cash discount ($26,200 account receivable − $1,200 reduction due to sales return = $25,000 × 0.01 = $250). The discount will reduce the amount of the receivable due to JPS. Also, the net amount of sales is $250 less than the original sale.[2] Accordingly, the discount reduces assets and equity. The decrease in net sales acts to reduce the amount of net income. Cash flow is not affected. A cash discount that is extended by the seller is frequently called a **sales discount.**

Event 9a
Sales Discount

Collected Balance Due on Account Receivable Generated in Event No. 6

After we take the sales return and the sales discount into account, the remaining balance in Accounts Receivable due from the merchandise sold in Event No. 6 is $24,750 ($26,200 gross sale − $1,200 sales return − $250 sales discount). The collection of this receivable increases the asset, Cash, and decreases the asset, Accounts Receivable. Total assets are unaffected The income statement is not affected by the collection of the receivable. However, the $24,750 cash inflow is shown in the operating activities section of the statement of cash flows.

Event 9b
Collection of Account Receivable

Purchased $14,000 of Merchandise Inventory under Credit Terms 2/10, n/30

The goods were shipped under freight terms FOB destination. Freight costs of $400 were paid in cash by the party responsible for the freight costs. *Since the freight terms are FOB destination, the seller is responsible, and JPS' accounts are not affected.* Accordingly, Merchandise Inventory and Accounts Payable will increase by $14,000. Net income and cash flow are not affected.

Event 10
Inventory Purchase

---

[2]As with sales returns and allowances, many companies record sales discounts in a separate contra account. While discounts are not reported separately in the income statement, knowledge of the extent to which customers are taking advantage of discount offerings is important for internal decision-making purposes, such as deciding whether the discount is too small to motivate prompt payment.

Paid Interest on Funds Borrowed in Event No. 5

Event 11a
Interest Payment

Assume that the 6-month term on the note issued in Event No. 5 has expired. Settling the liability is a two-step process. First, determine the amount of interest expense and pay this amount to the bank. Recall that the face value was $5,000, the term 6 months, and the interest rate 10% per year. Accordingly, the amount of interest expense is $250 ($5,000 × 0.10 × $\frac{6}{12}$). Since the term has expired, the interest is payable in cash. The payment acts to reduce assets (i.e., Cash) and equity (i.e., Retained Earnings). The recognition of interest expense causes a corresponding decrease in net income. The cash outflow is shown in the operating activities section of the statement of cash flows. Recall that while interest is shown as a nonoperating item on the income statement, it is shown as an operating item on the statement of cash flows.

Repaid Principal on Funds Borrowed in Event No. 5

Event 11b
Principal Payment

The second step requires a cash disbursement to repay the $5,000 principal amount of the note. This disbursement acts to reduce assets (i.e., Cash) and liabilities (i.e., Notes Payable). The repayment does not affect the income statement. The $5,000 cash outflow is shown in the financing activities section of the statement of cash flows.

Recognized $16,800 of Revenue on Sale of Merchandise That Cost $8,660

Event 12a
Sale of Inventory

The merchandise was sold under credit terms of 1/10, n/30. Freight terms were FOB shipping point. Freight costs of $275 were paid in cash by the party responsible. The effect of the revenue recognition on the balance sheet is to increase assets (i.e., Accounts Receivable) and equity (i.e., Retained Earnings). The event acts to increase revenue and net income. Since the sale was made on account, cash flow is not affected.

Recognized $8,660 of Cost of Goods Sold

Event 12b
Cost of Sale

To recognize the expense associated with the goods sold, $8,660 must be transferred from the Merchandise Inventory account to the Cost of Goods Sold account. The effect of the expense recognition on the balance sheet is to decrease assets (i.e., Inventory) and equity (i.e., Retained Earnings). The expense, cost of goods sold, increases and net income decreases. Cash flow is not affected. *Since the goods were delivered FOB shipping point, the buyer is responsible for the freight costs and JPS's accounts are not affected.*

Made $7,000 Cash Payment on Account Payable Generated in Event No. 10

Event 13
Payment of Account Payable

Assume that the payment was made after the discount period had expired. The effect of the event on the balance sheet is to decrease assets (i.e., Cash) and liabilities (i.e., Accounts Payable). The income statement is not affected. The $7,000 cash outflow is included in the operating activities section of the statement of cash flows.

Paid Cash for Selling and Administrative Expenses Amounting to $8,000

The effect of the event on the balance sheet is to decrease assets (i.e., Cash) and equity (i.e., Retained Earnings). The recognition of the selling and administrative expenses acts to decrease net income. The $8,000 cash outflow is shown in the operating activities section of the statement of cash flows.

Event 14
Selling and Administrative Expenses

Journal Entries and Ledger Accounts

Exhibit 5–7 shows the ledger T-accounts that reflect the accounting events just described. The exhibit includes the required closing entries. The ledger account balances are used to prepare the financial statements, which are shown in Exhibit 5–9. To confirm your understanding of the accounting process, trace the ledger account balances to the financial statements. It is also insightful to trace the totals contained in the horizontal statements model in Exhibit 5–6 to the financial statements in Exhibit 5–9.

Financial Statements

Exhibit 5–9 shows the 20X2 financial statements for JPS. Note especially the format of the income statement; it provides more information than a simple comparison of revenues and expenses. It matches particular expenses with particular revenues. More specifically, the computation of gross margin provides information about the relationship between the cost of goods sold and the selling price. This information facilitates comparisons between companies or between stores within the same company. Such comparisons permit investors and managers to assess the competitiveness of pricing strategies, to evaluate the effectiveness of management, and to anticipate the likelihood of continued performance. The income statement in Exhibit 5–9 (page 225) also distinguishes regular operating activities from peripheral nonoperating activities. The separation of operating from nonoperating activities promotes financial statement analysis. Analysts are able to distinguish recurring operating activities from items such as gains and losses, discontinued operating activities, and extraordinary items that are not likely to be repeated. Income statements that show these additional relationships are called **multistep income statements.** This title distinguishes them from the **single-step income statements** that display a single comparison of total revenues and total expenses. Exhibit 5–8 indicates that whereas most companies use a multistep format, many use the single-step approach.

> **L.O. 7**
>
> Compare and contrast single- and multistep income statements.

Note carefully that interest is classified as a nonoperating item on a *multistep income statement.* This treatment is inconsistent with the way interest is reported on the statement of cash flows. Recall that interest is reported as an operating activity on the *statement of cash flows.* When the Financial Accounting Standards Board (FASB) ruled on the classification of interest, there was considerable disagreement among accountants as to where it should be shown. Traditionally, interest had been shown as a nonoperating item. However, the FASB chose to depart from traditional practice by requiring that interest be reported as an operating item on the statement of cash flows. Unfortunately, the new requirement was not extended to the income statement. As a result, interest can be reported inconsistently as a nonoperating item on a multistep income statement and as an operating item on the statement of cash flows.

EXHIBIT 5–7
Ledger Account

Assets	=	Liabilities	+	Equity

Cash

Bal.	12,000	300	(2)
(5)	5,000	6,860	(4b)
(9b)	24,750	450	(7)
		250	(11a)
		5,000	(11b)
		7,000	(13)
		8,000	(14)
Bal.	13,890		

Account Receivable

(6a)	26,200	1,200	(8a)
(12a)	16,800	250	(9a)
		24,750	(9b)
Bal.	16,800		

Merchandise Inventory

Bal.	6,000	1,000	(3)
(1)	8,000	140	(4a)
(2)	300	12,300	(6b)
(8b)	800	8,660	(12b)
(10)	14,000		
Bal.	7,000		

Accounts Payable

(3)	1,000	8,000	(1)
(4a)	140	14,000	(10)
(4b)	6,860		
(13)	7,000		
		7,000	Bal.

Note Payable

(11b)	5,000	5,000	(5)
		0	Bal.

Contributed Capital

	15,000	Bal.

Retained Earnings

	3,000	Bal.
	12,690	(cl.)
	15,690	Bal.

Sales Revenue

(8a)	1,200	26,200	(6a)
(9a)	250	16,800	(12a)
(cl.)	41,550		
		0	Bal.

Cost of Goods Sold

(6b)	12,300	800	(8b)
(12b)	8,660	20,160	(cl.)
Bal.	0		

Transportation-out

(7)	450	450	(cl.)
Bal.	0		

Selling and Admin. Expenses

(14)	8,000	8,000	(cl.)
Bal.	0		

Interest Expense

(11a)	250	250	(cl.)
Bal.	0		

Total Assets	=	Total Liabilities	+	Total Equity
$37,690		$7,000		$30,690

Real-world companies frequently use income statement formats that are not purely single-step or multistep. For example, a company that uses a single-step format may choose to show income tax expenses as a separate item from other expenses. Alternatively, a company may choose to show the computation of gross margin but then include interest expense with other expenses. To verify the existence of alternative reporting formats, return to Exhibit 5–1. Which company (i.e., Nordstrom or Estee Lauder) uses a reporting format that more closely resembles a single-step format? Clearly, Estee Lauder's income statement includes more steps than the statement produced by Nordstrom. For example, notice that Estee Lauder shows a separate computation for gross margin, while Nordstrom lists the cost of goods sold with other expenses. The Nordstrom statement very closely approximates the single-step format.

Periodic Inventory Method

Under certain conditions, it is impractical to record inventory transactions as they occur. For example, consider the operations of a fast-food restaurant. If records were maintained perpetually, it would be necessary to transfer costs from the Inventory account to the Cost of Goods Sold account each time a hamburger, order of fries, soft drink, or any other food item was sold. Obviously, recording each item at the point of sale would be impractical without the availability of sophisticated computer equipment. The periodic inventory method offers a practical approach to recording inventory transactions in a low-technology, high-turnover environment.

Under the periodic method, the cost of goods sold is determined at the end of the period rather than at the point of sale. Indeed, the Inventory account is *not* affected by purchases or sales of inventory. When goods are purchased, the cost is recorded in a purchases account, and no entry is made to reduce inventory when goods are sold. Purchase returns and allowances, purchase discounts, and transportation-in are recorded in separate accounts. The amount of cost of goods sold is determined by subtracting the amount of ending inventory from the total cost of goods available for sale. The amount of ending inventory is determined by making a year-end physical count. Goods that are not in stock at the end of the period are assumed to have been sold. This is the same logic used in earlier chapters to determine the amount of supplies used during an accounting period.

It is important to note that the perpetual and periodic inventory methods represent alternative procedures for recording the same information. The amounts of cost of goods sold and ending inventory reported in the financial statements will be the same regardless of which method is applied. For comparative purposes, Exhibit 5–10 shows the general journal entries used under the periodic inventory

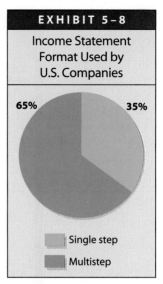

EXHIBIT 5–8

Income Statement Format Used by U.S. Companies

65%   35%

■ Single step
■ Multistep

Data Source: AICPA, *Accounting Trends and Techniques,* 1998.

L.O. 8

Understand the primary features of the periodic inventory system.

EXHIBIT 5–9						
Financial Statements						
Income Statement		**Balance Sheet**		**Statement of Cash Flows**		
Net Sales	$41,550	Assets		**Operating Activities**		
Cost of Goods Sold	(20,160)	Cash	$13,890	Inflow from Customers	$24,750	
Gross Margin	21,390	Accounts Rec.	16,800	Outflow for Inventory	(14,160)	
Less: Operating Exp.		Merchandise Inv.	7,000	Outflow for Trans.-out	(450)	
Sell. and Admin. Exp	(8,000)	Total Assets	$37,690	Outflow for S&A Exp.	(8,000)	
Transportation-out	(450)			Outflow for Interest	(250)	
Operating Income	12,940	Liabilities		Net Cash Inflow from Oper.	1,890	
Non-operating Items		Accounts Payable	$ 7,000			
Interest Expense	(250)	Equity		Investing Activities	0	
Net Income	$12,690	Contributed Capital	15,000	Financing Activities		
		Retained Earnings	15,690	Inflow from Note Pay.	5,000	
		Total Equity	30,690	Outflow to Repay Debt	(5,000)	
		Total Liab. and Equity	$37,690	Net Cash flow from Fin.	0	
				Net Change in Cash	1,890	
				Beginning Cash Bal	12,000	
				Ending Cash Bal.	$13,890	

EXHIBIT 5–10

General Journal Entries

Event No.	Account Title	Debit	Credit
1	Purchases	8,000	
	Accounts Payable		8,000
2	Transportation-in	300	
	Cash		300
3	Accounts payable	1,000	
	Purchase Returns and Allowances		1,000
4(a)	Accounts Payable	140	
	Purchase Discounts		140
4(b)	Accounts Payable	6,860	
	Cash		6,860
5	Cash	5,000	
	Notes Payable		5,000
6	Accounts Receivable	26,200	
	Sales Revenue		26,200
7	Transportation-out	450	
	Cash		450
8	Sales	1,200	
	Accounts Receivable		1,200
9(a)	Sales	250	
	Accounts Receivable		250
9(b)	Cash	24,750	
	Accounts Receivable		24,750
10	Purchases	14,000	
	Accounts Payable		14,000
11(a)	Interest Expense	250	
	Cash		250
11(b)	Notes Payable	5,000	
	Cash		5,000
12	Accounts Receivable	16,800	
	Sales Revenue		16,800
13	Accounts Payable	7,000	
	Cash		7,000
14	Operating Expenses	8,000	
	Cash		8,000
ADJ.	Cost of Goods Sold	20,160	
	Inventory	1,000	
	Purchase Returns and Allowances	1,000	
	Purchase Discounts	140	
	Purchases		22,000
	Transportation-in		300
CL	Sales Revenue	41,550	
	Cost of Goods Sold		20,160
	Transportation-out		450
	Operating Expenses		8,000
	Interest Expense		250
	Retained Earnings		12,690

method to record the accounting events for JPS for the 20X2 accounting period. Observe carefully that the amount of cost of goods sold is recorded in an adjusting entry. This entry transfers the various product costs to the Cost of Goods Sold account and adjusts the Inventory account to reflect the amount of inventory on hand at the end of the accounting period. As its name implies, accountants using the *periodic method* record changes in the balance of the Inventory and Cost of Goods Sold accounts at the end of the accounting period.

Schedule of Cost of Goods Sold

Since under the periodic method the cost of goods sold is not determined at the point of sale, it must be computed at the end of the period. The following logic is used to make the computation. First, calculate the cost of goods available for sale. This computation includes the amount of beginning inventory, plus the cost of all purchases, less any purchase returns and allowance, less purchase discounts, plus the cost of transportation-in. The result represents the total cost of all merchandise inventory that could have been sold to customers (i.e., the *cost of goods available for sale*). The next step is to subtract the amount of inventory that is on hand at the end of the accounting period from the cost of goods available for sale. The result is the amount of *cost of goods sold.*

Exhibit 5–11 is the computation of cost of goods sold for JPS's 20X2 accounting period. The **schedule of cost of goods sold** is used for internal reporting purposes and is not shown in the formal financial statements made available to the public. The amount of cost of goods sold is reported as a single line item on the income statement in exactly the same manner as demonstrated for the perpetual inventory. Indeed, the financial statements in Exhibit 5–9 will be the same regardless of whether JPS used the perpetual or periodic method to account for inventory transactions.

EXHIBIT 5–11	
Schedule of Cost of Goods Sold	
Beginning Inventory	$ 6,000
Purchases	22,000
Purchase Returns and Allowances	(1,000)
Purchase Discounts	(140)
Transportation-in	300
Cost of Goods Available for Sale	27,160
Ending Inventory	(7,000)
Cost of Goods Sold	$20,160

Lost, Damaged, or Stolen Merchandise

Although the *perpetual inventory system* is designed to capture information as it occurs, some events are not detectable at the time of occurrence. For example, when a shoplifter steals merchandise, the loss cannot be recorded until it is discovered, which usually occurs sometime after the theft has taken place. Also, customers or employees may not report damage to merchandise at the time of its occurrence. Finally merchandise may be lost or misplaced. Again, the loss cannot be recorded until it is discovered. Discovery of lost, damaged, or stolen merchandise is normally accomplished by taking a physical count of the merchandise on hand at the end of the accounting period and comparing that amount with the book balance in the Inventory account.

When a discrepancy between the book balance and the physical count of inventory is discovered, an adjusting entry is needed to correct the book balance. If

L.O. 9

Understand how lost, damaged, or stolen inventory affects financial statements.

goods have been lost, damaged, or stolen, the book balance will be higher than the actual amount of inventory on hand. In this case, the adjusting entry acts to reduce assets and equity. More specifically, the Inventory account is reduced, and an expense for the amount of the lost, damaged, or stolen inventory is recognized.

Adjustment for Lost, Damaged, or Stolen Inventory

To illustrate, assume that Midwest Merchandising Company uses the perpetual inventory method. Furthermore, assume that the end-of-period physical count reveals $23,500 of merchandise on hand while the Inventory account contains a $24,000 balance. The effect of the inventory write-down on the financial statements is shown here. The event acts to decrease assets (i.e., Inventory) and equity (i.e., Retained Earnings). The write-down increases expenses and thereby decreases net income. Cash flow is not affected.

Assets	=	Liab.	+	Equity	Rev.	−	Exp.	=	Net Inc.	Cash Flow
(500)	=	n/a	+	(500)	n/a	−	500	=	(500)	n/a

The following entry is used to record the transaction in the general journal:

Account Title	Debit	Credit
Inventory Loss (Cost of Goods Sold)	500	
Inventory		500

Theoretically, the inventory loss is an operating expense. However, such losses are normally immaterial in the amount and are treated as additions to the amount of cost of goods sold for external reporting purposes. In a *periodic inventory system*, lost, damaged, or stolen merchandise is included in the cost of goods sold as part of the computational process. Since lost, damaged, or stolen merchandise would not be included in the year-end physical count, these goods are assumed to have been sold when the cost of goods sold is computed by subtracting ending inventory from cost of goods available for sale. From a managerial perspective, this is a major disadvantage of the periodic system. Since the periodic system does not separate the cost of lost, damaged, or stolen merchandise from the cost of goods sold, the amount of the inventory loss is unknown. Without knowing the amount of the inventory loss, management cannot make informed decisions regarding the cost/benefit trade-offs of various security systems.

Financial Analysis for Merchandising Companies

Merchandising companies are in a very competitive business. A consulting enterprise may shelter itself from competition by hiring personnel whose expertise cannot be duplicated. A manufacturing company may hold a patent to a product that gives the company exclusive rights to produce it. Merchandise companies, however, usually sell products that are available for sale by other companies. Merchandise sold at Wal-Mart usually is sold at Kmart as well, and many customers shop where the prices are lowest. Because of the competitive nature of their business, merchan-

reality bytes

"Closed for Inventory Count" is a sign you frequently see on retail stores sometime during the month of January. As indicated in the chapter, companies using the periodic inventory method do not record inventory transactions at the time of sale. Accordingly, the amount of inventory on hand is unknown at any point in time. Even if companies use a perpetual inventory system, the amount of inventory on hand may be unknown because of lost, damaged, or stolen goods. The only way to determine the amount of inventory on hand is to count it. Why count it in January? Christmas shoppers and many after-Christmas sales shoppers are satiated by mid-January, leaving the stores low on both merchandise and customers. Accordingly, stores have less merchandise to count and "lost sales" are minimized during January. Companies that do not depend on seasonal sales (e.g., plumbing supplies wholesale business) may choose to count inventory at some other time during the year. Indeed, counting inventory is not a revenue-generating activity. It is a necessary evil that should be conducted when it least disrupts operations.

dising companies watch their *margins* very carefully. One such margin is the *gross margin,* introduced earlier in the chapter. The gross margin is also called *gross profit.*

Common Size Financial Statements

Chapter 3 introduced ratios as a meaningful way to compare accounting information for a large company to that of a small company. It was shown that raw accounting numbers alone can be misleading. Suppose that Smith Company has a 10% return on assets while Jones Company is able to return only 8% on its invested assets. Furthermore, assume that Smith Company has $1,000,000 of assets while Jones Company has $2,000,000. Under these circumstances, Smith Company would report less income ($1,000,000 × 0.10 = $100,000) than Jones Company ($2,000,000 × 0.08 = $160,000) even though Smith Company was doing a better job of investing its assets. Similar problems can arise when a company tries to compare its financial statements from the current period to those of prior periods. How good is a $1,000,000 increase in net income? Certainly not as good if the company is Intel as it would be if the company were a small local computer store. To facilitate comparisons between companies or between periods, ratios can be used to prepare financial statements on a percentage basis. These are called **common size financial statements.** The discussion in this chapter focuses on *common size income statements.*

To prepare a common size income statement, each account balance on the statement, or at least those of interest, are converted to a percentage of sales. Thus, net sales are always 100%. Next, the cost of gods sold is divided by sales to determine the cost of goods sold percentage, and so on down the income statement, with each item being converted to a percentage by dividing it by net sales. Exhibit 5–12 demonstrates a common size income statement using data from the 20X2 income statement shown in Exhibit 5–9 for JPS.

L.O. 10

Use common size financial statements to evaluate managerial performance.

EXHIBIT 5–12		
JUNE'S PLANT SHOP		
Comon Size income Statement*		
For the Year Ended 20x2		
Net Sales	$41,550	100.00%
Cost of Goods Sold	(20,160)	(48.52)
Gross Margin	21,390	51.48
Less: Operating Expenses		
Selling and Administrative Expenses	(8,000)	(19.25)
Transportation-out	(450)	(1.08)
Operating Income	12,940	31.14
Nonoperating Items		
Interest Expense	(250)	(.60)
Net Income	$12,690	30.54%

*Percentages do not add exactly because they have been rounded.

L.O. 11

Use ratio analysis to evaluate managerial performance.

Gross Margin Percentage

Perhaps the most important percentage on the common size income statement is that for gross margin. Users of accounting information often compute this ratio even when common size statements are not prepared. It is often called the **gross margin percentage** and is defined as

$$\frac{\text{Gross Margin}}{\text{Net Sales}}$$

The gross margin percentage can indicate a lot about a retailer. For example, it provides some indication as to a company's pricing strategy. Companies with low margins have a small spread between their cost and their sales price. In other words, they price their merchandise low in relation to its cost. For example, assume that two stores purchase the same type of inventory item for resale. Suppose that the item costs $100. Store A sells the item for $130 while store B charges $140. Store A's gross margin percentage is 23.1% ($30 ÷ $130), store B's percentage is 28.6% ($40 ÷ $140). Accordingly, lower margins suggest lower sales prices.

Associated Press AP

Real-World Data

Exhibit 5–13 shows the 1997 gross margin percentages and return on sales ratios for six companies. Three of these companies—Kmart, Wal-Mart, and Neiman Marcus—sell a variety of consumer goods; the other three companies sell office products.

Note that the retailers of consumer goods have a wide range of gross margin percentages. As expected, the upscale retailer, Neiman Marcus, has a much higher profit margin than the discount retailers. The profit margins also show that Wal-Mart, which claims to be the "low-price leader," does appear to be charging lower prices than its competitor, Kmart.

It is possible that Wal-Mart's lower profit margin is attributable to higher acquisition costs. In other words, Wal-Mart could be paying more to obtain its inventory. This condition would also lead to a lower spread, assuming that the two stores sold inventory for the same prices. However, it is not likely that Wal-Mart pays more for inventory than Kmart. Due to its size, Wal-Mart is usually able to obtain favorable pricing through quantity discounts (i.e., price reductions given when a customer buys large quantities of goods). Accordingly, the most logical explanation for the lower gross margin percentage is that Wal-Mart is selling its goods for lower prices. Given the competitive nature of the merchandising business, lower prices should translate to higher sales. Indeed, Wal-Mart has experienced phenomenal growth in sales during the past two decades.

In contrast to the stores selling consumer goods, Exhibit 5–13 reveals that the gross margin percentages for three leading merchandisers of office products are almost equal.

Return on Sales

Low prices motivate high sales, but there is a limit as to how low a company can go. The gross profit percentage must be high enough to cover the cost of other expenses that are necessary to operate the stores. Employees must be paid. A retailer must also pay for utilities, rent, office equipment, furnishings, taxes, and a variety of other operating activities that consume resources. If Wal-Mart sells its goods at lower prices, this means that the company will have less money to pay for other expenses. Does this mean that Wal-Mart will also have relatively lower profits? Another ratio from the common size income statement that can help answer this question is the **net income percentage.** This percentage is called **return on sales** and is determined as follows:

$$\frac{\text{Net Income}}{\text{Net Sales}}$$

Recall from Chapter 1 that if a company has unusual items, using *income from continuing operations* to compute ratios may be more appropriate than using net income.

Even though Kmart had a slightly higher gross margin percentage than Wal-Mart in 1997 (21.9% versus 20.8%), Wal-Mart had a much higher return on sales than Kmart (2.99% versus 0.77%). Accordingly, the data suggest that Kmart is selling its products for a higher price and is spending more to operate its business. This analysis suggests that one way Wal-Mart is able to sell for less is by exercising effective control over its operating expenses.

EXHIBIT 5-13		
Industry/Company	**Gross Margin %**	**Return on Sales**
Department Stores		
Kmart	21.9%	0.77%
Wal-Mart	20.8	2.99
Neiman Marcus	31.9	4.13
Office Supplies		
Office Depot	23.4	2.38
Office Max	23.1	2.38
Staples	24.1	2.53

Use of Common Size Financial Statements

The previous discussion focused on the use of common size income data to make comparisons among companies. Investors, creditors, and managers also find it useful to make comparisons of a particular company's performance over different periods. To illustrate, assume that June's Plant Shop decides to relocate its store to an upscale shopping mall with a wealthier customer base. June realizes that she will have to pay more for rent but believes that she will be able to cover the higher cost by selling her merchandise at higher prices. June changes location on January 1, 20X3. Exhibit 5-14 shows common size income statements for 20X2 and 20X3. Comparisons between these two income statements can provide insight as to whether June's strategy was successful.

An analysis of the common size statements suggests that June's strategy did indeed increase the profitability of her business. By increasing prices, June was able to increase the absolute dollar value of sales by $8,310 ($49,860 − $41,550). Notice that operating expenses increased as expected. They now constitute 25% of sales instead of 19%. Although this constitutes a 6% increase in operating expenses, it is more than offset by the increase in the gross margin rate. Gross profit in 20X3 was 9% higher than in 20X2 (60% − 51%), which verifies the fact that June was able to raise her prices. Transportation cost remained relatively stable. Interest cost were higher, implying that it was necessary to borrow more funds to

L.O. 12 Understand the cost of financing inventory.

EXHIBIT 5–14

JUNE'S PLANT SHOP
Common Size Income Statements*

	20X2		20X3	
Net Sales	$41,550	100%	$49,860	100%
Cost of Goods Sold	(20,160)	49	(19,944)	(40)
Gross Margin	21,390	51	29,916	60
Less: Operating Expenses				
Selling and Administrative Expenses	(8,000)	(19)	(12,465)	(25)
Transportation-out	(450)	(1)	(500)	(1)
Operating Income	12,940	31	16,951	34
Nonoperating Items				
Interest Expense	(250)	(1)	(400)	(1)
Net Income	$12,690	30%	$16,551	33%

*All percentages have been rounded to the nearest whole percentage point. Percentages do not add exactly because they have been rounded.

support the higher operating expenses. However, neither transportation nor interest costs changed drastically enough to affect the measurement in percentage terms. The overall impact of the new strategy is apparent in the net income percentage, which increased from 30 to 33%. Accordingly, profitability increased as expected.

Merchandise Inventory Financed

Suppose a store purchases inventory in October to be sold during the Christmas season. Assume sales are made on account so that cash from the sale is collected in January or February of the next year. Since the cash from the sale is collected 3 or 4 months after the goods were purchased, how will the company get the money to pay for the inventory? One answer is to borrow the money. The company could pay for the merchandise in October with money borrowed from a bank. The bank could be repaid when the cash collections from sales come in during January and February.

The obvious drawback to obtaining a loan to pay for inventory is that interest expense is incurred on the borrowed funds. However, other alternative sources of financing inventory would also be expensive. If the owner's money is used, then these funds cannot be invested elsewhere. For example, the owner's money could be deposited in an interest-earning savings account. The loss of interest earned is called an **opportunity cost;** it is effectively a financing cost that is just as real as the interest expense. Net income falls regardless of whether you incur expenses or lose revenue.

A third alternative is to purchase the inventory on account. However, when purchases are made on account, the seller usually charges the buyer an interest fee. This charge may be "hidden" in the form of higher prices. So while interest costs are lower, the cost of goods sold is higher. As indicated earlier in this chapter, many companies recognize financing costs by offering buyers the opportunity to receive cash discounts by paying for purchases within a short time immediately following the sale. In summary, any way you look at it, merchandisers incur significant inventory financing costs.

There is no way to eliminate the cost of financing inventory, but accounting information can help companies minimize this cost. As much as possible, businesses should reduce the time for which goods stay in inventory before being sold. Ratios that facilitate the management of inventory turnover are explained in Chapter 8. Companies should also try to shorten the time it takes to get customers to pay for the goods they purchase. This relates to managing accounts receivable turnover, which is explained in Chapter 7. Later chapters discuss efforts to control inventory costs; this chapter provided a clear explanation of the need for such control.

A LOOK

BACK

This chapter introduced accounting for *merchandising companies,* which earn a profit by selling inventory at a price that is higher than the cost of goods. Merchandising companies include retail companies (companies that sell goods to the final consumer) and *wholesale companies* (companies that sell to other merchandising companies). The products sold by merchandising companies are called *inventory.* The costs to purchase the inventory, to receive it, and to make inventory ready for sale are known as *product costs,* which are first accumulated in an Inventory account (balance sheet asset account) and then recognized as cost of goods sold (income statement expense account) in the period in which goods are sold. The purchase and sale of inventory can be recognized at the time goods are bought and sold (perpetual method) or at the end of the accounting period (periodic method).

Accounting for inventory includes the treatment of cash discounts, transportation costs, and returns and allowances. The cost of inventory is the list price less any *cash discount* offered by the seller. Since the gross method of accounting for discounts mixes interest cost (i.e., cash discounts) with product cost, it is theoretically inferior to the net method, which separates product cost from interest costs. The cost of freight paid to acquire inventory (*transportation-in*) is considered to be a product cost. The cost of freight paid to deliver inventory to customers (*transportation-out*) is a selling expense. *Sales returns and allowances* are subtracted from sales revenue to determine the amount of *net sales* that is shown on the income statement. Purchase returns and allowances act to reduce product cost. Theoretically, the cost of lost, damaged, or stolen inventory is an operating expense. However, these costs are usually immaterial in amount and are frequently reported as part of cost of goods sold on the income statement.

Some companies show product costs separately from general, selling, and administrative costs on the income statement. Cost of goods sold is subtracted from sales revenue to determine the *gross margin.* General, selling, and administrative expenses are subtracted from gross margin to determine the amount of income from continuing operations. This format is called a *multistep income statement.* Other companies report income under a *single-step format.* In this case, the cost of goods sold is listed along with general, selling, and administrative items in a single expense category that is subtracted in total from revenue to determine income from operations.

Merchandising businesses operate in a highly competitive environment. They must manage their operations closely to remain profitable. Managers of merchandising businesses frequently use *common size financial statements* (statements presented on a percentage basis) and ratio analysis to monitor their operations. Percentages (common size financial statements) permit comparisons among companies of different size. Although a $1 million increase in sales may be good for a small company and bad for a large company, a 10% increase represents an increment that is common to any size company. The two most common ratios used by merchandising companies are the *gross margin percentage* (gross margin ÷ net sales) and the *net income percentage* (net income ÷ net sales). Interpreting these ratios requires an understanding of industry practice. For example, a discount store such as Wal-Mart would be expected to have a much lower gross margin percentage than an upscale store such as Neiman Marcus.

Managers should be aware of the financing cost associated with carrying inventory. By investing funds in inventory, a firm loses the opportunity to invest them in interest-bearing assets. Accordingly, the financing cost of inventory is frequently called an *opportunity cost*. To minimize financing costs, a company should minimize the amount of inventory it carries, the length of time the inventory is held, and the time required to collect accounts receivable.

A LOOK

FORWARD

To this point, the text has covered the basic accounting cycle for service and merchandising businesses. The remainder of the book takes a closer look at specific accounting issues. For example, Chapter 6 examines internal control and accounting for cash. In Chapter 6 you will learn the accounting practices and procedures that companies use to protect their cash and other assets. You will learn to account for petty cash (small disbursements of cash) and to accomplish a bank reconciliation. Furthermore, you will learn to classify assets as being short or long term in nature. Finally, you will learn to use a ratio to assess the liquidity (the ability to satisfy short-term obligations) of a business.

KEY TERMS

Allowance   Reduction in the selling price of certain goods that have been extended to the buyer because the goods have been determined to be defective or of lower quality than the buyer ordered. An allowance frequently encourages a buyer to keep merchandise that would otherwise be returned. *(p. 219)*

Cash Discount   A discount given on merchandise sold to encourage prompt payment. These discounts are given by the sellers of the merchandise and represent a sales discount to the seller when they are used and a purchase discount to the purchaser of the merchandise.   *(p. 219)*

Common Size Financial Statements   Financial statements that are prepared using ratios in which the information is stated as percentages. This allows a better comparison of period-to-period and company-to-company financial data, since all information is placed on a common basis. *(p. 229)*

Cost of Goods Available for Sale   The total costs paid to obtain goods and to make them ready for sale, including the cost of beginning inventory plus purchases and transportation-in costs, less purchase returns and allowances and purchase discounts.   *(p. 210)*

Cost of Goods Sold   The total cost incurred for the goods sold during a specific accounting period. *(p. 210)*

FOB Destination (Free on Board)   The term that designates the seller as the responsible party for freight costs (i.e., transportation-in costs). *(p. 217)*

FOB Shipping Point (Free on Board)   The term that designates the buyer as the responsible party for freight costs (i.e., transportation-in costs). *(p. 217)*

Gross Margin   The difference between sales revenue and cost of goods sold. It is the amount a company makes from selling goods before operating expenses are subtracted.   *(p. 210)*

Gross Margin Percentage   Gross margin stated as a percentage of sales. This gross margin percentage is computed by dividing gross margin by net sales. The gross margin percentage is the amount of each dollar of sales that is profit before any operating expenses are deducted.   *(p. 230)*

Inventory   A supply of goods that are in the process of being made or are finished and ready for sale. The term can also be used to describe stockpiles of goods that are used in the business (i.e., office supplies, cleaning supplies).   *(p. 209)*

Merchandise Inventory   A supply of finished goods held for resale to customers.   *(p. 209)*

Merchandising Businesses   Companies that buy and sell merchandise inventory.   *(p. 210)*

Multistep Income Statement   Income statement format that matches particular revenue items with related expense items and distinguishes between recurring operating activities and nonoperating items such as gains and losses, discontinued operations, and extraordinary items that are not likely to recur.   *(p. 223)*

Net Income Percentage   Another term for return on sales. Refer to return of sales for the definition.   *(p. 231)*

Net Sales   Sales that have been reduced to reflect returns from customers and allowances or cash discounts given to customers.   *(p. 220)*

Opportunity Cost   The income that is given up by choosing one alternative over another. For example, a working student will forgo an hour's work time to attend class. The forgone wage is an opportunity cost.   *(p. 232)*

Period Costs   Costs that cannot be directly traced to products. Period costs are usually recognized as expenses in the period in which they are incurred.   *(p. 210)*

Periodic Inventory Method   Method of accounting for changes in the Inventory account only at the end of the accounting period.   *(p. 213)*

Perpetual Inventory Method   Method of accounting for inventories that increases the Inventory account each time merchandise is purchased and decreases each time merchandise is sold.   *(p. 213)*

Product Cost   Inventory costs that are directly traceable to the product, including the cost to acquire goods or make them ready for sale.   *(p. 210)*

Purchase Discount   A reduction in the gross price of merchandise that is extended under the condition that the purchaser pay cash for the merchandise within a stated time (i.e., usually within 10 days of the date of the sale).   *(p. 219)*

Retail Companies   Companies that sell goods to the final consumer.   *(p. 210)*

Return on Sales   The amount of net income generated by $1 of sales. The percentage is computed by dividing net income by net sales.   *(p. 231)*

Sales Discount   Cash discount extended by the seller of goods to encourage prompt payment. When the buyer of the goods takes advantage of the discount and pays less than the original selling price, the difference between the selling price and the cash collected is the sales discount.   *(p. 221)*

Schedule of Cost of Goods Sold   A computation that is used to determine the amount of the cost of goods sold under the periodic inventory system. The schedule is an internal report that is not shown in the formal financial statements.   *(p. 227)*

Selling and Administrative Costs   Costs that cannot be directly traced to products and are recognized as expenses in the period in which they are incurred. Examples include advertising expense and office expense.   *(p. 210)*

Single-Step Income Statement   A single comparison between total revenues and total expenses.   *(p. 223)*

Transportation-in (Freight-in)   The cost of freight on goods purchased under terms FOB shipping point. This freight cost is usually added to the cost of inventory and is a product cost.   *(p. 217)*

Transportation-out (Freight-out)   Freight cost for goods delivered to customers under terms FOB destination. Transportation-out is a period cost and is expensed when it is incurred.   *(p. 220)*

2/10, n/30   A term indicating that the seller will give the purchaser a 2% discount on the gross invoice price if the purchaser pays cash for the merchandise within 10 days from date of purchase.   *(p. 219)*

Wholesale Companies   Companies that sell to other businesses.   *(p. 210)*

QUESTIONS

1. Define *inventory.* What items might be included in inventory?

2. Define *merchandise inventory.* Distinguish between inventory and merchandise inventory. What are the types of costs that are included in the Merchandise Inventory account?

3. What is the difference between a product cost and a period cost?

4. How is the cost of goods available for sale determined?

5. What portion of cost of goods available for sale is shown on the balance sheet? What portion is shown on the income statement?

6. When are period costs expensed? When are product costs expensed?

7. If CarCo had net sales of $750,000, goods available for sale of $575,000, and cost of goods sold of $495,000, what is CarCo's gross margin? What amount of inventory will be shown on Car Co's balance sheet?

8. Explain the difference between a perpetual inventory system and a periodic inventory system. Discuss the advantages of each system. Is it necessary to take a physical inventory with both systems? Why or why not?

9. What are the effects of the following types of transactions on the accounting equation? List the financial statements that are affected. (Assume that the perpetual inventory method is used.)
   a. Acquisition of cash capital from the owners.
   b. A contribution of inventory by an owner of a company.
   c. The purchase of inventory with cash by a company.
   d. The sale of inventory for cash.

10. Western Merchandising Company sold inventory that cost $6,000 cash for $10,000 cash. How does this event affect the accounting equation? What financial statements and accounts are affected? (Assume that the perpetual inventory method is used.)

11. If goods are shipped FOB shipping point, which party (i.e., the buyer or the seller) is responsible for the shipping costs?

12. Define *transportation-in*. Is it a product or a period cost?

13. Keller Cellular Co. paid $80 for freight on merchandise that it had purchased for resale to customers (transportation-in) and paid $135 for freight on merchandise delivered to customers (transportation-out). What account is debited for the $80 payment? What account is debited for the $135 payment?

14. What is the purpose of allowances granted to the buyer of a company's merchandise?

15. Beams Department Store purchased goods with the terms 2/10, n/30. What do these terms mean?

16. Northern Discount Stores incurred a $5,000 cash cost. How would the accounting treatment of this cost differ if the cash were paid for inventory versus commissions paid to sales personnel?

17. What is the purpose of giving a cash discount to charge customers?

18. Define *transportation-out*. Is it a product cost or a period cost for the seller?

19. Explain the difference between purchase returns and sales returns. How do purchase returns affect the financial statements of both buyer and seller? How do sales returns affect the financial statements of both buyer and seller?

20. How is net sales determined?

21. What is the difference between a multistep income statement and a single-step income statement?

22. What is the purpose of preparing a schedule of cost of goods sold?

23. Why does the periodic inventory system create a major disadvantage for management in accounting for lost, stolen, or damaged goods?

24. What is the advantage of using common size statements to present financial information for several accounting periods?

25. What information is provided by the return-on-sales ratio?

EXERCISES

When the instructions for *any* exercise or problem call for the preparation of an income statement, use the multistep format unless otherwise indicated.

EXERCISE 5-1
L.O. 1, 3, 5

Comparison of Merchandising Company and Service Company

The following information is available for two different types of businesses for the accounting period. John's Management Consulting is a service business that provides consulting services to small businesses. Demi's Dive Shop is a merchandising business that sells diving gear to college students.

Data for John's Management Consulting
1. Borrowed $10,000 from the bank to start the business.
2. Provided $8,000 of services to customers and collected $8,000 cash.
3. Paid salary expense of $5,200.

Data for Demi's Dive Shop
1. Borrowed $10,000 from the bank to start the business.

2. Purchased $6,500 inventory for cash.
3. Inventory costing $4,100 was sold for $8,000 cash.
4. Paid $1,100 cash for operating expenses.

Required

a. Prepare an income statement, balance sheet, and statement of cash flows for each of the companies.
b. What is different about the income statements of the two businesses?
c. What is different about the balance sheets of the two businesses?
d. How are the statements of cash flow different for the two businesses?

Effect of Inventory Transactions on Journals, Ledgers, and Financial Statements—Perpetual Method

EXERCISE 5-2
L.O. 3, 5

Debra Jones started a small merchandising business in 20X6. The business experienced the following events during its first year of operation. Assume that Jones used the perpetual inventory method.

1. Acquired $15,000 cash from Jones to begin operations.
2. Purchased inventory costing $11,000 cash.
3. Sold inventory costing $8,500 for $12,000 cash.

Required

a. Record the events in general journal format.
b. Post the entries to T-accounts.
c. Prepare an income statement (remember to use the multistep format), statement of changes in equity, balance sheet, and statement of cash flows for the 20X6 accounting period.

Effect of Inventory Transactions on the Income Statement and Statement of Cash Flows—Perrpetual Method

EXERCISE 5-3
L.O. 3, 5

During 20X7, Rockyford Merchandising Company purchased $25,000 of inventory on account. The company sold inventory on account that cost $18,000 for $28,000. Cash payments on accounts payable amounted to $15,000. There was $25,000 cash collected from accounts receivable. Rockyford also paid $4,000 cash for operating expenses. Assume that Rockyford started the accounting period with $24,000 in cash and contributed capital.

Required

a. Identify the events described in the preceding paragraph and record them in a horizontal statements model like the following one:

Assets.				= Liab. +	Equity		Rev.	– Exp.	= Net Inc.	Cash Flow
Cash	+	Accts. Rec.	+ Inv.	= A. Pay.	C.Cap.	+ Ret. Earn.				
24,000	+	n/a	+ n/a	= n/a	+ 24,000	+ n/a	n/a	– n/a	= n/a	n/a

b. What is the balance of accounts receivable at the end of 20X7?
c. What is the balance of accounts payable at the end of 20X7?
d. What are the amount of gross margin and the amount of net income for 20X7?
e. Determine the amount of net cash flow from operating activities.
f. Explain any differences in net income and net cash flow from operating activities.

Inventory Transactions Recorded in the General Journal and Entries Posted to T-Accounts—Perpetual Method

EXERCISE 5-4
L.O. 5

Sara's Beauty Supply experienced the following events during 20X6:

1. Acquired $5,000 cash from the owners.

2. Purchased inventory for $3,500 cash.

3. Sold inventory costing $2,600 for $3,900 cash.

4. Paid $300 for advertising expense.

Required

    a. Record the general journal entries for the preceding transactions.

    b. Post each of the entries to appropriate T-accounts.

    c. Prepare a trial balance to verify the equality of debits and credits..

EXERCISE 5-5
L.O. 6

Either the buyer or seller can be responsible for freight cost. The responsible party can be identified by analyzing the freight terms FOB shipping point or FOB destination.

Required

Determine which party, buyer or seller, is responsible for freight charges in each of the following situations:

    a. Sold merchandise, freight terms, FOB shipping point.

    b. Sold merchandise, freight terms, FOB destination.

    c. Purchased merchandise, freight terms, FOB shipping point.

    d. Purchased merchandise, freight terms, FOB destination.

EXERCISE 5-6
L.O. 3, 5

Effect of Sales Returns and Allowances and Freight Costs on the Journal, Ledger, and Financial Statements—Perpetual Method

Ace Company began the accounting period with $6,500 cash, $35,000 inventory, $20,000 contributed capital, and $21,500 retained earnings. During the accounting period, Ace experienced the following account events:

1. Sold merchandise costing $30,200 for $50,100 on account to Cole's General Store.

2. Delivered the goods to Cole under terms FOB destination. Freight costs amounted to $1,300 cash.

3. Received returned damaged goods from Cole. The goods cost Ace $2,800 and were sold to Cole for $4,400.

4. Granted Cole a $1,700 allowance for other damaged goods that Cole agreed to keep.

5. Collected partial payment of $28,000 cash from accounts receivable.

Required

    a. Record the transactions in general journal format.

    b. Open general ledger T-accounts with the appropriate beginning balances and post the journal entries to the T-accounts.

    c. Prepare an income statement, balance sheet, and statement of cash flows.

    d. Why would Ace grant the $1,700 allowance to Cole? Whom does this benefit more?

EXERCISE 5-7
L.O. 3

Effect of Purchase Returns and Allowances and Freight Costs on the Journal, Ledger, and Financial Statements—Perpetual Method

The trial balance for Best Gift Shop as of January 1 was as follows:

Account Titles	Debit	Credit
Cash	$16,000	
Inventory	6,000	
Contributed Capital		$20,000
Retained Earnings		2,000
Total	$22,000	$22,000

The following events affected the company during the accounting period:

1. Purchased merchandise on account that cost $11,000.

2. Purchased goods FOB shipping point with freight cost of $500 cash.

3. Returned $1,600 of damaged merchandise for credit on account.

4. Agreed to keep other damaged merchandise for which the company received a $700 allowance.
5. Sold merchandise that cost $8,000 for $15,500 cash.
6. Delivered merchandise to customers under terms FOB destination with freight costs amounting to $400 cash.
7. Paid $8,000 on the merchandise purchased in Event No. 1.

Required

    a. Record the transactions in general journal format.
    b. Open general ledger T-accounts with the appropriate beginning balances, and post the journal entries to the T-accounts.
    c. Prepare an income statement, balance sheet, and statement of cash flows. (Assume that closing entries have been made.)
    d. Explain why a difference does or does not exist between net income and net cash flow from operating activities.

Product Costs Accounted for—Perpetual Inventory System

EXERCISE 5-8
L.O. 2, 5

Which of the following would be debited to the Inventory account for a merchandising business using the perpetual inventory system?

Required

1. Purchase of inventory.
2. Allowance received for damaged inventory.
3. Transportation-out.
4. Purchase discount.
5. Transportation-in.
6. Purchase of a new computer to be used by the business.

Effect of Product Cost and Period Cost—Horizontal Statements Model

EXERCISE 5-9
L.O. 2, 3, 5

Fun Sporting Goods experienced the following transactions for the 20X3 accounting period:

1. Acquired $5,000 cash from the owner to start the business.
2. Purchased $28,000 of inventory on account.
3. Received goods purchased in Event No. 2 FOB shipping point. Freight cost of $300 paid in cash.
4. Returned $1,200 of goods purchased in Event No. 1 because of poor quality.
5. Sold inventory on account that cost $16,500 for $28,700.
6. Paid freight cost on the goods sold in Event No. 5 of $120. The goods were shipped FOB destination. Cash was paid for the freight cost.
7. Collected $23,500 cash from accounts receivable.
8. Paid $20,000 cash on accounts payable.
9. Paid $550 for advertising expense.
10. Paid $1,000 cash for insurance expense.

Required

    a. Which of these transactions would be classified as period (i.e., selling and administrative) costs? Which would be classified as product costs? Events that do not pertain to the incurrence of cost should be classified as not applicable (n/a).
    b. Record each event in a horizontal statements model like the following one. The first event is recorded as an example.

Assets.				= Liab. +	Equity		Rev. – Exp. = Net. Inc.	Cash Flow
Cash	+	Acct. Rec.	+ Inv.	= A. Pay. +	C.Cap.	+ Ret. Earn.		
5,000	+	n/a	+ n/a	= n/a +	5,000	+ n/a	n/a – n/a = n/a	5,000 FA

EXERCISE 5-10   **Cash Discounts and Purchase Returns**
L.O. 3, 6   On March 6, 20X4, Kwon's Imports purchased $6,200 of merchandise from the Lamp Exchange with the terms of 2/10, n/45. On March 10, Kwon returned $1,200 of the merchandise to the Lamp Exchange for credit. Kwon paid cash for the merchandise on March 15, 20X4.

Required

  a. What is the amount of the check that Kwon must write to the Lamp Exchange on March 15?

  b. Prepare the journal entries for these transactions.

  c. How much must Kwon pay for the merchandise purchased if the payment is not made until March 20, 20X4?

  d. Why would the Lamp Exchange sell merchandise with the terms 2/10, n/45?

EXERCISE 5-11   **Effect of Cash Discounts on the Journal, Ledger, and Financial Statements—Perpetual**
L.O. 5, 6   **Method**
Gravel Sales was started in 20X5. The company experienced the following accounting events during its first year of operation:

  1. Started business when it acquired $30,000 cash from the owner.

  2. Purchased merchandise costing $18,000 on account under terms 2/10, n/30.

  3. Paid off the account payable within the discount period.

  4. Sold inventory on account that cost $10,000 for $15,000. Credit terms were 1/20, n/30.

  5. Collected cash from the account receivable within the discount period.

  6. Paid $3,800 cash for operating expenses.

Required

  a. Record the transactions in general journal format.

  b. Open general ledger T-accounts, and post the journal entries to the T-accounts.

  c. Record the events in a horizontal statements model like the following one.

Assets.				= Liab. +		Equity		Rev. – Exp. = Net Inc.	Cash Flow
Cash	+	Accts. Rec.	+ Inv.	= A. Pay. +	C. Cap.	+ Ret. Earn.			

  d. What is the amount of gross margin for the period? What is the net income for the period?

  e. Why would Gravel sell merchandise with the terms 1/20, n/30?

  f. What do the terms 2/10, n/30 mean to Gravel?

EXERCISE 5-12   **Effect of Inventory Losses—Perpetual Method**
L.O. 3, 5   Tech Merchandising experienced the following events during its first year of operation:

  1. Started the business when it acquired $40,000 cash from the owners.

  2. Paid $28,000 cash to purchase inventory.

  3. Sold inventory costing $21,500 for $34,200 cash.

  4. Physically counted inventory indicating that inventory of $5,800 was on hand at the end of the accounting period.

Required

  a. Open appropriate ledger T-accounts, and record the events in the accounts.

  b. Prepare an income statement and balance sheet.

  c. Explain how differences could arise between the book balance and the physical count of inventory. Why is being able to determine whether differences exist useful to management?

Determination of the Effect of Inventory Transactions on the Account Equation—Perpetual Method

Adams Sales Company experienced the following events:

1. Purchased merchandise inventory for cash.
2. Purchased merchandise inventory on account.
3. Sold merchandise inventory on account. Label the revenue recognition 3a and the expense recognition 3b.
4. Returned merchandise purchased on account.
5. Sold merchandise inventory for cash. Label the revenue recognition 5a and the expense recognition 5b.
6. Paid cash on accounts payable within the discount period.
7. Paid cash for selling and administrative expenses.
8. Collected cash from accounts receivable.
9. Paid cash for transportation-out.
10. Paid cash for transportation-in.

Required

Identify each event as an asset source (AS), asset use (AU), asset exchange (AE), or claims exchange (CE). Also explain how the occurrence of each event affects the financial statements by placing a + for increase, − for decrease, or n/a for not affected under each of the components in the following statements model. Assume that the perpetual inventory method is used. The first event is recorded as an example.

Event No.	Event Type	Assets	=	Liab.	+	Equity	Rev.	−	Exp.	=	Net Inc.	Cash Flow
1	AE	+ −	=	n/a	+	n/a	n/a	−	n/a	=	n/a	− OA

Effect of Inventory Transactions on the Income Statement and Balance Sheet—Periodic Method

Roberto Diaz is the owner of Joy Bridal Shop. At the beginning of the year, Diaz had $2,100 in inventory. During the year, Diaz purchased inventory that cost $10,500. At the end of the year, inventory on hand amounted to $4,400.

Required

Calculate the following:

a. Cost of goods available for sale during the year.
b. Cost of goods sold for the year.
c. Amount of inventory that would appear on the year-end balance sheet.

Single-Step and Multistep Income Statements

The following information was taken from the accounts of Smart Foods, a small grocery store. The accounts are listed in alphabetical order, and all have a normal balance.

Accounts Payable	$300
Accounts Receivable	350
Accumulated Depreciation	100
Advertising Expense	200
Cash	410
Contributed Capital	200
Cost of Goods Sold	450
Interest Expense	70
Merchandise Inventory	150
Prepaid Rent	40
Retained Earnings	510
Sales Revenue	800
Salaries Expense	130
Supplies Expense	55

Required

First, prepare an income statement using the single-step approach. Then prepare another income statement using the multistep approach.

EXERCISE 5-16
L.O. 4

Determination of Cost of Goods Sold—Periodic Method

Surf Fun Retailers uses the periodic inventory method to account for its inventory transactions. The following account titles and balances were drawn from Surf Fun's records: Beginning balance in inventory, $12,450; purchases, $153,200; purchase returns and allowances, $4,800; sales, $340,000; sales returns and allowances, $3,160; freight-in, $1,080; and operating expenses, $25,700. A physical count of merchandise indicated that $14,650 of merchandise was on hand at the end of the accounting period.

Required

a. Prepare a schedule of cost of goods sold.

b. Prepare a multistep income statement.

EXERCISE 5-17
L.O. 8

Basic Transactions—Periodic Method, Single Cycle

The following transactions apply to Sundial Gift Shop for 20X7.

1. Acquired $67,000 cash from the owners to open the business.

2. Acquired capital contribution of $5,000 of gift merchandise from Shana Justin, one of the owners, who had acquired the merchandise prior to opening the shop.

3. Purchased $87,000 of inventory on account.

4. Paid $5,500 for advertising expense.

5. Sold inventory for $155,000.

6. Paid a $16,000 salary to a part-time salesperson.

7. Paid $70,000 on accounts payable (see Event No. 3).

8. Physically counted inventory, which indicated that $14,000 of inventory was on hand at the end of the accounting period.

Required

a. Record each of these transactions in general journal form.

b. Post each of the transactions to ledger T-accounts.

c. Prepare an income statement, statement of changes in equity, balance sheet, and statement of cash flows for 20X7.

d. Prepare the necessary closing entries at the end of 20X7, and post the entry to the appropriate T-accounts.

e. Prepare an after-closing trial balance.

f. Discuss an advantage of using the periodic method instead of the perpetual method.

g. Why is the capital acquired from the owner on the statement of changes in equity different from the owner contribution in the cash flow from financing activities section of the cash flow statement?

EXERCISE 5-18
L.O. 3, 5, 12

Determination of Cost of Financing Inventory

On January 1, 20X8, B.J. Duke started a small sailboat merchandising business that he named BJ's Sails. The company experienced the following events during the first year of operation:

1. Started the business when Duke borrowed $50,000 from his parents. He issued a 1-year note dated January 1, 20X8, to them. The note carried a 7% annual rate of interest.

2. Paid $40,000 cash to purchase inventory.

3. Sold a sailboat that cost $18,000 for $34,000 on account.

4. Collected $14,000 cash from accounts receivable.

5. Paid $5,000 for operating expenses.

6. Recognized accrued interest on the note payable on December 31.

Required

 a. Record the transactions in general journal format.

 b. Open general ledger T-account, and post the journal entries to the T-accounts.

 c. Prepare an income statement, balance sheet, and statement of cash flows. (Assume that year-end closing entries have been made.)

 d. "Since B.J. sold inventory for $34,000, he will be able to repay more than half of the $50,000 loan from his parents when it comes due on January 1, 20X9." Do you agree with this statement? Why or why not?

Inventory and Cash Discounts Financed

EXERCISE 5-19
L.O. 6, 12

Amy Wallace came to you for advice. She has just purchased a large amount of inventory with the terms 2/10, n/60. The amount of the invoice is $130,000. She is currently short on cash but has good credit. She can borrow the money at the appropriate time to take advantage of the discount. The annual interest rate is 7% if she decides to borrow the money. Wallace is sure she will have the necessary cash by the due date of the invoice (but not by the discount date).

Required

 a. For how long would Wallace need to borrow the money in order to take advantage of the discount?

 b. How much money would Wallace need to borrow?

 c. Write a memo to Wallace and outline the most cost-effective strategy for her to follow. Include in your memo the amount of savings from the alternative you suggest.

PROBLEMS—SERIES A

Basic Transactions for Three Accounting Cycles—Perpetual Method

PROBLEM 5-1A
L.O. 3, 5

Garden Company was started in 20X7 when it acquired $40,000 cash from the owner. The following data summarize the company's first 3 years' operating activities. Assume that all transactions were cash transactions.

	20X7	20X8	20X9
Purchases of Inventory	$30,000	$45,000	$ 65,000
Sales	51,000	73,000	110,000
Cost of Goods Sold	27,000	39,000	70,000
Selling and Administrative Expenses	20,000	26,000	36,000

Required

Prepare an income statement and balance sheet for each fiscal year. (*Hint:* It may be helpful to record the transaction data for each accounting period in T-accounts before you attempt to prepare the statements for that period.)

Identification of Product and Period Costs

PROBLEM 5-2A
L.O. 2

Required

Indicate whether each of the following costs is a product cost or a period (i.e., selling and administrative) cost:

 a. Transportation-in.

 b. Insurance on the office building.

 c. Purchase of office supplies.

 d. Costs incurred to improve the quality of goods available for sale.

 e. Purchase of goods for resale.

 f. Salaries of salespersons.

g. Advertising costs.

h. Transportation-out.

i. Interest paid on a note payable.

j. Salary of the company president.

PROBLEM 5-3A

L.O. 2

Identification of Freight Costs

Required

For each of the following events, determine the amount of freight paid by The Magictree Shop. Also indicate whether the freight cost would be classified as a product or period (i.e., selling and administrative) cost.

a. Purchased inventory with freight costs of $520. The goods were shipped FOB destination.

b. Sold merchandise to a customer. Freight costs were $250. The goods were shipped FOB destination.

c. Purchased additional merchandise with freight costs of $245. The merchandise was shipped FOB shipping point.

d. Shipped merchandise to customers with freight terms FOB shipping point. The freight costs were $70.

PROBLEM 5-4A

L.O. 3, 5

Effect of Inventory Transactions on the Income Statement and the Statement of Cash Flows— Perpetual Method

The following transactions were completed by City Sales in May 20X9.

May   1   Acquired $50,000 cash from the owners.

1   Purchased $30,000 of merchandise on account with terms 2/10, n/30.

2   Paid $600 cash for freight costs to obtain merchandise purchased on May 1.

4   Sold merchandise that cost $22,000 for $37,000 to customers on account with the terms 1/10, n/30.

4   Returned $2,500 of defective merchandise from the May 1 purchase for credit on account.

10   Paid cash for the balance due on the merchandise purchased on May 1.

13   Received cash from customers of May 4 sale in settlement of one-half of the account balance.

31   Collected the balance due on accounts receivable from May 4 sale.

31   Paid selling expenses of $3,900.

Required

a. Record each event in a horizontal statements model like the following one. The first event is recorded as an example.

Assets.			= Liab. +	Equity		Rev. – Exp = Net Inc.	Cash Flow
Cash +	Accts. Rec. +	Inv.	= A. Pay. +	C. Cap. +	Ret. Earn.		
50,000 +	n/a +	n/a +	n/a +	50,000 +	n/a	n/a – n/a = n/a	50,000 FA

b. Record each of the transactions in general journal form.

c. Post each of the transactions to the appropriate general ledger T-account.

d. Prepare an income statement for the month ending May 31.

e. Prepare a statement of cash flows for the month ending May 31.

f. Explain why there is a difference between net income and cash flow from operations.

Comprehensive Cycle Problem—Perpetual Method

The following information was drawn from the records of Prime Star Company:

1. At the beginning of the period, the company had cash of $4,200, inventory of $1,000, contributed capital of $4,000, and retained earnings of $1,200.
2. Prime Star Company purchased inventory on account from Gates Company under terms 2/10, n/30. The inventory cost $2,800. The merchandise was delivered under terms FOB shipping point. Freight costs, which were paid in cash, amounted to $250.
3. Prime Star Company returned $200 of the inventory that it had purchased because the inventory was damaged in transit. Gates Company agreed to pay the return freight cost.
4. Prime Star Company paid the amount due on its account payable to Gates Company within the cash discount period.
5. Prime Star Company sold inventory that had cost $3,000 for $4,500. The sale was made on account under terms 2/10, n/45.
6. One of Prime Star's customers returned merchandise to the company. The merchandise had originally cost $260 and had been sold to the customer for $420 cash. The customer was paid $420 cash for the returned merchandise.
7. Prime Star Company delivered goods under terms FOB destination. Freight costs, which were paid in cash, amounted to $300.
8. Prime Star Company collected the amount due on the accounts receivable within the discount period.
9. A physical count indicated that $900 of inventory was on hand at the end of the accounting period.

Required

a. Starting with Event No. 2, identify each event as an asset source (AS), asset use (AU), asset exchange (AE), or claims exchange (CE). Also explain how the occurrence of each event affects the financial statements by placing a + for increase, − for decrease, or n/a for not affected under each of the components in the following statements model. Assume that the perpetual inventory method is used. When an event has more than one component, use letters to distinguish the effects of each component. The first event (Event No. 2) is recorded as an example.

Event No.	Event Type	Assets	=	Liab.	+	Equity	Rev.	−	Exp.	=	Net Inc.	Cash Flow
2a	AS	+	=	+	+	n/a	n/a	−	n/a	=	n/a	n/a
2b	AE	+ −	=	n/a	+	n/a	n/a	−	n/a	=	n/a	− OA

b. Record the transactions in general journal format.
c. Open ledger T-accounts and post the transactions in the accounts.
d. Prepare an income statement, statement of changes in equity, balance sheet, and statement of cash flows.
e. Record the closing entries, and prepare an after-closing trial balance.

PROBLEM 5-6A
L.O. 7, 8

Preparation of Schedule of Cost of Goods Sold and Multistep and Single-Step Income Statements—Periodic Method

The following account titles and balances were taken from the adjusted trial balance of TCO Sales Co. The company uses the periodic inventory method.

Account Title	Balance
Sales Returns and Allowances	$ 4,500
Income Taxes	7,400
Miscellaneous Expense	800
Transportation-out	1,200
Sales	139,500
Advertising Expense	5,500
Salaries Expense	15,800
Transportation-in	3,450
Purchases	80,000
Interest Expense	720
Merchandise Inventory, January 1	10,150
Sales Discounts	810
Rent Expense	10,000
Merchandise Inventory, December 31	8,100
Purchase Returns and Allowances	2,900
Depreciation Expense	1,420

Required

a. Prepare a schedule to determine the amount of cost of goods sold.

b. Prepare a multistep income statement.

c. Prepare a single-step income statement.

PROBLEM 5-7A
L.O. 8

Comprehensive Cycle Problem—Periodic Method

The following trial balance is for Dan's Furniture as of January 1, 20X9:

Account Title	Debit	Credit
Cash	$13,000	
Accounts Receivable	2,000	
Merchandise Inventory	25,000	
Accounts Payable		$2,000
Notes Payable		3,000
Contributed Capital		18,500
Retained Earnings		16,500
Totals	$40,000	$40,000

The following events occurred in 20X9. Assume that Dan's uses the periodic inventory method.

1. Purchased land for $10,000 cash and a building for $45,000 by paying $5,000 cash and issuing a 20-year note with an annual interest rate of 8%. The building has a 40-year estimated life with no residual value.

2. Purchased merchandise on account for $63,000 with the terms 1/10, n/45.

3. Purchased merchandise for which freight cost was $500 cash shipped FOB shipping point.

4. Returned $1,800 of defective merchandise purchased in Event No. 2.

5. Sold merchandise for $43,000 cash.

6. Sold merchandise on account for $60,000 under terms 2/10, n/30.

7. Paid cash within the discount period for accounts payable balance due on merchandise purchased in Event No. 2.

8. Paid $5,800 cash for selling expenses.

9. Collected part of the balance due from accounts receivable. Collections were made after the discount period on $30,000 of the receivable. Collections were made during the discount period on $25,000 of receivables.

10. Paid cash to the bank for 1 full year's interest on the note issued in Event No. 1.

11. Paid $5,000 on the principal of the note issued in Event No. 1.

12. Recorded 1 full year's depreciation on the building purchased in Event No. 1.

13. A physical count indicated that $13,800 of inventory was on hand at the end of the accounting period.

Required

    a. Record these transactions in a general journal.

    b. Post the transactions to appropriate ledger T-accounts.

    c. Prepare an income statement, statement of changes in equity, balance sheet, and statement of cash flows.

Use of Common Size Income Statements to Make Comparisons

The following income statements were drawn from the annual reports of Edison Company:

PROBLEM 5-8A
L.O. 10

	20X1*	20X2*
Net Sales	$74,507	$80,000
Cost of Goods Sold	(28,317)	(34,400)
Gross Margin	$46,190	$45,600
Less: Operating Expenses		
Selling and Administrative Expenses	(43,210)	(40,800)
Net Income	$2,980	$4,800

*All figures are reported in thousands of dollars.

Required

The president's message contained in the company's annual report states that the company increased profitability by decreasing prices and controlling operating expenses. Write a memorandum indicating whether you agree with the president's statement. Support your answer by preparing common size income statements and making appropriate references to the differences between 20X1 and 20X2.

PROBLEMS—SERIES B

Basic Transactions for Three Accounting Cycles—Perpetual Method

Picnic Company was started in 20X7 when it acquired $20,000 from the owners. The following data summarize the company's first 3 years' operating activities. Assume that all transactions were cash transactions.

PROBLEM 5-1B
L.O. 3, 5

	20X7	20X8	20X9
Purchases of Inventory	$ 9,800	$12,000	$18,500
Sales	14,100	17,500	26,000
Cost of Goods Sold	7,150	9,500	15,000
Selling and Administrative Expenses	4,600	6,200	7,400

Required

Prepare an income statement and balance sheet for each fiscal year. (*Hint:* It may be helpful to record the transaction data for each accounting period in T-accounts before you attempt to prepare the statements for that period.)

PROBLEM 5-2B
L.O. 2

Identification of Product and Period Costs

Required

Indicate whether each of the following costs is a product cost or a period cost:

a. Purchase of cleaning supplies for the office.
b. Freight paid on goods purchased for resale.
c. Salary paid to the director of marketing.
d. Freight paid on goods sold to customer's FOB destination.
e. Utilities expense incurred for office building.
f. Depreciation on office equipment.
g. Insurance on vans used to deliver goods to customers.
h. Salaries of the sales supervisors.
i. Monthly maintenance expense for copier.
j. Purchase of goods for resale.

PROBLEM 5-3B
L.O. 2

Identification of Freight Cost

Required

For each of the following events, determine the amount of freight paid by Stan's Body Shop. Also indicate whether the freight is classified as a product or period cost.

a. Purchased inventory with freight costs of $550. The goods were shipped under freight terms FOB destination.
b. Sold merchandise to a customer. Freight costs were $200. The goods were shipped under freight terms FOB shipping point.
c. Purchased additional merchandise with freight terms FOB shipping point. The freight costs were $190.
d. Shipped merchandise to customers with freight terms FOB destination. The freight costs were $100.

PROBLEM 5-4B
L.O. 3, 5

Effect of Inventory Transactions on the Income Statement and the Statement of Cash Flows—Perpetual Method

The following transactions were completed by Bluebird Company in September 20X9:

Sept.   1 Acquired $30,000 cash from the owner.
       1 Purchased $18,000 of merchandise on account with the terms 2/10, n/30.
       5 Paid $800 cash for freight cost to obtain merchandise purchased on September 1.
       8 Sold merchandise that cost $4,500 for $8,800 to customers on account with the terms 1/10, n/30.
       8 Returned $900 of defective merchandise from the September 1 purchase to the supplier.
     10 Paid cash for the balance due on the merchandise purchased on September 1.
     15 Received cash from customers of September 8 sale in settlement of one-half of the account balances.
     30 Collected the balance due on accounts receivable from September 8 sales.
     30 Paid $1,720 cash for selling expenses.

Required

a. Record each event in a statements model like the following one. The first event is recorded as an example.

Assets.				= Liab. +	Equity		Rev. – Exp. = Net Inc.			Cash Flow
Cash	+	Accts. Rec.	+ Inv.	= A. Pay. +	C. Cap.	+ Ret. Earn.				
30,000	+	n/a	+ n/a	= n/a +	30,000	+ n/a	n/a –	n/a =	n/a	30,000 FA

b. Record each of these transactions in general journal form.

c. Post each of the transactions to the appropriate general ledger T-accounts.

d. Prepare an income statement for the month ending September 30.

e. Prepare a statement of cash flows for the month ending September 30.

f. Explain why there is a difference between net income and cash flow from operations.

Comprehensive Cycle Problem—Perpetual Method

The following information was drawn from the records of Denton Company:

PROBLEM 5-5B
L.O. 3, 5, 9

1. At the beginning of the period, the company had cash of $4,300, inventory of $9,000, contributed capital of $10,000, and retained earnings of $3,300.

2. Denton Company purchased inventory on account from Duke Company under terms 1/10, n/30. The inventory cost $2,200. The merchandise was delivered under terms FOB shipping point. Freight costs that were paid in cash amounted to $110.

3. Denton Company returned $200 of the inventory that it had purchased because the inventory was damaged in transit. Duke Company agreed to pay the return freight cost.

4. Denton Company paid the amount due on its account payable to Duke Company within the cash discount period.

5. Denton Company sold inventory that had cost $3,000 for $5,500. The sale was made on account under terms 2/10, n/45.

6. One of Denton's customers returned merchandise to Denton Company. The merchandise originally cost $400 and was sold to the customer for $710 cash. The customer was paid $710 cash for the returned merchandise.

7. Denton Company delivered goods under terms FOB destination. Freight costs that were paid in cash amounted to $60.

8. Denton Company collected the amount due on the account receivable within the discount period.

9. A physical count indicated that $7,970 of inventory was on hand at the end of the accounting period.

Required

a. Starting with Event No. 2, identify each event as an asset source (AS), asset use (AU), asset exchange (AE), or claims exchange (CE). Also explain how the occurrence of each event would affect the financial statements by placing a + for increase, − for decrease, or n/a for not affected under each of the components in the following statements model. Assume that the perpetual inventory method is used. When an event has more than one component, use letters to distinguish the effects of each component. The first event (Event No. 2) is recorded as an example.

Event No.	Event Type	Assets	=	Liab.	+	Equity	Rev.	−	Exp.	=	Net Inc.	Cash Flow
2a	AS	+	=	+	+	n/a	n/a	−	n/a	=	n/a	n/a
2b	AE	+ −	=	n/a	+	n/a	n/a	−	n/a	=	n/a	− OA

b. Record the transactions in general journal format.

c. Open ledger T-accounts, and post the transaction in the accounts.

d. Prepare an income statement, a statement of changes in equity, a balance sheet, and a statement of cash flows.

e. Record the closing entries, and prepare a trial balance.

PROBLEM 5-6B
L.O. 7, 8

Preparation of a Schedule of Cost of Goods Sold and Multistep and Single-Step Income Statements—Periodic Method

The following account titles and balances were taken from the adjusted trial balance of Neon Sales Co. The company uses the periodic inventory method.

Account Title	Balance
Advertising Expense	$ 12,800
Depreciation Expense	3,000
Income Taxes	10,700
Interest Expense	5,000
Merchandise Inventory, January 1	18,000
Merchandise Inventory, December 31	20,100
Miscellaneous Expense	800
Purchases	130,000
Purchase Returns and Allowances	2,700
Rent Expense	14,000
Salaries Expense	53,000
Sales	290,000
Sales Discounts	13,500
Sales Returns and Allowances	8,000
Transportation-in	5,500
Transportation-out	10,800

Required

a. Prepare a schedule to determine the amount of cost of goods sold.

b. Prepare a multistep income statement.

c. Prepare a single-step income statement.

PROBLEM 5-7B
L.O. 8

Comprehensive Cycle Problem—Periodic Method

The following trial balance is for Easy Communications Systems as of January 1, 20X5:

Account Title	Debit	Credit
Cash	$14,000	
Accounts Receivable	9,000	
Merchandise Inventory	60,000	
Accounts Payable		$ 5,000
Notes Payable		20,000
Contributed Capital		50,000
Retained Earnings		8,000
Total	$83,000	$83,000

The following events occurred in 20X5. Assume that Easy Communications uses the periodic inventory method.

1. Purchased land for $8,000 cash and a building for $45,000 by paying $5,000 cash and issuing a 20-year note with an annual interest rate of 8%. The building has a 40-year estimated life with no residual value.

2. Purchased merchandise on account for $23,000 with the terms 2/10, n/30.

3. The merchandise purchased was shipped FOB shipping point for $230 cash.

4. Returned $2,000 of defective merchandise purchased in Event No. 2.

5. Sold merchandise for $27,000 cash.

6. Sold merchandise on account for $50,000 under terms 1/20, n/30.

7. Paid cash within the discount period for accounts payable balance due on merchandise purchased in Event No. 2.

8. Paid $1,200 cash for selling expenses.
9. Collected part of the balances due from accounts receivable. Collections were made after the discount period on $12,000 of the receivable. Collections were made during the discount period on $35,000 of receivables.
10. Paid cash to the bank for 1 full year's interest on the note issued in Event No. 1.
11. Paid $2,000 on the principal of the note issued in Event No. 1.
12. Recorded 1 full year's depreciation on the building purchased in Event No. 1.
13. A physical count indicated that $30,000 of inventory was on hand at the end of the account period.

Required

a. Record these transactions in a general journal..

b. Post the transactions to appropriate ledger T-accounts.

c. Prepare an income statement, a statement of changes in equity, a balance sheet, and a statement of cash flows as of the end of the year.

Use of Common Size Income Statements to Make Comparisons

PROBLEM 5-8B
L.O. 10

The following income statements were drawn from the annual reports of Libbey Company:

	20X1*	20X2*
Net Sales	$302,900	$370,500
Cost of Goods Sold	(217,400)	(264,700)
Gross Margin	85,500	105,800
Less: Operating Expense		
Selling and Administrate Expenses	(40,800)	(58,210)
Net Income	$ 44,700	$ 47,590

*All dollar amounts are reported in thousands.

The president's message contained in the company's annual report states that the company has implemented a strategy to increase market share by spending more on advertising. The president indicated that prices held steady and sales grew as expected. Write a memo indicating whether you agree with the president's statements. How has the strategy affected profitability? Support your answer by measuring growth in sales and selling expenses. Also prepare common size income statements and make appropriate references to the differences between 20X1 and 20X2.

analyze, communicate, think

BUSINESS APPLICATIONS CASE   **Gateway 2000 Annual Report**   ACT 5-1

Required

Using the Gateway 2000 financial statements in Appendix B, answer the following questions:

a. What is Gateway's gross profit percentage for 1996 and 1997?

b. What was Gateway's return on sales for 1996 and 1997?

c. Ignoring taxes, what would Gateway's 1997 return on sales have been if it had not incurred the $113,842,000 "nonrecurring expenses?"

d. Gateway's gross profit percentage was lower for 1997 than for 1996. Ignoring taxes, how much higher would its 1997 net income have been if the gross profit percentage for 1997 had been the same as for 1996?

ACT 5-2

GROUP EXERCISE   **Multistep Income Statement**

The following quarterly information is given for Reebok for the year ended 1997 (amounts shown are in thousands).

	First Quarter	Second Quarter	Third Quarter	Fourth Quarter
Net Sales	$930,041	$841,059	$1,009,053	$863,446
Gross Margin	356,229	323,511	370,211	299,599
Net Income	40,184	20,322	73,968	645

Required

a. Divide the class into groups and organize the groups into four sections. Assign each section one quarter of the financial information.

(1) Each group should compute the cost of goods sold and operating expenses for the specific quarter assigned to their section and prepare a multistep income statement for the quarter.

(2) Each group should compute the gross margin percentage and cost of goods sold percentage for their specific quarter.

(3) Have a representative of each group put that quarter's sales, cost of goods sold percentage, and gross margin percentage on the board.

Class Discussion

b. Have the class discuss the change in each of these items from quarter to quarter and provide some logical explanation as to why the change might have occurred. Which was the best quarter and why?

ACT 5-3

REAL WORLD CASE   **Identification of Companies Based on Financial Statement Information**

The following is selected information from the 10-K reports of four companies. This information is for the 1997 fiscal year. The four companies, in alphabetical order, are: BellSouth Corporation, a telephone company that operates in the southeastern United States; Caterpillar, Inc., a manufacturer of heavy machinery; Dollar General Corp., a company that owns Dollar General Stores, which are discount stores; and Tiffany & Company, which operates high-end jewelry stores. The data for the companies, presented in the order of the amount of their sales in millions of dollars, are as follow:

	A	B	C	D
Sales	$20,561	$18,110	$2,627.3	$1,017.6
Cost of Goods Sold	6,254	13,374	1,885.2	453.4
Net Earnings	3,261	1,665	144.6	72.8
Inventory or	n/a	2,603	632.0	386.4
Materials and Supplies	398	n/a	n/a	n/a
Accounts Receivable	4,750	3,331	0.0	99.5
Total Assets	36,301	20,756	914.8	827.1

Required

Based on these financial data and your knowledge and assumptions about the nature of the businesses that the companies operate, determine which data relate to which companies. Write a memorandum explaining the rationale for your decisions. Be sure to include a discussion of which ratios you used in your analysis, and show the computations of these ratios in your memorandum.

BUSINESS APPLICATIONS CASE   **Use of Ratios to Make Comparisons**   ACT 5-4

The following income statements were drawn from the annual reports of James Company and Brenda Company.

	James	Brenda
Net Sales	$ 45,000	$ 75,500
Cost of Goods Sold	(33,750)	(41,525)
Gross Margin	11,250	33,975
Less: Selling and Admin. Expenses	(9,000)	(26,425)
Net Income	$ 2,250	$ 7,550

*All figures are reported in thousands of dollars

Required

a. One of the companies is a high-end retailer that operates in exclusive shopping malls. The other operates discount stores located in low-cost stand-alone buildings. Identify the high-end retailer and the discounter. Support your answer with appropriate ratios.

b. If James and Brenda have equity of $19,500 and $99,600, respectively, which company is the more profitable business?

BUSINESS APPLICATIONS CASE   **Use of Common Size Statements and Ratios**   ACT 5-5
to Make Comparisons

At the end of 20X3, the following information is available for Carly and Taylor companies:

	Carly	Taylor
Sales	$2,000,000	$2,000,000
Cost of Goods Sold	1,400,000	1,200,000
Operating Expenses	300,000	400,000
Total Assets	2,400,000	2,400,000
Owners' Equity	1,000,000	1,500,000

Required

a. Prepare a common size financial statement for each company.

b. Compute the return on assets and return on equity for each company.

c. Which company is more profitable from the owner's perspective?

d. One company is a high-end retailer, and the other operates a discount store. Which is the discounter? Support your selection by making reference to the appropriate ratios.

WRITTEN ASSIGNMENT, CRITICAL THINKING   **Effect of Sales Returns**   ACT 5-6
on Financial Statements

Dixon Farm and Garden Equipment reported the following sales information for 20X7:

Net Sales of Equipment	$2,450,567
Other Income	6,786
Cost of Goods Sold	1,425,990
Selling, General, and Administrative Expense	325,965
Depreciation and Amortization	3,987
Net Operating Income	$ 701,411

Selected information from the balance sheet:

Cash and Marketable Securities	$113,545
Inventory	248,600
Accounts Receivable	82,462
Property, Plant, and Equipment—net	335,890
Other Assets	5,410
Total Assets	$785,907

Assume that a major customer returned a large order to Dixon on December 31, 20X7. The amount of the sale had been $146,800 with a cost of sales of $94,623. The return was recorded in the books on January 1, 20X8. The company president does not want to correct the books. He argues that it makes no difference as to whether the return is recorded in 20X7 or 20X8. Either way, the return has been duly recognized.

Required

a. Assume that you are the CFO for Dixon Farm and Garden Equipment Co. Write a memo to the president explaining how the omission of the entry on December 31, 20X7, could cause the financial statements to be misleading to investors and creditors. Explain how the omission of the return from the customer would affect net income and the balance sheet.

b. Why might the president want to record the return on January 1, 20X8, instead of December 31, 20X7?

c. Would the failure to record the customer return violate the AICPA Code of Professional Conduct? (See Exhibit 2–7 in Chapter 2.)

d. If the president of the company refuses to correct the financial statements, what action should you take?

ACT 5-7   **ETHICAL DILEMMA**   **Wait Until I Get Mine**

Ada Fontanez is the president of a large company that owns a chain of athletic shoe stores. The company was in dire financial condition when she was hired 3 years ago. In an effort to motivate Fontanez, the board of directors included a bonus plan as part of her compensation package. According to her employment contract, on January 15 of each year, Fontanez is paid a cash bonus equal to 5% of the amount of net income reported on the preceding December 31 income statement. Fontanez was sufficiently motivated. Through her leadership, the company prospered. Her efforts were recognized throughout the industry, and she received numerous lucrative offers to leave the company. One offer was so enticing that she decided to change jobs. Her decision was made in late December 20X5. However, she decided to resign effective February 1, 20X6, to ensure the receipt of her January bonus. On December 31, 20X5, the chief accountant, Walter Smith, advised Fontanez that the company had a sizable quantity of damaged inventory. A warehouse fire had resulted in smoke and water damage to approximately $600,000 of inventory. The warehouse was not insured, and the accountant recommended that the loss be recognized immediately. After examining the inventory, Fontanez argued that it could be sold as *damaged goods* to customers at reduced prices. Accordingly, she refused to allow the write-off the accountant recommended. She stated that so long as she is president, the inventory stays on the books at cost. She told the accountant that he could take up the matter with the new president in February.

Required

a. How would an immediate write-off of the damaged inventory affect the December 31, 20X5, income statement, balance sheet, and statement of cash flows?

b. How would the write-off affect Fontanez's bonus?

c. If the new president is given the same bonus plan, how will his or her bonus be affected by Fontanez's refusal to recognize the loss?

d. Assuming that the damaged inventory is truly worthless, comment on the ethical implications of Fontanez's refusal to recognize the loss in the 20X5 accounting period.

e. Assume that the damaged inventory is truly worthless and that you are Smith. How would you react to Fontanez's refusal to recognize the loss?

EDGAR DATABASE   Analyzing Alcoa's Profit Margins

ACT 5-8

Instructions for using EDGAR are in Appendix A. Using the most current 10-K annual report available on EDGAR, answer the following questions about Aluminum Company of America (Alcoa). Type in *Aluminum* as the company name when you search EDGAR.

Required

a. What was Alcoa's gross margin percentage for the most current year?

b. What was Alcoa's gross margin percentage for the previous year? Has it changed significantly?

c. What was Alcoa's return-on-sales percentage for the most current year?

d. What percentage of Alcoa's total sales for the most current year was from operations in the United Sates?

e. Comment on the appropriateness of comparing Alcoa's gross margin with that of Ford Motor Company. If Ford has a higher/lower margin, does that mean that Ford is a better managed company?

SPREADSHEET ANALYSIS   Use of Excel

ACT 5-9

The following accounts, balances, and other financial information are drawn from the records of Vong Company for the year 20X4:

Net Sales Revenue	$18,800	Beginning Contributed Capital	$ 9,000
Unearned Revenue	2,600	Land	8,000
Accounts Receivable	6,000	Certificate of Deposit	10,000
Cost of Goods Sold	6,000	Interest Revenue	100
Inventory	5,000	Interest Receivable	100
Accounts Payable	5,800	Distributions	1,500
Notes Payable	6,000	Beginning Retained Earnings	8,500
Interest Expense	550	Capital Acquired from Owners	3,000
Accrued Interest Payable	550	Cash	7,200
Supplies	50	Gain on Sale of Land	1,050
Supplies Expense	750	Loss on Sale of Property	(50)
Office Equipment	3,500	Salaries Expense	1,400
Depreciation Expense	500	Accrued Salaries Payable	400
Accumulated Depreciation	1,000	Rent Expense	1,100
Transportation-out Expense	500	Prepaid Rent	100
Miscellaneous Operating Expense	4,500		

The Cash account revealed the following cash flows:

Received cash from advances from customers	$ 2,600
Purchased office equipment	(3,500)
Received cash from owner contributions	3,000
Collected cash from accounts receivable	3,800
Purchased land	(8,000)
Received cash from borrowing funds	6,000
Paid cash for rent	(1,200)
Sold land	10,000
Paid cash for distributions	(1,500)
Paid cash for operating expenses	(1,000)
Purchased certificate of deposit	(10,000)

Required

Use an Excel spreadsheet to construct a multistep income statement, statement of changes in equity, balance sheet, and statement of cash flows for the year ended 20X4.

ACT 5-10   SPREADSHEET ANALYSIS   **Mastery of Excel**

At the end of 20X4, the following information is available for Short and Wise Companies:

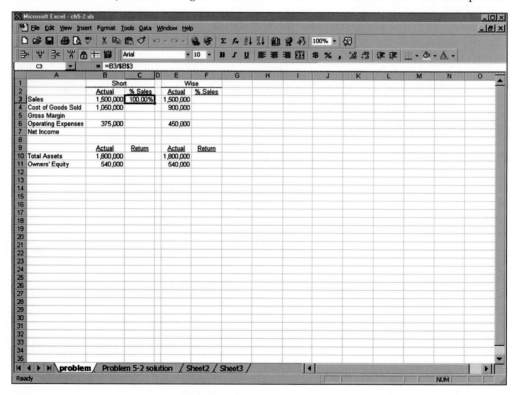

Required

a. Set up the spreadsheet shown here. Complete the income statements by using Excel formulas.

b. Prepare a common size financial statement for each company by completing the % Sales columns.

  c.   One company is a high-end retailer, and the other operates a discount store. Which is the discounter? Support your selection by referring to the common size statements.

  d.   Compute the return on assets and return on equity for each company.

  e.   Which company is more profitable from the owners' perspective?

  f.   Assume that a shortage of goods by suppliers is causing cost of goods sold to increase 10% for each company. Change the respective cost of goods sold balances in the Actual income statement column for each company. Note the new calculated amounts on the income statement and in the ratios. Which company's profits and returns are more sensitive to inventory price hikes?

Spreadsheet Tip

(1) Cell C3 (% Sales) can be copied down the income statement if the formula in cell C3 designates Sales (cell B3) as a fixed number. Designate a number as fixed by positioning $ signs within the cell address. Notice that the formula for C3 is =B3/B3.

6 Internal Control and Accounting for Cash

the **curious** accountant

In 1997 CUC and HFS merged to form Cendant Corporation. Cendant operates numerous businesses in different industries, including Avis rental cars, Century 21 Real Estate, and Days Inn. Its businesses also include discount shopping and travel clubs.

On April 15, 1998, the company announced that earnings of the then combined companies had been overstated during the prior three years. At that time, it estimated that 1997 net income would need to be restated downward by $100 to $115 million. In July, the company reported that nonexistent revenues had been recorded from 1995 to 1997 for an estimated $300 million; by September, this estimate had increased to $500 million. After a thorough review of its accounting records, Cendant revised its 1997 earnings downward by approximately $272.6 million; what had originally been reported as $55.4 million of net income became $217.2 million of net loss. Within six months of the initial disclosure of accounting irregularities, the price of Cendant's stock had declined by approximately 75% of its previous value. How could the accounting system at such a large and sophisticated company allow such large misstatements of revenues and earnings?

©Tom Pantages

The successful operation of a business enterprise requires control. How can upper management of a major retailer such as Wal-Mart know that all its stores will open at a certain time? How can the president of General Motors rest assured that the numbers in the company's financial reports accurately reflect the company's operating activities? How can the owner of a small restaurant be confident that the wait staff is not giving food to friends and relatives? The answer to each of these questions is "by exercising effective control over the enterprise." The policies and procedures used to provide *reasonable assurance* that the objectives of an enterprise will be accomplished are called **internal controls.**[1]

Internal controls can be divided into two categories: accounting controls and administrative controls. **Accounting controls** are composed of procedures designed to safeguard the assets and ensure that the accounting records contain reliable information. **Administrative controls** concern the evaluation of performance and the assessment of the degree of compliance with company policies and public laws.

[1]*AICPA Professional Standards*, vol. 1, sec. 320, par. 6 (June 1, 1989).

L.O. 1

Explain the types and purposes of internal control.

L.O. 2

Identify the key elements of a strong system of internal control.

Key Features of Internal Control Systems

The mechanics of internal control systems vary from company to company. However, most systems include a common set of general policies and procedures that have proved effective in accounting practice. The more prevalent features of a strong system of internal controls are now discussed.

Separation of Duties

There should be a clear **separation of duties.** The likelihood of fraud or theft is reduced if it becomes necessary to collude with others to accomplish an offense. For example, a person selling seats to a movie may be tempted to pocket some of the money received from customers who enter the theater. This temptation is reduced if the person staffing the box office is required to issue tickets that are then collected by a different employee as people come into the theater. The ticket stubs collected by a different employee could be compared with the cash receipts, and any cash shortages would become readily apparent. Furthermore, friends and relatives of the ticket agent would be precluded from entering the theater without paying. Theft or unauthorized entry would require collusion between the ticket agent and the usher who collects the tickets. Both individuals would have to be dishonest enough to agree to steal from the the-ater's owner, yet trustworthy enough to convince each other that they could keep the embezzlement secret. Clearly, the opportunity for crime is less than it would be if a single individual were permitted to sell the tickets and allow access to the theater.

Whenever possible, the functions of *authorization, recording,* and *custody* should be exercised by separate individuals. For example, one person should authorize the purchase of inventory, a second person should keep the records, and a third person should manage the warehouse in which the goods are stored. With this design, each person acts as a check on the other two. If the purchasing agent agreed to permit a supplier to deliver fewer goods than were ordered, the accountant would notice that the quantities on the purchase order were larger than the quantities shown on the receiving report prepared by the warehouse supervisor. Accordingly, the likelihood of errors and embezzlement is minimized when duties are separated.

Quality of Employees

Employees should be competent. A business is only as good as the people who run it. Cheap labor is not a bargain if the quality of output is so inferior as to require rework. A job done once at a cost of $6 per performance is less expensive than one that has to be done twice at a cost of $4 per performance. Employees should be adequately trained to perform a variety of tasks. The ability of employees to substitute for one another prevents disruptions that occur when co-workers are absent due to illnesses, vacations, or other commitments. The capacity to rotate jobs also relieves boredom and increases respect for the contributions of other employees. Every business should strive to maximize the productivity of each and every employee. Ongoing training programs represent an essential ingredient in a strong system of internal controls.

Bonded Employees

The adage "the best defense is a good offense" is especially true when it comes to hiring employees. The best way to ensure honesty is to hire employees with *high personal integrity.* Employers should screen job applicants through interviews, background checks, and recommendations that prior employers or educators provided. Even the best screening programs may fail to identify character weaknesses. Indeed, many frauds are perpetuated by employees who have had long records of exemplary service prior to the commission of crime. In other words, some employees with impeccable records at the time of employment can change after they have been hired. Accordingly, employees in positions of trust should be bonded. A **fidelity bond** is insurance that the company buys to protect itself from loss due to employee dishonesty. When a firm bonds an employee, the bonding company runs a check on the employee. This check is another review of the employee in addition to the verification performed by the hiring firm. Furthermore, the insurance company covers losses that the firm incurs when it is proved that such losses occurred due to the illegal actions of a bonded employee.

Periods of Absence

Employees should be required to take extended vacations and should be periodically rotated. An employee may be able to cover up illegal or unscrupulous activities while being present in the work environment. However, such activities are likely to be discovered in the employee's absence. Consider the case of a collection agent for a city's parking meter division. If the same agent always covers the same area, there is no basis for comparing that employee's collection pattern with patterns of other individuals. However, if the routes are altered, or if someone else covers the route while the regular agent is on vacation, improprieties may be discovered when the replacement agent reports different levels of cash receipts. For example, an embezzlement was discovered when a meter reader who had covered the same route for several years with no vacation became sick. When the substitute reported more money each day than the regular reader usually reported, management checked past records. It was found that the sick meter reader had been understating the cash receipts and pocketing the difference between the actual and reported collections. If management had required vacations or rotated the routes, the embezzlement would have been discovered much earlier.

Procedures Manual

There should be proper procedures for processing transactions. The procedures for processing transactions should be carefully designed so as to promote accuracy and to affect reasonable control. For example, a clerk should be instructed to prepare a check only after he or she receives a copy of the invoice and notification from the receiving department that the goods involved in the payment have arrived in acceptable condition. Furthermore, the check signer should not sign the check unless it is accompanied by adequate supporting documents. In this way, the check signer ensures that the clerk has followed the proper procedures in preparing the check. These and other appropriate accounting procedures should be establish in a **procedures manual.** The manual should be constantly updated, and periodic reviews should be conducted to ensure that the procedures outlined in the manual are being followed by employees.

Authority and Responsibility

Clear lines of authority and responsibility should be established. Motivation is maximized when individuals are given authority to act on their own judgment. Reasonable caution is exercised when employees are held accountable for their actions. Individuals often disagree on which course of action is most likely to lead to the accomplishment of the objectives of an organization. Businesses operate more effectively if clear lines of authority are established before disputes arise. Accordingly, businesses should prepare a manual that establishes a definitive *chain of command*. The authority manual should provide guidance for both specific and general authorizations. **Specific authorizations** outline the limitations that apply to different levels of management. For example, a production supervisor may be able to authorize overtime, and the plant manager authorizes the acquisition of production equipment. These authorizations apply to specific positions within the organization. In contrast, **general authority** applies across different levels of management. It includes making decisions regarding items such as credit limits for customers, the class (i.e., coach or first class) of employees' flights on business trips, the price ranges for purchases, and the names of vendors from which goods and services may be acquired.

Prenumbered Documents

You have probably seen signs in stores that offer rewards to customers for reporting clerks who do not provide sales receipts. The signs read something like this: "If you fail to receive a valid sales receipt, your purchase is free." Without a record of sales transactions, management has no means of knowing how much money should be in the cash register. Accordingly, clerks could sell merchandise and keep the proceeds for themselves. Likewise, if management does not control the supply of unused sales receipts, clerks could give customers receipts but fail to report the fact that a receipt had been used. Again, management would be left in the dark, and the clerk could steal the proceeds from the unrecorded sales transaction. However, if clerks are required to use a supply of prenumbered sales receipts, the number of sales transactions can be determined by identifying the number of missing receipts. Accordingly, the use of *prenumbered documents* can diminish the likelihood of embezzlement.

Prenumbered forms should be used for all important documents such as purchase orders, receiving reports, invoices, and checks. The forms should be as simple and easy to use as possible to reduce errors. Also, the documents should allow for a signature by authorized personnel. For example, credit sales slips should be signed by the customer making the purchase. These procedures leave no doubt as to who made the purchase. Thus, the likelihood of unauthorized transactions is reduced.

Physical Control

There should be adequate physical control over assets. While most people would not think of leaving cash lying around, they are frequently more careless with respect to other valuable assets. Employees walk away with billions of dollars of business assets each year. To limit losses, inventory should be kept in a storeroom and not released without proper authorization. Serial numbers on equipment should be recorded along with the name of the individual to whom the equipment was assigned. Unannounced physical counts should be conducted to ensure that the equipment remains in the business. Certificates of deposit and marketable securities should be kept in fireproof vaults. Access to these vaults should be limited to authorized personnel. These procedures protect the documents from fire and limit access to only those individuals who have the appropriate security clearance to handle the documents.

In addition to safeguarding assets, there should be physical control over the accounting records. The accounting journals, ledgers, and supporting documents should be kept in a fireproof safe. Only personnel responsible for recording transactions into the journals should have access to them. With limited access, there is less chance that someone will change the records to hide fraud or embezzlement.

Performance Evaluations

There should be independent verification of performance because few people can evaluate their own performance objectively. Independent verification is essential. For example, someone other than the person who has control over the inventory should take a physical count of inventory. This count should be compared with the accounting records. Discrepancies could alert management to the fact that inventory is being lost, stolen, or damaged. Internal and external audits serve as independent verification of performance. These auditors should appraise the effectiveness of the internal control system as well as verify the accuracy of the accounting records. In addition, the external auditors attest to the application of generally accepted accounting principles in the reporting process.

A system of internal controls is designed to prevent errors and fraud. However, no system is perfect or foolproof. Internal controls can be circumvented by collusion among employees. Two or more employees working together can hide embezzlement by covering for each other. For example, if an embezzler goes on vacation, illegal activity will not be reported by a replacement who is in collusion with the embezzler. No system can prevent all fraud. However, a good system of internal controls minimizes illegal or unethical activities by reducing temptation and increasing the likelihood of early detection.

Internal Control in Computer Systems

The basic internal control features discussed earlier apply to both manual and computer systems. The use of computers does not negate the need to hire competent employees with high personal integrity. Persons in positions of trust should still be bonded. The segregation and rotation of duties remain important, and the physical control of assets continues as a high priority. Indeed, computers often require special environmental features such as climate control and sophisticated electric circuitry. Accordingly, the use of computers provides an added dimension that increases the need for internal controls rather than reduces its importance. Some of the additional control requirements are as follows:

L.O. 3

Identify special internal controls for computer systems.

1. Computers do not think independently. They are neutral to the size of numbers. They would treat a $1,000,000 sales order in exactly the same manner as a $100 sales order. Accordingly, *tests of reasonableness* must be built into the operating programs. For example, programs could be designed to require a coded access number prior to initiating delivery orders for sales transactions in excess of $10,000 to motivate human scrutiny of major sales transactions. Similar controls should be incorporated to ensure that human logic remains an active component of business operations.

2. Significant technical expertise may be required to design and run the programs that operate an automated accounting system. Accordingly, the computer programmers may be more knowledgeable than the auditors who are assigned the task of monitoring the programmers' performance. Background checks and fidelity bonding for the programmers may be important under these circumstances.

3. Documentary evidence may be diminished in computer-based accounting systems. Information is usually stored on magnetic disks and therefore is unobservable to the human eye. These data can be easily destroyed or manipulated without the traditional traces that facilitate detection. Auditors may be required to **audit around the computer** to test the system. This expression is used to describe a procedure in which the auditor provides input that is expected to result in a designated output. The system is tested by comparing the actual output with the expected output. If actual output is consistent with expectations, then the procedure provides evidence of accurate processing. Differences signal the need for further investigation. For example, instead of analyzing a computer program to determine whether it was designed to compute payroll tax correctly, the auditor could input the gross salary of a test case and analyze the tax figures generated by the program to see if it is operating appropriately.

4. It may be more difficult to control access to sensitive data in automated accounting systems. Hackers have the ability to gain unauthorized access to highly sophisticated computer systems. Large quantities of data can be transferred across phone lines, thereby permitting thieves to commit their crimes without leaving the security of their own work environment. Care must be taken to control access to the system. Passwords and other screening devices should be employed to reduce the risk of unauthorized access to computer programs and data files.

5. It is important to maintain proper documentation regarding the development and operation of the computer programs used in the business. Without proper documentation, the operation of the system becomes dependent on the knowledge base of a particular programmer. If the programmer becomes ill or otherwise incapacitated, the operating system becomes dysfunctional as well. Many small businesses find the use of standard commercial programs to be a cost-effective alternative to writing their own programs. You do not have to build a car to obtain the benefits of automotive transportation; you simply buy, lease, or rent an automobile. Likewise, you do not have to write a computer program to obtain the benefits of an automated accounting system. Many existing commercial programs meet the needs of most small businesses. These programs provide proper documentation and technical support at affordable prices.

6. Finally, it is critically important to safeguard the programs and databases. Programs and databases are easily destroyed or sabotaged. Backup files should be maintained in a fireproof vault in a separate location to minimize the danger associated with lost or damaged programs and data files.

Based on the company's public disclosures, many inappropriate accounting practices were used at the CUC portion of Cendant Corporation. On October 15, 1998, Henry R. Silverman, CEO of Cedant, was interviewed on CNN. When he was asked how the fraudulent activities were not detected before the merger of the two companies was finalized, he responded, "Our financial system is based on trust. . . . We have to rely upon, really, the honor system. . . . Our system is very vulnerable to fraud because it is based on trust. . . . We can't do . . . polygraphs of every management that you happen to do business with. . . ."

Perhaps some or all of the irregularities at CUC and Cendant should have been detected earlier by the companies' internal controls and/or independent auditors; the courts will answer those questions ultimately. Nevertheless, Mr. Silverman's answer has a certain degree of truth. No system of internal controls can prevent all fraud from occurring if several members of management decide to work together to circumvent those controls.

If you wish to read a detailed report by Cendant's audit committee regarding these matters, using EDGAR, download Cendant's 8-K report that was filed with the SEC on August 28, 1998. Instructions for using EDGAR are contained in Appendix A of this book.

Accounting for Cash

Cash is broadly defined for financial statement purposes. Generally, **cash** includes currency and other items that are payable *on demand*, such as checks, money orders, bank drafts, and certain savings accounts. Savings accounts that require substantial penalties for early withdrawal should be classified as *investments* rather than as cash. Furthermore, postdated checks or IOUs represent *receivables* and should not be accounted for as cash. In practice, most companies use captions that highlight the fact that items other than currency are included in the cash classification. Exhibit 6–1 includes a list of the most frequently used balance sheet titles that include the word *cash*.

> **L.O. 4**
>
> Identify special internal controls for cash.

The amount of cash on hand must be closely monitored to ensure the viability and profitability of the business. There must be enough cash available to pay employees, suppliers, and creditors as amounts become due. When a company fails to pay legal debts, the creditors can force the business into bankruptcy. While the availability of cash is critical, management should avoid the accumulation of excess idle cash. The failure to invest excess cash in earning assets adversely affects profitability. Cash inflows and outflows must be properly managed to prevent a shortage or surplus of cash.

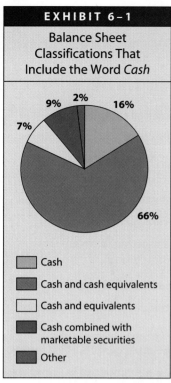

EXHIBIT 6–1

Balance Sheet Classifications That Include the Word *Cash*

2%
9%
7%
16%
66%

☐ Cash
☐ Cash and cash equivalents
☐ Cash and equivalents
☐ Cash combined with marketable securities
☐ Other

Data Source: AICPA, *Accounting Trends and Techniques*, 1998.

Controlling Cash

Cash more than any other asset requires strict adherence to internal control procedures. It has universal appeal. Relatively small amounts of high-denomination currency can be used to represent significant amounts of value. Furthermore, specific identification as to who owns currency is difficult to prove. In most cases, possession equates to ownership. Because of these qualities, cash is highly susceptible to theft and must be kept under close scrutiny. Cash is most susceptible to embezzlement at the points of receipt and disbursement. The following procedures should be employed to reduce the likelihood of theft.

Cash Receipts

A record of all cash receipts should be prepared immediately. If cash receipts are recorded in a timely and accurate manner, missing amounts of money can be detected by comparing the actual balances of cash with the book balances. Customers should be given written copies of the receipts that evidence payment. This practice results in a control on the receipts clerk by the customer. A customer usually reviews the receipt to ensure that she or he has been given credit for the amount paid and calls any errors to the clerk's attention.

Cash receipts should be deposited in a bank or other financial institution on a timely basis. Cash collected late in the day should be deposited in a night depository. Every effort should be made to minimize the amount of cash on hand. Large amounts of cash not only place the business at risk of loss from theft but also place the employees in danger of being harmed by criminals who attempt to rob the company.

Cash Payments

To effectively control cash, a company should make all disbursements by check, thereby providing a record of cash payments. All checks should be prenumbered and kept under lock. When checks are prenumbered, lost or stolen checks are easily identifiable by comparing the supply of unwritten and canceled checks with the list of prenumbered checks. If checks are kept locked and under the care of a responsible person, then there is less opportunity for unauthorized disbursements.

The duties of approving disbursements, signing checks, and recording transactions should be separated. If one person is authorized to approve, sign, and record checks, then it is easy for that person to falsify supporting documents, write a check, and record it in the records. By separating these three duties, the check signer reviews the documentation provided by the approving agent before signing the check. Likewise, the recording clerk reviews the work of both the approval agent and the signer when information is input to the accounting records. Again, collusion is required in order to circumvent the system of controls created by the separation of these duties.

Supporting documents with authorized approval signatures should be required when checks are presented to the check signer. Supporting documents prove an actual need for payment. Before the payment is approved, invoice amounts should be checked and the payee verified as being a legitimate vendor. Thus, the authorized approval signature acts as a check on the documents submitted by the payables clerk. Both the supporting documents and an authorized

approval help deter the payables clerk from creating fake documents with the disbursement being made to a friend or fictitious business. Also, the approver serves as a check on the accuracy of the work of the payables clerk.

Supporting documents should be marked *Paid* when the check is signed. If the documents are not indelibly marked, they could be retrieved from the file and resubmitted for a second payment. A payables clerk could work with the payee to share in any extra cash paid out by submitting the same supporting invoices for a second payment.

All spoiled and voided checks should be defaced and retained. An employee may claim that a certain check was written for an incorrect amount and therefore thrown away. Unless there is physical proof of the existence of the check, the firm has no way of knowing if the clerk is telling the truth or if he or she stole the check. To prevent this uncertainty, all spoiled and voided checks should be kept.

Checking Account Documents

The previous section clearly established the need for businesses and individuals to use checking accounts. The following are the four main types of forms associated with a bank checking account:

Signature Card

A bank **signature card** contains the bank account number and the signatures of the people authorized to write checks on the account. The form is retained in the bank's files. If a bank employee is unfamiliar with the signature on a check that is presented to the bank for payment, she or he can refer to the signature card to verify the signature for that particular account.

Deposit Ticket

Each deposit of cash or checks is accompanied by a **deposit ticket,** which normally contains the account number and the name of the account. The depositor fills in the amount of currency, coins, and checks deposited. The total of all currency, coins, and checks deposited is noted on the deposit ticket.

Bank Check

A written check involves three parties: (1) the person or business writing the check (i.e., the payer), (2) the bank on which the check is drawn, and (3) the person or business to whom the check is made payable (i.e., the payee). **Checks** are often multicopy, prenumbered forms, with the name of the business issuing them preprinted on the face. A remittance notice is usually attached to the check. This portion of the check gives the payer space in which to establish a record that identifies why the check is being written (e.g., what invoices are being paid), the amount being disbursed, and the date of payment. When signed by the person whose signature is on the signature card, the check authorizes the bank to transfer the face amount of the check from the payer's account to the payee.

Bank Statement

Periodically, the bank sends the depositor a **bank statement.** It is important to note that the bank statement is presented from the bank's point of view. Since the bank is obligated to pay back the money that customers have deposited in their accounts, a checking account is a liability to the bank. Accordingly, the checking account carries a credit balance on the bank's books. **Bank statement debit memos** describe transactions that reduce the balance of the bank's liability (i.e., the customer's account). **Bank statement credit memos** describe activities that increase the bank's liability (i.e., the customer's account balance). To avoid confusion, remember that the checking account is an asset (i.e., cash) to the depositor. Accordingly, a *debit memo* listed in the bank statement requires a *credit entry* to the Cash account on the depositor's books.

The information contained in the bank statement normally includes (a) the balance of the account at the beginning of the period, (b) additions created by customer deposits made during the period, (c) other additions described in credit memos (e.g., earned interest), (d) subtractions made for the payment of checks drawn on the account during the period, (e) other subtractions described in debit memos (e.g., service charges), (f) a running balance of the account, and (g) the balance of the account at the end of the period. Examples of these items are referenced with the letters in parentheses in the example of a bank statement in Exhibit 6–2. Normally, the canceled checks or copies of them are enclosed with the bank statement.

Reconciliation of the Bank Statement

L.O. 5

Prepare a bank reconciliation.

Usually the balance shown on the bank statement differs from the balance shown in the Cash account on the depositor's books. The difference is normally attributable to timing. For example, a depositor deducts the amount of a check from the account immediately after writing the check. However, the bank has no knowledge of the check until the payee presents it for payment, which may occur several weeks or even months after the check is written. Similarly, there may be a delay between the time when a bank adjusts a depositor's account and the time when the customer becomes aware that the adjustment was made. For example, a customer may not be aware that the bank deposited interest in or subtracted service charges from his or her account until the customer receives and reads the bank statement. Accordingly, the bank statement may reflect a balance larger or smaller than the balance recorded in the depositor's books. The following items cause the balance on the bank statement to be larger than the balance shown in the depositor's cash account:

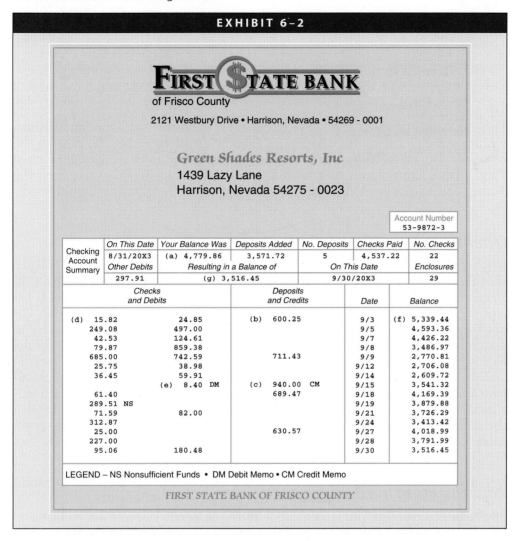

EXHIBIT 6-2

FIRST STATE BANK
of Frisco County

2121 Westbury Drive • Harrison, Nevada • 54269 - 0001

Green Shades Resorts, Inc
1439 Lazy Lane
Harrison, Nevada 54275 - 0023

Account Number
53-9872-3

Checking Account Summary	On This Date	Your Balance Was	Deposits Added	No. Deposits	Checks Paid	No. Checks
	8/31/20X3	(a) 4,779.86	3,571.72	5	4,537.22	22
	Other Debits	Resulting in a Balance of			On This Date	Enclosures
	297.91	(g) 3,516.45			9/30/20X3	29

Checks and Debits			Deposits and Credits		Date	Balance
(d) 15.82	24.85		(b) 600.25		9/3	(f) 5,339.44
249.08	497.00				9/5	4,593.36
42.53	124.61				9/7	4,426.22
79.87	859.38				9/8	3,486.97
685.00	742.59		711.43		9/9	2,770.81
25.75	38.98				9/12	2,706.08
36.45	59.91				9/14	2,609.72
	(e) 8.40 DM		(c) 940.00 CM		9/15	3,541.32
61.40			689.47		9/18	4,169.39
289.51 NS					9/19	3,879.88
71.59	82.00				9/21	3,726.29
312.87					9/24	3,413.42
25.00			630.57		9/27	4,018.99
227.00					9/28	3,791.99
95.06	180.48				9/30	3,516.45

LEGEND – NS Nonsufficient Funds • DM Debit Memo • CM Credit Memo

FIRST STATE BANK OF FRISCO COUNTY

1. **Outstanding checks.** These are disbursements that have been properly recorded as cash deductions on the payer's books. However, the amounts have not been deducted from the payer's bank account because the checks have not yet been presented by the payee to the bank for payment (i.e., the checks have not "cleared" the bank).

2. Deposits made by the bank. These are additions to the depositor's account made directly by the bank. They may be the result of collections made by the bank on behalf of the depositor or of interest paid to the depositor by the bank.

Alternatively, the balance reported on the bank statement may be less than the balance recorded in the depositor's books. This may be due to the following causes:

1. **Service charges.** These are fees charged by the bank for services performed or as a penalty for the depositor's failing to maintain a specified minimum cash balance throughout the period.

2. **Deductions for non-sufficient-funds (NSF) checks.** These are checks that were deposited. However, when the checks were submitted for payment to the bank on which they were drawn, the accounts did not

have enough funds to cover the amount of the checks. When such checks are returned, they must be deducted from the depositor's bank account.

3. **Deposits in transit.** These are deposits that have been recorded by the depositor on the accounting records but have not yet been recorded by the bank.

Additionally, there may be differences between the bank statement's cash balance and the depositor's cash balance due to errors by either the bank or the depositor. For example, the bank may pay a check written by a customer named *Turpen* from the account of a customer named *Turpin*. In this case, both the Turpen and Turpin bank statements would be incorrect. All errors should be corrected immediately.

Determining True Cash Balance

A schedule is preapproved to reconcile the differences between the cash balance shown on the bank statement and the cash balance recorded in the depositor's accounting records. This schedule is called a **bank reconciliation statement.** It begins with the cash balance reported by the bank as of the statement date (i.e., the **unadjusted bank balance**). The schedule then lists the adjustments necessary to determine the amount of cash that the depositor actually has as of the date of the bank statement. The actual cash balance is called the **true cash balance.** The true cash balance is determined a second time by making adjustments to the **unadjusted book balance.** The bank statement is reconciled when the true cash balance determined from the perspective of the unadjusted *bank* balance agrees with the true cash balance determined from the perspective of the unadjusted *book* balance. The procedures necessary to arrive at the *true cash balance* from the two different perspectives are outlined here.

Adjustments to the Bank Balance

Step 1 in determining the true balance from the perspective of the bank statement is to compare the deposit tickets with deposits shown in the depositor's records. Any deposits recorded on the depositor's books but not yet recorded by the bank are, as noted, deposits in transit. Since deposits are frequently made in the night depository or on the day following the receipt of cash, this is a frequent occurrence. Deposits in transit have not been recorded by the bank, and therefore they are added to the unadjusted bank balance to arrive at the true cash balance.

Step 2 is to sort the checks returned with the bank statement into numerical sequence. These checks are then compared with checks listed in the depositor's cash records, and the amounts are verified. After verification of all the checks returned with the bank statement, there may be some checks that were issued by the depositor but not presented to the bank for payment. These *outstanding checks* must be deducted from the unadjusted bank balance to determine the true cash balance. A **certified check** is a check guaranteed by a bank to be a check drawn on an account having sufficient funds. Whereas a regular check is deducted from the customer's account when it is presented for payment, a certified check is deducted from the customer's account when the bank certifies that the check is good. Accordingly, all certified checks have been deducted by the bank in the determination of the unadjusted bank balance, whether they have cleared the bank or remain outstanding as of the date of the bank statement. For this reason, it is not necessary to deduct *outstanding certified checks* from the unadjusted bank balance to determine the true balance of cash.

Adjustments to the Book Balance

The unadjusted book balance must be adjusted to reflect the credit and debit memos shown in the bank statement. Credit memo items such as earned interest are added to the unadjusted book balance, and debit memo items such as service charges are subtracted from it. Non-sufficient-funds checks must be subtracted from the unadjusted book balance to determine the true cash balance.

Correction of Errors

Errors can affect the determination of the true cash balance from the perspective of either the bank statement or the depositor's books. If an error is found on the bank statement, the bank should be notified immediately, and the adjustment is made to the unadjusted bank balance to determine the true cash balance. In contrast, errors made by the depositor require adjustments to the book balance in order to arrive at the true cash balance.

Illustration of the Reconciliation Statement

The following example illustrates the process of preparing the bank reconciliation statement for Green Shades Resorts, Inc. (GSRI). Recall that Exhibit 6–2 is the bank statement for GSRI. Exhibit 6–3 represents the completed bank reconciliation statement. The items included in the reconciliation statement are now described.

EXHIBIT 6–3

GREEN SHADES RESORT, INC.
Bank Reconciliation Statement
September 30, 20X3

Unadjusted Bank Balance, September 30, 20X3			$3,516.45
Add: Deposits in Transit			724.11
Bank Error: Check drawn on Green Valley Resorts Charged to GSRI			25.00
Less: Outstanding Checks			

Check No.	Date	Amount
639	Sept. 18	$ 13.75
646	Sept. 20	29.00
672	Sept. 27	192.50

Total	(235.25)
True Cash Balance, Sept 30, 20X3	$4,030.31

Unadjusted Book Balance, September 30, 20X3		$3,361.22
Add: Receivable Collected by Bank		940.00
Error Made by Accountant (Check no. 633 recorded as $63.45 instead of $36.45)		27.00
Less: Bank Service Charges		(8.40)
NSF Check		(289.51)
True Cash Balance, September 30, 20X3		$4,030.31

Adjustments to Bank Balance

As of September 30, 20X3, the bank statement shows an unadjusted balance of $3,516.45. Assume that a review of the bank statement discloses two adjustments that must be added to this amount. First, assume that a review of the deposit tickets indicated that there was $724.11 of deposits in transit. Second, assume that an examination of the returned checks disclosed that a $25 check written by Green Valley Resorts had been deducted from GSRI's bank account. Since the bank erroneously deducted this amount from GSRI's account, the amount must be added back to the unadjusted bank balance to arrive at the true balance.

Finally, assume that the returned checks included in the bank statement were sorted and compared to the cash records and that three checks were outstanding. Since these checks have not yet been deducted from GSRI's bank account, the unadjusted bank balance must be reduced. Exhibit 6–3 assumes that the amount of the outstanding checks was $235.25. After this deduction is made, the true cash balance is $4,030.31.

Adjustments to Book Balance

As indicated in Exhibit 6–3, GSRI's unadjusted book balance as of September 30, 20X3, amounted to $3,361.22. This balance does not accurately reflect GSRI's true cash balance because of four unrecorded accounting events: (1) The bank collected a $940 account receivable for GSRI, (2) GSRI's accountant made a $27 recording error, (3) the bank charged GSRI an $8.40 service fee, and (4) GSRI accepted a $289.51 check from a customer who did not have sufficient funds to cover the check. Each event requires an adjustment to GSRI's accounting records. The adjustments and their effects on the financial statements are now explained.

Adjustment 1   Recording the $940 receivables collection acts to increase Cash and reduce Accounts Receivables. The event is an asset exchange transaction. The effect of the collection on GSRI's financial statements follows:

Assets			= Liab.	+ Equity	Rev.	– Exp.	= Net Inc.	Cash Flow	
Cash	+	Acct. Rec.							
940	+	(940)	= n/a	+ n/a	n/a	– n/a	= n/a	940	OA

Adjustment 2   Assume that the $27 recording error occurred because GSRI's accountant made a transposition error when recording check no. 633. The check was written to pay utilities expense in the amount of $36.45 but was recorded as a $63.45 disbursement. Since cash payments are overstated by $27.00 ($63.45 − $36.45), this amount must be added back to GSRI's cash balance and deducted from the Utilities Expense account. Since the deduction causes the Utilities Expense account to decline, the Net Income increases. The effects on the financial statements are shown next:

Assets	= Liab.	+ Equity	Rev.	– Exp.	= Net Inc.	Cash Flow	
27	= n/a	+ 27	n/a	– (27)	= 27	27	OA

Adjustment 3   The $8.40 service charge is a typical expense item that reduces assets, equity, income, and cash flow. The effects are shown here:

Assets	= Liab.	+ Equity	Rev.	– Exp.	= Net Inc.	Cash Flow	
(8.40)	= n/a	+ (8.40)	n/a	– 8.40	= (8.40)	(8.40)	OA

The $289.51 NSF check reduces GSRI's cash balance. GSRI increased its Cash account when it originally accepted the customer's check. Now GSRI must reduce its Cash account because there is not enough money in the customer's bank account to pay the check. GSRI will try to collect the money directly from the customer. In the meantime, GSRI will show the amount due as an account receivable. Accordingly, the adjusting entry required to record the NSF check is an asset exchange transaction. The Cash account decreases, and the Accounts Receivable account increases. The effect on GSRI's financial statements is as follows:

Adjustment 4

Assets			= Liab.	+ Equity	Rev.	− Exp.	= Net Inc.	Cash Flow
Cash	+	Acct. Rec.						
(289.51)	+	289.51	= n/a	+ n/a	n/a	− n/a	= n/a	(289.51) OA

Determination of the True Cash Balance

Two of the adjustments act to increase the unadjusted cash balance. The other two adjustments act to decrease the unadjusted balance. After the adjustments have been recorded, the Cash account reflects the true cash balance of $4,030.31 ($3,361.22 unadjusted cash balance + $940.00 receivable collection + $27.00 recording error − $8.40 service charge − $289.51 NSF check). Since the true balance determined from the perspective of the bank account agrees with the true balance determined from the perspective of GSRI's books, the bank statement has been successfully reconciled with the accounting records.

Cash Balance Updated

The journal entries required for the four adjustments described are as follows:

Account Title	Debit	Credit
Cash	940.00	
Accounts Receivable		940.00
To record the account receivable collected by the bank		
Cash	27.00	
Utilities Expense		27.00
To correct error on recording check no. 633		
Bank Service Charge Expense	8.40	
Cash		8.40
To record service charge expense		
Accounts Receivable	289.51	
Cash		289.51
To establish receivable due from customer who		
wrote the bad check		

Cash Short and Over

Sometime errors are made when employees are collecting cash or making change to customers. If these errors occur, then the amount of money in the cash register will not agree with the amount of cash receipts recorded on the cash register tape. For example, suppose that when a customer paid for $17.95 of merchandise with a $20 bill, the sales clerk returned $3.05 in change instead of the correct amount of $2.05. If, at the end of the day, the cash register tape shows total receipts of $487.50, the cash drawer contains only $486.50. The actual cash balance is less than the expected cash balance by $1. Any shortage of cash or excess of cash is recorded in a special account named **Cash Short and Over.** In this example, the shortage is recorded in the following journal entry:

Account Title	Debit	Credit
Cash	486.50	
Cash Short and Over	1.00	
Sales		487.50

A debit to the Cash Short and Over account indicates a cash shortage that represents an expense. An overage of cash is considered revenue and is recorded by crediting the Cash Short and Over account. As with other expense and revenue items, the balance of the Cash Short and Over account is closed to the Retained Earnings account.

Petty Cash Funds

Although it is best to make all disbursements by check, it may be more practical and convenient to make certain small payments in cash. Payments for postage, delivery charges, taxi fares, employees' supper money, and other small items are frequently made with cash. To allow for these small payments and still keep effective control over cash disbursements, a company may establish a **petty cash fund.** The fund is established for some specified dollar amount, such as $300, and is controlled by one employee, called the *petty cash custodian.*

Petty cash funds are usually maintained on an **imprest basis,** which means that the cash disbursed is replenished on a periodic basis. The fund is created by drawing a check on the regular checking account, cashing it, and giving the currency to a petty cash custodian. The custodian normally keeps the cash under lock and key. In other words, the establishment of a petty cash fund merely transfers cash from a bank account to a safety box inside the company offices. As such, the event is an asset exchange. The Cash account decreases, and the Petty Cash account increases. The effect on the financial statements and the journal entry required to record the event are as follows:

Assets			= Liab.	+ Equity	Rev.	− Exp.	= Net Inc.	Cash Flow
Cash	+	Petty Cash						
(300)	+	300	= n/a	+ n/a	n/a	− n/a	= n/a	n/a

Account Title	Debit	Credit
Petty Cash	300.00	
Cash		300.00

The amount of the petty cash fund depends on what it is used for, how often it is used, and how often it is replenished. It should be large enough to handle disbursements for a reasonable time, such as a week or a month.

When money is disbursed from the petty cash fund, the custodian should fill out a petty cash **voucher,** such as the one in Exhibit 6–4. Any supporting documents, such as an invoice, restaurant bill, or parking fee receipt, should be attached to the petty cash voucher. The person who receives the cash should always sign the voucher as evidence of the receipt. At any time, the total of the amounts recorded on the petty cash vouchers plus the remaining coin and

EXHIBIT 6–4

Petty cash voucher no. _____

To: _____ Date _____ , 20 ____

Explanation: Account No. _____   Amount _____

Approved by _____   Received by _____

currency should equal the balance of the petty cash ledger account. *There is no journal entry made in the accounting records at the time when petty cash funds are disbursed.* The effect on financial statements is recorded at the time when the petty cash fund is replenished (i.e., at the time when additional cash is put into the petty cash safety box).

When the amount of cash in the petty cash fund is relatively low, the fund should be replenished. To accomplish the replenishment, the petty cash vouchers are totaled, and a check for this amount is issued to the bank to obtain the currency needed to return the fund to its full balance. For example, suppose the petty cash fund is replenished at a time when the total amount of petty cash vouchers equals $216. The vouchers can be classified according to different types of expenses or listed in total as miscellaneous expense. Assuming that the Miscellaneous Expense Account is used in this example, the journal entries to record the replenishment of the funds are as follows:

Account Title	Debit	Credit
Miscellaneous Expense	216.00	
Petty Cash		216.00
To record expenses paid from the petty cash fund		
Petty Cash	216.00	
Cash		216.00
To replenish the petty cash fund		

Note that the effect of the entries could have been recorded in a more efficient manner. Since the debit to the Petty Cash account is offset by the credit, a single entry debiting Miscellaneous Expense and crediting Cash would have the same effect on the accounts. Indeed, the entry more frequently used in practice to record the replenishment of petty cash appears as follows:

Account Title	Debit	Credit
Miscellaneous Expense	216.00	
Cash		216.00

The replenishment affects the financial statements in the same manner as any other cash expense. It acts to reduce assets, equity, income, and cash flow. The effects are shown here:

Assets	=	Liab.	+	Equity	Rev.	−	Exp.	=	Net Inc.	Cash Flow	
(216)	=	n/a	+	(216)	n/a	−	216	=	(216)	(216)	OA

If the vouchers and their amounts are separated as postage—$66, delivery charges—$78.40, taxi fares—$28, and supper money—$43.60, then the journal entry to replenish the fund could be recorded as follows:

Account Title	Debit	Credit
Postage Expense	66.00	
Delivery Expense	78.40	
Taxi Fares Expense	28.00	
Employee Meal Expense	43.60	
Cash		216.00

Once the vouchers are checked, the fund replenished, and the journal entry recorded, the vouchers should be indelibly marked *Paid* so that they cannot be reused.

Sometimes, cash shortages and overages are discovered when a physical count is taken of the money in the petty cash fund. Suppose that a physical count reveals $212.30 in petty cash vouchers and only $87 in cash. Assuming a normal petty cash balance of $300, the journal entries necessary to record the replenishment are as follows:

Account Title	Debit	Credit
Miscellaneous Expense	212.30	
Cash Short and Over	.70	
Petty Cash		213.00
To record expenses paid from the petty cash fund		
Petty Cash	213.00	
Cash		213.00
To replenish the petty cash fund		

If a cash shortage or overage does not occur frequently and it is an insignificant amount, then the shortage or overage may be included in miscellaneous expense.

Assessment of the Level of Liquidity

Current versus Noncurrent

L.O. 7

Prepare a classified balance sheet.

Assets have been defined as items that have probable future economic benefits to a business, and *liabilities* as the creditors' claim on some of those assets. However, not all assets and liabilities are the same; a significant distinguishing feature relates to their liquidity. The more quickly an asset is converted to cash, the more *liquid* it is. This is important because companies usually pay their bills with cash. Land and buildings are valuable assets, but they cannot be used to pay this month's electric bill.

Why not keep all assets in cash or liquid investments? Because investments in liquid assets usually do not earn as much money as investments in other assets. Thus, a company must try to maintain a proper balance between liquid assets (so it can pay its bills) and nonliquid assets (so it can earn a good return).

This distinction is so important that accountants organize items on the balance sheet according to liquidity. There are two major classes of assets: *current* and *noncurrent*. Current items are also referred to as *short term* and noncurrent items as *long term*. A **current (short-term) asset** is one that will be converted to cash or consumed within 1 year or an operating cycle, whichever is longer. For example, accounts receivable are usually expected to be collected (i.e., converted to cash) within 1 year. Therefore, they are classified as current.

An **operating cycle** is defined as the average time it takes a business to convert cash to inventory, inventory to accounts receivable, and accounts receivable back to cash. Graphically, it can be shown as follows:

L.O. 8

Identify the length of an operating cycle.

Operating cycles for most businesses are less than 1 year, but they can be longer. Consider the time it takes a construction company to build and sell a house—this time could easily exceed 1 year. Ratios that help measure the length of a company's operating cycle are introduced in Chapters 7 and 8. However, unless there is strong evidence to the contrary, assume that operating cycles are less than 1 year. Accordingly, the 1-year rule usually prevails with respect to the classification of current assets.

Based on the definition of *current* as explained here, the typical current assets section of a balance sheet includes the following items:

Current Assets
   Cash
   Marketable Securities
   Accounts Receivable
   Short-Term Notes Receivable
   Interest Receivable
   Inventory
   Supplies
   Prepaids

Given the definition of current assets, it seems logical that a **current (short-term) liability** would be one that must be repaid within 1 year or an operating cycle. This is almost always correct. However, this definition places some surprising accounts in the category of current liabilities. If a company issues bonds[2] that are to be repaid in 20 years, the bonds are included in long-term liabilities (i.e., until they have been outstanding for 19 years). After 19 years, the 20-year bonds become due within 1 more year and are classified as a current liability on the balance sheet.

---

[2]*Bonds* are certificates issued to creditors that evidence a company's obligation to pay interest and return of principal on borrowed funds. They are normally issued to the general public in exchange for the receipt of borrowed money. Bonds usually carry long terms to maturity, with 20 years being typical. Chapter 10 of this book is devoted almost exclusively to the accounting treatment of bonds. More detailed information is provided there. At this point, all that is necessary for your comprehension of the subject matter under discussion is to know that bonds represent a form of long-term debt. Companies that issue bonds receive cash that they are obligated to repay at a future date. In the interim, they pay interest to the creditors for the privilege of using the borrowed funds.

There is an exception to the general rule for determining which liabilities should be listed as short term. If a business does not plan to use any of its current assets to repay a debt, then that debt is listed as long term even if it is due within 1 year. How can debt be repaid without using current assets? Assume that the 20-year bonds referred to are now due within the next year. The company may plan to issue new 20-year bonds (long-term debt) and use the proceeds from those bonds to repay the old bonds. In this case, the currently maturing debt is classified as long term. This situation is referred to as *refinancing short-term debt on a long-term basis.*

Liabilities typically found in the current section of a balance sheet include the following:

Current Liabilities
    Accounts Payable
    Short-Term Notes Payable
    Wages Payable
    Taxes Payable
    Interest Payable

Balance sheets that distinguish between current and noncurrent items are called **classified balance sheets.** To enhance the usefulness of accounting information, most real-world balance sheets are classified. However, there is no requirement to present information in this fashion. Exhibit 6–5 is an example of a classified balance sheet.

Liquidity versus Solvency

Liquidity, as explained, deals with the ability to generate short-term cash flows. **Solvency** is the ability to repay liabilities in the long run. Liquidity and solvency are both important to the survival of a business, but one may be more important to a particular user than the other. If a bank is considering loaning a company money that must be repaid in 6 months, obviously the bank is concerned more with the company's liquidity. An investor thinking of purchasing the company's 20-year bonds is interested in the company's solvency as well as its liquidity because a company that cannot pay its bills in the short term will not be around to repay the bonds 20 years from now.

Current Ratio

L.O. 9

Use the current ratio to assess the level of liquidity.

Financial statement users calculate several ratios in the process of making the comparisons needed to evaluate a company's liquidity and solvency. The debt-to-assets ratio introduced in Chapter 3 is one tool used to examine solvency. The primary ratio used to evaluate liquidity is the **current ratio,** defined as

Current Assets

Current Liabilities

Since current assets normally exceed current liabilities, this ratio usually produces a result larger than 100%. Many individuals find large percentages difficult to interpret. Accordingly, the current ratio is frequently expressed as a decimal rather than as a percentage. For example, a company with $250 in current assets and $100 in current liabilities has a current ratio of 2.5 to 1 ($250 ÷ $100 = $2.50 in current assets for every $1 in current liabilities). This is, of course, the

EXHIBIT 6–5

LIMBAUGH COMPANY
Classified Balance Sheet
As of December 31, 20X6

Assets			
Current Assets			
Cash		$ 20,000	
Accounts Receivable		35,000	
Inventory		230,000	
Prepaid Rent		3,600	
Total Current Assets			$288,600
Property, Plant, and Equipment			
Office Equipment	$ 80,000		
Less: Accumulated Depreciation	(25,000)	55,000	
Building	340,000		
Less: Accumulated Depreciation	(40,000)	300,000	
Land		120,000	
Total Property, Plant, and Equipment			475,000
Total Assets			$763,600
Liabilities and Owner's Equity			
Current Liabilities			
Accounts Payable		$ 32,000	
Notes Payable		120,000	
Salaries Payable		32,000	
Unearned Revenue		9,800	
Total Current Liabilities			$193,800
Long-Term Liabilities			
Note Payable			100,000
Total Liabilities			293,800
Equity			
Contributed Capital		200,000	
Retained Earnings		269,800	469,800
Total Liabilities and Equity			$763,600

same as saying that current assets are 250% of current liabilities. However, as stated earlier, traditional practice tends to favor the decimal expression. Accordingly, this book uses that format when making reference to the current ratio.

Real-World Data

The current ratio is one of the most commonly used ratios to analyze accounting information. Current ratios can be too high, suggesting that the company has more assets available to pay current liabilities than are needed. This result would suggest that earnings could probably be improved by converting some of the short-term assets to longer-term investments that yield a higher return. Indeed, given the desire for profit maximization, you are likely to find more real-world companies with ratios that are too low than with those that are too high.

EXHIBIT 6-6			
Industry	Company	Current Ratio	Debt-to-Assets Ratio
Banking	American Express	1.75	0.92
	NationsBank	1.11	0.92
Grocery Stores	Kroger	0.90	1.12
	Safeway	0.80	0.75
Building Supplies	Home Depot	1.82	0.36
	Lowes	1.46	0.50

Exhibit 6–6 presents the 1997 current ratios and debt-to-assets ratios expressed in decimal format for six real-world companies from three different industries.

Which of these companies is exposed to the highest level of financial risk? Clearly, the answer is Kroger because it has a debt-to-assets ratio of more than 100%. This means it has more liabilities than assets! Notice that the banks have higher debt-to-assets ratios and lower current ratios than those of the companies in the building supplies business. Does this mean that banks are more risky investments? Not necessarily; since the companies are in different industries, one

focus on

international issues

Why Are These Balance Sheets Backward?

many of the differences in accounting rules used around the world would be difficult to detect by merely comparing financial statements from companies in different countries. For example, if a balance sheet for a U.S. company and one for a U.K. company both report an asset called *land,* it might not be clear if the reported amounts were computed by using the same measurement rules or different measurement rules. Did both companies use historical cost as a basis for measurement? Perhaps not, but this would be difficult to determine by merely comparing balance sheets from two countries.

However, one difference between financial reporting in the United Kingdom and the United States that is very obvious is the arrangement of assets on the balance sheet. In this chapter, we explain that U.S. GAAP require current assets to be shown first and noncurrent assets second; the same is true of liabilities. In the United Kingdom, noncurrent assets appear first, followed by current assets; however, liabilities are shown in the same order as in the United States. In other countries (e.g., France), both assets and liabilities are shown with noncurrent items first. The accounting rules of some countries require that equity be shown before liabilities; this is the opposite of the U.S. GAAP. Therefore, to someone who learned accounting in the United States, the balance sheets of companies from some countries may appear "backward" or "upside down."

No matter in what order the assets, liabilities, and equity accounts are arranged on a company's balance sheet, one accounting concept is true throughout the free world:

Assets = Liabilities + Equity

must be careful when comparing ratios. Banks traditionally have very high debt-to-asset ratios, so those of American Express and NationsBank are not unusual. Remember that financial leverage can increase profitability if the return on invested funds exceeds the cost of interest, so high debt levels can be productive if a company operates in a relatively stable industry.

Finally, note that the debt-to-assets ratios for the companies tend to be "grouped by industry," with Kroger being an obvious exception. Current ratios do vary somewhat among different industries, but they probably do not vary as much as the debt-to-asset ratios. Why? Because all companies, regardless of how they finance their total assets, must keep sufficient current assets on hand to repay current liabilities.

A LOOK

BACK

The policies and procedures used to provide reasonable assurance that the objectives of an enterprise will be accomplished are called *internal controls*, which can be subdivided into two categories: accounting controls and administrative controls. *Accounting* controls are composed of procedures designed to safeguard the assets and ensure that the accounting records contain reliable information. *Administrative controls* are designed to evaluate performance and the degree of compliance with company policies and public laws. While the mechanics of internal control systems vary from company to company, the more prevalent features include the following:

1. *Separation of Duties.* Whenever possible, the functions of authorization, recording, and custody should be exercised by separate individuals.

2. *Quality of Employees.* Employees should be qualified to competently perform the duties that are assigned to them. The enterprise must establish hiring practices to screen out unqualified candidates. Furthermore, procedures should be established to ensure that employees receive the appropriate training necessary to maintain competence.

3. *Bonded Employees.* Employees in sensitive positions should be covered by a fidelity bond that provides insurance to reimburse losses that are due to illegal actions committed by employees.

4. *Periods of Absence.* Employees should be required to take extended absences from their jobs so that they are not always present to hide unscrupulous or illegal activities.

5. *Procedures Manual.* To promote compliance, the procedures for processing transactions should be clearly described in a manual.

6. *Authority and Responsibility.* To motivate employees and promote effective control, clear lines of authority and responsibility should be established.

7. *Prenumbered Documents.* Numbered documents minimize the likelihood of missing or duplicate documents. Accordingly, prenumbered forms should be used for all important documents such as purchase orders, receiving reports, invoices, and checks.

8. *Physical Control.* Locks, fences, security personnel, and other physical devices should be employed to safeguard assets.

9. *Performance Evaluation.* Because few people can evaluate their own performance objectively, independent performance evaluations should be performed. Substandard performance will likely persist unless employees are encouraged to take corrective action.

10. *Internal Control in Computer Systems.*   The basic internal control features discussed are applicable to computer systems as well as manual systems.

Because cash is so important to businesses and because some persons find it tempting to steal, much of the discussion of internal controls in this chapter related specifically to cash controls. Special procedures should be employed to control the receipts and payments of cash. One of the most common control devices is the use of *checking accounts.*

Bank statements should be compared with internal accounting records through a procedure known as a *bank reconciliation.* One common way to accomplish a reconciliation is to determine the true cash balance based on both bank and book records. Typical items shown on a bank reconciliation include the following:

Unadjusted Bank Balance	xxx	Unadjusted Book Balance	xxx
Add:		Add:	
Deposits in Transit	xxx	Interest Revenue	xxx
		Collection of Receivables	xxx
Subtract:		Subtract:	
Outstanding Checks	xxx	Bank Service Charges	xxx
		NSF Checks	xxx
True Cash Balance	xxx	True Cash Balance	xxx

Attaining equality between the two true cash balances provides evidence of accuracy in the accounting for cash transactions.

Another commonly used internal control device for the protection of cash is a *petty cash* fund. Normally, an employee who is designated as the petty cash custodian is entrusted with a small amount of cash. The custodian reimburses employees for small expenditures made on behalf of the organization and collects receipts from the employees at the time of the reimbursement. At any point in time, the receipts plus the remaining cash should equal the amount of funds entrusted to the custodian. Journal entries to recognize the expenses incurred are made at the time the fund is replenished.

Finally, the chapter discussed the assessment of organizational *liquidity.* The *current ratio* is determined by dividing current assets by current liabilities. The higher the ratio, the more liquid the organization.

A LOOK

FORWARD

The material in Chapters 6 through 11 is organized primarily in the order of the arrangement of a classified balance sheet, which was discussed in this chapter. This chapter presented several issues related to accounting for cash; Chapter 7 addresses issues related to accounting for accounts receivable, and so on, until Chapter 11, which addresses issues related to accounting for equity. Owners' equity is the final section of a classified balance sheet.

KEY TERMS

Accounting Controls Procedures designed to safeguard the assets and to ensure the accuracy and reliability of the accounting records and reports. *(p. 259)*

Administrative Controls Procedures designed to evaluate performance and the degree of compliance with the firm's policies and public laws. *(p. 259)*

Audit Around the Computer The procedure in which auditors provide input that is expected to result in a designated output. The system is then tested by comparing the actual output with the expected output. *(p. 264)*

Bank Reconciliation Statement A statement that identifies and notes the differences between the cash balance reported by the bank and the cash balance as it appears in the firm's accounting records. *(p. 270)*

Bank Statement A statement issued by the bank (usually monthly) that denotes all activity in the bank account for that period. *(p. 268)*

Bank Statement Credit Memo A memo that describes an activity that increases the account balance. *(p. 268)*

Bank Statement Debit Memo A memo that describes an activity that decrease the account balance. *(p. 268)*

Cash Coins, currency, checks, balances in checking and certain savings accounts, money orders, bank drafts, certificates of deposit, and other items that are payable on demand. *(p. 265)*

Cash Short and Over An account used to record the amount of cash shortages or overages. Shortages are considered expenses and overages, revenues. *(p. 274)*

Certified Check A check that is guaranteed by a bank to be a check drawn on an account having funds sufficient to pay the check. *(p. 270)*

Checks Prenumbered forms, sometimes multicopy, with the name of the business issuing them preprinted on the face, indicating to whom they are paid, the amount of the payment, and the transaction date. *(p. 268)*

Classified Balance Sheet Balance sheet that distinguishes between current and noncurrent items. *(p. 278)*

Current (Short-Term) Asset An asset that will be converted to cash or consumed within 1 year or an operating cycle, whichever is longer. *(p. 276)*

Current (Short-Term) Liability Obligation that is due within 1 year or an operating cycle, whichever is longer. *(p. 277)*

Current Ratio The relationship between current assets and current liabilities. It is determined by dividing current assets by current liabilities, with the result expressed in decimal format. *(p. 278)*

Deposit Ticket A bank form that accompanies checks and cash deposited into a bank account. This form normally contains the account number, name of the account, and space to record the checks and cash being deposited. *(p. 267)*

Deposits in Transit Deposits recorded on a depositor's books but not received and recorded by the bank. *(p. 270)*

Fidelity Bond An insurance policy that the company buys to protect itself from loss due to employee dishonesty. *(p. 261)*

General Authority The policies and procedures that apply across different levels of management. For example, everyone flies coach class. *(p. 262)*

Imprest Basis A description of the periodic replenishment of a fund to maintain it at its specified original amount. *(p. 274)*

Internal Controls The policies and procedures of a company used to provide reasonable assurance that the objectives of an enterprise will be accomplished. *(p. 259)*

Liquidity The ability to convert assets to cash quickly and meet short-term obligations. *(p. 278)*

Non-Sufficient-Funds (NSF) Check A customer's check that was deposited but returned by the bank on which it was drawn because the customer did not have enough funds in the account to cover the check. *(p. 269)*

Operating Cycle The time required to turn cash into inventory, inventory into receivables, and receivables back to cash. *(p. 277)*

Outstanding Checks   Checks recorded as deductions from the depositor's cash book balance but not presented to the bank for payment.   *(p. 269)*

Petty Cash Fund   A small amount of cash set aside in a fund to cover small outflows for which writing checks is not practical.   *(p. 274)*

Procedures Manual   A manual that sets forth the accounting procedures to be followed.   *(p. 261)*

Separation of Duties   Whenever possible, the functions of authorization, recording, and custody should be carried out by separate individuals.   *(p. 260)*

Service Charges   Fees charged by the bank for services performed or a penalty for the depositor's failing to maintain a specified minimum cash balance throughout the period.   *(p. 269)*

Signature Card   A bank form that contains the bank account number and the signatures of the people authorized to write checks on the account.   *(p. 267)*

Solvency   The ability of a business to repay liabilities in the long run.   *(p. 278)*

Specific Authorizations   The policies and procedures that apply to designated levels of management. For example, the right to approve overtime pay may apply only to the plant manager.   *(p. 262)*

True Cash Balance   The actual balance of cash owned by a company at the close of business on the date of the bank statement.   *(p. 270)*

Unadjusted Bank Balance   The ending cash balance reported by the bank as of the date of the bank statement.   *(p. 270)*

Unadjusted Book Balance   The balance of the Cash account as of the date of the reconciliation, before any adjustments are made.   *(p. 270)*

Voucher   An internally generated document that includes spaces for recording transaction data and designated authorizations.   *(p. 274)*

QUESTIONS

1. What are the policies and procedures called that are used to provide reasonable assurance that the objectives of an enterprise will be accomplished?
2. What is the difference between accounting controls and administrative controls?
3. What are several features of a strong internal control system?
4. What is meant by *separation of duties*? Give an illustration.
5. What are the attributes of a high-quality employee?
6. What is a fidelity bond? Explain its purpose.
7. Why is it important that every employee periodically take an extended leave of absence or vacation?
8. What are the purpose and importance of a procedures manual?
9. What is the difference between specific and general authorizations?
10. What is the purpose of prenumbered documents (i.e., checks, invoices, receipts)?
11. What procedures are important in the physical control of assets and accounting records?
12. What is the purpose of independent verification of performance?
13. What are the six control requirements for computer systems discussed in this chapter? Explain each.
14. What items are considered cash?
15. Why is cash more susceptible to theft or embezzlement than other assets?
16. Giving written copies of receipts to customers can help prevent what type of illegal acts?
17. What are several procedures that can help to protect cash receipts?
18. What are several procedures that can help protect cash disbursements?
19. What effect does a debit memo in a bank statement have on the Cash account? What effect does the credit memo in a bank statement have on the Cash account?
20. What information is normally contained in a bank statement?

21. Why might a bank statement reflect an unadjusted balance that is larger than the balance recorded in the depositor's books? What could cause the unadjusted bank balance to be smaller than the book balance?

22. What is the purpose of a bank reconciliation?

23. What is an outstanding check?

24. What is a deposit in transit?

25. What is a certified check?

26. How is an NSF check accounted for in the accounting records?

27. What is the purpose of the Cash Short and Over account?

28. What is the purpose of a petty cash fund?

29. What type of expenditures are usually made from a petty cash fund?

30. What is the difference between a current asset and a noncurrent asset?

31. What are some of the most common current assets?

32. What does the term *operating cycle* mean?

33. What are some of the more common current liabilities?

34. What is a classified balance sheet?

35. What is the difference between the liquidity and the solvency of a business?

36. How is the arrangement of assets and liabilities on financial statements different for the United States, the United Kingdom, and France?

37. The higher the current ratio, the better the company's financial condition. Do you agree or disagree with this statement? Explain your position.

38. Does a high (80 to 95%) debt-to-assets ratio mean that a business is in financial difficulty? What types of businesses traditionally operate with high debt-to-assets ratios?

EXERCISES

Features of a Strong Internal Control System

EXERCISE 6-1
L.O. 2

Required

List and explain the nine features of a strong internal control system described in this chapter.

Internal Controls for a Computer System

EXERCISE 6-2
L.O. 3

Required

The basic internal control features apply to computer systems, but additional controls are necessary. List and explain the six control requirements for computers discussed in this chapter.

Features of Internal Control Procedures for Cash

EXERCISE 6-3
L.O. 4

Required

List and discuss effective internal control procedures that apply to cash.

Internal Control Procedures to Prevent Embezzlement

EXERCISE 6-4
L.O. 1, 2

Hazel Motl was in charge of the returns department at the Tax Software Company. She was responsible for evaluating returned merchandise. She sent merchandise that was reusable back to the warehouse, where it was restocked in the supply of inventory. Motl was also responsible for taking the merchandise that she determined to be defective to the city dump for disposal. She had agreed to buy a friend a tax planning program at a discount through her contacts at work. That is when the idea came to her. She could simply classify one of the reusable returns as defective and bring it home instead of taking it to the dump. She did so and made a quick $150. She was happy, and her friend was ecstatic; he was able to buy a $400 software package for only $150. He told his friends about the deal, and soon Motl had a regular set of customers. She was caught when a retail store owner complained to the marketing manager that his pricing strategy was being undercut by Tax's direct sales to the public. The marketing manager was suspicious because Tax had no direct marketing program. When the outside sales were ultimately traced back to Motl, the company discovered that it had lost over $10,000 in sales revenue to her criminal activity.

Required

Identify an internal control procedure that could have prevented the company's losses. Explain how the procedure would have stopped the embezzlement.

EXERCISE 6-5
L.O. 1, 2

Internal Control Procedures to Prevent Deception

Emergency Care Medical Centers (ECMC) hired a new physician, Ken Major, who was an immediate success. Everyone loved his bedside manner. He could charm the most cantankerous patient. Indeed he was a master salesman as well as an expert physician. Unfortunately, Major misdiagnosed a case that resulted in serious consequences to the patient. The patient filed suit against ECMC. In preparation for the defense, ECMC's attorneys discovered that Major was indeed an exceptional salesman. He had worked for several years as district marketing manager for a pharmaceutical company. In fact, he was not a physician at all! He had changed professions without going to medical school. He had lied on his application form. His knowledge of medical terminology had enabled him to fool everyone. ECMC was found negligent and lost a $3 million lawsuit.

Required

Identify the relevant internal control procedures that could have prevented the company's losses. Explain how these procedures would have prevented Major's deception.

EXERCISE 6-6
L.O. 5

Treatment of NSF Check

The bank statement of Louis & Clark Supplies contained a $250 NSF check that one of L&C's customers had written to pay for supplies purchased.

Required

a. Show the effects of recognizing the NSF check on the financial statements by recording the appropriate amounts in a horizontal statements model like the following one:

Assets			= Liab. + Equity	Rev. − Exp. = Net Inc.	Cash Flow
Cash	+	Accts. Rec.			

b. Is the recognition of the NSF check on L&C's books an asset source, use, or exchange transaction?

c. Suppose the customer redeems the check by giving L&C $280 cash in exchange for the bad check. The additional $30 paid a service fee charged by L&C. Show the effects on the financial statements in the horizontal statements model in part a.

d. Is the receipt of cash referenced in part c an asset source, use, or exchange transaction?

EXERCISE 6-7
L.O. 5

Adjustments to the Balance per the Books

Required

From the following list of items, identify those that are added to or subtracted from the unadjusted *book balance* to arrive at the true cash balance. Distinguish the additions from the subtractions by placing a + beside the items that are added to the unadjusted book balance and a − beside those that are subtracted from it. The first item is recorded as an example.

Items to Be Considered	Book Balance Adjusted?	Added or Subtracted?
Charge for Checks	Yes	—
NSF Check from Customer		
Note Receivable Collected by the Bank		
Outstanding Checks		
Credit Memo		
Interest Revenue		
Deposits in Transit		
Debit Memo		
Service Charge		

Adjustments to the Balance per the Bank

Required

From the following list of items, identify those that are added to or subtracted from the unadjusted *bank balance* to arrive at the true cash balance. Distinguish the additions from the subtractions by placing a + beside the items that are added to the unadjusted book balance and a − beside those that are subtracted from it. The first item is recorded as an example.

Items to Be Considered	Bank Balance Adjusted?	Added or Subtracted?
NSF Check from Customer	No	n/a
Interest Revenue		
Bank Service Charge		
Outstanding Checks		
Deposits in Transit		
Debit Memo		
Credit Memo		
Certified Checks		
Petty Cash Voucher		

Adjustment of the Cash Account

As of June 30, 20X4, the bank statement showed an ending balance of $13,679.85. The unadjusted Cash account balance was $13,283.75. The following information is available:

1. Deposit in transit, $1,476.30.
2. Credit memo in bank statement for interest earned in June, $35.
3. Outstanding check, $1,843.74.
4. Debit memo for service charge, $6.34.

Required

    a. Determine the true cash balance by preparing a bank reconciliation on June 30, 20X4, using the preceding information.

    b. Record the adjusting entries necessary to correct the unadjusted book balance in general journal format.

Determination of the True Cash Balance, Starting with the Unadjusted Bank Balance

The following information is available for Hull Company for the month of June:

1. The unadjusted balance per the bank statement on June 30 was $64,714.35.
2. Deposits in transit on June 30 amounted to $1,464.95.
3. A debit memo was included with the bank statement for a service charge of $25.38.
4. A $4,745.66 check written in June had not been paid by the bank.
5. Bank statement included a $944 credit memo for the collection of a note. The principal of the note was $859, and the interest collected amounted to $85.

Required

Determine the true cash balance as of June 30. (*Hint:* It is not necessary to use all of the preceding items to determine the true balance.)

Determination of the True Cash Balance, Starting with the Unadjusted Book Balance

Stuart Company had an unadjusted cash balance of $4,450 as of May 31. The company's bank statement, which was also dated May 31, contained a $38 NSF check that was written by one of Stuart's customers. There were $548.60 in outstanding checks and $143.74 in deposits in transit as of May 31. According to the bank statement, service charges amounted to $30 and the bank collected a $450 note receivable for Stuart. The bank statement also showed $18 of interest revenue earned by Stuart.

Required

Determine the true cash balance as of May 31. (*Hint:* It is not necessary to use all of the preceding items to determine the true balance.)

EXERCISE 6-12

L.O. 6

Effect of Establishing a Petty Cash Account

Evans Transfer Company established a $300 petty cash fund on January 1, 20X3.

Required

a. Is the establishment of the petty cash fund an asset source, use, or exchange transaction?

b. Record the establishment of the petty cash fund in a horizontal statements model like the following one:

Assets		= Liab. + Equity	Rev. − Exp. = Net Inc.	Cash Flow
Cash	+ Petty Cash			

c. Record the establishment of the fund in general journal format.

EXERCISE 6-13

L.O. 6

Effect of Petty Cash Events on the Financial Statements

Top Gun, Inc., established a petty cash fund of $100 on January 2. On January 31, the fund contained cash of $16.75 and vouchers for the following cash payments:

Postage	$34.68
Office Supplies	18.43
Printing Expense	7.40
Transportation Expense	23.92

The four distinct accounting events affecting the petty cash fund for the period were (1) establishment of the fund, (2) reimbursements made to employees, (3) recognition of expenses, and (4) replenishment of the fund.

Required

a. Record each of the four events in a horizontal statements model like the following example. In the Cash Flow column, indicate whether the item is an operating activity (OA), investing activity (IA), or a financing activity (FA). The letters n/a indicate that an element was not affected by the event.

Assets		= Liab. + Equity	Rev. − Exp. = Net Inc.	Cash Flow
Cash	+ Petty Cash			

b. Record the events in general journal entry format.

EXERCISE 6-14

L.O. 6

Determination of the Amount of Petty Cash Expense

Consider the following events:

1. A petty cash fund of $250 was established on April 1, 20X6.

2. Employees were reimbursed when they presented petty cash vouchers to the petty cash custodian.

3. On April 30, 20X6, the petty cash account contained vouchers totaling $184.93 plus $59.84 of currency.

Required

Answer the following questions:

a. How did the establishment of the petty cash fund affect (i.e., increase, decrease, or have no effect on) total assets?

b. What is the amount of total petty cash expenses to be recognized during April?

c. When are petty cash expenses recognized (i.e., at the time of establishment, reimbursement, or replenishment)?

Preparation of a Classified Balance Sheet

EXERCISE 6-15
L.O. 7

Required

Use the following information to prepare a classified balance sheet:

Accounts Receivable	$24,300
Accounts Payable	11,000
Cash	21,984
Contributed Capital	24,000
Land	25,000
Long-Term Notes Payable	23,000
Merchandise Inventory	32,000
Retained Earnings	45,284

Operating Cycle

EXERCISE 6-16
L.O. 8

Selma Co. sells gifts and novelty items mostly on account. Selma Co. takes an average of 96 days to sell its inventory and an average of 36 days to collect the accounts receivable.

Required

a. Draw a diagram of the operating cycle for Selma Co.

b. Compute the length of the operating cycle based on the information given.

PROBLEMS—SERIES A

Use of Internal Control to Restrict Illegal or Unethical Behavior

PROBLEM 6-1A
L.O. 1, 3, 4

Required

For each of the following "less than honest" acts, describe one or more internal control procedures that could have prevented (or helped prevent) the problems.

Never took a vacation 3 yrs audit

a. Everyone in the office has noticed what a dedicated employee Jennifer Reidel is. She never misses work, not even for a vacation. Reidel is in charge of the petty cash fund. She transfers funds from the company's bank account to the petty cash account on an as-needed basis. During a surprise audit, the petty cash fund was found to contain fictitious receipts. Over a 3-year period, Reidel had used more than $4,000 of petty cash to pay for personal expenses.

b. Bill Bruton was hired as the vice president of the manufacturing division of a corporation. His impressive resume listed a master's degree in business administration from a large state university and numerous collegiate awards and activities, when in fact Bruton had only a high school diploma. In a short time, the company was in poor financial condition because of his inadequate knowledge and bad decisions. *bank found check*

c. Havolene Manufacturing has good internal control over its manufacturing materials inventory. However, office supplies are kept on open shelves in the employee break room. The office supervisor has noticed that he is having to order paper, tape, staplers, and pens on an increasingly frequent basis.

Preparation of a Bank Reconciliation

PROBLEM 6-2A
L.O. 5

Wilma Clark is the owner of a card shop, Top Star. The following cash information is available for the month of August.

As of August 31, the bank statement shows a balance of $16,000. The August 31 unadjusted balance of the Cash account of Top Star was $15,000. A review of the bank statement reveals the following information:

1. A deposit of $2,260 on August 31, 20X6, does not appear on the August bank statement.

2. It was discovered that a check for payment of baseball cards was correctly written and paid by the bank for $4,040 but was recorded on the books as $4,400.

3. When checks written during the month were compared with those paid by the bank, three checks amounting to $3,000 were found to be outstanding.

4. A debit memo for $100 was included in the bank statement for the purchase of a new supply of checks.

Required

    a. Prepare a bank reconciliation for the month of August showing the true cash balance.

    b. Prepare any necessary journal entries to adjust the books to the true cash balance.

PROBLEM 6-3A
L.O. 5

Missing Information in a Bank Reconciliation

The following data apply to Green Light Auto Supply, Inc., for May 20X7.

1. Balance per the bank on May 31: $8,000.

2. Deposits in transit not recorded by the bank: $975.

3. Bank error; check written by Allen Auto Supply was drawn on Green Light Auto Supply, $650.

4. The following checks written and recorded by Green Light Auto Supply were not included in the bank statement:

3013	$ 385
3054	735
3056	1,900

5. Note of $500 collected by the bank.

6. Service charge for collection of note of $10.

7. Accountant recorded a check written for $188 as $888 in the cash disbursements journal to pay for the May utilities expense.

8. Bank service charge in addition to the collection fee, $25.

9. Customer checks returned by the bank as NSF, $125.

Required

Determine the amount of the unadjusted cash balance per Green Light Auto Supply's books.

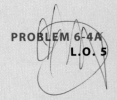

PROBLEM 6-4A
L.O. 5

Bank Reconciliation Requiring Adjustments to the Cash Account

Required

Determine whether the following items included in Doug's bank reconciliation will require adjusting or correcting entries on Doug's books. When an entry is required, record it in general journal format.

    a. An $877 deposit was recorded by the bank as $778.

    b. Four checks totaling $450 written during the month of January were not included with the January bank statement.

    c. A $54 check written to Office Max for office supplies was recorded in the general journal as $45.

    d. The bank statement indicated that the bank had collected a $330 note for Doug.

    e. Doug's recorded $500 of receipts on January 31, 20X6, which was deposited in the night depository of the bank. These deposits were not included in the bank statement.

    f. Service charges of $22 for the month of January were listed on the bank statement.

    g. The bank charged a $297 check drawn on Dougal Restaurant to Doug's account. The check was included in Doug's bank statement.

h.   A check of $31 was returned to the bank because of insufficient funds and was
noted on the bank statement. Doug received the check from a customer and
thought that it was good when he deposited it into his account.

Bank Reconciliation Requiring Adjustments to the Cash Account   PROBLEM 6-5A

The following information is available for Cooters Garage for March 20X2:   L.O. 5

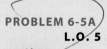

BANK STATEMENT

HAZARD STATE BANK
215 MAIN STREET
HAZARD, GA 30321

Cooters Garage   Account number
629 Main Street   62-00062
Hazard, GA 30321   March 31, 20X2

Beginning balance 3/1/20X2	$15,000.00
Total deposits and other credits	7,000.00
Total checks and other debits	6,000.00
Ending balance 3/31/20X2	16,000.00

Checks and Debits		Deposits and Credits	
Check No.	Amount	Date	Amount
1462	$ 1,163.00	March 1	$ 1,000.00
1463	62.00	March 2	1,340.00
1464	1,235.00	March 6	210.00
1465	750.00	March 12	1,940.00
1466	1,111.00	March 17	855.00
1467	964.00	March 22	1,480.00
DM	15.00	CM	175.00
1468	700.00		

The following is a list of checks and deposits recorded on the books of Cooters Garage for
March 20X2:

Date	Check No.	Amount of Check	Date	Amount of Deposit
March 1	1463	$ 62.00	March 1	$1,340.00
March 5	1464	1,235.00	March 5	210.00
March 6	1465	750.00		
March 9	1466	1,111.00	March 10	1,940.00
March 10	1467	964.00		
March 14	1468	70.00	March 16	855.00
March 19	1469	1,500.00	March 19	1,480.00
March 28	1470	102.00	March 29	2,000.00

Other Information

1.   Check no. 1462 was outstanding from February.
2.   A credit memo for collection of accounts receivable was included in the bank
statement.
3.   All checks were paid at the correct amount.
4.   The bank statement included a debit memo for service charges.
5.   The February 28 bank reconciliation showed a deposit in transit of $1,000.
6.   Check no. 1468 was for the purchase of equipment.
7.   The unadjusted Cash account balance at March 31 was $16,868.

Required

    a. Prepare the bank reconciliation for Cooters Garage for the month of March.

    b. Record in general journal form any necessary entries to the Cash account to adjust to the true cash balance.

PROBLEM 6-6A

L.O. 5

Effect of Adjustments to Cash on the Accounting Equation

After reconciling its bank account, Monroe Company made the following adjusting entries:

Entry No.	Account title	Debit	Credit
1	Cash	845	
	Accounts Receivable		845
	To record bank collection		
2	Cash	44	
	Interest Revenue		44
	To record interest revenue		
3	Service Charge Expense	35	
	Cash		35
	To record bank service charge		
4	Accounts Receivable, D. Beat	174	
	Cash		174
	To record NSF check from Beat		
5	Cash	20	
	Supplies Expense		20
	To correct overstatement of expense		

Required

Identify the type of event as asset source (AS), asset use (AU), asset exchange (AE), or claims exchange (CE) that is depicted in each journal entry. Also explain how each entry affects the accounting equation by placing a + for increase, − for decrease, or n/a for not affected under each component of the accounting equation. The first event is recorded as an example.

						Equity		
Event No.	Type of Event	Assets	=	Liabilities	+	Contributed Capital	+	Retained Earnings
1	AE	+ −		n/a		n/a		n/a

PROBLEM 6-7A

L.O. 2, 4, 5

Bank Reconciliation and Internal Control

Following is a bank reconciliation for Betts Company for the month of June 20X5:

	Cash Account	Bank Statement
Balance as of 5/31/X5	$1,618	$3,000
Deposit in Transit		600
Outstanding Checks		(1,507)
Note Collected by Bank	2,000	
Bank Service Charge	(25)	
NSF Check	(1,500)	
Adjusted Cash Balance as of 6/30/X5	$2,093	$2,093

When reviewing the bank reconciliation, Betts's auditor was unable to locate any reference to the NSF check on the bank statement. Furthermore, the clerk who reconciles the bank statement and records the adjusting entries could not find the actual NSF check that should have been included in the bank statement. Finally, there was no specific reference in the accounts receivable subsidiary account indicating the party who had written the check.

Required

a. Prepare the adjusting entry that the clerk would have made to record the NSF check.

b. Assume that the clerk who prepares the bank reconciliation and records the adjusting entries also makes bank deposits. Explain how the clerk could use a fictitious NSF check to hide the theft of cash.

c. How could Betts Company avoid the theft of cash that is covered by the use of fictitious NSF checks?

Petty Cash Fund

PROBLEM 6-8A
L.O. 6

Caragan Co. established a petty cash fund by issuing a check for $250 and appointing Ty Peninder as petty cash custodian. Peninder had vouchers for the following petty cash payments during the month:

Stamps	$14.00
Miscellaneous Expense	25.00
Employee Supper Money	75.00
Taxi Fare	80.00
Window-Washing Service	22.00

There was $32.00 of currency in the petty cash box at the time it was replenished.

Required

a. Prepare all general journal entries necessary to (1) establish the fund, (2) reimburse employees, (3) recognize expenses, and (4) replenish the fund. (*Hint:* Journal entries may not be required for all the events.)

b. Explain how the Cash Short and Over account required in this case will affect the income statement.

c. Identify the type of event as asset source (AS), asset use (AU), asset exchange (AE), or claims exchange (CE) that is depicted in each journal entry recorded in part *a*.

d. Record the effects of the events in part *a* on the financial statements using the horizontal statements model like the following one. In the Cash Flow column, indicate whether the item is an operating activity (OA), investing activity (IA), or financing activity (FA). The letters n/a indicate that an element was not affected by the event.

Assets			= Liab. + Equity	Rev. − Exp. = Net Inc.	Cash Flow
Cash	+	Petty Cash			

Classified Balance Sheet and Multistep Income Statement

PROBLEM 6-9A
L.O. 7

Required

Use the following information to prepare a classified balance sheet and a multistep income statement:

Accounts Receivable	$ 3,000
Contributed Capital	34,000
Salaries Expense	104,000
Interest Expense	2,500
Cash	10,000
Accounts Payable	900
Retained Earnings	38,000
Accumulated Depreciation	5,000
Unearned Revenue	8,000
Land	45,000
Salaries Payable	1,700
Cost of Goods Sold	150,000
Supplies	450
Note Receivable (Long-Term)	5,000
Inventory	8,000
Office Equipment	52,000
Gain on Sale of Equipment	5,000
Interest Receivable (Short-Term)	200
Operating Expenses	17,000
Sales Revenue	300,000
Prepaid Rent	8,000
Interest Payable (Short-Term)	600
Notes Payable (Long-Term)	43,450
Interest Revenue	400

PROBLEMS—SERIES B

PROBLEM 6-1B
L.O. 1, 2, 4

Use of Internal Control to Restrict Illegal or Unethical Behavior

Required

For each of the following "less than honest" acts, describe one or more internal control procedures that could have prevented (or helped prevent) the problems.

a. Paula Wissel, the administrative assistant in charge of payroll, created a fictional employee, wrote weekly checks to the "employee," and then personally cashed the checks for her own benefit.

b. Larry Kent, the receiving manager of Southern Lumber, created a fictitious supplier, named F&M Building Supply. F&M regularly billed Southern Lumber for supplies purchased. Kent had printed shipping slips and billing invoices with the name of the fictitious company and opened a post office box as the mailing address. Kent simply prepared a receiving report and submitted it for payment to the accounts payable department. The accounts payable clerk then paid the invoice when it was received because Kent acknowledged receipt of the supplies.

c. Holly Baker works at a local hobby shop and usually operates the cash register. She has developed a habit of giving discounts to her friends. When they come by she rings a lower price or does not charge the friend for some of the material purchased. At first, Baker thought she would get caught, but no one seemed to notice. Indeed, she has become so sure that there is no way for the owner to find out that she has started taking home some supplies for her own personal use.

PROBLEM 6-2B
L.O. 5

Preparation of a Bank Reconciliation

Darnell Bradshaw is the owner of a construction business, Home Builders Inc. The following cash information is available for the month of October, 20X1.

As of October 31, the bank statement shows a balance of $8,000. The October 31 unadjusted balance of the Cash account of Home Builders Inc. was $8,580. A review of the bank statement reveals the following information:

1. A deposit of $2,000 on October 31, 20X1, does not appear on the October 31 bank statement.

2. A debit memo for $50 was included in the bank statement for the purchase of a new supply of checks.

3. When checks written during the month were compared with those paid by the bank, three checks amounting to $1,200 were found to be outstanding.

4. It was discovered that a check for payment of equipment was correctly written and paid by the bank for $3,030 but was recorded on the books as $3,300.

Required
 a. Prepare a bank reconciliation for the month of October showing the true cash balance.
 b. Prepare any necessary journal entries to adjust the books to the true cash balance.

Missing Information in a Bank Reconciliation

PROBLEM 6-3B
L.O. 5

The following data apply to Harrison Flying Service for April 20X7:

1. Balance per the bank on April 30, $10,000.

2. Deposits in transit not recorded by the bank, $1,000.

3. Bank error; check written by Harrison Office Supply was drawn on Harrison Flying Service, $800.

4. The following checks written and recorded by Harrison Flying Service were not included in the bank statement:

2012	$ 220
2052	380
2055	1,700

5. Note collected by the bank, $450.

6. Service charge for collection of note, $15.

7. Accountant recorded a check written for $548 as $845 in the cash disbursements journal to pay for April's utilities expense.

8. Bank service charge in addition to the collection fee, $40.

9. NSF checks returned by the bank, $250.

Required
Determine the amount of the unadjusted cash balance per Harrison Flying Service books.

Bank Reconciliation Requiring Adjustments to the Cash Account

PROBLEM 6-4B
L.O. 5

Required
Determine whether the following items included in Kelvin Kline's bank reconciliation require adjusting or correcting entries on Kline's books. When an entry is required, record it in general journal format.

 a. The depositor wrote an $880 certified check that was still outstanding as of the closing date of the bank statement.
 b. The bank collected an $8,000 of Kline accounts receivable. Kline had instructed his customers to send their payments directly to the bank.
 c. The bank mistakenly gave Klipper credit for a $500 deposit made by Kline.
 d. Deposits in transit amounted to $4,550.
 e. Kline's bank statement contained a $375 NSF check. Kline received the check from a customer and included it in one of his bank deposits.
 f. The bank statement indicated that Kline earned $75 interest revenue.
 g. Kline's accountant mistakenly recorded a $156 check that was written to purchase supplies as $651.
 h. Bank service charges for the month amounted to $40.

i. The bank reconciliation process disclosed the fact that $1,000 had been stolen from Kline's business.

j. Outstanding checks amounted to $1,500.

PROBLEM 6-5B
L.O. 5

Bank Reconciliation Requiring Adjustments to the Cash Account

The following information is available for Sea Breeze Hotel for November 20X5:

Bank Statement

STATE BANK

Bolta Vista, NV 10001

The Seabreeze Hotel
10 Main Street
Bolta Vista, NV 10001

Account number
12-4567
November 30, 20X5

Beginning balance 10/31/20X5	$ 8,831
Total deposits and other credits	29,075
Total checks and other debits	23,906
Ending balance 11/30/20X5	14,000

Checks and Debits		Deposits and Credits	
Check No.	Amount	Date	Amount
2350	$3,761	November 1	$1,102
2351	1,643	November 10	6,498
2352	8,000	November 15	4,929
2354	2,894	November 21	6,174
2355	1,401	November 26	5,963
2357	6,187	November 30	2,084
DM	20	CM	2,325

The following is a list of checks and deposits recorded on the books of the SeaBreeze Hotel for November 20X5:

Date	Check No.	Amount of Check	Date	Amount of Deposit
November 2	2351	$1,643	November 8	$6,498
November 4	2352	8,000	November 14	4,929
November 10	2353	1,500	November 21	6,174
November 10	2354	2,894	November 26	5,963
November 15	2355	1,401	November 29	2,084
November 20	2356	745	November 30	3,550
November 22	2357	6,187		

Other Information

1. Check no. 2350 was outstanding from October.
2. Credit memo was for collection of notes receivable.
3. All checks were paid at the correct amount.
4. Debit memo was for printed checks.
5. The October 31 bank reconciliation showed a deposit in transit of $1,102.
6. The unadjusted Cash account balance at November 30 was $13,000.

Required

a. Prepare the bank reconciliation for Sea Breeze Hotel for the month of November.
b. Record in general journal form any necessary entries to the Cash account to adjust to the true cash balance.

Effect of Adjustments to Cash on the Accounting Equation

After reconciling its bank account, Magee Tractor Company made the following adjusting entries:

Entry No.	Account Titles	Debit	Credit
1	Rent Expense	35	
	Cash		35
	To correct understatement of expense		
2	Service Charge Expense	15	
	Cash		15
	To record bank service charge		
3	Cash	175	
	Accounts Receivable		175
	To record bank collection		
4	Cash	40	
	Interest Revenue		40
	To record interest revenue		
5	Accounts Receivable, K. Wilson	250	
	Cash		250
	To record NSF check from Wilson		

Required

Identify the type of event as asset source (AS), asset use (AU), asset exchange (AE), or claims exchange (CE) that is depicted in each journal entry. Also explain how each entry affects the accounting equation by placing a + for increase, − for decrease, or n/a for not affected under each component of the accounting equation. The first event is recorded as an example.

						Equity	
Event No.	Type of Event	Assets	=	Liabilities	+	Contributed Capital	− Retained Earnings
1	AU	−		n/a		n/a	−

Bank Reconciliation and Internal Control

Following is a bank reconciliation for Ross's Coffee Shop for the month of May 20X6:

	Cash Account	Bank Statement
Balance as of 5/31/X6	$25,000	$22,000
Deposit in Transit		4,250
Outstanding Checks		(465)
Note Collected by Bank	1,815	
Bank Service Charge	(30)	
Automatic Payment on Loan	(1,000)	
Adjusted Cash Balance as of 5/31/X6	$25,785	$25,785

Because of limited funds, Ross's Coffee Shop employed one accountant responsible for receiving cash, recording receipts and disbursements, preparing deposits, and preparing the bank reconciliation. The accountant left the company on June 8, 20X6, after preparing the preceding statement. His replacement compared the checks returned with the bank statement to the cash disbursements journal and found the total of outstanding checks to be $5,000.

Required

a. Prepare a corrected bank reconciliation statement.

b. What is the total amount of cash missing, and how was the difference between the "true cash" per the bank and the "true cash" per the books hidden on the reconciliation prepared by the former employee?

c. What could Ross's Coffee Shop do to avoid "missing" cash in the future?

PROBLEM 6-8B **Petty Cash Fund**

L.O. 6 The following data pertain to the petty cash fund of Morris Company:

1. The petty cash fund was created on an imprest basis at $100 on March 1.

2. On March 31, a physical count revealed $8.00 in currency and coins, vouchers authorizing meal allowances totaling $42.00, vouchers authorizing purchase of postage stamps of $32.00, and vouchers for payment of delivery charges of $20.00.

Required

a. Prepare all general journal entries necessary to (1) establish the fund, (2) reimburse employees, and (3) replenish the fund as of March 31. (*Hint:* Journal entries may not be required for all three events.)

b. Explain how the Cash Short and Over account required in this case affects the income statement.

c. Identify the type of event as asset source (AS), asset use (AU), asset exchange (AE), or claims exchange (CE) that is depicted in each journal entry recorded in part *a*.

d. Record the effects on the financial statements of the events in part *a*, using a horizontal statements model like the following one. In the Cash Flow column, indicate whether the item is an operating activity (OA), investing activity (IA), or financing activity (FA). The letters n/a indicate that an element was not affected by the event.

Assets			= Liab. + Equity	Rev. − Exp. = Net Inc.	Cash Flow
Cash	+	Petty Cash			

PROBLEM 6-9B **Classified Balance Sheet and Multistep Income Statement**

L.O. 7

Required

Use the following information to prepare a classified balance sheet and a multistep income statement:

Accounts Receivable	$ 4,000
Contributed Capital	41,000
Salaries Expense	118,000
Interest Expense	12,200
Cash	3,600
Accounts Payable	1,000
Retained Earnings	42,000
Accumulated Depreciation	4,800
Unearned Revenue	9,600
Land	50,000
Salaries Payable	1,800
Cost of Goods Sold	174,000
Supplies	500
Note Receivable (Long-Term)	6,000
Inventory	9,000
	(cont'd)

Office Equipment	58,000
Gain on Sale of Equipment	6,400
Interest Receivable (Short-Term)	240
Operating Expenses	19,000
Sales Revenue	340,000
Prepaid Rent	9,600
Interest Payable (Short-Term)	740
Interest Revenue	420
Notes Payable (Long-Term)	40,000

analyze, communicate, think

BUSINESS APPLICATIONS CASE   **Gateway 2000 Annual Report**   **ACT 6-1**

Required

Using the Gateway 2000 financial statements in Appendix B, answer the following questions:

a. What is Gateway's current ratio as of December 31, 1997?

b. Which of Gateway's current assets had the largest balance at December 31, 1997?

c. What percentage of Gateway's total assets consisted of current assets?

d. Did Gateway's creditors require the company to maintain certain levels of financial ratios? (*Hint:* See Note 2-a on page 28 of the "Annual Report".)

GROUP ASSIGNMENT   **Analysis of Financial Statements**   **ACT 6-2**

The following selected information was taken from the annual reports of three companies: Southwest Airlines, Pier 1 Imports, and Wendy's. Information is given in thousands of dollars.

	Company 1	Company 2	Company 3
Accounts Receivable	$ 76,530	$ 4,128	$ 66,755
Accounts Payable	160,891	105,541	107,157
Other Current Liabilities	707,622	4,845	105,457
Allowance for Depreciation	1,375,631	138,179	537,910
Cash	623,343	32,280	234,262
Property, Plant, and Equipment	4,811,324	355,015	1,803,410
Inventories	0	220,013	35,633
Retained Earnings	1,632,115	118,721	839,215
Stockholders' Contributed Capital	376,903	204,327	345,019
Other Current Assets	108,543	29,057	44,904
Other Long-Term Assets	4,051	67,954	294,626
Long-Term Liabilities	1,370,629	136,834	544,832

Required

a. Organize the class into three sections and divide each section into groups of three to five students. Assign Company 1 to groups in section 1, Company 2 to groups in section 2, and Company 3 to groups in section 3.

Group Tasks

1. Identify the company that is represented by the financial data assigned to your group.

2. Prepare a classified balance sheet for the company assigned to your group.

3. Select a representative from a group in each section and put the balance sheet on the board.

Class Discussion

    b. Discuss the balance sheets of each company and the rationale for matching the financial information with the company.

ACT 6-3

REAL WORLD CASE   **Whose Numbers Are They Anyway?**

The following excerpt, sometimes referred to as *management's statement of responsibility,* was taken from JC Penney's 10-K report for the fiscal year ended January 31, 1998. The authors have italicized and numbered selected portions of the excerpt.

Company Statement on Financial Information (partial)

    [1] *The Company is responsible for the information presented in this Annual Report.* The consolidated financial statements have been prepared in accordance with generally accepted accounting principles and are considered to present fairly in all material respects the Company's results of operations, financial position, and cash flows. Certain amounts included in the consolidated financial statements are estimated based on currently available information and judgment as to the outcome of future conditions and circumstances. . . .

    The Company's system of internal controls is supported by written policies and procedures and supplemented by a staff of internal auditors. **[2]** *This system is designed to provide reasonable assurance, at suitable costs,* that assets are safeguarded and that transactions are executed in accordance with appropriate authorization and are recorded and reported properly. The system is continually reviewed, evaluated, and where appropriate, modified to accommodate current conditions. *Emphasis is placed on the careful* **[3]** *selection,* **[4]** *training, and development of professional managers.*

    An organizational alignment that is premised upon appropriate **[5]** *delegation of authority* and **[6]** *division of responsibility* is fundamental to this system. **[7]** *Communication programs are aimed at assuring that established policies and procedures are disseminated and understood* throughout the company.

    The consolidated financial statements have been audited by independent auditors whose report appears below. This audit was conducted in accordance with generally accepted auditing standards, which include the consideration of the Company's internal controls to the extent necessary to form an independent opinion on the consolidated financial statements prepared by management.

    The Audit committee of the Board of Directors is composed solely of directors who are not officers or employees of the Company. . . .

Required

Assume that a colleague, who has never taken an accounting course, asks you to explain JC Penney's "company statement on financial information." Write a memorandum that explains each of the numbered portions of the material. When appropriate, include examples to explain these concepts of internal control to your colleague.

ACT 6-4

BUSINESS APPLICATIONS CASE   **Use of the Current Ratio**

	Hyper-Rom Inc.	Web Toys, Inc.
Current Assets	$60,000	$90,000
Current Liabilities	37,000	72,000

Required

    a. Compute the current ratio for each company.

    b. Which company has the greater likelihood of being able to pay its bills?

    c. Assuming that both companies have the same amount of total assets, speculate as to which company would produce the higher return-on-assets ratio.

BUSINESS APPLICATIONS CASE
Using Current Ratios to Make Comparisons

The following accounting information exists for Kinlaw and Parker companies at the end of 20X6:

Account Title	Kinlaw	Parker
Cash	$ 20,000	$ 35,000
Wages Payable	25,000	35,000
Merchandise Inventory	35,000	70,000
Building	80,000	100,000
Accounts Receivable	30,000	45,000
Bonds Payable	90,000	120,000
Land	65,000	50,000
Accounts Payable	30,000	50,000
Revenue	220,000	270,000
Expenses	190,000	245,000

Required

a. Identify the current assets and current liabilities, and compute the current ratio for each company.

b. Assuming that all assets and liabilities are listed here, compute the debt-to-assets ratio for each company.

c. Determine which company has the greatest financial risk in both the short term and the long term.

WRITING ASSIGNMENT **Internal Control Procedures**

Alison Marsh was a trusted employee of Small City State Bank. She was involved in everything. She worked as a teller, she accounted for the cash at the other teller windows, and she recorded many of the transactions into the accounting records. She was so loyal that she never would take a day off, even when she was really too sick to work. She routinely worked late to see that all the day's work was posted into the accounting records. She would never take even a day's vacation because they might need her at the bank. Tick and Tack CPAs were hired to perform an audit, the first complete audit that had been done in several years. Marsh seemed somewhat upset by the upcoming audit. She said that everything had been properly accounted for and that the audit was a needless expense. When Tick and Tack examined some of the bank's internal control procedures, it discovered problems. In fact, as the audit progressed, it became apparent that a large amount of cash was missing. There had been numerous adjustments to customer accounts with credit memorandums, and many of the transactions had been posted several days late. In addition, there were numerous cash payments for "office expenses." When the audit was complete, it was determined that more than $200,000 of funds was missing or improperly accounted for. All fingers pointed to Marsh. The bank's president, who was a close friend of Marsh, was bewildered. How could this type of thing happen at our bank?

Required

Prepare a written memo to the bank president, outlining the procedures that should be followed to prevent this type of problem in the future.

ETHICAL DILEMMA **See No Evil, Hear No Evil, Report No Evil**

Cindy Putman recently started her first job as an accounting clerk with the Wheeler Company. When reconciling Wheeler's bank statement, Putman discovered that the bank had given the company a $42,245 credit for a deposit made in the amount of $24,245. As a result, the bank account was overstated by $18,000. Putman brought the error to the attention of Ed Wheeler, who told her to reconcile the two accounts by subtracting the amount of the error from the unadjusted bank balance. Wheeler told Putman, "Don't bother informing the bank. They'll find the mistake soon enough." Three months later, Putman was still having to include the bank error in the bank reconciliation. She was convinced that the bank would not find the mistake and asked Wheeler what to do. He told Putman that it was not her job to correct bank mistakes. He told her to adjust the company books by making a debit to Cash and a credit to Retained Earnings. He said "We can always reverse the entry if the bank discovers the mistake." Putman was uneasy about this solution. Wheeler told her that his years of business experience had taught him to *go with the flow*. He said, "Sometimes you win, sometimes you lose. I'm sure that we have made mistakes that were to our disadvantage, and no one ever told us about them. We just got a good break. Keep quiet and share in the good fortune." At the end of the month, Putman discovered a $500 cash bonus included in her paycheck. She had been working hard, and she rationalized that she deserved the bonus. She told herself that it had nothing to do with the treatment of the bank error. Anyway, she thought that Wheeler was probably right. The bank would eventually find the mistake, she could reverse the adjusting entry, and everything would be set straight.

Two years later, a tax auditor for the Internal Revenue Service (IRS) discovered the adjusting entry that debited Cash and credited Retained Earnings for $18,000. The IRS agent charged Wheeler Company with income tax evasion. Being unable to identify the source of the increase in cash, the agent concluded that the company was attempting to hide revenue by making direct credits to retained earnings. Wheeler denied any knowledge of the entry. He told the agent that Putman rarely brought anything to his attention. He said that Putman was the independent sort who had probably made an honest mistake. He pointed out that at the time the entry was made, Putman had little experience.

Later in a private conversation, Wheeler told Putman to plead ignorance and that they both would get off the hook. He said that if she did not keep quiet, they would go down together. He reminded her of the $500 bonus. Wheeler told Putman that accepting payment to defraud the IRS constituted a crime that would land her in jail. Putman was shocked that Wheeler would not tell the truth. She had expected some loyalty from him, and it was clear that she was not going to get it.

Required

Answer the following questions:

   a. Explain how the direct credit to retained earnings understated net income.

   b. What course of action would you advise Putman to take?

   c. Why was Putman foolish to expect loyalty from Wheeler?

   d. Suppose Putman had credited Miscellaneous Revenue instead of Retained Earnings and the company had paid income taxes on the $18,000. Under these circumstances, the bank error would never have been discovered. Is it OK to hide the error from the bank if it is reported on the tax return?

ACT 6-8

EDGAR DATABASE   **Analyzing Pep Boys' Liquidity**

Required

Using the most current 10-K available on EDGAR, answer the following questions about Pep Boys, Manny, Moe & Jack, for the most recent year reported. Type in *Pep Boys* as the company name when you search EDGAR. Instructions for using EDGAR are in Appendix A.

   a. What is Pep Boys' current ratio?

   b. Which of Pep Boys' current assets had the largest balance?

   c. What percentage of Pep Boys' total assets consisted of current assets?

   d. Did Pep Boys have any "currently maturing" long-term debt included in current liabilities on its balance sheet?

   e. If Pep Boys' were a company that manufactured auto parts rather than a retailer of auto parts, how do you think its balance sheet would be different?

SPREADSHEET ASSIGNMENT   **Use of Excel**

ACT 6-9

At the end of 20X5, the following accounting information is available for Bainbridge and Crist Companies.

	A	B	C	D	E	F	G	H	I	J	K
	Classified Balance Sheet	Bainbridge	Crist		Multistep Income Statement	Bainbridge	Crist				
1											
2	**Assets**										
3					Sales	500,000	575,000				
4	**Current Assets**				Cost of Goods Sold	170,000	200,000				
5	Cash	18,000	22,500		Gross Margin	330,000	375,000				
6	Accounts Receivable	19,000	19,500		Operating Expenses	285,000	345,000				
7	Inventory	14,000	18,000		Net Income	45,000	30,000				
8	Total Current Assets	51,000	60,000								
9											
10	**Property, Plant and Equipment**				**RATIOS**						
11	Land	52,500	50,000		Current Ratio	1.46	0.85				
12	Building	135,000	120,000		Debt to Total Assets	46.12%	82.83%				
13	Total Property, Plant and Equipment	187,500	170,000		Equity to Total Assets	53.88%	17.17%				
14					Gross Margin Percentage	66.00%	65.22%				
15	Total Assets	238,500	230,000		Return on Sales	9.00%	5.22%				
16					Return on Assets	18.87%	13.04%				
17	**Liabilities**				Return on Equity	35.02%	75.95%				
18	**Current Liabilities**										
19	Accounts Payable	20,000	52,500								
20	Wages Payable	15,000	18,000								
21	Total Current Liabilities	35,000	70,500								
22											
23	**Long-Term Liabilities**										
24	Notes Payable	75,000	120,000								
25											
26	Total Liabilities	110,000	190,500								
27											
28	**Equity**										
29	Contributed Capital	30,000	9,500								
30	Retained Earnings	98,500	30,000								
31											
32	Total Equity	128,500	39,500								
33											
34	Total Liabilities and Equity	238,500	230,000								
35											

Required

a. Set up the preceding spreadsheet. Complete the balance sheet and income statement. Use Excel formulas for rows that "total" on the balance sheet, and gross margin and net income on the income statement.

b. Calculate the designated ratios using Excel formulas.

c. Which company is more likely to be able to pay its current liabilities?

d. Which company carries a greater financial risk?

e. Which company is more profitable from the owners' perspective?

f. Based on profitability alone, which company performed better?

g. Assume that sales increased 10% and that the additional sales were made on account. Adjust the balance sheet and income statement for the effects. Notice that Retained Earnings will also need to be adjusted to keep the balance sheet in balance. What is the resultant effect on the ratios?

h. Return the financial statements to the original data. Assume that operating expenses increased 10% and that the additional expenses were acquired on credit. Adjust the financial statements for the effects. Notice that Retained Earnings must be adjusted to keep in balance. What is the resultant effect on the ratios?

SPREADSHEET ANALYSIS   **Mastery of Excel**

ACT 6-10

Refer to Problem 6-9A.

Required

Complete the classified balance sheet and multistep income statement on an Excel spreadsheet.

7 Accounting for Accruals—Advanced Topics
Receivables and Payables

1 Understand the importance of offering credit terms to customers.

2 Explain how the allowance method of accounting for bad debts affects financial statements.

3 Understand how the direct write-off method of accounting for bad debts affects financial statements.

4 Explain how accounting for credit card sales affects financial statements.

5 Explain how accounting for warranty obligations affects financial statements.

6 Understand how discount notes and related interest charges affect financial statements.

7 Understand the cost of financing credit sales.

the **curious** accountant

Suppose that Eckerd Drugs orders supplies from Merck & Co., Inc. Assume that Eckerd offers to (1) pay for the supplies on the day it receives them from Merck (i.e., a cash purchase) or (2) pay for them 45 days later (i.e., a purchase on account). Assume that Merck is absolutely sure Eckerd will pay its account when due. Why should Merck care if the sale is made to Eckerd Drugs for cash or on account?

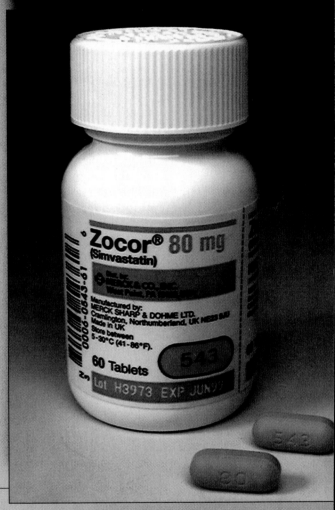

Associated Press AP MERCK & CO.

Many people are impulse buyers. A particular mix of environmental setting and emotional condition sparks an immediate urge to purchase. If people are forced to wait, because of a lack of funds, the mix of environment and emotion shifts and the desire to buy may dissipate. In recognition of this phenomenon, merchants offer credit terms that permit the customer to "buy now and pay later." By offering credit, businesses are able to increase their sales. The offsetting disadvantage of this strategy occurs when some customers are unable or unwilling to pay their bills. However, the widespread availability of credit attests to the fact that the advantages of increased sales generally outweigh the disadvantages arising from the associated bad debts.

When a company permits one of its customers to buy now and pay later, the expected future receipt is called an **account receivable.** Typically, amounts due from accounts receivable are relatively small, and the terms to maturity are short. Collection on most accounts receivable occurs within 30 days. When a longer credit term is necessary or when the amount of the receivable is large, a note evidencing a credit agreement between the parties involved is usually exchanged. The note specifies the maturity date, rate of interest, and other credit terms. Receivables evidenced by such notes are called **notes receivable.** Accounts and notes receivable are shown as assets on the balance sheet. For every receivable listed on one company's books, there is a corresponding obligation listed on another company's books. In other words, if one company expects to collect, another company expects to pay. Current obligations to make future economic sacrifices such as cash payments are frequently called **payables.** Accounts and notes payable[1] are shown as liabilities on the balance sheet.

L.O. 1

Understand the importance of offering credit terms to customers.

Receivables and payables represent future expected cash receipts or payments. However, most companies do not expect to receive the full face value of their receivables because they know that some of their customers will be unable or unwilling to pay the amounts due. Companies recognize this fact by reporting receivables at face value less an allowance for accounts whose collection is doubtful. The **net realizable value** (i.e., amount actually expected to be collected) is the amount added in the computation of total assets. In contrast, payables are normally carried at face value because companies operate under the **going concern assumption.** Since companies believe that they will continue to operate (i.e., they are going concerns), they assume they will be responsible for paying the full balance of their obligations. Accordingly, it is customary to carry receivables at net realizable value and payables at face value on the balance sheet.

The practice of reporting the net realizable value of receivables in the financial statements is commonly called the **allowance method of accounting for bad debts.** The following section demonstrates the application of the allowance method for a company named Allen's Tutoring Services.

Accounting Events Affecting the 20X1 Period

L.O. 2

Explain how the allowance method of accounting for bad debts affects financial statements.

Allen's Tutoring Services was started as a part-time venture by an individual named Mark Allen. Allen is a bright, young college student who started the tutoring service during his sophomore year. The following section illustrates three accounting events that affected Allen's Tutoring Services during its first year of operation. As you read, try to anticipate the effect of each event on the financial statements. Then check the accuracy of your expectation by looking at the statements model following the transaction. You will learn more rapidly if you think about the possible effects of each transaction *before* you read the results. To facilitate your analysis of the illustration, the transaction data are referenced by the event number.

Recognized $14,000 of Service Revenue Earned on Account during 20X1

Event 1
Revenue Recognition

By this point, you should be familiar with this type of event. It is an asset source transaction. Allen's Tutoring Services obtains assets (i.e., Accounts Receivable) by providing services to its customers. Accordingly, both assets and equity (i.e.,

---

[1]Notes payable can be classified as short term or long term, depending on the time to maturity. Short-term notes mature within 1 year or the operating cycle, whichever is longer. Notes with longer maturities are classified as long-term notes. This chapter focuses on accounting for short-term notes; accounting for long-term notes is discussed in Chapter 10.

Retained Earnings) increase. The event increases revenue and net income. Cash flow is not affected. These effects are shown in the following horizontal statements model:

Event No.	Assets	=	Liab.	+	Equity	Rev.	−	Exp.	=	Net Inc.	Cash Flow
1	14,000	=	n/a	+	14,000	14,000	−	n/a	=	14,000	n/a

Collected $12,500 Cash from Accounts Receivable in 20X1

This event is an asset exchange transaction. One asset, Cash, increases; and another asset, Accounts Receivable, decreases. The total amount of assets is unchanged. Net income is not affected because the revenue was recognized in the previous transaction. The cash inflow is shown in the operating activities section of the statement of cash flows.

Event 2
Collection of Receivable

Event No.	Assets			=	Liab.	+	Equity	Rev.	−	Exp.	=	Net Inc.	Cash Flow
	Cash	+	Accts. Rec.										
2	12,500	+	(12,500)	=	n/a	+	n/a	n/a	−	n/a	=	n/a	12,500 OA

Recognized Bad Debts Expense for Accounts Expected to Be Uncollectible in the Future

Event 3
Recognizing Bad Debts Expense

The ending balance in the receivable account is $1,500 ($14,000 of revenue on account − $12,500 of collections). Although Allen's Tutoring Services hopes to collect the full $1,500 in 20X2, the company is not likely to do so because some of its customers may not pay the amounts due. Accordingly, the $1,500 receivables balance does not represent the amount of cash that is truly expected to be collected. While Allen's Tutoring Services is reasonably certain that some of its customers will not pay, the actual amount of uncollectible accounts cannot be known until the future period when the customers default (i.e., refuse to pay). Even so, the company can make a reasonable *estimate* of the amount of receivables that will be uncollectible.

Suppose that Allen's Tutoring Services believes that $75 of the receivables is uncollectible. To improve accuracy, the company can recognize the anticipated future write-down of receivables in the current accounting period. Specifically, the company records a year-end adjusting entry that recognizes **bad debts expense,** thereby reducing the book value of total assets and equity (i.e., Retained Earnings). Like any other expense recognition transaction, the adjusting entry for bad debts expense reduces the amount of reported net income. The statement of cash flow is not affected. The effects of the recognition of bad debts expense are shown in the following horizontal statements model:

Event No.	Assets	=	Liab.	+	Equity	Rev.	−	Exp.	=	Net Inc.	Cash Flow
3	(75)	=	n/a	+	(75)	n/a	−	75	=	(75)	n/a

The amount of receivables that are expected to be uncollectible ($75) is accumulated in a contra asset account called **Allowance for Doubtful Accounts.** The difference between the amount in accounts receivable and the contra allowance account is called the *net realizable value of receivables*. In this case, the net realizable value of receivables is:

Accounts Receivable	$1,500
Less: Allowance for Doubtful Accounts	(75)
Net Realizable Value of Receivables	$1,425

The *net realizable value* of receivables represents the amount of receivables the company believes it will actually collect. Most companies disclose the amount of the allowance account as well as the net realizable value of receivables in their balance sheets. However, a significant number of companies show only the net balance. Some typical alternative balance sheet captions that could be used to report accounts receivable for Allen's Tutoring Services are shown here:

Alternative 1
Accounts Receivable	$1,500
Less Allowance for Doubtful Accounts	(75)
Total	$1,425

Alternative 2
Trade Accounts Receivable, Less Allowance of $75	$1,425

Alternative 3
Receivables, Less Allowance for Losses of $75	$1,425

Alternative 4
Accounts and Notes Receivable, net	$1,425

Alternative 5
Accounts Receivable	$1,425

As the different captions indicate, companies use a variety of terms and formats in reporting the amount of receivables in the balance sheet. Exhibit 7–1 provides insight regarding the most frequently used captions.

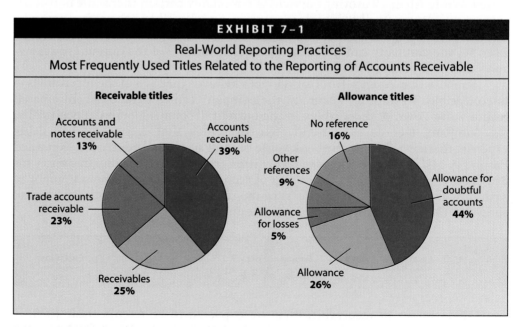

EXHIBIT 7–1

Real-World Reporting Practices
Most Frequently Used Titles Related to the Reporting of Accounts Receivable

Receivable titles

- Accounts and notes receivable 13%
- Accounts receivable 39%
- Trade accounts receivable 23%
- Receivables 25%

Allowance titles

- No reference 16%
- Other references 9%
- Allowance for losses 5%
- Allowance for doubtful accounts 44%
- Allowance 26%

Data source: AICPA, *Accounting Trends and Techniques,* 1998.

Ledger T-Accounts

Exhibit 7–2 shows ledger T-accounts for the business events experienced by Allen's Tutoring Services. The exhibit includes the entry used to close the revenue and expense accounts at the end of the 20X1 accounting period. The closing entry is an equity exchange transaction, with some equity accounts decreasing while others increase. The amount of total equity is not affected by the closing entry. Also, the income statement and the statement of cash flows are not affected by the closing entry. The ledger account balances are used to prepare the financial statements shown in Exhibit 7–3. To confirm your understanding of the accounting treatment for bad debts, trace the transactions to the ledger accounts and the account balances to the financial statements. The relevant accounting events are summarized here for your convenience:

1. Earned $14,000 of revenue on account.
2. Collected $12,500 cash from accounts receivable.
3. Adjusted the accounts to reflect management's belief that $75 of the receivable balance would be uncollectible.
4. Closed the revenue and expense accounts. The letters *cl* are used as a posting reference for the closing entries.

Financial Statements

The practice of estimating bad debts improves the accuracy of the 20X1 financial statements in two important ways. First, the net realizable value of accounts receivable is shown on the balance sheet. This presentation lets the statement users see not only the gross amount of receivables but also the amount that Allen's Tutoring Services actually expects to collect ($1,500 − $75 = $1,425). Furthermore, the amount of bad debts expense (that is, $75) is shown in the 20X1 income statement along with the revenue that was recognized when receivables

EXHIBIT 7–2

General Ledger

Cash		=	Liabilities	+	Retained Earnings	
(2) 12,500			0 Bal.			13,925 (cl)
Bal. 12,500						13,925 Bal.

Accounts Receivable					Service Revenue	
(1) 14,000	12,500 (2)				(cl) 14,000	14,000 (1)
Bal. 1,500						0 Bal.

Allowance for Doubtful Accounts					Bad Debts Expense	
	75 (3)				(3) 75	75 (cl)
	75 Bal.				Bal. 0	

EXHIBIT 7–3

Financial Statements for 20X1

Income Statement		Balance Sheet			Statement of Cash Flows	
Service Revenue	$14,000	Assets			**Operating Activities**	
Bad Debts Exp.	(75)	Cash		$12,500	Inflow from Customers	$12,500
Net Income	$13,925	Accounts Receivable	$1,500		**Investing Activities**	0
		Less: Allowance	(75)			
		Net Realizable Value		1,425	**Financing Activities**	0
		Total Assets		$13,925	Net Change in Cash	12,500
					Plus: Beginning Cash Balance	0
		Equity				
		Retained Earnings		$13,925	Ending Cash Balance	$12,500

were recorded. Since the associated revenues and expenses are shown on the same income statement, the allowance method improves matching and provides a better measure of managerial performance. As you continue to review the statements in Exhibit 7–3, observe carefully that the amount of cash flow from operations ($12,500) is different from the amount of net income ($13,925) because only cash collections are reported in the statement of cash flows, whereas the income statement includes revenues earned on account less the estimated amount of bad debts expense.

Estimation of Bad Debts Expense

In the case of Allen's Tutoring, we simply provided the estimated amount of uncollectible accounts. How do real-world accountants make such estimates? Most accountants start by reviewing their company's credit history. They ask, how much of our accounts receivable were we unable to collect in the past? A convenient way to express the answer to this question is to state the amount of uncollectible accounts as a percentage of the accounts receivable balance. To illustrate, assume that Tannon Company was unable to collect $10,000 of $200,000 in accounts receivable. Accordingly, Tannon's uncollectible accounts amounted to 5% of the receivables balance ($10,000 ÷ $200,000).

Before the historical percentage is applied to the current receivables balance, it is normally adjusted for new circumstances that are anticipated to be experienced in the future. For example, the percentage could be lowered if the company plans to apply more rigorous approval standards to new credit applicants. Alternatively, the percentage may be increased if economic forecasts signal a downturn in the economy that would make future defaults more likely. Once the expected percentage of uncollectible accounts is determined, it is applied to the balance in the receivables account at the end of the current period, in order to obtain an estimate of the amount of these receivables that will be uncollectible in the future.

Due to more stringent credit standards and projections of economic stability, Tannon's management believes that the company can reduce the level of uncollectible accounts from 5 to 4.5% of the current accounts receivable balance. Assuming a year-end receivables balance of $280,000, the balance in Allowance for Doubtful Accounts should be $12,600 ($280,000 × 0.045). Under these circumstances, the company's current balance sheet reflects a net realizable value of receivables of $267,400 ($280,000 accounts receivable − $12,600 allowance).

Determining the estimated percentage of uncollectible accounts may be particularly difficult when a company is in its first year of operation because there is no credit history upon which to base the estimate. In this case, it is necessary to consult with trade associations or business associates (i.e., other people in the same industry who do have experience) to develop a reasonable estimate of the expected losses.

Accounting Events Affecting the 20X2 Period

Now we discuss eight accounting events that occurred during the 20X2 accounting cycle. As in the previous section, you should anticipate the effect of each event on the financial statements prior to reviewing the appropriate statements model. An accounting textbook should not be merely read; it should be worked. Read the book with pencil in hand. Anticipate the results, trace the transactions, and verify the numbers. You will learn more by *doing* accounting than by *reading* about it. So do the accounting as you read the text.

> **L.O. 2**
> Explain how the allowance method of accounting for bad debts affects financial statements.

Wrote Off an Uncollectible Account Receivable

Event 1
Write-Off of an Uncollectible Account Receivable

Since the impact of recognizing bad debts was shown in the 20X1 financial statements, the actual *write-off of uncollectible accounts* does not affect the balance sheet. At the time when a specific account is determined to be uncollectible, the balance of the account is removed from the Receivables account and from the Allowance for Bad Debts account. Accordingly, the event constitutes an asset exchange transaction. Total assets, liabilities, and equity are the same immediately after the write-off in 20X2. Likewise, the income statement and the statement of cash flows are not affected by a write-off of an uncollectible account. To illustrate, assume that one of Allen's Tutoring Services' customers refuses to pay a $70 receivable balance. Allen's Tutoring Services has tried in every way to collect the amount due and has determined that regardless of further efforts, the funds are not collectible now or in the future. Accordingly, Allen's has decided to write off the account. The effect on the financial statements is shown in the following horizontal statements model:

Event No.	Assets			=	Liab.	+	Equity	Rev.	–	Exp.	=	Net Inc.	Cash Flow
	Acct. Rec.	–	Allow.										
1	(70)	–	(70)	=	n/a	+	n/a	n/a	–	n/a	=	n/a	n/a

As indicated, the write-off is an asset exchange transaction. The decrease in Accounts Receivable is offset by a reduction in the balance of the allowance account. Note that while the balances in accounts receivable and the allowance account decrease, the net realizable value of receivables—and therefore total assets—remains unchanged.

	Before Write-Off	After Write-Off
Accounts Receivable	$1,500	$1,430
Allowance for Doubtful Accounts	(75)	(5)
Net Realizable Value	$1,425	$1,425

Invested in a Note Receivable

Event 2
Investment in Note Receivable

After taking an accounting course, Mark Allen becomes concerned about the growing balance in his company's Cash account. He realizes that he could improve his company's profitability by investing some of the idle cash. Accordingly, on May 1, 20X2, Allen loans $12,000 cash to another student who is starting a business of her own. The borrower issues a 9% interest-bearing note to Allen. The note carries 1-year term. The loan represents an investment by Allen's Tutoring Services. One asset account, *Cash*, decreases; another asset account, *Notes Receivable*, increases. Total assets are unchanged. The income statement is unaffected by the event. The cash outflow is shown in the investing activities section of the statement of cash flows. These effects are reflected in the statements model:

Event No.	Assets			=	Liab.	+	Equity	Rev.	–	Exp.	=	Net Inc.	Cash Flow	
	Cash	+	Note Rec.											
2	(12,000)	+	12,000	=	n/a	+	n/a	n/a	–	n/a	=	n/a	(12,000)	IA

Provided $10,000 of Tutoring Services on Account during the 20X2 Accounting Period

Event 3
Revenue Recognition

Assets (i.e., Accounts Receivable) and equity (i.e., Revenue) increase. The recognition of revenue acts to increase net income. Cash flow is not affected. The effects on the financial statements are shown here:

Event No.	Assets	=	Liab.	+	Equity	Rev.	–	Exp.	=	Net Inc.	Cash Flow
3	10,000	=	n/a	+	10,000	10,000	–	n/a	=	10,000	n/a

Collected $8,430 Cash from Accounts Receivable

Event 4
Collection of Account Receivable

The balance in the Cash account increases, and the balance in the receivables account decreases. Total assets are unaffected. Net income is not affected because revenue was recognized previously. The cash inflow is shown in the operating activities section of the statement of cash flows:

Event No.	Assets		=	Liab.	+	Equity	Rev.	−	Exp.	=	Net Inc.	Cash Flow
	Cash	+ Acct. Rec.										
4	8,430	+ (8,430)	=	n/a	+	n/a	n/a	−	n/a	=	n/a	8,430 OA

Recovered a Bad Debt That Was Previously Written Off

Occasionally, a company receives payment from a customer whose account was previously written off. When this occurs, the customer's account should be reestablished and the collection should be recorded in ordinary fashion. This practice reflects a complete record of activity that may be useful in the event the customer requests additional credit at some future date or in case the company is asked to provide a credit history of the customer to a credit bureau, bank, or some other interested party. To illustrate, assume that Allen's Tutoring Services receives a $10 cash payment from a customer whose account had previously been written off. The first step is to reestablish the receivable and allowance accounts that were written off. The effect is simply the reverse of a write-off. Accounts receivable increases, and the allowance account increases. Since the allowance is a contra asset account, the increase in this account offsets the increase in the receivables account, and total assets are unchanged. Net income and cash flow are unaffected. These effects are shown here:

Event 5
Recovery of Bad Debt: Reestablishment of Receivable

Event No.	Assets		Assets	=	Liab.	+	Equity	Rev.	−	Exp.	=	Net Inc.	Cash Flow
	Acct. Rec.	−	Allow.										
5	10	−	10	=	n/a	+	n/a	n/a	−	n/a	=	n/a	n/a

Collected Reestablished Receivable

The collection of $10 is treated as any other collection of a receivable account. The Cash account increases, and the receivables account decreases.

Event 6
Recovery of Bad Debt: Collection of Receivable

Event No.	Assets		Assets	=	Liab.	+	Equity	Rev.	−	Exp.	=	Net Inc.	Cash Flow
	Cash	+	Acct. Rec.										
6	10	+	(10)	=	n/a	+	n/a	n/a	−	n/a	=	n/a	10 OA

Recognized Bad Debts Expense for 20X2

Assume that Allen estimates that 5% of the year-end accounts receivable balance will be uncollectible. As shown in Exhibit 7–4, the receivables account contained a $3,000 balance at the December 31, 20X2, fiscal closing date. Accordingly, the allowance account should contain a $150 balance ($3,000 × 0.05) *after* the adjusting entry to record bad debts expense is posted. Prior to the 20X2 adjustment for bad debts expense, the allowance account contains a $15 balance ($75 beginning balance − $70 write-off + $10 recovery of bad debt). Accordingly, it is necessary to add $135 ($150 − $15) to the allowance account to arrive at the desired $150 ending balance. To add $135 to the balance in the allowance account, it is necessary to recognize that amount of bad debts expense in the year-end adjusting entry. The recognition of the $135 bad debts expense acts to decrease assets (i.e., net realizable value of receivables) and equity (i.e., retained earnings). The

Event 7
Adjustment for Recognition of Bad Debts Expense

recognition of the expense acts to decrease the amount of net income. The statement of cash flows is not affected. The effects on the financial statements are shown here:

Event No.	Assets			=	Liab.	+	Equity	Rev.	−	Exp.	=	Net Inc.	Cash Flow
	Acct. Rec.	−	Allow.										
7	n/a	−	135	=	n/a	+	(135)	n/a	−	135	=	(135)	n/a

Recognized Interest Revenue on Note Receivable

Event 8
Recognition of
Interest Revenue

Recall that on May 1, 20X2, Allen's Tutoring Services invested $12,000 in a note receivable with a 1-year term and a 9% annual rate of interest. By December 31, 20X2, the note will have earned $720 ($12,000 × 0.09 × [8 ÷ 12]). The recognition of the earned interest acts to increase assets (i.e., Interest Receivable) and equity (i.e., Retained Earnings). The recognition of revenue acts to increase net income. Cash flow is not affected. The effects on the financial statements are shown here:

Event No.	Assets	=	Liab.	+	Equity	Rev.	−	Exp.	=	Net Inc.	Cash Flow
8	720	=	n/a	+	720	720	−	n/a	=	720	n/a

Ledger T-Accounts

Exhibit 7–4 shows ledger T-accounts for the 20X2 business events experienced by Allen's Tutoring Services. The exhibit includes the entry used to close the revenue and expense accounts at the end of the 20X2 accounting period. The ledger account balances are used to prepare the financial statements shown in Exhibit 7–5. The relevant accounting events are summarized for your convenience.

✓ 1. Wrote off a $70 uncollectible account receivable.
✓ 2. Invested $12,000 in note receivable.
3. Earned $10,000 of tutoring service revenue on account.
4. Collected $8,430 cash from accounts receivable.
5. Reestablished a $10 account receivable that had previously been written off.
6. Collected $10 from the reestablished receivable.
7. Adjusted accounts to recognize $135 of estimated bad debts expense.
8. Adjusted accounts to recognize $720 of accrued interest revenue.
9. Closed the revenue and expense accounts. The letters *cl* are used as a posting reference for the closing entries.

Analysis of Financial Statements

Exhibit 7–5 shows the relevant financial statements. Observe carefully that the amount of bad debts expense (that is, $135) is different from the ending balance of the allowance account (that is, $150). Recall that the allowance account had a $15 balance just prior to the time that the 20X2 adjusting entry for bad debts expense was made. This balance existed because the estimate for uncollectible accounts in 20X1 was overstated. In 20X1, Allen's Tutoring Services estimated that there would be $75 of uncollectible accounts when, in fact, only $70 of accounts was

EXHIBIT 7–4

General Ledger

Assets	=	Liabilities	+	Equity

Cash			=	Liabilities		+	Retained Earnings	
Bal.	12,500	12,000 (2)			0 Bal.		13,925	Bal.
(4)	8,430						10,585	(cl)
(6)	10						24,510	Bal.
Bal.	8,940							

Accounts Receivable

Bal.	1,500	70	(1) ✓
(3)	10,000	8,430	(4)
(5)	10	10	(6)
Bal.	3,000		

Service Revenue

(cl)	10,000	10,000	(3)
		0	Bal.

Allowance for Doubtful Accounts

(1) ✓	70	75	Bal.
		10	(5)
		135	(7)
		150	Bal.

Interest Revenue

(cl)	720	720	(8)
		0	Bal.

Bad Debts Expense

(7)	135	135	(cl)
Bal.	0		

Notes Receivable

(2)	12,000	

Interest Receivable

(8)	720	

EXHIBIT 7–5

Financial Statements for 20X2

Income Statement		Balance Sheet			Statement of Cash Flows	
Service Revenue	$10,000	Assets			**Operating Activities**	
Bad Debts Exp.	(135)	Cash		$ 8,940	Inflow from	
		Accounts Receivable	$3,000		Customers	$ 8,440
Operating Income	9,865	Less: Allowance	(150)		**Investing Activities**	(12,000)
Interest Revenue	720					
		Net Realizable Value		2,850	**Financing Activities**	0
Net Income	$10,585	Note Receivable		12,000		
		Interest Receivable		720	Net Change in Cash	(3,560)
					Plus: Beginning Cash	
		Total Assets		$24,510	Balance	12,500
					Ending Cash Balance	$ 8,940
		Equity				
		Retained Earnings		$24,510		

written off and $10 of those accounts was recovered, resulting in a net loss of uncollectible accounts of only $60. Accordingly, the expense for 20X1 was overstated by $15. However, if no estimate had been made, the amount of bad debts expense would have been understated by $60. Although the allowance method does not result in perfection, it does improve the accuracy of the financial statements. The $15 of overstated expenses in 20X1 is offset by an adjustment to the bad debts expense in 20X2. Although Allen's Tutoring Services estimates that $150 of the 20X2 accounts receivable balance will be uncollectible, the amount of bad debts expense shown in the 20X2 income statement is only $135. Since there were no distributions, ending retained earnings are computed as last year's retained earnings plus this year's net income (that is, $13,925 + $10,585 = $24,510). Once again, the cash flow from operations ($8,440) is different from the amount of net income ($10,585) because the statement of cash flows does not include the effects of revenues earned on account or the recognition of bad debts expense.

Recognition of Bad Debts under the Direct Write-Off Method

If the amount of uncollectible accounts is immaterial, bad debts expense can be recognized at the time when accounts are determined to be uncollectible. This method is called the **direct write-off method** of accounting for bad debts. Since the direct write-off method does not make an allowance for uncollectible accounts, it overstates the net realizable value of receivables on the balance sheet. Therefore, the method does not comply with generally accepted accounting principles. However, if the amount of uncollectible accounts is insignificant, the overstatement is tolerated as a fair trade-off for the recording convenience offered by the direct write-off method. This is an example of the application of the materiality concept. The reporting of immaterial items does not have to conform to GAAP.

No estimates, allowance account, or adjusting entries are needed under the direct write-off method. Simply record the bad debts as they occur. Sales or services on account are recognized in the customary fashion in the period in which goods or services are provided. Bad debts expense is then recognized in the period in which a particular account is determined to be uncollectible. To illustrate, assume that the following events apply to Dr. Price's optical services company.

Event 1
Recognition of Revenue on Account

During 20X1, the company provides $50,000 of services on account. The effects of this event on the financial statements are shown here:

Event No.	Assets	=	Liab.	+	Equity	Rev.	−	Exp.	=	Net Inc.	Cash Flow
1	50,000	=	n/a	+	50,000	50,000	−	n/a	=	50,000	n/a

The following entry is used to record the transaction in the general journal:

Account Title	Debit	Credit
Accounts Receivable	50,000	
Service Revenue		50,000

Event 2
Recognition of Bad Debts Expense

Assume that Price determines in 20X2 that one of his customers who owes $200 for services delivered in 20X1 is unable to pay the amount due. The write-off of the account results in the recognition of bad debts expense in 20X2, even though the associated revenue was recognized in 20X1. In other words, the expense is recognized in the year in which an account is determined to be uncollectible. Accuracy is compromised because revenues are not matched with related expenses. As indicated earlier, such inaccuracies are tolerated only to the extent that they are deemed to be immaterial. The effect of the write-off of the uncollectible account on the financial statements is as follows:

Event No.	Assets	=	Liab.	+	Equity	Rev.	−	Exp.	=	Net Inc.	Cash Flow
2	(200)	=	n/a	+	(200)	n/a	−	200	=	(200)	n/a

The only entry required to recognize bad debts is made in 20X2. This entry is shown here in general journal format:

Account Title	Debit	Credit
Bad Debt Expense	200	
Accounts Receivable		200

Accounting for Credit Card Sales

The effective management of credit is an involved task that can be very expensive in terms of time and money. Not only will a company incur bad debts expense but also it must incur considerable clerical costs. Creditworthiness must be established for each customer, and detailed records of each transaction must be maintained. Many businesses have chosen to pass these costs on to financial institutions that service the merchant's credit sales for a fee that typically ranges between 2 and 8% of gross sales.

L.O. 4

Explain how accounting for credit card sales affects financial statements.

The financial institution (i.e., credit card company) provides the customer with a plastic card that permits the cardholder to charge purchases at various retail outlets. When a sale is made, the seller records the transactions on an invoice the customer signs. The invoice is forwarded to the credit card company, which immediately pays the merchant. The service charge is deducted from the gross amount of the invoice, and the merchant is paid the net balance (i.e., gross invoice less credit card discount) in cash. The credit card company collects the amount of the gross sales directly from the customer. Therefore, the merchant is able to avoid the risk of bad debts as well as the cost of maintaining credit records. To illustrate, assume that the following events apply to Joan Wilson's consulting practice.

Wilson accepts a credit card as payment for $1,000 of services rendered to one of her customers. Assume that the credit card company charges a 5% fee for handling the credit ($1,000 × 0.05 = $50). Income increases by the amount of revenue ($1,000) and decreases by the amount of the credit card expense ($50). Accordingly, net income increases by $950. The event acts to increase assets (i.e., Account Receivable due from the credit card company) and equity (i.e., Retained Earnings) by $950. Cash flow is not affected. The effect of the event on the financial statements is as follows:

Event 1
Recognition of Revenue and Expense on Credit Card Sale

Event No.	Assets	=	Liab.	+	Equity	Rev.	−	Exp.	=	Net Inc.	Cash Flow
1	950	=	n/a	+	950	1,000	−	50	=	950	n/a

The following entry is used to record the transaction in the general journal:

Account Title	Debit	Credit
Account Receivable—Credit Card Company	950	
Credit Card Expense	50	
Service Revenue		1,000

The collection of the receivable due from the credit card company is treated as any other collection of a receivable. When Wilson collects the net amount of $950 ($1,000 − $50) from the credit card company, one asset account increases (i.e., Cash) and another asset account decreases (i.e., Accounts Receivable). Total assets are not affected. The *income statement* is not affected by the transaction. There is a $950 cash inflow shown in the operating activities section of the *statement of cash flows.* The effect of the collection on the financial statement elements is shown here:

Event No.	AssetsAssets			= Liab.	+ Equity	Rev.	− Exp.	= Net Inc.	Cash Flow	
	Cash	+	Acct. Rec.							
2	950	+	(950)	= n/a	+ n/a	n/a	− n/a	= n/a	950	OA

The following entry is used to record the transaction in the general journal.

Account Title	Debit	Credit
Cash	950	
Accounts Receivable		950

Warranty Obligations

Global competition has forced most companies to guarantee customer satisfaction. A promise to correct a deficiency or dissatisfaction in quality, quantity, or performance is called a **warranty.** Warranties take many forms. Usually, they provide a guaranty that extends over some specified period after the point of sale. Within this period, the seller promises to replace or repair defective products without charge. Many companies promise satisfaction or "your money back." Some even offer double or triple money-back guarantees. Although the obligations stemming from warranties may be uncertain as to amount, timing, or customer, they usually represent legal liabilities that must be recognized in the accounts.

To demonstrate the accounting treatment for warranty obligations, assume that Perfect Picture Frame (PPF) Company had cash of $2,000, inventory of $6,000, contributed capital of $5,000, and retained earnings of $3,000 on January 1, 20X5. The 20X5 accounting period is affected by three accounting events: (1) sale of merchandise, (2) recognition of warranty obligations to customers who purchased the merchandise, and (3) settlement of a warranty claim made by a customer.

Sold Merchandise That Cost $4,000 for $7,000 Cash

In the statements model shown here, the sale is referenced with the notation 1a and the cost of the sale as 1b. The recognition of sales revenue acts to increase assets and equity. Net income also increases. The statement of cash flows includes a $7,000 cash inflow in the operating activities section. The recognition of expense (i.e., cost of goods sold) acts to decrease assets and equity. Net income also decreases. Cash flow is not affected by the expense recognition. The effects on the financial statements are indicated here:

Event No.	Assets			= Liab.	+ Equity	Rev.	− Exp.	= Net Inc.	Cash Flow	
	Cash	+	Inven.							
1	7,000		n/a	= n/a	+ 7,000	7,000	− n/a	= 7,000	7,000	OA
1	n/a		(4,000)	= n/a	+ (4,000)	n/a	− 4,000	= (4,000)	n/a	

Guaranteed the Merchandise Sold in Event No. 1 to Be Free from Defects for a 1-Year Period following the Date of Sale

While the exact amount of future warranty claims is unknown, PPF must inform financial statement users of the obligation that the company has incurred. Accordingly, it is necessary for PPF to estimate the amount of the liability and to include that estimate in the current period's financial statements. Assume that the warranty obligation is estimated to be $100. Recognizing this obligation acts to increase liabilities (i.e., Warranties Payable) and reduce equity (i.e., Retained Earnings). The recognition of the warranty expense acts to reduce net income. The statement of cash flows is not affected by the recognition of the obligation and corresponding expense. The effects on the financial statements are shown here:

Event 2
Recognition of Warranty Expense

Event No.	Assets	=	W. Pay.	+	Equity	Rev.	−	Exp.	=	Net Inc.	Cash Flow
2	n/a	=	100	+	(100)	n/a	−	100	=	(100)	n/a

Paid $40 Cash to Repair Defective Merchandise Returned by Customers

Note carefully that the payment for the repair is not an expense. The expense was recognized in the period in which the sale was made (i.e., at the time the Warranty Payable account was created). Accordingly, rather than being an expense, the cash payment acts to reduce the Warranty Payable account. Therefore, the payment reduces the asset (i.e., Cash) and liabilities (i.e., Warranty Payable). The income statement is not affected by the repairs payment. However, there is a $40 cash outflow shown in the operating activities section of the statement of cash flows.

Event 3
Settlement of Warranty Obligation

Event No.	Assets	=	W. Pay.	+	Equity	Rev.	−	Exp.	=	Net Inc.	Cash Flow
3	(40)	=	(40)	+	n/a	n/a	−	n/a	=	n/a	(40) OA

Ledger T-Accounts and Financial Statements

Exhibit 7–6 presents ledger T-accounts for the business events experienced by PPF. The exhibit includes the entry used to close the revenue and expense accounts at the end of the 20X5 accounting period. The ledger account balances are used to prepare the financial statements shown in Exhibit 7–7. The relevant accounting events are summarized below for your convenience.

Transactions for 20X5
1. Sold merchandise that cost $4,000 for $7,000 cash.
2. Recognized a $100 warranty obligation and the corresponding expense.
3. Paid $40 to satisfy a warranty claim.
4. Closed the revenue and expense accounts. The letters *cl* are used as a posting reference for the closing entries.

Accounting for Discount Notes

Up to this point, all notes payable have been assumed to be **interest-bearing notes.** At maturity, the amount due is the *face value* of the note *plus accrued interest.* In contrast, **discount notes** have the interest included in the face value of the note.

L.O. 6

Understand how discount notes and related interest charges affect financial statements.

EXHIBIT 7–6

General Ledger

Assets	=	Liabilities	+	Equity

Cash

Bal.	2,000	40	(3)
(1a)	7,000		
Bal.	8,960		

Inventory

Bal.	6,000	4,000	(1b)
Bal.	2,000		

Warranties Payable

(3)	.40	100	(2)
		60	Bal.

Contributed Capital

	5,000	Bal.

Retained Earnings

	3,000	Bal.
	2,900	(cl)
	5,900	Bal.

Sales Revenue

(cl)	7,000	7,000	(1a)
		0	Bal.

Cost of Goods Sold

(1b)	4,000	4,000	(cl)
Bal.	0		

Warranty Expense

(2)	100	100	(cl)
Bal.	0		

EXHIBIT 7–7

Financial Statements for 20X5

Income Statement		Balance Sheet		Statement of Cash Flows	
Sales	$7,000	Assets		**Operating Activities**	
Cost of Goods	(4,000)	Cash	$ 8,960	Inflow from Customers	$7,000
		Inventory	2,000	Outflow for Warranty	(40)
Gross Margin	3,000				
Warranty Exp.	(100)	Total Assets	$10,960	Net Inflow from Oper.	6,960
Net Income	$2,900	Liabilities		**Investing Activities**	0
		Warranties Payable	$ 60	**Financing Activities**	0
		Equity		Net Change in Cash	6,960
		Contributed Capital	5,000	Plus: Beginning Cash Balance	2,000
		Retained Earnings	5,900		
				Ending Cash Balance	$8,960
		Total Liab. and Equity	$10,960		

Accordingly, a $5,000 face value discount note is repaid with a $5,000 cash payment at maturity. This payment includes principal and accrued interest. To illustrate, assume that the following four events apply to Beacon Management Services.

Started Beacon Management Services by Issuing a $10,000 Face Value Discount Note to State Bank on March 1, 20X1

Event 1
Borrowing by Issuing a Discount Note

The note carried a 9% *discount rate* and a 1-year term to maturity. As with interest-bearing notes, the **issuer of the note** gives the promissory note in

reality bytes

Most electrical appliances come with a manufacturer's warranty that obligates the manufacturer to pay for defects that occur during some designated period of time after the point of sale. Why would Circuit City issue warranties that obligate it to pay for defects that occur after the manufacturer's warranty has expired? Warranties are in fact insurance policies that generate profits. Indeed, the Circuit City Group reported that the gross dollar sales from extended warranty programs were 5.5 percent of its total sales in fiscal year 1998. Even more important, Circuit City notes that gross profit margins on products sold with extended warranties are higher than the gross profit margins on products sold without extended warranties. It should be noted that warranties produce revenues for manufacturers as well as retailers. The only difference is that the revenues generated from manufacturer's warranties are embedded in the sales price. Indeed, products with longer, more comprehensive warranties usually sell at higher prices than products with shorter, less extensive warranties.

encer Grant/Photo Edit

exchange for the receipt of cash. The first step in accounting for the discount note is to divide the face amount between the discount and the principal (i.e., amount borrowed). The discount is computed by multiplying the face value of the note by the interest rate by the time period. In this case, the discount is $900 ($10,000 × 0.09). The amount borrowed is determined by subtracting the discount from the face value of the note ($10,000 − $900 = $9,100). Accordingly, in this case the **principal** (i.e., the amount of cash borrowed) is $9,100, and the **discount** (i.e., the amount of interest to be incurred over the term of the loan) is $900. In summary, *on the issue date,* assets and total liabilities increase by the amount borrowed (i.e., the $9,100 principal). The *income statement* is not affected by the borrowing transaction on the issue date. There is a $9,100 cash inflow shown in the financing activities section of the *statement of cash flows.* These effects are shown here:

Event No.	Assets	=	Liab.	+	Equity	Rev.	−	Exp.	=	Net Inc.	Cash Flow
1	9,100	=	9,100	+	n/a	n/a	−	n/a	=	n/a	9,100 FA

For internal record-keeping purposes, the amount of the discount is normally contained in a separate account titled **Discount on Notes Payable.** This account is a **contra liability account.** It is subtracted from the Notes Payable account to determine the carrying value of the liability. The *carrying value,* also known as the *book value,* gets its name from the fact that it is the amount at which the liability is shown (i.e., carried) on the books. In this case, Beacon's ledger contains the Notes Payable account with a $10,000 credit balance and the Discount on Notes Payable account with a $900 debit balance. The carrying value is computed as follows:

Notes Payable	$10,000
Discount on Notes Payable	(900)
Carrying Value of Liability	$ 9,100

Incurred $8,000 of Cash Operating Expenses

Event 2
Recognition of Operating Expenses

The payment for these expenses acts to reduce assets and equity. The effect of the event on the income statement is to increase expenses and decrease net income. The cash outflow is shown in the operating activities section of the statement of cash flows. These effects are shown here:

Event No.	Assets	=	Liab.	+	Equity	Rev.	−	Exp.	=	Net Inc.	Cash Flow
2	(8,000)	=	n/a	+	(8,000)	n/a	−	8,000	=	(8,000)	(8,000) OA

Recognized $12,000 of Cash Revenue

Event 3
Recognition of Revenue

The recognition of the revenue acts to increase assets and equity. The amount of net income increases. The cash inflow is shown in the operating activities section of the statement of cash flows. These effects follow.

Event No.	Assets	=	Liab.	+	Equity	Rev.	−	Exp.	=	Net Inc.	Cash Flow
3	12,000	=	n/a	+	12,000	12,000	−	n/a	=	12,000	12,000 OA

Recognized Accrued Interest Expense

Event 4
Adjustment for Accrued Interest

On December 31, 20X1, Beacon is required to adjust the accounting records to reflect the accrual of 10 months of interest for the 20X1 accounting period. Interest expense accrues at the rate of $75 per month ($900 discount ÷ 12 = $75). Accordingly, $750 ($75 × 10) of interest is accrued as of December 31. The reduction in equity caused by the recognition of the interest expense is balanced by an increase in liabilities. The increase in liabilities is accomplished by reducing the contra liability account, *Discount on Note Payable.* Recall that the carrying value of the liability was $9,100 (that is, $10,000 face value less $900 discount) on the day the note was issued. The entry to record the accrued interest expense removes $750 from the discount account, leaving a $150 balance ($900 − $750) remaining after the adjusting entry is posted. The practice of converting the discount to interest expense over a designated period is referred to as the **amortization** of the discount. After 10 months of amortization, the carrying value of the liability shown on the December 31, 20X1, balance sheet in Exhibit 7–9 is $9,850 ($10,000 face value − the $150 discount). The effect of the interest recognition on the income statement is to increase expenses and decrease net income by $750. The statement of cash flows is not affected by the accrual. Cash is paid for the interest at the maturity date. The effects of the adjusting entry for accrued interest expense are shown here:

Event No.	Assets	=	Liab.	+	Equity	Rev.	−	Exp.	=	Net Inc.	Cash Flow
4	n/a	=	750	+	(750)	n/a	−	750	=	(750)	n/a

Ledger T-Accounts and Financial Statements

Exhibit 7–8 shows ledger T-accounts for the business events experienced by Beacon Management Services. The exhibit includes the entry used to close the revenue and expense accounts at the end of the 20X1 accounting period. The ledger account balances are used to prepare the financial statements shown in Exhibit 7–9. The relevant accounting events are summarized here for your convenience.

1. Issued a $10,000 face value discount note with a 9% discount rate.
2. Paid $8,000 cash for operating expenses.
3. Earned $12,000 cash revenue.
4. Recognized $750 of accrued interest expense.
5. Closed the revenue and expense accounts. The letters *cl* are used as a posting reference for the closing entries.

EXHIBIT 7–8

General Ledger

Assets	=	Liabilities	+	Equity

Cash		=	Notes Payable		+	Retained Earnings	
(1) 9,100	8,000 (2)			10,000 (1)			3,250 (cl)
(3) 12,000			**Discount on Note Payable**				3,250 Bal.
Bal. 13,100							

Discount on Note Payable

(1)	900	750	(4)
Bal.	150		

Service Revenue

(cl)	12,000	12,000	(3)
		0	Bal.

Operating Expense

(2)	8,000	8,000	(cl)
Bal.	0		

Interest Expense

(4)	750	750	(cl)
Bal.	0		

EXHIBIT 7–9

Financial Statements for 20X1

Income Statement		Balance Sheet			Statement of Cash Flows	
Service Revenue	$12,000	Assets			**Operating Activities**	
Operating Exp.	(8,000)	Cash		$13,100	Inflow from Customers	$12,000
		Liabilities			Outflow for Expenses	(8,000)
Operating Income	4,000	Notes Payable	$10,000		Net Inflow from Oper.	4,000
Interest Exp.	(750)	Less: Disc. on Note Pay.	(150)		**Investing Activities**	0
					Financing Activities	
Net Income	$3,250	Total Liabilities		$ 9,850	Inflow from Creditors	9,100
		Equity				
		Retained Earnings		3,250	Net Change in Cash	13,100
					Plus: Beginning Cash Balance	0
		Total Equity and Liab.		$13,100	Ending Cash Balance	$13,100

L.O. 6

Understand how discount notes and related interest charges affect financial statements.

Accounting Events Affecting the 20X2 Period

This section introduces four accounting events that apply to Beacon's 20X2 accounting cycle.

Recognized 2 Months of Accrued Interest

Event 1
Accrual of Interest for 20X2

Since the note carried a 1-year term, 2 months of interest have to be accrued at the maturity date on February 28, 20X2. Since interest expense accrues at the rate of $75 per month ($900 discount ÷ 12 = $75), there is $150 ($75 × 2) of interest expense accrued in 20X2. The recognition of the interest acts to increase liabilities (i.e., reduce the discount account to zero) and decrease equity. The effect of the recognition on the income statement is to increase expenses and decrease net income by $150. The statement of cash flows is not affected by the transaction. These effects are shown here:

Event No.	Assets	=	Liab.	+	Equity	Rev.	−	Exp.	=	Net Inc.	Cash Flow
1	n/a	=	150	+	(150)	n/a	−	150	=	(150)	n/a

Repaid Face Value on Discount Note Payable

Event 2
Payment of Face Value

The face value ($10,000) of the note is due on the maturity date. The repayment of the note is an asset use transaction causing assets and liabilities to decrease. The income statement is not affected by the event. The $10,000 cash payment includes $900 for interest and $9,100 for principal. Accordingly, there is a $900 outflow shown in the operating activities section and a $9,100 outflow shown in the financing activities section of the statement of cash flows. These effects are shown here:

Event No.	Assets	=	Liab.	+	Equity	Rev.	−	Exp.	=	Net Inc.	Cash Flow	
2	(10,000)	=	(10,000)	+	n/a	n/a	−	n/a	=	n/a	(900)	OA
											(9,100)	FA

Recognized $13,000 of Cash Revenue

Event 3
Revenue Recognition

Assets and equity increase as a result of the recognition. Net income also increases. The cash inflow is shown in the operating activities section of the statement of cash flows. These effects are shown here:

Event No.	Assets	=	Liab.	+	Equity	Rev.	−	Exp.	=	Net Inc.	Cash Flow	
3	13,000	=	n/a	+	13,000	13,000	−	n/a	=	13,000	13,000	OA

Incurred $8,500 of Cash Operating Expenses

Event 4
Recognition of Operating Expenses

This event causes assets and equity to decrease. Net income also decreases. The cash outflow is shown in the operating activities section of the statement of cash flows. These effects are shown here:

Event No.	Assets	=	Liab.	+	Equity	Rev.	−	Exp.	=	Net Inc.	Cash Flow
4	(8,500)	=	n/a	+	(8,500)	n/a	−	8,500	=	(8,500)	8,500 OA

Ledger T-Accounts and Financial Statements

Exhibits 7–10 and 7–11 present the relevant ledger T-accounts and financial statements, respectively. Notice in Exhibit 7–11 that the balance in liabilities is zero because both interest and principal have been paid, leaving Beacon with no obligations as of the 20X2 fiscal closing date. Retained earnings includes the total of net income for 20X1 and 20X2. This result occurs because all income was retained in the business since no distributions were made to owners during 20X1 and 20X2.

EXHIBIT 7–10

General Ledger

Assets	=	Liabilities	+	Equity

Cash = **Notes Payable** + **Retained Earnings**

Bal.	13,100	10,000	(2)	(2)	10,000	10,000 Bal.	3,250	Bal.
(3)	13,000	8,500	(4)				4,350	(cl)
Bal.	7,600						7,600	Bal.

Discount on Note Payable

Bal.	150	150	(1)

Service Revenue

(cl)	13,000	13,000	(3)

Operating Expense

(4)	8,500	8,500	(cl)
Bal.	0		

Interest Expense

(1)	150	150	(cl)
Bal.	0		

EXHIBIT 7–11

Financial Statements for 20X2

Income Statement		Balance Sheet		Statement of Cash Flows	
Service Revenue	$13,000	Assets		**Operating Activities**	
Operating Exp.	(8,500)	Cash	$7,600	Inflow from Customers	$13,000
				Outflow for Expenses	(8,500)
Operating Income	4,500	Liabilities	$ 0	Outflow for Interest	(900)
Interest Exp.	(150)			Net Inflow from Oper.	3,600
		Equity			
Net Income	$ 4,350	Retained Earnings	7,600	**Investing Activities**	0
				Financing Activities	
		Total Liab. & Equity	$7,600	Outflow to Creditors	(9,100)
				Net Change in Cash	(5,500)
				Plus: Beginning Cash Bal.	13,100
				Ending Cash Balance	$ 7,600

Real-World Credit Costs

Costs of Managing Accounts Receivable

Why do companies sell goods on credit or *on account?* Why not simply require all customers to pay cash for the goods and services they receive? There are two good reasons that a business might allow customers to buy now and pay later. First, as explained earlier, experience has shown that people will buy more goods if credit sales are available. Second, if a business sells goods to other companies, it may be necessary for the selling company to give the buying company time to generate the cash needed to pay for the goods purchased.

To illustrate, assume that Mattel sells toys to Toys R Us. If the goods are delivered (sold) to Toys R Us on September 1, they may not be resold to retail customers until October or November. If Mattel gives Toys R Us 60 days to pay for the goods, Toys R Us can use the money it receives from selling the goods to its customers to pay Mattel. For many small companies that do not have cash available to pay up front, buying on credit is the only way to obtain the inventory that they need. If a manufacturer or wholesaler wants to sell to these customers, *sales on account* are the only means possible.

Costs of Making Credit Sales

Although the policy of allowing customers to buy goods on account may generate more sales, and more gross profit, it is not without additional costs. One such cost is obvious. Some customers may never pay their bills. Bad debts constitute a major cost of extending credit. Other costs are more subtle. As mentioned earlier, there is the cost of keeping the records related to accounts receivable. These costs can be significant. Large companies have entire departments devoted to managing their accounts receivable. For these companies, it may cost literally millions of dollars to buy the equipment and pay the staff necessary to operate their accounts receivable departments. Finally, there is an implicit interest charge associated with the extension of credit. When a customer is allowed to delay payment, the creditor loses the opportunity to use the amount due. Indeed, many real-world companies sell their receivables for less than the full amount due in order to obtain cash. The difference between the face value of the receivables and the amount of cash collected from the sale of the receivables is equivalent to the discount interest.

Exhibits 7–12 and 7–13 are excerpts from the annual report of Tyco International Ltd. These excerpts provide insight as to the costs of credit incurred by real-world companies. First, note that the 1997 balance sheet shows $107.7 million balance in the company's Allowance for Doubtful Accounts. Bad debts of more that $10.7 million certainly constitute a significant cost of credit. In addition, footnote 5 (Exhibit 7–13) indicates that the company has an agreement to sell some of its accounts receivable. The receivables are sold at a discount. The amount of the discount for the 1997 accounting period was $10.4 million. Footnote 5 also indicates that new receivables will be sold to the bank to replace those that the bank has eliminated through collections. Since the new receivables will be sold at a discount, the interest will be a continuing expense incurred by the company. It is interesting to note that while the discount is, in fact, an interest cost, the footnote indicates that Tyco has chosen to include this cost in the selling, general, and administrative expense category on the income statement. Real-world reporting includes a great deal of diversity with respect to the classification of amounts. Reading the footnotes should expand your appreciation for diversity as well as your understanding of the costs of credit.

EXHIBIT 7–12

TYCO INTERNATIONAL LTD.
Consolidated Balance Sheets
At September 30
(in millions, except share data)

Consolidated Balance Sheets

	September 30	
	1997	**1996**
Current Assets		
Cash and Cash Equivalents	$ 369.8	$ 324.2
Receivables, Less Allowance for Doubtful Accounts of $107.7 in 1997 and $84.2 in 1996	1,912.3	1,288.4
Contracts in Progress	138.3	131.6
Inventories	1,124.8	946.5
Deferred Income Taxes	389.4	144.9
Prepaid Expenses and Other Current Assets	174.2	217.4
Total Current Assets	4,108.8	3,053.0
Property, Plant, and Equipment, net	2,924.0	2,590.9
Goodwill and Other Intangible Assets, net	2,933.2	2,439.0
Long-Term Investments	108.5	100.6
Deferred Income Taxes	144.0	67.2
Other Assets	228.5	220.6
Total Assets	$10,447.0	$8,471.3
Current Liabilities		
Loans Payable and Current Maturities of Long-Term Debt	$ 250.0	$ 587.9
Accounts Payable	1,012.0	722.0
Accrued Expenses and Other Current Liabilities	2,005.7	1,016.9
Contracts in Process—Billings in Excess of Costs	141.4	153.3
Deferred Revenue	152.3	146.1
Income Taxes	403.5	121.2
Deferred Income Taxes	26.9	12.9
Total Current Liabilities	3,991.8	2,760.3
Long-Term Debt	2,480.6	1,878.4
Other Long-Term Liabilities	497.5	419.6
Deferred Income Taxes	47.7	124.4
Total Liabilities	7,017.6	5,182.7
Shareholders' Equity		
Common Shares, $.20 par value, 750,000,000 shares authorized: 536,357,498 shares outstanding in 1997 and 481,045,721 shares outstanding in 1996	107.3	96.2
Capital in Excess		
Share Premium	2,041.3	1,081.0
Contributed Surplus, net of deferred compensation of $2.2 in 1997 and $31.4 in 1996	2,305.7	2,168.8
Currency Translation Adjustment	(161.6)	(42.5)
Accumulated Deficit	(863.3)	(14.9)
Total Shareholders' Equity	3,429.4	3,288.6
Total Liabilities and Shareholders' Equity	$10,447.0	$8,471.3

EXHIBIT 7–13

Partial Footnote 5: Sale of Accounts Receivable

The Company has an agreement under which one of its operating subsidiaries sells a defined pool of trade accounts receivable . . . . The proceeds of sale are less than the face amount of accounts receivable sold by an amount that approximates the purchaser's financing costs of issuing its own commercial paper backed by these accounts receivable. The discount from the face amount is accounted for as a loss on the sale of receivables of $10.4 million, $12.1 million, and $8.2 million during Fiscal 1997, 1996 and 1995, respectively, and has been included in the selling, general and administrative expense in the Company's Consolidated Statement of Operations. The operating subsidiary, as servicing agent for the purchaser, retains collection and administrative responsibilities for the participating interests in the defined pool.

Average Number of Days to Collect Accounts Receivable

The longer it takes a company to collect accounts receivable, the higher the cost to the company. As explained earlier, when a company extends credit, it loses the opportunity to invest funds elsewhere, and the longer the funds are not available, the greater the lost income. Also, experience has shown that the older an account receivable becomes, the less likely it is to be collected. Finally, taking longer to collect an account typically means that more money is spent on salaries, equipment, and supplies used in the process of trying to collect it. Accordingly, businesses are very interested in knowing the time it takes to collect their receivables. They want to know if they are taking more or less time to collect receivables than they took in past periods, or how their collection period compares to the collection periods of their competitors. Ratio analysis can help managers convert absolute dollar values to common units of measure that enable them to make such comparisons.

Two ratios are available to help a company's management, or other users, express the collection period in common measurement units. The first is the **accounts receivable turnover ratio.** It is defined as [2]

$$\frac{\textbf{Sales}}{\textbf{Accounts Receivable}}$$

Dividing a company's sales by its accounts receivable tells how many times the accounts receivable balance is "turned over" (i.e., turned into cash) each year. The more rapid the turnover, the shorter the collection period. The problem with this ratio is that it is hard to interpret because it does not provide a measure in units of time. Therefore, the accounts receivable turnover ratio is often taken one step further to determine the **average number of days to collect accounts receivable,** sometimes called the *average collection period.* This is computed as

$$\frac{\textbf{365 days}}{\textbf{Accounts Receivable Turnover Ratio}}$$

This ratio tells the user how many days, on average, it takes a company to collect its accounts receivable. Since longer collection periods equate to higher costs, shorter periods are obviously more desirable. To illustrate the computation of the *average number of days to collect accounts receivable* ratio for Allen's Tutoring Services, refer to the 20X2 financial statements in Exhibit 7–5. On average,

---

[2]To be more correct, technically, the ratio should be computed using only credit sales and average accounts receivable. Often, however, credit sales alone are not given in published financial statements. Average accounts receivable, if desired, is easily computed as ([beginning receivables + ending receivables] ÷ 2). For the purposes of this course, use the simpler ratio defined here (sales ÷ accounts receivable).

the company takes 104 days to collect its receivables. This collection period can be computed in two steps:

1. Accounts receivable turnover is 3.509 ($10,000 ÷ $2,850).
2. Average number of days to collect receivables is 104 (365 ÷ 3.509).

In the preceding computations, the net realizable value of accounts receivable is used because that is the amount typically shown in published financial statements. The results would not have been materially different had total accounts receivable been used.

Real-World Data

What is the collection period for real-world companies? The answer depends on the industry in which the company operates. Exhibit 7–14 shows the average number of days to collect receivables for seven companies in three different industries.

		EXHIBIT 7–14
Industry	**Company**	**Average Number of Days to Collect Receivables**
Fast Food	McDonald's	16
	Wendy's	11
	Starbucks	9
Drugstores	Eckerd	7
	Rite Aid	9
Wine	Chalone	52
	Mondavi	60

focus on
international issues

A Rose by Any Other Name . . .

If a person who studied U.S. GAAP wanted to look at the financial statements of a non-U.S. company, choosing statements of a company from another English-speaking country might seem logical. Presumably, this would eliminate language differences, and only the differences in GAAP would remain. Unfortunately, this is not true.

When an accountant in the United States uses the term *turnover*, she or he is usually thinking of a financial ratio, such as the accounts receivable turnover ratio. However, in the United Kingdom, the term *turnover* refers to what U.S. accountants call *sales*. U.K. balance sheets do not usually show an account named *Inventory*; rather, they use the term *Stocks*. In the United States, accountants typically use the term *stocks* to refer to certificates representing ownership in a corporation. Finally, if an accountant or banker from the United Kingdom should ever ask you about your *gearing ratio*, he or she probably is not interested in your bicycle, but in your debt-to-assets ratio.

Note that there is significant variation in the collection periods among different industries. Also note that the fast-food companies do have accounts receivable, which may seem odd to some readers because these restaurants require customers to pay cash when purchasing hamburgers or coffee. The accounts receivable for McDonald's, Wendy's, and Starbucks exist because these companies sell goods to restaurants that are independent franchisees, so the money is owed to McDonald's by individual restaurants, not by the individual who purchases a Happy Meal.

Are the collection periods for Mondavi and Chalone Wine Group too long? The answer depends on their credit policies. If they are selling goods to customers for net 30 days terms, then there may be reason for concern. But if they allow customers 60 days to pay and the cost of this policy has been built into their pricing structure, then there is little need for concern.

In Chapter 6, the operating cycle was defined as the average time it take a company to go from cash to inventory to accounts receivable and back to cash. The *average number of days to collect accounts receivable* is a measure of the time necessary to complete part of this cycle. A method for computing the remainder of the cycle is explained in Chapter 8.

A LOOK

BACK

Accounting for receivables and payables was introduced first in Chapter 2. This chapter presented several more challenging issues related to short-term receivables and payables. More specifically, the chapter discussed the *allowance method of accounting for bad debts.* The allowance method seeks to measure the amount of accounts that an organization actually expects to collect. The amount expected to be collected is called the *net realizable value* of receivables. It is determined by subtracting the amount in the *Allowance for Bad Debts* from the gross amount of accounts receivable (i.e., Accounts Receivable − Allowance for Bad Debts = net realizable value). The difference between the year-end balance in the allowance account and the amount of receivables expected to be uncollectible is recognized as *bad debts expense.*

The allowance method of accounting for bad debts is compared to the *direct write-off method,* which recognizes bad debts expense when an account is determined to be uncollectible. The method is conceptually invalid because it overstates the value of accounts receivable shown on the balance sheet and it fails to properly match revenue and expense. However, the method is simple to apply. It is used when the amount of bad debts is considered to be insignificant. When the amount of bad debts is immaterial, the benefits derived from recording convenience are considered to be more important than conceptual accuracy.

This chapter also discussed accounting for *warranty obligations.* The amount of warranty expense is recognized in the period in which the sale is made or service provided. The associated warranty obligation is shown as a liability on the balance sheet until the future period in which the obligation is settled.

The chapter also introduced a new method of measuring interest. *Discount notes* include the interest at their face value. The borrower is given an amount of cash that is less than the face value of the note. For example, a borrower signing a $5,000, 8% note would receive $4,600 ($5,000 − [$5,000 × 0.08]). The $400 difference between the amount borrowed ($4,600) and the amount repaid ($5,000) is interest.

Finally, the chapter discussed the costs of making credit sales. In addition to bad debts, interest is a major cost of financing receivables. Determining the length of the collection period provides a measure of the quality of receivables. Short collection periods usually indicate low amounts of uncollectible accounts and interest cost. Long collection periods imply higher costs. The collection period can be measured in two steps. First, determine the *accounts receivable turnover ratio* by dividing sales by the accounts receivable balance. Next, determine the *average number of days to collect accounts receivable* by dividing the number of days in the year (365) by the accounts receivable turnover ratio.

A LOOK FORWARD

It is especially important that you understand how to account for discount notes. Chapter 10 presents topics related to long-term debt that are very similar to accounting issues related to discount notes. Understanding how to account for discount notes is *essential* if you are to understand the topics covered in Chapter 10.

This chapter also discussed the costs associated with the collection of accounts receivable. Specifically, the longer it takes to collect receivables, the higher the cost of financing those receivables. Chapter 8 presents several topics associated with accounting for inventory. One of these topics concerns the costs associated with holding inventory, which is similar to the financing costs associated with the collection of receivables.

KEY TERMS

Accounts Receivable The expected future receipt when a company permits one of its customers to *buy now and pay later.* Usually the amount is small with a short term to maturity. *(p. 305)*

Accounts Receivable Turnover Ratio Measures how fast accounts receivable are turned into cash. It is computed by dividing sales by accounts receivable. *(p. 328)*

Allowance for Doubtful Accounts A contra asset account that contains an amount equal to the accounts receivable that are expected to be uncollectible. *(p. 307)*

Allowance Method of Accounting for Bad Debts A method of accounting for bad debts in which bad debts are estimated and expensed in the same period in which the corresponding sales are recognized. The receivables are reported at net realizable value (i.e., the amount that is expected to be collected in cash in the financial statements). *(p. 306)*

Amortization The practice of converting the discount on a note to interest expense over a designated period. *(p. 322)*

Average Number of Days to Collect Accounts Receivable The length of the average collection for accounts receivable. It is computed by dividing 365 (or 366) by the accounts receivable turnover. *(p. 328)*

Bad Debts Expense A decrease in assets to recognize the expense associated with uncollectible accounts receivable. The amount of the expense recognized may be estimated under the allowance method, or it may represent actual losses under the direct write-off method. *(p. 307)*

Contra Liability Account An account that is shown in the liability section of the balance sheet but that has a normal debit balance. Its balance reduces total liabilities. A discount on a Note Payable is an example of a contra liability account. *(p. 321)*

Direct Write-off Method The practice of recognizing bad debts expense only when accounts are determined to be uncollectible. *(p. 316)*

Discount The amount of interest that is included in the face of a note. The discount (interest) is subtracted from the face amount of the note to determine the amount of cash borrowed. *(p. 321)*

Discount Notes Notes that have the interest included their face value. *(p. 319)*

Discount on Notes Payable A contra liability account that is subtracted from the Notes Payable account to determine the carrying value of the liability. *(p. 321)*

Going Concern Assumption The assumption that a company will continue to operate indefinitely. Under this assumption, a company is expected to pay its obligations and should therefore carry those obligations at their full face value in the financial statements. *(p. 306)*

Interest-Bearing Notes Notes that require the payment of the face value plus accrued interest at maturity. *(p. 319)*

Issuer of the Note The party borrowing the cash. *(p. 320)*

Net Realizable Value Face amount of receivable less an allowance for accounts whose collection is doubtful (i.e., amount actually expected to be collected). *(p. 306)*

Notes Receivable   Represent amounts owed to a business evidenced by notes. The notes usually specify the maturity date, rate of interest, and other credit terms.   *(p. 305)*

Payables   Current obligations to make future economic sacrifices such as cash payments.   *(p. 306)*

Principal   The amount of cash actually borrowed.   *(p. 321)*

Warranty   A promise to correct a deficiency or dissatisfaction in quality, quantity, or performance of a product or service sold.   *(p. 318)*

QUESTIONS

1. What is the difference between accounts receivable and notes receivable?

2. What is meant by the *net realizable value* of receivables?

3. Explain what is meant by the *going concern* assumption. How does it affect the way accounts receivable versus accounts payable are shown in financial statements?

4. What is the difference between the allowance method and the direct write-off method of accounting for bad debts?

5. What is the most common format for reporting accounts receivable on the balance sheet? What information does this method provide instead of showing only the net amount?

6. What are two ways in which estimating bad debts improves the accuracy of the financial statements?

7. Why is it necessary to make an entry to reinstate a previously written off account before the collection is recorded?

8. What are some of the factors taken into consideration in estimating the amount of uncollectible accounts?

9. What is the effect of recognizing bad debts expense on the accounting equation?

10. What is the effect of writing off an uncollectible account receivable on the accounting equation when the allowance method is used? When the direct write-off method is used?

11. How does the recovery of a bad debt affect the income statement when the allowance method is used? How does the recovery of a bad debt affect the statement of cash flows when the allowance method is used?

12. What is the advantage of using the allowance method of accounting for bad debts? What is the advantage of using the direct write-off method?

13. When is it acceptable to use the direct method of accounting for bad debts?

14. Why is it generally beneficial for a business to accept credit cards as payment for goods and services even when the fee charged by the credit card company is substantial?

15. What types of costs do businesses avoid when they accept credit cards as compared with making credit sales?

16. What does the term *warranty* mean?

17. What effect does the recognition of warranty expense have on the balance sheet? On the income statement?

18. When is the warranty cost shown on the statement of cash flows?

19. What is the difference between an interest-bearing note and a discount note?

20. How is the carrying value of a discount note computed?

21. Will the effective rate of interest be the same on a $10,000 face value, 12% interest-bearing note and a $10,000 face value, 12% discount note? Is the amount of cash received upon making these two loans the same? Why or why not?

22. How does the *amortization* of a discount affect the income statement, balance sheet, and statement of cash flows?

23. What is the effect on the accounting equation of borrowing $8,000 by issuing a discount note that carries a 10% discount rate and a 1-year term to maturity? What is the effect on the accounting equation of the periodic amortization of the discount? What is the effect on the accounting equation of the payment of the face value of the note at maturity?

24. What type of account is Discount on Notes Payable?

25. How is the accounts receivable turnover computed? What information does the ratio provide?

26. How is the average number of days to collect accounts receivable computed? What information does it provide?

27. Is accounting terminology standard in all countries? What term is used in the United Kingdom to refer to *sales?* What term is used to refer to *inventory?* What is a *gearing ratio?* Is it important to know about these differences?

EXERCISES

Effect of Recognizing Bad Debts Expense on Financial Statements—Allowance Method

Scott Cleaning Service was started on January 1, 20X4. The company experienced the following events during its first year of operation.

Events Affecting 20X4

1. Provided $10,000 of services on account.
2. Collected $8,000 cash from accounts receivable.
3. Adjusted the accounting records to reflect the expectation that 5% of the ending receivable balance would be uncollectible.

Events Affecting 20X5

1. Wrote off $80 account receivable that was determined to be uncollectible.
2. Provided $12,000 of services on account.
3. Collected $9,000 cash from accounts receivable.
4. Adjusted the accounting records to reflect the expectation that 5% of the ending receivable balance would be uncollectible.

Required

a. Draw an accounting equation and record the events for 20X4 in T-accounts under the appropriate categories.

b. Prepare an income statement, balance sheet, statement of changes in equity, and statement of cash flows for the 20X4 accounting period.

c. Repeat the requirements in parts a and b for the 20X5 accounting period.

Analysis of Financial Statement Effects of Accounting for Bad Debts under the Allowance Method

Businesses using the allowance method for the recognition of bad debts expense commonly experience four accounting events:

1. Recognition of revenue on account.
2. Collection of cash from accounts receivable.
3. Recognition of bad debts expense through a year-end adjusting entry.
4. Write-off of uncollectible accounts.

Required

Show the effect of each event on the elements of the financial statement, using a horizontal statements model like the one shown here. Use the following coding scheme to record your answers: increase is +, decrease is −, not affected is n/a. In the cash flow column, indicate whether the item is an operating activity (OA), investing activity (IA), or financing activity (FA). The first transaction is entered as an example.

Event No.	Assets	=	Liab.	+	Equity	Rev.	−	Exp.	=	Net Inc.	Cash Flow
1	+		n/a		+	+		n/a		+	n/a

Analysis of Account Balances for a Company Using the Allowance Method of Accounting for Bad Debts

The following account balances were drawn from the records of Purvis Company.

	Beginning Balance	Ending Balance
Accounts Receivable	1,000	1,200
Allowance for Bad Debts	50	75

During the account period, Purvis recorded $5,000 of revenue on account. Also the company wrote off a $60 account receivable.

Required

  a. Determine the amount of cash collected from receivables.

  b. Determine the amount of bad debts expense recognized during the period.

EXERCISE 7-4   **Effect of Recovering a Receivable Previously Written Off**
L.O. 2   The accounts receivable balance of Shoebox Shoestore at December 31, 20X6, was $77,000.
Also on that date, the balance in the allowance for doubtful accounts was $2,784. During
20X7, bad accounts amounting to $3,240 were written off as uncollectible. In addition,
Shoebox unexpectedly collected $876 of receivables that were written off in a previous ac-
counting period. Sales on account during 20X7 amounted to $196,000, and cash collections
from receivables amounted to $188,000. Uncollectible accounts were estimated to be 5%
of the ending accounts receivable balance.

Required

(*Hint:* It may be helpful to post the transactions to T-accounts before you complete the
requirements).

  a. Based on the preceding information, compute (after adjustment):

  (1) Balance of allowance for doubtful accounts at December 31, 20X7.

  (2) Balance of accounts receivable at December 31, 20X7.

  (3) Net realizable value of accounts receivable at December 31, 20X7.

  b. What amount of bad debts expense will be recorded for 20X7?

  c. Explain how the recovery of the $876 receivable affected the accounting equation.

EXERCISE 7-5   **Accounting for Bad Debts—Allowance versus Direct-Write-Off Method**
L.O. 2, 3   James Auto Parts sells new and used auto parts. Although a majority of its sales are cash
sales, it makes a significant amount of credit sales. During 20X8, its first year of operations, James Auto Parts experienced the following transactions:

Credit Sales	$310,000
Cash Sales	565,000
Collections of Accounts Receivable	285,000
Uncollectible Accounts Charged Off during the Year	275

Required

  a. Assume that James Auto Parts uses the allowance method for accounting for bad
debts and estimates that 3% of its accounts receivable balance will not be collectible. Answer the following questions:

  (1) What is the accounts receivable balance at December 31, 20X8?

  (2) What is the ending balance of allowance for doubtful accounts at December 31,
20X8, after all entries and adjusting entries are made?

  (3) What is the amount of bad debt expense for 20X8?

  (4) What is the net realizable value of accounts receivable at December 31, 20X8?

  b. Assume that James Auto Parts uses the direct write-off method of accounting for
bad debts. Answer the following questions:

  (1) What is the accounts receivable balance at December 31, 20X8?

  (2) What is the amount of bad debt expense for 20X8?

  (3) What is the net realizable value of accounts receivable at December 31, 20X8?

EXERCISE 7-6   **Accounting for Bad Debts—Direct Write-Off Method**
L.O. 3   Johnson's Bass Shop has mostly a cash business, but does have a small number of sales on
account. Consequently, the direct write-off method is used to account for bad debts.
During 20X6 Johnson's Bass Shop earned $9,000 of cash revenue and $1,000 of revenue on
account. Cash operating expenses amounted to $7,000. After numerous attempts to collect
a $65 account receivable from Boris Shilov, the account was determined to be uncol-
lectible in 20X7.

Required

a. Record the effects of (1) cash revenue, (2) revenue on account, (3) cash expenses, and (4) write-off of the uncollectible account on the financial statements using a horizontal statements model like the one shown here. When you record amounts in the Cash Flow column, indicate whether the item is an operating activity (OA), investing activity (IA), or financing activity (FA). The letters n/a indicate that an element is not affected by the event.

Assets			=	Liab.	+	Equity	Rev.	−	Exp.	=	Net Inc.	Cash Flow
Cash	+	Acct. Rec.										

b. What was the amount of net income reported on the 20X6 income statement?

c. Prepare the general journal entries for the four accounting events listed in requirement *a*.

Effect of Credit Card Sales on Financial Statements

EXERCISE 7-7
L.O. 4

Colorado Hunting Lodge provided $60,000 of services during 20X6. All customers paid for the services with credit cards. Colorado turned the credit card receipts over to the credit card company immediately. The credit card company paid Colorado cash in the amount of face value less a 5% service charge.

Required

a. Record the credit card sales and the subsequent collection of accounts receivable in a horizontal statements model like the one shown here. When you record amounts in the Cash Flow column, indicate whether the item is an operating activity (OA), investing activity (IA), or financing activity (FA). The letters n/a indicate that an element is not affected by the event.

Assets			=	Liab.	+	Equity	Rev.	−	Exp.	=	Net Inc.	Cash Flow
Cash	+	Acct. Rec.										

b. Answer the following questions:

(1) What is the amount of total assets at the end of the accounting period?

(2) What is the amount of revenue recognized on the income statement?

(3) What is the amount of cash flow from operating activities shown on the statement of cash flows?

(4) Why would Colorado Hunting Lodge accept credit cards instead of providing direct credit to its customers? In other words, why would Colorado be willing to pay 5% of sales to have the credit card company handle its sales on account?

Credit Card Sales Recorded

EXERCISE 7-8
L.O. 4

Duck Hill Company accepted credit cards in payment of merchandise sold in the amount of $2,450 during March 20X6. The credit card company charged Duck Hill a 3% handling fee. The credit card company paid Duck Hill as soon as the invoices were received.

Required

a. Prepare the general journal entry to record the sale of the merchandise.

b. Prepare the general journal entry for the collection of the receivable from the credit card company.

c. Based on this information alone, what is the amount of net income earned during the month of March?

EXERCISE 7-9
L.O. 5

Effect of Warranties on Income and Cash Flow

To support herself while attending school, Wendy Chang sold computers to other students. During her first year of operation, she sold computers that had cost her $90,000 cash for $105,000 cash. She provided her customers with a 1-year warranty against defects in parts and labor. Based on industry standards, she estimated that warranty claims would amount to 6% of sales. During the year she was forced to pay $150 cash to replace a defective keyboard.

Required

Prepare an income statement and statement of cash flows for Chang's first year of operation. Explain the difference between net income and the amount of cash flow from operating activities.

EXERCISE 7-10
L.O. 5

Effect of Warranty Obligations and Payments on Financial Statements

The Lawnmower Company provides a 120-day parts-and-labor warranty on all merchandise it sells. Lawnmower estimates the warranty expense for the current period to be $700. During the period a customer returned a product that cost $298 to repair.

Required

a. Show the effects of these transactions on the financial statements using a horizontal statements model like the example shown here. Use a + to indicate increase, a − for decrease, and the letters n/a for not affected. Also in the Cash Flow column, indicate whether the item is an operating activity (OA), investing activity (IA), or financing activity (FA).

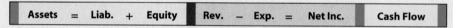

Assets	=	Liab.	+	Equity	Rev.	−	Exp.	=	Net Inc.	Cash Flow

b. Prepare the journal entry to record the warranty expense for the period.
c. Prepare the journal entry to record the payment of the actual repair costs.
d. Discuss the advantage of estimating the amount of warranty expense.

EXERCISE 7-11
L.O. 6

Effect of a Discount Note on Financial Statements

Michael Tebett started a moving company on January 1, 20X6. On March 1, 20X6, Tebett borrowed cash from a local bank by issuing a 1-year $100,000 face value note with annual interest based on a 10% discount. During 20X6, Tebett provided services for $27,500 cash.

Required

Answer the following questions. (*Hint:* It may be helpful to record the events in T-accounts prior to answering the questions.)

a. What is the amount of total liabilities on the 20X6 balance sheet?
b. What is the amount of net income on the 20X6 income statement?
c. What is the amount of cash flow from operating activities on the 20X6 statement of cash flows?
d. Provide the general journal entries necessary to record the issuance of the note on March 1, 20X6; the recognition of accrued interest on December 31, 20X6; and the repayment of the loan on February 28, 20X7.

EXERCISE 7-12
L.O. 6

Assessment of Effective Interest Rate on Discount versus Interest-Bearing Notes

Direll Birdsong borrowed money by issuing two notes on January 1, 20X6. The financing transactions are described here.

1. Borrowed funds by issuing a $15,000 face value discount note to State Bank. The note had a 10% discount rate and a 1-year term to maturity and was paid off on January 1, 20X7.
2. Borrowed funds by issuing a $15,000 face value, interest-bearing note to Community Bank. The note carried a 10% stated rate of interest and a 1-year term to maturity and was paid off on January 1, 20X7.

Required

a. Show the effects of issuing the two notes on the financial statements using separate horizontal financial statement models like the ones here. Record the transaction amounts under the appropriate categories. Also in the Cash Flow column, indicate whether the item is an operating activity (OA), investing activity (IA), or financing activity (FA). Record only the events occurring on the date of issue. Do not record accrued interest or the repayment at maturity.

Discount Note

Assets	=	Liabilities			+	Equity		Rev.	–	Exp.	=	Net Inc.		Cash Flow
Cash	=	Notes Pay.	–	Disc. on Notes Pay.	+	Ret. Ear.								

Interest-Bearing Note

Assets	=	Liabilities	+	Equity		Rev.	–	Exp.	=	Net Inc.		Cash Flow
Cash	=	Notes Pay.	+	Ret. Ear.								

b. What is the total amount of interest to be paid on each note?

c. What amount of principal (i.e., cash) was borrowed on each note?

d. Which note has a higher effective interest rate? Support your answer with appropriate computations.

Accounting Events for a Discount Note Recorded

Marque Dollar issued a $20,000 face value discount note to First Bank on June 1, 20X6. The note carried a 12% discount rate and a 1-year term to maturity.

Required

Prepare general journal entries for the following:

a. The issuance of the note on June 1, 20X6.

b. The adjustment for accrued interest at the end of the fiscal year, December 31, 20X6.

c. The interest expense for 20X7 and the repayment of the principal on May 31, 20X7.

Comprehensive Single-Cycle Problem

The following post-closing trial balance was drawn from the accounts of Python Steel Co. (PSC), as of December 31, 20X6.

	Debit	Credit
Cash	$ 2,000	
Accounts Receivable	10,000	
Allowance for Doubtful Accounts		$ 500
Inventory	20,000	
Accounts Payable		5,000
Contributed Capital		10,000
Retained Earnings		16,500
Totals	$32,000	$32,000

Transactions for 20X7

1. PSC acquired an additional $2,000 cash from the owners.

2. PSC purchased $40,000 of inventory on account.

3. PSC sold inventory that cost $38,000 for $64,000. The sale was made on account.

4. The products sold were warrantied, and PSC estimated future warranty costs to amount to 5% of sales.

5. The company wrote off $400 of uncollectible accounts.

6. On September 1, PSC issued a $5,000 face value, 8% discount note. The note carried a 1-year term.

7. PSC paid $1,000 cash to satisfy warranty claims.

8. PSC paid $8,000 cash for operating expenses.

9. The company collected $66,600 cash from accounts receivable.

10. A cash payment of $34,000 was made to settle accounts payable.

11. The company paid a $1,000 cash distribution to the owners.

12. Bad debts are estimated to be 4% of accounts receivable.

Required

a. Open T-accounts and record the beginning balances and the effects of the accounting events described.

b. Prepare an income statement, statement of changes in equity, balance sheet, and statement of cash flows for 20X7.

PROBLEMS—SERIES A

PROBLEM 7-1A
L.O. 2

Accounting for Bad Debts—Two Cycles under the Allowance Method

The following transactions apply to Stanford & Son's for 20X6, the first year of operation:

1. Recognized $255,000 of service revenue earned on account.

2. Collected $159,000 from accounts receivable.

3. Adjusted the accounts to recognize bad debts expense. Stanford uses the allowance method for accounting for bad debts and estimates that 4% of the year-end accounts receivable will be uncollectible.

The following transactions apply to Stanford & Sons for 20X7:

1. Recognized $408,000 of service revenue earned on account.

2. Collected $411,000 from accounts receivable.

3. Determined that $1,800 of accounts receivable was uncollectible and wrote it off.

4. Collected $600 of the bad debt that had previously been written off.

5. Paid $126,000 cash for operating expense.

6. Adjusted the accounts to recognize bad debts expense for 20X7. Stanford estimates that 3% of the year-end balance of accounts receivable will be uncollectible.

Required

Complete all the following requirements for 20X6 and 20X7. All requirements for 20X6 should be completed prior to beginning the requirements for 20X7.

a. Identify the type of each of these transactions (i.e., asset source, asset use, asset exchange, or claims exchange).

b. Show the effect of each of the transactions on the elements of the financial statements using a horizontal statements model like the one shown here. Use the following coding scheme to record your answers: increase is +, decrease is −, and not affected n/a. The first transaction is entered as an example. Also in the Cash Flow column, indicate whether the item is an operating activity (OA), investing activity (IA), or financing activity (FA). (*Hint:* Closing entries do not affect the statements model.)

Event No.	Assets	=	Liab.	+	Equity	Rev.	−	Exp.	=	Net Inc.	Cash Flow
1	+		n/a		+	+		n/a		+	n/a

c. Prepare the entries in general journal form, and post to the appropriate T-accounts (begin 20X7 with the ending T-account balance from 20X6).

d. Prepare the balance sheet, statement of changes in equity, income statement, and statement of cash flows.

e. Prepare closing entries and an after-closing trial balance. Post the entries to the appropriate T-accounts.

Determination of Account Balances and Preparation of Journal Entries—Allowance Method of Accounting for Bad Debts

PROBLEM 7-2A
L.O. 2

During the first year of operation, 20X2, Martin's Appliance recognized $292,000 of service revenue on account. At the end of 20X2, the accounts receivable balance was $57,400. Even though this is his first year in business, the owner believes he will collect all but about 4% of the ending balance.

Required

a. What amount of cash was collected by Martin's during 20X2?

b. Assuming the use of an allowance system to account for bad debts, what amount should Martin record as bad debts expense in 20X2?

c. Prepare the journal entries to

  (1) Record service revenue on account.

  (2) Record collection of accounts receivable.

  (3) Record the entry to recognize bad debts expense.

d. What is the net realizable value of receivables at the end of 20X2?

e. Show the effect of these transactions listed in part c on the financial statements by recording the appropriate amounts in a horizontal statements model like the one shown here. When you record amounts in the Cash Flow column, indicate whether the item is an operating activity (OA), investing activity (IA), or financing activity (FA). The letters n/a indicate that an element is not affected by the event.

Assets			=	Liab.	+	Equity	Rev.	−	Exp.	=	Net Inc.	Cash Flow
Cash	+	Accts. Rec.	−	Allow.								

Accounting for Credit Card Sales, Warranties, and Bad Debts—Direct Write-Off Method

PROBLEM 7-3A
L.O. 3, 4, 5

Buzz Company had the following transactions for 20X5:

1. The business was started when it acquired $300,000 cash from the owners.

2. Buzz purchased $1,050,000 of merchandise for cash in 20X5.

3. During the year, the company sold merchandise for $1,450,000. The merchandise cost $780,000. Sales were made under the following terms:

$580,000	Cash sales
430,000	Credit card sales (The credit card company charges a 4% handing fee.)
440,000	Sales on account

4. The company collected all the amount due from the credit card company.

5. The company collected $320,000 of accounts receivable.

6. Buzz used the direct write-off method for bad debts expense and determined that $3,600 of the accounts receivable was uncollectible.

7. Buzz gives a 1-year warranty on equipment it sells and estimates that the warranty expense for 20X5 will be $3,000.

8. The company paid $96,000 cash for selling and administrative expenses.

Required

    a. Show the effect of each of the transactions on the elements of the financial statements, using a horizontal statements model like the one shown here. Use the following coding scheme to record your answers: increase is +, decrease is −, and not affected is n/a. The first transaction is entered as an example. (*Hint:* Closing entries do not affect the statements model.)

Event No.	Assets	=	Liab.	+	Equity	Rev.	−	Exp.	=	Net Inc.	Cash Flow
1	+		n/a		+	n/a		n/a		n/a	+ FA

    b. Prepare the general journal entries for each of the transactions, and post them to the appropriate T-accounts.

    c. Prepare an income statement, statement of changes in equity, balance sheet, and statement of cash flows for 20X5.

PROBLEM 7-4A
L.O. 6

Accounting for a Discount Note across Two Accounting Cycles

Lisa Brown opened an accounting practice named Brown & Company in 20X6. The following summary of transactions occurred during 20X6:

1. Issued a $100,000 face value discount note to Cummin National Bank on August 1, 20X6. The note carried a 10% discount rate with a 1-year term to maturity.
2. Recognized cash revenue of $168,000.
3. Incurred and paid $66,000 of operating expenses.
4. Adjusted the books to recognize accrued interest at December 31, 20X6.
5. Prepared the necessary closing entries at December 31, 20X6.

The following summary of transactions occurred in 20X7:

1. Recognized $592,000 of cash revenue.
2. Incurred and paid $208,000 of operating expenses.
3. Repaid the face value of the note and recognized the accrued interest for 20X7.
4. Prepared the necessary closing entries at December 31, 20X7.

Required

    a. Show the effect of each of the transactions on the elements of the financial statements using a horizontal statements model like the one shown here. Use the following coding scheme to record your answers: increase is +, decrease is −, and not affected is n/a. The first transaction is entered as an example. (*Hint:* Closing entries do not affect the statements model.)

Event No.	Assets	=	Liab.	+	Equity	Rev.	−	Exp.	=	Net Inc.	Cash Flow
1	+		+		n/a	n/a		n/a		n/a	+ FA

    b. Prepare the entries in general journal form for the transactions for 20X6 and 20X7, and post to the appropriate T-accounts.

    c. Prepare an income statement, statement of changes in equity, balance sheet, and statement of cash flows for 20X6 and 20X7.

PROBLEM 7-5A
L.O. 3–6

Effect of Transactions on the Elements of Financial Statements

Required

For each of the following independent transactions, identify the type of event as asset source (AS), asset use (AU), asset exchange (AE), or claims exchange (CE). Also explain how the occurrence of each event affects assets, liabilities, equity, net income, and cash flow by

placing a + for increase, − for decrease, and n/a for not affected under each of the categories. The first two events are recorded as examples.

Event No.	Type of Event	Assets	Liabilities	Contributed Capital	Retained Earnings	Net Income	Cash Flow
a	AE	+ −	n/a	n/a	n/a	n/a	−
b	AS	+	n/a	n/a	+	+	n/a

a. Paid cash for equipment.
b. Sold merchandise at a price above cost. Accepted payment by credit card. The credit
    card company charges a user fee. The invoice has not yet been presented to the
    credit card company for collection.
c. Submitted receipts to credit card company and collected cash.
d. Incurred a gain when equipment was sold for cash.
e. Provided services for cash.
f. Paid cash to satisfy warranty obligations.
g. Paid cash for salaries expense.
h. Recovered a bad debt that was previously written off (assume direct write-off
    method is used to account for bad debts.)
i. Paid cash to creditors on account.
j. Issued a discount note to State Bank.
k. Provided services on account.
l. Wrote off an uncollectible account (assume direct write-off method).
m. Amortized 3 months of the discount on a note payable.
n. Collected cash from customers on account.
o. Recognized warranty expense.

Classified Balance Sheet and a Multistep Income Statement

PROBLEM 7-6A
L.O. 2, 5, 6

Required

Use the following information below to prepare a classified balance sheet and a multistep
income statement. (*Hint:* Some of the items will *not* appear on either statement, and ending retained earnings must be calculated.)

Operating Expenses	$ 87,500	Cash	$ 22,200
Land	45,000	Interest Receivable (short term)	620
Accumulated Depreciation	37,500	Cash Flow from Investing Activities	100,000
Accounts Payable	57,500	Allowance for Doubtful Accounts	5,000
Unearned Revenue	55,600	Interest Payable (short term)	2,200
Warranties Payable (short term)	1,620	Discount on Note Payable	3,000
Equipment	75,000	Sales Revenue	495,000
Notes Payable (long term)	132,500	Bad Debts Expense	13,500
Salvage Value of Equipment	5,000	Interest Expense	30,000
Distributions	10,000	Accounts Receivable	112,500
Warranty Expenses	4,200	Salaries Payable	11,500
Beginning Retained Earnings	23,000	Supplies	2,000
Interest Revenue	5,200	Prepaid Rent	12,000
Gain on Sale of Equipment	8,000	Contributed Capital	50,000
Inventory	153,500	Cost of Goods Sold	178,600
Notes Receivable (short term)	15,000	Salaries Expense	120,000

PROBLEM 7-7A
L.O. 2, 5, 6

Missing Information

The following information was drawn from the accounts of Black Angus Company:

Account Title	Beginning Balance	Ending Balance
Accounts Receivable	$20,000	$24,000
Allowance for Doubtful Accounts	1,300	1,400
Warranties Payable	2,400	2,000
Note Payable	30,000	30,000
Discount on Note Payable	1,800	1,200

Required

a. There was $160,000 of sales on account during the accounting period. Write-offs of uncollectible accounts amounted to $1,200. What is the amount of cash collected from accounts receivable? What is the amount of bad debts expense shown on the income statement? What is the net realizable value of receivables at the end of the accounting period?

b. Warranty expense for the period amounted to $1,800. How much cash is paid to settle warranty claims?

c. What is the amount of interest expense recognized during the period? How much cash is paid for interest? What is the book value of the discount note that will be shown on the year-end balance sheet?

PROBLEM 7-8A
L.O. 2, 4–6

Comprehensive Accounting Cycle Problem

The following trial balance was prepared for The Pro Cycle Shop on December 31, 20X6, after the closing entries were posted:

Account Title	Debit	Credit
Cash	$ 59,000	
Accounts Receivable	86,000	
Allowance for Doubtful Accounts		$ 5,000
Inventory	345,000	
Accounts Payable		71,000
Contributed Capital		360,000
Retained Earnings		54,000
Totals	$490,000	$490,000

Pro Cycle had the following transactions in 20X7:

1. Purchased merchandise on account for $210,000.
2. Sold merchandise on account for $240,000 that cost $144,000.
3. Sold $120,000 of merchandise for cash that had cost $72,000.
4. Sold merchandise for $90,000 to credit card customers. The merchandise cost $54,000. The credit card company charges a 4% processing fee.
5. Collected $263,000 cash from accounts receivable.
6. Paid $270,000 cash on accounts payable.
7. Paid $67,000 cash for selling and administrative expenses.
8. Collected cash for all the amount due from the credit card company.
9. Issued a $24,000 face value discount note with a 10% discount rate and a 1-year term to maturity.
10. Wrote off $3,600 of accounts as uncollectible.

11. Made the following adjusting entries:
    a. Expected 6% of the ending accounts receivable balance not to be collectible.
    b. Recorded 7 months of interest on the discount note at December 31, 20X7.
    c. Estimated warranty expense to be $1,800.

Required

a. Prepare general journal entries for these transactions; post the entries to the appropriate T-accounts; and prepare an income statement, a statement of changes in equity, a balance sheet, and a statement of cash flows for the 20X7 accounting period.
b. Compute the net realizable value of Accounts Receivable at December 31, 20X7.
c. If Pro Cycle used the direct write-off method, what amount of bad debt expense would be shown on the income statement?

PROBLEMS—SERIES B

Accounting for Bad Debts—Two Cycles under the Allowance Method

PROBLEM 7-1B
L.O. 2

The following transactions apply to Hunt Consulting for 20X6, the first year of operation:
1. Recognized $40,000 of service revenue earned on account.
2. Collected $34,000 from accounts receivable.
3. Adjusted accounts to recognize bad debts expense. Hunt uses the allowance method for accounting for bad debts and estimates that 5% of year-end accounts receivable will be uncollectible.

The following transactions apply to Hunt Consulting for 20X7:
1. Recognized $51,500 of service revenue on account.
2. Collected $47,500 from accounts receivable.
3. Determined that $150 of the accounts receivable was uncollectible and wrote it off.
4. Collected $12 of the bad debt that was written off previously.
5. Paid $36,500 cash for operating expense.
6. Adjusted accounts to recognize bad debts expense for 20X7. Hunt estimates that 4% of the year-end balance of accounts receivable will be uncollectible.

Required

Complete all the following requirements for 20X6 and 20X7. All requirements for 20X6 should be completed prior to beginning the requirements for 20X7.

a. Identify the type of each of these transactions (i.e., asset source, asset use, asset exchange, or claims exchange).
b. Show the effect of each of the transactions on the elements of the financial statements, using a horizontal statements model like the one shown here. Use the following coding scheme to record your answers: increase is +, decrease is −, and not affected is n/a. Also, in the Cash Flow column, indicate whether the item is an operating activity (OA), investing activity (IA), or financing activity (FA). The first transaction is entered as an example. (*Hint:* Closing entries do not affect the statements model.)

Event No.	Assets	=	Liab.	+	Equity	Rev.	−	Exp.	=	Net Inc.	Cash Flow
1	+		n/a		+	+		n/a		+	n/a

c. Prepare the entries in general journal form, and post to the appropriate T-accounts (begin 20X7 with the ending T-accounts balance from 20X6).

d. Prepare the balance sheet, statement of changes in equity, income statement, and statement of cash flows.

e. Prepare closing entries and an after-closing trial balance. Post the entries to the appropriate T-accounts.

PROBLEM 7-2B
L.O. 2

Determination of Accounting Balances and Preparation of Journal Entries—Allowance Method of Accounting for Bad Debts

The following information is available for Book Barn Company's sales on account and accounts receivable:

Accounts Receivable Balance, January 1, 20X7	$ 172,800
Allowance for Doubtful Accounts, January 1, 20X7	5,184
Sales on Account, 20X7	1,269,800
Collection on Accounts Receivable, 20X7	1,284,860

After several collection attempts, Book Barn wrote off $4,500 of accounts that could not be collected. Book Barn estimates that 4% of the ending accounts receivable balance will be uncollectible.

Required

a. Compute the following amounts:

(1) Using the allowance method, the amount of bad debts expense for 20X7.

(2) Net realizable value of receivable at the end of 20X7.

b. Record the general journal entries to:

(1) Record sales on account for 20X7.

(2) Record cash collections from accounts receivable for 20X7.

(3) Write off the accounts that are not collectible.

(4) Record the estimated bad debts expense for 20X7.

c. Explain why the bad debts expense amount is different from the amount that was written off as uncollectible.

PROBLEM 7-3B
L.O. 3–5

Accounting for Credit Card Sales, Warranties, and Bad Debts—Direct Write-Off Method

Logan's Supply Company had the following transactions for 20X4:

1. Acquired a $70,000 cash contribution of capital from the owners.

2. Purchased $240,000 of merchandise for cash in 20X4.

3. Sold merchandise that cost $190,000 for $370,000 during the year under the following terms:

$100,000	Cash Sales
250,000	Credit Card Sales (The credit card company charges a 3% handling fee.)
20,000	Sales on Account

4. Collected all the amount due from the credit card company.

5. Collected $16,000 of accounts receivable.

6. Used the direct write-off method for bad debts expense and determined that $240 of the accounts receivable was uncollectible.

7. Gives a 1-year warranty on equipment it sells and estimates that the warranty expense for 20X4 will be $650.

8. Paid selling and administrative expenses of $53,000.

Required

a. Show the effect of each of the transactions on the elements of the financial statements, using a horizontal statements model like the one shown here. Use the following coding scheme to record your answers: increase is +, decrease is −, and not affected is n/a. The first transaction is entered as an example. (*Hint:* Closing entries do not affect the statements model.)

Event No.	Assets	=	Liab.	+	Equity	Rev.	−	Exp.	=	Net Inc.	Cash Flow
1	+		n/a		+	n/a		n/a		n/a	+ FA

b. Prepare the general journal entries for each of the transactions, and post them to the appropriate T-accounts.

c. Prepare an income statement, statement of changes in equity, balance sheet, and statement of cash flows for 20X4.

Accounting for a Discount Note—Two Accounting Cycles

PROBLEM 7-4B
L.O. 6

Stark Corp. was started in 20X1. The following summary of transactions occurred during 20X1:

1. Issued a $40,000 face value discount note to Golden Savings Bank on April 1, 20X1. The note carried a 9% discount rate with a 1-year term to maturity.
2. Incurred and paid $118,000 cash for selling and administrative expenses.
3. Recognized revenue from services performed for cash, $176,000.
4. Amortized the discount at the end of the year, December 31, 20X1.
5. Prepared the necessary closing entries at December 31, 20X1.

The following is a summary of transactions that occurred in 20X2:

1. Recognized $292,000 of service revenue in cash.
2. Incurred and paid $198,000 for selling and administrative expenses.
3. Repaid the face value of the note and amortized the remainder of the discount note for 20X2.

Required

a. Show the effect of each of the transactions on the elements of the financial statements, using a horizontal statements model like the one shown here. Use the following coding scheme to record your answers: increase is +, decrease is −, and not affected is n/a. The first transaction is entered as an example. (*Hint:* Closing entries do not affect the statements model.)

Event No.	Assets	=	Liab.	+	Equity	Rev.	−	Exp.	=	Net Inc.	Cash Flow
1	+		+		n/a	n/a		n/a		n/a	+ FA

b. Prepare the entries in general journal form for these transactions for 20X1 and 20X2, and post to the appropriate T-accounts.

c. Prepare an income statement, statement of changes in equity, balance sheet, and statement of cash flows for 20X1 and 20X2.

Effect of Transactions on the Elements of Financial Statements

PROBLEM 7-5B
L.O. 3–5

Required

For each of the following independent transactions, identify the type of event as asset source (AS), asset use (AU), asset exchange (AE), or claims exchange (CE). Also explain how the occurrence of each event affects assets, liabilities, equity, net income, and cash flow by placing a + for increase, − for decrease, or n/a for not affected under each of the categories. The first event is recorded as an example.

Event No.	Type of Event	Assets	Liabilities	Contributed Capital	Retained Earnings	Net Income	Cash Flow
a	AS	+	n/a	n/a	+	+	+

a. Provided services for cash.
b. Paid cash for salaries expense.
c. Provided services on account.
d. Wrote off an uncollectible account (assume direct write-off method).
e. Collected cash from customers on account.
f. Recovered a bad debt that was previously written off (assume direct write-off method).
g. Paid cash for equipment.
h. Recognized warranty expense.
i. Sold merchandise at a price above cost. Accepted payment by credit card. The credit card company charges a user fee. The invoice has not yet been presented to the credit card company for collection.
j. Incurred a gain when equipment was sold for cash.
k. Paid cash to satisfy warranty obligations.
l. Submitted receipts to credit card company and collected cash.
m. Issued a discount note to First National Bank.
n. Paid cash to creditors on account.
o. Amortized 3 months of the discount on a note payable.

PROBLEM 7-6B
L.O. 2, 5, 6

Classified Balance Sheet and Multistep Income Statement

Required

Use the following information to prepare a classified balance sheet and a multistep income statement. (*Hint:* Some of the items will *not* appear on either statement, and ending retained earnings must be calculated.)

Salaries Expense	$ 96,000	Interest Receivable (short term)	$ 500
Contributed Capital	40,000	Beginning Retained Earnings	10,400
Notes Receivable (short term)	12,000	Warranties Payable (short term)	1,300
Allowance for Doubtful Accounts	4,000	Gain on Sale of Equipment	6,400
Accumulated Depreciation	30,000	Operating Expenses	70,000
Discount on Note Payable	2,400	Cash Flow from Investing Activities	80,000
Notes Payable (long term)	106,000	Prepaid Rent	9,600
Salvage Value of Building	4,000	Land	36,000
Interest Payable (short term)	1,800	Cash	17,800
Bad Debts Expense	10,800	Inventory	122,800
Supplies	1,600	Accounts Payable	46,000
Equipment	60,000	Interest Expense	24,000
Interest Revenue	4,200	Salaries Payable	9,200
Sales Revenue	396,000	Unearned Revenue	52,600
Distributions	8,000	Cost of Goods Sold	143,000
Warranty Expense	3,400	Accounts Receivable	90,000

PROBLEM 7-7B
L.O. 2, 5, 6

Missing Information

The following information was drawn from the accounts of Merrimac Company:

Account Title	Beginning Balance	Ending Balance
Accounts Receivable	$30,000	$28,000
Allowance for Doubtful Accounts	2,000	1,800
Warranties Payable	3,600	3,000
Note Payable	40,000	40,000
Discount on Note Payable	2,400	1,600

Required

a. There was $240,000 in sales on account during the accounting period. Write-offs of uncollectible accounts amounted to $1,600. What is the amount of cash collected from accounts receivable? What is the amount of bad debts expense shown on the income statement? What is the net realizable value of receivables at the end of the accounting period?

b. Warranty expense for the period amounted to $1,100. How much cash was paid to settle warranty claims?

c. What is the amount of interest expense recognized during the period? How much cash is paid for interest? What is the book value of the discount note that will be shown on the year-end balance sheet?

Comprehensive Accounting Cycle Problem

PROBLEM 7-8B
L.O. 3–6

The following trial balance was prepared for Rex's Auto Sales and Service on December 31, 20X2, after the closing entries were posted.

Account Title	Debit	Credit
Cash	$ 87,100	
Accounts Receivable	17,800	
Inventory	94,600	
Accounts Payable		$ 44,000
Contributed Capital		90,000
Retained Earnings		65,500
Totals	$199,500	$199,500

Rex's had the following transactions in 20X3:

1. Purchased merchandise on account for $390,000.
2. Sold merchandise on account for $522,000 that cost $364,000.
3. Performed $44,000 of services for cash.
4. Sold merchandise for $26,400 to credit card customers. The merchandise cost $18,600. The credit card company charges a 5% processing fee.
5. Collected $504,000 cash from accounts receivable.
6. Paid $396,000 cash on accounts payable.
7. Paid $150,000 cash for selling and administrative expenses.
8. Collected cash for all the amount due from the credit card company.
9. Issued a $60,000 face value discount note with an 8% discount rate and a 1-year term to maturity.
10. Wrote off $450 of accounts as uncollectible (use the direct write-off method).
11. Made the following adjusting entries:
    a. Recorded 3 months' interest on the discount note at December 31, 20X3.
    b. Estimated warranty expense to be $3,090.

Required

Prepare general journal entries for these transactions; post the entries to the appropriate T-accounts; and prepare an income statement, a statement of changes in equity, a balance sheet, and a statement of cash flows for the 20X3 accounting period.

analyze, communicate, think

BUSINESS APPLICATIONS CASE   **Gateway 2000 Annual Report**   ACT 7-1

Required

Using the Gateway 2000 financial statements in Appendix B, answer the following questions:

a. What was the average number of days to collect accounts receivable for the year ended December 1997?

b. Approximately what percentage of Gateway's accounts receivable as of December 31, 1997, does the company think will not be collected (see Note 10)?

c. What percentage of Gateway's current assets at December 31, 1997, was represented by accounts receivable?

ACT 7-2

GROUP ASSIGNMENT   Missing Information

The following selected financial information is available for three companies:

	Marsh	Brawn	Dole
Total Sales	$125,000	$210,000	?
Cash Sales	?	26,000	$120,000
Credit Sales	40,000	?	75,000
Accounts Receivable, January 1, 20X8	6,200	42,000	?
Accounts Receivable, December 31, 20X8	5,600	48,000	7,500
Allowance for Doubtful Accounts, January 1, 20X8	?	?	405
Allowance for Doubtful Accounts, December 31, 20X8	224	1,680	?
Bad Debt Expense, 20X8	242	1,200	395
Uncollectible Accounts Charged Off	204	1,360	365
Collections of Accounts Receivable, 20X8	?	?	75,235

Required

a. Organize the class in three sections and divide each section into groups of three to five students. Assign one of the companies to each of the sections.

Group Task

(1) Determine the missing amounts for your company.

(2) Determine the percentage of accounts receivable that is estimated to be uncollectible for 20X7 and 20X8 for your company.

(3) Determine the percentage of total sales that are credit sales for your company.

(4) Determine the accounts receivable turnover for your company.

Class Discussion

b. Have a representative of each section put the missing information on the board and explain how it was determined.

c. Which company has the highest percentage of sales that are credit sales?

d. Which company is doing the best job of collecting its accounts receivable? What procedures and policies can a company use to better collect its accounts receivable?

ACT 7-3

REAL-WORLD CASE   Time Needed to Collect Accounts Receivable

Presented here are the average-days-to-collect-accounts-receivable ratios for four companies in different industries. The data are for 1997.

Boeing (aircraft manufacturer)	24 days
Chrysler (automobile manufacturer)	12
Heilig-Meyers (furniture retailer)	151
PepsiCo (soft-drink producer)	37

Required

Write a brief memorandum that provides possible explanations to each of the following questions:

a. Why would a company that manufactures cars (Chrysler) collect its accounts receivable faster than a company that sells furniture (Heilig-Meyers)? Remember that Chrysler sells cars to dealerships, not to individual customers.

b. Why would a company that manufactures and sells large airplanes (Boeing) collect its accounts receivable faster than a company that sells soft drinks (PepsiCo)?

Average Number of Days to Collect Accounts Receivable to Make Comparisons

The following information was drawn from the accounting records of Infotel, Inc., and Next-tec Company.

Account Title	Infotel Inc.	Next-tec Company
Accounts Receivable Balance	$ 90,000	$ 60,000
Sales	873,000	738,000

Required

a. Determine the average number of days to collect accounts receivable for each company.
b. Which company is likely to incur a larger amount of costs associated with the extension of credit?
c. Identify and discuss some of the costs associated with the extension of credit.
d. Explain why a company would be willing to accept the costs of extending credit to its customers.

The following accounting information exists for Quick-Mart and Express Foods companies at the end of 20X7.

	Quick-Mart	Express Foods
Cash	$ 25,000	$ 80,000
Accounts Receivable	120,000	215,000
Allowance for Doubtful Accounts	5,000	15,000
Merchandise Inventory	85,000	130,000
Accounts Payable	90,000	180,000
Cost of Goods Sold	585,000	650,000
Building	215,000	125,000
Sales	800,000	1,000,000

Required

a. For each company, compute the gross profit percentage and the average number of days to collect accounts receivable (use the net realizable value of receivables to compute the average days to collect accounts receivable).
b. In relation to cost, which company is charging more for its merchandise?
c. Which company is likely to incur higher financial costs associated with the granting of credit to customers? Explain the reasons for your answer.
d. Which company appears to have more restrictive credit standards when authorizing credit to its customers? (*Hint:* There is no specific answer to this question. You are expected to use your judgment and general knowledge of ratios to answer this question.)

Mark Jones is opening a men's clothing store in University City. He has some of the necessary funds to lease the building and purchase the inventory but will need to borrow between $45,000 and $50,000. He has talked with two lending agencies that have offered the money according to the following terms:

1. Jones can borrow the money from Bank No. 1 by issuing a $50,000, 1-year note with an interest rate of 10%.
2. Jones can borrow the money from Bank No. 2 by issuing a $50,000 face value discount note. The note will carry a 9.5% discount rate and a 1-year term to maturity.

Jones does not understand very much about financial matters but wants the best alternative. He has come to you for advice.

Required

Write a memo to Jones explaining the difference in the two types of notes. Also advise him as to which is the best alternative and why. Include in your explanation the true cost of each of the loans.

ACT 7-7

ETHICAL DILEMMA   **What They Don't Know Won't Hurt Them, Right?**

Alonzo Saunders owns a small training services company that is experiencing growing pains. The company has grown rapidly by offering liberal credit terms to its customers. While his competitors require payment for services provided within 30 days, Saunders permits his customers to delay payment for up to 90 days. This extended delay allows his customers time to fully evaluate the training that employees receive before being required to pay for that training. Saunders guarantees satisfaction. If the customer is unhappy, the customer does not have to pay. Saunders works with reputable companies, he provides top-quality training, and he rarely encounters dissatisfied customers. However, the long collection period has left Saunders with a cash flow problem. Although he has a large accounts receivable balance, he needs cash to pay the current bills. He has recently negotiated a loan agreement with National Bank of Brighton County that should solve his cash flow problems. A condition of the loan is that the accounts receivable be pledged as collateral for the loan. The bank agreed to loan Saunders 70% of the value of his receivables balance. The current balance in the receivables account is approximately $100,000, thereby giving him access to $70,000 cash. Saunders feels very comfortable with this arrangement because he estimates that he needs approximately $60,000, which is well within the range permitted by the bank.

Unfortunately, on the day Saunders was scheduled to execute the loan agreement, he heard a rumor that his largest customer was experiencing financial problems and was considering the declaration of bankruptcy. The customer owed Saunders $45,000. Saunders immediately called the company's chief accountant and was told "off the record" that the rumor was true. The accountant advised Saunders that the company had a substantial level of negative net worth and that most of the valuable assets were collateralized against bank loans. He said that, in his opinion, Saunders was unlikely to be able to collect the balance due. Saunders's immediate concern was the impact that the situation would have on his loan agreement with the bank. Removing the receivable from the collateral pool would leave only $55,000 in the pool and thereby reduce his available credit to $38,500 ($55,000 × 70%). Even worse, the recognition of the bad debts expense would so adversely affect his income statement that the bank might decide to reduce the available credit by lowering the percentage of receivables allowed under the current loan agreement.

As Saunders heads for the bank, he wonders how he will make ends meet. If he cannot obtain the cash he needs, he will soon be declaring bankruptcy himself. He wonders whether he should even tell the bank about the bad debt or just let the bank discover the situation after the fact. He knows that he will have to sign an agreement attesting to the quality of the receivables at the date of the loan. However, he reasons that the information he received is off the record and that therefore he *may not* be legally bound to advise the bank of the condition of the receivables balance. He wishes that he had gone to the bank before he called to confirm the rumor.

Required

a.   Assuming that Saunders uses the direct write-off method of accounting for bad debts, explain how the $45,000 write-off of the uncollectible account affects his financial statements.

b.   Should Saunders advise the bank of the condition of the receivables? What are the ethical implications associated with telling or not telling the bank about the uncollectible account?

ACT 7-8

EDGAR DATABASE   **Analyzing Maytag's Accounts Receivable**

Required

Using the most current 10-K available on EDGAR, answer the following questions about Maytag Company for the most recent year reported. Instructions for using EDGAR are in Appendix A.

a. What was Maytag's average days to collect accounts receivable?

b. What percentage of accounts receivable did Maytag estimate would not be collected?

c. Did Maytag provide any information about warranties that it provides to customers? If so, what information was provided? (*Hint:* Look in the accrued liabilities footnote.)

d. Maytag Company manufactures products under brand names other than *Maytag.* What are these brand names?

e. Does it appear that Maytag's warranty costs have been decreasing or increasing? Explain some reasons this may have occurred.

SPREADSHEET ANALYSIS   **Use of Excel**   ACT 7-9

Set up the following spreadsheet comparing Vong and Crist Companies.

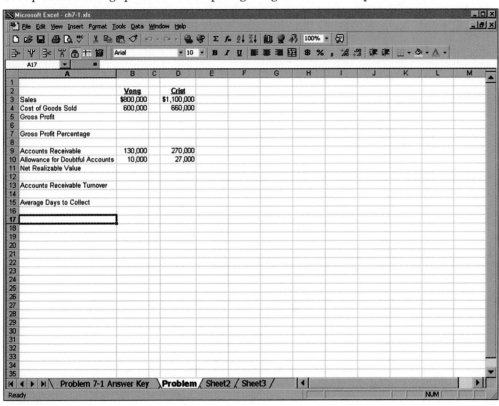

Required

a. For each company compute gross profit, gross profit percentage, net realizable value, accounts receivable turnover, and average days to collect.

b. In relation to cost, which company is charging more for its merchandise?

c. Which company is likely to incur higher financial costs associated with granting credit to customers? Explain the reasons for your answer.

d. Which company appears to have more restrictive credit standards when authorizing credit to customers? How do you know?

SPREADSHEET ANALYSIS   **Mastery of Excel**   ACT 7-10

Refer to Problem 7-6A.

Required

Prepare the financial statements using an Excel spreadsheet.

8 Asset Valuation
Accounting for Investments and Inventories

1 Identify certain assets that are shown on the balance sheet at market value.

2 Explain how accounting for investment securities differs when the securities are classified as held-to-maturity, trading, or available-for-sale.

3 Explain how different inventory cost flow methods (i.e., specific identification, FIFO, LIFO, and weighted-average) affect financial statements.

4 Demonstrate the computational procedures for FIFO, LIFO, and weighted-average.

5 Apply the lower-of-cost-or-market rule to inventory valuation.

6 Demonstrate how to make inventory estimates.

7 Understand the effect of inventory errors on financial statements.

8 Explain the importance of inventory turnover to a company's profitability.

9 Demonstrate how to compute a company's operating cycle.

the **curious** accountant

As of December 31, 1994, Sears Roebuck and Co. held significant investments in *equity securities* (i.e., financial instruments that designate ownership interests in other companies). These securities had cost Sears approximately $4,281 million. The market value of the securities was $4,852 million. In other words, the securities had a market value that was $571 million above their cost. Which of the amounts (i.e., historical cost or market value) was included in the computation of total assets appearing on Sears's 1994 balance sheet? Which value, market or historical cost, do you believe *should* be reported in the financial statements?

©Spencer Grant/Photo Edit

Just Jeans, Inc., is a retail company that makes and sells denim clothes. The company recently purchased $1,000,000 worth of uniquely styled denim jackets. They had leather collars and cuffs with a worn look that gave them a distinctive rugged appearance. Although the buyer was confident the jackets would sell for twice their cost, the marketing manager expressed doubts as to whether her staff could sell them at any price. She said, "These jackets are so worn, they are ready for the trash bin." On the same day that the inventory was purchased, Just Jeans bought $1,000,000 of marketable securities. Three weeks later, the jackets arrived at the warehouse. Suppose that on the date of arrival, you are asked to determine the market value of the inventory and the securities. Which asset could be valued with a higher degree of accuracy?

Clearly, inventory valuation involves subjective judgment. First, you have to decide which market value you are trying to determine: the market value of the wholesale price (i.e., replacement value) or the market value of the retail price (i.e., exit value). If the jackets do not sell well, they may not be reproduced and therefore will not even have a replacement value. On the other hand the exit value is determined by customer demand, which can be best predicted by use of a crystal ball. Indeed, it is the subjective nature of valuation that has caused the widespread acceptance of the historical cost concept. Most accountants recognize market value information as being more relevant to decision makers. Accountants use historical cost only because they have no objective means of determining current market values.

Investment securities offer a rare opportunity for accountants to report market value information because established markets (e.g., the New York Stock Exchange) provide timely, unbiased measures of value. Marketable securities are bought and sold daily. The best estimate of the market value of an investment security is the most current price paid in the open market. Accordingly, the market value of securities can be established by simply looking at the closing prices of those securities on the company's fiscal closing date. Indeed, the availability of reliable information has led the Financial Accounting Standards Board to mandate market value accounting for a significant portion of the investment securities held by most companies.[1] This means that many investment securities are shown on the balance sheet at their current market value rather than at their historical cost.

Types of Investment Securities

L.O. 1

Identify certain assets that are shown on the balance sheet at market value.

A financial investment occurs when one entity gives assets or services to another entity in exchange for a certificate known as a *security.* The entity that gives the assets and receives the security certificate is called the **investor.** The entity that receives the assets or services and gives the security certificate is called the **investee.** This chapter discusses accounting practices that apply to securities held by investors.

There are two primary types of investment securities: debt securities and equity securities. An investor receives a **debt security** when assets or services *are loaned* to the investee. In general, a debt security describes the investee's obligation to return the assets and to pay interest for the use of the assets. Common types of debt securities include bonds, notes, certificates of deposit, and commercial paper. An *equity security* is acquired when an investor *gives* assets or services to an investee in exchange for an *ownership interest* in the investee. An equity security usually describes the rights of ownership, including the right to influence the operations of the investee and to share in profits or losses that accrue from those operations. The most common types of equity securities are common stock and preferred stock. In summary, **investment securities** are certificates that describe the rights and privileges that investors receive when they loan or give assets or services to investees.

Transactions between the investor and the investee constitute the **primary securities market.** There is a **secondary securities market** in which investors exchange (i.e., buy and sell) investment securities with other investors. Securities that regularly trade in established secondary markets are called **marketable securities.** Investee companies are affected by secondary-market transactions only to the extent that their obligations are transferred to a different party. For example, assume that Tom Williams, (i.e., investor) loans assets to American Can Company (i.e., investee). Williams receives a bond (i.e., investment security) from American Can that describes American Can's obligation to return assets and pay interest to Williams. This exchange represents a primary securities market transaction. Now assume that in a secondary-market transaction Williams sells his investment security (i.e., bond) to Tina Tucker. American Can Company is affected by this transaction only to the extent that the company's obligation transfers from Williams to Tucker. In other words, American Can's obligation to repay

---

[1]*Statement of Financial Accounting Standards No. 115,* "Accounting for Certain Investments in Debt and Equity Securities" (Norwalk, CT: FASB, May 1993), par 7–12.

principal and interest does not change. The only thing that changes is the party to whom American Can makes payments. Accordingly, *an investee's financial statements do not change when the securities it has issued to an investor are traded in the secondary market.*

The **market value,** sometimes called *fair value,* of an investor's securities is established by the prices at which they sell in the secondary markets. For financial reporting purposes, fair value is established as the closing (i.e., last) price paid for an identical security on the investor's fiscal closing date. Whether securities are reported at market value or historical cost depends on whether the investor intends to sell or hold the securities. Generally accepted accounting principles require companies to classify their investments into one of three categories: (1) held-to-maturity securities, (2) trading securities, and (3) available-for-sale securities.

Held-to-Maturity Securities

Since ownership interest in equity securities has no maturity date, the held-to-maturity classification applies only to debt securities. Debt securities should be classified as held-to-maturity securities if the investor has a *positive intent* and the *ability* to hold the securities until the maturity date. **Held-to-maturity securities** are reported in the financial statements at *amortized cost* (i.e., historical cost adjusted for the amortization of discounts or premiums). Recall from your experience with discount notes that amortized cost approaches the face value of a security as the security moves toward its maturity date. Since an investor receives the face value of a debt security at the maturity date, amortized cost is considered the best measure of value for held-to-maturity securities.

Trading Securities

Both debt and equity securities can be classified as *trading securities.* **Trading securities** are bought and sold for the purpose of generating profits on the short-term appreciation of stock and/or bond prices. They are usually traded within a 3-month span. Trading securities are shown on the balance sheet at the market value existing on the investor's fiscal closing date.

Available-for-Sale Securities

All marketable securities that are not classified as held-to-maturity or trading securities must be classified as **available-for-sale securities.** These securities are also shown on the balance sheet at market value as of the investor's fiscal closing date.

Note that two of the three classifications require market value reporting, which is a clear exception to the historical cost concept. Other exceptions to the use of historical cost measures for asset valuation are discussed in later sections of this chapter.

L.O. 2
Explain how accounting for investment securities differs when the securities are classified as held-to-maturity, trading, or available-for-sale.

Reporting Events That Affect Investment Securities

Four distinct accounting events affect marketable investment securities. These events and their effects on financial statements are illustrated in the following section. The illustration assumes that Arapaho Company is an investor company that started the accounting period with $10,000 in cash and contributed capital.

Paid Cash to Purchase $9,000 of Marketable Investment Securities

Event 1
Investment Purchase

This is an asset exchange event. One asset (i.e., cash) decreases, and another asset (i.e., investment securities) increases. The income statement is not affected. The $9,000 cash outflow is shown as either an operating activity or an investing activity, depending on how the securities are classified. Since *trading securities* are short-term assets that are regularly traded for the purpose of producing income, cash flows from the purchase or sale of these securities are shown in the operating activities section of the statement of cash flows. In contrast, cash flows associated with the purchase or sale of securities classified as *held-to-maturity* or *available-for-sale* are shown in the investing activities section of the statement of cash flows. These alternative treatments are shown in the following statements model. Once again, the only difference between the treatments lies in the classification of the cash outflow shown on the statement of cash flows.

Event No.	Type	Assets			=	Liab.	+	Equity	Rev.	−	Exp.	=	Net Inc.	Cash Flow
		Cash	+	Inv. Sec.										
1	Held	(9,000)	+	9,000	=	n/a	+	n/a	n/a	−	n/a	=	n/a	(9,000) IA
1	Trading	(9,000)	+	9,000	=	n/a	+	n/a	n/a	−	n/a	=	n/a	(9,000) OA
1	Available	(9,000)	+	9,000	=	n/a	+	n/a	n/a	−	n/a	=	n/a	(9,000) IA

Earned $1,600 of Cash Investment Revenue

Event 2
Recognition of
Investment Revenue

Investment revenue is treated the same regardless of whether the securities are classified as held-to-maturity, trading, or available-for-sale. The revenue comes in two primary forms. Earnings from equity investments is called **dividends.** Revenue from debt securities is called **interest.** Both types have the same impact on the financial statements. The recognition of the investment revenue acts to increase assets and equity. Likewise, net income increases. The cash inflow from investment revenue is shown in the operating activities section of the statement of cash flows regardless of how the investment securities are classified.

Event No.	Assets	=	Liab.	+	Equity	Rev.	−	Exp.	=	Net Inc.	Cash Flow
2	1,600	=	n/a	+	1,600	1,600	−	n/a	=	1,600	1,600 OA

Sold Securities That Cost $2,000 for $2,600 Cash

Event 3
Sale of Investment
Securities

This event results in the recognition of a $600 realized gain that acts to increase total assets and equity. More specifically, the Cash account increases by $2,600, and the Investment Securities account decreases by $2,000, thereby resulting in a $600 increase in total assets. The $600 realized gain is shown on the income statement, thereby increasing net income and ultimately retained earnings. The $600 gain is not shown separately on the statement of cash flows. Instead, the entire $2,600 cash inflow is shown in one section of the statement of cash flows. Cash inflows from the sale of held-to-maturity and available-for-sale securities are classified as investing activities. Cash flows associated with trading securities are included in operating activities. These effects are shown on the next page.

an **answer** for the curious accountant

As the opening section of this chapter implies, Sears Roebuck and Co. included the *market value* of its equity securities in the computation of the amount of total assets appearing on the company's 1994 balance sheet. Exhibit 8–1 shows Sears's balance sheet. Note that some of the company's investments are carried at market value while others are shown at cost. For example, some fixed-income securities (i.e., debt securities) are classified as *available-for-sale* and are shown at fair value, and other fixed-income securities are classified as *held-to-maturity* and are carried at amortized cost. The reasoning behind this apparent conflicting treatment is a key topic in this chapter. This chapter provides many interesting insights regarding the valuation of assets in real-world reports.

Event No.	Type	Assets			=	Liab.	+	Equity	Rev. or Gain	–	Exp. or Loss	=	Net Inc.	Cash Flow	
		Cash	+	Inv. Sec.											
3	Held	2,600	+	(2,000)	=	n/a	+	600	600	–	n/a	=	600	2,600	IA
3	Trading	2,600	+	(2,000)	=	n/a	+	600	600	–	n/a	=	600	2,600	OA
3	Available	2,600	+	(2,000)	=	n/a	+	600	600	–	n/a	=	600	2,600	IA

Recognized $700 Unrealized Gain

After Event 3, the historical cost of Arapaho's portfolio of remaining investment securities is $7,000 ($9,000 purchased less $2,000 sold). Assume that at Arapaho's fiscal closing date, these securities have a market value of $7,700. This means that Arapaho has experienced a $700 *unrealized* gain on its investment. This type of gain (i.e., sometimes called a *paper profit*) is classified as an **unrealized gain** because the securities have not been sold. The treatment of unrealized gains and losses in the financial statements depends on whether the securities are classified as held-to-maturity, trading, or available-for-sale.

Unrealized gains and losses on securities classified as *held-to-maturity* are not recognized in the financial statements. Accordingly, the balance sheet, income statement, and statement of cash flows are not affected by unrealized gains or losses. Even so, many companies choose to disclose the market value of the securities as part of the narrative description or in the footnotes that accompany the statements. Regardless of the disclosure, the amount of amortized cost is included in the computation of the amount of total assets shown on the balance sheet.

Investments classified as trading securities are shown in the financial statements at market value. This means that *unrealized gains and losses* on *trading securities* are recognized. In this case, the $700 gain acts to increase the carrying value of the investment securities. The gain acts to increase net income, which in turn acts to increase retained earnings. Cash flow is not affected by unrealized gains and losses.

Event 4
Market Value
Adjustment

EXHIBIT 8–1

SEARS ROEBUCK AND CO.
Consolidated Statements of Financial Position
(in millions)

	December 31	
	1994	1993
Assets		
Investments (note 7)		
Fixed Income Securities		
Available-for-Sale, at Fair Value (Amortized Cost $30,733 and $28,549)	$30,033	$30,955
Held-to-Maturity, at Amortized Cost (Fair Value $7,869 and $8,857)	8,008	7,933
	38,041	38,888
Equity Securities, at Fair Value (Cost $4,281 and $3,626)	4,852	4,555
Mortgage Loans	3,234	3,563
Real estate	815	747
Total investments	46,942	47,753
Receivables		
Retail Customer	18,201	15,906
Insurance Premium Installment and Other Receivables	3,768	4,113
Total Receivables	21,969	20,019
Cash and Invested Cash	1,421	1,819
Merchandise Inventories	4,044	3,518
Property and Equipment, net	5,041	5,223
Deferred Income Taxes (Note 10)	3,334	2,369
Other Assets	5,872	5,490
Net Assets of Discontinued Operations (Note 5)	473	452
Separate Accounts	2,800	2,282
Total Assets	$91,896	$88,925
Liabilities		
Insurance Reserves	$40,136	$37,444
Long-Term Debt (Note 12)	10,854	11,640
Short-Term Borrowings (Note 12)	6,190	4,636
Unearned Revenues	7,259	7,009
Postretirement Benefits (Note 11)	3,413	3,302
Accounts Payable and Other Liabilities	8,509	8,614
Separate Accounts	2,800	2,282
Total Liabilities	79,161	74,927
Minority Interest	1,934	2,334
Commitments and Contingent Liabilities (Notes 9, 13, 14, 16, 17)		
Shareholders' Equity (Note 17)		
Preferred Shares ($1 Par Value, 50 Shares Authorized)		
8.88% Preferred Shares, First Series (3.25 Shares Issued and Outstanding)	325	325
Series A Mandatorily Exchangeable Preferred Shares (7.1875 Shares Issued and Outstanding)	1,236	1,236
Common Shares ($.75 Par Value, 1,000 Shares Authorized, 351.7 and 350.8 Shares Outstanding)	294	294
Capital in Excess of Par Value	2,385	2,354
Retained Income	8,918	8,163
Treasury Stock (at Cost)	(1,690)	(1,704)
Deferred ESOP Expense (Note 11)	(558)	(614)
Unrealized Net Capital Gains (Note 7)	32	1,674
Cumulative Translation Adjustments	(141)	(64)
Total Shareholders' Equity	10,801	11,664
Total Liabilities and Shareholders' Equity	$91,896	$88,925

Unrealized gains and losses are also recognized on investment securities classified as *available-for-sale*. However, an important distinction exists with respect to how the unrealized gains and losses affect the financial statements. *Unrealized gains and losses on available-for-sale securities* are shown on the balance sheet but *are not* recognized in the determination of net income.[2] With respect to the balance sheet, the $700 gain acts to increase the carrying value of the investment securities. A corresponding increase is shown in a separate equity account titled *Unrealized Gain/Loss on Available-for-Sale Securities*. The statement of cash flows is not affected by the recognition of unrealized gains and losses on *available-for-sale* securities.

Clearly, the effect of unrealized gains and losses on Arapaho's financial statements is determined by whether the investment securities are classified as held-to-maturity, trading, or available-for-sale. The effects associated with each alternative treatment are shown here:

Event No.	Type	Assets	=	Liab.	+	Equity				Rev. or Gain	−	Exp. or Loss	=	Net Inc.	Cash Flow
		Inv. Sec.				Ret. Earn.	+	Unreal. Gain							
4	Held	n/a	=	n/a	+	n/a	+	n/a		n/a	−	n/a	=	n/a	n/a
4	Trading	700	=	n/a	+	700	+	n/a		700	−	n/a	=	700	n/a
4	Available	700	=	n/a	+	n/a	+	700		n/a	−	n/a	=	n/a	n/a

Financial Statements

As the preceding discussion implies, the financial statements of Arapaho Company are affected by not only the business events relating to its security transactions but also the accounting treatment that is applied to those events. In other words, the same economic events are reflected differently in the financial statements depending on whether the securities are classified as held-to-maturity, trading, or available-for-sale. Exhibit 8–2 contains the financial statements for Arapaho that are prepared under each investment classification alternative. Statements under Alternative 1 are prepared under the assumption that Arapaho classifies its investment securities as held-to-maturity. Alternative 2 assumes the investments are classified as trading securities . Alternative 3 assumes an available-for-sale classification.

The amount of net income reported under the trading securities category is $700 higher than that reported under the held-to-maturity and available-for-sale categories because unrealized gains and losses on the trading securities are recognized on the income statement. Similarly, total assets are $700 higher under the trading category than they are under the held-to-maturity category. This too is a result of the recognition of the $700 unrealized gain on the trading securities. Note that this gain is also recognized on the balance sheet when the securities are classified as available-for-sale. Even though the gain is not shown on the income statement, it does appear on the balance sheet in a special equity account titled *Unrealized Gain on Investment Securities*. Accordingly, total assets and equity

L.O. 2

Explain how accounting for investment securities differs when the securities are classified as held-to-maturity, trading, or available-for-sale.

---

[2]*Statement of Financial Accounting Standards No. 130* permits companies to show unrealized gains and losses on available-for-sale securities as additions to or subtractions from net income with the result being titled *comprehensive income*. Alternatively, the unrealized gains and losses can be shown on a separate statement or as part of the statement of changes in equity.

EXHIBIT 8-2

ARAPAHO COMPANY
Comparative Financial Statements

Income Statements

Investment Securities Classified as	Held	Trading	Available
Investment Revenue	$ 1,600	$ 1,600	$ 1,600
Realized Gain	600	600	600
Unrealized Gain		700	
Net Income	$ 2,200	$ 2,900	$ 2,200

Balance Sheets

	Held	Trading	Available
Assets			
Cash	$ 5,200	$ 5,200	$ 5,200
Investment Securities, at Cost			
(Market Value $7,700)	7,000		
Securities, at Market (Cost $7,000)		7,700	7,700
Total Assets	$12,200	$12,900	$12,900
Equity			
Contributed Capital	$10,000	$10,000	$10,000
Retained Earnings	2,200	2,900	2,200
Unrealized Gain on Investment Securities			700
Total Equity	$12,200	$12,900	$12,900

Statements of Cash Flows

	Held	Trading	Available
Operating Activities			
Cash Inflow from Investment Revenue	$ 1,600	$ 1,600	$ 1,600
Outflow to Purchase Securities		(9,000)	
Inflow from Sale of Securities		2,600	
Net Cash Inflow from Operations	1,600	(4,800)	1,600
Investing Activities			
Outflow to Purchase Securities	(9,000)		(9,000)
Inflow from Sale Securities	2,600		2,600
Financing Activities*	0	0	0
Net Increase (Decrease) in Cash	(4,800)	(4,800)	(4,800)
Beginning Cash Balance	10,000	10,000	10,000
Ending Cash Balance	$ 5,200	$ 5,200	$ 5,200

*The $10,000 capital acquisition is assumed to have occurred prior to the start of the accounting period.

are higher under the available-for-sale category than they are under the held-to-maturity category. The statements of cash flows reflect the fact that purchases and sales of trading securities are classified as operating activities while purchases and sales of available-for-sale and held-to-maturity securities are considered investing activities. Exhibit 8–3 shows the important reporting difference associated with the three classifications of investment securities.

EXHIBIT 8-3					
Investment Category	Types of Securities	Types of Revenue Recognized	Reported on Balance Sheet at	Recognition of Unrealized Gains and Losses on the Income Statement	Cash Flow from Purchase or Sale of Securities Classified As
Held-to-Maturity	Debt	Interest	Amortized Cost	No	Investing Activity
Trading	Debt and Equity	Interest and Dividends	Market Value	Yes	Operating Activity
Available-for-Sale	Debt and Equity	Interest and Dividends	Market Value	No	Investing Activity

Alternative Reporting Practices for Equity Securities

Depending on the amount of equity securities owned, an investor can exercise *significant influence* over an investee company. Indeed, an investor can obtain enough equity securities to gain *control* of the investee. The previous discussion regarding accounting requirements for equity securities assumed that the investor did not control or significantly influence the investee. Alternative accounting requirements apply to securities owned by investors who exercise significant influence over or control of an investee company. Determining the level of influence that an investor exercises over an investee frequently requires significant judgment. Accountants have established percentage thresholds to facilitate their assessment of an investor's ability to influence or control the operations of an investee. Unless there is evidence to the contrary, investors owning more than 20% of the stock of an investee company are assumed to have a significant influence on the investee. Investors owning more than 50% of the stock of an investee company are assumed to have control over the investee. These percentage guidelines can be overridden when other classification criteria such as interlocking directorates, joint management, technological dependence, product dependence, and so on indicate that the percentages do not accurately reflect the level of influence. The accounting treatment applied to equity investment securities differs depending on the level of the investor's ability to influence or control the operating, investing, and financing activities of the investee.

As previously demonstrated, investors who do not have a significant influence (i.e., they own 20% or less of the stock of the investee) account for their investments in equity securities at market value. Investors exercising significant influence (i.e., they own 20 to 50% of the investee's stock) must account for their investments under the **equity method.** A detailed discussion of the equity method is beyond the scope of this text. However, *you should be aware that investments carried under the equity method represent a measure of the book value of the investee rather than the cost or market value.*

Investors who have a controlling interest (i.e., own more than 50% of the investee's stock) in an investee company are required to issue a set of **consolidated financial statements.** The company that holds the controlling interest is referred to as the **parent company,** and the company that is controlled is called the **subsidiary company.** Usually, the parent and subsidiary companies maintain separate accounting records. However, a parent company is also required to report to the public its accounting data along with that of its subsidiaries in a single set of combined financial statements. These consolidated statements represent a separate accounting entity composed of the parent and its subsidiaries. Accordingly for a parent company that owns one subsidiary, there will be three sets of financial statements: statements for the parent company, statements for the subsidiary company, and statements for the consolidated entity.

the **curious** accountant

On June 5, 1998, the workers at a Flint, Michigan, metal stamping plant of General Motors went on strike. This plant manufactured parts used in General Motors's 29 automobile assembly plants. Within 4 days, the strike at this plant caused GM to close 8 of its 29 automobile assembly plants due to a shortage of parts. Within 2 weeks after the beginning of the strike, GM had closed 23 of its 29 automobile assembly plants as well as several other plants that manufactured other automobile parts. Considering the enormous costs of having to stop production at its assembly plants, why does GM not keep a larger inventory of parts available so that a strike at one plant will not cause most assembly plants to stop production within 2 weeks?

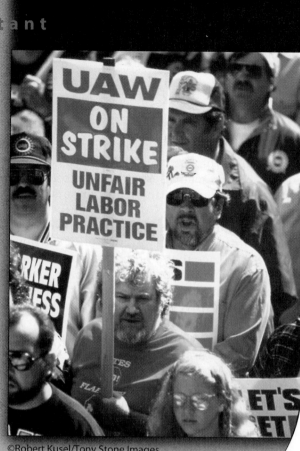

©Robert Kusel/Tony Stone Images

Valuation of Inventory Assets

The previous section introduced market value as an alternative to historical cost for the valuation of certain investment securities shown on a company's balance sheet. You were shown how securities are written up when the market value increases and written down when the market value decreases. In contrast, *inventory* is reported on the balance sheet at the *lower of cost or market*. This means that inventory can be written down when the market value decreases, but it is not written up when the market value increases. The first step in applying the lower-of-cost-or-market rule is to determine the cost of the inventory.

L.O. 3

Explain how different inventory cost flow methods (i.e., specific identification, FIFO, LIFO, and weighted average) affect financial statements.

Inventory Cost Flow Methods

The process of determining the cost of inventory was simplified in our introduction to inventory concepts in Chapter 5 by the assumption that the cost per unit remained constant. In practice, different prices may be paid for identical inventory items, thereby requiring a decision as to which costs to allocate to cost of goods sold versus ending inventory. For example, assume that Baker Company paid cash to purchase two inventory items. The first item was purchased at a cost of $100; the second was purchased sometime later for $110. Except for cost, both items are identical. Suppose that the items are mixed together so that Baker is unable to determine which item was purchased first. If Baker sells one of the inventory items, which cost should be removed from the Inventory account and charged to cost of goods sold? There are several **inventory cost flow methods** that offer alternative solutions to this problem. The four common methods for assigning product costs to the income statement are (1) specific identification; (2) first-in, first-out (FIFO); (3) last-in, first-out (LIFO); and (4) weighted-average. Each cost flow method is explained in the following discussion.

Specific Identification

If the two inventory items Baker Company purchased were tagged when they were purchased so that the specific cost of each item could be identified, then the actual cost of the item sold could be charged to cost of goods sold. When the inventory consists of low-priced, high-turnover goods such as food items, the record-keeping task necessary for **specific identification** can become burdensome. Think of the work required to maintain a record of the specific cost of each food item in a grocery store. Another potential disadvantage of the specific identification method is that it provides the opportunity to manipulate the income statement. By selecting which items to deliver to customers, management can control the cost of goods sold expense and thereby manipulate the amount of net income reported in the financial statements. Even so, specific identification is frequently used for high-priced, low-turnover items such as automobiles. Here the record keeping is minimal, and customer demands for specific products limit management's ability to select the merchandise being sold.

First-In, First-Out (FIFO)

The **first-in, first-out (FIFO) cost flow method** assumes that the cost of the items purchased *first* should be assigned to cost of goods sold. Under FIFO, the cost of goods sold by Baker Company is $100.

Last-In, First-Out (LIFO)

The **last-in, first-out (LIFO) cost flow method** requires that the cost of the *last* items purchased be charged to cost of goods sold. Under this method, the cost of goods sold for Baker Company is $110.

Weighted Average

Under the **weighted-average cost flow method,** the average unit cost of the inventory is determined by totaling the costs incurred and dividing by the number of units ([100 + 110] ÷ 2 = 105). The average unit cost is then multiplied by the number of units sold, and the result is charged to cost of goods sold. In the Baker Company case, $105 is assigned to the cost of goods sold.

Physical Flow

It is important to note that the preceding discussion referred to the *flow of costs* through the accounting records. The **physical flow of goods** is an entirely separate consideration. Goods are usually moved physically on a FIFO basis, which means that the first merchandise in (i.e., the oldest merchandise) is the first merchandise to be delivered to customers. The last items in (i.e., the newest goods) are retained by the business. Obviously, this procedure is necessary to keep inventories from becoming filled with dated merchandise. However, note that while the *physical flow* of goods is being conducted on a FIFO basis, the *flow of costs* can have an entirely different basis, such as LIFO or weighted average.

Effect of Cost Flow on Financial Statements

Effect on Income Statement

The cost flow method a company uses can have a significant effect on the amount of gross margin reported in the income statement. To demonstrate this point, assume that Baker Company sold the inventory item under discussion for $120. The amounts of gross margin under the FIFO, LIFO, and weighted-average cost flow assumptions are shown in the following table:

	FIFO	LIFO	Weighted-Average
Sales	$120	$120	$120
Cost of Goods Sold	100	110	105
Gross Margin	$ 20	$ 10	$ 15

Note that the amount of gross margin reported under FIFO is double the amount reported under LIFO. This result occurs even though the accounting events described by each cost flow method are identical. In each case, the same inventory items were bought and sold. As with investment securities, *companies experiencing identical economic events with respect to the purchase and sale of inventories can report significantly different results in their financial statements.* Financial analysis requires an understanding of reporting practices as well as economic relationships.

Effect on Balance Sheet

Since total product costs are allocated between costs of goods sold and ending inventory, the type of cost flow method used affects the balance sheet as well as the income statement. For example, since FIFO transfers the first cost to the income statement, it leaves the last costs on the balance sheet. Similarly, by transferring the last cost to the income statement, LIFO leaves the first costs in ending inventory. The weighted-average method uses the average cost per unit to determine the amount of both cost of goods sold and ending inventory. The amount of ending inventory reported on the balance sheet for each of the three cost flow methods is shown in the following table:

	FIFO	LIFO	Weighted-Average
Ending Inventory	$110	$100	$105

All three methods are used extensively in business practice. Indeed, the same company may use one cost flow method for some of its products and different cost flow methods for other products. Exhibit 8–4 depicts the relative use of the different cost flow methods among U.S. companies.

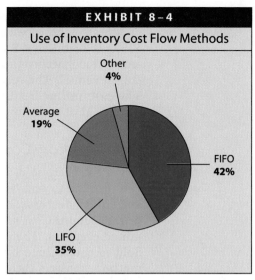

EXHIBIT 8–4

Use of Inventory Cost Flow Methods

Other 4%

Average 19%

FIFO 42%

LIFO 35%

Data source: AICPA, *Accounting Trends and Techniques,* 1998.

Inventory Cost Flow under a Perpetual System

Multiple Layers with Multiple Quantities

To facilitate your understanding of the different cost flow methods, the preceding example used a simplified case that included only two cost layers ($100 and $110), with one inventory item in each layer. The following information is used to demonstrate a more interesting situation that includes multiple layers, with different quantities in each layer. The underlying allocation concepts remain unchanged and should facilitate your understanding of the more complex situation.

Suppose that the accounting records of The Mountain Bike Company (TMBC) contained the following account balances as of January 1, 20X6: Cash $12,000, Inventory $2,000, Contributed Capital $6,000, and Retained Earnings $8,000. During 20X6, TMBC made two cash purchases of inventory. The following table shows the detailed records of the beginning inventory balance and the two purchases:

L.O. 4

Demonstrate the computational procedures for FIFO, LIFO, and weighted-average.

Jan. 1	Beginning Inventory	10 units @ $200	=	$ 2,000
Mar. 18	First Purchase	20 units @ $220	=	4,400
Aug. 21	Second Purchase	25 units @ $250	=	6,250
	Total Cost of the 55 Bikes Available for Sale			$12,650

Assume that in October 20X6, TMBC sold 43 bikes at a price of $350 per bike. Also assume that TMBC incurred $2,600 of cash operating expenses during 20X6. Finally assume that the company paid cash for income taxes at a rate of 30% of net income. Accordingly, there are five events that affected the company during the 20X6 accounting period: (1 and 2) the cash purchases of inventory, (3) the cash sale of inventory, (4) the cash payment of operating expenses, and (5) the cash payment of taxes. Exhibit 8–5 shows the effect of each event on the financial statements under three different inventory cost flow assumptions: FIFO, LIFO, and weighted-average. The exhibit also assumes that TMCB uses a *perpetual inventory* system.

As shown in Exhibit 8–5, on page 367, purchases of inventory are treated exactly the same under FIFO, LIFO, and weighted-average assumptions. In each case, the purchase constitutes an asset exchange. The asset, *inventory,* increases and the asset, *cash,* decreases. Total assets are unaffected. Although the income statement is not affected, the cash outflow is shown in the operating activities section of the statement of cash flows.

Events 1 and 2
Purchase of Inventory

Event 3a
Sale of Inventory

As with purchases, the treatment of sales revenue is not affected by the flow of inventory cost. Note that under all three cost flow methods, sales amounted to $15,050 (43 bikes × $350 per bike). The sale represents a source of assets. The effect of recognizing the sales revenue is to increase assets (i.e., cash) and equity (i.e., revenue). The recognition of the sales revenue acts to increase net income. The cash inflow from the sale is shown in the operating activities section of the statement of cash flows.

FIFO Inventory Cost Flow

Event 3b
Cost of Sale

When goods are sold, the cost of those goods is transferred from the Inventory account to the Cost of Goods Sold account. Accordingly, the assets (i.e., inventory) and equity decrease. The decrease in equity results from the increase in the expense account *Cost of Goods Sold*, which reduces net income and ultimately retained earnings. The *amount* to be transferred from Inventory to Cost of Goods Sold is determined by the type of cost flow method that is applied. The FIFO method transfers the cost of the *first 43 bikes* that came into TMBC to the Cost of Goods Sold account. This allocation occurs no matter which bikes were actually sold. Remember, physical flow and cost flow are totally separate events. The first 43 bikes acquired by TMBC include the 10 bikes that were in the beginning inventory (i.e., these were left over from purchases made in the prior period) plus the 20 bikes that were purchased in March and 13 of the bikes purchased in August. Panel 1, Exhibit 8–5 shows the cost of goods sold expense recognition. The expense recognition acts to decrease net income. There is no effect on cash flow at this time. The effect on cash flow occurred at the time the inventory was purchased. The amount of the recognition ($9,650) is computed as follows:

Jan. 1	Beginning Inventory	10 units @ $200	=	$2,000
Mar. 18	First Purchase	20 units @ $220 ·	=	4,400
Aug. 21	Second Purchase	13 units @ $250	=	3,250
	Total Cost of the 43 Bikes Sold			$9,650

LIFO Inventory Cost Flow

As indicated in Panel 2, Exhibit 8–5, the amount of cost transferred from Inventory to Cost of Goods Sold under a LIFO system is $10,210. This amount is determined by computing the cost of the *last 43 bikes* acquired by TMBC as shown:

Aug. 21	Second Purchase	25 units @ $250	=	$ 6,250
Mar. 18	First Purchase	18 units @ $220	=	3,960
	Total Cost of the 43 Bikes Sold			$10,210

Weighted-Average Cost Flow

To compute the amount of cost of goods sold under the weighted-average method, it is necessary to begin by calculating the weighted-average cost per unit. This is determined by dividing the *total cost of goods available-for-sale* by the *total number of goods available-for-sale*. In the case of TMBC, the weighted-average cost per unit is $230 ($12,650 ÷ 55). The weighted-average cost of goods sold is then determined by multiplying the cost per unit by the number of units sold ($230 × 43 = $9,890). Panel 3, Exhibit 8–5 shows the cost of goods sold expense recognition.

EXHIBIT 8–5

Effect of Events on Financial Statements

Panel 1: FIFO Cost Flow

Event No.	Balance Sheet					Income Statement				Statement of Cash Flows	
	Assets		=	Equity							
	Cash	+ Inventory	=	Cont. Cap.	+ Ret. Earn.	Rev.	− Exp.	= Net Inc.			
Bal.	12,000	+ 2,000	=	6,000	+ 8,000	0	− 0	= 0		0	
1	(4,400)	+ 4,400	=	n/a	+ n/a	n/a	− n/a	= n/a		(4,400)	OA
2	(6,250)	+ 6,250	=	n/a	+ n/a	n/a	− n/a	= n/a		(6,250)	OA
3(a)	15,050	+ n/a	=	n/a	+ 15,050	15,050	− n/a	= 15,050		15,050	OA
3(b)	n/a	+ (9,650)	=	n/a	+ (9,650)	n/a	− 9,650	= (9,650)		n/a	
4	(2,600)	+ n/a	=	n/a	+ (2,600)	n/a	− 2,600	= (2,600)		(2,600)	OA
5	(840)	+ n/a	=	n/a	+ (840)	n/a	− 840	+ (840)		(840)	OA
Bal.	12,960	+ 3,000	=	6,000	+ 9,960	15,050	− 13,090	= 1,960		960	NC

Panel 2: LIFO Cost Flow

Event No.	Balance Sheet					Income Statement				Statement of Cash Flows	
	Assets		=	Equity							
	Cash	+ Inventory	=	Cont. Cap.	+ Ret. Earn.	Rev.	− Exp.	= Net Inc.			
Bal.	12,000	+ 2,000	=	6,000	+ 8,000	0	− 0	= 0		0	
1	(4,400)	+ 4,400	=	n/a	+ n/a	n/a	− n/a	= n/a		(4,400)	OA
2	(6,250)	+ 6,250	=	n/a	+ n/a	n/a	− n/a	= n/a		(6,250)	OA
3(a)	15,050	+ n/a	=	n/a	+ 15,050	15,050	− n/a	= 15,050		15,050	OA
3(b)	n/a	+ (10,210)	=	n/a	+ (10,210)	n/a	− 10,210	= (10,210)		n/a	
4	(2,600)	+ n/a	=	n/a	+ (2,600)	n/a	− 2,600	= (2,600)		(2,600)	OA
5	(672)	+ n/a	=	n/a	+ (672)	n/a	− 672	= (672)		(672)	OA
Bal.	13,128	+ 2,440	=	6,000	+ 9,568	15,050	− 13,482	= 1,568		1,128	NC

Panel 3: Weighted-Average Cost Flow

Event No.	Balance Sheet					Income Statement				Statement of Cash Flows	
	Assets		=	Equity							
	Cash	+ Inventory	=	Cont. Cap.	+ Ret. Earn.	Rev.	− Exp.	= Net Inc.			
Bal.	12,000	+ 2,000	=	6,000	+ 8,000	0	− 0	= 0		0	
1	(4,400)	+ 4,400	=	n/a	+ n/a	n/a	− n/a	= n/a		(4,400)	OA
2	(6,250)	+ 6,250	=	n/a	+ n/a	n/a	− n/a	= n/a		(6,250)	OA
3(a)	15,050	+ n/a	=	n/a	+ 15,050	15,050	− n/a	= 15,050		15,050	OA
3(b)	n/a	+ (9,890)	=	n/a	+ (9,890)	n/a	− 9,890	= (9,890)		n/a	
4	(2,600)	+ n/a	=	n/a	+ (2,600)	n/a	− 2,600	= (2,600)		(2,600)	OA
5	(768)	+ n/a	=	n/a	+ (768)	n/a	− 768	= (768)		(768)	OA
Bal.	13,032	+ 2,760	=	6,000	+ 9,792	15,050	− 13,258	= 1,792		1,032	NC

The payment of operating expenses is not affected by the inventory cost flow method. Accordingly, in all cases, the $2,600 of operating expenses act to reduce assets (i.e., Cash) and equity (i.e., retained earnings). The expense recognition acts to decrease net income. The cash outflow is shown in the operating activities section of the statement of cash flows.

Since the inventory cost flow method affects the amount of cost of goods sold, it will also affect the amount of net income and, therefore, the amount of income tax expense. While the *amount* of the tax due (i.e., net income before tax $\times$ tax rate) will vary depending on which cost flow method is applied, the *effect* of the tax expense on the financial statements will be the same under all three methods. In each case, the tax expense will act to reduce assets (i.e., cash) and equity (i.e., retained earnings). The expense recognition acts to decrease net income. The cash outflow is shown in the operating activities section of the statement of cash flows.

Effect of Cost Flow on Financial Statements

L.O. 3

Explain how
different inventory cost flow
methods (i.e.,
specific identification, FIFO, LIFO,
and weighted-
average) affect
financial
statements.

Exhibit 8–6 contains an income statement, balance sheet, and statement of cash flows for each of the three cost flow assumptions. Look at these financial statements, and decide which cost flow method you would recommend that TMBC use in its published financial statements. The initial recommendation that most people make is FIFO. Indeed, FIFO produces the highest amount of net income as well as the largest balance in the ending inventory. Accordingly, assets and income look better under FIFO. However, a closer look reveals that net cash inflow is lower under FIFO because more income taxes must be paid on the higher amount of reported net income. Recall that except for taxes, the economic circumstances are identical under all three methods. In other words, the only real economic difference between FIFO and LIFO is the fact that FIFO requires the payment of more taxes. Under these circumstances, TMBC should use the LIFO method.

It is important to note that when LIFO is used, tax law requires companies to use that method for financial reporting as well as for tax reporting. In other words, if a company uses LIFO on its tax return, then that company is legally bound to use that method in its published financial statements. This is the *one area* in which the Internal Revenue Service dictates consistency between financial and tax reporting.

You may wonder if the advantages of reporting the more positive financial image under FIFO outweigh the disadvantage of having to pay more taxes. Given an optimistic report of more assets and higher income, would investors not be more interested in the company even if TMBC had to pay more income taxes? Research suggests that investors are not deceived by spurious reporting procedures. They make investment decisions on the basis of economic substance regardless of how it is presented in financial statements. Accordingly, investors would be more attracted to TMBC if it used LIFO. More value stays in the business under LIFO because fewer assets (i.e., cash) are used to pay taxes. Sophisticated investors understand the illusions that can be created by the selection of favorable reporting practices and are not taken in by the reporting of false profits.

Note that FIFO produces higher reported income and assets than LIFO only in an environment of rising prices (i.e., inflationary conditions). In an inflationary environment, the most recent prices are the highest prices. The oldest prices (i.e., first-in prices) are the lowest prices. Since FIFO assigns the oldest prices to the income statement, expenses (i.e., cost of goods sold) are lower and net income is higher. Also, the newest (i.e., highest) prices are retained in ending inventory, thereby resulting in a higher amount of reported assets. Notice that this condition

EXHIBIT 8–6

TMBC COMPANY
Comparative Financial Statements

Income Statements

	FIFO	LIFO	Weighted Average
Sales	$15,050	$15,050	$15,050
Cost of Goods Sold	(9,650)	(10,210)	(9,890)
Gross Margin	5,400	4,840	5,160
Operating Expenses	(2,600)	(2,600)	(2,600)
Income before Taxes (IBT)	2,800	2,240	2,560
Income Tax Expense (IBT × .30)	(840)	(672)	(768)
Net Income	$ 1,960	$ 1,568	$ 1,792

Balance Sheets

	FIFO	LIFO	Weighted Average
Assets			
Cash	$12,960	$13,128	$13,032
Inventory	3,000	2,440	2,760
Total Assets	$15,960	$15,568	$15,792
Equity			
Contributed Capital	$ 6,000	$ 6,000	$ 6,000
Retained Earnings	9,960	9,568	9,792
Total Equity	$15,960	$15,568	$15,792

Statements of Cash Flows

	FIFO	LIFO	Weighted Average
Operating Activities			
Cash Inflow from Customers	$15,050	$15,050	$15,050
Cash Outflow for Inventory	(10,650)	(10,650)	(10,650)
Cash Outflow for Operating Expenses	(2,600)	(2,600)	(2,600)
Cash Outflow for Tax Expenses	(840)	(672)	(768)
Net Cash Inflow from Operations	960	1,128	1,032
Investing Activities	0	0	0
Financing Activities	0	0	0
Net Increase in Cash	960	1,128	1,032
Beginning Cash Balance	12,000	12,000	12,000
Ending Cash Balance	$12,960	$13,128	$13,032

reverses in an environment characterized by falling prices (i.e., deflationary conditions) such as firms in the computer industry experience. Under conditions of deflation, the oldest prices are the highest prices, and the newest prices are the lowest prices. Accordingly, FIFO assigns the first-in (i.e., oldest and highest) costs to the income statement and the newest (i.e., lowest) to the balance sheet, which means that in a deflationary economy, FIFO results in the reporting of lower amounts of income and assets than would be reported under LIFO. This explains why some firms choose to report under FIFO instead of LIFO. Also, in many cases the magnitude of changing prices is too small to materially affect cash flows and thus does not affect the selection of the cost flow method employed.

Inventory Cost Flow When Sales and Purchases Occur Intermittently

In the previous sections, all purchases were made before any of the goods were sold. This section addresses sales transactions that occur intermittently with purchases. To illustrate, assume that the following table describes the beginning inventory, purchases, and sales transactions for Sharon Sales Company (SSC) during 20X8:

Date	Transaction	Description
Jan. 1	Beginning Inventory	100 units @ $20.00
Feb. 14	Purchased	200 units @ $21.50
Apr. 5	Sold	220 units @ $30.00
June 21	Purchased	160 units @ $22.50
Aug. 18	Sold	100 units @ $30.00
Sept. 2	Purchased	280 units @ $23.50
Nov. 10	Sold	330 units @ $30.00

INV 740

Total sales 640

1390   35,980

focus on

international issues

The Influence of Tax Accounting on GAAP

As noted earlier in this chapter, a U.S. company can use LIFO for income tax purposes only if it also uses LIFO for GAAP purposes. This is an unusual situation because tax accounting in the United States is separate and distinct from financial reporting under GAAP, which means that the Internal Revenue Service has no formal power to control GAAP. In the case of LIFO, however, the IRS has an indirect influence on the inventory method that a company chooses for financial reporting. The tax accounting rules of most other countries do not allow the use of the LIFO cost flow method, even if the country's GAAP did allow its use. If U.S. tax rules did not al-

low the use of LIFO under any circumstances, how many companies would use it for financial reporting? Very few!

The separation between tax accounting and GAAP accounting that exists in the United States does not exist in many other countries. In some countries, a company cannot deduct a cost for tax purposes unless the same cost is shown as an expense on the company's GAAP–based income statement. In other words, the unusual situation that exists in the United States only for the use of LIFO is the general rule in many countries. Countries whose tax laws greatly influence GAAP reporting include France, Germany, and Japan.

FIFO Cost Flow

Exhibit 8–7 contains the supporting computations for the determination of the amounts of cost of goods sold and inventory, assuming that SSC uses a FIFO cost flow. Note that the inventory is maintained in layers. Each time a sales transaction occurs, the unit cost contained in the first layer is applied to the number of goods sold. If there are not enough items in the first layer to cover the total number of units sold, the unit cost of the next layer is applied to the remaining number of goods sold. For example, the cost of 220 units of inventory sold on April 5 is determined by adding the cost of 100 units of inventory in the first layer (i.e., beginning inventory) to the cost of 120 units of inventory contained in the second layer. Accordingly, the cost of goods sold for this transaction is $4,580 (100 units @ $20.00 + 120 units @ $21.50). As shown in Exhibit 8–7, the cost of goods sold for subsequent sales transactions is computed in a similar fashion.

The computation of gross margin for the 20X8 accounting period under a FIFO cost flow is shown here:

Sales (650 units @ $30 each)	$19,500
Cost of Goods Sold	14,365
Gross Margin	$ 5,135

Weighted-Average and LIFO Cost Flows

When we attempt to apply LIFO or the weighted-average cost flow method to intermittent sales and purchase transactions, a problem emerges at the point of the first sales event. For example, LIFO requires that the cost of the *last items* purchased *during the period* be charged to cost of goods sold. This is not possible because the period is not over and the last items have not been purchased at the time the first sale is made. Accountants frequently solve this problem by recording only the quantities of sales and purchases on a perpetual basis, enabling them to obtain many of the benefits of a perpetual inventory system even when cost data are unavailable. For example, management can identify the quantity of lost,

EXHIBIT 8–7

Sales and Purchase Transactions under FIFO Cost Flow

Date	Purchase Units	Purchase Cost	Purchase Total	COGS Units	COGS Cost	COGS Total	Inventory Units	Inventory Cost	Inventory Total
Jan. 1							100 @ 20.00	=	$2,000
Feb. 14	200 @ 21.50	=	$4,300				200 @ 21.50	=	$4,300
Apr. 5				100 @ 20.00	=	$ 2,000			
				120 @ 21.50	=	$ 2,580	80 @ 21.50	=	$1,720
June 21	160 @ 22.50	=	$3,600				160 @ 22.50	=	$3,600
Aug. 18				80 @ 21.50	=	$ 1,720			
				20 @ 22.50	=	$ 450	140 @ 22.50	=	$3,150
Sept. 2	280 @ 23.50	=	$6,580				280 @ 23.50	=	$6,580
Nov. 10				140 @ 22.50	=	$ 3,150			
				190 @ 23.50	=	$ 4,465	90 @ 23.50	=	$2,115
				Total COGS	=	$14,365	Ending Bal.	=	$2,115

©Dick Durrance II/Woodfin
Camp & Associates

To avoid spoilage, most companies use a first-in, first-out (FIFO) approach for the flow of physical goods. The older goods (i.e., first units purchased) are sold before the newer goods are sold. For example, Kroger and other food stores stack older merchandise at the front of the shelf where customers are more likely to pick it up first. As a result, merchandise is sold before it becomes spoiled. However, when spoilage is not an issue, convenience may dictate the use of the last-in, first-out (LIFO) method. Examples of products that frequently move on a LIFO basis include rock, gravel, dirt, or other nonwasting assets. Indeed, rock, gravel, and dirt are normally stored in piles that are unprotected from weather. New inventory is simply piled on top of the old. Inventory that is sold is taken from the top of the pile because it is convenient to do so. Accordingly, the last inventory purchased is the first inventory sold. Regardless of whether the flow of physical goods is accomplished on a LIFO or FIFO basis, costs can flow differently. The flow of inventory through the physical facility is a separate issue from the flow of costs through the accounting system.

damaged, or stolen goods, and it can determine when it is time to reorder merchandise. At the end of the accounting period, when complete information about purchases and sales is available, costs are assigned to the quantity data that have been maintained perpetually. Although a complete discussion of weighted-average and LIFO cost flow approaches is beyond the scope of this text, be aware that the potential problems associated with intermittent sales are manageable. Indeed, weighted average and LIFO are used by many companies that experience intermittent sales and purchase transactions.

Inventory Cost Flow in a Periodic System

Recall that under the *periodic inventory method*, inventory records are not changed when goods are purchased or sold. The amount of ending inventory is determined by taking a physical count of goods on hand at the end of the accounting period. Furthermore, the amount of *cost of goods sold* is computed by subtracting the amount of *ending inventory* from *cost of goods available-for-sale*. Accordingly, the assignment of cost focuses on the measurement of ending inventory. To illustrate, assume the same facts as those used for Sharon Sales Company in the previous section. For your convenience, these data are repeated in Exhibit 8–8. Although the facts are the same, the data have been arranged in a different order to reflect the use of a periodic as opposed to perpetual inventory system.

Exhibit 8–9 shows the computations for the allocation of the *cost of goods available-for-sale* between *ending inventory* and *cost of goods sold* under

EXHIBIT 8–8					
Sales and Purchase Transactions for Sharon Sales Company					
Date	Transaction		Description	Cost of Goods Available for Sale	Sales
Jan. 1	Beg. Inventory		100 units @ $20.00 =	$ 2,000	
Feb. 14	Purchased		200 units @ $21.50 =	4,300	
Apr. 5	Sold	220	units @ $30.00 =		$ 6,600
June 21	Purchased		160 units @ $22.50 =	3,600	
Aug. 18	Sold	100	units @ $30.00 =		3,000
Sept. 2	Purchased		280 units @ $23.50 =	6,580	
Nov. 10	Sold	330	units @ $30.00 =		9,900
	Totals	650	740	$16,480	$19,500

the FIFO, LIFO, and weighted-average cost flow methods. All three methods are shown because the periodic method does not involve the computational problems associated with the perpetual method. According to the data in Exhibit 8–8, 740 inventory items were available-for-sale (beginning inventory of 100 units + purchases of 640 units).

EXHIBIT 8–9			
Allocation of Cost of Goods Available for Sale under a Periodic Inventory System			
	FIFO	LIFO	Weighted Average
Cost of Goods Available for Sale	$16,480	$16,480	$16,480
Less: Ending Inventory	(2,115)	(1,800)	(2,004)
Cost of Goods Sold	$14,365	$14,680	$14,476

Since 650 items were sold, ending inventory contains 90 units. FIFO transfers the *first* costs to cost of good sold and thereby leaves the *last* costs in ending inventory. Accordingly, ending inventory under FIFO is $2,115 (90 × $23.50). LIFO allocates the last costs to cost of goods sold, leaving the *first* costs in ending inventory. Ending inventory under LIFO is $1,800 (90 × $20). Finally, the weighted-average unit cost of $22.27 ($16,480 ÷ 740) times 90 units of inventory yields an ending inventory balance of $2,004 (rounded to the nearest dollar).

Remember that the perpetual and periodic accounting procedures represent two different approaches for arriving at the same end result; only the method of computation differs. This fact can be verified by comparing the cost of goods sold and the balance in ending inventory in Exhibit 8–7 with the amounts under the FIFO column in Exhibit 8–9.

Lower-of-Cost-or-Market Rule

To this point, the discussion has been directed toward the flow of inventory costs. Once the cost of ending inventory has been determined, accounting practice requires that it be compared with the current market value and that the inventories be carried at the *lower-of-cost-or-market value.* For the purposes of this comparison, *market* is defined as the amount that would have to be paid to replace the merchandise. Regardless of whether a decline in market value to a point below cost is due to physical damage, deterioration, obsolescence, or a general decline in the level of prices, the resultant loss must be recognized in the current period.

L.O. 5

Apply the lower-of-cost-or-market rule to inventory valuation.

EXHIBIT 8-10

Determination of Ending Inventory at Lower of Cost or Market

Item	Quantity (a)	Unit Cost (b)	Unit Market (c)	Total Cost (a × b)	Total Market (a × c)	Lower of Cost or Market
A	320	$21.50	$22.00	$ 6,880	$ 7,040	$ 6,880
B	460	18.00	16.00	8,280	7,360	7,360
C	690	15.00	14.00	10,350	9,660	9,660
D	220	20.50	23.00	4,510	5,060	4,510
				$30,020	$29,120	$28,410

The **lower-of-cost-or-market rule** can be applied to (1) each individual inventory item, (2) major classes or categories of inventory, or (3) the entire stock of inventory in aggregate. The most common practice is the individualized application. To illustrate the application to individual inventory items, assume that Wilson Office Supply Company purchased 100 calculators at a cost of $14 each. If the current replacement cost of the calculators is above $14, then the ending inventory is carried at cost (100 × $14 = $1,400). However, if some form of technological advance permits the manufacturer to reduce the unit price of the calculators to $11, then the replacement cost to Wilson will fall below the historical cost and the carrying value of the inventory will be written down to $1,100 (100 × $11). Exhibit 8–10 demonstrates the computation of ending inventory for a company that has four different inventory items.

In the case presented in Exhibit 8–10, the company is required to reduce the $30,020 historical cost of its ending inventory to $28,410. This $1,610 reduction causes a decline in the amount of the company's gross margin for the period. The procedure used to reflect the inventory write-down in the accounts will depend on whether the company uses the perpetual or periodic inventory system. If the perpetual system is used, the effect of the write-down and the journal entry necessary to record it are as follows:

Assets	=	Liab.	+	Equity	Rev.	−	Exp.	=	Net Inc.	Cash Flow
(1,610)	=	n/a	+	(1,610)	n/a	−	1,610	=	(1,610)	n/a

Account Title	Debit	Credit
Cost of Goods Sold (Inventory Loss)	1,610	
Inventory		1,610

Conceptually, the loss should be shown as an operating expense on the income statement. However, if the amount is immaterial, it can be included in the cost of goods sold.

Under the periodic method, the amount of ending inventory is shown at the lower of cost or market in the schedule of cost of goods sold. By lowering the ending inventory, cost of goods is increased. These relationships are shown in the following schedule of cost of goods sold:

Schedule of Cost of Goods Sold

Beginning Inventory	xxx
Plus: Purchases	xxx
Cost of Goods Available for Sale	xxx
Less: Ending Inventory	(xxx)
Cost of Goods Sold	xxx

Lower amount reported here results in a
higher amount reported here

As the preceding schedule indicates, when ending inventory is shown at the lower of cost or market, any loss is automatically included in the cost of goods sold. By increasing the cost of goods sold, net income and ultimately equity are reduced, which balances against the reduction in assets (i.e., inventory). Cash flow is not affected by the write-down.

Estimating the Ending Inventory Balance

Under the *perpetual inventory system*, the best estimate of the amount of inventory on hand at any time is the book balance in the Inventory account. Recall that the book balance is increased when purchases are made and is decreased when goods are sold. As a result, if records are maintained accurately, the balance in the Inventory account should be equal to the amount of goods on hand except for unrecorded items such as lost, damaged, or stolen goods. In contrast, the Inventory account is not altered when goods are purchased or sold under the periodic system. Accordingly, it may be necessary to estimate the amount of inventory on hand at various times when a company is using the periodic inventory system.

Estimates of the amount of inventory are necessary when a company wants to prepare monthly or quarterly financial statements but does not want to incur the expense of undertaking a physical count of goods on hand. Also, estimates may be needed to support insurance claims when inventory has been destroyed by fire, storms, or other natural disasters. Finally, estimates of inventory can be used to evaluate the accuracy of a physical count of goods. One common method used to estimate the amount of inventory is called the *gross margin method.*

The **gross margin method** assumes that the percentage of gross margin to sales remains relatively stable from one accounting period to the next. Information regarding the amount of sales and the cost of goods available-for-sale is drawn from the general ledger. Furthermore, the percentage of gross margin to sales is determined on the basis of the historical relationship between these two accounts (e.g., the average of the last 5 years' sales is divided into the average gross margin for the same 5-year period). The percentage is then multiplied by the amount of sales for the current period to estimate the current period's gross margin. The estimated gross margin is subtracted from sales in order to compute the amount of estimated cost of goods sold. The estimated cost of goods sold is then subtracted from the cost of goods available-for-sale to arrive at the estimated ending inventory.

To illustrate, assume that the information in Exhibit 8–11 is drawn from the accounting records of the T-Shirt Company.

The cost of the estimated ending inventory can be computed as follows:

1. Estimate the amount of gross margin by multiplying the gross margin percentage by the sales ($22,000 × .25 = $5,500).

L.O. 6

Demonstrate how to make inventory estimates.

EXHIBIT 8–11

THE T-SHIRT COMPANY
Schedule for Estimating the Ending Inventory Balance
For the Period Ending June 30, 20X2

Beginning Inventory	$ 5,100	
Purchases	18,500	
Goods Available for Sale		$23,600
Sales through June 30, 20X2	22,000	
Less: Estimated Gross Margin	?	
Estimated Cost of Goods Sold		?
Estimated Ending Inventory		$?

*Historically, gross margin has amounted to approximately 25% of sales.

2. Estimate the amount of the cost of goods sold by subtracting the estimated gross margin from sales ($22,000 − $5,500) = $16,500).

3. Estimate the amount of ending inventory by subtracting the estimated cost of goods sold from the amount of goods available-for-sale ($23,600 − $16,500 = $7,100).

Effect of Inventory Errors on Financial Statements

L.O. 7

Understand the effect of inventory errors on financial statements.

Inventory is one of the largest assets that appear on the balance sheets of most merchandising businesses. It constitutes the lifeblood of a business. If it sells, the business thrives; if it does not, the business dies. It is frequently used to collateralize loans. Accordingly, both investors and creditors are keenly interested in the character and content of a company's inventory. Under conditions of adversity, managers may be tempted to misrepresent the financial condition of their companies by manipulating the balance of the Inventory account. Indeed, some of the most significant frauds in the history of business involved the falsification of inventory records. It is critically important that business students become aware of the effects of inventory errors (legitimate or otherwise) on financial statements.

Errors under a Periodic System

The financial condition of a company can be severely misrepresented by merely overstating the amount of ending inventory in the year-end physical count under a periodic system. The overstatement of ending inventory causes an understatement of cost of goods sold and thereby a corresponding overstatement of net income. The overstatement of net income causes an overstatement of retained earnings, which creates the increase in equity that balances with the overstated value of the inventory. To illustrate, assume that McCrary Merchandising overstates its year-end inventory balance by $1,000. As indicated in the following schedule, this overstatement causes the understatement of cost of goods sold:

	Ending Inventory Is Accurate	Ending Inventory Is Overstated	
Beginning Inventory	$ 4,000	$ 4,000	
Purchases	6,000	6,000	
Cost of Goods Available for Sale	10,000	10,000	
Ending Inventory	(3,000)	(4,000)	1,000 Overstated
Cost of Goods Sold	$ 7,000	$ 6,000	1,000 Understated

The understatement of cost of goods sold results in the overstatement of gross margin, as indicated in the following income statement:

	Ending Inventory Is Accurate	Ending Inventory Is Overstated	Effect on Cost of Goods Sold
Sales	$11,000	$11,000	
Cost of Goods Sold	(7000)	(6,000)	1,000 Understated
Gross Margin	$ 4,000	$ 5,000	1,000 Overstated

On the balance sheet, assets (i.e., Inventory) and equity (i.e., Retained Earnings) are overstated as follows:

	Ending Inventory Is Accurate	Ending Inventory Is Overstated	
Assets			
Cash	$1,000	$ 1,000	
Inventory	3,000	4,000	1,000 Overstated
Other Assets	5,000	5,000	
Total Assets	$9,000	$10,000	
Equity			
Contributed Capital	$5,000	$ 5,000	
Retained Earnings	4,000	5,000	1,000 Overstated
Total Equity	$9,000	$10,000	

Since the current period's ending inventory becomes the next period's beginning inventory, the error in the current period reverses itself in the succeeding period. Net income for the current period is overstated, and net income of the succeeding period is understated.

The retained earnings at the end of the second period are stated correctly as a result of the counterbalancing errors shown on the income statements:

McCLARY MERCHANDISING Schedule of Cost of Goods Second Accounting Period		
Beginning Inventory	$4,000	1,000 Overstated
Purchases	xxx	
Cost of Goods Available for Sale	xxx	1,000 Overstated
Ending Inventory	(xxx)	
Cost of Goods Sold	$ xxx	1,000 Overstated

Income Statement		
Sales	$xxx	
Cost of Goods Sold	(xxx)	1,000 Overstated
Gross Margin	$xxx	1,000 Understated

According to this, the first period's overstatement of net income is offset by the second period's understatement. Accordingly, the balance sheet reported at the end of the second period is not affected by the error made in the first period.

Errors Under a Perpetual System

Large inventory errors are more likely to be discovered under the perpetual system because the book balance can be compared to the physical count. Since the two balances should be the same except for differences caused by lost, damaged, or stolen goods, major differences would be investigated and their cause identified. Nevertheless, mistakes can still occur. For example, suppose that a company failed to count $5,000 of inventory on hand at the end of the accounting period. Since the inventory was not counted, it would be assumed to be lost or stolen, and the company would record an inventory loss. As a result, expenses (i.e., cost of goods sold or inventory loss) would be overstated. The ending balance in the Inventory account would be understated, as would net income and retained earnings. The inventory and retained earnings would continue to be understated until such time as the error was discovered and corrected.

Understanding How Length of the Operating Cycle Affects Profitability

L.O. 8

Explain the importance of inventory turnover to a company's profitability.

The importance of the gross margin percentage to the management of merchandising companies was discussed in Chapter 5. While it is certainly important to know the difference between what a product costs and its selling price, more information is needed to assess the desirability of selling individual inventory items. To illustrate, assume that a grocery store sells two brands of kitchen cleansers, Zjax and Cosmos. Zjax costs $1 and sells for $1.25, resulting in a gross margin of $.25 ($1.25 − $1). Cosmos costs $1.20 and sells for $1.60, resulting in a gross margin of $.40 ($1.60 − $1.20). Accordingly, Zjax has a 20% gross margin percentage ($.25 ÷ $1.25), while Cosmos has a 25% margin ($.40 ÷ $1.60). Does this mean that it is more desirable to stock Cosmos than Zjax? Not if you can sell significantly more cans of Zjax than Cosmos. Suppose the lower price results in higher customer demand for Zjax. Indeed, the manager of the grocery store expects that during the coming year, the store can sell 7,000 units of Zjax but only 3,000 units of Cosmos. Under these circumstances, Zjax will return a total gross profit of $1,750 (7,000 units × $.25 per unit), while Cosmos will return only $1,200 (3,000 units × $.40 per unit). Accordingly, it is important to consider how rapidly inventory sells as well as the spread between cost and selling price.

Average Number of Days to Sell Inventory

The measure of how fast inventory sells is called **inventory turnover,** and it is defined as follows:

$$\frac{\underline{\text{Cost of Goods Sold}}}{\text{Inventory}}$$

The result of this computation is the number of times the balance in the Inventory account is turned over (i.e., sold) each year. As with the accounts receivable turnover ratio, the inventory turnover ratio may be somewhat difficult to interpret because it does not provide a measure in units of time. To alleviate this problem, the inventory turnover ratio is often taken one step further to determine the average number of days required to sell inventory. The **average days in inventory ratio** (sometimes called **average number of days to sell inventory ratio**) is computed as

$$\frac{365}{\text{Inventory Turnover}}$$

As indicated, a retailer's success from selling inventory depends on a combination of two factors: gross margin and inventory turnover. The most desirable scenario is an inventory system with a high margin that turns over rapidly. However, due to competition, companies often focus on one of these elements more than on the other. For example, *discount merchandisers* offer lower prices in the hope that they can stimulate rapid sales. In contrast, *specialty stores* often require larger gross margins to compensate for the fact that their goods sell more slowly. Specialty stores often offer something such as better service to persuade customers that the higher prices are justified.

Will a person buy a high-quality camera at Kmart or at a local camera shop? It depends on whether price or service is more important to that individual. A person needing considerable advice about which model to choose may be willing to pay the camera shop's higher price to get more professional help. So, although decisions about pricing, advertising, service, and so on, are often thought of as marketing decisions, they cannot be made properly without understanding the interaction between the gross margin percentage and inventory turnover.

Real-World Data

The discussion of operating cycles that began in Chapter 6 and continued in Chapter 7 can now be completed. The length of a company's operating cycle is the sum of its average number of days to sell inventory plus its average number of days to collect accounts receivable.

Exhibit 8–12 shows operating cycles for seven real-world companies. These numbers are for 1997.

What is the significance of operating cycles of different lengths? Recall from Chapter 6 that the operating cycle for a business is the time required for the business to get back the cash that it invested in inventory. As previously explained, the longer this takes, the more it costs the company. Notice from Exhibit 8–12

L.O. 9

Demonstrate how to compute a company's operating cycle.

EXHIBIT 8–12				
Industry	Company	Average Days in Inventory	Average Days to Collect Receivables	Length of Operating Cycle
Fast-Food	McDonald's	4	16	20
	Wendy's	9	11	20
	Starbucks	50	9	59
Drugstores	Eckerd	87	7	94
	Rite Aid	119	9	128
Wine	Chalone	555	52	607
	Mondavi	341	60	401

that Rite Aid's operating cycle was 34 days longer than Eckerd's. All other things being equal, approximately how much did this extra month increase Rite Aid's costs compared to Eckerd's? Assume that Rite Aid could invest excess cash at 8% (or alternatively, assume that it pays 8% to finance its inventory and accounts receivable). Using accounting information provided in Rite Aid's 1997 financial statements, we can determine the solution as follows:

Rite Aid's Investment in Inventory	×	Interest Rate	×	Time	=	Cost
$3,061,211,000	×	8%	×	34/365	=	$22,812,000

Based on the assumed 8% cost of money, the extra month it takes Rite Aid to get back its investment in inventory costs the company $22.8 million per operating cycle. Based on 2.85 cycles per year (365 ÷ 128) the extended operating cycle costs Rite Aid $65 million annually. After the effects of income taxes are included, reducing its operating cycle by 34 days increases Rite Aid's net income by over 12%! The preceding certainly is a rough estimate, but it clearly demonstrates that it is important for businesses to monitor the length of their operating cycles.

There are other costs of having excess inventory besides the financing cost explained in the preceding paragraphs. The more inventory a company maintains, the more expense it will incur for storage and insurance and the more likely its inventory will be damaged or stolen during storage. Of course, carrying too little inventory can result in lost sales, so constant monitoring is necessary to ensure that the proper level of inventory is on hand.

Returning to the data in Exhibit 8–12, why do Mondavi and Chalone take so long to sell their inventories? Because both companies produce wine. Wine must be aged before it can be sold, so much of the time spent in inventory is really a part of the production process. In the "wine world," Chalone is considered a higher-quality wine than most of the wine that Mondavi produces, which is the result, in part, of the almost 7 additional months it ages its wines.

Finally, why does Starbucks hold its inventory so much longer than the other two fast-food businesses? Starbuck's main inventory is coffee. Prior to being roasted, coffee, unlike hamburgers, can be held for long periods without its quality deteriorating. Furthermore, very little coffee is grown in the United States (Hawaii is the only state that produces coffee). Starbucks cannot wait until the last minute to order its inventory. This problem is further complicated by the fact

an **answer** for the curious accountant

As explained, the cost of carrying inventory can be very high. General Motors and many other companies have decided that the costs of closing plants due to potential strikes are lower than the costs of carrying excessive inventory at all times. The strategy of carrying as little inventory as pos-

sible is referred to as a *just-in-time* (JIT) inventory system. As indicated by its name, JIT systems attempt to obtain inventory *just in time* for it to be used or sold, thereby eliminating the need for large stockpiles of parts and products.

that coffee is harvested during only one season of the year. Cattle can be processed into hamburgers year-round.

Once again, note that to understand a company, you must understand the industry in which that company operates. Understanding the accounting procedures used to prepare its financial statements is only part of the task.

Effects of Cost Flow on Ratio Analysis

As demonstrated earlier in the chapter, the inventory cost flow assumption that a company uses affects its cost of goods sold and thereby its gross margin, net income, and retained earnings. The method selected also affects the cost assigned to ending inventory, which in turn affects current assets and total assets. Financial statement analysis is also affected if it is based on ratios that use any of the items mentioned in their computation. Therefore, almost every ratio discussed in this book is affected. Previously defined ratios that are affected include the following:

Current ratio

Debt-to-assets ratio

Return-on-assets ratio

Return-on-equity ratio

Return-on-sales ratio

Gross margin percentage

Average days to sell inventory

The magnitude of the effect of different cost flow methods on some of these ratios may be immaterial. For a large business, the difference in total assets that results from its decision to use LIFO versus FIFO probably will be small. Therefore, the effect on the debt-to-assets ratio will be small. The effect of LIFO versus FIFO on the current ratio, however, might be more pronounced. It is important for financial statement users to be aware that a company's choice of accounting methods may significantly affect the users' analysis of its accounting information.

Generally accepted accounting principles require companies to classify their investments in marketable securities into one of three categories: (1) *held-to-maturity securities,* (2) *trading securities,* and (3) *available-for-sale securities.* Since equity securities have no maturity date the held-to-maturity category applies only to debt securities. Securities classified as held-to-maturity are reported at amortized cost. Unrealized gains or losses are not recognized. Both debt and equity securities can be classified as trading securities or available-for-sale securities. Securities in both of these categories are reported on the balance sheet at market value. Unrealized gains and losses on trading securities are reported on the income statement. On available-for-sale securities unrealized gains and losses are reported in a variety of ways. The most common practice is to bypass the income statement and show the unrealized gains and losses as direct equity adjustments on the balance sheet. Alternatively, unrealized gains and losses on available-for-sale securities can be shown as additions to or subtractions from net income with the result being titled **comprehensive income.** In addition, the unrealized gains and losses can be shown on a separate statement or as part of the statement of changes in equity.

Chapter 5 introduced the basic issues associated with accounting for inventory and cost of goods sold. This chapter expanded the subject to include a discussion of inventory cost flow methods including first-in, first-out (i.e., FIFO), last-in, first-out (i.e., LIFO), and weighted average. Under *FIFO,* the cost of the items purchased first is shown on the income statement, and the cost of the items purchased last is shown on the balance sheet. Under *LIFO,* the cost of the items purchased last is shown on the income statement, and the cost of the items purchased first is shown on the balance sheet. Under the *weighted-average method,* the average cost of inventory is shown on the income statement and the balance sheet.

Generally accepted accounting principles often allow companies to account for the same types of events in different ways. The different cost flow assumptions presented in this chapter—FIFO, LIFO, and weighted average—are excellent examples of alternative accounting procedures allowed by GAAP. Persons who use financial information must be aware of the accounting alternatives available for a given event and the effects that choosing one method over another have on companies' financial statements and ratios.

This chapter also completed the discussion of the operating cycle, which began in Chapter 6. The measure of how fast inventory sells is called *inventory turnover;* it is computed by dividing cost of goods sold by inventory. The result of this computation is the number of times the balance in the Inventory account is turned over each year. The *average number of days in inventory ratio* can be determined by dividing the number of days in a year (i.e., 365) by the inventory turnover ratio.

Chapter 9 discusses accounting for long-term assets such as buildings and equipment. Although this topic is very different from accounting for inventory that a company purchases to sell to customers, it is similar in that GAAP allows different companies to use different accounting methods to account for the same types of events. The lives of accounting students would be easier if all companies had to use the same accounting methods. However, accounting methods used by different companies in the real world are probably becoming even more diverse. Thus, it is important that users of financial information consider these differences when making decisions.

Available-for-Sale Securities   Marketable securities that are not properly classified as held-to-maturity or trading securities.   *(p. 355)*

Average Days in Inventory Ratio (sometimes called **Average Number of Days to Sell Inventory Ratio**)   A measure representing the average number of days that inventory stays in stock before being sold.   *(p. 379)*

Comprehensive Income   The amount of net income plus or minus unrealized gains or losses.   *(p. 382)*

Consolidated Financial Statements   Financial statements that represent the combined operations of a parent company and its subsidiaries.   *(p. 361)*

Debt Security   The type of security acquired by loaning assets to the investee company.   *(p. 354)*

Dividends   Earnings from equity investments.   *(p. 356)*

Equity Method   A method of accounting for investments in marketable equity securities. The equity method is required when the investor owns 20% to 50% of the investee company. The amount of investments carried under the equity method represents a measure of the book value of the investee rather than the cost or market value of the investment security.   *(p. 361)*

First-In, First-Out (FIFO) Cost Flow Method   The inventory cost flow method that assumes that the first items purchased are the first items sold for the purpose of computing the cost of goods sold.   *(p. 363)*

Gross Margin Method   The method of estimating ending inventory that assumes that the percentage of gross margin to sales remains relatively stable from one accounting period to the next.   *(p. 375)*

Held-to-Maturity Securities   Debt securities that are intended to be held until maturity.   *(p. 355)*

Interest   As used in this chapter the term means revenue from debt securities.   *(p. 356)*

Inventory Cost Flow Methods   Assumptions about which goods have been sold and which goods remain in inventory for the purpose of allocating cost between cost of goods sold and inventory.   *(p. 363)*

Inventory Turnover   The ratio of cost of goods sold to inventory that indicates how many times a year the average inventory is sold (turned over).   *(p. 379)*

Investee   The company that receives assets or services and gives a security certificate in exchange.   *(p. 354)*

Investment Securities   Certificates that describe the rights and privileges that investors receive when they loan or give assets or services to investees.   *(p. 354)*

Investor   The company or individual who gives assets or services and receives a security certificate in exchange.   *(p. 354)*

Last-In, First-Out (LIFO) Cost Flow Method   The inventory cost flow method that assumes that the last items purchased are the first items sold for the purpose of computing costs of goods sold.   *(p. 363)*

Lower-of-Cost-or-Market Rule   The accounting practice that dictates inventories be carried on the books at market value if the value of the product has declined below its cost, regardless of the cause.   *(p. 374)*

Market Value   The value at which securities sell in the secondary market; also called *fair value*.   *(p. 355)*

Marketable Securities   Securities that are readily traded in the secondary securities market.   *(p. 354)*

Moving Average   The method of computing average product cost in which the average cost of inventory items is recomputed each time a purchase is made.   (*see* **Weighted-Average Inventroy Method** *p. 363)*

Parent Company   A company that holds a controlling interest (more than 50% ownership) in another company.   *(p. 361)*

Physical Flow of Goods   The movement of the physical goods through the business. This is normally a FIFO flow, so that the first goods purchased are the first goods delivered to customers, thereby reducing the likelihood of obsolete inventory.   *(p. 363)*

Primary Securities Market   The market made up of transactions between the investor and investee.   *(p. 354)*

Secondary Securities Market   The market made up of transactions of securities between investors.   *(p. 354)*

Specific Identification   The inventory method that allocates costs between cost of goods sold and ending inventory by making reference to the cost of the specific goods being sold or retained in the business.   *(p. 363)*

Subsidiary Company   A company that is controlled (more than 50% ownership) by another company.   *(p. 361)*

Trading Securities   Securities that are bought and sold for the purpose of generating profit from the short-term appreciation in the price of stock and bond prices.   *(p. 355)*

Unrealized Gain/Loss   The paper gain/loss on investment securities that has not yet been realized. It is not realized until the security is sold or otherwise disposed of.   *(p. 357)*

Weighted-Average Inventory Method   The inventory cost flow method in which the cost allocated between inventory and cost of goods sold is based on the average cost per unit. Average cost per unit is determined by dividing total costs of goods available-for-sale during the accounting period by total units available-for-sale during the period. If the average is recomputed each time a purchase is made, the result is called a *moving average*.   *(p. 363)*

QUESTIONS

1. Why is historical cost information generally used in the preparation of financial statements?

2. What are some situations in which the Financial Accounting Standards Board requires the use of market value information for financial reporting?

3. What is an example of an asset that is easily valued at fair market value? What is an example of an asset that is difficult to value at fair market value?

4. What are the two primary types of investment securities?

5. What is a debt security? Give an example.

6. What is an equity security? Give an example.

7. What is the difference between the primary securities market and the secondary securities market?

8. What are marketable securities?

9. Generally Accepted Accounting Principles require companies to classify investment securities into three categories. What are they? Define them.

10. When must the equity method be used to account for investments for financial statement reporting?

11. What are the four cost flow methods discussed in this chapter? Define each.

12. What are some advantages and disadvantages of the specific identification method of accounting for inventory?

13. What are some advantages and disadvantages of using the FIFO method of inventory valuation?

14. What are some advantages and disadvantages of using the LIFO method of inventory valuation?

15. In an inflationary period, which inventory cost flow method will produce the largest net income? Explain.

16. In an inflationary period, which inventory cost flow method will produce the largest amount of total assets on the balance sheet? Explain.

17. What is the difference in the flow of cost and the physical flow of goods?

18. Does the choice of cost flow method (i.e., FIFO, LIFO, or weighted average) affect the cash flow statement? Explain.

19. Assume that Key Co. purchased 1,000 units of merchandise in its first year of operations for $25 per unit. The company sold 850 units for $40. What is the amount of cost of goods sold using FIFO? LIFO? Weighted average?

20. Assume that Key Co. purchased 1,500 units of merchandise in its second year of operation for $27 per unit. Its beginning inventory was determined in Question 19. Assuming that 1,500 units are sold, what is the amount of cost of goods sold using FIFO? LIFO? Weighted average?

21. Refer to Questions 19 and 20. Which method would you prefer to use for financial statements? For tax reporting? Explain.

22. In an inflationary period, which cost flow method, FIFO or LIFO, produces the larger cash flow? Explain.

23. Which inventory cost flow method produces the largest net income in a deflationary period?

24. How is the weighted-average cost per unit computed by using a moving-average cost flow?

25. What is the difference between a periodic inventory system and a perpetual inventory system?

26. How does the phrase *lower-of-cost-or-market* value apply to inventory valuation?

27. If some merchandise declined in value because of damage or obsolescence, what effect will the lower-of-cost-or-market rule have on the income statement? Explain.

28. What are three situations in which estimates of the amount of inventory may be useful or even necessary?

29. Under which inventory system, periodic or perpetual, is it easier to manipulate net income if it is so desired?

30. Why is it sometimes necessary to estimate ending inventory?

31. If the amount of goods available-for-sale is $123,000, the amount of sales is $130,000, and the gross margin is 25% of sales, what is the amount of ending inventory?

32. Assume that inventory is overstated by $1,500 at the end of 20X1. What effect will this have on the 20X1 income statement? The 20X1 balance sheet? The 20X2 income statement? The 20X2 balance sheet? (Assume that the periodic inventory method is used.)

33. What information does inventory turnover provide?

34. What is an example of a business that would have a high inventory turnover? A low inventory turnover?

35. How is a company's operating cycle computed?

EXERCISES

Identifying Asset Values for Financial Statements

EXERCISE 8-1
L.O. 1

Required

For each of the following assets, indicate whether it should be valued at fair market value (FMV), lower-of-cost-or-market (LCM), or historical cost (HC) on the balance sheet. For certain assets historical cost may be called amortized cost (AC.)

Asset	FMV	LCM	HC/AC
Land			
Trading Securities			
Cash			
Held-to-Maturity Securities			
Buildings			
Available-for-Sale Securities			
Office Equipment			
Inventory			
Supplies			

Accounting for Investment Securities

EXERCISE 8-2
L.O. 2

Milano Bros. purchased $30,000 of marketable securities on March 1, 20X4. On the company's fiscal closing date, the securities had a market value of $27,000. During 20X4, Milano recognized $10,000 of revenue and $3,000 of expenses.

Required

a. Record a +, −, or n/a in a horizontal statements model to show how the purchase of the securities affects the financial statements, assuming that the securities are classified as (1) held-to-maturity, (2) trading, or (3) available-for-sale. When you record amounts in the Cash Flow column, indicate whether the item is an operating activity (OA), investing activity (IA), or financing activity (FA). Record only the effects of the purchase event.

Event No.	Type	Cash	+	Inv. Sec.	=	Liab.	+	Equity	Rev.	−	Exp.	=	Net Inc.	Cash Flow
1	Held													
2	Trading													
3	Available													

b. Determine the amount of net income that would be reported on the 20X4 income statement, assuming that the marketable securities are classified as (1) held-to-maturity, (2) trading, or (3) available-for-sale.

EXERCISE 8-3   **Effect of Investment Securities on Financial Statements**

L.O. 2   The following information was available for Electra Electronics for 20X2.

1. Purchased $75,000 of marketable investment securities.
2. Earned $4,500 of cash investment revenue in 20X2.
3. Sold securities for $15,000 that cost $12,500 during 20X2.
4. The value of the remaining securities at December 31, 20X2, was $50,000.

Required

a. Record the four events in a statements model like the following example. Use a separate model for each classification, including: (1) held-to-maturity, (2) trading, and (3) available-for-sale. The first event for the first classification is shown as an example.

Held-to-Maturity

Event No.	Cash	+	Inv. Sec.	=	Liab.	+	Ret. Earn.	+	Unreal. Gain.	Rev. or Gains	–	Exp. Or Loss	=	Net. Inc.	Cash Flow
1	(75,000)	+	75,000	=	n/a	+	n/a	+	n/a	n/a	–	n/a	=	n/a	(75,000) IA

b. What is the amount of net income under each of the three classifications?
c. What is the change in cash flow from operating activities under each of the three assumptions?
d. Are the answers to parts b and c different? Why or why not?

EXERCISE 8-4   **Preparing Financial Statements for Investment Securities**

L.O. 2   Wilson, Inc., began 20X1 with $40,000 in cash and contributed capital. The company engaged in the following investment transactions during 20X1:

1. Purchased $20,000 of marketable investment securities.
2. Earned $600 cash from investment revenue.
3. Sold investment securities for $8,000 that cost $6,000.
4. Purchased $9,000 of additional marketable investment securities.
5. Determined that the investment securities had a value of $24,000 at the end of 20X1.

Required

Use a vertical statements model to prepare income statements, balance sheets, and statements of cash flow for Wilson, Inc., under each of the following assumptions: (a) held-to-maturity, (b) trading, and (c) available-for-sale.

EXERCISE 8-5   **Differences for Marketable Investment Securities Reported**

L.O. 2   Complete the following table for the three categories of marketable investment securities:

Investment Category	Types of Securities	Types of Revenue Recognized	Value Reported on Balance Sheet at	Recognition of Unrealized Gains and Losses on the Income Statement	Cash Flow from Purchase or Sale of Securities Is Classified as
Held-to-maturity	Debt	Interest	Amortized Cost	No	Investing Activity
Trading					
Available-for-Sale					

EXERCISE 8-6   **Effect of Inventory Cost Flow Assumption on Financial Statements**

L.O. 2   **Required**

For each of the following situations, fill in the blank with *FIFO, LIFO,* or *weighted average*.

a. _____ would produce the highest amount of assets in an inflationary environment.
b. _____ would produce the highest amount of net income in an inflationary environment.

c. ____ would produce the lowest amount of assets in an inflationary environment.

d. ____ would produce the highest amount of assets in a deflationary environment.

e. ____ would produce the lowest amount of net income in a deflationary environment.

f. ____ would produce the same unit cost for assets and cost of goods sold in an inflationary environment.

g. ____ would produce the lowest amount of net income in an inflationary environment.

h. ____ would produce an asset value that was the same regardless of whether the environment was inflationary or deflationary.

Allocating Product Cost between Cost of Goods Sold and Ending Inventory—Single Purchase

Lauren Co. started the year with no inventory. During the year, Lauren purchased two identical inventory items. The inventory was purchased at different times. The first purchase cost $1,500 and the other, $2,000. One of the items was sold during the year.

EXERCISE 8-7
L.O. 3, 4

Required

Based on this information, how much product cost would be allocated to cost of goods sold and ending inventory on the year-end financial statements, assuming

a. FIFO?

b. LIFO?

c. weighted-average cost flows?

Allocating Product Cost between Cost of Goods Sold and Ending Inventory—Multiple Purchases

Randall Company sells clocks that are used in business offices. The beginning inventory for one of its clocks was 100 units at $20 per unit. During the year, Randall made two batch purchases of this clock. The first was a 150-unit purchase at $30 per unit; the second was a 200-unit purchase at $34 per unit. During the period, 260 clocks were sold.

EXERCISE 8-8
L.O. 3, 4

Required

Determine the amount of product costs that would be allocated to cost of goods sold and ending inventory, assuming that Randall uses

a. FIFO

b. LIFO

c. weighted-average cost flows

Effect of Inventory Cost Flow (FIFO, LIFO, and Weighted-Average) on Determination of Gross Margin

The following information pertains to Appleton Company for 20X5.

EXERCISE 8-9
L.O. 3, 4

Beginning Inventory	50 units @ $10
Units Purchased	275 units @ $40

Ending inventory consisted of 5 units. Appleton sold 320 units at $75 each. All purchases and sales were made with cash.

Required

a. Compute the gross margin for Appleton Company using the following cost flow assumptions: (1) FIFO, (2) LIFO, and (3) weighted average.

b. What is the dollar amount of difference in net income from using FIFO versus LIFO? (Ignore income tax considerations.)

c. Determine the cash flow from operating activities, using each of the three cost flow assumptions listed in part a. Do not consider the effect of income taxes. Explain why there are no differences in these cash flows.

EXERCISE 8-10
L.O. 4

Effect of Inventory Cost Flow on Ending Inventory Balance

Spencer Sales had the following transactions for cameras for 20X4, its first year of operations.

Jan.	20	Purchased 450 units @ $10	=	$4,500
Apr.	21	Purchased 200 units @ $12	=	2,400
July	25	Purchased 100 units @ $20	=	2,000
Sept.	19	Purchased 75 units @ $15	=	1,125

During the year, Spencer Sales sold 725 cameras for $40 each.

Required

a. Compute the amount of ending inventory that would be shown on the balance sheet, assuming the following cost flow assumptions: (1) FIFO, (2) LIFO, and (3) weighted average.

b. Compute the difference in gross margin using the FIFO and LIFO cost flow assumptions.

EXERCISE 8-11
L.O. 3, 4

Saving Income Tax by Shifting from FIFO to LIFO

The following information pertains to the inventory of the Fortune Company:

Jan. 1	Beginning Inventory	500 units @ $20
Apr. 1	Purchased	2,500 units @ $22
Oct. 1	Purchased	800 units @ $28

During the year, Fortune sold 3,400 units of inventory at $40 per unit and incurred $34,000 of operating expenses. Fortune currently uses the FIFO method but is considering a change to LIFO. All transactions are cash transactions. Assume a 30% income tax rate.

Required

a. Prepare an income statement under FIFO and LIFO.

b. Determine the amount of income taxes that Fortune would save if the company changed cost flow methods.

c. Determine the amount of cash flow from operating activities under FIFO and LIFO.

d. Explain why cash flow from operating activities is higher under FIFO when that cost flow method produced the lower gross margin.

EXERCISE 8-12
L.O. 3, 4

Effect of FIFO versus LIFO on Income Tax Expense

Tool Trade Company had sales of $250,000 for 20X6, its first year of operation. On April 2, the company purchased 200 units of product at $350 per unit. On September 1, an additional 150 units were purchased for $375 per unit. The company had 100 units on hand at the end of the year. The company's income tax rate is 40%. All transactions are cash transactions.

Required

a. The paragraph above describes five accounting events, including (1) a sales transaction, (2) the first purchase of inventory, (3) a second purchase of inventory, (4) the recognition of cost of goods sold expense, and (5) the payment of income tax expense. Record the amounts of each event in a horizontal statements model like the following example, assuming first a FIFO and then a LIFO cost flow.

Effect of Events on Financial Statements			
Panel 1: FIFO Cost Flow			
Event No.	Balance Sheet	Income Statement	Statement of Cash Flows
	Cash + Inventory = Cont. Cap. + Ret. Earn.	Rev. − Exp. = Net Inc.	
Panel 2: LIFO Cost Flow			
Event No.	Balance Sheet	Income Statement	Statement of Cash Flows
	Cash + Inventory = Cont. Cap. + Ret. Earn.	Rev. − Exp. = Net Inc.	

b. Compute the amount of net income, assuming a FIFO cost flow.

c. Compute the amount of net income, assuming a LIFO cost flow.

d. Explain the difference, if any, in the amount of income tax expense that will be paid using the two cost flow assumptions.

e. How does the use of the FIFO versus the LIFO cost flow assumption affect the statement of cash flows?

Recording Inventory Transactions under the Perpetual Method—Intermittent Sales and Purchases

EXERCISE 8-13
L.O. 4

The following inventory transactions apply to Price Company for 20X4.

Jan.	1	Purchased	250 units @ $20
Apr.	1	Sold	125 units @ $35
Aug.	1	Purchased	400 units @ $22
Dec.	1	Sold	500 units @ $38

The beginning inventory amounted to 175 units at $22 per unit. All transactions are cash transactions.

Required

a. Provide the journal entries necessary to record these transactions, assuming that Price uses a FIFO cost flow with a perpetual system.

b. Compute the ending balance in the Inventory account.

Effect of Cost Flow on Ending Inventory—Intermittent Sales and Purchases

EXERCISE 8-14
L.O. 4

Water Valley, Inc., had the following series of transactions for 20X7:

Date		Transaction	Description
Jan.	1	Beginning Inventory	50 units @ $40
Mar.	15	Purchased	200 units @ $48
May	30	Sold	170 units @ $80
Aug.	10	Purchased	275 units @ $50
Nov.	20	Sold	340 units @ $80

Required

a. Determine the number and dollar amount of inventory at the end of the year, assuming that FIFO cost flow is applied on a perpetual basis.

b. Write a memo explaining why Water Valley, Inc., would have difficulty applying the LIFO method on a perpetual basis. Include a discussion of how these difficulties could be overcome.

Lower-of-Cost-or-Market Rule—Perpetual Method

EXERCISE 8-15
L.O. 5

The following information is available for Wacky Widgets Co.'s ending inventory for the current year.

Item	Quantity	Unit Cost	Unit Market Value
P	100	$ 8	$ 6
D	50	9	8
S	20	12	13
J	15	10	9

Required

a. Determine the value of the ending inventory, using the lower-of-cost-or-market rule applied to (1) each individual inventory item and (2) the total inventory in aggregate.

b. Prepare any necessary journal entries, assuming that loss of value is immaterial. Wacky Widgets Co. uses the perpetual inventory method.

EXERCISE 8-16
L.O. 5

Lower-of-Cost-or-Market Rule—Periodic Method

Highland Company carries three inventory items. The following information applies to the ending inventory:

Item	Quantity	Unit Cost	Unit Market Value
O	200	$20	$18
J	250	30	28
R	175	10	15

Required

a. Determine the ending inventory that will be carried on the balance sheet, assuming that Highland applies the lower-of-cost-or-market rule to individual inventory items.

b. Explain how the write-down would be recorded under the periodic inventory method.

EXERCISE 8-17
L.O. 6

Estimating Ending Inventory—Periodic Method

A substantial part of the inventory of Danny's Sporting Goods was recently destroyed when the roof collapsed during a rainstorm. It is necessary to estimate the amount of loss from the storm for insurance reporting and financial statement purposes. Danny's used the periodic inventory method. The following is available from Danny's books:

Beginning Inventory	$ 50,000
Purchases to Date of Storm	200,000
Sales to Date of Storm	275,000

The value of undamaged inventory counted was $4,000. Historically Danny's gross margin percentage amounted to approximately 20% of sales.

Required

Estimate the following:

a. Gross margin
b. Cost of goods sold
c. Ending inventory
d. Amount of lost inventory

EXERCISE 8-18
L.O. 6

Estimating Ending Inventory—Perpetual Method

Julie Milano owned a small company that sold garden equipment. The equipment items were expensive, and a perpetual system was maintained for control purposes. Even so, lost, damaged, and stolen merchandise normally amounted to 5% of the inventory balance. On June 14, Milano's warehouse was destroyed by fire. Just prior to the fire, the accounting records contained a $338,000 balance in the Inventory account. However, inventory costing $42,000 had been sold and delivered to customers but had not been recorded in the books at the time of the fire. The fire did not affect the showroom, which contained inventory that cost $75,000.

Required

Estimate the amount of inventory destroyed by fire.

EXERCISE 8-19
L.O. 7

Effect of Inventory Error on Financial Statements—Perpetual Method

The Careless Company failed to count $20,000 of inventory in its 20X7 year-end physical count.

Required

Explain how this error will affect Careless's 20X7 financial statements, assuming that the Careless Company uses the perpetual inventory method.

Effect of Inventory Error on Elements of Financial Statements—Periodic Method

The ending inventory for Tedall Co. was understated by $5,200 for the year 20X5.

EXERCISE 8-20
L.O. 7

Required

Tell whether each of the following amounts was overstated, understated, or not affected by the error.

Item No.	Year	Amount
1	20X5	Beginning Inventory
2	20X5	Purchases
3	20X5	Goods Available for Sale
4	20X5	Cost of Goods Sold
5	20X5	Gross Margin
6	20X5	Net Income
7	20X6	Beginning Inventory
8	20X6	Purchases
9	20X6	Goods Available for Sale
10	20X6	Cost of Goods Sold
11	20X6	Gross Margin
12	20X6	Net Income

PROBLEMS—SERIES A

Effect of Marketable Investment Securities on Financial Statements

The following transactions pertain to Brogan's Trucking Co. for 20X7:

PROBLEM 8-1A
L.O. 1, 2

1. Started business when it acquired $15,000 cash from the owner, Heather Brogan.
2. Provided $50,000 of services for cash.
3. Invested $12,000 in marketable investment securities.
4. Paid $17,000 of operating expense.
5. Received $400 investment income from the securities.
6. Invested an additional $16,000 in marketable investment securities.
7. Made a $1,000 cash distribution to the owner.
8. Sold investment securities that cost $6,000 for $6,400.
9. Received $900 in investment income.
10. Determined the value of the investment securities at the end of the year to be $20,000.

Required

Use a vertical model to prepare an income statement, balance sheet, and statement of cash flows, assuming that the marketable investment securities were classified as (a) held-to-maturity, (b) trading, and (c) available-for-sale. (*Hint:* It may be helpful to record the events in T-accounts prior to preparing the financial statements.)

Effect of Different Inventory Cost Flow Methods on Financial Statements

The accounting records of Pete's Parts Shop reflected the following balances as of January 1, 20X7.

PROBLEM 8-2A
L.O. 3, 4

Cash	$25,400
Beginning Inventory	28,000 (200 units @ $140)
Contributed Capital	21,500
Retained Earnings	31,900

The following five transactions occurred in 20X7:

1. First purchase (cash)   120 units @ $150
2. Second purchase (cash)   140 units @ $165
3. Sales (all cash)   400 units @ $225
4. Paid $15,000 cash for operating expenses.
5. Paid cash for income tax at the rate of 25% of net income.

Required

a. Compute the cost of goods sold and ending inventory, assuming (1) FIFO cost flow, (2) LIFO cost flow, and (3) weighted-average cost flow.

b. Compute the amount of net income and income tax paid, assuming (1) FIFO cost flow, (2) LIFO cost flow, and (3) weighted-average cost flow.

c. Use a vertical model to prepare the 20X7 balance sheet, income statement, and statement of cash flows under FIFO, LIFO, and weighted average. (*Hint:* It may be helpful to record the events under an accounting equation before preparing the statements.)

PROBLEM 8-3A
L.O. 4

Allocating Product Costs between Cost of Goods Sold and Ending Inventory—Intermittent Purchase and Sales of Merchandise

Franky's Fences had the following sales and purchase transactions during 20X8. Beginning inventory consisted of 60 items at $175 each. The company uses a FIFO cost flow applied to a perpetual inventory system.

Date	Transaction	Description
Mar. 5	Purchased	50 items @ $185
Apr. 10	Sold	40 items @ $225
June 19	Sold	50 items @ $225
Sept. 16	Purchased	50 items @ $195
Nov. 28	Sold	35 items @ $235

Required

a. Provide the general journal entries necessary to record the inventory transactions.

b. Calculate the gross margin that would appear on the 20X8 income statement.

c. Determine the balance of ending inventory that would appear on the 20X8 balance sheet.

PROBLEM 8-4A
L.O. 5

Inventory Valuation Based on Lower-of-Cost-or-Market Rule

At the end of the year, Troglin Parts & Service has the following items in inventory:

Item	Quantity	Unit Cost	Unit Market Value
P1	80	$40	$45
P2	60	30	33
P3	100	70	65
P4	50	65	70

Required

a. Determine the amount of ending inventory, using the lower-of-cost-or-market rule applied to each individual inventory item.

b. Provide the general journal entry necessary to write down the inventory according to part *a*. Assume that Troglin Parts & Service uses the perpetual inventory method.

c. Determine the amount of ending inventory, assuming that the lower-of-cost-or-market rule is applied to the total inventory in aggregate.

d. Provide the general journal entry necessary to write down the inventory according to part *c*. Assume that Troglin Parts & Service uses the perpetual inventory method.

e. Explain how an inventory loss would be recognized when the periodic inventory method is used.

Estimating Ending Inventory—Gross Margin Method

PROBLEM 8-5A
L.O. 6

Fran's Fun House had its inventory destroyed by a hurricane on October 6 of the current year. Fortunately, the accounting records were at the home of one of the owners and were not damaged. The following information was available for the period of January 1 through October 6:

Beginning Inventory	$ 81,000
Purchases through October 6	340,000
Sales through October 6	570,000

Gross margin for Fran's Fun House has traditionally been 30% of sales.

Required

a. For the period ending October 6, compute the following:

  (1) Estimated gross margin.

  (2) Estimated cost of goods sold.

  (3) Estimated inventory at October 6.

b. Assume that $10,000 of the inventory was not damaged. What is the amount of the loss?

c. Explain how the estimation process would have differed if Frank's Fun House had used the perpetual inventory method.

Estimating Ending Inventory—Gross Margin Method

PROBLEM 8-6A
L.O. 6

Don's Deli wishes to produce quarterly statements, but a physical count of inventory is taken only at year end. The following historical data were taken from the records of 20X6 and 20X7:

	20X6	20X7
Net Sales	$120,000	$140,000
Cost of Goods Sold	62,000	73,000

At the end of the first quarter of 20X8, the ledger of Don's Deli had the following account balances:

Sales	$113,000
Sale Discounts	5,000
Purchases	82,000
Transportation-in	4,000
Transportation-out	10,000
Beginning Inventory	25,000

Required

Using the information provided, estimate the following for the first quarter of 20X8:

a. Gross margin

b. Ending inventory

PROBLEM 8-7A
L.O. 7

Effect of Inventory Errors on Financial Statements

The following income statement was prepared for Eddie's Fireworks for the year 20X6:

EDDIE'S FIREWORKS Income Statement For the Year Ended December 31, 20X6	
Sales	$140,000)
Cost of Goods Sold	(77,200)
Gross Margin	62,800
Operating Expenses	(40,900)
Net Income	$ 21,900

After the year-end audit, the following errors were discovered:

1. A $2,000 payment for repairs was erroneously charged to the Cost of Goods Sold account. (Assume that the perpetual inventory method is used.)

2. Sales to customers for $500 at December 31, 20X6, were not recorded on the books for 20X6. Also, the $300 cost of these goods was not recorded. The error was not discovered in the physical count because the goods had not been delivered.

3. A mathematical error was made in determining ending inventory. Ending inventory was understated by $1,800. (The Inventory account was written down in error.)

Required

Determine the effect, if any, of each of the errors on the following items. Give the dollar amount of the effect and whether it would increase (+), would decrease (−), or would not affect (n/a) the amount. The first item is recorded as an example.

Error No. 1	Amount of Error	Effect
Sales 20X6	n/a	n/a
Ending Inventory, December 31, 20X6		
Gross Margin, December 31, 20X6		
Beginning Inventory, January 1, 20X7		
Cost of Goods Sold, 20X6		
Net Income, 20X6		
Retained Earnings, December 31, 20X6		
Total Assets, December 31, 20X6		

Error No. 2	Amount of Error	Effect
Sales 20X6	$500	Decrease
Ending Inventory, December 31, 20X6		
Gross Margin, December 31, 20X6		
Beginning Inventory, January 1, 20X7		
Cost of Goods Sold, 20X6		
Net Income, 20X6		
Retained Earnings, December 31, 20X6		
Total Assets, December 31, 20X6		

Error No. 3	Amount of Error	Effect
Sales 20X6	n/a	n/a
Ending Inventory, December 31, 20X6		
Gross Margin, December 31, 20X6		
Beginning Inventory, January 1, 20X7		
Cost of Goods Sold, 20X6		
Net Income, 20X6		
Retained Earnings, December 31, 20X6		
Total Assets, December 31, 20X6		

Comprehensive Horizontal Statements Model

The following independent events were experienced by Planet Popcorn Co.

PROBLEM 8-8A
L.O. 2, 3

1. Acquired cash capital from the owners.
2. Paid cash to purchase marketable securities classified as available-for-sale.
3. Paid cash to purchase inventory.
4. Experienced unrealized gain on marketable securities that were classified as trading securities.
5. Experienced unrealized gain on marketable securities that were classified as available-for-sale securities.
6. Experienced unrealized gain on marketable securities that were classified as held-to-maturity securities.
7. Wrote down inventory to comply with lower-of-cost-or-market rule. (Assume that the company used the perpetual inventory system.)
8. Estimated the ending inventory balance under the perpetual inventory system.
9. Recognized cost of goods sold under FIFO.
10. Recognized cost of goods sold under LIFO.

Required

a. Show the effect of each event on the elements of the financial statements using a horizontal statements model like the following one. Use the following coding scheme to record your answers: increase (+), decrease (−), and not affected (n/a). In the Cash Flow column, indicate whether the item is an operating activity (OA), investing activity (IA) or financing activity (FA). The first transaction is entered as an example.

Event No.	Assets	=	Liab.	+	Equity	Rev. or Gain	−	Exp. or Loss	=	Net Inc.	Cash Flow
1	+		n/a		+	n/a		n/a		n/a	+ FA

b. Explain why there is or is not a directional difference in the way Event Nos. 9 and 10 affect the financial statements model.

PROBLEMS—SERIES B

Effect of Marketable Investment Securities on Financial Statements

The following transactions pertain to Tia's Answering Service for 20X7:

PROBLEM 8-1B
L.O. 1, 2

1. Started business when it acquired $20,000 cash from the owner, Tia Perez.
2. Provided $60,000 of services for cash.
3. Invested $20,000 in marketable investment securities.
4. Paid $19,000 of operating expense.
5. Received $400 of investment income from the securities.

6. Invested an additional $12,000 in marketable investment securities.
7. Made a $2,000 cash distribution to the owner.
8. Sold investment securities that cost $5,000 for $6,300.
9. Received another $1,000 in investment income.
10. Determined the value of the investment securities at the end of the year to be $40,000.

Required

Use a vertical model to prepare a 20X7 income statement, balance sheet, and statement of cash flows, assuming that the marketable investment securities were classified as (a) held-to-maturity, (b) trading, and (c) available-for-sale. (*Hint:* It may be helpful to record the events in T-accounts prior to preparing the financial statements.)

PROBLEM 8-2B
L.O. 3, 4

Effect of Different Inventory Cost Flow Methods on Financial Statements

The accounting records of Phil's Photography, Inc., reflected the following balances as of January 1, 20X7:

Cash	$22,000
Beginning Inventory	16,500 (150 units @ $110)
Contributed Capital	14,300
Retained Earnings	24,200

The following five transactions occurred in 20X6:
1. First purchase (cash)   120 units @ $85
2. Second purchase (cash)   200 units @ $100
3. Sales (all cash)   300 units @ $185
4. Paid $12,000 cash for operating expenses.
5. Paid cash for income tax at the rate of 40% of net income.

Required

    a. Compute the cost of goods sold and ending inventory, assuming (1) FIFO cost flow, (2) LIFO cost flow, and (3) weighted-average cost flow.

    b. Compute the amount of net income and income tax paid, assuming (1) FIFO cost flow, (2) LIFO cost flow, and (3) weighted-average cost flow.

    c. Use a vertical model to prepare the 20X6 balance sheet, income statement, and statement of cash flows under FIFO, LIFO, and weighted average. (*Hint:* It may be helpful to record the events under an accounting equation before preparing the statements.)

PROBLEM 8-3B
L.O. 4

Allocating Product Costs between Cost of Goods Sold and Ending Inventory—Intermittent Purchase and Sales of Merchandise

Tutti Frutti, Inc., had the following sales and purchase transactions during 20X6. Beginning inventory consisted of 80 items at $120 each. Tutti Frutti uses a perpetual inventory system with a FIFO cost flow.

Date	Transaction	Description
Mar. 5	Purchased	80 items @ $125
Apr. 10	Sold	60 items @ $245
June 19	Sold	70 items @ $245
Sept. 16	Purchased	60 items @ $130
Nov. 28	Sold	55 items @ $255

Required

a. Provide the general journal entries necessary to record the inventory transactions.

b. Calculate the gross margin that would appear on the 20X6 income statement.

c. Determine the balance of ending inventory that would appear on the 20X6 balance sheet.

Inventory Valuation Based on Lower-of-Cost-or-Market Rule

PROBLEM 8-4B
L.O. 5

At the end of the year, Powder's Donut Shop had the following items in inventory:

Item	Quantity	Unit Cost	Unit Market Value
D1	60	$30	$35
D2	30	55	50
D3	44	40	55
D4	40	50	35

Required

a. Determine the amount of ending inventory, using the lower-of-cost-or-market rule applied to each individual inventory item.

b. Provide the general journal entry necessary to write down the inventory according to part a. Assume that Powder's Donut Shop used the perpetual inventory method.

c. Determine the amount of ending inventory, assuming that the lower-of-cost-or-market rule is applied to the total inventory in aggregate.

d. Provide the general journal entry necessary to write down the inventory according to part c. Assume that Powder's Donut Shop used the perpetual inventory method.

e. Explain how the inventory loss would be recognized if Powder's Donut Shop used the periodic inventory method.

Estimating Ending Inventory—Gross Margin Method

PROBLEM 8-5B
L.O. 6

Jolly Mermaid had its inventory destroyed by a hurricane on September 21 of the current year. The accounting records were stored in an off-site location and were not damaged. The following information was available for the period of January 1 through September 21:

Beginning Inventory	$ 68,000
Purchases through September 21	350,000
Sales through September 21	520,000

The gross margin for Jolly Mermaid has traditionally been 25% of sales.

Required

a. For the period ending September 21, compute the following:

(1) Estimated gross margin.

(2) Estimated cost of goods sold.

(3) Estimated inventory at September 21.

b. Assume that $8,000 of the inventory was not damaged. What is the amount of the loss?

c. Explain how the estimation process would have differed if Jolly Mermaid had used the perpetual inventory method.

PROBLEM 8-6B
L.O. 6

Estimating Ending Inventory—Gross Margin Method

Washington Company wants to produce quarterly statements, but a physical count of inventory is taken only at year end. The following historical data were taken from the records of 20X4 and 20X5:

	20X4	20X5
Net Sales	$140,000	$200,000
Cost of Goods Sold	62,000	90,000

At the end of the first quarter of 20X6, the ledger of Washington Company had the following account balances:

Sales	$240,000
Sales Discounts	10,000
Purchases	160,000
Transportation-in	4,000
Transportation-out	6,000
Beginning Inventory	60,000

Required

Using the information provided, estimate the following for the first quarter of 20X6:

a. Gross margin

b. Ending inventory

PROBLEM 8-7B
L.O. 7

Effect of Inventory Errors on Financial Statements

The following income statement was prepared for PTO Company for the year 20X2:

PTO COMPANY Income Statement For the Year Ended December 31, 20X2	
Sales	$69,000
Cost of Goods Sold	(38,640)
Gross Margin	30,360
Operating Expenses	(9,100)
Net Income	$21,260

After the year-end audit, the following errors were discovered.

1. A $1,400 payment for repairs was erroneously charged to the Cost of Goods Sold account. (Assume that the perpetual inventory method is used.)

2. Sales to customers for $2,400 at December 31, 20X2, were not recorded on the books for 20X2. Also, the $1,344 cost of these goods was not recorded. The error was not discovered in the physical count because the goods had not been delivered.

3. A mathematical error was made in determining ending inventory. Ending inventory was understated by $1,200. (The Inventory account was written down in error.)

Required

Determine the effect, if any, of each of the errors on the following items. Give the dollar amount of the effect and whether it would increase (+), would decrease (−), or would not affect (n/a) the amount. The effect on sales is recorded as an example.

Error No. 1	Amount of Error	Effect
Sales 20X2	n/a	n/a
Ending Inventory, December 31, 20X2		
Gross Margin, December 31, 20X2		
Beginning Inventory, January 1, 20X3		
Cost of Goods Sold, 20X2		
Net Income, 20X2		
Retained Earnings, December 31, 20X2		
Total Assets, December 31, 20X2		

Error No. 2	Amount of Error	Effect
Sales 20X2	$2,400	Decrease
Ending Inventory, December 31, 20X2		
Gross Margin, December 31, 20X2		
Beginning Inventory, January 1, 20X3		
Cost of Goods Sold, 20X2		
Net Income, 20X2		
Retained Earnings, December 31, 20X2		
Total Assets, December 31, 20X2		

Error No. 3	Amount of Error	Effect
Sales 20X2	n/a	n/a
Ending Inventory, December 31, 20X2		
Gross Margin, December 31, 20X2		
Beginning Inventory, January 1, 20X3		
Cost of Goods Sold, 20X2		
Net Income, 20X2		
Retained Earnings, December 31, 20X2		
Total Assets, December 31, 20X2		

Comprehensive Horizontal Statements Model

PROBLEM 8-8B
L.O. 2, 3

The following independent events were experienced by Sato's Dairy.

1. Acquired cash capital from owners.
2. Purchased inventory on account.
3. Paid cash to purchase marketable securities classified as trading.
4. Experienced unrealized loss on marketable securities that were classified as trading securities.
5. Experienced unrealized loss on marketable securities that were classified as available-for-sale securities.
6. Experienced unrealized loss on marketable securities that were classified as held-to-maturity securities.
7. Wrote down inventory to comply with lower-of-cost-or-market rule. (Assume that the company used the perpetual inventory system.)
8. Estimated the ending inventory balance under the periodic inventory system.
9. Recognized cost of goods sold under FIFO.
10. Recognized cost of goods sold under weighted-average method.

Required

a. Show the effect of each event on the elements of the financial statements, using a horizontal statements model like the following one. Use the following coding scheme to record your answers: increase (+), decrease (−), and not affected (n/a). In the Cash Flow column, indicate whether the item is an operating activity (OA), investing activity (IA), or financing activity (FA). The first transaction is entered as an example.

Event No.	Assets	=	Liab.	+	Equity	Rev. or Gain	−	Exp. or Loss	=	Net Inc.	Cash Flow
1	+		n/a		+	n/a		n/a		n/a	+ FA

b. Explain why there is or is not a directional difference in the way Event Nos. 9 and 10 affect the financial statements model.

analyze, communicate, think

ACT 8-1

BUSINESS APPLICATIONS CASE   **Gateway 2000 Annual Report**

Required

Using the Gateway 2000 financial statements in Appendix B, answer the following questions:

a. What are the inventory turnover ratio and average number of days in inventory for the year ended December 31, 1997?

b. What cost flow method(s) did Gateway use to account for inventory?

c. In 1997, Gateway's inventory represented 21% of its total current assets. This is a much lower percentage than many companies have. For example, at Lands' End, a direct marketer of clothing, inventory represented 81% of current assets in 1997. Why does Gateway have a lower investment in inventory than other companies such as Lands' End?

ACT 8-2

GROUP ASSIGNMENT   **Inventory Cost Flow**

The accounting records of The Radio Company showed the following balances at January 1, 20X8:

Cash	$15,000
Beginning Inventory (200 units @ $45, 60 units @ $48)	11,880
Contributed Capital	10,000
Retained Earnings	16,880

Transactions for 20X8 were as follows:

Purchased 100 units @ $50 per unit.
Sold 220 units @ $80 per unit.
Purchased 250 units @ $52 per unit.
Sold 300 units @ $90 per unit.
Paid operating expense of $3,200.
Paid income tax expense. The income tax rate is 30%.

Required

a. Organize the class into three sections, and divide each section into groups of three to five students. Assign each section one of the cost flow methods, FIFO, LIFO, or weighted average.

Group Tasks

Determine the amount of ending inventory, cost of goods sold, gross margin, and net income after income tax for the cost flow method assigned to your section.

Class Discussion

b. Have a representative of each section put its income statement on the board. Discuss the effect that each cost flow method has on assets (ending inventory), net income, and cash flows. Which method is preferred for tax reporting? For financial reporting? What restrictions are placed on the use of LIFO for tax reporting?

REAL-WORLD CASE

ACT 8-3

Evaluating the Cost Savings from Managing Inventory More Efficiently

This chapter reported earlier that in its 1997 fiscal year, Starbucks Coffee took 50 days to sell its inventory. This is a significant improvement over its 1995 fiscal year, when it held inventory an average of 126 days before it was sold. Additional information about Starbucks for 1997 and 1995 is presented here (all dollar amounts are in thousands):

	1995	1997
Average Number of Days to Sell Inventory	126	50
Average Inventory on Hand	n/a	$101,448
Sales	$465,213	$966,946
Cost of Goods Sold	$360,064	$741,323
Net Income	$26,102	$57,412
Approximate Number of Stores	800	1,270
Income Tax Rate	39.5%	38.5%

Required

a. Assume that Starbucks paid an average of 6% interest on money that it borrowed during 1997. Determine how much the company saved in inventory financing costs, *after taxes*, in 1997 by selling its inventory in 50 days versus the 126 days it was holding inventory during 1995. In other words, how much lower would Starbucks' 1997 net income have been if it had maintained 126 days of sales in inventory rather than 50? Show your computations in good form. (*Hint:* You may want to refer to the discussion of Rite Aid versus Eckerd in the chapter to help with this analysis.)

b. Using your answer for part *a* and based on the *average profit generated per store at Starbucks in 1995* (which must be computed), answer the following question. The increase in net income resulting from the more efficient management of inventory produced the same increase in income as if Starbucks had opened what number of new stores?

c. Will Starbucks be able to improve the efficiency with which it manages its inventory from 1997 to 1999 as much as it did from 1995 to 1997?

BUSINESS APPLICATIONS CASE

ACT 8-4

Using the Average-Days-to-Sell-Inventory Ratio to Make a Lending Decision

Bradford's Wholesale Fruits has applied for a loan. Bradford's has agreed to use its inventory to collateralize the loan. The company currently has an inventory balance of $289,000. The cost of goods sold for the past year was $7,518,000. The average shelf life for the fruit that Bradford's sells is 10 days, after which time it begins to spoil and must be sold at drastically reduced prices to dispose of it rapidly. The company had maintained steady sales over the past 3 years and expects to continue at current levels for the foreseeable future.

Required

Based on your knowledge of inventory turnover, write a memo that describes the quality of the inventory as collateral for the loan.

ACT 8-5

BUSINESS APPLICATIONS CASE   Using Ratios to Make Comparisons

The following accounting information exists for Thompson Hardware and Old Town Hardware at the end of 20X8. The only difference between the two companies is that Thompson uses FIFO while Old Town uses LIFO.

	Thompson Hardware	Old Town Hardware
Cash	$ 90,000	$ 90,000
Accounts Receivable	350,000	350,000
Merchandise Inventory	270,000	220,000
Accounts Payable	240,000	240,000
Cost of Goods Sold	1,350,000	1,400,000
Building	450,000	450,000
Sales	2,000,000	2,000,000

Required

a. Compute the gross margin percentage for each company, and identify the company that *appears* to be charging the higher prices in relation to its costs.

b. For each company, compute the inventory turnover ratio and the average days to sell inventory. Identify the company that *appears* to be incurring the higher inventory financing cost.

c. Provide a logical explanation for the fact that the company with the lower gross margin percentage has the higher inventory turnover ratio.

d. Compute the length of the operating cycle for each company. Explain why short operating cycles are more desirable than long operating cycles.

ACT 8-6

WRITING ASSIGNMENT   Marketable Securities in Financial Statements

The following information is taken from the annual report of The Equitable Companies at December 31, 1997, for its fixed securities (amounts given in millions):

	Amortized Cost	Gross Unrealized Gains	Gross Unrealized Losses	Estimated Fair Value
Investments				
Available-for-Sale	$19,107.1	$951.3	$ 79.9	$ 19,978.5
Held-to-Maturity	143.0	21.7	.4	164.3
Trading securities	16,521.9	13.8	0.0	16,535.7

Required

a. Using the preceding information, what amounts would be shown on the balance sheet for the period ending December 31, 1997?

b. Write a memo to the shareholders explaining why some investments are shown at cost and others are shown at market value. Explain how the values of these investments would be shown at market value. Also explain how gains and losses of the various types of securities are shown in the financial statements.

ETHICAL DILEMMA   **Show Them Only What You Want Them to See**

Clair Coolage is the chief accountant for a sales company called Far Eastern Imports. The company has been highly successful and is trying to increase its capital base by attracting new investors. The company operates in an inflationary environment and has been using LIFO inventory cost flow in order to minimize its net earnings and thereby reduce its income taxes. Katie Bailey, the vice president of finance, asked Coolage to estimate the change in net earnings that would occur if the company switched to FIFO. After reviewing the company's books, Coolage estimated that pretax income would increase by $1,200,000 if the company adopted a FIFO cost flow. However, the switch would result in approximately $400,000 of additional taxes. The overall effect would result in an increase of $800,000 in net earnings. Bailey told Coolage to avoid the additional taxes by preparing the tax return on a LIFO basis but to make up a set of statements on a FIFO basis to be distributed to potential investors.

Required

a. Comment on the legal and ethical implications of Bailey's decision.

b. How will the switch to FIFO affect Far Eastern's balance sheet?

c. If Bailey reconsiders and makes a decision to switch to FIFO for tax purposes as well as financial reporting purposes, net income will increase by $800,000. Comment on the wisdom of paying $400,000 in income taxes to obtain an additional $800,000 of net income.

EDGAR DATABASE   **Analyzing Inventory at Gap Company**

Required

Using the most current 10-K available on EDGAR, answer the following questions about Gap Company. Instructions for using EDGAR are in Appendix A.

a. What was the average amount of inventory per store? Use *all* stores operated by Gap, not just those called *The Gap.* (*Hint:* The answer to this question must be computed. The number of stores in operation at the end of the most recent year can be found in the MD&A of the 10-K.)

b. How many *new* stores did Gap open during the year?

c. Using the quarterly financial information contained in the 10-K, complete the following chart.

Quarter	Sales During Each Quarter
1	$
2	
3	
4	

d. Referring to the chart in part *c*, provide an explanation of why Gap's sales vary so widely throughout its fiscal year. Do you believe that Gap's inventory level varies throughout the year in relation to sales?

SPREADSHEET ANALYSIS   **Using Excel**

At the beginning of January 1, 20X5, the accounting records of Bronco Boutique reported the following balances:

Cash	$1,000
Inventory	2,250 (150 units @ $15)
Contributed Capital	2,000
Retained Earnings	1,250

During January, Bronco Boutique entered into five cash transactions:

1. Purchased 120 units of inventory @ $16 each.
2. Purchased 160 units of inventory @ $17 each.
3. Sold 330 units of inventory @ $30 each.
4. Incurred $1,700 of operating expenses.
5. Paid for income tax at the rate of 30% of net income before taxes.

Required

a. Set up rows 1 through 10 of the following spreadsheet to compute cost of goods sold and ending inventory, assuming (1) FIFO, (2) LIFO, and (3) weighted-average cost flows. Notice that the FIFO cost flow has already been completed for you. Although not shown, columns O through W will be used to complete the LIFO and weighted-average cost flow computations. Be sure to use formulas for all calculations.

Cost of Goods Available For Sale					**FIFO Ending Inventory**			**FIFO Cost of Goods Sold**			**LIFO Ending Inventory**		
	Units	Unit Price	Total Cost		Units	Unit Price	Total Cost	Units	Unit Price	Total Cost	Units	Unit Price	Total Cost
Beginning Inventory	150	$15	$2,250					150	$15	$2,250			
First Purchase (cash)	120	$16	$1,920					120	$16	$1,920			
Second Purchase)cash)	160	$17	$2,720		100	$17	$1,700	60	$17	$1,020			
Total Cost of Goods Available for Sale	430		$6,890		100		$1,700	330		$5,190			
Average Cost			$16.02		Check:	EI + CGS	430 Units						
						EI + CGS	$6,890 Total Cost						

Income Statements	FIFO	LIFO	WEIGHTED AVERAGE
Sales (330 units @ $30 each) (cash)	$9,900		
Cost of Goods Sold	5,190		
Gross Margin	4,710		
Operating Expenses (cash)	1,700		
Net Income Before Taxes	3,010		
Income Tax Expense (30%) (cash)	903		
Net Income	$2,107		

Statement of Cash Flows	FIFO
Cash from Operating Activities:	
Cash received from Customers	$9,900
Cash paid for Inventory Purchased	(4,640)
Cash paid for Operating Expenses	(1,700)
Cash paid for Income Taxes	(903)
Net Cash Flow from Operations	2,657
Beginning Cash	1,000
Ending Cash	$3,657

b. In rows 13 through 31, compute the amount of net income and net cash flow from operations under FIFO, LIFO, and weighted average. Notice that the FIFO column has been provided as an example.

ACT 8-10   SPREADSHEET ASSIGNMENT   **Mastering Excel**

Required

Complete ACT 8-5 using an Excel spreadsheet. Excel problem ACT 7-9 may be used as a resource for structuring the spreadsheet.

9 Long-Term Operational Assets

LEARNING OBJECTIVES
AFTER COMPLETING THIS CHAPTER, YOU SHOULD BE ABLE TO:

1 Understand why some businesses generate high revenue with few operational assets.

2 Distinguish between tangible and intangible assets.

3 Identify different types of long-term operational assets.

4 Determine the cost of long-term operational assets.

5 Explain how expense recognition (i.e., depreciation) affects financial statements throughout the life cycle of a tangible asset.

6 Determine how a gain or loss from the disposal of long-term operational assets affects financial statements.

7 Understand how different depreciation methods affect the amount of expense recognized in a particular accounting period.

8 Identify tax issues related to long-term operational assets.

9 Understand how revising estimates affects financial statements.

10 Explain how continuing expenditures for operational assets affect financial statements.

11 Explain how expense recognition for natural resources (i.e., depletion) affects financial statements.

12 Explain how expense recognition for intangible assets (i.e., amortization) affects financial statements.

13 Understand how GAAP can adversely affect the ability of U.S. companies to attract international capital.

14 Understand how expense recognition choices and industry characteristics affect financial performance measures.

the **curious** accountant

In the normal course of operations, most companies acquire long-term assets each year. The way in which a company hopes to make money with these assets varies for the type of business and the asset acquired.

During 1997, Georgia-Pacific Corporation made cash acquisitions of property and equipment of $717 million and cash acquisitions of timber and timberlands of $182 million. How does Georgia-Pacific plan to use each type of asset to produce earnings for the company? Should the accounting treatment for trees differ from the accounting treatment for trucks?

©1991 Earl Roberge/Photo Researchers

Long-term operational assets are the resources businesses use to produce revenue. The size of a company's operational assets relative to the income it generates by using them will depend on the nature of its operating activity. For example, a trucking company requires substantial investments in physical equipment to move freight from one destination to another. In contrast, a firm of attorneys uses intellectual rather than physical assets to meet the needs of its clients. Accordingly, law offices tend to generate significantly more revenue per dollar invested in operational assets than do trucking companies.

How long is a *long-term?* There is no definitive time limit. However, as noted earlier, assets that are used in more than one accounting period are usually considered long term. The cost of long-term assets is normally recognized as an expense in the accounting periods in which the asset is used. In other words, you do not expense the total cost of long-term assets in a single year; instead, you spread the expense recognition over the life of the assets. There are several types of long-term assets, and different terms are used to describe the process of expense recognition for each type. For example, Delta Airlines *depreciates* its planes, while Exxon *depletes* its oil reserves. This chapter teaches you how to classify costs into one of several long-term asset categories and explains how to account for the utilization of these assets from the date of purchase to their final disposal.

L.O. 1
Understand why some businesses generate high revenue with few operational assets.

L.O. 2
Distinguish between tangible and intangible assets.

L.O. 3
Identify different types of long-term operational assets.

Classifications of Long-Term Operational Assets

Long-term assets are either tangible or intangible. **Tangible assets** are those that are "able to be touched" and include equipment, machinery, natural resources, and land. **Intangible assets** may be represented by pieces of paper or contracts that appear tangible; however, the true value of an intangible asset lies in the rights and privileges extended to its owners. For example, a *patent* is a legal right granting its owner an exclusive privilege to produce and sell a commodity that has one or more unique features. Accordingly, inventors who own intangible patent rights can protect their inventions by seeking legal recourse against anyone who attempts to profit by copying their innovations.

Tangible Long-Term Assets

Property, Plant, and Equipment

Property, plant, and equipment is a category whose assets are sometimes called *plant assets* or *fixed assets.* Examples of property, plant, and equipment include furniture, cash registers, machinery, delivery trucks, computers, mechanical robots, and buildings. Rather than recording all these assets in a single account, each company uses subcategories to satisfy its particular needs for information. One company may include all office machinery in one account, whereas another company might divide office equipment into computers, desks, chairs, and so on. As indicated in earlier chapters, the process of expense recognition for property, plant, and equipment is called **depreciation.**

Natural Resources

Mineral deposits, oil and gas reserves, reserves of timber, mines, and quarries are known as **natural resources.** They are sometimes called *wasting assets* because their value "wastes away" as the resources are removed. The balance sheet classification for natural resources as long-term assets sometimes conflicts with the way in which these assets are expensed. Conceptually, natural resources are inventories. Indeed, these assets are frequently expensed through the cost of goods sold. However, they are classified as long-term assets because (1) the resource deposits generally have long lives, (2) the accounting treatment is very similar to that for other long-term assets, and (3) practice and convention have made this the acceptable treatment. The process of expense recognition for natural resources is called *depletion.*

Land

Land is classified in a separate category from other property for one major reason: Land is not subject to depreciation or depletion. It is considered to have an infinite life. In other words, land is not destroyed through the process of its use. When buildings or natural resources are purchased simultaneously with land, the amount paid must be carefully divided between the land and the other assets because of the nondepreciable nature of the land.

Intangible Assets

Intangible assets may be classified into two groups: those that are specifically identifiable and can be acquired individually and those that arise from the purchase of a group of assets and cannot be attributed to any one asset.

L.O. 3

Identify different types of long-term operational assets.

Specifically Identifiable Intangible Assets

This category includes patents, trademarks, franchises, copyrights, and other privileges extended by government agencies. The costs of acquiring these assets may range from relatively insignificant legal fees to huge sums paid for fast-food franchises. Later in this chapter we look at several of these intangibles on an individual basis, but the accounting treatment is basically the same for each. The process of expense recognition for the cost of intangible assets is called **amortization.**

Goodwill

Goodwill refers to the benefits resulting from purchasing a company with a good reputation, an established clientele, a favorable business location, or other features that provide an above-average profit potential. For example, a fast-food restaurant with the name *McDonald's* will likely produce higher revenues than another restaurant named *Joe's*, even if both have the same physical asset base. An investor will have to pay more to acquire a business with above-average profit potential than to acquire an identical set of assets that are separated from the favorable business conditions. Like other intangible assets, this extra amount, or goodwill, is amortized (i.e., expensed) over its useful life.

Determining the Cost of Long-Term Assets

The **historical cost concept** requires that assets be recorded at the amount paid for them. This amount includes the purchase price plus whatever costs are necessary to obtain the asset and prepare it for its intended use. As years go by, the historical cost may begin to bear little relation to the current value of the asset for several reasons: (1) Depreciation may not approximate the use of the asset, (2) inflation may change the value of the dollar, or (3) the value of the asset itself may increase or decrease. Because of these factors, many critics have suggested that companies be allowed to revalue their assets periodically so as to reflect the assets' current values. However, due to a lack of objective measurement techniques, most long-term assets are still reported at historical cost in the primary financial statements.

L.O. 4

Determine the cost of long-term operational assets.

   While the cost of an asset includes all expenditures that are normally necessary to obtain it and prepare it for its intended use, *payments for fines, damages, and so on, are not considered normal costs of acquiring an asset* and are therefore not included. Some of the more common costs associated with particular types of assets include the following:

   Purchase of buildings: (1) purchase price, (2) sales taxes, (3) title search and transfer documents, (4) real estate fees and attorney's fees, and

(5) remodeling costs.

Purchase of land: (1) purchase price, (2) sales taxes, (3) title search and transfer documents, (4) real estate and attorney's fees, and (5) removal of old buildings, and (6) grading.

Purchase of equipment: (1) purchase price (less discounts), (2) sales taxes, (3) delivery costs, (4) installation, and (5) costs to adapt to intended use.

Basket Purchase Allocation

L.O. 4

Determine the cost of long-term operational assets.

A **basket purchase** is the acquisition of several assets in a single transaction. Often a single price is assigned to that purchase, and the acquiring company must determine how much of that price should be assigned to each asset. This can be done by using the **relative fair market value method.**

Assume that Beatty Company purchased a building and plot of land for $240,000 cash. A real estate appraiser was called in and determined the fair market value of each to be as follows:

Building	$270,000
Land	90,000
Total	$360,000

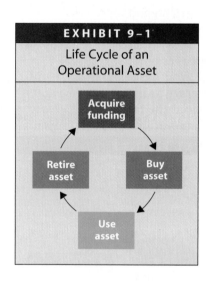

EXHIBIT 9–1

Life Cycle of an Operational Asset

Acquire funding

Retire asset

Buy asset

Use asset

Beatty paid less than the appraised values but can still use these values to determine a reasonable basis for assigning the total cost to the two assets. The appraisal indicated that the land is worth 25% (90,000/360,000) of the total value, and the building, 75% (270,000/360,000). Applying these percentages to the actual purchase price results in the following cost allocation:

Building	0.75 × $240,000 =	$180,000
Land	0.25 × $240,000 =	60,000
Total		$240,000

Life Cycle of Operational Assets

The life cycle of an operational asset begins with the effort to obtain the financing necessary to acquire it. The next step is to acquire the asset (i.e., invest the funds). The asset is then used to produce revenue. The final step is to retire the asset. The use and retirement of the asset should generate enough funds to replace the asset and to provide a reasonable return on the invested funds. Exhibit 9–1 depicts the life cycle of an operational asset.

L.O. 5

Explain how expense recognition (i.e., depreciation) affects financial statements throughout the life cycle of a tangible asset.

Accounting for Operational Assets throughout the Life Cycle

The acquisition of capital results in an increase in assets and equity. Once the financing has been acquired, the funds are invested in an asset. The cost of the asset is then systematically expensed over its useful life. In prior chapters, the

an **answer** for the curious accountant

Equipment is a long-term asset that is used for the purpose of producing revenue. The portion of the equipment that is used each accounting period is recognized as depreciation expense. Accordingly, the expense recognition for the cost of equipment is spread over the useful life of the asset. Timber, however, is not used until the trees are grown. Conceptually, the cost of the trees should be treated as inventories and expensed as cost of goods sold at the time the products made from trees are sold. Even so, some timber companies recognize a periodic

charge called *depletion* in a manner similar to that used for depreciation.

Accounting for unusual long-term assets such as timber requires an understanding of specialized "industry practice" accounting rules that are beyond the scope of this course. Be aware that many industries have unique accounting problems, and business managers in such industries must make the effort to understand specialized accounting rules that relate to their companies.

expense recognition phase for tangible assets was spread equally over the life of the asset. This method of depreciating an asset is called **straight-line depreciation.** Straight-line depreciation is appropriate when an asset is used evenly over its life. However, not all assets are used evenly. Some assets may be used much more rapidly when they are new and less frequently as they grow older. These assets require **accelerated depreciation methods,** which charges more of the cost of the asset to expense in the early years of the asset's useful life. Other assets may be used extensively in one accounting period, infrequently in the next, and extensively again in another accounting period. In other words, their use varies from one accounting period to the next. Accordingly, meth-

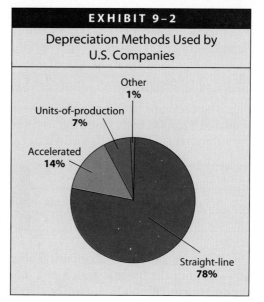

EXHIBIT 9–2

Depreciation Methods Used by
U.S. Companies

Other
1%

Units-of-production
7%

Accelerated
14%

Straight-line
78%

Data source: AICPA, *Accounting Trends and Techniques,* 1998

ods other than straight line are needed to accurately reflect the use of many assets. The next section of this chapter reviews straight-line depreciation and introduces two new methods, the *double-declining balance* and *units-of-production methods.* Exhibit 9–2 shows the different depreciation methods that U.S. companies use. The double-declining balance is an accelerated depreciation method.

Methods of Depreciation

L.O. 5

Explain how expense recognition (i.e., depreciation) affects financial statements throughout the life cycle of a tangible asset.

To demonstrate how different depreciation methods affect expense recognition over the life cycle, we trace the events of Dryden Enterprises for a 5-year time span. Dryden was started on January 1, 20X1, when it acquired a $25,000 cash contribution of capital from its owners. Immediately after the acquisition of capital, Dryden purchased a van. The van had a list price of $23,500. Dryden was able to obtain a 10% cash discount from the dealer. However, the van was delivered FOB shipping point, and Dryden agreed to pay an additional $250 for transportation costs. Dryden also paid $2,600 to have the van customized to make it more appealing as a rental vehicle. Accordingly, the amount to be capitalized in the Van account is computed as follows:

List Price	$23,500	
Less: Cash Discounts	(2,350)	$23,500 × 0.10
Plus: Transportation Costs	250	
Plus: Cost of Customization	2,600	
Total	$24,000	

The van has an estimated **salvage value** of $4,000 and an **estimated life** of 4 years. The revenue stream is expected to be distributed evenly over the van's useful life at a rate of $8,000 per year. The effects of the accounting treatment during the four phases of the life cycle are now discussed.

Straight-Line Depreciation

Given that the revenue is expected to flow smoothly over the asset's useful life, it is logical to assume that the asset will be used evenly over its life. Accordingly, straight-line depreciation is appropriate.

Life-Cycle Phase 1

The first phase of the life cycle is the acquisition of capital. In this case, Dryden acquired $25,000 cash from the owners. The effect of this capital acquisition on the financial statements is shown here:

Assets				=	Equity			Rev.	−	Exp.	=	Net Inc.	Cash Flow
Cash	+	Van	− A. Dep.	=	C. Cap	+	Ret. Earn.						
25,000	+	n/a	− n/a	=	25,000	+	n/a	n/a	−	n/a	=	n/a	25,000 FA

Clearly, the capital acquisition affects the balance sheet and statement of cash flows but not the income statement. These effects should be traced to the financial statements in Exhibit 9–3. Notice that the financing activities section of the statement of cash flows shows a cash inflow from capital acquisitions amounting to $25,000. Also the balance sheet shows a $25,000 balance in the equity section under the Contributed Capital account. Since the balance sheet accounts reflect the cumulative effect of events that have occurred from a company's inception, the $25,000 in contributed capital appears in the statements throughout the life cycle. In contrast, the statement of cash flows reflects activities for a particular accounting period. Accordingly, the inflow from the capital acquisition appears only once during the 20X1 accounting period. The cash balance shown in the balance sheet is not equal to $25,000 because the Cash account is affected by other events during 20X1.

EXHIBIT 9–3

Financial Statements under Straight-Line Depreciation

DRYDEN ENTERPRISES
Financial Statements

Income Statements

	20X1	20X2	20X3	20X4	20X5
Rent Revenue	$ 8,000	$ 8,000	$ 8,000	$ 8,000	$ 0
Depreciation Expense	(5,000)	(5,000)	(5,000)	(5,000)	0
Operating Income	3,000	3,000	3,000	3,000	0
Gain	0	0	0	0	500
Net Income	$ 3,000	$ 3,000	$ 3,000	$ 3,000	$ 500

Balance Sheets

	20X1	20X2	20X3	20X4	20X5
Assets					
Cash	$ 9,000	$17,000	$25,000	$33,000	$37,500
Van	24,000	24,000	24,000	24,000	0
Accumulated Depreciation	(5,000)	(10,000)	(15,000)	(20,000)	0
Total Assets	$28,000	$31,000	$34,000	$37,000	$37,500
Equity					
Contributed Capital	$25,000	$25,000	$25,000	$25,000	$25,000
Retained Earnings	3,000	6,000	9,000	12,000	12,500
Total Equity	$28,000	$31,000	$34,000	$37,000	$37,500

Statements of Cash Flows

	20X1	20X2	20X3	20X4	20X5
Operational Activities					
Inflow from Customers	$ 8,000	$ 8,000	$ 8,000	$ 8,000	$ 0
Investing Activities					
Outflow to Purchase Van	(24,000)				
Inflow from Sale of Van					4,500
Financing Activities					
Inflow from Capital Acquisition	25,000				
Net Change in Cash	9,000	8,000	8,000	8,000	4,500
Beginning Cash Balance	0	9,000	17,000	25,000	33,000
Ending Cash Balance	$ 9,000	$17,000	$25,000	$33,000	$37,500

Life-Cycle Phase 2

The second phase of the life cycle is the investment in the operational asset (i.e., purchase of the van). The purchase price was previously computed as $24,000 cash. The effect of the investment on the financial statements is shown here:

Assets				=	Equity			Rev.	–	Exp.	=	Net Inc.	Cash Flow	
Cash	+	Van	– A. Dep.	=	C. Cap.	+	Ret. Earn.							
(24,000)	+	24,000	– n/a	=	n/a	+	n/a	n/a	–	n/a	=	n/a	(24,000)	IA

The investment is an asset exchange transaction involving a cash payment. As such, it affects the balance sheet and the statement of cash flows. Refer to Exhibit 9–3 to see how the effects of this event appear on the financial statements.

Note that the cash outflow is shown one time in 20X1 under the investing activities section of the statement of cash flows. However, the cost of the asset is shown on the balance sheet as $24,000 throughout the entire life cycle (20X1–20X4). The historical cost is removed from the asset account when the van is retired in 20X5.

Life-Cycle Phase 3

The use of the asset results in the generation of $8,000 revenue per year. The wear and tear on the asset are reflected in the recognition of depreciation expense. The amount of the depreciation expense calculated on a straight-line basis is determined by subtracting the salvage value from the original cost and dividing the difference by the useful life. This computation results in the recognition of $5,000 ([$24,000 − $4,000] ÷ 4) of depreciation expense each year. The expense recognition is shown in a **contra asset account** titled **Accumulated Depreciation.** The effects of the revenue and expense recognition on the financial statements are shown here. In order to save space, the events are shown only once. In fact, they would occur four times—once for each year the asset is in use.

Assets				=	Equity			Rev.	−	Exp.	=	Net Inc.	Cash Flow
Cash	+	Van	−	A. Dep.	=	C. Cap.	+	Ret. Earn.					
8,000	+	n/a	−	n/a	=	n/a	+	8,000	8,000	−	n/a	=	8,000	8,000 OA
n/a	+	n/a	−	5,000	=	n/a	+	(5,000)	n/a	−	5,000	=	(5,000)	n/a

The revenue event affects all three statements. Depreciation expense affects the balance sheet and the income statement but not the statement of cash flows. Recall that the cash paid for the van was spent on January 1, 20X1. The total cash outflow is shown in the investing section of the statement of cash flows. Accordingly, the cash flow consequences have already been recognized and therefore are not affected by the recognition of depreciation expense. This is the meaning of the statement "depreciation is a noncash expenditure." Depreciation represents the use of the physical asset rather than the expenditure of cash.

Once again, the events should be traced to the financial statements in Exhibit 9–3. As shown in the statement of cash flows, the revenue stream produces $8,000 of cash per year for 4 years (20X1–20X4). Accordingly, the use (i.e., rental) of the van provided $32,000 of cash ($8,000 × 4) over its life cycle. Note that the depreciation expense is shown in the income statement but does not affect the statement of cash flows. (The reason for this effect was explained in the previous paragraph.) Observe here that the effects of depreciation occur throughout the life cycle of the asset. Indeed, it is interesting to note that the depreciation expense stays at $5,000 each year, whereas the Accumulated Depreciation account grows from $5,000 to $10,000 to $15,000 and finally to $20,000 between 20X1 and 20X4.

L.O. 6

Determine how a gain or loss from the disposal of operational assets affects financial statements.

Life-Cycle Phase 4

The final stage in the life cycle of an operational asset is the retirement of the asset and its removal from the company's records. This occurs on January 1, 20X5, when Dryden sells the van for $4,500 cash. The effect of this event on the financial statements is shown on the following page. Since the book value at the time of the sale was only $4,000, Dryden recognizes a $500 gain ($4,500 − $4,000).

Assets			=	Equity			Rev. or Gain	−	Exp. or Loss	=	Net Inc.	Cash Flow
Cash	+ Van	− A. Dep.	=	C. Cap	+	Ret. Earn.						
4,500	+ (24,000)	− (20,000)	=	0	+	500	500	−	0	=	500	4,500 IA

Tracing the effects of these events to the financial statements in Exhibit 9–3 provides interesting insights as to how businesses recover their invested funds. Although the gain shown on the income statement is only $500, the amount of cash inflow is $4,500. This amount is shown as an inflow in the investing activities section of the statement of cash flows. The gain is not shown separately on the statement of cash flows but instead is included in the $4,500 shown in the investing section. The total cash inflow from using and retiring the van amounts to $36,500 ([$8,000 revenue × 4 years] + $4,500 salvage value), which means that Dryden not only recovered the cost of the asset ($24,000) but also generated a $12,500 return on its investment. In other words, over its life cycle, the operational asset generated $12,500 more than it cost ($36,500 − $24,000). This is consistent with the total amount of net income that was earned over the life cycle. Accordingly, the difference between income and cash flow is shown to be a matter of timing. Other interesting insights include the fact that the amount of the ending balance in the Retained Earnings account is equal to the sum of the amounts of net income that appear on the 20X1 through 20X5 income statements. This result occurs because all earnings were retained in the business. No distributions were made to the owners.

Recording Procedures

Exhibit 9–4 shows the general journal entries required to record the transactions over the life cycle.

Double-Declining Balance Depreciation

Assume the same set of facts as those just presented with one exception. Suppose that Dryden believes that customer demand for the van will diminish over time. When the van is new, it looks more attractive, drives better, and is less susceptible to breakdowns. Accordingly, more people will want to use the van when it is new. As it ages, fewer and fewer people will be willing to rent the vehicle. As a result, the van will be used less frequently as time goes by. Since the purpose of depreciation is to reflect asset use, the amount of depreciation expense should be higher when the van is new and should decline as the van ages. A method of depreciation known as **double-declining balance depreciation** is specifically designed to recognize larger amounts of depreciation in the earlier stages of an asset's life and progressively lower levels of expense as the asset ages. Since the double-declining balance method recognizes depreciation expense more rapidly than the straight-line method, it is sometimes referred to as an *accelerated depreciation method.* The amount of depreciation to recognize under the double-declining balance method can be determined by performing three simple computations.

L.O. 5

Explain how expense recognition (i.e. depreciation) affects financial statements throughout the life cycle of a tangible asset.

1. **Determine the straight-line rate.** If the asset is depreciated evenly over its useful life, the portion depreciated each year can be determined by dividing the full use (100%) by the expected useful life of the asset. For example, since Dryden's van was expected to have a 4-year useful life, the straight-line rate is 25% (100% ÷ 4 years) per year.

EXHIBIT 9–4		
General Journal Entries		
Account Title	**Debit**	**Credit**
Cash	25,000	
Contributed Captial		25,000
Entry on January, 20X1, to record capital acquistion		
Van	24,000	
Cash		24,000
Entry on January 1, 20X1, to record investment in van		
Cash	8,000	
Revenue		8,000
Revenue Recognition entries on December 31, 20X1–20X5		
Depreciation Expense	5,000	
Accumulated Depreciation		5,000
Expense recognition entries on December 31, 20X1–20X5		
Cash	4,500	
Accumulated Depreciation	20,000	
Van		24,000
Gain of Sale of Van		500
Entry on January 1, 20X5, to record asset disposal		

2. **Determine the double-declining balance rate.** Multiply the straight-line rate by 2 (i.e., *double* the rate). The double-declining-balance rate for the van is 50% (25% × 2).

3. **Apply the double-declining balance rate to the book value.** Multiply the double-declining-balance rate by the book value of the asset *at the beginning of the period* (i.e., **book value** being historical cost less the amount of *accumulated depreciation*).

Applying the computations to Dryden's van will produce the following schedule of charges for the years 20X1 through 20X4:

Year	Book Value at Beginning of Period	×	Double the Straight-Line Rate	=	Annual Depreciation Expense	
20X1	($24,000 − $0)	×	0.5	=	$12,000	
20X2	($24,000 − $12,000)	×	0.5	=	6,000	
20X3	($24,000 − $18,000)	×	0.5	=	~~3,000~~	2,000
20X4	($24,000 − $20,000)	×	0.5	=	~~2,000~~	0

Computations for the third year are complicated by the fact that *the book value of an asset cannot be depreciated below its salvage value.* Since the van cost $24,000 and had a $4,000 salvage value, the total amount of cost to be depreciated is $20,000 ($24,000 − $4,000). Since $18,000 ($12,000 + $6,000) of the cost is depreciated in the first 2 years, only $2,000 ($20,000 − $18,000) more can be depreciated. Accordingly, the $3,000 formula value is ignored in year 3 because it exceeds the $2,000 maximum. Similarly, the formula value for 20X4 is ignored because the maximum allowable depreciation was charged in the first 3 years.

Exhibit 9–5 is a full set of financial statements prepared under the assumption that Dryden is using double-declining-balance depreciation. Trace the depreciation charges shown in the exhibit to the financial statements. Observe how the amount of depreciation expense is larger in the earlier years and smaller in the later years of the asset's life. Since the van is used more during the early years, it is logical to assume higher amounts of revenue during those years. We presume a revenue stream of $15,000, $9,000, $5,000, and $3,000 for the years 20X1, 20X2, 20X3, and 20X4, respectively. These amounts are reflected in the statements in Exhibit 9–5.

Since the use of the asset is directly related to the production of revenue, the double-declining-balance method smoothes the amount of net income reported on the income statement. The high revenues produced by the extensive use of the

EXHIBIT 9–5

Financial Statements under Double-Declining Balance Depreciation

DRYDEN ENTERPRISES
Financial Statements

Income Statements

	20X1	20X2	20X3	20X4	20X5
Rent Revenue	$15,000	$ 9,000	$ 5,000	$ 3,000	$ 0
Depreciation Expense	(12,000)	(6,000)	(2,000)	0	0
Operating Income	3,000	3,000	3,000	3,000	0
Gain	0	0	0	0	500
Net Income	$ 3,000	$ 3,000	$ 3,000	$ 3,000	$ 500

Balance Sheets

	20X1	20X2	20X3	20X4	20X5
Assets					
Cash	$16,000	$25,000	$30,000	$33,000	$37,500
Van	24,000	24,000	24,000	24,000	0
Accumulated Depreciation	(12,000)	(18,000)	(20,000)	(20,000)	0
Total Assets	$28,000	$31,000	$34,000	$37,000	$37,500
Equity					
Contributed Capital	$25,000	$25,000	$25,000	$25,000	$25,000
Retained Earnings	3,000	6,000	9,000	12,000	12,500
Total Equity	$28,000	$31,000	$34,000	$37,000	$37,500

Statements of Cash Flows

	20X1	20X2	20X3	20X4	20X5
Operating Activities					
Inflow from Customers	$15,000	$ 9,000	$ 5,000	$ 3,000	$ 0
Investing Activities					
Outflow to Purchase Van	(24,000)				
Inflow from Sale of Van					4,500
Financing Activities					
Inflow from Capital Acquisition	25,000				
Net Change in Cash	16,000	9,000	5,000	3,000	4,500
Beginning Cash Balance	0	16,000	25,000	30,000	33,000
Ending Cash Balance	$16,000	$25,000	$30,000	$33,000	$37,500

asset in the first years are offset by high expenses that reflect the corresponding level of asset use. Similarly, declining levels of use produce lower levels of expense as well as revenue. As a result, net income remains constant at a level of $3,000 per year.

How does accelerated depreciation improve financial reporting? Compare the income figures in Exhibit 9–5 with the outcome that would have occurred had Dryden used the straight-line method. Given the revenue stream in Exhibit 9–5, a constant $5,000 per year depreciation charge would have resulted in reported net income of $10,000, $4,000, $0, and − $2,000 for 20X1, 20X2, 20X3, and 20X4, respectively. These figures suggest a state of steadily declining economic viability, while in fact the company is performing as expected. As a result, use of straight-line depreciation would have provided a false impression of managerial performance. As this discussion implies, financial reporting provides a more accurate representation of business activity when expense recognition is closely aligned with asset use.

Effects during Other Phases of the Life Cycle

The effects of acquiring the financing, investing the funds, and retiring the asset are not changed by the method of depreciation. Accordingly, descriptions of the effects of the accounting events in these life-cycle phases are the same as under the straight-line approach. If you need reinforcement in this area, review the appropriate sections in the previous coverage. Similarly, the recording procedures are not affected by the depreciation method. Different depreciation methods affect only the amounts of the transactions, not the accounts included in the entries. To avoid redundancy, the general journal entries are not shown for the double-declining balance or the units-of-production depreciation methods.

Units-of-Production Depreciation

L.O. 5

Explain how expense recognition (i.e. depreciation) affects financial statements throughout the life cycle of a tangible asset.

Given the need to match expense recognition with asset use, a third depreciation method has been developed to reflect asset use that fluctuates from one accounting period to another. For example, suppose that Dryden experiences a demand for rentals that is dependent on general economic conditions. In a robust economy, travel increases and the demand for renting the van is high. In a stagnant economy, demand for van rentals declines. Accordingly, the pattern of asset use varies from one accounting period to the next, depending on the state of the economy. Under these circumstances, it is more reasonable to use some measure of total production, rather than time, as the basis for determining the amount of depreciation. For a van, the number of miles driven may represent a reasonable measure of total production. If the asset to be depreciated were a saw used to cut pieces of wood into baseball bats, an appropriate measure of total production would be the number of bats that the saw was expected to produce during its useful life. In other words, the basis for measuring production depends on the nature of the asset being depreciated.

To illustrate the computation of depreciation under the **units-of-production** method, assume that Dryden measures asset use according to the number of miles that the van is driven each year. Furthermore, assume that Dryden expects the van to have a useful life of 100,000 miles. The first step in determining the amount of depreciation expense is the computation of the cost per unit of production. In the case of the van, the amount can be determined by dividing the total depreciable cost (historical cost − salvage value) by the number of units of total expected productive capacity (100,000 miles). Accordingly, the cost per mile is $0.20 ([$24,000 cost − $4,000 salvage] ÷ 100,000 miles). The depreciation expense is computed by multiplying the cost per mile by the number of miles driven. Based on mileage records that show the van was driven 40,000 miles, 20,000 miles, 30,000 miles, and 15,000 miles in 20X1, 20X2, 20X3, and 20X4, respectively, Dryden developed the following schedule of depreciation charges.

Year	Cost Per Mile (a)	Miles Driven (b)	Depreciation Expense (a × b)
20X1	$.20	40,000	$8,000
20X2	.20	20,000	4,000
20X3	.20	30,000	6,000
20X4	.20	15,000	~~3,000~~ 2,000

As with the double-declining balance method, the asset's book value cannot be depreciated below the salvage value. Since $18,000 of cost is depreciated in the first 3 years of operation, and since total depreciable cost is $20,000 ($24,000 cost − $4,000 salvage), only $2,000 ($20,000 − $18,000) of cost is charged to depreciation in year 4, even though the application of the computational formula suggests a $3,000 charge. As the preceding table indicates, the general formula for determining the amount of units-of-production depreciation is as follows:

$$\frac{\text{Cost} - \text{Salvage Value}}{\text{Total Estimated Units of Production}} \times \begin{array}{c} \textbf{Units of Production} \\ \textbf{in Current} \\ \textbf{Accounting Period} \end{array} = \begin{array}{c} \textbf{Annual} \\ \textbf{Depreciation} \\ \textbf{Expense} \end{array}$$

Exhibit 9–6 is a full set of financial statements that assume that Dryden uses units-of-production depreciation. Again, it is logical to assume that revenue will fluctuate with asset use. The exhibit assumes that Dryden collected cash revenue of $11,000, $7,000, $9,000, and $5,000 for 20X1, 20X2, 20X3, and 20X4, respectively. Notice that the revenue pattern fluctuates with the depreciation charges, thereby resulting in a constant amount of $3,000 per year of reported net income.

Comparing the Methods

Note that the total amount of depreciation expense recognized under all three methods was $20,000. The different depreciation methods affect the timing of recognition but not the total amount of cost to be recognized. The different methods simply assign the $20,000 to different accounting periods. Exhibit 9–7 is a graphical depiction of the three methods. Each method offers unique opportunities to match expense recognition with asset use. As indicated earlier, matching asset use with expense recognition is desirable because it improves the capacity of financial reports to more accurately describe managerial performance.

Income Tax Considerations

Although matching asset use with revenue recognition is important for the assessment of managerial performance, it is not a meaningful consideration for the payment of income taxes. Here the objective is to minimize the tax expense by reporting the highest amount of depreciation permissible under the law. The

L.O. 7

Understand how different depreciation methods affect the amount of expense recognized in a particular accounting period.

L.O. 8

Identify tax issues related to long-term operational assets.

EXHIBIT 9–6

Financial Statements under Units-of-Production Depreciation

DRYDEN ENTERPRISES
Financial Statements

Income Statements

	20X1	20X2	20X3	20X4	20X5
Rent Revenue	$11,000	$ 7,000	$ 9,000	$ 5,000	$ 0
Depreciation Expense	(8,000)	(4,000)	(6,000)	(2,000)	0
Operating Income	3,000	3,000	3,000	3,000	0
Gain	0	0	0	0	500
Net Income	$ 3,000	$ 3,000	$ 3,000	$ 3,000	$ 500

Balance Sheets

Assets					
Cash	$12,000	$19,000	$28,000	$33,000	$37,500
Van	24,000	24,000	24,000	24,000	0
Accumulated Depreciation	(8,000)	(12,000)	(18,000)	(20,000)	0
Total Assets	$28,000	$31,000	$34,000	$37,000	$37,500
Equity					
Contributed Capital	$25,000	$25,000	$25,000	$25,000	$25,000
Retained Earnings	3,000	6,000	9,000	12,000	12,500
Total Equity	$28,000	$31,000	$34,000	$37,000	$37,500

Statements of Cash Flows

Operating Activities					
Inflow from Customers	$11,000	$ 7,000	$ 9,000	$ 5,000	$ 0
Investing Activities					
Outflow to Purchase Van	(24,000)				
Inflow from Sale of Van					4,500
Financing Activities					
Inflow from Capital Acquisition	25,000				
Net Change in Cash	12,000	7,000	9,000	5,000	4,500
Beginning Cash Balance	0	12,000	19,000	28,000	33,000
Ending Cash Balance	$12,000	$19,000	$28,000	$33,000	$37,500

maximum depreciation currently allowed under tax law is computed under an accelerated depreciation method known as the **Modified Accelerated Cost Recovery System (MACRS)**; MACRS specifies the length of useful life permitted for designated categories of assets. For example, under the law, a 5-year useful life must be used for automobiles, light trucks, technological equipment, and other similar types of assets. In contrast, a 7-year life has to be used for office furniture, fixtures, and many types of conventional machinery. In total, the law classifies depreciable property into one of six categories: 3-year property, 5-year property, 7-year property, 10-year property, 15-year property, and 20-year property. Tables have been established for each category that specify the percentage of cost that can be expensed (i.e., deducted) in determining the amount of taxable income. A tax table for 5- and 7-year property is shown here as an example:

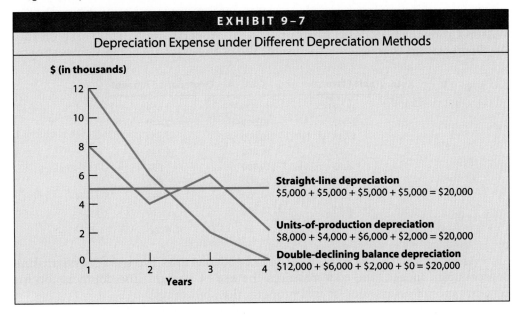

EXHIBIT 9–7

Depreciation Expense under Different Depreciation Methods

Straight-line depreciation
$5,000 + $5,000 + $5,000 + $5,000 = $20,000

Units-of-production depreciation
$8,000 + $4,000 + $6,000 + $2,000 = $20,000

Double-declining balance depreciation
$12,000 + $6,000 + $2,000 + $0 = $20,000

Year	5-Year Property, %	7-Year Property, %
1	20.00	14.29
2	32.00	24.49
3	19.20	17.49
4	11.52	12.49
5	11.52	8.93
6	5.76	8.92
7		8.93
8		4.46

The amount of depreciation that can be deducted each year for tax purposes is determined by multiplying the cost of a depreciable asset by the percentage shown in the table. For example, the depreciation expense for year 1 of a 7-year property asset is determined by multiplying the cost of the property by 14.29%. Year 2's depreciation is found by multiplying the cost by 24.49%.

The tables contain some apparent inconsistencies. For example, if MACRS is an accelerated depreciation method, why is less depreciation permitted in year 1 than in years 2 and 3? Also, why is depreciation computed in year 6 for property with a 5-year life and in year 8 for property with a 7-year life? In fact, these conditions are the logical consequence of what is known as the **half-year convention.** Taxpayers purchase assets at different times during any single tax period. Indeed, given the number of U.S. taxpayers, someone buys an asset every single day of the year. Accordingly, to accurately measure asset use for all taxpayers, the tax code would have to include 365 tables (i.e., one table beginning with each day of the year) for each class of property. Given the six classes of property, the code would have to include 2,190 tables (365 × 6). Obviously, the accurate measurement of asset use is an impractical goal. To eliminate this potential problem, the tax law ignores the specific dates of acquisition and disposal. Instead, the code requires one-half year's depreciation to be charged in the year in which an asset is acquired and one-half year's depreciation in the year of disposal. Accordingly, the percentages shown in the table for the first and last year represent amounts of depreciation for one-half year instead of the actual time of usage.

To illustrate the computation of depreciation under MACRS, assume that Wilson Company purchased furniture (7-year-property) for $10,000 cash on July 21. Depreciation charges over the useful life of the asset are computed as shown:

Year	Table Factor, %	×	Cost	=	Depreciation Amount
1	14.29		10,000		$ 1,429
2	24.49		10,000		2,449
3	17.49		10,000		1,749
4	12.49		10,000		1,249
5	8.93		10,000		893
6	8.92		10,000		892
7	8.93		10,000		893
8	4.46		10,000		446
Total over useful life					$10,000

As an alternative to MACRS, the tax code permits the use of straight-line depreciation. Indeed, the code requires the use of straight-line depreciation for certain types of assets such as real property (i.e., buildings).

To minimize taxes and to provide a meaningful representation of managerial performance, companies may calculate depreciation twice: once for financial reporting purposes and once for tax returns. There are no requirements that force consistency between depreciation methods reported in the financial statements and those used on the income tax return. For example, straight-line depreciation may be used in the financial statements presented to stockholders and creditors, while MACRS is used on the tax return. Under these circumstances, taxes are reduced because higher depreciation charges would be shown on the tax return. However, it is important to note that in later years, taxes will be higher because under MACRS the amount of depreciation declines as the asset becomes older (i.e., under accelerated depreciation, the higher charges in early years are offset by lower charges in later years). Accordingly, taxes are not avoided but are delayed instead. The amounts of taxes delayed for future payment are called **deferred taxes.** Deferred taxes are shown on the balance sheet after the presentation of liabilities and before the presentation of equity. Although deferring taxes is not as good as never having to pay them, the delay is still advantageous because of the opportunity to invest the money in assets that produce revenue during the period of the delay.

Revision of Estimates

L.O. 9

Understand how revising estimates affects financial statements.

When an estimate of salvage, life, or total production is revised during the use of the asset, nothing is done to correct the previously reported figures. There are so many estimates used in accounting that revisions are considered a normal part of business. The new information is simply incorporated into any present and future calculations.

To illustrate, assume that McGraw Company purchased an asset on January 1, 20X3, for $50,000. The machine was estimated to have a useful life of 8 years and a salvage value of $3,000. McGraw used the straight-line depreciation method and determined the annual depreciation charge according to the following formula:

$$(\$50,000 - \$3,000) \div 8 \text{ years} = \$5,875 \text{ per year}$$

Using these assumptions, consider the possibility of two different revisions occurring in the fifth year. At the beginning of the fifth year, the amount in accumulated depreciation is $23,500 ($5,875 × 4), making the book value $26,500 ($50,000 − $23,500). Each revision should be considered separately from the other.

Revision of Life

If McGraw revised the expected life to 14 years rather than 8 years, the asset would now be expected to last 10 more years rather than 4 more years. Salvage remains at $3,000, so computation of each remaining year's depreciation is

$$(\$26,500 \text{ book value} - \$3,000 \text{ salvage}) \div 10\text{-year remaining life} = \$2,350$$

Revision of Salvage

If the original expected life remained the same but the salvage value were revised to $6,000, the depreciation charge for each of the remaining 4 years would be

$$(\$26,500 \text{ book value} - \$6,000 \text{ salvage}) \div 4\text{-year remaining life} = \$5,125$$

Notice that it was not important when the company revised its estimates during the year. The entire year's depreciation was considered changed.

Continuing Expenditures for Plant Assets

Over the life of an asset, it is often necessary or advisable to make expenditures to maintain or improve the asset's productivity. These expenditures fall into two classifications: those that are expensed and those that are capitalized.

L.O. 10

Understand how continuing expenditures for operational assets affect financial statements.

Costs That Are Expensed

When an expenditure that is necessary to keep the asset in good working order is made, it is expensed in the period in which it is incurred. These costs consist of such things as routine maintenance and minor repairs. Extending the example for the machine owned by McGraw Company, we assume that $500 was spent to lubricate and replace minor parts of the machine. The effect of the expenditure on the financial statements and the journal entry necessary to record it are as follows:

Assets	=		Equity		Rev.	−	Exp.	=	Net Inc.	Cash Flow
Cash	=	C. Cap.	+	Ret. Earn.						
(500)	=	0	+	(500)	0	−	500	=	(500)	(500) OA

Account Title	Debit	Credit
Repairs Expense	500	
Cash		500

Costs That Are Capitalized

Capital expenditures are usually substantial amounts spent to improve the quality or extend the life of an asset. As such, these expenses affect the remainder of the asset's life and should not be treated as an expense of the current accounting period. Capital expenditures are accounted for in one of two possible ways, depending on whether the cost incurred is considered to *improve the quality* or *extend the life* of the asset. In practice, it is often difficult to determine exactly which effect an expenditure will have. Thus, the selection of which approach to use is often a matter of judgment.

Improving Quality

When an expenditure is deemed to have improved the quality of an asset, the cost is added to the asset's historical cost, and this extra amount ends up being expensed over the remainder of the asset's life through the process of depreciation. Continuing with the McGraw Company example, we assume that a major expenditure costing $4,000 is made in the fifth year. The expenditure acts to improve the productive capacity of the company's machine. Recall that the asset originally cost $50,000, had an estimated salvage of $3,000, and had a predicted life of 8 years. If we assume straight-line depreciation, the amount in accumulated depreciation at the beginning of the fifth year is $23,500 ($5,875 × 4), making the book value $26,500 ($50,000 − $23,500). The effect of the $4,000 expenditure on the financial statements and the journal entry necessary to record it are as follows:

Assets				=	Equity			Rev.	−	Exp.	=	Net Inc.	Cash Flow	
Cash	+	Mach.	−	A. Dep.	=	C. Cap.	+	Ret. Earn.						
(4,000)	+	4,000	−	n/a	=	n/a	+	n/a	n/a	−	n/a	=	n/a	(4,000)	IA

Account Title	Debit	Credit
Machine	4,000	
Cash		4,000

After we recognize the effects of the expenditure, the machine contains a $54,000 balance, resulting in a book value of $30,500 ($54,000 − $23,500). The depreciation charges for the remaining 4 years are calculated as follows:

($30,500 book value − $3,000 salvage) ÷ 4-year remaining life = $6,875

Extending Life

When a company undertakes a capital expenditure that extends the life of the asset but not its quality, it is theoretically objectionable to increase the cost of the asset. Instead, the expenditure is looked on as canceling some of the depreciation that has already been charged to expense. The event is still an asset exchange. Cash decreases, and the book value of the machine increases. The increase in the book value of the machine is accomplished by reducing the amount in the contra asset account, Accumulated Depreciation. To illustrate, assume that instead of increasing productive capacity, McGraw's $4,000 expenditure had merely extended the useful life of the machine by 2 years. The effect of the event on the financial statements and the journal entry necessary to record it are as follows:

Assets				=	Equity			Rev.	−	Exp.	=	Net Inc.	Cash Flow	
Cash	+	Mach.	− A. Dep.	=	C. Cap.	+	Ret. Earn.							
(4,000)	+	n/a	− (4,000)	=	n/a	+	n/a	n/a	−	n/a	=	n/a	(4,000)	IA

Account Title	Debit	Credit
Accumulated Depreciation—Machine	4,000	
Cash		4,000

Notice that the book value is now the same as if the $4,000 had been added to the Machine account ($50,000 cost − $19,500 adjusted balance in accumulated depreciation = $30,500). Depreciation expense for each of the remaining 6 years is calculated as follows:

($30,500 book value − $3,000 salvage) ÷ 6-year remaining life = $4,583.33

Natural Resources

Natural resources are recorded in the books at the cost of acquisition. Other costs frequently capitalized in natural resource accounts include the cost of exploration necessary to locate resources and payments for corresponding geographic surveys and estimates.

Depletion is a process of expense recognition[1] that systematically allocates the cost of natural resources to expense. The units-of-production method is the most common method used to calculate depletion. The cost of the natural resource is divided by the total estimated number of units to be extracted to produce a charge per unit. If Apex Coal Mining paid $4,000,000 cash to purchase a mine with an estimated 16,000,000 tons of coal, the unit charge is $.25 per ton ($4,000,000 ÷ 16,000,000). If Apex mines 360,000 tons of coal in the first year, the depletion charge is $90,000 (360,000 × $.25). The depletion of a natural resource has the same effect on the accounting equation as other expense recognition events. Assets (in this case, a *coal mine*) decrease and equity decreases because the depletion expense reduces net income and ultimately retained earnings. The effect on the financial statements and the journal entries necessary to record the acquisition and depletion of the coal mine are as follows:

Assets			=	Equity			Rev.	−	Exp.	=	Net Inc.	Cash Flow	
Cash	+	Coal Mine	=	C. Cap.	+	Ret. Earn.							
(4,000,000)	+	4,000,000	=	n/a	+	n/a	n/a	−	n/a	=	n/a	(4,000,000)	IA
n/a	+	(90,000)	=	n/a	+	(90,000)	n/a	−	90,000	=	(90,000)	n/a	

---

[1]In practice, the depletion charge is considered a product cost and allocated between inventory and cost of goods sold. This text adopts the simplifying assumption that all resources are sold in the same accounting period in which they are extracted. Accordingly, the full amount of the depletion charge is expensed in the period in which the resources are extracted.

Account Title	Debit	Credit
Coal Mine	4,000,000	
Cash		4,000,000
Depletion Expense	90,000	
Coal Mine		90,000

The decrease in the asset, coal mine, could have been shown in a contra account titled *Allowance for Depletion*. When the Allowance for Depletion account is used, it has the same relationship with natural resources as the Accumulated Depreciation account has with property, plant, and equipment. However, most companies follow the practice of deducting the amount of depletion directly from the asset account. Accordingly, this book emphasizes the direct deduction approach.

Intangible Assets

Intangible assets provide rights, privileges, and special opportunities to businesses. As with other long-term operational assets, intangibles are capitalized in asset accounts at historical cost and are systematically expensed over their useful lives. The expense recognition process for intangible assets is called *amortization*. It is helpful to note that *amortization*, *depletion*, and *depreciation* are simply different terms used to describe the expense allocation process applied to different types of assets. There are two classes of intangibles: those that are specifically identifiable and goodwill.

Specifically Identifiable Intangibles

Some of the more common, specifically identifiable intangible assets include trademarks, patents, copyrights, and franchises. The common and unique features of each of these assets are now discussed.

Intangible assets are normally amortized (expensed) on a straight-line basis. In determining how much to expense each year, the company must consider three possible lifetimes: (1) the legal life of the intangible, (2) the useful life of the intangible, and (3) a 40-year maximum amortization period imposed by GAAP. *An intangible asset should be amortized over the shortest of these three possible lives.*

To illustrate, assume that Flowers Industries pays $44,000 cash to purchase a patent. Although the patent has a legal life of 17 years, Flowers estimates that it will be useful for only 11 years. Furthermore, the patent is also subject to the limits of accounting practice, which restrict the lives of all intangibles to a period of no more than 40 years. The annual charge is $4,000 ($44,000 ÷ 11 years). The effect of the purchase of the patent and its amortization on the financial statements and the journal entries necessary to record the events are as follows.

Assets			=	Equity			Rev.	−	Exp.	=	Net Inc.	Cash Flow
Cash	+	Patent	=	C. Cap.	+	Ret. Earn.						
(44,000)	+	44,000	=	n/a	+	n/a	n/a	−	n/a	=	n/a	(44,000) IA
n/a	+	(4,000)	=	n/a	+	(4,000)	n/a	−	4,000	=	(4,000)	n/a

Account Title	Debit	Credit
Patent	44,000	
Cash		44,000
Amortization Expense, Patent	4,000	
Patent		4,000

Notice that the patent was credited directly. This is the usual method; however, an allowance account can be used if the company so desires. Popular practice is to reduce the asset account directly, and for that reason this book adheres to this method for examples and problems.

We just discussed the general accounting practices for the acquisition and amortization of intangibles. Each type of intangible has different characteristics and purposes; some of the unique features of the more common intangible assets are now described.

Trademarks

A **trademark** is a name or symbol that identifies a company or an individual product. Some trademarks that you may be familiar with are the Polo emblem, the name *Coca-Cola*, and the slogan, "You can be sure if it's Westinghouse." Trademarks are registered with the federal government and have an indefinite legal lifetime. Therefore, they are usually amortized over the 40-year life dictated by GAAP.

The costs to be capitalized include those required to develop the trademark and those incurred to defend it. When trademarks are purchased, the amount of the purchase price is capitalized in the Trademark account. Companies want their trademarks to become familiar but fear the situation in which the trademark begins to be treated as the generic name for a product. Companies in this predicament expend large amounts to protect the trademark, including legal fees and extensive advertising programs to educate consumers. Some well-known trademarks that have been subject to this problem are Coke, Xerox, Kleenex, and Vaseline.

Patents

As previously indicated, a **patent** is an exclusive right to produce and sell a commodity that has one or more unique features. Patents granted by the U.S. Patent Office have a legal life of 17 years. Patents may be purchased, leased, or developed within the company. When a patent is developed by a company, the question arises as to what costs should be capitalized in the Patent account. Clearly, the legal costs associated with obtaining and defending the patent are capitalized. What about the research and development costs incurred to make the product that is being patented? Product research and development is frequently unsuccessful; companies spend hundreds of millions of dollars on research projects that lead nowhere. Because it is difficult to determine which research development costs will produce future revenues, GAAP requires that these costs be expensed in the period in which they are incurred. Accordingly, the costs capitalized in the Patent account are usually limited to a purchase price and/or legal fees.

Copyrights

A **copyright** protects the writings, musical compositions, and other works of art for the exclusive benefit of the creator or persons assigned the right by the creator. The cost of a copyright includes the purchase price or the legal costs associated with obtaining and defending the copyright. Copyrights are granted by the federal government for a period defined as the life of the creator plus 50 years. A radio commercial could use a Bach composition as background music with no legal ramifications; however, if "Streets of Philadelphia" were desired instead, royalties would have to be paid to Bruce Springsteen or to the assigned owner of the copyright. Often the cost of a copyright is expensed very early because future royalties may be uncertain.

focus on international issues

U.S. GAAP: A Competitive Disadvantage?

here are many differences among the accounting rules of different countries, but perhaps none cause as much concern to companies involved in global competition as the rules related to accounting for goodwill and research and development (R&D).

Suppose that company A pays $300,000 to purchase company B's assets. Furthermore, suppose company B's assets have a market value of only $200,000. In the United States, the $100,000 difference is classified as *goodwill*. It is capitalized in an intangible asset account and amortized (expensed) over its useful life. In the United Kingdom, the treatment could be very different. A U.K. company is allowed to "charge" the entire $100,000 *directly against retained earnings* in the year of the purchase. Normally, a cost is placed in an asset account and then expensed. When the expense is recognized, net income decreases and retained earnings decreases. Under the U.K. approach, you simply skip the income statement. You do not recognize an expense. Instead, you make a direct reduction to retained earnings. As a result, goodwill does not affect a U.K. company's current or future income statements. Based on income statement analysis, company A would look more profitable if it used U.K. GAAP than if it used U.S. GAAP.

Next, suppose company X is a pharmaceutical company that spends $10 million on the R&D of a new drug. Under U.S. GAAP, the company is required to expense the $10 million immediately. In Japan, the company is allowed to capitalize the cost in an asset account and then to expense it gradually over the useful life of the asset. Accordingly, in the year in which R&D costs are incurred, a U.S. company reports more expense and less income than its Japanese counterpart.

Some businesspeople believe that U.S. GAAP can put U.S. companies at a competitive disadvantage in the search for capital. Certainly, the rules pertaining to goodwill and R&D demonstrate how U.S. companies may be forced to report lower earnings. Foreign companies that report higher earnings may be able to attract international investors who would otherwise invest in U.S. companies. Keep in mind that well-informed business professionals know how different accounting rules affect a company's financial statements. If they believe that U.S. GAAP cause a company's earnings to be understated, they take this into consideration when making investment decisions.

Franchises

Franchises are exclusive rights to sell products or perform services in certain geographic areas. Franchises may be granted by governments or private business. An example of a franchise granted by the federal government is a broadcasting license. Fast-food restaurant chains, private labels such as Healthy Choice, and real estate offices are examples of private business franchises. Franchises can cost hundreds of thousands and even millions of dollars. These costs are capitalized in an asset account and amortized over the life of the asset. The legal and useful lives of a franchise are frequently difficult to define. Furthermore, when the cost of a franchise is small, amortization charges based on a 40-year accounting life become immaterial. Accordingly, judgment is often crucial to the establishment of an amortization schedule for franchise costs.

Goodwill

Goodwill is the added value of a business that is attributable to favorable factors such as reputation, location, and superior products. To better understand goodwill, consider the most popular restaurant in your town. If the owner sold the restaurant, do you think the purchase price would simply be the total value of the chairs, tables, kitchen equipment, and building? Certainly not, because much of the restaurant's value lies in its popularity, in other words, its ability to generate a high return.

Calculation of goodwill can be very complex; here we present a very simple example to illustrate how it is determined. Suppose that the accounting records of a restaurant named Bendigo's show assets of $200,000, liabilities of $50,000, and equity of $150,000. A food services company that wants to acquire the restaurant agrees to purchase it by assuming the liabilities and paying the owner $300,000 cash. The amount of goodwill acquired can be determined by subtracting the fair market value of the assets on the day of purchase from the amount paid to acquire them. In this case, the amount paid includes $50,000 of liabilities that were assumed plus $300,000 cash. Assume that an independent appraiser assessed the fair market value of the assets as $280,000 on the date of purchase. Under these circumstances, the amount of goodwill purchased is $70,000 ([$50,000 + $300,000] − $280,000). The effect of the purchase on the financial statements of the buyer is shown here:

Assets			=	Liab.	+	Equity	Rev.	−	Exp.	=	Net Inc.	Cash Flow
Cash	+ Rest. Assets	+ Goodwill										
(300,000) +	280,000	+ 70,000	=	50,000	+	n/a	n/a	−	n/a	=	n/a	(300,000) IA

The journal entry required to record the acquisition of the restaurant follows:

Account Title	Debit	Credit
Restaurant Assets	280,000	
Goodwill	70,000	
Cash		300,000
Liabilities		50,000

reality bytes

In October 1998, Clorox Company agreed to pay $1.6 billion to purchase First Brands Corporation. First Brands is the company that sells Glad plastic bags and STP oil treatment, among other products. At the time, First Brands' balance sheet showed net assets (i.e., assets minus liabilities) of approximately $620 million. Why would Clorox pay the owners of First Brands more than 2 times the book value of the assets shown on the company's balance sheet? Clorox was willing to pay more than the book value for First Brands Corporation for two reasons. First, the value of the assets on First Brands' balance sheet represents the historical cost of the assets (i.e., the amount First Brands paid to obtain the assets). The current market value of these assets may be higher than the historical cost, especially for assets such as the trademarks for Glad and STP. Second, Clorox probably believed that First Brands had *goodwill* that enables a company to use its assets in a manner that will provide above-average earnings. In other words, Clorox was buying a hidden asset not shown on First Brands' books.

©John S. Reid

Note that the fair market value of the restaurant assets represents the historical cost to the new owner. Accordingly, it becomes the basis for future depreciation charges.

Balance Sheet Presentation

In this chapter, you learned about the acquisition, expense allocation, and disposal of a wide range of long-term assets. Exhibit 9–8 is a typical balance sheet that exemplifies many of the assets discussed.

Understanding How Expense Recognition Affects Financial Performance Measures

L.O. 14

Understand how expense recognition choices and industry characteristics affect financial performance measures.

It should be clear from the preceding discussion that the amount of expense recognized in any particular accounting period depends on which allocation method (straight line, accelerated, or units of production) a company uses. Ideally, a company should use the method that best matches the pattern of asset use. More expense should be recognized in periods in which the assets are used extensively. Smaller amounts should be recognized in periods in which assets

EXHIBIT 9–8			
Balance Sheet Presentation of Operational Assets			
Balance Sheet			
Long-Term Assets			
Plant and Equipment			
Buildings	$4,000,000		
Less: Accumulated Depreciation	(2,500,000)	$1,500,000	
Equipment	1,750,000		
Less: Accumulated Depreciation	(1,200,000)	550,000	
Total Plant and Equipment			$2,050,000
Land			850,000
Natural Resources			
Mineral Deposits (Less: Depletion)		2,100,000	
Oil Reserves (Less: Depletion)		890,000	
Total Natural Resources			2,990,000
Intangibles			
Patents		38,000	
Goodwill		175,000	
Total Intangible Assets			213,000
Total Long-Term Assets			$6,103,000

are used infrequently. Unfortunately, the pattern of asset use may be uncertain when the expense recognition method is selected. Since asset use occurs in the future, different managers may have different opinions about how assets will be used. As a result, managers of different companies may use different expense recognition methods for similar assets. Accordingly, companies affected by an identical set of economic circumstances could produce significantly different financial statements.

Effect of Judgment and Estimation

As a simple example, assume that two companies, Alpha and Zeta, are affected by the same set of economic events in 20X1 and 20X2. Both generate revenue of $50,000 and incur cost of goods sold of $30,000 during each year. In 20X1, each company pays $20,000 for an asset with an expected useful life of 5 years and no salvage value. How will the companies' financial statements differ if one uses straight-line depreciation and the other uses the double-declining balance method? To answer this question, begin by computing the depreciation expense for both companies for 20X1 and 20X2.

If Alpha Company uses straight-line depreciation, the amount of depreciation for 20X1 and 20X2 is computed as follows:

(Cost − Salvage) ÷ No. of Years = Depreciation Expense per Year
($20,000 − $0) ÷   5   = $4,000

In contrast, if Zeta Company uses the double-declining balance method, Zeta recognizes the following amounts of depreciation expense for 20X1 and 20X2:

(Cost − Accumulated Depreciation) × 2 × (Straight-Line Rate) = Depreciation Expense

20X1	($20,000 − $0)	×	(2 × [1 ÷ 5])	=	$8,000
20X2	($20,000 − $8,000)	×	(2 × [1 ÷ 5])	=	$4,800

Based on these computations, the income statements for the two companies appear as follows:

Income Statements					
	20X1		**20X2**	
	Alpha Co.	**Zeta Co.**	**Alpha Co.**	**Zeta Co.**
Sales	$50,000	$50,000	$50,000	$50,000
Cost of Goods Sold	(30,000)	(30,000)	(30,000)	(30,000)
Gross Margin	20,000	20,000	20,000	20,000
Depreciation Expense	(4,000)	(8,000)	(4,000)	(4,800)
Net Income	$16,000	$12,000	$16,000	$15,200

The relevant sections of the balance sheets are as follows:

Plant Assets					
	20X1		**20X2**	
	Alpha Co.	**Zeta Co.**	**Alpha Co.**	**Zeta Co.**
Asset	$20,000	$20,000	$20,000	$20,000
Accumulated Depreciation	(4,000)	(8,000)	(8,000)	(12,800)
Book Value	$16,000	$12,000	$12,000	$ 7,200

Clearly, the depreciation method selected by each company affects its expenses and thus its net income and retained earnings. The method used also affects the accumulated depreciation, which in turn affects the book value of plant assets and total assets. Financial statement analysis is affected if it is based on ratios whose computations use any of the items mentioned. Previously defined ratios that are affected include the (1) debt-to-assets ratio, (2) return-on-assets ratios, (3) return-on-equity ratio, and (4) return-on-sales ratio.

Choosing the depreciation method is not the only aspect of expense recognition that can vary for two companies. The companies may also make different assumptions about the useful lives and salvage values of plant assets. Thus, even if the same depreciation method is used, depreciation expenses may still differ. To illustrate, assume that both Delta Airlines and United Airlines buy an airplane that costs $40 million and both decide to use straight-line depreciation. Delta might choose to depreciate the plane over 15 years while United may choose 20 years. If salvage value is expected to be negligible, the depreciation expense per year for each airplane is

	(Cost − Salvage)	÷	**Estimated Life**	=	**Depreciation Expense**
Delta	($40 million − $0)	÷	15	=	$2.7 million
United	($40 million − $0)	÷	20	=	$2.0 million

Based on these numbers, Delta's depreciation expense is 33% higher than United's for the next 15 years. This difference could have a significant impact on the companies' financial statements and the ratios used to evaluate financial performance. Although the performance measures are affected, the real economic substance as measured by cash flow is not affected. Accordingly, an uninformed user may conclude that performance differences exist when, in fact, they do not.

Users of accounting information must be aware of all accounting policies a company uses before that company's financial statements and financial ratios can be analyzed. For this reason, companies that wish to have their statements audited are required to disclose all significant accounting policies such as depreciation and inventory cost flow methods used. This disclosure is usually provided in the footnotes that accompany the financial statements.

Effect of Industry Characteristics

Financial performance measures can also be affected by industry characteristics. Some businesses use more depreciable assets than other businesses. For example, companies in manufacturing industries rely on heavy machinery, while insurance companies use human capital. Accordingly, manufacturing companies can be expected to have relatively higher depreciation charges than insurance companies. The ability to evaluate a company's financial performance requires an understanding of the industry in which it operates. To illustrate how the type of industry can affect financial reporting, review the information in Exhibit 9–9. This exhibit compares the ratio of sales to property, plant, and equipment for two companies for each of three different industries. These data are for 1997.

The table indicates that for every $1 invested in property, plant, and equipment, Lehman Brothers produced $56.55 of sales. In contrast, Southern Co. produced only $.53 in sales for each $1 it invested in operational assets. In other words, the higher the investment in operational assets, the lower the ratio.

Considering the amount of equipment required to produce and deliver electricity, it is not surprising that utility companies have a much lower ratio of sales to property, plant, and equipment than stock brokerage companies do. However, it might be surprising to some readers that the ratio for airlines is more than 3 times higher than that for utility companies. Given the investment in airplanes, we expect that airline companies would have a smaller ratio. Passengers flying on an airline tend to underestimate the investment in human capital because they see only the crew plus a few employees inside the air terminal. Airlines have many employees, such as reservation agents, schedulers, baggage handlers, and mechanics, whom most passengers do not see.

L.O. 1

Understand why some businesses generate high revenue with few operational assets.

©Jim Pickerall 1992/ Stock Boston

EXHIBIT 9–9		
Industry Data Reflecting the Use of Operational Assets		
Industry	**Company**	**Sales ÷ Property, Plant, and Equipment**
Stock Brokerage	Lehman Brothers	56.55 times
	Merrill Lynch	15.30
Airlines	Delta	1.76
	United	1.61
Utilities	Amer. Electric	0.53
	Southern Co.	0.53

A failure to understand that financial statements reflect industry characteristics can lead to a misinterpretation of managerial performance. For example, the fact that an insurance company uses fewer operational assets than a utility company is not an indication that insurance companies are better managed. Rather, it means that the two companies operate in different business environments. When you use financial ratios for performance evaluation, it is critically important that you compare ratios of companies from the same industry. Also, do not forget that even within the same industry, companies may use different expense recognition methods and may reach different conclusions regarding the estimated useful lives and salvage values of their operational assets. Financial statement analysis requires not only an understanding of the technical aspects of accounting but also the ability to assess the reasonableness of management's judgments.

A LOOK

BACK

In Chapter 3 you learned that the primary objective of depreciation is to match the cost of a long-term operational asset with the revenues that the asset is expected to generate. Chapter 9 showed how this basic concept can be extended to natural resources, through depletion, and to intangible assets, through amortization. This chapter also explained how different methods can be used to account for the same event (e.g., straight-line versus double-declining balance depreciation). Accordingly, companies experiencing the exact same business events could produce different financial statements. The alternative accounting methods for depreciating, depleting, or amortizing assets include the (1) straight-line, (2) double-declining-balance, and (3) units-of-production methods.

The *straight-line method* recognizes the same amount of expense during each accounting period. The amount of the expense to recognize is determined by the formula ([cost − salvage] ÷ number of years of useful life). The *double-declining balance method* recognizes proportionately larger amounts of expense in the early years of an asset's useful life and increasingly smaller amounts of expense in the later years of the asset's useful life. The formula for calculating expense based on the double-declining balance method is (book value at beginning of period × double the straight-line rate). The *units-of-production method* recognizes expense in direct proportion to the number of units produced during an accounting period. The amount of expense to recognize each period is computed by the formula ([cost − salvage] ÷ total estimated units of production = allocation rate × units of production in current accounting period).

The chapter also discussed *MACRS depreciation*, which is a tax treatment. MACRS is an accelerated method that is not acceptable under GAAP rules for public reporting. Accordingly, a company may use MACRS depreciation for tax purposes and straight-line or one of the other methods for public reporting. As a result, differences may exist in the amount of tax expense and the amount of tax liability. Such differences are called *deferred taxes.*

Chapter 9 covered the accounting treatment for *changes in estimates* such as the useful life or the salvage value. Under these circumstances, the amount of depreciation recognized previous to the change in estimate is not affected. Instead, the remaining book value of the asset is expensed over its remaining useful life.

Three types of costs occur after an asset has been placed into service. These costs include maintenance, quality improvement, and extensions of useful life. *Maintenance costs* are expensed in the period in which they are incurred. *Costs that improve the quality* of an asset are added to the cost of the asset, thereby increasing the book value and the amount of future depreciation charges. *Costs that extend the useful life* of an asset are subtracted from the asset's Accumulated Depreciation account, thereby increasing the book value and the amount of future depreciation charges.

A LOOK FORWARD

In Chapter 10 we leave the assets section of the balance sheet and investigate some interesting issues related to accounting for long-term liabilities. As you will learn, tax issues are also important when considering the consequences of borrowing money.

KEY TERMS

Accelerated Depreciation Methods Depreciation methods that recognize depreciation expense more rapidly in the early stages of an asset's life than in the later stages of the asset's life. *(p. 411)*

Accumulated Depreciation A contra asset account that indicates the sum of all depreciation expenses recognized for an asset since the date of acquisition. *(p. 414)*

Amortization A method to systematically allocate the costs of intangible assets to expense over their useful lives. *(p. 409)*

Basket Purchase The acquisition of several assets in a single transaction, with no specific cost attributed to each asset. *(p. 410)*

Book Value The original cost of an asset minus any accumulated depreciation. Alternatively, the undepreciated amount to date. *(p. 416)*

Capital Expenditures (on an existing asset) Substantial amounts of funds spent to improve the quality or to extend the life of an asset. *(p. 424)*

Contra Asset Account An account that has the effect of reducing the asset account with which it is associated. *(p. 414)*

Copyright The protection of writings, musical compositions, and other works of art for the exclusive use of the creator or persons assigned the right by the creator. *(p. 428)*

Deferred Taxes Taxes that are not paid until future years because of the difference in accounting methods selected for financial statements and methods required for tax purposes (i.e., a company may select straight-line depreciation for financial statement reporting but will be required to use MACRS for tax reporting). *(p. 422)*

Depletion A method to systematically allocate the costs of natural resources to expense over their useful lives. *(p. 425)*

Depreciation A method to systematically allocate the costs of tangible assets to expense over their useful lives. *(p. 408)*

Double-Declining Balance Depreciation A depreciation method that recognizes larger amounts of depreciation in the early stages of an asset's life and progressively smaller amounts as the asset ages. *(p. 415)*

Estimated Life The time for which an asset is expected to be used by a business. *(p. 412)*

Franchise The exclusive right to sell products or perform services in certain geographic areas. *(p. 429)*

Goodwill The added value of a successful business that is attributable to factors that enable the business to earn above-average profits. Such factors include reputation, location, and superior products. Stated differently, it is the excess paid for an existing business over the appraised value of the net assets. *(p. 429)*

Half-Year Convention The tax rule that requires 6 months of depreciation expense be taken in the year of purchase of the asset and the year of disposal regardless of the purchase date. *(p. 421)*

Historical Cost Concept The accounting concept that requires assets to be recorded and carried on the books at the amount paid for them. *(p. 409)*

Intangible Assets Assets that may be represented by pieces of paper or contracts that appear tangible; however, the true value of the intangible asset lies in the rights and privileges extended to its owners. *(p. 408)*

Long-Term Operational Assets Assets that are used by a business to generate revenue. The condition of being used distinguishes them from assets that are sold (inventory) and assets that are held (investments). *(p. 407)*

Modified Accelerated Cost Recovery System (MACRS) The prescribed method of depreciation for tax purposes that provides the maximum depreciation expense deduction under the tax law. *(p. 420)*

Natural Resources Mineral deposits, oil and gas reserves, reserves of timber, mines, and quarries are examples of natural assets, sometimes called *wasting assets* because their value "wastes away" as the resources are removed. *(p. 408)*

Patent A legal right granted by the U.S. Patent Office ensuring a company, or an individual, the exclusive right to a product or process. *(p. 427)*

Property, Plant, and Equipment A category of assets, sometimes called *plant assets*, used to produce products or to carry on the administrative and selling functions of a business. Assets in this category include machinery and equipment, buildings, and land. *(p. 408)*

Relative Fair Market Value A method of assigning value to individual assets acquired in a basket purchase. Each asset is assigned a percentage of the total price paid for all the assets. The percentage assigned is equal to the market value of a particular asset divided by the total of the market values of all the assets acquired in the basket purchase. *(p. 410)*

Salvage Value The estimated recoverable amount to be received at the time the asset is removed from service. *(p. 412)*

Straight-Line Depreciation The method of depreciation that allocates the cost of an asset to expense in equal amounts over the life of the asset. *(p. 411)*

Tangible Assets Assets that can be "touched," such as equipment, machinery, natural resources, and land. *(p. 408)*

Trademark A name or symbol that identifies a company or an individual product. *(p. 427)*

Units-of-Production Depreciation A method of depreciation that is based on a measure of production rather than a measure of time. For example, an automobile may be depreciated based on the expected miles to be driven rather than on a specific number of years. *(p. 418)*

QUESTIONS

1. What is the difference in the functions of long-term operational assets and investments?
2. What is the difference between tangible and intangible assets? Give an example of each.
3. What is the difference between goodwill and specifically identifiable intangible assets?
4. Define *depreciation*. What kind of asset is depreciated?
5. Why are natural resources called *wasting assets*?
6. Is land a depreciable asset? Why or why not?
7. Define *amortization*. To what kind of assets does amortization apply?
8. Explain the historical cost concept as it applies to long-term operational assets. Why is the book value of an asset likely to be different from the current market value of the asset?
9. What are the different kinds of expenditures that might be included in the recorded cost of a building?
10. What is a basket purchase of assets? When a basket purchase is made, how is cost assigned to individual assets?
11. What is the life cycle of a long-term operational asset?
12. Explain straight-line, units-of-production, and double-declining balance depreciation. When is it appropriate to use each of these depreciation methods?
13. What effect does the recognition of depreciation expense have on total assets? On total equity?
14. Does the recognition of depreciation expense affect the statement of cash flows? Why or why not?
15. MalMax purchased a depreciable asset. What would be the difference in total assets at the end of the first year if MalMax chooses straight-line depreciation versus double-declining balance?
16. John Smith mistakenly expensed the cost of a long-term tangible fixed asset. Specifically, he charged the cost of a truck to a delivery expense account. How will this error affect the income statement and the balance sheet in the year in which the mistake is made?
17. What is *salvage value*?
18. What type of account (classification) is accumulated depreciation?
19. Why is depreciation that has been recognized over the life of the asset shown in a contra account? Why not just reduce the asset account?
20. Assume that a piece of equipment cost $5,000 and had accumulated depreciation recorded of $3,000. What is the book value of the equipment? Is the book value equal to the fair market value of the equipment? Explain.

21. Why may a company choose to depreciate one piece of equipment using the double-declining balance method and another piece of equipment using straight-line depreciation?

22. Explain MACRS depreciation. When is it appropriate to use MACRS depreciation?

23. Does the method of depreciation required to be used for tax purposes reflect the use of a piece of equipment? Can you use double-declining balance depreciation for tax purposes?

24. Define *deferred taxes*. Where does the account *Deferred Taxes* appear in the financial statements?

25. Why may it be necessary to revise the estimated life of a plant asset? When the estimated life is revised, does it affect the amount of depreciation per year? Why or why not?

26. How do you account for capital expenditures made to improve the quality of a capital asset? Would your answer change if the expenditure extended the life of the asset but did not improve quality? Explain.

27. When a long-term operational asset is sold for a gain, how is the balance sheet affected? Is the statement of cash flows affected? If so, how?

28. Define *depletion*. What is the most commonly used method of computing depletion?

29. List several of the most common intangible assets. How is the life determined that is to be used to compute amortization?

30. What are some differences among U.S. GAAP and GAAP of other countries?

31. How do differences in expense recognition and industry characteristics affect financial performance measures?

EXERCISES

Unless specifically stated, income tax considerations should be ignored in all exercises and problems.

Using Long-Term Operational Assets in a Business

EXERCISE 9-1
L.O. 3

Required

Give some examples of long-term operational assets that each of the following companies is likely to own: *(a)* Memphis Transit Authority, *(b)* Princess Cruise Lines, *(c)* Redd Pest Control, and *(d)* Arkansas Diamond Mining Company.

Identifying Long-Term Operational Assets

EXERCISE 9-2
L.O. 3

Required

Which of the following items should be classified as long-term operational assets?

a.	Cash	*g.*	Inventory
b.	Buildings	*h.*	Patent
c.	Production machinery	*i.*	Tract of timber
d.	Accounts receivable	*j.*	Land
e.	Certificate of deposit (6 months)	*k.*	Computer
f.	Franchise	*l.*	Goodwill

Classifying Tangible and Intangible Assets

EXERCISE 9-3
L.O. 2

Required

Identify each of the following long-term operational assets as either tangible (T) or intangible (I).

a.	Plant warehouse	*g.*	Delivery van
b.	Drill press	*h.*	Land
c.	Patent	*i.*	Franchise
d.	Oil well	*j.*	Computer
e.	Desk	*k.*	Copyright
f.	Goodwill	*l.*	Copper mine

EXERCISE 9-4   **Determining the Cost of an Asset**
L.O. 4   Southwest Lumber Co. purchased an electronic saw used to cut various types and sizes of logs. The saw had a list price of $70,000. The seller agreed to provide a 5% discount because Southwest paid cash. Delivery terms were FOB shipping point. Freight cost amounted to $400. Southwest had to hire an individual to operate the saw. The operator was trained to run the saw for a one-time training fee of $500. The operator was paid an annual salary of $20,000. The cost of the company's theft insurance policy increased by $1,100 per year as a result of the acquisition of the saw. The asset had a 4-year useful life and an expected salvage value of $5,000.

Required

Determine the cost amount to be capitalized in an asset account for the purchase of the saw.

EXERCISE 9-5   **Allocating Costs on the Basis of Relative Market Values**
L.O. 4   Pine Company purchased a building and the land upon which the building is situated for a total cost of $500,000 cash. The land was appraised at $150,000 and the building at $450,000.

Required

a.   What is the technical terminology applied to this acquisition?
b.   Determine the amount of cost to be assigned to the land and the amount to be assigned to the building.
c.   Would the company recognize a gain on the purchase? Why or why not?
d.   Record the purchase in a statements model like the following one.

Assets			=	Liab.	+	Equity	Rev.	−	Exp.	=	Net Inc.	Cash Flow
Cash	+ Land	+ Building										

EXERCISE 9-6   **Allocating Costs for a Basket Purchase**
L.O. 4   Bushby Company purchased a restaurant building, land, and equipment for $350,000. Bushby paid $50,000 in cash and issued a 20-year, 8% note to First Bank for the balance. The appraised value of the assets was as follows:

Land	$ 80,000
Building	200,000
Equipment	120,000
Total	$400,000

Required

a.   Compute the amount to be recorded on the books for each of the assets.
b.   Record the purchase in a horizontal statements model like the following one.

Assets				=	Liab.	+ Equity	Rev.	−	Exp.	=	Net Inc.	Cash Flow
Cash	+ Land	+ Building	+ Equip.									

c.   Prepare the general journal entry required to record the purchase.

EXERCISE 9-7   **Effect of Double-Declining Balance Depreciation on Financial Statements**
L.O. 5   Star Communications Company was started by acquiring $100,000 cash from the owners. The company purchased an asset that cost $80,000 cash on January 1, 20X1. The asset had an expected useful life of 4 years and an estimated salvage value of $10,000. Star Communications earned $46,000 and $32,500 of cash revenue during 20X1 and 20X2, respectively. Star Communications uses double-declining balance depreciation.

Required

Prepare an income statement, balance sheet, and statement of cash flows for 20X1 and 20X2. Use a vertical statements format. (*Hint:* It may be helpful to record the events in T-accounts prior to preparing the statements.)

Events Related to the Acquisition, Use, and Disposal of a Tangible Plant Asset—Straight-Line Depreciation

EXERCISE 9-8
L.O. 5, 6

Drew's Pizza purchased a delivery van on January 1, 20X1, for $24,000. In addition, Drew's had to pay sales tax and title fees of $800. The van is expected to have a 5-year life with an expected salvage value of $4,000.

Required

a. Using the straight-line method, compute the depreciation expense for 20X1 and 20X2.

b. Prepare the general journal entries to record the 20X1 depreciation.

c. Assume that the van was sold on January 1, 20X4, for $18,000. Prepare the journal entry for the sale of the van in 20X4.

Computing and Recording Straight-Line versus Double-Declining Balance Depreciation

EXERCISE 9-9
L.O. 7

At the beginning of 20X1, Precision Company purchased a new computerized drill press for $24,000. It is expected to have a 4-year life with a $2,000 salvage value.

Required

a. Compute the depreciation for each of the 4 years, assuming that the company uses

(1) Straight-line depreciation

(2) Double-declining-balance depreciation

b. Record the purchase of the drill press and the depreciation expense for the first year under straight-line and double-declining-balance methods in a financial statements model like the following one:

Assets			=	Equity		Rev.	–	Exp.	=	Net Inc.	Cash Flow
Cash	+ Drill Press	– A. Dep.	=	C. Cap.	+ Ret. Earn.						

c. Prepare the journal entries to recognize depreciation for each of the 4 years, assuming that the company uses

(1) Straight-line depreciation

(2) Double-declining balance depreciation

Effect of the Disposal of Plant Assets on the Financial Statements

EXERCISE 9-10
L.O. 6

A plant asset with a cost of $15,000 and accumulated depreciation of $12,500 is sold for $3,600.

Required

a. What is the book value of the asset at the time of sale?

b. What is the amount of gain or loss on the disposal?

c. How would the event affect net income (increase, decrease, no effect) and by how much?

d. How would the event affect the amount of total assets shown on the balance sheet (increase, decrease, no effect) and by how much?

e. How would the event affect the statement of cash flows (inflow, outflow, no effect) and in what section?

Double-Declining Balance and Units-of-Production Depreciation: Gain or Loss on Disposal

EXERCISE 9-11
L.O. 6, 7

Sandy's Service Co. purchased a new color copier at the beginning of 20X6 for $32,000. It is expected to have a 4-year useful life and a $3,000 salvage value. The expected copy production is estimated at 1,820,000 copies. Actual copy production for the 4 years was as follows:

20X6	560,000
20X7	550,000
20X8	370,000
20X9	460,000
Total	1,940,000

The copier was sold at the end of 20X9 for $4,500.

Required

a. Compute the depreciation expense for each of the 4 years, using double-declining balance depreciation.

b. Compute the depreciation expense for each of the 4 years, using units-of-production depreciation. (Round cost per unit to 3 decimals)

c. Calculate the amount of gain or loss from the sale of the asset under each of the depreciation methods.

EXERCISE 9-12
L.O. 8

Computing Depreciation for Tax Purposes

Vision Computer Company purchased $90,000 of equipment on November 1, 20X1.

Required

a. Compute the amount of depreciation expense that is deductible under MACRS for 20X1 and 20X2, assuming that the equipment is classified as 7-year property.

b. Compute the amount of depreciation expense that is deductible under MACRS for 20X1 and 20X2, assuming that the equipment is classified as 5-year property.

EXERCISE 9-13
L.O. 9

Revision of Estimated Useful Life

On January 1, 20X1, Duncan Milling Co. purchased a compressor and related installation equipment for $24,000. It had a 3-year estimated life with a $3,000 salvage value. Straight-line depreciation was used. At the beginning of year 3, Duncan revised the expected life of the asset to 4 years rather than 3 years. The salvage value was revised to $2,000.

Required

Compute the depreciation expense for each of the 4 years.

EXERCISE 9-14
L.O. 10

Distinguishing between Maintenance Costs and Capital Expenditures

David's Cleaning Service has just completed a minor repair on a service truck. The repair cost was $550, and the book value prior to the repair was $4,400. In addition, the company spent $5,000 to replace the roof on a building. The new roof extended the life of the building by 5 years. Prior to the roof replacement, the general ledger reflected the Building account at $80,000 and its Accumulated Depreciation account at $38,500.

Required

After the work was completed, what book value should appear on the balance sheet for the delivery truck and the building?

EXERCISE 9-15
L.O. 10

Effect of Maintenance Costs versus Capital Expenditures on Financial Statements

Yucon Construction Company purchased a forklift for $53,000 cash. It had an estimated useful life of 4 years and a $3,000 salvage value. At the beginning of the third year of use, the company spent an additional $5,000 that was related to the equipment. The company's financial condition just prior to this purchase is shown in the following statements model.

Assets			=	Equity			Rev.	−	Exp.	=	Net Inc.	Cash Flow
Cash	+ Forklift	− A. Dep.	=	C. Cap.	+	Ret. Earn.						
6,000	+ 53,000	− (25,000)	=	12,000	+	22,000	n/a	−	n/a	=	n/a	n/a

Required

Record the $5,000 expenditure in the statements model under each of the following *independent* assumptions:

a. The expenditure was made to cover the cost of routine maintenance.
b. The expenditure was made to prolong the life of the forklift.
c. The expenditure was made to improve the operating capacity of the forklift.

Effect of Maintenance Costs versus Capital Expenditures on Financial Statements

EXERCISE 9-16
L.O. 10

On January 1, 20X1, Sun Power Company overhauled four of its turbine engines that generate power for its customers. The overhaul resulted in a slight increase in the capacity of the engines to produce power. However, overhauls occur regularly at 2-year intervals and have been treated as maintenance expense in the past. Management is considering whether to capitalize this year's $26,000 cash cost in the engine asset account or to expense it as a maintenance expense. Assume that the engines have a remaining useful life of 2 years and no expected salvage value. Assume straight-line depreciation.

Required
a. Determine the amount of additional depreciation expense recognized in 20X1 and 20X2 if the cost is capitalized in the engine account.
b. Determine the amount of expense recognized in 20X1 and 20X2 if the cost is recognized as maintenance expense.
c. Determine the effect of the overhaul on cash flow from operating activities for 20X1 and 20X2 if the cost is capitalized and expensed through depreciation charges.
d. Determine the effect of the overhaul on cash flow from operating activities for 20X1 and 20X2 if the cost is recognized as maintenance expense.

Computing and Recording Depletion Expense

EXERCISE 9-17
L.O. 11

Central Sand and Gravel paid $450,000 to acquire 600,000 cubic yards of sand reserves. The following statements model reflects the financial condition just prior to the purchase of the sand reserves. The company extracted 300,000 cubic yards of sand in year 1 and 250,000 cubic yards in year 2.

Assets			=	Equity			Rev.	−	Exp.	=	Net Inc.	Cash Flow
Cash	+	Sand. Res.	=	C. Cap.	+	Ret. Earn.						
600,000	+	n/a	=	600,000	+	n/a	n/a	−	n/a	=	n/a	n/a

Required
a. Compute the depletion charge per unit.
b. Record the acquisition of the sand reserves and the depletion expense for years 1 and 2 in a financial statements model like the preceding one.
c. Prepare the general journal entries to record the depletion expense for years 1 and 2.

Computing and Recording the Amortization of Intangibles

EXERCISE 9-18
L.O. 12

Phoenix Manufacturing paid cash to purchase the assets of an existing company. Among the assets purchased were the following items:

Patent with 6 remaining years of legal life	$24,000
Goodwill with a 40-year accounting life	$60,000

Phoenix's financial condition just prior to the purchase of these assets is shown in the following statements model:

Assets					=	Liab.	+	Equity	Rev.	−	Exp.	=	Net Inc.	Cash Flow
Cash	+	Patent	+	Goodwill										
90,000	+	n/a	+	n/a	=	n/a	+	90,000	n/a	−	n/a	=	n/a	n/a

Required
a. Compute the annual amortization for these items.

b. Record the purchase of the assets and the related amortization for year 1 in a horizontal statements model like the preceding one.

c. Prepare the journal entries to record the purchase of the preceding assets and the related amortization for year 1.

EXERCISE 9-19   **Computing and Recording Goodwill**

L.O. 14   Fran Wallace purchased the business Alpha Peripherals for $300,000 cash and assumed all liabilities at the date of purchase. The books of Alpha show assets of $250,000, liabilities of $30,000, and equity of $220,000. An appraiser assessed the fair market value of the physical assets at $270,000 at the date of purchase. Wallace's financial condition just prior to the purchase is shown in the following statements model:

Assets			=	Liab.	+	Equity	Rev.	–	Exp.	=	Net Inc.	Cash Flow
Cash	+	Assets	+	Goodwill								
400,000	+	n/a	+	n/a	=	n/a	+	400,000	n/a	–	n/a	=	n/a	n/a

Required

a. Compute the amount of goodwill purchased.

b. Record the purchase in a financial statements model like the preceding one. Also record the amortization of goodwill for year 1 in the statements model. Goodwill is amortized using a 40-year life.

c. Prepare the journal entry for year 1 to record the amortization of goodwill.

PROBLEMS—SERIES A

PROBLEM 9-1A   **Accounting for Acquisition of Assets Including a Basket Purchase**

L.O. 4   Moon Co., Inc., made several purchases of long-term assets in 20X9. The details of each purchase are presented here.

New Office Equipment

1. List price: $30,000; terms: 2/10, n/30, paid within discount period.
2. Transportation-in: $800.
3. Installation: $1,100.
4. Damage during unloading: $500.
5. Six months later: routine maintenance, $150.

Basket Purchase of Copier, Typewriters, and Calculators for $9,000 with Fair Market Values

1. Copier, $5,000.
2. Typewriters, $3,000.
3. Calculators, $2,000.

Land for New Warehouse with an Old Building Torn Down

1. Purchase price, $100,000.
2. Demolition of building, $5,000.
3. Lumber sold from old building, $3,500.
4. Grading in preparation for new building, $7,000.
5. Construction of new building, $250,000.

Required

In each of these cases, determine the amount of cost to be capitalized in the asset account.

PROBLEM 9-2A   **Accounting for Depreciation over Multiple Accounting Cycles—Straight-Line Depreciation**

L.O. 5, 6   Dandy Company started business by acquiring $30,000 cash from the owners on January 1, 20X1. The cash received by the company was immediately used to purchase a $30,000 asset that had a $6,000 salvage value and an expected useful life of 4 years. The asset was used to produce the following revenue stream (assume that all revenue transactions are for cash). At the beginning of the fifth year, the asset was sold for $6,800 cash. Dandy used straight-line-depreciation.

	20X1	20X2	20X3	20X4	20X5
Revenue	$7,600	$7,200	$6,500	$6,000	$0

Required

Prepare an income statement, statement of changes in equity, balance sheet, and statement of cash flows as of the end of each of the five accounting periods. Present the statements in the form of a vertical statements model.

Purchase, Use, and Disposal of Tangible Asset—Three Accounting Cycles and Straight-Line Depreciation

PROBLEM 9-3A
L.O. 5, 9, 10

The following transactions relate to We-Haul Towing Service: Assume that the transactions regarding the purchase of the wrecker and any capital improvements occur on January 1.

20X7

1. Acquired $20,000 cash from the owners.
2. Purchased a used wrecker for $13,000 with an estimated useful life of 3 years and a $1,000 salvage value.
3. Paid sales tax on the wrecker of $900.
4. Collected $8,800 in towing fees.
5. Paid $1,500 for gasoline and oil.
6. Recorded straight-line depreciation on the wrecker for 20X7.
7. Closed the revenue and expense accounts to Retained Earnings for 20X7.

20X8

1. Paid for a tune-up for the wrecker's engine, $700.
2. Bought four new tires, $600.
3. Collected $9,000 in towing fees.
4. Paid $2,100 for gasoline and oil.
5. Recorded straight-line depreciation for 20X8.
6. Closed the revenue and expense accounts to Retained Earnings for 20X8.

20X9

1. Paid to overhaul the engine, $700, which extended the life of the wrecker to a total of 4 years.
2. Paid for gasoline and oil, $1,800.
3. Collected $15,000 in towing fees for 20X9.
4. Recorded straight-line depreciation for 20X9.
5. Closed the revenue and expense accounts for 20X9.

Required

a. Use a horizontal statements model like the following one to show the effect of these transactions on the elements of financial statements. Place a plus sign under the elements that increase, a minus sign under the elements that decrease, and the letters n/a under elements that are not affected. The first event is recorded as an example.

20X7 Event No.	Assets	=	Liabilities	+	Equity		Net Inc.	Cash Flow
1	+		n/a		+		n/a	+ FA

b. Use a vertical model to prepare financial statements for 20X7, 20X8, and 20X9. (*Hint:* It may be helpful for you to record the transactions in T-accounts before attempting to prepare the financial statements.)

PROBLEM 9-4A **Calculating Depreciation Expense Under Four Different Methods**
L.O. 6, 7 Flextron, Inc., manufactures sporting goods. The following information applies to a machine purchased on January 1, 20X1:

Purchase Price	$35,000
Delivery Cost	$1,000
Installation Charge	$500
Estimated Life	5 years
Estimated Units	70,000
Salvage Estimate	$1,500

During 20X1, the machine produced 13,000 units and during 20X2, it produced 10,500 units.

Required

Determine the amount of depreciation expense for 20X1 and 20X2 under each of the following methods:

a. Straight-line.

b. Double-declining balance.

c. Units-of-production.

d. MACRS, assuming that the machine is classified as 7-year property.

PROBLEM 9-5A **Effect of Straight-Line versus Double-Declining-Balance Depreciation on the Recognition of**
L.O. 5, 6, 7 **Expense and Gains or Losses**

Marianne's Office Service purchased a new computer system in 20X8 for $54,000. It is expected to have a 5-year useful life and a $4,000 salvage value. The company feels the equipment will be used more extensively in the early years.

Required

a. Calculate the depreciation expense for each of the 5 years, assuming the use of straight-line depreciation.

b. Calculate the depreciation expense for each of the 5 years, assuming the use of double-declining balance depreciation.

c. Would the choice of one depreciation method over another produce a different amount of cash flow for any year? Why or why not?

d. Assume that Marianne's Office Service sold the computer system at the end of the fourth year for $15,000. Compute the amount of gain or loss under each depreciation method.

e. Explain any differences in gain or loss due to using the different methods.

PROBLEM 9-6A **Computing and Recording Units-of-Production Depreciation**
L.O. 5, 6 Telecommunications & Transportation (T&T) purchased assembly equipment for $350,000 on January 1, 20X1. T&T's financial condition immediately prior to the purchase is shown in the following horizontal statements model:

Assets				=	Equity			Rev.	–	Exp.	=	Net Inc.	Cash Flow
Cash	+	Equip.	–	A. Dep.	=	C. Cap.	+	Ret. Earn.					
400,000	+	n/a	–	n/a	=	400,000	+	n/a	n/a	–	n/a	=	n/a	n/a

The equipment is expected to have a useful life of 500,000 machine hours with an estimated salvage value of $10,000. Actual machine-hour use was as follows:

20X1	160,000
20X2	165,000
20X3	175,000
20X4	140,000
20X5	60,000

Required

a. Compute the depreciation for each of the 5 years, assuming the use of units-of-production depreciation.

b. Assume that T&T earns $160,000 of cash revenue during 20X1. Record the purchase of the equipment and the recognition of the revenue and the depreciation expense for the first year in a financial statements model like the preceding one.

c. Assume that T&T sold the equipment at the end of the fifth year for $5,000. Record the general journal entry for the sale.

Determining the Effect of Depreciation Expense on Financial Statements

PROBLEM 9-7A
L.O. 7

Three different companies purchased a truck on January 1, 20X1, for $20,000. Each truck is expected to last 4 years or 100,000 miles. Salvage value is estimated to be $5,000. All three trucks are driven 33,000 miles in 20X1, 21,000 miles in 20X2, 20,000 miles in 20X3, and 30,000 miles in 20X4. Each of the three companies earns $15,000 of cash revenue during each of the four accounting periods. Company A uses straight-line depreciation, company B uses double-declining balance depreciation, and company C uses units-of-production depreciation.

Required

Answer each of the following questions. Ignore the effects of income taxes.

a. Which company will report the highest amount of net income during 20X1?

b. Which company will report the lowest amount of net income during 20X4?

c. Which company will have the highest book value reported on the 20X3 balance sheet?

d. Which company will have the highest amount of retained earnings reported on the 20X4 balance sheet?

e. Which company will have the lowest amount of cash flow from operating activities reported on the 20X3 statement of cash flows?

Accounting for Depletion

PROBLEM 9-8A
L.O. 9, 11

Delta Company engages in the exploration and development of many types of natural resources. In the last 2 years, the company has engaged in the following activities:

Jan. 1, 20X1   Purchased a silver mine estimated to contain 50,000 tons of silver ore for $800,000.

July 1, 20X1   Purchased a tract of timber for $1,000,000. The timber was estimated to yield 1,000,000 board feet of lumber and the residual value of the land was apportioned at $100,000.

Feb. 1, 20X2   Purchased a gold mine for $900,000 estimated to yield 12,000 tons of gold-veined ore.

Sept. 1, 20X2   Purchased an oil reserve for $680,000. The reserve was estimated to contain 95,000 barrels of oil, of which 10,000 would be unprofitable to pump.

Required

a. Prepare the journal entries necessary to account for the following:

(1) The 20X1 purchases.

(2) Depletion on the 20X1 purchases, assuming that 6,000 tons of silver are mined and 500,000 board feet of lumber are cut.

(3) The 20X2 purchases.

(4) Depletion on the four natural resource assets, assuming that 10,000 tons of silver ore, 250,000 board feet of lumber, 2,000 tons of gold ore, and 25,000 barrels of oil are extracted.

b. Prepare the portion of the December 31, 20X2, balance sheet dealing with natural resources.

c. Assume that in 20X3 the estimates revealed that only 8,000 tons of gold ore remain. Prepare the depletion entry in 20X3 to account for the extraction of 3,000 tons of gold ore.

PROBLEM 9-9A   **Recording Continuing Expenditures for Plant Assets**

L.O. 5, 6, 9, 10   Red Hall, Inc., had the following transactions recorded over the life of a piece of equipment purchased in 20X1:

Jan.	1, 20X1	Purchased equipment for $80,000. The equipment is estimated to have a 5-year life and $5,000 salvage value and is to be depreciated using the straight-line method.
Dec.	31, 20X1	Recorded depreciation expense for 20X1.
Sept.	30, 20X2	Incurred routine repairs costing $750.
Dec.	31, 20X2	Recorded depreciation expense for 20X2.
Jan.	1, 20X3	Made an adjustment costing $3,000 to the equipment. It improved the quality of the output but did not affect the life estimate.
Dec.	31, 20X3	Recorded depreciation expense for 20X3.
June	1, 20X4	Incurred $620 cost to oil and clean the equipment.
Dec.	31, 20X4	Recorded depreciation expense for 20X4.
Jan.	1, 20X5	Had the equipment completely overhauled at a cost of $8,000. The overhaul was estimated to extend the total life to 7 years.
Dec.	31, 20X5	Recorded depreciation expense for 20X5.
Oct.	1, 20X6	Received and accepted an offer of $18,000 for the equipment.

Required

a. Use a horizontal statements model like the following one to show the effect of these transactions on the elements of financial statements. Place a plus sign under the elements that increase, a minus sign under the elements that decrease, and the letters n/a under the elements that are not affected. The first event is recorded as an example.

Date	Assets	=	Liabilities	+	Equity	Net. Inc.	Cash Flow
Jan. 1, 20X1	+ −		n/a		n/a	n/a	− IA

b. Determine the amount of depreciation expense to be recognized on the income statements for the years 20X1 through 20X5.

c. Determine the amount of book value (i.e., cost − accumulated depreciation) that will appear on the balance sheets for the years 20X1 through 20X5.

d. Determine the amount of the gain or loss to be recognized on the disposal of the equipment on October 1, 20X6.

PROBLEM 9-10A   **Continuing Expenditures with Statements Model**

L.O. 9, 10   Tri-Star Company owned a service truck that was purchased at the beginning of 20X7 for $10,000. It had an estimated life of 3 years and an estimated salvage value of $1,000. Tri-Star uses straight-line depreciation. Its financial condition as of January 1, 20X9, is shown in the following financial statements model:

Assets				=		Equity			Rev.	−	Exp.	=	Net Inc.	Cash Flow
Cash	+	Truck	− A. Dep.	=	C. Cap.	+	Ret. Earn.							
7,000	+	10,000	− 6,000	=	2,000	+	9,000	n/a	−	n/a	=	n/a	n/a

In 20X9, Tri-Star spent the following amounts on the truck:

Jan.	4	Overhauled the engine for $2,000. The estimated life was extended 1 additional year, and the salvage value was revised to $2,000.
July	6	Obtained oil change and transmission service, $80.
Aug.	7	Replaced the fan belt and battery, $180.
Dec.	31	Purchased gasoline for the year, $2,500.
	31	Recognized 20X9 depreciation expense.

Required

a. Record the 20X9 transactions in a statements model like the preceding one.

b. Prepare journal entries for the 20X9 transactions.

Accounting for Intangible Assets

Green Vision purchased Atlantic Transportations Co. for $1,200,000. The fair market value of the assets purchased were as follows. No liabilities were assumed.

Equipment	$400,000
Land	100,000
Building	400,000
Franchise (10-year life)	20,000

Required

a. Calculate the amount of goodwill purchased.

b. Prepare the necessary journal entries to record the amortization of the franchise fee and goodwill at the end of year 1. Assume goodwill is amortized over 40 years.

PROBLEMS—SERIES B

Accounting for Acquisition of Assets Including a Basket Purchase

Optima Company made several purchases of long-term assets in 20X9. The details of each purchase are presented here.

New Office Equipment

1. List price: $25,000; terms: 1/10, n/30 paid within discount period.
2. Transportation-in: $900.
3. Installation: $650.
4. Damage during unloading: $450.
5. Eight months later: routine maintenance, $90.

Basket Purchase of Office Furniture, Copier, Computers, and Laser Printers for $40,000 with Fair Market Values

1. Office furniture, $6,000.
2. Copier, $6,000.
3. Computers, $28,000.
4. Laser printers, $10,000.

Land for New Headquarters with Old Barn Torn Down

1. Purchase price, $60,000.
2. Demolition of barn, $3,000.
3. Lumber sold from old barn, $2,000.
4. Grading in preparation for new building, $6,000.
5. Construction of new building, $180,000.

Required

In each of these cases, determine the amount of cost to be capitalized in the asset account.

Accounting for Depreciation over Multiple Accounting Cycles

Belle Company began operations when it acquired $25,000 cash from the owners on January 1, 20X5. The cash received by the company was immediately used to purchase a $25,000 asset that had a $3,000 salvage value and an expected useful life of 4 years. The asset was used to produce the following revenue stream (assume all revenue transactions are for cash). At the beginning of the fifth year, the asset was sold for $2,500 cash. Belle used straight-line depreciation.

	20X5	20X6	20X7	20X8	20X9
Revenue	$6,000	$6,200	$6,500	$7,000	$0

Required

Prepare an income statement, statement of changes in equity, balance sheet, and statement of cash flows as of the end of each of the five accounting periods.

PROBLEM 9-3B
L.O. 4, 5, 9, 10

Purchase, Use, and Disposal of Tangible Asset—Three Accounting Cycles and Double-Declining Balance Depreciation

The following transactions relate to Easy Solutions Services: Assume that the transactions regarding the purchase of the computer and any capital improvements occur on January 1.

20X7

1. Acquired $50,000 cash from the owners.
2. Purchased a computer system for $15,000. It has an estimated useful life of 5 years with a $3,000 salvage value.
3. Paid $500 sales tax on computer system.
4. Collected $20,000 in data entry fees from clients.
5. Paid $800 in service fees for computers.
6. Recorded double-declining balance depreciation on computer system for 20X7.
7. Closed the revenue and expense accounts to Retained Earnings for 20X7.

20X8

1. Paid $550 for repairs to computer system.
2. Bought a case of toner cartridges for the printers that are part of the computer system, $600.
3. Collected $30,000 in data entry fees from clients.
4. Paid $900 in service fees for computers.
5. Recorded double-declining balance depreciation for 20X8.
6. Closed the revenue and expense accounts to Retained Earnings for 20X8.

20X9

1. Paid $2,500 to upgrade the computer system, which extended the life of the system to 6 years.
2. Paid $800 in service fees for computers.
3. Collected $35,000 in data entry fees from clients.
4. Recorded double-declining balance depreciation for 20X9.
5. Closed the revenue and expense accounts for 20X9.

Required

a. Use a horizontal statements model like the following one to show the effect of these transactions on the elements of financial statements. Place a plus sign under the elements that increase, a minus sign under the elements that decrease, and the letters n/a under elements that are not affected. The first event is recorded as an example.

20X6 Event No.	Assets	= Liabilities	+ Equity	Net Inc.	Cash Flow
1	+	n/a	+	n/a	+ FA

b. Use a vertical model to prepare financial statements for 20X7, 20X8, and 20X9. (*Hint:* It may be helpful for you to record the transactions in T-accounts before attempting to prepare the financial statements.)

Calculating Depreciation Expense under Four Different Methods

Clark Service Company purchased a copier on January 1, 20X8, for $5,000. An additional $200 was paid for delivery charges. The copier was estimated to have a life of 4 years or 1,000,000 copies. Salvage was estimated at $1,200. The copier produced 230,000 copies in 20X8 and 250,000 in 20X9.

Required

Compute the amount of depreciation expense for Clark Service Company for calendar years 20X8 and 20X9, using these methods:

a. Straight-line.

b. Units-of-production.

c. Double-declining balance.

d. MACRS, assuming that the copier is classified as 5-year property.

Effect of Straight-Line versus Double-Declining Balance Depreciation on the Recognition of Expense and Gains or Losses

Speedy Laundry Services purchased a new steam press machine in 20X1 for $38,000. It is expected to have a 5-year useful life and a $3,000 salvage value. Speedy feels the equipment will be used more extensively in the early years.

Required

a. Calculate the depreciation expense for each of the 5 years, assuming the use of straight-line depreciation.

b. Calculate the depreciation expense for each of the 5 years, assuming the use of double-declining balance depreciation.

c. Would the choice of one depreciation method over another produce a different amount of annual cash flow for any year? Why or why not?

d. Assume that Speedy Laundry Services sold the steam press machine at the end of the third year for $20,000. Compute the amount of gain or loss under each depreciation method.

Computing and Recording Units-of-Production Depreciation

More Corporation purchased a delivery van for $35,000 in 20X7. More's financial condition immediately prior to the purchase is shown in the following horizontal statements model:

Assets				=	Equity			Rev.	−	Exp.	=	Net Inc.	Cash Flow
Cash	+ Equip.	− A. Dep.	=		C. Cap.	+	Ret. Earn.						
50,000	+ n/a	− n/a	=		50,000	+	n/a	n/a	−	n/a	=	n/a	n/a

The van is expected to have a useful life of 150,000 miles with an estimated salvage value of $5,000. Actual mileage was as follows:

20X7	50,000
20X8	70,000
20X9	58,000

Required

a. Compute the depreciation for each of the 3 years, assuming the use of units-of-production depreciation.

b. Assume that More earns $21,000 of cash revenue during 20X7. Record the purchase of the equipment and the recognition of the revenue and the depreciation expense for the first year in a financial statements model like the preceding one.

c. Assume that More sold the van at the end of the third year for $4,000. Record the general journal entry for the sale.

PROBLEM 9-7B

L.O. 7

Determining the Effect of Depreciation Expense on Financial Statements

Three different companies purchased machines on January 1, 20X5, for $60,000. Each machine is expected to last 5 years or 200,000 hours. Salvage value is estimated to be $4,000. All three machines are operated for 50,000 hours in 20X5, 55,000 hours in 20X6, 40,000 hours in 20X7, 44,000 hours in 20X8, and 31,000 hours in 20X9. Each of the three companies earns $30,000 of cash revenue during each of the 5 accounting periods. Company A uses straight-line depreciation, company B uses double-declining-balance depreciation, and company C uses units-of-production depreciation.

Required

Answer each of the following questions. Ignore the effects of income taxes.

a. Which company will report the highest amount of net income during 20X5?

b. Which company will report the lowest amount of net income during 20X7?

c. Which company will have the highest book value reported on the 20X7 balance sheet?

d. Which company will have the highest amount of retained earnings reported on the 20X8 balance sheet?

e. Which company will have the lowest amount of cash flow from operating activities reported on the 20X7 statement of cash flows?

PROBLEM 9-8B

L.O. 9, 11

Accounting for Depletion

Pacific Exploration Corporation engages in the exploration and development of many types of natural resources. In the last 2 years, the company has engaged in the following activities:

Jan. 1, 20X7   Purchased a coal mine estimated to contain 200,000 tons of coal for $720,000.

July 1, 20X7   Purchased a tract of timber for $1,800,000. The timber was estimated to yield 3,000,000 board feet of lumber and the residual value of the land was apportioned at $150,000.

Feb. 1, 20X8   Purchased a silver mine estimated to contain 30,000 tons of silver for $900,000.

Aug. 1, 20X8   Purchased an oil reserve for $880,000. The reserve was estimated to contain 250,000 barrels of oil, of which 30,000 would be unprofitable to pump.

Required

a. Prepare the journal entries necessary to account for the following:

(1) The 20X7 purchases.

(2) Depletion on the 20X7 purchases, assuming that 80,000 tons of coal are mined and 1,100,000 board feet of lumber are cut.

(3) The 20X8 purchases.

(4) Depletion on the four reserves, assuming that 62,000 tons of coal, 1,450,000 board feet of lumber, 9,000 tons of silver, and 78,000 barrels of oil are extracted.

b. Prepare the portion of the December 31, 20X8, balance sheet dealing with natural resources.

c. Assume that in 20X9 the estimates revealed that only 50,000 tons of coal remain. Prepare the depletion entry in 20X9 to account for the extraction of 35,000 tons of coal.

PROBLEM 9-9B

L.O. 5, 6, 9, 10

Recording Continuing Expenditures for Plant Assets

Summit, Inc., had the following transactions recorded over the life of a piece of equipment purchased in 20X2:

Jan. 1, 20X2   Purchased equipment for $24,000. The equipment is estimated to have a 5-year life and $4,000 salvage value and is to be depreciated using the straight-line method.

Dec. 31, 20X2	Recorded depreciation expense for 20X2.
May 5, 20X3	Incurred routine repairs costing $350.
Dec. 31, 20X3	Recorded depreciation expense for 20X3.
Jan. 1, 20X4	Made an adjustment costing $3,000 to the equipment. It improved the quality of the output, but did not affect the life estimate.
Dec. 31, 20X4	Recorded depreciation expense for 20X4.
Mar. 1, 20X5	Incurred $250 cost to oil and clean the equipment.
Dec. 31, 20X5	Recorded depreciation expense for 20X5.
Jan. 1, 20X6	Had the equipment completely overhauled at a cost of $5,600. The overhaul was estimated to extend the total life to 7 years.
Dec. 31, 20X6	Recorded depreciation expense for 20X6.
July 1, 20X7	Received and accepted an offer of $9,500 for the equipment.

Required

a. Use a horizontal statements model like the following one to show the effect of these transactions on the elements of financial statements. Place a plus sign under the elements that increase, a minus sign under the elements that decrease, and the letters n/a under elements that are not affected. The first event is recorded as an example.

Date	Assets	=	Liabilities	+	Equity	Net. Inc.	Cash Flow
Jan. 1, 20X2	+ −		n/a		n/a	n/a	− IA

b. Determine the amount of depreciation expense to be recognized on the income statements for the years 20X2 through 20X6.

c. Determine the amount of the book value (i.e., cost − accumulated depreciation) that will appear on the balance sheets for the years 20X2 through 20X6.

d. Determine the amount of the gain or loss to be recognized on the disposal of the equipment on July 1, 20X7.

Accounting for Continuing Expenditures

PROBLEM 9-10B
L.O. 9, 10

K&C Manufacturing paid $26,000 to purchase a computerized assembly machine on January 1, 20X1. The machine had an estimated life of 8 years and a $4,000 salvage value. K&C's financial condition as of January 1, 20X5, is shown in the following financial statements model.

Assets				=	Equity			Rev.	−	Exp.	=	Net Inc.	Cash Flow
Cash	+	Mach.	− A. Dep.	=	C. Cap.	+	Ret. Earn.						
15,000	+	26,000	− 11,000	=	8,000	+	22,000	n/a	−	n/a	=	n/a	n/a

K&C Manufacturing made the following expenditures on the computerized assembly machine in 20X5.

Jan. 2	Added an overdrive mechanism for $6,000 that would improve the overall quality of the performance of the machine but would not extend the life. The salvage was revised to $3,000.
Aug. 1	Performed routine maintenance, $920.
Oct. 2	Replaced some computer chips (considered routine), $620.
Dec. 31	Recognized 20X5 depreciation expense.

Required

a. Record the 20X5 transactions in a statements model like the preceding one.

b. Prepare journal entries for the 20X5 transactions.

PROBLEM 9-11B **Accounting for Intangible Assets**
L.O. 12 Gardenia Company purchased a fast-food restaurant for $1,395,000. The fair market value of the assets purchased was as follows. No liabilities were assumed.

Equipment	$600,000
Land	250,000
Building	155,000
Franchise (5-year life)	150,000

Required
a. Calculate the amount of goodwill purchased.
b. Prepare the necessary journal entries to record the amortization of the franchise fee and goodwill at the end of year 1. Assume goodwill is amortized over 40 years.

analyze, communicate, think

ACT 9-1   **BUSINESS APPLICATIONS CASE**   **Gateway 2000 Annual Report**

Required
Using the Gateway 2000 financial statements in Appendix B, answer the following questions:
a. What method of depreciation does Gateway use?
b. What type of intangible assets does Gateway have?
c. What does Gateway estimate the useful lives of its intangible assets to be?
d. What percentage of Gateway's "identifiable" assets are located in areas other than the Americas? (*Hint:* See Note 12.)

ACT 9-2   **GROUP ASSIGNMENT**   **Different Depreciation Methods**

Barker's Bakery makes cakes, pies, and other pastries that are sold to local grocery stores. The company experienced the following transactions during 20X8.
1. Started business when it acquired $60,000 cash from the owners.
2. Purchased bakery equipment for $46,000.
3. Had sales in 20X8 amounting to $42,000.
4. Paid $8,200 of cash for supplies used to make food products.
5. Incurred other operating expense of $12,000 for 20X8.
6. Recorded Depreciation assuming the equipment had a 4-year life and a $6,000 salvage value. MACRS recovery period is 5 years.
7. Paid income tax. The rate is 30%.

Required
a. Organize the class into three sections and divide each section into groups of 3 to 5 students. Assign each section a depreciation method: straight line, double declining balance, or MACRS.

Group Task
Prepare an income statement and balance sheet using the preceding information and the depreciation method assigned to your group.

Class Discussion
b. Have a representative of each section put its income statement on the board. Are there differences in net income? In the amount of income tax paid? How will these differences in the amount of depreciation expense change over the life of the asset?

REAL-WORLD CASE   Different Numbers for Different Industries

The following ratios are for four companies in different industries. Some of these ratios have been discussed in the textbook; others have not, but their names explain how the ratio was computed. The four sets of ratios, presented randomly, are as follows:

Ratio	Company 1	Company 2	Company 3	Company 4
Current assets ÷ total assets	76%	46%	20%	14%
Operating cycle	309 days	340 days	24 days	50 days
Return on assets	5.9%	14.4%	5.1%	10.0%
Gross margin	28.0%	81.8%	20.0%	35.9%
Sales ÷ property, plant and equipment	5.5 times	3.0 times	2.2 times	1.4 times
Sales ÷ current assets	1.0 times	1.8 times	8.3 times	7.0 times
Sales ÷ number of full-time employees	$368,733	$254,146	$28,632	$454,912

These are the four companies to which these ratios relate, listed in alphabetical order:

Anheuser Busch Companies, Inc., produces beer and related products. Its fiscal year-end was December 31, 1997.

Darden Restaurants, Inc., operates restaurants, including Red Lobster and The Olive Garden. Its fiscal year-end was May 31, 1998.

Deere & Company manufactures heavy equipment for construction and farming. Its fiscal year-end was October 31, 1997.

Pfizer, Inc., is a pharmaceutical company. Its fiscal year-end was December 31, 1997.

Required

Match each company with a set of the ratios. Write a memorandum explaining your decisions.

BUSINESS APPLICATIONS CASE

Effect of Depreciation on the Return-on-Assets Ratio

Freedom Publishing Company was started on January 1, 20X1, when it acquired a $60,000 cash contribution from the owners. The company immediately purchased a printing press that cost $60,000 cash. The asset had an estimated salvage value of $4,000 and an expected useful life of 8 years. Freedom used the asset during 20X1 to produce $20,000 of cash revenue. Assume that these were the only events affecting Freedom Publishing Company during 20X1.

Required

(*Hint:* It may be helpful if you prepare an income statement and a balance sheet prior to completing the following requirements.)

a. Compute the return-on-assets ratio as of December 31, 20X1, under the assumption that Freedom Publishing Company uses the straight-line depreciation method.

b. Recompute the ratio under the assumption that Freedom uses the double-declining-balance method.

c. Which depreciation method makes it *appear* that Freedom is utilizing its assets more effectively?

BUSINESS APPLICATIONS CASE   Effect of Depreciation on Financial Statement Analysis—Straight Line versus Double-Declining Balance

Sabot Company and Danco Company experienced the exact same set of economic events during 20X1. Both companies purchased a machine on January 1, 20X1. If we do not consider the effects of this purchase, the accounting records of both companies contained the following accounts and balances.

As of January 1, 20X1	
Total Assets	$100,000
Total Liabilities	$ 40,000
Total Equity	$ 60,000
During 20X1	
Total Sales Revenue	$ 50,000
Total Expenses (not including depreciation)	$ 30,000

Liabilities were not affected by transactions in 20X1.

The machine purchased by each company cost $20,000 cash. The machines had expected useful lives of 5 years and estimated salvage values of $2,000. Sabot uses straight-line depreciation. Danco uses double-declining balance depreciation.

Required

a. For both companies, calculate the balances in the preceding accounts on December 31, 20X1, after the effects of the purchase and depreciation of the machine have been applied. (*Hint:* The purchase of the equipment is an asset exchange transaction that does not affect total assets. However, the effect of depreciating the machine changes the amounts in total assets, expense, and equity [i.e., retained earnings]).

b. Based on the new account balances determined in part *a*, calculate the following ratios for both companies:

(1) Debt-to-assets ratio

(2) Return-on-assets ratio

(3) Return-on-equity ratio

c. Disregarding the effects of income taxes, which company produced the higher increase in real economic wealth during 20X1?

ACT 9-6

WRITING ASSIGNMENT
Impact of Historical Cost in Asset Presentation on the Balance Sheet
Assume that you are examining the balance sheets of two companies and note the following information:

	Company A	Company B
Equipment	$1,130,000	$900,000
Accumulated Depreciation	(730,000)	(500,000)
Book Value	$ 400,000	$400,000

Sam Gulio, a student who has had no accounting courses, remarks that company A and company B have the same amount of equipment.

Required

In a short paragraph, explain to Gulio that the two companies do not have equal amounts of equipment. You may want to include in your discussion comments regarding the possible age of each company's equipment, the impact of the historical cost concept on balance sheet information, and the impact of different depreciation methods on book value.

ACT 9-7

ETHICAL DILEMMA   Good Standards/Bad People or Just Plain Bad Standards?
Eleanor Posey has been reading the financial statements of her fiercest competitor, Barron Bailey, who like herself owns a regionally based heating and cooling services company. The statements were given to her by a potential investor, Jim Featherson, who told her that the statements convinced him to put his investment money in Bailey's business instead of Posey's. Bailey's statements show a net income figure 10% higher than that reported by Posey's company. When analyzing the footnotes to the financial statements, Posey noticed

that Bailey depreciates all property, plant, and equipment on a straight-line basis. In contrast, she depreciates only her building on a straight-line basis. All her equipment is depreciated by the double-declining balance method, which she believes matches the pattern of use of equipment in the heating and cooling services business.

Posey arranges a meeting with Featherson in which she attempts to inform him of the effects of depreciation on financial statements. She explains that Bailey's reporting practices are deceptive. While Bailey's income figure is higher now, the situation will reverse in the near future because her depreciation charges will decline, whereas Bailey's will stay constant. She explains that Bailey may even have to report losses because declines in the use of equipment also translate to lower revenues. Featherson tells Posey that Bailey's financial statements were audited by a very respectable CPA and that the company received an unqualified opinion. He tells her that nobody can predict the future and that he makes his decisions on the basis of current facts.

After Featherson leaves, Posey becomes somewhat resentful of the rules of accounting. Reporting depreciation in the way that she and her accountant believe to be consistent with actual use has caused her to lose an investor with a significant base of capital. She writes a letter to the chairperson of the Financial Accounting Standards Board in which she suggests that the board establish a single depreciation method that is required to be used by all companies. She argues that this approach would be better for investors who know little about accounting alternatives. If all companies were required to use the same accounting rules, comparability would be significantly improved.

Required

Answer the following questions under the assumption that actual use is, in fact, greater in the earlier part of the life of equipment in the heating and cooling services business.

a. Are Posey's predictions regarding Bailey's future profitability accurate? Explain.

b. Comment on the ethical implications associated with Bailey's decision to depreciate his equipment according to the straight-line method.

c. Comment on Posey's recommendation that the FASB eliminate alternative depreciation methods to improve comparability.

d. Comment on Featherson's use of accounting information.

ACT 9-8

EDGAR DATABASE   Comparing Microsoft and Intel

Required

a. Using the EDGAR database, fill in the missing data in the following table, drawing on the most current 10-K reports available for Microsoft Corporation and Intel Corporation. The information about "percentages" must be computed; it is not included in the companies' 10-Ks. See Appendix A for instructions on using EDGAR. (*Note:* The percentages for current assets and property, plant, and equipment will not sum to 100.)

	Current Assets	Property, Plant, and Equipment	Total Assets
Microsoft			
Dollar Amount	$	$	$
% of Total Assets	%	%	100%
Intel			
Dollar Amount	$	$	$
% of Total Assets	%	%	100%

b. Briefly explain why these two companies have different percentages of their assets in current assets versus property, plant, and equipment.

ACT 9-9

Reporting to the IRS versus Financial Statement Reporting

Crist Company operates a lawn mowing service. Crist has chosen to depreciate its equipment for financial statement purposes using the straight-line method. However, to save cash in the short run, Crist has elected to use the MACRS method for income tax reporting purposes.

Required

a. Set up the following spreadsheet to reflect the two different methods of reporting. Notice that the first two years of revenues and operating expenses are provided.

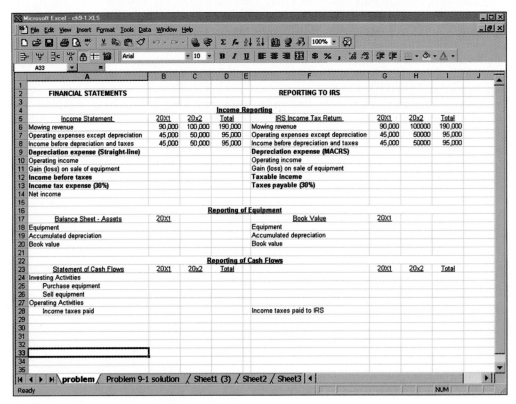

b. Enter in the effects of the following items for 20X1.

(1) At the beginning of 20X1, Crist purchased a lawn mower for $10,000 cash. Crist expects to use the mower for 5 years. Salvage value is estimated to be $2,000. As stated earlier, Crist uses the straight-line method of depreciation for financial statement purposes and the MACRS method for income tax purposes. Use formulas to calculate depreciation expense for each method.

(2) No equipment was sold during 20X1; therefore, no gain or loss would be reported this year.

(3) The income tax rate is 30%. To keep it simple, assume that the income tax payable was paid in 20X1.

(4) Complete the schedules for Income Reporting, Reporting of Equipment, and Reporting of Cash Flows for 20X1. Be sure to use formulas for all calculations.

c. Enter in the effects of the following items for 20X2.

(1) Crist used the mower for the entire 20X2 year. Enter 20X2 depreciation expense amounts for the Income Reporting section of your spreadsheet.

(2) At December 31, Crist sold the lawn mower for $7,000. Calculate the gain or loss on the sale for the Income Reporting section. Use formulas to make the calculations.

(3) The income tax rate is 30%. To keep it simple, assume that the income tax payable was paid in 20X2.

(4) Complete the schedules for Income Reporting and Reporting of Cash Flows for 20X2.

d. Calculate the Total columns for the Income Reporting and Reporting of Cash Flows sections.

e. Respond to the following.

(1) In 20X1, by adopting the MACRS method of depreciation for tax purposes instead of the straight-line method, what is the difference in the amount of cash paid for income taxes?

(2) In the long term, after equipment has been disposed of, is there any difference in total income under the two methods?

(3) In the long term, after equipment has been disposed of, is there any difference between total income tax expense and total income tax paid?

(4) Explain why Crist Company would use two different depreciation methods, particularly the straight-line method for the financial statements and an accelerated method (MACRS) for reporting to the IRS.

SPREADSHEET ASSIGNMENT **Alternative Methods of Depreciation**

ACT 9-10

Short Company purchased a computer on January 1, 20X1, for $5,000. An additional $100 was paid for delivery charges. The computer was estimated to have a life of 5 years or 10,000 hours. Salvage value was estimated at $300. During the 5 years, the computer was used as follows:

20X1	2,500 hours
20X2	2,400 hours
20X3	2,000 hours
20X4	1,700 hours
20X5	1,400 hours

Required

a. Prepare a 5-year depreciation schedule for the computer using the straight-line depreciation method. Be sure to use formulas for all computations including depreciation expense. Set up the following headings for your schedule:

		Beginning				Ending	
Year	Cost	Accumulated Depreciation	Book Value	Depreciation Expense	Cost	Accumulated Depreciation	Book Value

b. Prepare another 5-year depreciation schedule for the computer using the units-of-production method. Use (copy) the headings used in part a.

c. Prepare another 5-year depreciation schedule for the computer using the double-declining balance method. Use (copy) the headings used in part a.

d. Prepare another 5-year depreciation schedule for the computer using the MACRS method. Use (copy) the headings used in part a.

Spreadsheet Tip

After the year 20X1, enter subsequent dates automatically. Position the mouse in the lower right-hand corner of the highlighted cell "20X1" until a thin cross appears. Click and drag down four additional rows.

10 Accounting for Long-Term Debt

1 Comprehend the need for long-term debt financing.

2 Understand how the amortization of long-term notes affects financial statements.

3 Understand how a line of credit affects financial statements.

4 Describe the different types of bonds that companies issue.

5 Explain why bonds are issued at face value, a discount, or a premium.

6 Understand how bond liabilities and their related interest costs affect financial statements.

7 Explain how to account for bonds and their related interest costs.

8 Explain the advantages and disadvantages of debt financing.

9 Understand the time value of money.

Waste Management, Inc., had a net loss of $1.2 billion during its 1997 fiscal year. That same year, Waste Management had interest expense of $447 million. Does the fact that Waste Management had a net loss indicate that it probably was not able to pay the interest owed to its creditors?

Associated Press AP

Most businesses spend large sums of cash in the course of daily operations. They use cash to replace inventories, pay employees, settle liabilities, purchase supplies, obtain advertising, buy insurance, and so on. For most firms, expenditures for short-term operating activities consume only a portion of the funds needed to keep the business running. Expenditures for long-term operational assets, such as newer, more technologically advanced machinery or improved buildings and plant facilities require even larger amounts of cash. The need for cash is so exhaustive that most companies are forced to borrow some of the funds necessary to accomplish their goals and objectives.

A variety of options is available for the interest and principal payments associated with borrowed funds. Interest may be paid annually, semiannually, or monthly or may be added to the principal balance of the debt and paid at maturity. Interest rates may remain the same over the term of the loan or may fluctuate with market conditions. Rates that do not change over the life of a loan are called **fixed rates;** those that fluctuate are called **variable interest rates.** The principal (i.e., amount borrowed) may be repaid in one lump sum at the maturity date of the debt. Alternatively, the **amortization of the loan**[1] can occur over the life of

---

[1] The term *amortization* was used in Chapter 9 to describe the process of

the loan (i.e., paid systematically). Some debt instruments combine these options by amortizing a portion of the debt over the term of the loan with the remainder being due in full at maturity. This type of payment schedule is referred to as an *amortization with a* **balloon payment.** This chapter covers the major forms of debt refinancing and the options available for the payment of principal and interest.

Long-Term Notes Payable

L.O. 1

Comprehend the need for long-term debt financing.

Notes payable can be classified as short term or long term, depending on the time to maturity. As discussed in Chapter 7, short-term notes mature within 1 year or the operating cycle, whichever is longer. In contrast, long-term notes payable are used to satisfy financing needs for periods that range from 2 to 5 years. Most long-term loans are obtained from banks or other financial institutions, and they frequently require periodic payments of principal as well as interest. To illustrate, assume that Bill Blair obtained the cash needed to start a small business by issuing a $100,000 face value note to National Bank on January 1, 20X1. As with other debt-financing activities, the issue of a long-term note payable acts to increase assets (i.e., cash) and liabilities (i.e., notes payable). The income statement is not affected when the note is issued. The cash inflow is shown in the financing activities section of the statement of cash flows. The effects on the financial statements are shown here:

L.O. 2

Understand how the amortization of long-term notes affects financial statements.

Assets	=	Liab.	+	Equity		Rev.	−	Exp.	=	Net Inc.		Cash Flow	
100,000	=	100,000	+	n/a		n/a	−	n/a	=	n/a		100,000	FA

The note carried a 9% annual rate of interest and a 5-year term. Principal and interest are to be paid through a single $25,709 payment[2] made on December 31 of each year from 20X1 through 20X5. Exhibit 10–1 shows the allocation[3] of this payment to principal and interest. The amount of interest paid each year is determined by multiplying the outstanding principal balance of the loan by the 9% interest rate. The portion of the payment that is not used for interest acts to reduce the principal balance of the loan. For example, the first interest payment made on December 31, 20X1, amounts to $9,000 ($100,000 × 0.09). Accordingly, $16,709 ($25,709 − $9,000) is applied to reducing the principal balance of the loan. The second interest payment is computed by multiplying the new principal balance of $83,291 ($100,000 − $16,709) by the 9% interest rate. As a result, the payments for interest and principal reduction on December 31, 20X2, are $7,496

---

expense recognition by systematically allocating the *cost of intangible assets* over their useful lives. It will become apparent in this chapter that the word has a broader meaning that applies to a variety of allocation processes. Here the word is used to describe the systematic process of allocating the *principal repayment* over the life of a loan.

[2]The determination of the annual payment is based on the present value concepts presented in the appendix to this chapter.

[3]All computations are rounded to the nearest dollar. Rounding differences resulted in the necessity to add an additional dollar to the final payment in order to fully liquidate the liability.

EXHIBIT 10–1				
Amortization Schedule for Note Issued by Bill Blair				
Accounting Period	Principal Balance on Jan. 1	Cash Payment Dec. 31	Applied to Interest	Applied to Principal
20X1	$100,000	$25,709	$9,000	$16,709
20X2	83,291	25,709	7,496	18,213
20X3	65,078	25,709	5,857	19,852
20X4	45,226	25,709	4,070	21,639
20X5	23,587	25,710	2,123	23,587

($83,291 × 0.09) and $18,213 ($25,709 − $7,496), respectively. Allocations for the remaining three payments are computed in a similar way. Check your under-standing of the amortization schedule by doing the computations required to ex-tend the table for the 20X3 payment.

Notice that the amount allotted to interest declines each period while the amount allotted to principal increases because the amount borrowed declines as a portion of the principal is repaid each year. Since the amount borrowed de-clines, the amount of interest due on the debt also declines.

Although the amounts allotted to principal and interest are different for each accounting period, the effects of the annual payment on the financial state-ments are the same for each accounting period. With respect to the balance sheet, assets (i.e., cash) decrease. Liabilities decrease by the amount of the principal re-payment (see Exhibit 10-1, the column titled Applied to Principal). Similarly, the recognition of interest expense (see Exhibit 10-1, the column titled Applied to In-terest) acts to reduce equity (i.e., retained earnings). Net income decreases as a re-sult of the recognition of interest. The portion of the cash payment applied to principal should be shown in the financing activities section of the statement of cash flows. The portion of the cash payment applied to interest should be shown in the operating activities section. The effects on the 20X1 financial statements are shown here:

Assets	=	Liab.	+	Equity	Rev.	−	Exp.	=	Net Inc.	Cash Flow	
(25,709)	=	(16,709)	+	(9,000)	n/a	−	9,000	=	(9,000)	(9,000)	OA
										(16,709)	FA

Exhibit 10–2 shows income statements, balance sheets, and statements of cash flows for Blair's company for the accounting periods 20X1 through 20X5. Note the differences between Blair's income statements and its statements of cash flow. First, the $100,000 of borrowed funds is shown under the financing ac-tivities of the statement of cash flows but not shown on the income statement. Furthermore, only the interest portion of the annual $25,709 payment is shown on the income statement. In contrast, the whole payment is shown on the state-ment of cash flows (i.e., part in operating activities for interest expense and part in financing activities to reflect the principal payment).

With respect to the balance sheet, the amount in the Cash account decreases each year from 20X2 through 20X5 because the amount of cash paid for principal and interest ($25,709) is higher than the amount of cash collected from revenue

EXHIBIT 10–2

BLAIR COMPANY
Financial Statements

Income Statements

	20X1	20X2	20X3	20X4	20X5
Rent Revenue	$ 12,000	$12,000	$12,000	$12,000	$12,000
Interest Expense	(9,000)	(7,496)	(5,857)	(4,070)	(2,123)
Net Income	$ 3,000	$ 4,504	$ 6,143	$ 7,930	$ 9,877

Balance Sheets

Assets					
Cash	$ 86,291	$72,582	$58,873	$45,164	$31,454
Liabilities					
Note Payable	$ 83,291	$65,078	$45,226	$23,587	$ 0
Equity					
Retained Earnings	3,000	7,504	13,647	21,577	31,454
Total Liabilities and Equity	$ 86,291	$72,582	$58,873	$45,164	$31,454

Statements of Cash Flows

Operating Activities					
Inflow from Customers	$ 12,000	$12,000	$12,000	$12,000	$12,000
Outflow for Interest	(9,000)	(7,496)	(5,857)	(4,070)	(2,123)
Investing Activities	0	0	0	0	0
Financing Activities					
Inflow from Note Issue	100,000				
Outflow to Repay Note	(16,709)	(18,213)	(19,852)	(21,639)	(23,587)
Net Change in Cash	86,291	(13,709)	(13,709)	(13,709)	(13,710)
Plus: Beginning Cash Balance	0	86,291	72,582	58,873	45,164
Ending Cash Balance	$ 86,291	$72,582	$58,873	$45,164	$31,454

($12,000). The annual $13,709 net cash outflow ($12,000 − $25,709) causes the steady decline in the cash balance. Also note that the liability declines as time passes because the annual payment includes a principal reduction as well as an interest component. In other words, some of the debt is being paid off each year. Finally, note that the Retained Earnings account increases by the amount of net income each year. Since the company pays no distributions, all the income is retained in the business.

Security for Bank Loan Agreements

Bankers are interested in securing the collection of principal and interest. To ensure collection, they frequently require creditors to pledge designated assets as **collateral for loans.** For example, a bank usually holds legal title to automobiles that are purchased with the proceeds of its loans. If the creditor is unable to make principal and interest payments, the bank repossesses the car. The car is then sold to another individual, and the proceeds from the sale are used to pay the debt. In addition to collateral, bankers often include **restrictive covenants** in loan agreements. For example, a bank may restrict additional borrowing by requiring creditors to maintain a minimal debt-to-assets ratio. If the ratio rises above the designated level, the loan is considered in default and due immediately. Other common restrictions include limits on the payment of dividends to owners and salaries to management. Finally, banks often ask key personnel to provide copies of their personal tax returns and financial statements. The financial condition of key executives is important because they may be asked to pledge personal property as collateral for business loans.

Line of Credit

Another form of short- and intermediate-term credit many companies use is called a **line of credit.** A line of credit enables companies to borrow a limited amount of funds on an as-needed basis. As long as the company stays within the preapproved boundaries, funds can be obtained and repaid at will. The interest rate usually fluctuates in proportion to the bank's prime rate (i.e., the publicly announced rate that banks charge their best customers) or some standard base, such as the rate paid on 3-month U.S. Treasury bills (i.e., credit instruments issued by the U.S. government). The typical term of a line of credit is 1 year. In other words, the funds borrowed are due for repayment within 1 year. However, most lines of credit are renewable and for all practical purposes represent a relatively permanent source of financing. So, although they are classified on the balance sheet as short-term liabilities, frequently they are paid off, year after year, by simply renewing the credit agreement.

As indicated in Exhibit 10–3, line-of-credit agreements with banks, insurance companies, and other financial institutions are used widely in business. Approximately 90% of U.S. companies provide footnote disclosures regarding credit agreements and include information regarding the amount of the credit line, credit terms, and restrictive covenants.

To illustrate the use of a line of credit, assume that Terry Parker owns a wholesale jet ski distributorship. Parker borrows money through a line of credit to build up inventory levels in the spring. The funds are repaid in the summer months when sales generate cash inflow. Parker's line of credit carries a variable interest rate adjusted monthly to remain 2 percentage points above the bank's prime rate. The following table shows Parker's borrowing activity and interest charges for the current accounting period.

L.O. 3

Understand how a line of credit affects financial statements.

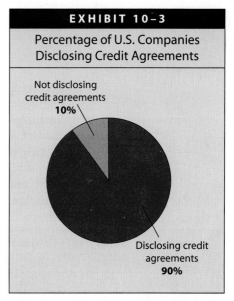

EXHIBIT 10–3

Percentage of U.S. Companies Disclosing Credit Agreements

Not disclosing credit agreements **10%**

Disclosing credit agreements **90%**

Data source: AICPA, *Accounting Trends and Techniques,* 1998.

Date	Amount Borrowed or (Repaid)	Loan Balance at End of Month	Effective Interest Rate per Month (%)	Interest Expense (Rounded to Nearest $1)
Mar. 1	$ 20,000	$ 20,000	0.09 ÷ 12	$150
Apr. 1	30,000	50,000	0.09 ÷ 12	375
May 1	50,000	100,000	0.105 ÷ 12	875
June 1	(10,000)	90,000	0.10 ÷ 12	750
July 1	(40,000)	50,000	0.09 ÷ 12	375
Aug. 1	(50,000)	0	0.09 ÷ 12	0

Waste Management, Inc., was able to make its interest payments in 1997 for two reasons. (1) Remember, interest is paid with cash, not accrual earnings. Many of the expenses on the company's income statement did not require the use of cash. Indeed, the company's statement of cash flows shows that net cash flow from operating activities, *after making interest payments,* was a positive $1.6 billion during 1997. (2) The net loss the company incurred was *after* interest expense had

been deducted. The capacity of operations to support interest payments is measured by the amount of earnings before interest deductions. For example, look at the 20X1 income statement for Blair Company in Exhibit 10–2. This statement shows only $3,000 of net income, but there was $12,000 of revenue available for the payment of interest. Similarly, Waste Management's 1997 net loss is not an indication of the company's ability to pay interest.

Each borrowing event (March 1, April 1, and May 1) is an asset source transaction. The asset account, *Cash,* increases, and the line-of-credit liability increases. Each repayment (June 1, July 1, and August 1) is an asset use transaction, with the assets and liabilities decreasing. The expense recognition for the payment of monthly interest is an asset use transaction. Cash decreases, and the corresponding increase in interest expense causes equity (i.e., retained earnings) to decrease. The effects of borrowing, repayment, and interest recognition on the financial statements follow:

Date	Assets	=	Liabilities	+	Equity	Rev.	−	Exp.	=	Net Inc.	Cash Flow	
Mar. 1	20,000	=	20,000	+	n/a	n/a	−	n/a	=	n/a	20,000	FA
31	(150)	=	n/a	+	(150)	n/a	−	150	=	(150)	(150)	OA
Apr. 1	30,000	=	30,000	+	n/a	n/a	−	n/a	=	n/a	30,000	FA
30	(375)	=	n/a	+	(375)	n/a	−	375	=	(375)	(375)	OA
May 1	50,000	=	50,000	+	n/a	n/a	−	n/a	=	n/a	50,000	FA
31	(875)	=	n/a	+	(875)	n/a	−	875	=	(875)	(875)	OA
June 1	(10,000)	=	(10,000)	+	n/a	n/a	−	n/a	=	n/a	(10,000)	FA
30	(750)	=	n/a	+	(750)	n/a	−	750	=	(750)	(750)	OA
July 1	(40,000)	=	(40,000)	+	n/a	n/a	−	n/a	=	n/a	(40,000)	FA
31	(375)	=	n/a	+	(375)	n/a	−	375	=	(375)	(375)	OA
Aug. 1	(50,000)	=	(50,000)	+	n/a	n/a	−	n/a	=	n/a	(50,000)	FA
31	n/a	=	n/a	+	n/a	n/a	−	n/a	=	n/a	n/a	

Bond Liabilities

One of the most common methods of obtaining long-term financing is through the issuance of bonds. The company that borrows money issues (i.e., gives) a *bond*, which describes the company's responsibilities to pay interest and repay the principal. *Since the borrower issues the bond, the borrower is called the* **issuer.**

There are advantages and disadvantages to obtaining funds through bond issues. An advantage is that companies are usually able to obtain longer-term commitments from bondholders than they can obtain from financial institutions. The typical term of a bond is 20 years, whereas term loans from banks are normally limited to a maximum of 5 years. Second, the amount of interest may be lower than the amount that banks or other financial institutions charge. Banks obtain much of the money that they use for making loans from their depositors. In other words, banks use the money that the public deposits in savings and checking accounts to make loans to their customers. Banks profit by charging a higher rate of interest on loans than they pay for deposits. For example, banks may pay 4% interest on a certificate of deposit and charge 9% for an auto loan. The 5% **spread** (9% − 4%) is used to pay the expenses of operating the bank and to provide a return to the owners of the bank. The spread can be avoided if a company is able to borrow directly from the public through a bond issue. Since bonds are not insured by the federal government, as bank deposits are, businesses have to pay more than the bank rate of interest to encourage the public to accept the risk of default (i.e., the failure to pay principal or interest). However, the huge sums of money that pass through the bond markets attest to the fact that the public is willing to accept a higher level of risk to obtain higher interest. Accordingly, companies frequently are able to borrow money by issuing bonds at lower rates of interest than they would have to pay to borrow money from banks or other financial institutions.

Regardless of whether interest is paid to banks or to bondholders, it is deductible in the determination of income for tax purposes. Thus, although interest acts to reduce income, part of the effect is offset because the company pays lower taxes. Furthermore, as discussed in earlier chapters, borrowing activities may even lead to earnings increases. If a firm can generate earnings of 14% on assets and can borrow money at only 10% interest, then the 4% differential actually increases the firm's profitability. As noted earlier, the concept of increasing earnings through debt financing is referred to as **financial leverage.** The concept has been a key element in the generation of wealth for many individuals and corporations. Finally, as with other forms of borrowing, inflation has an advantageous effect in that the debt is repaid with dollars that have less purchasing power than the dollars borrowed.

There are some very real disadvantages that often negate the advantages just listed. A firm is legally bound to pay the specified interest. In addition, there is a legal liability to repay the principal. Failure to satisfy these obligations can force companies into bankruptcy. If the company is forced to liquidate, the bondholders, like other creditors, have claims on the firm's assets that have priority over the claims of the owners. Even in financially sound companies, bondholders may impose conditions that restrict managers from taking actions that increase the risk of default. Accordingly, the freedom to run the business *any way you wish* may be diminished by the incurrence of debt.

Characteristics of Bonds

As stated previously, a **bond** is a written promise to pay a sum of money in the future to the bondholder. The amount to be paid at maturity is called the **face value** of the bond. In addition to paying the bondholder the face value of the bond at maturity, most bonds include a commitment to pay a **stated interest rate** at specified intervals over the life of the bond. The face value and stated rate of interest are set forth in a contract called a **bond indenture.** The bond indenture also specifies any special characteristics, such as forms of collateral (i.e., property pledged as security for a loan), the manner of payment, the timing of maturity, and *restrictive covenants,* which are designed to prohibit management from taking certain actions that place the bondholders at risk.

Security of Bonds

Bonds can be classified as either secured or unsecured; within each category there are different forms of indebtedness.

1. **Secured bonds** contain a clause that guarantees that the bondholders will be given certain identifiable assets in case of default. A common type of secured bond is a **mortgage bond,** which conditionally transfers title of a designated piece of property to the bondholder until the bond is paid.

2. **Unsecured bonds,** also known as **debentures,** are simply issued on the general credit of the organization. The holders of debentures share claims against the total assets of the company with other creditors. Often the bond indenture specifies the priority of debenture holders in relation to other creditors. **Subordinated debentures** have lower priority than other creditors, whereas **unsubordinated debentures** have equal claims.

The security of a bond is an important factor to potential investors. There is a trade-off between the risk of default and the magnitude of the return that a bondholder demands for lending money. To entice investors to purchase a bond with considerable risk, an organization must offer very high interest rates. To reduce risk and thereby lower interest rates, companies often include *restrictive covenants* in the bond indenture agreement. These covenants are designed to provide assurances to creditors regarding the payment of principal and interest. Like the covenants included in bank notes, restrictive covenants in bond indentures may limit the payment of dividends to owners or the salaries of key employees. Debt restrictions measured by financial ratios are also frequently included in bond covenants.

Manner of Interest Payment

Bonds also differ in the manner in which the issuer pays interest. They may be either *registered* or *unregistered.*

1. **Registered bonds** are those issued by most corporations. The firm keeps a record of the names and addresses of the bondholders and sends interest and maturity payments directly to the individuals on file. To transfer these bonds, the bond certificate must be endorsed, and notification of the change must be sent to the issuing corporation.

2. **Unregistered bonds,** also known as **bearer** or **coupon bonds** are commonly issued by municipalities. Interest payments are made to any

individual who redeems the coupon attached to the bond. Because no record of the purchaser is kept, coupon bonds are much like cash in that they are vulnerable to theft.

Timing of Maturity

The maturity date of bonds can be established in a variety of ways. Even bonds sold in a single issuance may mature in different ways.

1. **Term bonds** mature on a specified date in the future.
2. **Serial bonds** mature at specified intervals throughout the life of the total issuance. For example, bonds with a total face value of $1,000,000 may mature in increments of $100,000 every year for 10 years.

Often the bond indenture calls for the issuing corporation to annually set aside funds to ensure the availability of cash for the payment of the face value at the maturity date. The company makes payments into what is known as a **sinking fund.** This fund is usually managed by an independent trustee, often a bank, charged with the fiduciary responsibility of investing the funds until the bonds mature. At maturity, the funds and the proceeds from the investments are used to repay the debt.

Special Features

Many bonds have special features that make them more attractive to investors or that allow the issuing corporation more flexibility in its financing activities.

1. **Convertible bonds** may be exchanged by the bondholder for an ownership interest in the corporation. The bond indenture sets forth the conditions under which this exchange may take place. Usually, an investor agrees to accept a lower interest rate in the hope that the value of the ownership interest will increase.
2. **Callable bonds** allow the corporation to pay off the bonds before their maturity dates. This feature is desirable if interest rates decline. Under these circumstances, the company would borrow money at lower rates and use the proceeds to pay off the more expensive bonds. Obviously, the call feature is undesirable from the perspective of the bondholders, who do not want to give up their high-yield investment. To encourage investors to buy this type of bond, the bond indenture generally specifies a call price that exceeds the face value of the bonds. The difference between the call price and the face value is commonly referred to as a **call premium.**

Bond Rating

As indicated, many features affect the security of a bond. Several financial services, such as Moody's, analyze the risk of default and publish their ratings as guides to bond investors. The highest rating that can be achieved is AAA, the next highest AA, and so forth. Companies and government entities that issue bonds try to maintain high credit ratings because lower ratings force them to pay higher interest rates.

reality bytes

©Gernard Boutrit/Woodfin Camp & Associates

Livent has been described as a theatrical colossus. The company's credits include shows such as *Ragtime, Show Boat, Kiss of the Spider Woman, Parade,* and *Fosse.* In 1997, Livent sold $125 million of bonds to help finance its operations. Receiving a Standard and Poor's credit ranking of BB−, the bonds were classified as junk bonds. A **junk bond** is a bond issued by companies with credit ratings so low that they signal significant risk regarding the companies' ability to pay interest or return principal to the bondholder. Junk bonds are attractive to some investors because they normally pay interest at rates that are significantly higher than interest paid on lower-risk bonds. In most cases, companies do not default on their junk bonds. Accordingly, many investors are willing to accept additional risk to obtain high rates of interest. However, the risk should not be underestimated. Indeed, Livent filed for bankruptcy protection in 1998.

Bonds Issued at Face Value

Fixed-Rate, Fixed-Term, Annual Interest Bonds

L.O. 5

Explain why bonds are issued at face value, a discount, or a premium.

To illustrate the effects of a bond issue on the books of the borrower, assume that Marsha Mason needs cash in order to seize a business opportunity. Mason is aware of a company that needs a plot of land on which it can store its inventory of crushed stone. The company agreed to pay Mason $12,000 per year to lease the land that it needs. Mason knows of a suitable tract of land that could be purchased for $100,000. The only problem facing Mason is a lack of funds necessary to make the acquisition.

When Mason heard some of her friends complaining about the low interest rates that banks pay on certificates of deposit, she suggested that they invest in bonds instead of CDs. She then offered to sell her friends bonds that carried a 9% stated rate of interest payable in cash on December 31 of each year. To make the bonds an attractive alternative for her friends, Mason constructed a bond indenture that called for a 5-year term and provided the security of having the land pledged as collateral for the bonds.[4] Her friends were favorably impressed, and Mason issued the bonds to them on January 1, 20X1.

Mason used the funds to purchase the land and immediately entered into a contract to lease the land. The arrangement proceeded according to plan for the

---

[4]In practice, bonds are usually issued for large sums of money that often amount to hundreds of millions of dollars. Also, terms to maturity are normally long periods, with 20 years being common. Demonstrating issues of such magnitude is impractical for instructional purposes. The effects of bond issues can be illustrated more efficiently by using smaller amounts of debt with shorter maturities, such as that assumed in the case of Marsha Mason.

5-year term of the bonds. At the maturity date of the bond (December 31, 20X5), Mason was able to sell the land for its $100,000 book value and used the proceeds from the sale to repay the bond liability.

Effect of Events on Financial Statements

Six distinct accounting events are associated with Mason's business venture. These events are summarized here:

1. Received $100,000 cash from the issue of bonds at face value.
2. Invested proceeds from bond issue to purchase land costing $100,000 cash.
3. Earned $12,000 annual cash revenue from land lease.
4. Paid $9,000 annual interest on December 31 of each year.
5. Sold land for $100,000 cash.
6. Repaid bond principal to bondholders.

The effects of these events on Mason's financial statements are now discussed.

**Event 1
Bond Issue**

The bond issue, Event 1, is an asset source transaction. Assets (i.e., Cash) and liabilities (i.e., Bonds Payable) increase. The income statement is not affected. The $100,000 cash inflow is shown in the financing activities section of the statement of cash flows. The effect is shown here:

Assets	=	Liab.	+	Equity	Rev.	−	Exp.	=	Net Inc.	Cash Flow	
100,000	=	100,000	+	n/a	n/a	−	n/a	=	n/a	100,000	FA

**Event 2
Investment in Land**

Event 2 involves the $100,000 cash purchase of land, which is an asset exchange transaction. The asset account, *Cash*, decreases, and the asset account, *Land*, increases. The income statement is not affected. The cash outflow is shown in the investing activities section of the statement of cash flows. These effects are shown here:

Assets			=	Liab.	+	Equity	Rev.	−	Exp.	=	Net Inc.	Cash Flow	
Cash	+	Land	=										
(100,000)	+	100,000	=	n/a	+	n/a	n/a	−	n/a	=	n/a	(100,000)	IA

**Event 3
Revenue Recognition**

Event 3 recognizes the $12,000 cash revenue generated from the rental of the property. This event is repeated each year from 20X1 through 20X5. The event is an asset source transaction that results in an increase in assets and equity. The revenue recognition causes net income to increase. The cash inflow is shown in the operating activities section of the statement of cash flows. These effects are shown here:

Assets	=	Liab.	+	Equity	Rev.	−	Exp.	=	Net Inc.	Cash Flow	
12,000	=	n/a	+	12,000	12,000	−	n/a	=	12,000	12,000	OA

**Event 4
Expense Recognition**

Event 4 applies to the $9,000 ($100,000 × 0.09) cash payment of interest expense. This event is also repeated each year from 20X1 through 20X5. The interest payment is an asset use transaction. The Cash account decreases, and the recognition of interest expense causes a decrease in equity (i.e., Retained Earnings). The expense recognition causes net income to decrease. The cash outflow is shown in the operating activities section of the statement of cash flows. These effects are shown here:

Assets	=	Liab.	+	Equity	Rev.	−	Exp.	=	Net Inc.	Cash Flow	
(9,000)	=	n/a	+	(9,000)	n/a	−	9,000	=	(9,000)	(9,000)	OA

Event 5
Sale of Investment in Land

Event 5 occurs when the land is sold for $100,000 cash. The sale is an asset exchange transaction. The Cash account increases and the Land account decreases. Since there was no gain or loss on the sale, the income statement is not affected. The cash inflow is shown in the investing activities section of the statement of cash flows. These effects are shown here:

Assets			=	Liab.	+	Equity	Rev.	−	Exp.	=	Net Inc.	Cash Flow	
Cash	+	Land	=										
100,000	+	(100,000)	=	n/a	+	n/a	n/a	−	n/a	=	n/a	100,000	IA

Event 6
Payoff of Bond Liability

Finally, Event 6 concerns the repayment of the face value of the bond liability. This is an asset use transaction. The Cash and the Bonds Payable accounts decrease. The income statement is not affected. The cash outflow is shown in the financing activities section of the statement of cash flows:

Assets	=	Liab.	+	Equity	Rev.	−	Exp.	=	Net Inc.	Cash Flow	
(100,000)	=	(100,000)	+	n/a	n/a	−	n/a	=	n/a	(100,000)	FA

Financial Statements

L.O. 6

Understand how bond liabilities and their related interest costs affect financial statements.

Exhibit 10–4 shows the financial statements of Mason Company. The income statement is presented in a single-step format and therefore does not distinguish between operating and nonoperating items. Rent revenue and interest expense are constant across all accounting periods, resulting in the recognition of $3,000 of net income in each accounting period. With respect to the balance sheet, the Cash account increases by $3,000 each year because cash revenue exceeds cash paid for interest. The Land account stays at $100,000 from the date of purchase in 20X1 until the land is sold in 20X5. Similarly, Bonds Payable remains at $100,000 from the date of issue in 20X1 until the liability is paid off on December 31, 20X5.

It is interesting to compare the income statements for Bill Blair shown in Exhibit 10–2 with those of Mason Company shown in Exhibit 10–4. Note that in both cases, a face value of $100,000 cash was borrowed at a stated interest rate of 9%. Both companies also earned $12,000 revenue per year, yet Blair produced a total net income of $31,454 while Mason's net earnings for the same period were only $15,000. The difference is attributable solely to the additional interest that Mason was required to pay because no payment of principal was made until the maturity date. By repaying the loan more rapidly, Blair was able to lower its liabilities and thereby the amount of interest expense.

L.O. 7

Explain how to account for bonds and their related interest costs.

Recording Procedures

Exhibit 10–5 summarizes the general journal entries required to record the six events that Mason Company experienced.

EXHIBIT 10–4

**Financial Statements
Under the Assumption That Bonds Are Issued at Face Value**

Income Statements

	20X1	20X2	20X3	20X4	20X5
Rent Revenue	$ 12,000	$ 12,000	$ 12,000	$ 12,000	$ 12,000
Interest Expense	(9,000)	(9,000)	(9,000)	(9,000)	(9,000)
Net Income	$ 3,000	$ 3,000	$ 3,000	$ 3,000	$ 3,000

Balance Sheets

	20X1	20X2	20X3	20X4	20X5
Assets					
Cash	$ 3,000	$ 6,000	$ 9,000	$ 12,000	$ 15,000
Land	100,000	100,000	100,000	100,000	0
Total Assets	$103,000	$106,000	$109,000	$112,000	$ 15,000
Liabilities					
Bond Payable	$100,000	$100,000	$100,000	$100,000	$ 0
Equity					
Retained Earnings	3,000	6,000	9,000	12,000	15,000
Total Liabilities and Equity	$103,000	$106,000	$109,000	$112,000	$ 15,000

Statements of Cash Flows

	20X1	20X2	20X3	20X4	20X5
Operating Activities					
Inflow from Customers	$ 12,000	$ 12,000	$ 12,000	$ 12,000	$ 12,000
Outflow for Interest	(9,000)	(9,000)	(9,000)	(9,000)	(9,000)
Investing Activities					
Outflow to Purchase Land	(100,000)				
Inflow from Sale of Land					100,000
Financing Activities					
Inflow from Bond Issue	100,000				
Outflow to Repay Bond Liab.					(100,000)
Net Change in Cash	3,000	3,000	3,000	3,000	3,000
Beginning Cash Balance	0	3,000	6,000	9,000	12,000
Ending Cash Balance	$ 3,000	$ 6,000	$ 9,000	$ 12,000	$ 15,000

Bonds Issued at a Discount

Effective Interest Rate

At the time that bonds are issued, market conditions may force a company to pay more interest than the *stated rate* of interest. In other words, if the *stated rate* of interest is too low, no one will buy the bonds. The rate of interest that the issuer must pay to sell the bonds is called the *effective interest rate.* The **effective interest rate** reflects the true cost of borrowing. The amount of the effective rate is dictated by the availability of other investment opportunities. For example, if an investor can purchase a low-risk government bond that yields 8%, she or he will be willing to invest in a higher-risk corporate bond only if the return is higher than 8%. The rate that is available on a wide range of alternative investments is referred to as the **market interest rate.** Theoretically, the *effective rate* and the

L.O. 5

Explain why bonds are issued at face value, a discount, or a premium.

EXHIBIT 10–5				
Event No.	**Account Title**		**Debit**	**Credit**
1	Cash		100,000	
	Bonds Payable			100,000
	Entry on January 1, 20X1, to record bond issue			
2	Land		100,000	
	Cash			100,000
	Entry on January 1, 20X1, to record investment in land			
3	Cash		12,000	
	Revenue			12,000
	Revenue recognition entries on December 31, 20X1–20X5			
4	Interest Expense		9,000	
	Cash			9,000
	Expense recognition entries on December 31, 20X1–20X5			
5	Cash		100,000	
	Land			100,000
	Entry on January 1, 20X6, to record sale of land			
6	Bonds Payable		100,000	
	Cash			100,000
	Entry on January 1, 20X6, to record bond payment			

market rate for investments with similar levels of risk are equal at the time the bonds are issued. However, once the bonds have been sold, the *effective rate* becomes fixed by the price paid for the bonds, whereas the *market rate* continues to vary with the changing economic conditions.

The bond indenture requires that the cash payment for interest be determined by multiplying the *stated rate of interest by the face value* of the bond. In other words, the periodic cash payments for interest are fixed, which means that companies cannot adjust the effective interest rate by changing the periodic cash payments for interest. If a company wishes to adjust the effective rate of interest upward (i.e., pay more than the stated rate), it must do so by lowering the purchase price of the bonds. For example, a $1,000 face value bond may be issued for $900. At maturity, the investor who purchases the bond will receive $1,000 even though he or she paid only $900 to obtain the bond. The $100 differential represents an additional interest payment. In other words, the creditor (i.e., bond investor) will receive the regular cash payments for interest (i.e., stated rate times principal balance), plus the $100 difference between the face value ($1,000) and the price paid for the bond ($900).

When bonds are sold at an amount below their face value, the difference between the purchase price and the face value is called a **bond discount.** As indicated, bonds sell at a discount when the market rate of interest is higher than the stated rate on the issue date. To demonstrate the accounting treatment for bonds issued at a discount, assume the same facts as those presented in the preceding example involving Mason Company. One additional factor will be considered. Suppose that Mason's friends receive an offer to buy bonds from another entrepreneur willing to pay a rate of interest higher than the 9% stated rate contained in Mason's indenture. Although they feel some sense of commitment to Mason, they conclude that business decisions cannot be made on the basis of friendship. Mason is understanding and wants to provide a counteroffer. There is no time to change the bond indenture, so she states that she is willing to accept $95,000 for the bonds today and will still repay the full face value of $100,000 at the maturity date. The $5,000 differential makes her offer competitive, and the transaction for the bond issue is consummated immediately.

Bond Prices

In accounting terms, the bonds were sold *at a discount* for *a price of 95.* As this statement implies, *bond prices are normally expressed as a percentage of the face value* that is received when the bonds are sold. Amounts of less than 1 percentage point are usually expressed as a fraction. Therefore, a bond selling for 98¾ sells for 98.75% of the face value of the bond.

Mason Company Revisited

The next section revisits the Mason Company illustration. The same six events are examined under a new assumption: The bonds are issued at a discount. This assumption changes the amounts appearing on the financial statements. For example, Event 1 in year 20X1 reflects the fact that only $95,000 cash was obtained from the bond issue. Likewise, since there was only $95,000 available to invest in land, the illustration assumes that a less desirable piece of property was acquired. Accordingly, the property generated only $11,400 of rent revenue per year.

When bonds are issued at a discount, the amount of the discount is recorded in a contra liability account titled **Discount on Bonds Payable.** In this case, the $100,000 face value of the bonds is recorded in the Bonds Payable account. The $5,000 discount is shown in a separate contra account. As indicated in the following discussion, the contra account is subtracted from the face value to determine the **carrying value** (i.e., book value) of the bonds.

Bonds Payable	$100,000
Less: Discount on Bonds Payable	(5,000)
Carrying Value	$ 95,000

From Mason's perspective, her company borrowed only $95,000. When the $100,000 is paid at maturity, it will include a return of the $95,000 principal borrowed plus a $5,000 cash payment for interest. Mason will have to continue to make the annual $9,000 ($100,000 face value × 0.09 stated interest rate) cash payment for interest. The additional $5,000 of interest paid at maturity will cause the effective interest rate to be higher than the stated rate.

The bond issue is an asset source transaction with assets and total liabilities both increasing by $95,000. Net income is not affected. The cash inflow is shown in the financing activities section of the statement of cash flows. The effect of the bond issue on the financial statements and the journal entry required to record it are shown here:

Assets	=		Liabilities		+	Equity		Rev.	−	Exp.	=	Net Inc.	Cash Flow
Cash	=	Bonds Pay.	−	Discount	+	Equity							
95,000	=	100,000	−	5,000	+	n/a		n/a	−	n/a	=	n/a	95,000 FA

Account Title	Debit	Credit
Cash	95,000	
Discount on Bonds Payable	5,000	
Bonds Payable		100,000

L.O. 7

Explain how to account for bonds and their related interest costs.

Event 1
Issue of Bond Liability

In the financial statements, the $5,000 debit to the Discount account is off-set by the $100,000 credit to the Bonds Payable account. The remaining $95,000 credit balance represents the carrying value of the bond liability.

Event 2
Investment in Land

Event 2 involves the $95,000 cash purchase of land, which is an asset exchange transaction. The asset account, *Cash,* decreases, and the asset account, *Land,* increases. The income statement is not affected. The cash outflow is shown in the investing activities section of the statement of cash flows. These effects are shown here:

Assets			=	Liab.	+	Equity	Rev.	−	Exp.	=	Net Inc.	Cash Flow	
Cash	+	Land	=										
(95,000)	+	95,000	=	n/a	+	n/a	n/a	−	n/a	=	n/a	(95,000)	IA

Event 3
Revenue Recognition

Event 3 recognizes the $11,400 cash revenue generated from the rental of the property. This event is repeated each year from 20X1 through 20X5. The event is an asset source transaction that results in an increase in assets and equity. The revenue recognition causes net income to increase. The cash inflow is shown in the operating activities section of the statement of cash flows. These effects are shown here:

Assets	=	Liab.	+	Equity	Rev.	−	Exp.	=	Net Inc.	Cash Flow	
11,400	=	n/a	+	11,400	11,400	−	n/a	=	11,400	11,400	OA

Event 4
Expense Recognition

Although the interest associated with the $5,000 discount will be paid in one lump sum at maturity, it is systematically allocated to the Interest Expense account over the life of the bond. Under **straight-line amortization,** the amount of the discount recognized as expense in each accounting period is $1,000 ($5,000 discount ÷ 5 years). As a result, there is $10,000 of interest expense recognized in each accounting period. This figure is composed of $9,000 of stated interest plus $1,000 amortization of this bond discount. Compare this amount with the $9,000 charge for interest expense shown in the previous illustration when the bonds were sold at face value (i.e., no discount).

Recall that an expense is either a decrease in assets or an increase in liabilities. The $9,000 cash payment for interest is an asset use transaction. The $1,000 portion of interest expense recognition through the amortization of the discount is an equity exchange transaction. This transaction acts to increase liabilities. More specifically, amounts are removed from the Discount account and placed into the Interest Expense account. Since the Discount account is a contra liability account, reducing it acts to increase the carrying value of the bond liability. In summary, $10,000 of interest expense is recognized. The recognition of the interest expense causes equity (i.e., retained earnings) to decrease. The $10,000 decrease in retained earnings is offset by a $9,000 decrease in the Cash account and a $1,000 increase in the carrying value of the bond liability (i.e., a decrease in the Discount account). The effect of the interest expense recognition on the financial statements and the journal entry necessary to record it for each accounting period are as follows:

Assets	=	Liabilities			+	Equity	Rev.	−	Exp.	=	Net Inc.	Cash Flow	
Cash	=	Bonds Pay.	−	Discount									
(9,000)	=	n/a	−	(1,000)	+	(10,000)	n/a	−	10,000	=	(10,000)	(9,000)	OA

Account Title	Debit	Credit
Interest Expense	10,000	
Cash		9,000
Discount on Bonds Payable		1,000

Event 5 occurs when the land is sold for $95,000 cash. The sale is an asset exchange transaction. The Cash account increases and the Land account decreases. Since there was no gain or loss on the sale, the income statement is not affected. The cash inflow is shown in the investing activities section of the statement of cash flows. These effects are shown here:

Event 5
Sale of Investment in Land

Assets			=	Liab.	+	Equity	Rev.	−	Exp.	=	Net Inc.	Cash Flow	
Cash	+	Land	=										
95,000	+	(95,000)	=	n/a	+	n/a	n/a	−	n/a	=	n/a	95,000	IA

Finally, Event 6 concerns the repayment of the face value of the bond liability. This is an asset use transaction. The Cash and Bonds Payable accounts decrease. The income statement is not affected. The cash outflow is shown in the financing activities section of the statement of cash flows. The outflow associated with the repayment of the principal is $95,000. The remaining $5,000 represents an interest charge associated with the discount. In practice, the amount of the discount is frequently immaterial and is included in the financing activities section along with the principal payment:

Event 6
Payoff of Bond Liability

Assets	=	Liab.	+	Equity	Rev.	−	Exp.	=	Net Inc.	Cash Flow	
(100,000)	=	(100,000)	+	n/a	n/a	−	n/a	=	n/a	(95,000)	FA
										(5,000)	OA

Effect on Financial Statements

Exhibit 10–6 contains the financial statements that reflect Mason's business venture under the assumption that the bonds were issued at a discount. Note that the amount of net income is significantly lower than the amount reported in Exhibit 10–4, where it was assumed that the bonds were sold at face value. The lower income results from two factors. First, since the bonds were sold at a discount, there was less money to invest in land, and the lower investment (i.e., less desirable property was purchased) produced lower revenues. Second, the effective interest rate was higher than the stated rate, thereby resulting in higher expenses. Lower revenues coupled with higher expenses result in less profitability.

With respect to the balance sheet, note that the carrying value of the bond liability increases each year until the liability is equal to the face value of the bond on the December 31, 20X5, year-end closing date, which is logical because Mason is obligated to pay the full $100,000 at maturity. Also note that the amount of retained earnings ($7,000) on December 31, 20X5, is equal to the total amount of net income reported over the 5-year life of the business ($1,400 × 5). Again, this is logical because no distributions were made during the 5-year period. Accordingly, all earnings were retained in the business.

L.O. 6

Understand how bond liabilities and their related interest costs affect financial statements.

EXHIBIT 10–6
Financial Statements **Under the Assumption That Bonds Are Issued at a Discount**

Income Statements

	20X1	20X2	20X3	20X4	20X5
Rent Revenue	$ 11,400	$ 11,400	$ 11,400	$ 11,400	$11,400
Interest Expense	(10,000)	(10,000)	(10,000)	(10,000)	(10,000)
Net Income	$ 1,400	$ 1,400	$ 1,400	$ 1,400	$ 1,400

Balance Sheets

	20X1	20X2	20X3	20X4	20X5
Assets					
Cash	$ 2,400	$ 4,800	$ 7,200	$ 9,600	$ 7,000
Land	95,000	95,000	95,000	95,000	0
Total Assets	$ 97,400	$ 99,800	$102,200	$104,600	$ 7,000
Liabilities					
Bonds Payable	$100,000	$100,000	$100,000	$100,000	$ 0
Discount on Bonds Payable	(4,000)	(3,000)	(2,000)	(1,000)	0
Carrying Value of Bond Liab.	96,000	97,000	98,000	99,000	0
Equity					
Retained Earnings	1,400	2,800	4,200	5,600	7,000
Total Liabilities and Equity	$ 97,400	$ 99,800	$102,200	$104,600	$ 7,000

Statements of Cash Flows

	20X1	20X2	20X3	20X4	20X5
Operating Activities					
Inflow from Customers	$ 11,400	$ 11,400	$ 11,400	$ 11,400	$11,400
Outflow for Interest	(9,000)	(9,000)	(9,000)	(9,000)	(14,000)
Investing Activities					
Outflow to Purchase Land	(95,000)				
Inflow for Sale of Land					95,000
Financing Activities					
Inflow from Bond Issue	95,000				
Outflow to Repay Bond Liab.					(95,000)
Net Change in Cash	2,400	2,400	2,400	2,400	(2,600)
Beginning Cash Balance	0	2,400	4,800	7,200	9,600
Ending Cash Balance	$ 2,400	$ 4,800	$ 7,200	$ 9,600	$ 7,000

The differences between net income and cash flow are attributable to several factors. First, although $10,000 of interest expense is shown on the 20X1 income statement, only $9,000 of cash was paid for interest. The $1,000 differential is a result of the amortization of the bond discount. The cash outflow for the amortization of the discount is included in the $100,000 payment made at maturity. This payment is composed of $95,000 repayment of principal and $5,000 payment for interest.[5] Since there is a $9,000 cash payment for the interest expense

---

[5]In practice, many companies do not separate the discount from the principal for the presentation of information on the statement of cash flows. In other words, the entire face value of the bond liability is shown in the financing section of the statement of cash flows. While this practice is conceptually invalid, it is acceptable as long as the amounts are considered immaterial.

in 20X5, the total cash paid for interest is $14,000 ($9,000 based on the stated rate + $5,000 for discount). Even though $14,000 of cash is paid for interest in 20X5, only $10,000 is recognized as interest expense on the income statement. Although the total net cash inflow over the 5-year life of the business ($7,000) is equal to the total amount of net income reported for the same period, there are significant differences in the timing of the recognition of the interest expense and the cash outflows associated with it.

Effect of Semiannual Interest Payments

Up to this point, our examples assumed that interest payments were made on an annual basis. In practice, most bond indentures call for the payment of interest on a semiannual basis, which means that interest is paid in cash twice each year. If Marsha Mason's bond indenture had stipulated semiannual interest payments, her company would have had to make a $4,500 ($100,000 × 0.09 = $9,000 ÷ 2 = $4,500) cash payment for interest on June 30, 20X1, and December 31 of each year. The journal entries necessary to record interest for each year are as follows (the entries apply to the bonds issued at a discount):

L.O. 7

Explain how to account for bonds and their related interest costs.

Date	Account Title	Debit	Credit
June 30	Interest Expense	5,000	
	Discount on Bonds Payable		500
	Cash		4,500
Dec. 31	Interest Expense	5,000	
	Discount on Bonds Payable		500
	Cash		4,500

The same total amount of expenses is recognized and paid over the life of the bond. The difference centers on the timing of the cash payments. If the interest is paid semiannually, then cash outflow for interest is made earlier and more frequently. This is a disadvantage from the issuer's point of view because the capacity to use the cash is transferred to the investor earlier. Considering the financial advantages associated with delaying the cash payments, the issuer prefers to make payments annually. However, since investors have become accustomed to receiving semiannual interest collections, bonds that pay interest annually are more difficult to sell. Accordingly, most bonds in U.S. markets pay semiannual interest.

Bonds Issued at a Premium

When bonds are sold at an amount above their face value, the differential between the two amounts is called a **bond premium.** Bonds sell at a premium when the market rate of interest is below the stated rate. Bond premiums act to lower the effective interest rate to the market rate. Accordingly, they have the effect of lowering interest expense. For example, assume that Marsha Mason sold her bonds for 105. Mason would receive $105,000 cash when the bonds were issued. Even so, she is required to repay only the $100,000 face value of the bonds at the

L.O. 5

Explain why bonds are issued at face value, a discount, or a premium.

maturity date. The $5,000 difference between the amount received and the amount paid acts to reduce the amount of interest expense. The Premium on Bonds Payable account is shown on the balance sheet as an adjunct liability account (i.e., it adds to the carrying value of the bond liability). Accordingly, the bond liability would be shown on the balance sheet as indicated here:

Bonds Payable	$100,000
Plus: Premium on Bonds Payable	5,000
Carrying Value	$105,000

The effect of issuing the bonds at a premium on the financial statements is as follows:

Assets =	Liabilities		+ Equity	Rev. −	Exp. =	Net Inc.	Cash Flow
Cash =	Bond Pay. +	Premium					
105,000 =	100,000 +	5,000 +	n/a	n/a −	n/a =	n/a	105,000 FA

Note that the entire $105,000 cash inflow is shown under the financing activities section of the statement of cash flows even though the $5,000 premium pertains to interest. Conceptually, the premium is related to operating activities. However, in practice, the amounts associated with premiums are usually so small that they are considered immaterial. Accordingly, the entire cash inflow is normally classified as a financing activity.

The journal entries necessary to record the bond issue at a premium and the first interest payment are as follows (the entries assume an annual interest payment):

L.O. 7

Explain how to account for bonds and their related interest costs.

Date	Account Title	Debit	Credit
Jan. 1	Cash	105,000	
	Bonds Payable		100,000
	Premium on Bonds Payable		5,000
Dec 31	Interest Expense	8,000	
	Premium on Bonds Payable	1,000	
	Cash		9,000

Bond Redemptions

The previous exhibits for the bonds issued by Marsha Mason assumed that the bonds were redeemed on the maturity date. The bondholders were paid the face value of the bonds, and the bond liability was removed from the books. The discount or premium was fully amortized so these accounts no longer existed at the time the bonds were redeemed.

Often bonds with a *call provision* are redeemed prior to the maturity date. When this situation arises, the company must pay the bondholders the **call price,** which is an amount that is normally higher than the maturity value. For example, suppose that Mason's bond indenture includes a provision that enables her to call the bonds at a price of 103. Assume that her client refuses to renew the contract to rent the land at the end of 20X3. Accordingly, Mason is forced to sell the land and pay off the bonds. Using the data that assumes the bonds were sold for a discount, there is a $2,000 balance in the Discount on Bonds Payable account on January 1, 20X4 (see Exhibit 10–6 for details).

Mason is required to pay the bondholders $103,000 ($100,000 face value × 103 call price) to redeem the bonds. Since the book value of the bond liability is $98,000 ($100,000 face value − $2,000 remaining discount), Mason experiences a $5,000 loss ($103,000 redemption price − $98,000 book value) when the bonds are paid off. Accordingly, cash, the carrying value of the bond liability, and equity all decrease as a result of the redemption. The effect of the redemption on the financial statements is as follows:

Assets	=	Liabilities			+	Equity	Rev.	−	Exp.	=	Net Inc.	Cash Flow
Cash	=	Bond Pay.	−	Discount								
(103,000)	=	(100,000)	−	(2,000)	+	(5,000)	n/a	−	5,000	=	(5,000)	(103,000) FA

Note that the entire $103,000 cash outflow is shown under the financing activities section of the statement of cash flows. Conceptually, some of this amount is attributable to activities other than financing. However, in practice, the amounts not associated with financing are usually so small that they are considered immaterial. Accordingly, the entire cash outflow is classified as a financing activity.

The general journal entry necessary to record the bond redemption is shown here:

Account Title	Debit	Credit
Loss on Bond Redemption	5,000	
Bonds Payable	100,000	
Discount on Bonds Payable		2,000
Cash		103,000

The loss on redemption of bonds, if material, appears on Mason's income statement as an **extraordinary item.** Extraordinary items are set apart from operating income to highlight unusual items that are not likely to recur.

L.O. 7

Explain how to account for bonds and their related interest costs.

Tax Advantage Associated with Debt Financing

Two important concepts must be understood in order to compare debt financing with equity financing. The first is the concept of financial leverage, explained in Chapter 3. The second is the tax advantage of debt financing. Debt financing is said to have a tax advantage over equity financing because interest payments are deductible for the purpose of computing taxable income. In contrast, dividends are not deductible in the determination of taxable income. The effect of this difference is now described.

Suppose that $100,000 is needed to start Maduro Company. Assume that the company can be started by having investors contribute $100,000 to the business (i.e., equity financing). Alternatively, it can be started by borrowing $100,000 (debt financing). During the first year of operation, the company earns $60,000 of

L.O. 8

Explain the advantages and disadvantages of debt financing.

revenue and incurs $40,000 of expenses, not including interest. If investors finance the business, they are provided an $8,000 distribution. Alternatively, if the business is financed with debt, it is required to pay 8% annual interest (i.e., interest expense is $8,000). Assuming a 30% tax rate, which form of financing will produce the larger addition to retained earnings for the business? The answer can be computed as follows:

Computation of Addition to Retained Earnings		
	Equity Financing	**Debt Financing**
Revenue	$60,000	$60,000
Expense (excluding interest)	(40,000)	(40,000)
Earnings before Interest and Taxes	20,000	20,000
Interest (100,000 × 8%)	0	(8,000)
Pretax Income	20,000	12,000
Income Tax (30%)	6,000	3,600
Net Income	14,000	8,400
Distribution	(8,000)	0
Addition to Retained Earnings	$ 6,000	$ 8,400

Note that if the company is financed with debt, it produces $2,400 more retained earnings than if it is financed with equity because the interest expense is tax deductible. If equity financing is used, the company pays $6,000 of income taxes, whereas debt financing requires only $3,600 of income taxes. Accordingly, debt financing saved $2,400 of income tax expense. In other words, the effective cost (i.e., after-tax cost) of the debt is only $5,600 ($8,000 interest expense − $2,400 tax savings). In contrast, the $8,000 distribution is not tax deductible. As a result, it removes a full $8,000 from the amount of earnings to be retained in the business. In both cases, the investors or creditors receive $8,000. The difference lies in the fact that under debt financing, the Internal Revenue Service receives $2,400 less.

In general terms, the after-tax interest cost of debt can be computed as

Total Interest Expense × (1.0 − Tax Rate)

In the case of Maduro Company, this formula confirms the previous analysis. The after-tax cost of debt is computed to be

$8,000 × (1.0 − 0.30) = $5,600

The after-tax interest rate that Maduro is paying can be computed by using the same logic. It is 5.6% (8% × 0.70). In contrast, there is no difference in the before-tax and after-tax effects of an 8% distribution. This means that $1 of dividends cost the company a full $1 of retained earnings, while $1 of interest has an after-tax cost of only $.70 (i.e., assuming a 30% tax rate). All other things being equal, debt financing results in higher profitability than equity financing because it lowers the amount of taxes that must be paid. This conclusion assumes that the business is operating profitably. There can be no tax savings if there is no income because businesses that produce consistent losses pay no taxes.

EBIT and Ratio Analysis

Several ratios presented in this book use net income in their computations. In practice, some of these ratios are computed by using *earnings before interest and taxes* (EBIT) rather than net income. One such ratio is the *return-on-assets* (ROA)

ratio, explained in Chapter 3. The purpose of the ROA ratio is to measure how efficiently a business is using its assets. If net income is used in its computation rather than EBIT, the ratio may be distorted by the nature of the company's financing activities.

To illustrate, we return to the example of Maduro Company. Recall that Maduro plans to invest the $100,000 it receives in exactly the same manner regardless of whether it obtains the funds from equity or debt financing. Even so, the ROA ratio with net income as the numerator is 14% ($14,000 ÷ $100,000) under equity financing and only 8.4% ($8,400 ÷ $100,000) under debt financing. Since the assets are used in exactly the same manner regardless of how they are obtained, the difference between the 14% ROA and the 8.4% ROA ratios is due to financing strategy rather than asset management. The use of EBIT avoids this discrepancy and thereby provides a better measure of asset utilization. In the case of Maduro Company, the ROA ratio computed on the basis of EBIT is 20% ($20,000 ÷ $100,000), regardless of whether debt or equity financing is used. Since the assets are used in the same manner regardless of how they are financed, the measure of assets utilization should be the same regardless of the method of financing. Accordingly, the use of EBIT in the computation of the ROA ratio provides a better measure of asset utilization. However, for the sake of simplification, continue to use net income when you compute ratios unless instructed otherwise.

Times-Interest-Earned Ratio

Debt financing is not without disadvantages. The increased risk to a business that uses more debt versus less debt has been noted. Financial statement users have ratios that help assess this risk. One is the debt-to-assets ratio, explained in Chapter 3. Another is the **times-interest-earned ratio,** defined as

$$\frac{\textbf{EBIT}}{\textbf{Interest Expense}}$$

Because the amount of earnings before interest and taxes is available for the payment of interest, the times-interest-earned ratio must be based on EBIT, not on net income. This ratio tells *how many times* a company would be able to pay its interest by using the amount of earnings available to make interest payments. The higher the ratio, the less likely a company is to find itself in the unfortunate position of being unable to make its interest payments. Since the failure to pay interest can lead to bankruptcy, higher times-interest-earned ratios suggest lower levels of risk. Shown here are the times-interest-earned ratios and debt-to-assets ratios for six real-world companies. These numbers are for 1997.

Industry	Company	Times Interest Earned	Debt to Assets
Breakfast Cereal	Kellogg	9.35 times	.80
	Quaker Oats	−11.40	.91
Tools	Black & Decker	3.80	.67
	Stanley Works	−0.12	.65
Hotel	Four Seasons	5.74	.44
	Hilton Hotels	3.36	.57

Given that Quaker's and Stanley's times-interest-earned ratios are negative numbers, were the companies able to make the required interest payments to their creditors during 1997? The answer is yes. Remember, bills are paid with cash, not net income. The fact that the companies had no EBIT does not mean that the companies did not have cash provided by operations. This case demonstrates the fact that effective financial statement analysis cannot be accomplished on the basis of any single ratio or, for that matter, any set of ratios. Ratios must be used in conjunction with one another and with other information to make rational business decisions. A company with terrible ratios and a patent on a newly discovered drug that cures cancer may be a far better investment than a company with great ratios and a patent on a chemotherapy product that will soon be out of date. Remember that ratios are based on historical facts. They are useful only to the extent that history is likely to repeat itself.

A LOOK BACK

This chapter addressed the basic issues related to accounting for long-term debt. *Long-term notes* have a maturity period of between two to five years and usually require payments that include a return of principal plus interest. A *line of credit* enables companies to borrow a limited amount of funds on an as-needed basis. Although a line of credit normally carries a term of 1 year, companies frequently refinance, thereby extending the effective maturity data to the intermediate range of 5 or more years. Interest for a line of credit is normally paid on a monthly basis.

Long-term debt financing with terms exceeding 10 years is usually accomplished through the issue of *bonds*. Bond agreements normally commit a company to *semiannual interest* at an amount that is equal to a fixed percentage of the face value. The amount of interest required by the bond agreement is called the *stated interest rate*. If bonds are sold when the *market interest rate* is different from the stated interest rate, companies are required to issue the bonds at a price above or below the face value. They must do this to achieve an effective rate of interest that is consistent with market conditions. Selling bonds at a *discount* (i.e., below face value) increases the effective interest rate above the stated rate. Selling bonds at a *premium* decreases the effective rate of interest.

This chapter explained the tax advantages of using debt financing versus equity financing. Basically, interest is a *tax-deductible expense* that is subtracted prior to the determination of taxable income. In contrast, distributions to owners such as dividends are not deductible in the determination of taxable income.

A LOOK FORWARD

A company that needs long-term financing might choose to use debt, such as the types of bonds or term loans that were discussed in this chapter. Owners' equity is another source of long-term financing. Several equity alternatives are available, depending on the type of business organization the owners choose to establish. For example, a company could be organized as a sole proprietorship, partnership, or corporation. Chapter 11 presents some accounting issues related to equity transactions of each of these types of business structures.

APPENDIX

Time Value of Money
Future Value

L.O. 9

Understand the time value of money.

Suppose that you recently won a $10,000 cash prize in a local lottery. You decide to save the money in order to have funds available to obtain a masters of business administration (MBA) degree. You plan to enter the program 3 years from today. Assuming that you invest the money in an account that earns 8% annual interest, how much money will you have available in 3 years? The answer depends on whether your investment will earn *simple* or *compound* interest.

To determine the amount of funds available assuming that you earn 8% **simple interest,** multiply the principal balance by the interest rate to determine the amount of interest earned per year ($10,000 × .08 = $800). Next, multiply the amount of annual interest by the number of years for which the funds will be invested ($800 × 3 = $2,400). Finally, add the interest earned to the principal balance to determine the total amount of funds available at the end of the 3-year term ($10,000 principal + $2,400 interest = $12,400 cash available at the end of 3 years).

Most investors can increase their returns by reinvesting the income earned from their investments. For example, at the beginning of the second year, you will have available for investment not only the original $10,000 principal balance but also $800 of interest earned during the first year. In other words, you will be able to earn interest on the interest that you previously earned. The practice of earning interest on interest is called **compounding.** Assuming that you are able to earn 8% compound interest, the amount of funds available to you at the end of 3 years can be computed, as shown in Exhibit 10–7.

Obviously, you earn more with compound interest ($2,597.12 compound versus $2,400 simple). The number of computations required for **compound interest** can become cumbersome when the investment term is long. Fortunately, there are mathematical formulas, interest tables, and computer programs that reduce the computational burden. For example, a compound interest factor can be developed from the formula

$$(1 + i)^n$$

where i = interest
n = no. of periods

The value of the investment is determined by multiplying the compound-interest factor by the principal balance. The compound-interest factor for a 3-year term and an 8% interest rate is 1.259712 (1.08 × 1.08 × 1.08 = 1.259712). Assuming a $10,000 original investment, the value of the investment at the end of 3 years is $12,597.12 ($10,000 × 1.259712). This is, of course, the same amount that was computed in the previous illustration (see final figure in the New Balance column of Exhibit 10–7).

The mathematical formulas have been used to develop tables containing interest factors that can be used to determine the **future value** of an investment under a variety of interest rates and time periods. For example, Table I on page 488 contains the interest factor for an investment with a 3-year term earning 8% compound interest. To confirm this point, move down the column marked n to the third period. Next move across to the column marked 8%, where you will find the value 1.259712. This is identical to the amount computed by using the mathematical formula in the preceding paragraph. Here also, the value of the investment at the end of 3 years can be determined by multiplying the principal balance by the compound interest factor ($10,000 × 1.259712 = $12,597.12). These same factors and amounts can be determined through the use of computer programs contained in calculators and spreadsheet software.

Clearly, a variety of ways can be used to determine the future value of an investment, given a principal balance, interest rate, and term to maturity. In our case, we showed that your original investment of $10,000 would be worth $12,597 in 3 years, assuming an 8% compound interest rate. Suppose that you determine that this amount is insufficient to get you through the MBA program you want to complete. Indeed, assume that you believe you will need $18,000 3 years from today to sustain yourself while you finish the degree. Suppose your parents agree to cover the shortfall. They ask how much money you need today in order to have $18,000 3 years from now.

	EXHIBIT 10-7								
Year	Amount Invested	×	Interest Rate	=	Interest Earned	+	Amount Invested	=	New Balance
1	$10,000.00	×	0.08	=	$ 800.00	+	$10,000.00	=	$10,800.00
2	10,800.00	×	0.08	=	864.00	+	10,800.00	=	11,664.00
3	11,664.00	×	0.08	=	933.12	+	11,664.00	=	12,597.12
	Total Interest Earned			=	$2,597.12				

Present Value

The mathematical formula required to convert the future value of a dollar to its **present value** equivalent is

$$\frac{1}{(1 + i)^n}$$

where i = interest
n = no. of periods

For easy conversion, the formula has been used to develop Table II, titled Present Value of $1. At an 8% annual compound interest rate, the present value equivalent of $18,000 to be received 3 years from today is computed as follows: Move down the far-left column to the spot where n = 3. Next, move right to the column marked 8%. At this point, you should see the interest factor 0.793832. Multiplying this factor by the desired future value of $18,000 yields the present value result of $14,288.98 ($18,000 × 0.793832). This means that if you invest $14,288.98 (present value) today at an annual compound-interest rate of 8%, you will have the $18,000 (i.e., future value) you need to enter the MBA program 3 years from now.

If you currently have $10,000, you will need an additional $4,288.98 from your parents to make the required $14,288.98 investment that will yield the future value of $18,000 you need to enter the MBA program. In other words, having $14,288.98 today is the same thing as having $18,000 3 years from today, assuming you can earn 8% compound interest. To validate this conclusion, use Table I to determine the future value of $14,288.98, given a 3-year term and an 8% annual compound interest. As previously indicated, the future-value conversion factor under these conditions is 1.259712. Multiplying this factor by the $14,288.98 present value produces the expected future value of $18,000 ($14,288.98 × 1.259712 = $18,000). Accordingly, the factors in Table I can be used to convert present values to future values, and the corresponding factors in Table II are used to convert future values to present values.

Future Value Annuities

The previous examples described present and future values associated with a single lump-sum payment. Many financial transactions involve a series of payments. To illustrate, we return to the example in which you want to have $18,000 available 3 years from today. We continue the assumption that you can earn 8% compound interest. However, now we assume that you do not have $14,288.98 to invest today. Instead, you decide to save part of the money during each of the next 3 years. How much money must you save each year to have $18,000 at the end of 3 years? *The series of equal payments made over a number of periods in order to acquire a future value is called an* **annuity.** The factors contained in Table III titled Future Value of an Annuity of $1 can be used to determine the amount of the annuity needed to produce the desired $18,000 future value. The table is constructed so that future values can be determined by multiplying the conversion factor by the amount of the annuity. These relationships can be expressed algebraically as follows:

Amount of Annuity Payment × Table Conversion Factor = Future Value

To determine the amount of the required annuity payment in our example, first locate the future value conversion factor. In Table III, move down the first column on the left-hand side until you locate period 3. Next move to the right until you locate the column for the 8% interest rate. At this location you will see a conversion factor of 3.2464. This factor can be used to determine the amount of the annuity payment as indicated below:

Amount of Annuity Payment × Table Conversion Factor = Future Value

Amount of Annuity Payment = Future Value ÷ Table Conversion Factor

Amount of Annuity Payment = $18,000.00 ÷ 3.2464

Amount of Annuity Payment = $5,544.60

If you deposit $5,544.60 in an investment account at the end of each of the next 3 years,[6] the investment account balance will be $18,000, assuming your investment earns 8% interest compounded annually. This conclusion is validated by the following schedule.

---

[6]A payment made at the end of a period is known as an *ordinary annuity*. A payment made at the beginning of a period is called an *annuity due*. Tables are generally set up to assume ordinary annuities. Minor adjustments must be made when dealing with an annuity due. For the purposes of this text, we consider all annuities to be ordinary.

End of Year	Beg. Acct. Bal.	+	Interest Computation	+	Payment	=	End. Acct. Bal.
1	0	+	0	+	$5,544.60	=	$ 5,544.60
2	$ 5,544.60	+	$ 5,544.60 × 0.08 = $443.57	+	5,544.60	=	11,532.77
3	11,532.77	+	11,532.77 × 0.08 = 922.62	+	5,544.60	=	18,000.00*

*Total does not add exactly due to rounding.

Present Value Annuities

We previously demonstrated that a future value of $18,000 is equivalent to a present value of $14,288.98, given annual compound interest of 8% for a 3-year period. Accordingly, if the future value of a $5,544.60 annuity is equivalent to a future value of $18,000, that same annuity should have a present value of $14,288.98. We can test this conclusion by using the conversion factors shown in Table IV, Present Value of an Annuity of $1. The present value annuity table is constructed so that present values can be determined by multiplying the conversion factor by the amount of the annuity. These relationships can be expressed algebraically as follows:

Amount of Annuity Payment × Table Conversion Factor = Present Value

To determine the amount of the required annuity payment in our example, first locate the present value conversion factor. In Table IV, move down the first column on the left-hand side until you locate period 3. Next move to the right until you locate the column for the 8% interest rate. At this location you will see a conversion factor of 2.577097. This factor can be used to determine the amount of the annuity payment, as indicated:

Amount of Annuity Payment × Table Conversion Factor = Present Value
$5,544.60   ×   2.577097   = $14,288.97*

In summary, Tables III and IV can be used to convert annuities to future or present values for a variety of different assumptions regarding interest rates and time periods.

Business Applications
Long-Term Notes Payable

In the early part of this chapter, we considered a case in which Bill Blair borrowed $100,000 from National Bank. We indicated that Blair agreed to repay the bank through a series of annual payments (i.e., an *annuity*) in the amount of $25,709 each. How was this amount determined? Recall that Blair agreed to pay the bank 9% interest over a 5-year term. Under these circumstances, we are trying to find the annuity equivalent to the $100,000 present value that the bank is loaning Blair. The first step in determining the annuity (i.e., annual payment) is to locate the appropriate present value conversion factor from Table IV. At the fifth row under the column titled 9%, you will find the value 3.889651. This factor can be used to determine the amount of the annuity payment as indicated here:

Amount of Annuity Payment × Table Conversion Factor = Present Value
Amount of Annuity Payment = Present Value ÷ Table Conversion Factor
Amount of Annuity Payment = $100,000 ÷ 3.889651
Amount of Annuity Payment = $ 25,709

There are many applications in which debt repayment is accomplished through annuities. Common examples with which you are probably familiar include auto loans and home mortgages. Payment schedules for such loans may be determined from the interest tables, as demonstrated here. However, most real-world businesses have further refined the computational process through the use of sophisticated computer programs. The software program prompts the user to provide the relevant information regarding the present value of the amount borrowed, number of payments, and interest rate. Given this information and a few simple keystrokes, the computer program produces the amount of the amortization payment along with an amortization schedule showing the amounts of principal and interest payments over the life of the loan. Similar results can be accomplished with spreadsheet software applications such as Excel and Lotus. Even

---

*The 1 cent difference between this value and the expected value of $14,288.98 is due to rounding.

many handheld calculators have present and future value functions that enable users to quickly compute annuity payments for an infinite number of interest rate and time period assumptions.

Bond Liabilities Determine Price

We discussed the use of discounts and premiums as means of producing an effective rate of interest that is higher or lower than the stated rate of interest. For example, if the stated rate of interest is lower than the market rate of interest at the time the bonds are issued, the issuer can increase the effective interest rate by selling the bonds for a price lower than their face value. At maturity, the issuer will settle the obligation by paying the face value of the bond. The difference between the discounted bond price and the face value of the bond is additional interest. To illustrate, assume that Tower Company issues $100,000 face value bonds with a 20-year term and a 9% stated rate of annual interest. At the time the bonds are issued, the market rate of interest for bonds of comparable risk is 10% annual interest. For what amount would Tower Company be required to sell the bonds in order to move its 9% stated rate of interest to an effective rate of 10%?

Information from present value Tables II and IV is required to determine the amount of the discount required to produce a 10% effective rate of interest. First, we define the future cash flows that will be generated by the bonds. Based on the stated interest rate, the bonds will pay $9,000 ($100,000 face value $\times$ 0.09 interest) interest per year. This constitutes a 20-year annuity that should be discounted back to its present value equivalent. Also, at the end of 20 years, the bonds will require a single $100,000 lump-sum payment to settle the principal obligation. This amount must also be discounted back to its present value in order to determine the bond price. The computations required to determine the discounted bond price are shown here:

Present Value of Principal	$100,000 $\times$ 0.148644	= $14,864.40
	(Table II, $n = 20$, $i = 10$%)	
Present Value of Interest	$9,000 $\times$ 8.513564	= 76,622.08
	(Table IV, $n = 20$, $i = 10$%)	
Bond Price		$91,486.48

Tower Company bonds sell at an $8,513.52 discount ($100,000 − $91,486.48) to produce a 10% effective interest rate. Note carefully that in these computations, the stated rate of interest was used to determine the amount of cash flow, and the effective rate of interest was used to determine the table conversion factor.

Bond Liabilities: Effective Interest Method of Amortization

To this point, the straight-line method has been used to amortize bond discounts or premiums. This method is commonly used in practice because it is simple to apply and easy to understand. However, the method is theoretically deficient because it results in the recognition of a constant amount of interest expense while the carrying value of the bond liability fluctuates. Consider the discount on Tower Company bonds just discussed as an example. In this case, the amount of interest expense recognized each period is computed as follows:

Stated Rate of Interest	$100,000.00 $\times$ 0.09	= $9,000.00
Amortization of Discount	$ 8,513.52 ÷ 20	= 425.68
Interest Expense Recognized Each Accounting Period		= $9,425.68

As previously demonstrated, the amortization of the bond discount acts to increase the carrying value of the bond liability. Accordingly, under the straight-line method, the bond liability increases while the amount of interest expense recognized remains constant. Logically, the amount of interest expense should increase as the amount of liability increases. This rational relationship can be accomplished by applying the **effective interest rate method** to the amortization of bond discounts and premiums. The effective interest rate method is required when the result of its application will cause a material effect on the financial statements.

Under the effective interest rate method, the amount of interest expense recognized in the financial statements is determined by multiplying the effective rate of interest by the carrying value of the bond liability. The amount of the discount to be amortized is determined by the difference between the interest expense and the cash outflow, as defined by the stated rate of interest. The following schedule demonstrates the application of the effective interest rate method for the recognition of interest expense during the first 3 years that Tower Company bonds were outstanding.

End of Year	Cash Payment	Interest Expense	Discount Amortization	Carrying Value
1	$9,000[a]	$9,148.65[b]	$148.65[c]	$91,635.13[d]
2	9,000	9,163.51	163.51	91,798.64
3	9,000	9,179.86	179.86	91,978.50

[a]Cash outflow based on the stated rate of interest ($100,000 × 0.09).
[b]Effective interest rate times the carrying value (10 × $91,486.48).
[c]Interest expense minus cash outflow ($9,148.65 − $9,000.00).
[d]Previous carrying value plus portion of discount amortized ($91,486.48 + $148.65).

Notice that the effective interest rate method results in increasingly larger amounts of expense recognition as the carrying value of the bond liability increases. The effect of the expense recognition on the financial statements and the journal entry necessary to record it for the first accounting period are as follows:

Cash	=	Bond Liab.	+	Equity		Rev.	−	Exp.	=	Net Inc.		Cash Flow	
(9,000)	=	148.65*	+	(9,148.65)		n/a	−	9,148.65	=	(9,148.65)		(9,000)	OA

*The decrease in the amount of the discount acts to increase the bond liability.

Account Title	Debit	Credit
Interest Expense	9,148.65	
Cash		9,000.00
Discount on Bonds Payable		148.65

TABLE I
Future Value of $1

n	4%	5%	6%	7%	8%	9%	10%	12%	14%	16%	20%
1	1.040000	1.050000	1.060000	1.070000	1.080000	1.090000	1.100000	1.120000	1.140000	1.160000	1.200000
2	1.081600	1.102500	1.123600	1.144900	1.166400	1.188100	1.210000	1.254400	1.299600	1.345600	1.440000
3	1.124864	1.157625	1.191016	1.225043	1.259712	1.295029	1.331000	1.404928	1.481544	1.560896	1.728000
4	1.169859	1.215506	1.262477	1.310796	1.360489	1.411582	1.464100	1.573519	1.688960	1.810639	2.073600
5	1.216653	1.276282	1.338226	1.402552	1.469328	1.538624	1.610510	1.762342	1.925415	2.100342	2.488320
6	1.265319	1.340096	1.418519	1.500730	1.586874	1.677100	1.771561	1.973823	2.194973	2.436396	2.985984
7	1.315932	1.407100	1.503630	1.605781	1.713824	1.828039	1.948717	2.210681	2.502269	2.826220	3.583181
8	1.368569	1.477455	1.593848	1.718186	1.850930	1.992563	2.143589	2.475963	2.852586	3.278415	4.299817
9	1.423312	1.551328	1.689479	1.838459	1.999005	2.171893	2.357948	2.773079	3.251949	3.802961	5.159780
10	1.480244	1.628895	1.790848	1.967151	2.158925	2.367364	2.593742	3.105848	3.707221	4.411435	6.191736
11	1.539454	1.710339	1.898299	2.104852	2.331639	2.580426	2.853117	3.478550	4.226232	5.117265	7.430084
12	1.601032	1.795856	2.012196	2.252192	2.518170	2.812665	3.138428	3.895976	4.817905	5.936027	8.916100
13	1.665074	1.885649	2.132928	2.409845	2.719624	3.065805	3.452271	4.363493	5.492411	6.885791	10.699321
14	1.731676	1.979932	2.260904	2.578534	2.937194	3.341727	3.797498	4.887112	6.261349	7.987518	12.839185
15	1.800944	2.078928	2.396558	2.759032	3.172169	3.642482	4.177248	5.473566	7.137938	9.265521	15.407022
16	1.872981	2.182875	2.540352	2.952164	3.425943	3.970306	4.594973	6.130394	8.137249	10.748004	18.488426
17	1.947900	2.292018	2.692773	3.158815	3.700018	4.327633	5.054470	6.866041	9.276464	12.467685	22.186111
18	2.025817	2.406619	2.854339	3.379932	3.996019	4.717120	5.559917	7.689966	10.575169	14.462514	26.623333
19	2.106849	2.526950	3.025600	3.616528	4.315701	5.141661	6.115909	8.612762	12.055693	16.776517	31.948000
20	2.191123	2.653298	3.207135	3.869684	4.660957	5.604411	6.727500	9.646293	13.743490	19.460759	38.337600

TABLE II

Present Value of $1

n	4%	5%	6%	7%	8%	9%	10%	12%	14%	16%	20%
1	0.961538	0.952381	0.943396	0.934579	0.925926	0.917431	0.909091	0.892857	0.877193	0.862069	0.833333
2	0.924556	0.907029	0.889996	0.873439	0.857339	0.841680	0.826446	0.797194	0.769468	0.743163	0.694444
3	0.888996	0.863838	0.839619	0.816298	0.793832	0.772183	0.751315	0.711780	0.674972	0.640658	0.578704
4	0.854804	0.822702	0.792094	0.762895	0.735030	0.708425	0.683013	0.635518	0.592080	0.552291	0.482253
5	0.821927	0.783526	0.747258	0.712986	0.680583	0.649931	0.620921	0.567427	0.519369	0.476113	0.401878
6	0.790315	0.746215	0.704961	0.666342	0.630170	0.596267	0.564474	0.506631	0.455587	0.410442	0.334898
7	0.759918	0.710681	0.665057	0.622750	0.583490	0.547034	0.513158	0.452349	0.399637	0.353830	0.279082
8	0.730690	0.676839	0.627412	0.582009	0.540269	0.501866	0.466507	0.403883	0.350559	0.305025	0.232568
9	0.702587	0.644609	0.591898	0.543934	0.500249	0.460428	0.424098	0.360610	0.307508	0.262953	0.193807
10	0.675564	0.613913	0.558395	0.508349	0.463193	0.422411	0.385543	0.321973	0.269744	0.226684	0.161506
11	0.649581	0.584679	0.526788	0.475093	0.428883	0.387533	0.350494	0.287476	0.236617	0.195417	0.134588
12	0.624597	0.556837	0.496969	0.444012	0.397114	0.355535	0.318631	0.256675	0.207559	0.168463	0.112157
13	0.600574	0.530321	0.468839	0.414964	0.367698	0.326179	0.289664	0.229174	0.182069	0.145227	0.093464
14	0.577475	0.505068	0.442301	0.387817	0.340461	0.299246	0.263331	0.204620	0.159710	0.125195	0.077887
15	0.555265	0.481017	0.417265	0.362446	0.315242	0.274538	0.239392	0.182696	0.140096	0.107927	0.064905
16	0.533908	0.458112	0.393646	0.338735	0.291890	0.251870	0.217629	0.163122	0.122892	0.093041	0.054088
17	0.513373	0.436297	0.371364	0.316574	0.270269	0.231073	0.197845	0.145644	0.107800	0.080207	0.045073
18	0.493628	0.415521	0.350344	0.295864	0.250249	0.211994	0.179859	0.130040	0.094561	0.069144	0.037561
19	0.474642	0.395734	0.330513	0.276508	0.231712	0.194490	0.163508	0.116107	0.082948	0.059607	0.031301
20	0.456387	0.376889	0.311805	0.258419	0.214548	0.178431	0.148644	0.103667	0.072762	0.051385	0.026084

TABLE III

Future Value of an Annuity of $1

n	4%	5%	6%	7%	8%	9%	10%	12%	14%	16%	20%
1	1.000000	1.000000	1.000000	1.000000	1.000000	1.000000	1.000000	1.000000	1.000000	1.000000	1.000000
2	2.040000	2.050000	2.060000	2.070000	2.080000	2.090000	2.100000	2.120000	2.140000	2.160000	2.200000
3	3.121600	3.152500	3.183600	3.214900	3.246400	3.278100	3.310000	3.374400	3.439600	3.505600	3.640000
4	4.246464	4.310125	4.374616	4.439943	4.506112	4.573129	4.641000	4.779328	4.921144	5.066496	5.368000
5	5.416323	5.525631	5.637093	5.750739	5.866601	5.984711	6.105100	6.352847	6.610104	6.877135	7.441600
6	6.632975	6.801913	6.975319	7.153291	7.335929	7.523335	7.715610	8.115189	8.535519	8.977477	9.929920
7	7.898294	8.142008	8.393838	8.654021	8.922803	9.200435	9.487171	10.089012	10.730491	11.413873	12.915904
8	9.214226	9.549109	9.897468	10.259803	10.636628	11.028474	11.435888	12.299693	13.232760	14.240093	16.499085
9	10.582795	11.026564	11.491316	11.977989	12.487558	13.021036	13.579477	14.775656	16.085347	17.518508	20.798902
10	12.006107	12.577893	13.180795	13.816448	14.486562	15.192930	15.937425	17.548735	19.337295	21.321469	25.958682
11	13.486351	14.206787	14.971643	15.783599	16.645487	17.560293	18.531167	20.654583	23.044516	25.732904	32.150419
12	15.025805	15.917127	16.869941	17.888451	18.977126	20.140720	21.384284	24.133133	27.270749	30.850169	39.580502
13	16.626838	17.712983	18.882138	20.140643	21.495297	22.953385	24.522712	28.029109	32.088654	36.786196	48.496603
14	18.291911	19.598632	21.015066	22.550488	24.214920	26.019189	27.974983	32.392602	37.581065	43.671987	59.195923
15	20.023588	21.578564	23.275970	25.129022	27.152114	29.360916	31.772482	37.279715	43.842414	51.659505	72.035108
16	21.824531	23.657492	25.672528	27.888054	30.324283	33.003399	35.949730	42.753280	50.980352	60.925026	87.442129
17	23.697512	25.840366	28.212880	30.840217	33.750226	36.973705	40.544703	48.883674	59.117601	71.673030	105.930555
18	25.645413	28.132385	30.905653	33.999033	37.450244	41.301338	45.599173	55.749715	68.394066	84.140715	128.116666
19	27.671229	30.539004	33.759992	37.378965	41.446263	46.018458	51.159090	63.439681	78.969235	98.603230	154.740000
20	29.778079	33.065954	36.785591	40.995492	45.761964	51.160120	57.274999	72.052442	91.024928	115.379747	186.688000

TABLE IV

Present Value of an Annuity of $1

n	4%	5%	6%	7%	8%	9%	10%	12%	14%	16%	20%
1	0.961538	0.952381	0.943396	0.934579	0.925926	0.917431	0.909091	0.892857	0.877193	0.862069	0.833333
2	1.886095	1.859410	1.833393	1.808018	1.783265	1.759111	1.735537	1.690051	1.646661	1.605232	1.527778
3	2.775091	2.723248	2.673012	2.624316	2.577097	2.531295	2.486852	2.401831	2.321632	2.245890	2.106481
4	3.629895	3.545951	3.465106	3.387211	3.312127	3.239720	3.169865	3.037349	2.913712	2.798181	2.588735
5	4.451822	4.329477	4.212364	4.100197	3.992710	3.889651	3.790787	3.604776	3.433081	3.274294	2.990612
6	5.242137	5.075692	4.917324	4.766540	4.622880	4.485919	4.355261	4.111407	3.888668	3.684736	3.325510
7	6.002055	5.786373	5.582381	5.389289	5.206370	5.032953	4.868419	4.563757	4.288305	4.038565	3.604592
8	6.732745	6.463213	6.209794	5.971299	5.746639	5.534819	5.334926	4.967640	4.638864	4.343591	3.837160
9	7.435332	7.107822	6.801692	6.515232	6.246888	5.995247	5.759024	5.328250	4.946372	4.606544	4.030967
10	8.110896	7.721735	7.360087	7.023582	6.710081	6.417658	6.144567	5.650223	5.216116	4.833227	4.192472
11	8.760477	8.306414	7.886875	7.498674	7.138964	6.805191	6.495061	5.937699	5.452733	5.028644	4.327060
12	9.385074	8.863252	8.383844	7.942686	7.536078	7.160725	6.813692	6.194374	5.660292	5.197107	4.439217
13	9.985648	9.393573	8.852683	8.357651	7.903776	7.486904	7.103356	6.423548	5.842362	5.342334	4.532681
14	10.563123	9.898641	9.294984	8.745468	8.244237	7.786150	7.366687	6.628168	6.002072	5.467529	4.610567
15	11.118387	10.379658	9.712249	9.107914	8.559479	8.060688	7.606080	6.810864	6.142168	5.575456	4.675473
16	11.652296	10.837770	10.105895	9.446649	8.851369	8.312558	7.823709	6.973986	6.265060	5.668497	4.729561
17	12.165669	11.274066	10.477260	9.763223	9.121638	8.543631	8.021553	7.119630	6.372859	5.748704	4.774634
18	12.659297	11.689587	10.827603	10.059087	9.371887	8.755625	8.201412	7.249670	6.467420	5.817848	4.812195
19	13.133939	12.085321	11.158116	10.335595	9.603599	8.905115	8.364920	7.365777	6.550369	5.877455	4.843496
20	13.590326	12.462210	11.469921	10.594014	9.818147	9.128546	8.513564	7.469444	6.623131	5.928841	4.869580

KEY TERMS

Amortization of Loan Systematic repayment of the principal and interest over the life of the loan. *(p. 459)*

Annuity A series of equal payments made over a specified number of periods. *(p. 484)*

Balloon Payment The systematic payment (amortization) of a part of the debt over the term of the loan with the remainder due at maturity. *(p. 460)*

Bearer or **Coupon Bonds** Also called *unregistered bonds;* unregistered bonds in which interest and principal payments are made to anyone who holds and redeems the interest coupon. *(p. 466)*

Bond A form of long-term financing in which a company borrows funds from a number of lenders, called *bondholders*. Bonds are usually issued in denominations of $1,000. *(p. 466)*

Bond Discount The difference between the selling price and the face amount of a bond that is sold for less than the face amount. *(p. 472)*

Bond Indenture The bond contract that specifies the stated rate of interest and the face value of the bond. *(p. 466)*

Bond Premium The difference between the selling price and the face amount of the bond that is sold for more than the face amount. *(p. 477)*

Call Premium The difference between the call price (the price that must be paid for called bonds) and the face amount of the bond. *(p. 467)*

Call Price A specified price that must be paid for bonds that are called. The call price is usually higher than the face amount of the bonds. *(p. 478)*

Callable Bonds Bonds that include a feature allowing the issuer to pay them off prior to maturity. *(p. 467)*

Carrying Value The face amount of the loan less any unamortized bond discount or plus any unamortized bond premium. *(p. 473)*

Collateral for Loans Assets that are pledged as security for a loan. *(p. 462)*

Compound Interest The practice of reinvesting interest so that interest is earned on interest as well as on the initial principal. *(p. 483)*

Compounding The practice of earning interest on interest. *(p. 483)*

Convertible Bonds Bonds that can be converted (exchanged) to an ownership interest (stock) in the corporation. *(p. 467)*

Debenture An unsecured bond that is issued based on the general credit of the organization. *(p. 466)*

Discount on Bonds Payable A contra liability account that is used to record the amount of discount on a bond issue. *(p. 473)*

Effective Interest Rate Method (appendix) The method of amortizing bond discounts and premiums that computes interest on the actual amount of liability. As the liability increases or decreases, the amount of interest expense also increases or decreases. *(p. 486)*

Effective Interest Rate The yield rate of bonds, which is usually equal to the market rate of interest on the day the bonds are sold. *(p. 471)*

Extraordinary Items Items of income and expense that are unusual and rarely occur and that are set apart from operating income on the income statement. *(p. 479)*

Face Value The amount of the bond that is to be paid back (to the bondholders) at maturity. *(p. 466)*

Financial Leverage The concept of increasing earnings through debt financing. *(p. 465)*

Fixed Interest Rate An interest rate (charge for the use of money) that does not change over the life of the loan. *(p. 459)*

Future Value (appendix) The amount an investment will be worth at some point in the future, assuming a specified interest rate and assuming the interest is reinvested each period that it is earned. *(p. 483)*

Issuer of a Bond The party that issues the bond (the borrower). *(p. 465)*

Junk Bonds Bonds issued by companies with credit ratings so low that they signal a significant risk regarding the companies' ability to pay interest or return principal to the bondholder. *(p. 468)*

Line of Credit A preapproved credit arrangement with a lending institution in which a business can borrow money by simply writing a check up to the approved limit. *(p. 463)*

Long-Term Debt Debt that does not mature within 1 year or the operating cycle, whichever is longer. *(p. 459)*

Market Interest Rate The current interest rate that is available on a wide range of alternative investments. *(p. 471)*

Mortgage Bonds Type of secured bond that conditionally transfers title of a designated piece of property to the bondholder until the bond is paid. *(p. 466)*

Present Value (appendix) The current value of some investment amount that is expected to be received at some specified future time. *(p. 484)*

Registered Bonds Bonds for which the issuing company keeps a record of the names and addresses of the bondholders and pays interest and principal payments directly to the registered owner. *(p. 466)*

Restrictive Covenants Special provisions specified in the bond contract that are designed to prohibit management from taking certain actions that place bondholders at risk. *(p. 462)*

Secured Bonds Bonds that are secured by specific identifiable assets. *(p. 466)*

Serial Bonds Bonds that mature at specified intervals throughout the life of the total issue. *(p. 467)*

Simple Interest Interest computed by multiplying the principal by the interest rate by the number of periods. Interest earned in a period is not added to the principal, so that no interest is earned on the interest of previous periods. *(p. 483)*

Sinking Fund A fund to which the issuer annually contributes to ensure the availability of cash for the payment of the face amount on maturity date. *(p. 467)*

Spread The difference between the rate a bank pays to obtain money (e.g., interest paid on savings accounts) and the rate that the bank earns on money it lends to borrowers. *(p. 465)*

Stated Interest Rate The rate of interest specified in the bond contract that will be paid at specified intervals over the life of the bond. *(p. 466)*

Straight-Line Amortization The method of amortization that allocates bond discount or premium in equal amounts to each period over the life of the bond. *(p. 474)*

Subordinated Debentures Unsecured bonds that have a lower priority than general creditors; that is, these bonds are paid off after the general creditors are paid in the case of liquidation. *(p. 466)*

Term Bonds Bonds in an issue that mature on a specified date in the future. *(p. 467)*

Time Value of Money (appendix) The recognition that the present value of a promise to receive a dollar some time in the future is worth less than a dollar. For example, a person may be willing to pay $0.90 today for the entitlement to receive $1.00 one year from today. *(p. 482)*

Times-Interest-Earned Ratio A ratio that computes how many times a company would be able to pay its interest by using the amount of earnings available to make interest payments. This amount of earnings is net income before interest and income taxes. *(p. 481)*

Unregistered Bonds Also called *coupon* or *bearer bonds*; bonds for which no record of the holder of the bond is kept. *(p. 466)*

Unsecured Bonds Also known as *debentures*, bonds issued on the general credit of the organization. *(p. 466)*

Unsubordinated Debentures Unsecured bonds that have equal claims with the general creditors. *(p. 466)*

Variable Interest Rate An interest rate that fluctuates (may change) from period to period over the life of the loan. *(p. 459)*

QUESTIONS

1. What is the difference between classification of a note as short term or long term?

2. At the beginning of year 1, B Co. has a note payable of $72,000 that calls for an annual payment of $16,246, which includes both principal and interest. If the interest rate is 8%, what is the amount of interest expense in year 1 and in year 2? What is the balance of the note at the end of year 2?

3. What is the purpose of a line of credit for a business? Why would a company choose to obtain a line of credit instead of issuing bonds?

4. What are the primary sources of debt financing for most large companies?

5. What are some of the advantages of issuing bonds versus borrowing from a bank?

6. What are some of the disadvantages of issuing bonds?

7. Why can a company usually issue bonds at a lower interest rate than the company would pay if the funds were borrowed from a bank?

8. What effect does income tax have on the cost of borrowing funds for a business?

9. What is the concept of financial leverage?

10. Which type of bond, a secured or an unsecured bond, is likely to have a lower interest rate? Explain.

11. What is the function of restrictive covenants attached to bond issues?

12. Why are unregistered bonds (bearer or coupon bonds) more vulnerable to theft than registered bonds?

13. What is the difference between term bonds and serial bonds?

14. What is the purpose of establishing a sinking fund?

15. What is the call price of a bond? Is it usually higher or lower than the face amount of the bond? Explain.

16. If Roc Co. issued $100,000 of 5%, 10-year bonds at the face amount, what is the effect of the issuance of the bonds on the financial statements? What amount of interest expense will be recognized by Roc Co. each year?

17. What mechanism is used to adjust the stated interest rate to the market rate of interest?

18. When the effective interest rate is higher than the stated interest rate of a bond issue, will the bond sell at a discount or premium? Why?

19. What type of transaction is the issuance of bonds by a company?

20. What factors may cause the effective interest rate and the stated interest rate to be different?

21. If a bond is selling at 97.5, how much cash will the company receive from the sale of a $1,000 bond?

22. How is the carrying value of a bond computed?

23. Gay Co. has a balance in the Bonds Payable account of $25,000 and a balance in the Discount on Bonds Payable account of $5,200. What is the carrying value of the bonds? What is the total amount of the liability?

24. When the effective interest rate is higher than the stated interest rate, will interest expense be higher or lower than the amount of interest paid?

25. Assuming that the selling price of the bond and the fact value are the same, would the issuer of a bond rather make annual or semiannual interest payments? Why?

26. Rato Co. called some bonds and had a loss on the redemption of the bonds of $2,850. How is this amount shown on the income statement?

27. Which method of financing, debt financing or equity financing, is generally more advantageous from a tax standpoint? Why?

28. If a company has a tax rate of 30% and interest expense was $10,000, what is the after-tax cost of the debt?

29. Which type of financing, debt financing or equity financing, increases the risk factor of a business? Why?

30. What information does the times-interest-earned ratio provide?

31. What is the difference between simple and compound interest?

32. What is meant by the future value of an investment? How is it determined?

33. If you have $10,000 to invest at the beginning of year 1 at an interest rate of 8%, what will be the future value of the investment at the end of year 4?

34. What is meant by the present value of an investment? How is it determined?

35. Assume that your favorite aunt gave you $25,000, but you will not receive the gift until you are 25 years old. You are presently 22 years old. What is the current value of the gift, assuming an interest rate of 8%?

36. What is the present value of four payments of $4,000 each to be received at the end of each of the next 4 years, assuming an interest rate of 8%?

37. How does the effective interest method of bond amortization differ from the straight-line method of bond amortization? Which method is conceptually more correct?

EXERCISES

EXERCISE 10-1
L.O. 2

Understanding How Credit Terms Affect Financial Statements

Rubel Co. borrowed $40,000 from the National Bank by issuing a note with a 5-year term. Rubel has two options with respect to the payment of interest and principal. Option 1 requires the payment of interest only on an annual basis with the full amount of the principal being due at maturity. Option 2 calls for an annual payment that includes interest due plus a partial repayment of the principal balance. The effective annual interest rate on both notes is identical.

Required

Write a memo explaining how the two alternatives will affect (a) the carrying value of liabilities, (b) the amount of annual interest expense, (c) the total amount of interest that will be paid over the life of the note, and (d) the cash flow consequences.

Accounting for a Long-Term Note Payable with Annual Payment That Includes Interest and Principal

On January 1, 20X6, Craft Co. borrowed $120,000 cash from First Bank by issuing a 5-year, 8% note. The principal and interest are to be paid by making annual payments in the amount of $30,055. Payments are to be made December 31 of each year, beginning December 31, 20X6.

Required

Prepare an amortization schedule for the interest and principal payments for the 5-year period.

Long-Term Installment Notes Payable

Lee Chang started a business by issuing an $80,000 face value note to State National Bank on January 1, 20X6. The note carried a 10% annual rate of interest and a 5-year term. Payments of $21,104 are to be made each December 31 for 5 years.

Required

a. What portion of the December 31, 20X6, payment is applied to the following:

   (1) Interest expense

   (2) Principal

b. What is the principal balance on January 1, 20X7?

c. What portion of the December 31, 20X7, payment is applied to the following?

   (1) Interest expense

   (2) Principal

Amortization of a Long-Term Loan

A partial amortization schedule for a 10-year note payable issued on January 1, 20X4, is shown here:

Accounting Period	Principal Balance January 1	Cash Payment	Applied to Interest	Applied to Principal
20X4	$200,000	$32,547	$20,000	$12,547
20X5	187,453	32,547	18,745	13,802
20X6	173,651	32,547	17,365	15,182

Required

a. Using a financial statements model like the one shown here, record the appropriate amounts for the following two events:

   (1) January 1, 20X4, issuance of the note payable.

   (2) December 31, 20X4, payment on the note payable.

Event No.	Assets	=	Liab.	+	Equity	Rev.	−	Exp.	=	Net Inc.	Cash Flow
1											
2											

b. If the company earned $100,000 cash revenue and paid $50,000 in cash expenses in addition to the interest in 20X4, what is the amount of each of the following?

   (1) Net income for 20X4.

   (2) Cash flow from operating activities for 20X4.

   (3) Cash flow from financing activities for 20X4.

c. What is the amount of interest expense on this loan for 20X7?

EXERCISE 10-5   **Accounting for a Line of Credit**
L.O. 3   Rex Company has a line of credit with Federal Bank. Rex can borrow up to $200,000 at any time over the course of the 20X7 calendar year. The following table shows the prime rate expressed as an annual percentage along with the amounts borrowed and repaid during the first 3 months of 20X7. Rex agreed to pay interest at an annual rate equal to 2% above the bank's prime rate. Funds are borrowed or repaid on the first day of each month. Interest is payable in cash on the last day of the month. The interest rate is applied to the outstanding monthly balance. For example, Rex pays 6% (4% + 2%) annual interest on $80,000 for the month of February.

Month	Amount Borrowed or (Repaid)	Prime Rate for the Month, %
January	$50,000	3.0
February	30,000	4.0
March	(40,000)	4.5

Required
Provide all journal entries associated with Rex's line of credit for the first 3 months of 20X7.

EXERCISE 10-6   **Annual versus Semiannual Interest Payments**
L.O. 6   Samuels Company issued a $10,000 face value bond on January 1, 20X7. The bond carried an 8% stated rate of interest and a 6-year term. The bond was issued at face value. Interest is payable on an annual basis.

Required
Write a memo explaining whether the total cash outflow for interest will be more, less, or the same if the bonds accrue semiannual versus annual interest.

EXERCISE 10-7   **Determining the Amount of Cash Receipts from Bond Issues**
L.O. 5, 7
Required
Compute the cash proceeds from bond issues under the following terms. For each case, indicate whether the bond sold at a premium or discount.
   a. Star, Inc., issued $200,000 of 10-year, 8% bonds at 103.
   b. Moon Co. issued $80,000 of 5-year, 12% bonds at 95½.
   c. Sun Co. issued $100,000 of 5-year, 6% bonds at 101¾.
   d. Planet, Inc., issued $50,000 of 4-year, 8% bonds at 98.

EXERCISE 10-8   **Identifying the Relationship between the Stated Rate of Interest and the Market Rate**
L.O. 5   **of Interest**

Required
Indicate whether a bond will sell for a premium (P), discount (D), or face value (F) for each of the following conditions:
   a. _____ The market rate of interest is equal to the stated rate.
   b. _____ The market rate of interest is less than the stated rate.
   c. _____ The market rate of interest is higher than the market rate.
   d. _____ The stated rate of interest is higher than the market rate.
   e. _____ The stated rate of interest is less than the market rate.

EXERCISE 10-9   **Identifying Bond Premiums and Discounts**
L.O. 5
Required
In each of the following situations, state whether the bond will sell at a premium or discount.

a. Tenco issued $200,000 of bonds with a stated interest rate of 8%. At the time of issue, the market rate of interest for similar investments was 7%.

b. Tenco issued $100,000 of bonds with a stated interest rate of 8%. At the time of issue, the market rate of interest for similar investments was 9%.

c. Space Inc. issued callable bonds with a stated interest rate of 8%. The bonds were callable at 104. At the date of issue, the market rate of interest was 9% for similar investments.

Determining the Amount of Bond Premiums and Discounts

EXERCISE 10-10
L.O. 5

Required

For each of the following situations, calculate the amount of bond discount or premium, if any.

a. Jeff Co. issued $80,000 of 6% bonds at 102.

b. Bill, Inc., issued $50,000 of 10-year, 8% bonds for 98.

c. Will, Inc., issued $100,000 of 15-year, 9% bonds for 102¼.

d. Edd Co. issued $500,000 of 20-year, 8% bonds for 98¾.

Effect of a Bond Discount on Financial Statements—Annual Interest

EXERCISE 10-11
L.O. 6, 7

Mr. P. Company issued a $100,000 face value bond on January 1, 20X4. The bond carried an 8% stated rate of interest and a 5-year term. Interest is paid in cash annually, beginning December 31, 20X4. The bond was issued at a price of 96.

Required

a. Show the effect of (1) the bond issue, (2) amortization of the discount on December 31, 20X4, and (3) the December 31, 20X4, interest payment on the financial statements, using a horizontal statements model like the following one. Use the following coding scheme to record your answer: increase (+), decrease (−), and not affected (n/a).

Event No.	Assets	=	Liab.	+	Equity	Rev.	−	Exp.	=	Net Inc.	Cash Flow
1											
2											

b. Determine the amount of the carrying value (i.e., face value less discount or plus premium) of the bond liability as of December 31, 20X4.

c. Determine the amount of interest expense shown on the December 31, 20X4, income statement.

d. Determine the amount of the carrying value (i.e., face value less discount or plus premium of the bond liability as of December 31, 20X5.

e. Determine the amount of interest expense shown on the December 31, 20X5, income statement.

Effect of a Bond Premium on Financial Statements—Annual Interest

EXERCISE 10-12
L.O. 6, 7

Sterling Company issued a $100,000 face value bond on January 1, 20X4. The bond carried an 8% stated rate of interest and a 5-year term. Interest is paid in cash annually, beginning December 31, 20X4. The bond was issued at a price of 102.

Required

a. Show the effect of (1) the bond issue, (2) amortization of the premium on December 31, 20X4, and (3) the December 31, 20X4, interest payment on the financial statements using a horizontal statements model like the following one. Use the following coding scheme to record your answer: increase (+), decrease (−), and not affected (n/a).

Event No.	Assets	=	Liab.	+	Equity	Rev.	−	Exp.	=	Net Inc.	Cash Flow
1											
2											

b. Determine the amount of the carrying value (i.e., face value less discount or plus premium) of the bond liability as of December 31, 20X4.

c. Determine the amount of interest expense shown on the December 31, 20X4, income statement.

d. Determine the amount of the carrying value of the bond liability as of December 31, 20X5.

e. Determine the amount of interest expense shown on the December 31, 20X5, income statement.

EXERCISE 10-13
L.O. 6, 7

Effect of Bonds Issued at a Discount on Financial Statements—Semiannual Interest

Yard Supplies, Inc., issued $200,000 of 10-year, 6% bonds on July 1, 20X3, for 95. Interest is payable in cash semiannually on June 30 and December 31.

Required

a. Prepare the journal entries to record the issuance of the bonds and any necessary journal entries for 20X3 and 20X4. Post the journal entries to the appropriate T-accounts.

b. Prepare the liabilities section of the balance sheet for 20X3 and 20X4.

c. What is the amount of interest expense that will be reported on the financial statements for 20X3 and 20X4?

d. What is the amount of cash that will be paid for interest in 20X3 and 20X4?

EXERCISE 10-14
L.O. 6, 7

Recording Bonds Issued at Face Value and Associated Interest for Two Accounting Cycles—Annual Interest

On January 1, 20X1, Leslie Corp. issued $100,000 of 10-year, 9% bonds at their face amount. Interest is payable on December 31 of each year with the first payment due December 31, 20X1.

Required

Prepare the general journal entries for all events related to this information for 20X1 and 20X2.

EXERCISE 10-15
L.O. 6, 7

Recording Bonds Issued at a Discount—Annual Interest

On January 1, 20X5, Talley Co. issued $100,000 of 5-year, 8% bonds at 97½. Interest is payable annually on December 31. Discount is amortized by using the straight-line method.

Required

Prepare the journal entries to record these events for 20X5 and 20X6. Be sure to include any required year-end adjusting entries.

EXERCISE 10-16
L.O. 6, 7

Recording Bonds Issued at a Premium—Semiannual Interest

On January 1, 20X6, Chris Company issued $200,000 of 5-year, 12% bonds for 103. Interest is payable semiannually on June 30 and December 31. Premium is amortized by the straight-line method.

Required

Prepare the journal entries to record these events for 20X6 and 20X7. Be sure to include any required year-end adjusting entries.

One Complete Accounting Cycle: Bonds Issued at Face Value with Annual Interest

Niagra Company issued $1,000,000 of 10-year, 10% bonds on January 1, 20X4. The bonds were issued at face value. Interest is payable in cash on December 31 of each year. Niagra immediately invested the proceeds from the bond issue in land. The land was leased and thereby produced $140,000 of cash revenue, which was collected on December 31 of each year, beginning December 31, 20X4.

Required

a. Prepare the journal entries for these events, and post to the appropriate T-accounts for 20X4 and 20X5.

b. Prepare the income statement, balance sheet, and statement of cash flows for 20X4 and 20X5.

Recording Callable Bonds

Yang Co. issued $500,000 of 8%, 10-year, callable bonds on January 1, 20X5, for their face value. The call premium was 4% (i.e., bonds are callable at 104). Interest was payable annually on December 31. The bonds were called on December 31, 20X9.

Required

Prepare the journal entries to record the bond issue on January 1, 20X5, and the bond redemption on December 31, 20X9. Assume that all events associated with the accrual and payment of interest have been recorded correctly.

Determining the After-Tax Cost of Debt

The following 20X3 information is available for three companies:

	March Co.	May Co.	Pilot Co.
Face Value of Bonds Payable	$300,000	$600,000	$500,000
Interest Rate	10%	9%	8%
Income Tax Rate	40%	30%	35%

Required

a. Determine the before-tax interest cost for each company *in dollars*.

b. Determine the after-tax interest cost for each company *in dollars*.

c. Determine the after-tax interest cost for each company as *a percentage* of the face value of bonds.

Future Value and Present Value (Appendix)

Required

Using Tables I, II, III, or IV in the appendix, calculate the following:

a. The future value of $10,000 invested at 6% for 4 years.

b. The future value of five annual payments of $2,000 at 10% interest.

c. The amount that must be deposited today (present value) at 9% to accumulate $200,000 in 10 years.

d. The annual payment on a 5-year, 8%, $100,000 note payable.

Computing the Amount of Payment (Appendix)

Required

a. Marcy Shilov has just graduated from Ivory Tower University with a degree in theater. She wants to buy a new sports utility vehicle but does not know if she can afford the payments. Since Shilov knows that you have had an accounting course, she asks you to compute the annual payment on a $30,000, 10%, 5-year note. What would Shilov's annual payment be?

b. If Shilov can afford an annual payment of only $4,000, what price of vehicle should she look for, assuming an interest rate of 10% and a 5-year term?

EXERCISE 10-22
L.O. 9

Saving for a Future Value (Appendix)

Julie and Tom Yuppy are celebrating the birth of their son, Thomas Joseph Yuppy IV. They want to send Little Joe to the best university and know they must begin saving for his education right away. They project that Little Joe's education will cost $500,000.

Required

a. How much must the Yuppys set aside annually to accumulate the necessary $500,000 in 18 years? Assume an 8% interest rate.

b. If the Yuppys wish to make a one-time investment currently for Little Joe's education, how much must they deposit today, assuming an 8% interest rate?

EXERCISE 10-23
L.O. 9

Sale of Bonds at a Discount Using Present Value (Appendix)

Dixon Corporation sold $100,000 of its own 10%, 10-year bonds on January 1, 20X2, for a price that reflected a 9% market rate of interest. Interest is payable annually on December 31.

Required

a. What is the selling price of the bonds?

b. Prepare the journal entry for the issuance of the bonds.

c. Prepare the journal entry for the first interest payment on December 31, 20X2, using the effective interest rate method.

EXERCISE 10-24
L.O. 8

Effect of Semiannual Interest on Investment Returns (Appendix)

Required

Write a short memo explaining why an investor would find a bond that pays semiannual interest more attractive than one that pays annual interest.

PROBLEMS—SERIES A

PROBLEM 10-1A
L.O. 2

Effect of a Long-Term Note Payable on Financial Statements

On January 1, Macon Co. borrowed cash from Stellar Bank by issuing a $100,000 face value, 4-year term note that carried a 10% annual interest rate. The note is to be repaid by making cash payments of $31,547 that include both interest and principal on December 31 of each year. Macon invested the proceeds from the loan to purchase land that generated rental revenues of $40,000 cash per year.

Required

a. Prepare an amortization schedule for the 4-year period.

b. Prepare an income statement, balance sheet, and statement of cash flows for each of the 4 years. (*Hint:* It may be helpful for you to record the transactions for each year in T-accounts before beginning the preparation of the financial statements.)

c. Given that revenue is the same for each period, explain why net income becomes increasingly higher each year.

PROBLEM 10-2A
L.O. 3

Effect of a Line of Credit on Financial Statements

Moon Company has a line of credit with Lunar Bank. Moon can borrow up to $200,000 at any time over the course of the 20X6 calendar year. The following table shows the prime rate expressed as an annual percentage along with the amounts borrowed and repaid during 20X6. Moon agreed to pay interest at an annual rate equal to 2% above the bank's prime rate. Funds are borrowed or repaid on the first day of each month. Interest is payable in cash on the last day of the month. The interest rate is applied to the outstanding monthly balance. For example, Moon pays 7% (5% + 2%) annual interest on $100,000 for the month of January.

Month	Amount Borrowed or (Repaid)	Prime Rate for the Month (%)
January	$100,000	5
February	50,000	6
March	(40,000)	7
April through October	No change	No change
November	(80,000)	6
December	(20,000)	5

Moon earned $30,000 of cash revenue during the 20X6 accounting period.

Required

a. Prepare an income statement, balance sheet, and statement of cash flows for the 20X6 accounting period. (*Note:* Round computations to the nearest dollar.)

b. Write a memo to explain how the business was able to generate retained earnings when the owner contributed no assets to the business.

Accounting for a Bond Discount over Multiple Accounting Cycles

Mir Company was started when it issued bonds with a $400,000 face value on January 1, 20X5. The bonds were issued for cash at a price of 96. They had a 20-year term to maturity and carried an 8% annual interest rate payable on December 31 of each year. Mir Company immediately purchased land with the proceeds (i.e., cash received) from the bond issue. Mir leased the land for $50,000 cash per year. On January 1, 20X8, the company sold the land for $400,000 cash. Immediately after the sale of the land, Mir redeemed the bonds at a price of 98. Assume that no other accounting events occur during 20X8.

PROBLEM 10-3A
L.O. 6, 7

Required

Prepare an income statement, statement of changes in equity, balance sheet, and statement of cash flows as of the end of each of the 20X5, 20X6, 20X7, and 20X8 accounting periods. Assume that the company closes its books on December 31 of each year. Prepare the statements using a vertical statements format. (*Hint:* It may be helpful for you to record each year's transactions in T-accounts prior to the preparation of the financial statements.)

Recording and Reporting Bond Discount over Two Cycles

During 20X6 and 20X7, Jeno Corp. completed the following transactions relating to its bond issue. The corporation's fiscal year is the calendar year.

PROBLEM 10-4A
L.O. 5, 6, 7

20X6

Jan. 1 Issued $100,000 of 10-year, 10% bonds for $96,000. Interest is payable on December 31.

Dec. 31 Paid the interest on the bonds.

31 Recorded the bond discount amortization according to the straight-line method.

31 Closed the Interest Expense account.

20X7

Dec. 31 Paid the interest on the bonds.

31 Recorded the bond discount amortization using the straight-line method.

31 Closed the interest expense account.

Required

a. Was the market rate of interest more or less than the stated rate of interest? If Jeno had sold the bonds at face amount, what would be the amount of cash received?

b. Prepare the general journal entries for these transactions.

c. Prepare the liabilities section of the balance sheet for 20X6 and 20X7.

      d. Determine the amount of interest expense that will be reported on the income statements for 20X6 and 20X7.

      e. Determine the amounts of interest that will be paid in cash to the bondholder in 20X6 and 20X7.

PROBLEM 10-5A
L.O. 6, 7

Effect of a Bond Discount on the Elements of Financial Statements

Sherman Co. was formed when it acquired cash from its owners. The company then issued bonds at a discount on January 1, 20X3. Interest is payable on December 31 with the first payment made December 31, 20X3. On January 2, 20X3, Sherman Co. purchased a piece of land that produced rent revenue annually. The rent is collected on December 31 of each year, beginning December 31, 20X3. At the end of the 6-year period (January 1, 20X9), the land was sold for a gain, and the bonds were paid off at face value. A summary of the transactions for each year follows:

20X3

1. Acquired cash from owners.
2. Issued the 6-year bonds.
3. Purchased the land.
4. Received the land-lease income.
5. Amortized the bond discount at December 31.
6. Paid cash for the interest expense at the stated rate on December 31.
7. Prepared the December 31 closing entry for Rent Revenue.
8. Prepared the December 31 closing entry for Interest Expense.

20X4–20X8

9. Received the land-lease income.
10. Amortized the bond discount at December 31.
11. Paid cash for the interest expense at the stated rate on December 31.
12. Prepared the December 31 closing entry for Rent Revenue.
13. Prepared the December 31 closing entry for Interest Expense.

20X9

14. Sold the land for a gain.
15. Retired the bonds at face value.

Required

For each of these 15 transactions, identify the type of event as asset source (AS), asset use (AU), asset exchange (AE), or claims exchange (CE). Explain how the occurrence of each event affect assets, liabilities, equity, net income, and cash flow by placing a + for increase, − for decrease, or n/a for not affected under each of the categories. In the Cash Flow column, indicate whether the item is an operating activity (OA), investing activity (IA), or financing activity (FA). The first event is recorded as an example.

Event No.	Type of Event	Assets	Liabilities	Contributed Capital	Retained Earnings	Net Income	Cash Flow
1	AS	+	n/a	+	n/a	n/a	+ FA

PROBLEM 10-6A
L.O. 6, 7

Recording Transactions for Callable Bonds

JBC Corp. issued $300,000 of 20-year, 10%, callable bonds on January 1, 20X4, with interest payable on December 31. The bonds were issued at their face amount. The bonds are callable at 105. The fiscal year of the corporation ends December 31.

Required

a. Show the effect of the following events on the financial statements by recording the appropriate amounts in a horizontal statements model like the following one. In the Cash Flow column, indicate whether the item is an operating activity (OA), investing activity (IA), or financing activity (FA). The letters n/a indicate that an element was not affected by the event.

(1) Issued the bonds on January 1, 20X4.

(2) Paid interest due to bondholders on December 31, 20X4.

(3) On January 1, 20X9, JBC Corp. called the bonds. Assume that all interim entries have been recorded.

Event No.	Assets	=	Liab.	+	Equity	Rev.	−	Exp.	=	Net Inc.	Cash Flow
1											
2											
3											

b. Prepare journal entries for the three events listed in part a.

Effect of Debt Transactions on Financial Statements

There are three common accounting events associated with borrowing money through a bond issue:

1. Exchanging the bond for cash on the day of issue.
2. A cash payment for interest expense and amortization when applicable.
3. Repayment of principal at maturity.

PROBLEM 10-7A
L.O. 7

Required

a. Assuming the bonds are issued at face value, show the effect of each of the three events on the financial statements, using a horizontal statements model like the following one. Use the following coding scheme to record your answer: increase +, decrease −, and not affected n/a.

Event No.	Assets	=	Liab.	+	Equity	Rev.	−	Exp.	=	Net Inc.	Cash Flow
1											
2											
3											

b. Repeat the requirements shown for part a, but assume that the bonds are issued at a discount.

c. Repeat the requirements shown for part a, but assume that the bonds are issued at a premium.

Sale of Bonds at a Discount and Amortization Using the Effective Interest Method (Appendix)

On January 1, 20X4, Big Corp. sold $500,000 of its own 8%, 10-year bonds. Interest is payable annually on December 31. The bonds were sold to yield an effective interest rate of 9%.

PROBLEM 10-8A
L.O. 7, 9

Required

a. Using the information in the appendix, calculate the selling price of the bonds.

b. Prepare the journal entry for the issuance of the bonds.

c. Prepare the journal entry for the amortization of the bond discount and the payment of the interest at December 31, 20X4.

d. Calculate the amount of interest expense for 20X5.

PROBLEMS—SERIES B

PROBLEM 10-1B
L.O. 2

Effect of a Term Loan on Financial Statements

On January 1, Yates Co. borrowed cash from First City Bank by issuing an $80,000 face value, 3-year term note that carried an 8% annual interest rate. The note is to be repaid by making annual payments of $31,043 that include both interest and principal on December 31. Yates invested the proceeds from the loan in land that generated lease revenues of $36,000 cash per year.

Required

a. Prepare an amortization schedule for the 3-year period.

b. Prepare an income statement, balance sheet, and statement of cash flows for each of the 3 years. (*Hint:* It may be helpful for you to record the transactions for each year in T-accounts before beginning the preparation of the financial statements.)

c. Given that net income becomes increasingly higher each year, why does cash flow from operating activities remain constant?

PROBLEM 10-2B
L.O. 3

Effect of a Line of Credit on Financial Statements

Beacon Company has a line of credit with National Bank. Beacon can borrow up to $150,000 at any time over the course of the 20X3 calendar year. The following table shows the prime rate expressed as an annual percentage along with the amounts borrowed and repaid during 20X3. Beacon agreed to pay interest at an annual rate equal to 3% above the bank's prime rate. Funds are borrowed or repaid on the first day of each month. Interest is payable in cash on the last day of the month. The interest rate is applied to the outstanding monthly balance. For example, Beacon pays 7% (4% + 3%) annual interest on $80,000 for the month of January.

Month	Amount Borrowed or (Repaid)	Prime Rate for the Month (%)
January	$80,000	4
February	50,000	4
March	(30,000)	5
April through October	No change	No change
November	(60,000)	5
December	(40,000)	4

Beacon earned $18,000 of cash revenue during the 20X3 accounting period.

Required

a. Prepare an income statement, balance sheet, and statement of cash flows for the 20X3 accounting period.

b. Write a memo to explain how the business was able to generate retained earnings when the owner contributed no assets to the business.

PROBLEM 10-3B
L.O. 6, 7

Accounting for a Bond Premium over Multiple Accounting Cycles

Deleware Company was started when it issued bonds with $150,000 face value on January 1, 20X4. The bonds were issued for cash at a price of 105. They had a 15-year term to maturity and carried a 10% annual interest rate payable annually. Deleware immediately purchased land with the proceeds (i.e., cash received) from the bond issue. Deleware leased the land for $17,500 cash per year. On January 1, 20X7, the company sold the land for $160,000 cash. Immediately after the sale, Deleware repurchased its bonds (i.e., repaid the bond liability) at a price of 106. Assume that no other accounting events occurred in 20X7.

Required

Prepare an income statement, statement of changes in equity, and balance sheet as of the end of each of the 20X4, 20X5, 20X6, and 20X7 accounting periods. Assume that the company closes its books on December 31 of each year. Prepare the statements, using a vertical statements format. (*Hint:* It may be helpful for you to record each year's transactions in T-accounts prior to the preparation of the financial statements.)

Recording and Reporting a Bond Discount over Two Cycles—Semiannual Interest

During 20X2 and 20X3, Bing Co. completed the following transactions relating to its bond issue. The company's fiscal year ends on December 31.

20X2

Mar. 1 Issued $50,000 of 8-year, 9% bonds for $48,000. Interest is payable on March 1 and September 1, beginning September 1, 20X2.

Sept. 1 Paid the semiannual interest on the bonds.

Dec. 31 Recorded the accrued interest on the bonds.

     31 Recorded the bond discount amortization by the straight-line method.

     31 Closed the Interest Expense account.

20X3

Mar. 1 Paid the semiannual interest on the bonds.

Sept. 1 Paid the semiannual interest on the bonds.

Dec. 31 Recorded the accrued interest on the bonds.

     31 Recorded the bond discount amortization by the straight-line method.

     31 Closed the Interest Expense account.

Required

a. Was the market rate of interest more or less than the stated rate of interest? If the bonds had sold at face value, what amount of cash would Bing Co. have received?

b. Prepare the general journal entries for these transactions.

c. Prepare the liabilities section of the balance sheet for 20X2 and 20X3.

d. Determine the amount of interest expense that will be reported on the income statements for 20X2 and 20X3.

e. Determine the amounts of interest that will be paid to the bondholders in 20X2 and 20X3.

Effect of a Bond Premium on the Elements of Financial Statements

Weaver Land Co. was formed when it acquired cash from its owners. The company then issued bonds at a premium on January 1, 20X1. Interest is payable annually on December 31 of each year, beginning December 31, 20X1. On January 2, 20X1, Weaver Land Co. purchased a piece of land and leased it for an annual rental fee. The rent is received annually on December 31, beginning December 31, 20X1. At the end of the 8-year period (December 31, 20X8), the land was sold for a gain, and the bonds were paid off. A summary of the transactions for each year follows:

20X1

1. Acquired cash from the owners.
2. Issued the 8-year bonds.
3. Purchased the land.
4. Received the land-lease income.
5. Amortized the bond premium at December 31.
6. Paid cash for the interest expense at the stated rate on December 31.
7. Prepared the December 31 closing entry for Rent Revenue.
8. Prepared the December 31 closing entry for Interest Expense.

20X2–20X7

9. Received the land-lease income.
10. Amortized the bond premium at December 31.
11. Paid cash for the interest expense at the stated rate on December 31.
12. Prepared the December 31 closing entry for Rent Revenue.
13. Prepared the December 31 closing entry for Interest Expense.

20X8

14. Sold the land for a gain.
15. Retired the bonds at face value.

Required

For each of these 15 transactions, identify the type of event as asset source (AS), asset use (AU), asset exchange (AE), or claims exchange (CE). Explain how the occurrence of each event affects assets, liabilities, equity, net income, and cash flow by placing a + for increase, − for decrease, or n/a for not affected under each of the categories. In the Cash Flow column, indicate whether the item is an operating activity (OA), investing activity (IA), or financing activity (FA). The first event is recorded as an example.

Event No.	Type of Event	Assets	Liabilities	Contributed Capital	Retained Earnings	Net Income	Cash Flow
1	AS	+	n/a	+	n/a	n/a	+ FA

PROBLEM 10-6B
L.O. 6, 7

Recording Transactions for Callable Bonds

Cagle Co. issued $100,000 of 10-year, 10%, callable bonds on January 1, 20X1, with interest payable December 31. The bonds were issued at their face amount. The bonds are callable at 101½. The fiscal year of the corporation is the calendar year.

Required

a. Show the effect of the following events on the financial statements by recording the appropriate amounts in a horizontal statements model like the following one. When you record amounts in the Cash Flow column, indicate whether the item is an operating activity (OA), investing activity (IA), or financing activity (FA). The letters n/a indicate that an element was not affected by the event.

   (1) Issued the bonds on January 1, 20X1.
   (2) Paid interest due to bondholders on December 31, 20X1.
   (3) On January 1, 20X9, Cagle Co. called the bonds. Assume that all interim entries have been recorded.

Event No.	Assets	=	Liab.	+	Equity	Rev.	−	Exp.	=	Net Inc.	Cash Flow
1											
2											
3											

b. Prepare journal entries for the three events listed in part a.

PROBLEM 10-7B
L.O. 8

Effect of Debt Transactions on Financial Statements

Required

Show the effect of each of the following independent accounting events on the financial statements, using a horizontal statements model like the following one. Use the following coding scheme to record your answer: increase +, decrease −, and not affected n/a. The first event is recorded as an example.

Event No.	Assets	=	Liab.	+	Equity	Rev.	−	Exp.	=	Net Inc.	Cash Flow
1	+		+		n/a	n/a		n/a		n/a	+ FA

a. Borrowed funds using a line of credit.
b. Made an interest payment for funds that had been borrowed through a line of credit.

c. Made a cash payment on a note payable. The payment included a provision for interest and the partial repayment of principal.
d. Issued a bond at face value.
e. Made an interest payment on a bond that had been issued at face value.
f. Issued a bond at a discount.
g. Made an interest payment on a bond that had been issued at a discount.
h. Issued a bond at a premium.
i. Made an interest payment on a bond that had been issued at a premium.

Sale of Bonds at a Premium and Amortization Using the Effective Interest Rate Method (Appendix)

PROBLEM 10-8B
L.O. 7, 9

On January 1, 20X2, Sun Corp. sold $200,000 of its own 8%, 10-year bonds. Interest is payable annually on December 31. The bonds were sold to yield an effective interest rate of 7%. Sun Corp. uses the effective interest rate method.

Required

a. Using the data in the appendix, calculate the selling price of the bonds.
b. Prepare the journal entry for the issuance of the bonds.
c. Prepare the journal entry for the amortization of the bond premium and the payment of the interest on December 31, 20X4.
d. Calculate the amount of interest expense for 20X5.

analyze, communicate, think

BUSINESS APPLICATIONS CASE   Gateway 2000 Annual Report

ACT 10-1

Required

Using the Gateway 2000 financial statements in Appendix B, answer the following questions:

a. What was the primary type of long-term debt that Gateway had in 1997?
b. What was the maximum length to maturity of Gateway's long-term debt?
c. Why did Gateway choose not to include "warranty obligations" in current liabilities?
d. What was the maximum amount available to Gateway through its line of credit?

GROUP ASSIGNMENT   Missing Information

ACT 10-2

The following three companies issued the following bonds:

1. BIG, Inc., issued $100,000 of 8%, 5-year bonds for 101.5 on January 1, 20X6. Interest is payable annually on December 31.
2. CAR, Inc., issued $100,000 of 8%, 5-year bonds for 97 on January 1, 20X6. Interest is payable annually on December 31.
3. QVX, Inc., issued $100,000 of 8%, 5-year bonds for 105 on January 1, 20X6. Interest is payable annually on December 31.

Required

a. Organize the class into three sections and divide each section into groups of three to five students. Assign each of the sections one of the companies.

Group Tasks

(1) For your company compute the following amounts:
  (a) Cash proceeds from the bond issue.
  (b) Interest expense for 20X6.
  (c) Interest paid in 20X6.
(2) Prepare the liabilities section of the balance sheet as on December 31, 20X6.

Class Discussion

b. Have a representative of each section put the liabilities section for its company on the board.

c. Is the amount of interest expense different for the three companies? Why or why not?

d. Is the amount of interest paid different for each of the companies? Why or why not?

e. Is the amount of total liabilities different for each of the companies? Why or why not?

ACT 10-3

REAL-WORLD CASE   Using Accounting Numbers to Assess Creditworthiness

Standard & Poor's (S&P) and Moody's are two credit-rating services that evaluate the creditworthiness of various companies. Their "grading" systems are similar but not exactly the same. S&P's grading scheme works as follows: AAA is the highest rating, followed by AA, A, BBB, and so on. For each grade, a + or − may be used.

The following are selected financial data for four companies whose overall, long-term creditworthiness was rated by S&P. The date the company was rated by S&P is shown in parentheses. The companies, listed alphabetically, are as follows:

Advanced Micro Devices, Inc., is a company that manufactures semiconductors for memory circuits, logic circuits, and microprocessors.

Bristol-Myers Squibb Company is a very large pharmaceutical company.

Ethan Allen Interiors, Inc., is a national retailer of home furnishings.

Physicians Resource Group, Inc., began operations in 1995. As of April 6, 1998, the company operated a network of 130 eye care practices at 347 locations in 22 states.

Dollar amounts are in thousands except for Bristol-Myers, which is in millions.

	Net Income	Cash Flow from Operations	Current Ratio	Debt-to-Assets Ratio	Times-Interest-Earned-Ratio	Return-on-Assets Ratio
Advanced Micro Devices (4/10/98)						
1997	($21,090)	$398,815	1.62	0.42	(0.7)	(0.6%)
1996	(68,950)	73,237	1.76	0.36	(9.4)	(2.2%)
Bristol-Myers Squibb (4/24/98)						
1997	3,205	2,486	1.54	0.52	39.0	5.7%
1996	2,850	2,641	1.49	0.55	52.4	6.1%
Ethan Allen Interiors (6/18/98)						
1997	48,740	77,413	3.08	0.38	14.8	11.4%
1996	28,145	60,888	2.85	0.44	6.3	7.1%
Physicians Resource Group (8/25/98)						
1997	(41,323)	843	2.62	0.50	(4.9)	(7.7%)
1996	7,172	(15,966)	3.52	0.47	22.0	1.2%

Each company received a different credit rating by S&P. The grades awarded, in descending order, were AAA, BBB+, B, and CCC.

Required

Determine which grade was assigned to each company. Write a memorandum explaining the reason for your decisions.

BUSINESS APPLICATIONS CASE   **Using Ratios to Make Comparisons**   **ACT 10-4**

The following accounting information exists for Evans Furniture Co. and Wood-Tone, Inc., at the end of 20X1.

	Evans Furniture Co.	Wood-Tone, Inc.
Current Assets	$ 35,000	$ 35,000
Total Assets	200,000	200,000
Current Liabilities	20,000	15,000
Total Liabilities	150,000	120,000
Owners' Equity	50,000	80,000
Interest Expense	14,000	11,000
Tax Expense	12,000	13,200
Net Income	19,500	21,300

Required

a. Compute the following for each company: debt-to-assets, current, and times-interest-earned ratios (EBIT must be computed). Identify the company with the greater financial risk.

b. For each company, compute the return-on-equity and return-on-assets ratios. Use EBIT instead of net income to compute the return-on assets ratio. Identify the company that is managing its assets more effectively. Identify the company that is producing the higher return from the owner's perspective. Provide a logical explanation of how one company was able to produce a higher return on equity than the other.

BUSINESS APPLICATIONS CASE   **ACT 10-5**

Determining the Effects of Financing Alternatives on Ratios

Evergreen Industries has the following account balances:

Current Assets	$ 80,000	Current Liabilities	$ 50,000
Noncurrent Assets	170,000	Noncurrent Liabilities	120,000
		Owners' Equity	80,000

The company wishes to raise $100,000 in cash and is considering two financing options. Either it can sell $100,000 of bonds payable, or it can issue $100,000 of new common stock. To help in the decision process, Evergreen's management wants to determine the effects of each alternative on its current ratio and debt-to-assets ratio.

Required

a. Help Evergreen's management by completing the following chart:

Ratio	Currently	If Bonds Are Issued	If Stock Is Issued
Current Ratio			
Debt-to-Assets Ratio			

b. Assume that after the funds are invested, EBIT amounted to $40,000. Also assume that Evergreen pays $10,000 in dividends or $10,000 in interest, depending on which source of financing is used. Based on a 30% tax rate, determine the amount of the addition to retained earnings under each financing option.

ACT 10-6

WRITING ASSIGNMENT   Debt versus Equity Financing

On January 1, 20X3, Smith Company invested $50,000 in land that will produce annual rent revenue equal to 15% of the investment. The revenue is collected in cash at the end of each year, starting December 31, 20X3. Smith can obtain the cash necessary to purchase the land from two sources. First, funds can be obtained by issuing $50,000 at 10%, 5-year bonds at their face amount. Interest due on the bonds is payable on December 31 of each year with the first payment due on December 31, 20X3. Second, the $50,000 needed to invest in land can be obtained from equity financing. In this case, the owners (holders of the equity) will be paid a $5,000 annual distribution. Smith Company is in a 30% income tax bracket.

Required

a. Compute the amount of net income for 20X3 and 20X4 under the two alternative financing proposals.

b. Write a short memorandum explaining why one financing alternative provides more net income but less cash flow than the other.

ACT 10-7

ETHICAL DILEMMA   I Don't Want to Pay Taxes

Dana Harbert recently started a very successful small business. Indeed, the business had grown so rapidly that she was no longer able to finance its operations by investing her own resources in the business. She needed additional capital but had no more of her own money to put into the business. A friend, Gene Watson, was willing to invest $100,000 in the business. Harbert estimated that with Watson's investment, the company would be able to increase revenue by $40,000. Furthermore, she believed that operating expenses would increase by only 10%. Harbert and Watson agree that Watson's investment should entitle him to receive a cash distribution that is equal to 20% of net income. A set of forecasted statements with and without Watson's investment is presented here. (Assume that all transactions involving revenue, expense, and distributions are cash transactions.)

Financial Statements		
	Forecast 1 without Watson's Investment	**Forecast 2 with Watson's Investment**
Income Statement		
Revenue	$120,000	$160,000
Operating Expenses	(70,000)	(77,000)
Income before Interest and Taxes	50,000	83,000
Income Tax Expense (i.e., Effective Tax Rate Is 30%)	(15,000)	(24,900)
Net Income	$ 35,000	$ 58,100
Statement of Changes in Equity		
Beginning Retained Earnings	$ 15,000	$ 15,000
Plus: Net Income	35,000	58,100
Less: Distribution to Watson (20% of $58,100)	0	(11,620)
Ending Retained Earnings	$ 50,000	$ 61,480

(cont'd)

Financial Statements		
	Forecast 1 without Watson's Investment	**Forecast 2 with Watson's Investment**
Balance Sheets		
Assets (computations explained in following paragraph)	$400,000	$511,480
Liabilities	$ 0	$ 0
Equity		
Contributed Capital	350,000	450,000
Retained Earnings	50,000	61,480
Total Liabilities and Equity	$400,000	$511,480

The balance for assets in forecast 1 is computed as the beginning balance of $365,000 plus net income of $35,000. The balance for assets in forecast 2 is computed as the beginning balance of $365,000, plus the $100,000 cash investment, plus net income of $58,100, less the $11,620 distribution. Alternatively, total assets can be computed by determining the amount of total claims (i.e., total assets = total claims).

Harbert tells Watson that there would be a $3,486 tax advantage associated with debt financing. She says that if Watson is willing to become a creditor instead of an owner, she could pay him an additional $697.20 (that is, 20% of the tax advantage). Watson tells Harbert that he has no interest in participating in the management of the business, but Watson wants an ownership interest so as to guarantee that he will always receive 20% of the profits of the business. Harbert suggests that they execute a formal agreement in which Watson is paid 11.62% interest on his $100,000 loan to the business. This agreement will be used for income tax reporting. In addition, Harbert says that she is willing to establish a private agreement to write Watson a personal check for any additional amount necessary to make Watson's total return equal to 20% of all profits plus a $697.20 bonus for his part of the tax advantage. She tells Watson, "It's just like ownership. The only difference is that we call it debt for the Internal Revenue Service. If they want to have some silly rule that says if you call it debt, you get a tax break, then we are foolish if we don't call it debt. I will call it anything they want, just as long as I don't have to pay taxes on it."

Required

a. Construct a third set of forecasted financial statements (forecast 3) at 11.62% annual interest, assuming that Watson is treated as creditor (i.e., he loans the business $100,000).

b. Verify the tax advantage of debt financing by comparing the balances of the Retained Earnings account in forecast 2 and forecast 3.

c. If you were Watson, would you permit Harbert to classify the equity transaction as debt so as to provide a higher return to the business and to you?

d. Comment on the ethical implications of misnaming a financing activity for the sole purpose of reducing income taxes.

EDGAR DATABASE   Analyzing Long-Term Debt at Wendy's   **ACT 10-8**

Many companies have a form of debt called *capital leases.* A capital lease is created when a company agrees to "rent" an asset, such as equipment or a building, for such a long time that GAAP treats this "lease" as if the asset were purchased by using borrowed funds. Thus, a capital lease creates a liability for the company that acquired the leased asset because the company has promised to make payments to another company for several years in the future. If a company has any capital leases, it must disclose them in the footnotes to the financial statements and will sometimes disclose them in a separate account in the liabilities section of the balance sheet.

Required

Using the most current 10-K available on EDGAR, answer the following questions about Wendy's International. Type in *Wendy's* as the company name when you search EDGAR. Instructions for using EDGAR are in Appendix A.

a. What was Wendy's debt-to-assets ratio?

b. How much interest expense did Wendy's incur?

c. What amount of liabilities did Wendy's have as a result of capital leases?

d. What percentage of Wendy's long-term liabilities was the result of capital leases?

e. Many companies try to structure (design) leasing agreements so that their leases will *not* be classified as capital leases. Explain why a company such as Wendy's might want to avoid having capital leases.

ACT 10-9

SPREADSHEET ASSIGNMENT

On January 1, 20X1, Bainbridge Company borrowed $100,000 cash from a bank by issuing a 10-year, 9% note. The principal and interest are to be paid by making annual payments in the amount of $15,582. Payments are to be made December 31 of each year beginning December 31, 20X1.

	Loan Information					
Principal	100,000					
Interest Rate	9%					
Periods	10					
Payments	(15,582)					
			December 31			
	Beginning			Applied	Ending	
	Principal	Cash	Interest	To	Principal	
Year	Balance	Payment	Expense	Principal	Balance	
20X1	100,000	15,582	9,000	6,582	93,418	
20X2						
20X3						
20X4						
20X5						
20X6						
20X7						
20X8						
20X9						
20X10						
Totals						

Cell B6 = =PMT(B4,B5,B3)

Required

a. Set up the preceding spreadsheet. Notice that Excel can be set up to calculate the loan payment. If you're unfamiliar with this, see the following Spreadsheet Tips section. The Beginning Principal Balance (B12) and Cash Payment (C12) can be referenced from the Loan Information section. The interest rate used to calculate Interest Expense (D12) can also be referenced from the Loan Information section.

b. Complete the spreadsheet for the 10 periods.

c. In Row 23, calculate totals for Cash Payments, Interest Expense, and Applied to Principal.

d. Consider how the amounts would differ if Bainbridge were to borrow the $100,000 at different interest rates and time periods. The results of the original data (option 1) have been entered in the following schedule. In the spreadsheet, delete 9% and 10 from cells B4 and B5. Enter the data for the second option (8% and 10 years) in cells B4 and B5. Enter in the Payment and Total Interest in the schedule for the second option. Continue the same process for options 3 through 9 by deleting the prior rate and number of periods in the spreadsheet and entering in the next option's data. The number of years scheduled (rows 12 through 21) will have to be shortened for the 7-year options and lengthened for the 13-year options.

					Option				
	1	**2**	**3**	**4**	**5**	**6**	**7**	**8**	**9**
Rate	9%	8%	10%	9%	8%	10%	9%	8%	10%
Years	10	10	10	7	7	7	13	13	13
Payment		15,582							
Total Interest		55,820							

Spreadsheet Tips

1. Excel will calculate an installment loan payment. The interest rate (%), number of periods (nper), and amount borrowed or otherwise known as present value (PV) must be entered in the payment formula. The formula for the payment is =PMT(rate,nper,pv). The rate, number of periods, and amount borrowed (present value) may be entered in as actual amounts or referenced to other cells. In the preceding spreadsheet, the payment formula can be either =PMT(9%,10,100000) or =PMT(B4,B5,B3). In our case, the latter is preferred so that variables can be altered in the spreadsheet without also having to rewrite the payment formula. Notice that the payment is a negative number.

2. Using positive numbers is preferred in the amortization schedule. The loan payment (cell B6) in the Loan Information section shows up as a negative number. Any reference to it in the amortization schedule should be preceded by a minus sign to convert it to a positive number. For example, the formula in cell C12 for the Cash Payment is =−B6.

3. Recall that to copy a fixed number, a $ sign must be positioned before the column letter and row number. The complete formula then for cell C12 is =−B6.

ACT 10-10

SPREADSHEET ANALYSIS

Wise Company was started on January 1 when it issued 20-year, 10%, $200,000 face value bonds at a price of 90. Interest is payable annually at December 31 of each year. Wise immediately purchased land with the proceeds (i.e., cash received) from the bond issue. Wise leased the land for $27,000 cash per year. The lease revenue payments are due every December 31.

Required

Set up the following horizontal statements model onto a blank spreadsheet. The SCF Activity column is for the classifications operating, financing, or investing.

Microsoft Excel - dch10-2.xls									

	A	B	C	D	E	F	G	H	I	J	K
1		SCF				Bonds	Bond	Retained		Effect on	
2	Date	Activity	Cash	Land		Payable	Discount	Earnings		Net Income	
3	1-1-X1										
4	1-1-X1										
5	12-31-X1	OA	27,000					27,000		27,000	Lease Revenue
6	12-31-X1										
7											
8	20X1 Ending				=						Net Income
9											
10			Total Assets		=		Total Claims				
11											
12	20X2 Beginning										
13	12-31-X2										
14	12-31-X2										
15											
16	20X2 Ending										Net Income
17											
18			Total Assets				Total Claims				
19											
20	20X3 Beginning										
21	12-31-x3										
22	12-31-x3										
23											
24	20X3 Ending										Net Income
25											
26			Total Assets				Total Claims				
27											
28	20X4 Beginning										
29	1-1-X4										
30	1-1-X4										
31											
32	20X4 Ending										Net Income
33											
34			Total Assets				Total Claims				
35											

Problem 10-2 Answer Key / **Problem** / Pr 10-2 Key Effective

a. Enter the effects of the 20X1 transactions. Assume that both the interest and lease payments occurred on December 31. Notice that the entry for the lease has already been entered as an example. Calculate the ending balances.

b. Enter the effects of the 20X2 transactions. Assume that both the interest and lease payments occurred on December 31. Calculate the ending balances.

c. Enter the effects of the 20X3 transactions. Assume that both the interest and lease payments occurred on December 31. Calculate the ending balances.

d. On January 1, 20X4, Wise Company sold the land for $190,000 cash. Immediately after the sale of the land, Wise repurchased its bond at a price of 93. Assume that no other accounting events occurred during 20X4. Enter in the effects of the 20X4 balances. Calculate the ending balances.

Accounting for
Equity Transactions

1 Understand the primary characteristics of a sole proprietorship, partnership, and corporation.

2 Identify the different types of business organizations through the analysis of financial statements.

3 Explain the characteristics of major types of stock issued by corporations.

4 Understand the accounting treatment for different types of stock issued by corporations.

5 Explain the effects of treasury stock transactions on a company's financial statements.

6 Explain the effects of a declaration and payment of cash dividends on a company's financial statements.

7 Explain the effects of stock dividends and stock splits on a company's financial statements.

8 Understand how the appropriation of retained earnings affects financial statements.

9 Understand how accounting information can be useful in making stock investment decisions.

10 Understand accounting for not-for-profit entities and governmental organizations.

the **curious** accountant

Imagine that a rich uncle wanted to reward you for outstanding performance in your first accounting course, so he gave you $15,000 to invest in the stock of one company. You narrowed your choice to two companies. After reviewing their recent annual reports, you developed the following information:

Mystery Company A: This company has been in existence for about four years and has never made a profit; in fact, it had net losses totaling more than $36 million. Each year of its existence, its net loss has been much larger than the loss of the year before. This stock is selling for about $100 per share, so you can buy 150 shares. A friend told you it was a "sure winner."

Mystery Company B: This company has been in existence more than 100 years and has made a profit most years. In the most recent three years, its operating income totaled over $22 *billion,* and it paid dividends of over $9 *billion*. This stock is trading for about $75 per share, so you can buy 200 shares of it. Your friend said it was a stock "your grandfather should own."

The descriptions apply to real-world companies, the names of which are revealed later. Based on the information provided, which company's stock would you buy?

©Jon Riley/ Tony Stone Images

The three major forms of business organization are *sole proprietorship*, *partnership*, and *corporation*. These business structures evolved to meet the special needs of society at different times. The most basic form is the sole proprietorship. **Sole proprietorships** are owned by one person and are usually fairly small. Since the participants of any exchange of goods could be classified as proprietors, it is impossible to identify the first proprietorship in history.

The proprietorship was the dominant form of business for many years. Gradually, businesspeople realized the benefits that can be derived by joining together as partners to share their talents, their capital, and the risks of business. The **partnership** also dates back to some unidentifiable transaction occurring thousands of years ago. However, the real development of partnerships began around the 13th century during the Middle Ages. To defend and promote their interests, artisans formed professional associations called *guilds*. These guilds conducted extensive trade, often with one partner providing capital while another went in search of riches.

The roots of the **corporation** lie in the exploration of the New World. The need for large amounts of capital led to the sale of shares in trading companies such as the Dutch East India Company. The industrial revolution of the 19th century further influenced the proliferation of the corporate form of business. Vast sums of capital were needed to keep pace with increasing technology and mass production.

Formation of Business Organizations

Ownership Agreements

L.O. 1

Understand the primary charac-teristics of a sole proprietorship, partnership, and corporation.

Since proprietorships are owned by a single individual, there are no disputes re-garding who is ultimately responsible for making decisions or how profits are to be distributed. Accordingly, the process of establishing a sole proprietorship is usually as simple as obtaining a business license from local government authori-ties. In contrast, partnerships require clear communication of how authority, risks, and profitability will be shared among the partners. To minimize misun-derstandings and conflict, most partnerships are based on a **partnership agree-ment,** a legal document that defines the responsibilities of each partner and describes the division of income and losses. In addition to legal advice, the for-mation and operation of partnerships may require the services of accounting pro-fessionals. The distribution of profits is certainly affected by the measurement of profitability. Accordingly, partnerships may require the services of independent public accountants to ensure that records are kept in accordance with GAAP. Also, the application of tax regulations to partnerships may become so compli-cated that many partners are forced to seek professional advice.

The establishment of a corporation usually requires the assistance of legal and accounting professionals. Although individuals are permitted to file the doc-uments necessary to start a corporation, the process involves the completion of a fairly complex set of forms containing technical terminology. Accordingly, the fil-ing process may be perplexing to a layperson who is unfamiliar with business practice. Even so, the process is simple and methodical for professionals who are trained and experienced in the filing process. As a result, legal and accounting services for routine filings are usually well worth the customary fees charged.

A corporation is designated as a *separate legal entity* by the state in which it is incorporated. Each of the 50 states has its own laws governing this process; however, many have adopted the provisions of the Model Business Corporation Act, and standard procedures are followed by most states. The first step of incor-poration consists of an application filed with a state agency. This application is called the **articles of incorporation,** and it contains all the information required by state law. The most common information items required are (1) the name of the corporation and proposed date of incorporation; (2) the purpose of the corpo-ration; (3) the location of the business and its expected life (which can be *perpe-tuity,* meaning "endless"); (4) provisions for capital stock (i.e., the certificates that evidence an ownership interest in the corporation); and (5) the names and ad-dresses of the members of the first board of directors (i.e., the designated group of individuals with the ultimate authority for operating the business). If the articles are found to be in order, a charter of incorporation is issued, which establishes the legal existence of the corporation and is filed, along with the articles, in county records that are available to any person interested in reviewing them.

Regulation

Very few laws apply specifically to the operation of proprietorships and partner-ships. Corporations are a different story. The level of regulation applicable to cor-porations depends on the size and distribution of the company's ownership interest. The ownership interest in a corporation is normally evidenced by **stock**

certificates. When owners contribute assets to a corporation, the owners receive stock certificates that describe the rights and privileges accompanying the ownership interest. Since stock evidences ownership, owners are frequently called **stockholders.**

Ownership can be transferred from one individual to another by the exchange of stock certificates. As long as exchanges (i.e., the buying and selling of shares of stock) are limited to transactions between individuals, the company is defined as being a **closely held corporation.** However, once a corporation reaches a certain size, it may list its stock on a stock exchange such as the New York Stock Exchange or the American Stock Exchange. Trading on a stock exchange is limited to the stockbrokers who are members of the exchange. These brokers represent buyers and sellers who want to exchange stock certificates. The buyers and sellers pay the brokers commissions as compensation for completing the transactions. Although closely held corporations are relatively free from regulation, companies whose stock is traded on the exchanges by brokers are subject to an extensive set of rules and regulations.

Before the 1930s, trading on stock exchanges was relatively free of regulation. However, the stock market crash of 1929 and the subsequent Great Depression led to the passage of the **Securities Act of 1933** and the **Securities Exchange Act of 1934** designed to regulate the issuance of stock and to govern the exchanges. The laws created the Securities and Exchange Commission (SEC) to enforce the acts. As discussed previously, the SEC was given legal authority for the establishment of accounting policies to be followed by corporations registered on the exchanges. However, the SEC has generally deferred its rule-making authority to the accounting profession. Even so, it is important to realize that the only legal authority for accounting procedures does reside with the SEC. Indeed, the SEC has stepped in on several occasions when it felt that the profession was not properly regulating itself.

Advantages and Disadvantages of Different Forms of Business Organization

The owners of proprietorships and partnerships are held *personally accountable* for the actions that they take in the name of their businesses. Indeed, a partner is responsible not only for his or her own actions but also for the actions that any other partner takes on behalf of the partnership. In contrast, corporations are established as legal entities separate from their owners. Accordingly, corporations, rather than their owners, bear the responsibility for actions taken in the name of the company. These different levels of responsibility provide a unique set of advantages and disadvantages for each type of business structure. The next section compares and contrasts the advantages and disadvantages of proprietorships, partnerships, and corporations.

L.O. 1

Understand the primary characteristics of a sole proprietorship, partnership, and corporation.

Double Taxation

Because the corporation is an entity in itself, its profits are taxed by state and federal governments. This often gives rise to a situation known as *double taxation.* **Double taxation** refers to the fact that corporate profits that are distributed to

an **answer** for the curious accountant

Mystery Company A is Amazon.com, Inc. (as of the end of 1997). The company was incorporated in 1994, and on May 15, 1997, its stock was sold to the public in an *initial public offering* (IPO) at $18. The first day its stock traded on NASDAQ, it opened at $29; at the end of that day, it was selling for $23.50 per share. Obviously, the people trading Amazon.com's stock were not paying much attention to accounting data. Instead, they **were focusing on what the company *might* become, and many were simply speculating based on the hype the company's IPO had generated. The stock market does not always behave rationally. Mystery Company B is General Electric Company (as of the end of 1997).**

Of course, only the future will tell which company will be the better investment.

owners are taxed twice—once when the income appears on the corporation's income tax return and once when the distribution appears on the individual's return. For example, assume that a corporation in a 30% tax bracket earns pretax income of $100,000. The corporation is required to pay income tax of $30,000 ($100,000 × 0.30). If the corporation distributes the after-tax income of $70,000 ($100,000 − $30,000) to an individual who is also taxed at a 30% rate, that individual has to report the distribution on her or his income tax return and has to pay $21,000 ($70,000 × 0.30) of income taxes. Accordingly, a total of $51,000 of tax has to be paid on $100,000 of earned income. This equates to an effective tax rate of 51% ($51,000 ÷ $100,000).

Double taxation could be a great burden to small closely held corporations. Fortunately, tax laws permit the election of an "S Corporation," which allows closely held companies to be taxed as partnerships or proprietorships. Also, many states have recently enacted legislation that permits the formation of **limited liability companies (LLCs).** Although LLCs offer many of the benefits associated with corporate ownership, the Internal Revenue Service has, in general, permitted them to be taxed as partnerships. Since partnerships and proprietorships are not separate legal entities, they do not earn income in the names of their companies. Instead, the income generated by these businesses is considered to be earned by the owners and therefore is taxed only at the individual owner's tax rate. This is true regardless of whether the income is retained in the business or is distributed to the owners.

Regulation

Corporations do not exist in a natural state. Instead, they are created by government authorities. These authorities may restrict corporations from engaging in certain activities. Also, authorities frequently require corporations to make public disclosures that are not required of proprietorships or partnerships. For example, the Securities and Exchange Commission requires large publicly traded corporations to make a full set of audited financial statements available for public review. Staying in compliance with the multitude of regulations that apply to corporations can be complicated and expensive. Clearly, exposure to government regulation is a disadvantage of the corporate form of business organization.

Limited Liability

Given the consequences of double taxation and increased regulation, you may wonder why anyone would choose the corporate form of business structure over a partnership or proprietorship. One major reason is that the corporate form limits the potential liability an investor must accept in order to obtain an ownership interest in a business venture. Because a corporation is responsible for its own actions, creditors cannot lay claim to the owners' personal assets as payment for the company's debts. Also, plaintiffs must file suit against the corporation, not against its owners. As a result, the most that any owner of a corporation can lose is the amount that she or he has invested in the company. In contrast, the owners of proprietorships and partnerships are *personally liable* for actions taken in the names of their companies. The benefit of **limited liability** is one of the most significant reasons for the popularity of the corporate form of business organization.

Continuity

Unlike partnerships or proprietorships, which are terminated with the departure of their owners, a corporation's life may extend well beyond the time at which any particular shareholder decides to retire or sell his or her stock. **Continuity** of existence accounts for the fact that many corporations formed in the 1800s continue to thrive in today's economy.

Transferability

Since the ownership of a corporation is divided into small units that are represented by shares of stock, **transferability** of ownership interests can be accomplished with ease. Indeed, hundreds of millions of shares of stock representing ownership in corporations are bought and sold on the major stock exchanges daily. The operations of the firm are usually unaffected by the transfers, and owners of corporations are not burdened with the task of finding willing buyers for an entire business, as are the owners of proprietorships and partnerships. For example, think of the difference in difficulty of selling $1 million of Exxon stock versus that of selling a locally owned gas station. The stock could be sold on the New York Stock Exchange to a diverse group of investors within a matter of minutes. In contrast, it could take years to find an individual who is financially capable of and interested in owning a gas station.

Management Structure

Partnerships and proprietorships are usually operated by their owners. In contrast, there are three tiers of management authority in a corporate structure. The *owners* (i.e., stockholders) are perched at the highest level of the organization. These stockholders *elect* a **board of directors** to oversee the operations of the corporation. The directors then *hire* executives who manage the company. Since large corporations are able to offer high salaries and challenging career opportunities, often these companies are able to attract superior managerial talent. However, exceptional performance is not guaranteed, and the elimination of incompetent managers is sometimes complicated by a bureaucratic corporate structure. Firing the chief executive officer who is usually a member of the board of directors requires the approval of the majority of his or her peer directors. Furthermore, many of these directors may have self-interests that are served by the existing managerial team. Accordingly, the political implications of asking a chief executive to resign can become so distasteful that many individuals are reluctant to give the necessary approval. Corporations operating under such conditions are said to be experiencing **entrenched management.**

Ability to Raise Capital

Because corporations can be owned by millions of individuals, they have more opportunities to raise capital. Few individuals have the financial ability to establish a telecommunications network such as AT&T or a marketing distribution system such as Wal-Mart. However, by pooling the resources of millions of individuals through public stock and bond offerings, corporations generate the billions of dollars of capital necessary to make such massive investments. In contrast, the capital capacity of proprietorships and partnerships is bound by the financial condition of a relatively few private owners. Although these types of businesses can increase their resource base by borrowing, the amount that creditors are willing to lend them is usually limited by the size of the owners' net worth. The capacity to raise vast sums of capital is a primary reason that corporations are able to develop and market expensive new technologies more effectively than individuals operating other forms of business.

Appearance of Capital Structure in Financial Statements

L.O. 2

Identify the different types of business organizations through the analysis of financial statements.

Up to this point, we have used generic terms to reflect capital structure in financial statements. The term *equity* has been used to describe the total ownership interest in the business. This interest has been divided into two categories: (1) *contributed capital,* which represents owner investments, and (2) *retained earnings,* which provides a measure of the capital generated through operating activities. Although these two elements are present in all forms of business organization, they are shown in significantly different formats, depending on the type of business for which a set of financial reports is being prepared.

Presentation of Equity in Proprietorships

Contributed capital and retained earnings are combined in a single Capital account on the balance sheets of proprietorships. To illustrate, assume that Worthington Company was started on January 1, 20X1, when it acquired a $5,000 capital contribution from its owner, Phil Worthington. During the first year of operation, the company generated $4,000 of cash revenues, incurred $2,500 of cash expenses, and distributed $1,000 cash to the owner. Exhibit 11–1 shows the December 31, 20X1, financial statements for Worthington's company. Looking at the *capital statement* (sometimes called a statement of changes in equity), note

EXHIBIT 11–1

WORTHINGTON SOLE PROPRIETORSHIP
Financial Statements
As of December 31, 20X1

Income Statement		Capital Statement		Balance Sheet	
Revenue	$4,000	Beginning Capital Balance	$ 0	Assets	
Expenses	2,500	Plus: Investment by Owner	5,000	Cash	$5,500
Net Income	$1,500	Plus: Net Income	1,500	Worthington, Capital	$5,500
		Less: Withdrawal by Owner	(1,000)		
		Ending Capital Balance	$5,500		

that in accounting for proprietorships, distributions are called **withdrawals.** The other unique feature you should verify is the combination of the $5,000 capital acquisition and the retained earnings of $500 (that is, $1,500 net income − $1,000 withdrawal) into a single equity account called *capital*. More specifically, note the $5,500 (i.e., $5,000 + $500) balances in the Capital account on the capital statement and the balance sheet.

Presentation of Equity in Partnerships

The format for presenting partnership equity in financial statements is similar to that used for proprietorships. For example, the Capital account includes both acquired capital and retained earnings. The only significant difference is that a separate Capital account is used to reflect the amount of ownership interest of each partner in the business.

   To illustrate, assume that Sara Slater and Jill Johnson decided to form a partnership. The partnership acquired $2,000 of capital from Slater and $4,000 from Johnson. The partnership agreement called for an annual distribution equal to 10% of acquired capital The remaining amount of earnings was retained in the business and added to each partner's Capital account on an equal basis. The partnership was formed on January 1, 20X1. During 20X1, the company earned $5,000 of cash revenue and incurred $3,000 of cash expenses, resulting in net income of $2,000 ($5,000 − $3,000). In accordance with the partnership agreement, Slater received a $200 ($2,000 × 0.10) cash withdrawal, while Johnson's withdrawal was $400 ($4,000 × 0.10). The remaining $1,400 of income was retained in the business and divided equally, thereby resulting in a $700 addition to each partner's Capital account.

   Exhibit 11–2 shows the financial statements for the Slater and Johnson partnership. Again, note that the word *withdrawal* is used to label the distributions made to the owners. Also, note that the balance sheet contains a *separate Capital account* for each partner. Each Capital account includes the amount of the partner's invested Capital plus her proportionate share of the retained earnings.

Presentation of Equity in Corporations

Capital structures of corporations are considerably more complicated than proprietorships and partnerships. The remainder of this chapter is devoted to some of the more prevalent features of the corporate structure.

			EXHIBIT 11–2				

SLATER AND JOHNSON PARTNERSHIP
Financial Statements
As of December 31, 20X1

Income Statement		Capital Statement		Balance Sheet	
Revenue	$5,000	Beginning Capital Balance	$ 0	Assets	
Expenses	3,000	Plus: Investment by Owner	6,000	Cash	$7,400
Net Income	$2,000	Plus: Net Income	2,000		
		Less: Withdrawal by Owner	(600)	Slater, Capital	$2,700
		Ending Capital Balance	$7,400	Johnson, Capital	4,700
				Total Capital	$7,400

Characteristics of Capital Stock

L.O. 3

Explain the characteristics of major types of stock issued by corporations.

A number of terms are associated with stock. Some terms are used to identify different values that are commonly assigned to stock; other terms pertain to the number of shares that a corporation has the authority to issue versus the number that it has actually issued. There are also terms that describe different classes of stock. These terms are used to distinguish the rights and privileges that may be assigned to the different owners of the same corporation (i.e., not all stockholders are treated the same). Knowledge of the meanings of these terms is essential to an understanding of the accounting practices used to report on the events that affect the ownership interest in corporations.

focus on international issues

Who Provides the Financing?

he accounting rules in a country are affected by who provides financing to businesses in that country. Equity (versus debt) financing is the largest source of financing for most businesses in the United States. The stock (i.e., equity ownership) of most large U.S. companies is said to be *widely held*. This means that many different institutional investors (e.g., pension funds) and individuals own stock. At the other extreme is a country in which the government owns most industries. In-between might be a country in which large banks provide a major portion of business financing, such as Japan or Germany.

It is well beyond the scope of this course to explain specifically how a country's GAAP are affected by who provides the financing of the country's major industries. Nevertheless, a businessperson should be aware that the source of a company's financing affects the financial reporting that it must do. Do not assume that business practices or accounting rules in other countries are like those in the United States.

Par Value

Many states require the assignment of a **par value** to stock. Historically, par value has represented the maximum liability of the investor. Likewise, when the par value is multiplied by the number of shares of stock issued, the resulting figure represents the minimum amount of assets that should be maintained as protection for creditors. This figure is known as the amount of **legal capital.** To ensure that the legal capital is maintained, many states require that a purchaser pay at least the par value when a share of stock is initially purchased from a corporation. To minimize the amount of assets that owners are required to maintain in the business, many corporations issue stock with very low par values, often $1 or less. Therefore, legal capital as defined by par value has come to have very little relevance to investors or creditors. As a result of this situation, many states allow the issuance of no-par stock.

Stated Value

No-par stock may have a stated value. Like par value, the **stated value** is an amount that is arbitrarily assigned by the board of directors to the stock. Accordingly, it also has little relevance to investors and creditors. For accounting purposes, par value stock and stock with a stated value are treated exactly the same. When stock has no par or stated value, there are slight differences in treatment. These differences will be made clear when the procedures necessary for the recognition of par values in financial statements are covered later in this chapter.

Other Valuation Terminology

The price that must be paid to purchase a share of stock is called the **market value.** There is no relationship between market value and par value. The sales price of a share of stock may be more or less than the par value. Another term that is frequently associated with stock is *book value.* The **book value per share** is determined by dividing the total stockholders' equity (i.e., assets − liabilities) by the number of shares of stock. The book value is different from the market value because equity is primarily measured in historical dollars rather than in current values.

Stock: Authorized, Issued, and Outstanding

Several terms are used to distinguish the number of shares of stock available for issue from those that have been issued to stockholders. **Authorized stock** refers to the number of shares that the corporation is approved to issue by the state. When blocks of stock are sold to the public, they become **issued stock.** Often, for reasons that we discuss later, a corporation may buy back some of its own stock. This stock is called **treasury stock,** and although it remains issued, it is no longer outstanding. Thus, **outstanding stock** is defined as stock owned by outside parties, or total issued stock minus treasury stock. For example, assume that a company that is authorized to issue 150 shares of stock issues 100 shares and then buys 20 shares of treasury stock. There are 150 shares authorized, 100 shares issued, and 80 shares outstanding.

Classes of Stock

The corporate charter defines the number of shares of stock authorized, the par value, and the classes of stock that a corporation can issue. Although there are many variations in the types of stock that may be sold, most issues can be classified as either common or preferred. If only one class of stock is issued, it is known as **common stock.** Common stockholders generally possess several rights, including these five: (1) the right to buy and sell stock, (2) the right to share in the distribution of profits, (3) the right to share in the distribution of corporate assets in the case of liquidation, (4) the right to vote on significant matters that affect the corporate charter, and (5) the right to participate in the selection of directors. Common stockholders are considered the true owners of a corporation. On one hand, they bear the ultimate risk of losing their investment if the company is forced to liquidate; on the other hand, they are the primary beneficiaries when a corporation prospers.

Preferred Stock

Holders of **preferred stock** receive some form of preferential treatment relative to common stockholders. To receive special privileges in some areas, preferred stockholders often give up rights in other areas. Usually, preferred stockholders have no right to vote at stockholders' meetings, and the size of the distributions they are entitled to receive is frequently limited. Some of the common preferences assigned to preferred stockholders are as follows:

1. **Preference as to assets.** Often there is a liquidation value associated with preferred stock. In case of bankruptcy, the amount of liquidation value must be paid to the preferred stockholders before distributions can be made to common stockholders. However, the preferred stockholder claims still fall behind those of the creditors.

2. **Preference as to dividends.** Distributions given to stockholders are commonly called **dividends.** Preferred shareholders are frequently guaranteed the right to receive dividends before common stockholders. The amount of the preferred dividend is normally stated on the stock certificate. It may be stated in an absolute dollar value per share (say, $5 per share) or as a percentage of the par value. Most preferred stock has **cumulative dividends,** meaning that if a corporation is unable to pay the preferred dividend in any year, the dividend is not lost but begins to accumulate. Cumulative dividends that have not been paid are called **dividends in arrears.** Once the firm is able to pay dividends, the arrearages must be paid first. Noncumulative preferred stock is not seen often because much of the attraction of purchasing preferred stock is lost if past dividends do not accumulate.

To illustrate the effects of preferred dividends, consider this situation. Dillion Incorporated has the following shares of stock outstanding:

Preferred Stock, 4%, $10 Par	10,000 shares
Common Stock, $10 Par	20,000 shares

Assume that the preferred stock dividend is 2 years in arrears. If Dillion distributes $22,000 to the two classes, how much will each receive? The answer will differ, depending on whether the preferred stock is cumulative.

Allocation of Distribution for Cumulative Preferred Stock		
	To Preferred	**To Common**
Dividends in Arrears	$ 8,000	$ 0
Current Year's Dividends	4,000	10,000
Total Distribution	$12,000	$10,000

Allocation of Distribution for Noncumulative Preferred Stock		
	To Preferred	**To Common**
Dividends in Arrears	$ 0	$ 0
Current Year's Dividends	4,000	18,000
Total Distribution	$4,000	$18,000

The yearly dividend for preferred stock is $4,000, calculated as $0.04 \times \$10$ par $\times$ 10,000 shares. If the preferred stock is cumulative, the $8,000 in arrears must be paid first. The $4,000 for the current year's dividend is paid next. The remaining $10,000 goes to common stockholders. If the preferred stock is noncumulative, the $8,000 of dividends from past periods is ignored. This year's preferred dividend is paid first, with the remainder going to common.

Several of the other features that may be considered for preferences are the right to participate in distributions beyond those established as the amount of the preferred dividend, the right to convert preferred stock to common stock or to bonds, and the potential for having the preferred stock called (i.e., repurchased) by the corporation. A detailed discussion of these topics is left to more advanced courses. Although the majority of the U.S. companies do not include preferred stock in their corporate structures, a significant number of companies do issue preferred shares (see Exhibit 11–3 for details).

Accounting for Stock Transactions on the Day of Issue

Stock Issued at Par Value

Recording the initial issue of stock differs slightly, depending on whether the stock has a par value, has a stated value, or is no-par stock. When either a par or stated value exists, this amount is recorded in the stock account. Any amount above the par or stated value is recorded in the **Paid-in Excess account.** Accordingly, the total amount invested by the owners is divided between two separate equity accounts. To illustrate, assume that during 20X1, Nelson Incorporated issues 100 shares of

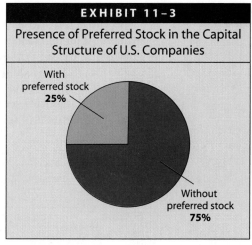

EXHIBIT 11–3

Presence of Preferred Stock in the Capital Structure of U.S. Companies

With preferred stock **25%**

Without preferred stock **75%**

Data source: AICPA, *Accounting Trends and Techniques,* 1998.

$10 par common stock for $22 per share. The event acts to increase assets and stockholders' equity by $2,200 ($22 × 100 shares). The increase in stockholders' equity is divided into two parts, with one part representing the $1,000 of par value (i.e., 100 shares × $10 per share) and the remaining $1,200 ($2,200 − $1,000) pertaining to the additional amount that was paid in excess of the par value. The income statement is not affected. The $2,200 cash inflow is shown in the financing activities section of the statement of cash flows. The effects on the financial statements and the journal entry necessary to record the event are as follows:

Assets	=	Liab.	+		Equity		Rev.	−	Exp.	=	Net Inc.	Cash Flow	
Cash	=	Liab.	+	C. Stk.	+	Paid-in Excess							
2,200	=	n/a	+	1,000	+	1,200	n/a	−	n/a	=	n/a	2,200	FA

Account Title	Debit	Credit
Cash	2,200	
Common Stock, $10 Par Value		1,000
Paid-in Capital in Excess of Par Value—Common		1,200

The legal capital of the corporation is $1,000, which is the par value of the common stock. The number of shares issued can be easily determined by dividing the total amount in the common stock account by the par value ($1,000 ÷ $10 = 100 shares). One final note concerns the title of the paid-in capital in excess of Par or Stated Value account. The *paid-in* terminology applied to this account sometimes confuses the fact that the full amount that has been *paid in* by the investors is $2,200. Note that the amount in the Common Stock account is also paid-in capital and that the amount in the *Paid-in Excess* account represents only the additional amount above the par value.

Stock Classification

Nelson Incorporated obtains authorization to issue 400 shares of class B, $20 par value common stock. The company issues 150 shares of this stock at $25 per share. The event acts to increase assets and stockholders' equity by $3,750 ($25 × 150 shares). The increase in stockholders' equity is divided into two parts, with one representing the $3,000 of par value (150 shares × $20 per share) and the remaining $750 ($3,750 − $3,000) pertaining to the additional amount paid in excess of the par value. The income statement is not affected. The $3,750 cash inflow is shown in the financing activities section of the statement of cash flows. The effects on the financial statements and the journal entry necessary to record the event are as follows:

Assets	=	Liab.	+		Equity		Rev.	−	Exp.	=	Net Inc.	Cash Flow	
Cash	=	Liab.	+	C. Stk.	+	Paid-in Excess							
3,750	=	n/a	+	3,000	+	750	n/a	−	n/a	=	n/a	3,750	FA

Account Title	Debit	Credit
Cash	3,750	
Common Stock, Class B, $20 Par Value		3,000
Paid-in Capital in Excess of Par Value—Common		750

As the preceding event suggests, companies can have numerous classes of common stock. The specific rights and privileges associated with each class are described in the individual stock certificates.

Stock Issued at Stated Value

Assume that Nelson issues another 100 shares of a second class of stock. This stock is preferred stock with a stated value of $10 per share. The preferred stock pays a 7% cumulative dividend. Assume here also that the stock is issued at a price of $22 per share. The effect on the financial statements is identical to that described for the issue of the $10 par value common stock. The journal entry changes only to reflect the name of the different class of stock.

Assets	=	Liab.	+		Equity		Rev.	−	Exp.	=	Net Inc.	Cash Flow	
Cash	=	Liab.	+	P. Stk. +	Paid-in Excess								
2,200	=	n/a	+	1,000 +	1,200		n/a	−	n/a	=	n/a	2,200	FA

Account Title	Debit	Credit
Cash	2,200	
Preferred Stock, $10 Stated Value, 7% cumulative		1,000
Paid-in Capital in Excess of Stated Value—Preferred		1,200

Stock Issued at No-Par Value

When no-par stock is issued (i.e., no par or stated values are assigned to the stock), then the entire amount is assigned to the capital stock account. Assume that Nelson Incorporated issues 100 shares of a third class of stock. This stock is no-par stock and is once again sold at $22 per share. As in the previous two examples, the event acts to increase assets and stockholders' equity by $2,200. The effects on the financial statements and the journal entry required to record the event are shown here:

Assets	=	Liab.	+		Equity		Rev.	−	Exp.	=	Net Inc.	Cash Flow	
Cash	=	Liab.	+	C. Stk. +	Paid-in Excess								
2,200	=	n/a	+	2,200 +	n/a		n/a	−	n/a	=	n/a	2,200	FA

Account Title	Debit	Credit
Cash	2,200	
Common Stock, No Par		2,200

Financial Statement Presentation

Exhibit 11–4 shows the balance sheet of Nelson Incorporated immediately after the four issues of stock just described. The exhibit assumes that Nelson earned and retained $5,000 of cash income during 20X1. Notice that the stock accounts are presented first, followed by the presentation of the paid-in excess accounts. Another popular format is to group accounts by the type of stock classification,

EXHIBIT 11–4

NELSON INCORPORATED
Balance Sheet
As of January 1, 20X1

Assets	
Cash	$15,350
Stockholders' Equity	
Preferred Stock, $10 Stated Value, 7% cumulative,	
300 shares authorized, 100 issued and outstanding	$ 1,000
Common Stock, $10 Par Value, 250 shares authorized,	
100 issued and outstanding	1,000
Common Stock, Class B, $20 Par Value, 400 shares authorized	
150 issued and outstanding	3,000
Common Stock, No Par, 150 shares authorized, 100 issued	
and outstanding	2,200
Paid-in Capital in Excess of Stated Value—Preferred	1,200
Paid-in Capital in Excess of Par—Common	1,200
Paid-in Capital in Excess of Par—Class B Common	750
Total Paid-in Capital	10,350
Retained Earnings	5,000
Total Paid-in Capital	$15,350

with the paid-in excess accounts shown along with their associated stock accounts. A properly constructed stockholders' equity section includes complete descriptions of the stock classifications, as shown in Exhibit 11–4. However, in practice many companies simply combine the different classes of stock into a single account and provide the detailed information in footnotes to the financial statements. Do not be confused by the fact that a wide variety of reporting formats are used in practice.

Stockholder Equity Transactions after the Day of Issue

Treasury Stock

L.O. 5

Explain the effects of treasury stock transactions on a company's financial statements.

When a company buys its own stock, the stock purchased is called *treasury stock.* Why would a company buy its own stock? There are many possible reasons. Some of the more common reason are (1) to have stock available to give employees in stock option plans, (2) to accumulate stock in preparation for a merger or business combination, (3) to reduce the number of shares outstanding in order to increase earnings per share, (4) to keep the price of the stock high when it appears to be falling, and (5) to avoid a hostile takeover (i.e., the shares are removed from the open market and so are not available to the individuals who are attempting to obtain enough voting shares to gain control of the company).

Conceptually, treasury stock is a return of invested capital to the owner whose stock is being purchased. In other words, it is the reverse of a capital acquisition. When a business acquires capital by issuing stock, the assets and equity of the business increase. When a business returns capital to owners by purchasing its stock from them, the assets and equity of the business decrease. To illustrate, assume that during 20X1, Nelson Incorporated buys back 50 shares of the $10 par value common stock that was sold in the first issue of stock for $22 per share. Assume that the stock is bought back at a price of $20 per share. The purchase of treasury stock is an asset use transaction. Assets and equity decrease by the amount of the cost of the purchase ($20 × 50 shares = $1,000). The income statement is not affected. The cash outflow is shown in the financing activities section of the statement of cash flows. The effects on the financial statements and the journal entry necessary to record the event are as follows:

Assets	=	Liab.	+	Equity			Rev.	−	Exp.	=	Net Inc.	Cash Flow
Cash	=	Liab.	+	Other Equity Accts.	−	Treasury Stk.						
(1,000)	=	n/a	+	n/a	−	1,000	n/a	−	n/a	=	n/a	(1,000) FA

Account Title	Debit	Credit
Treasury Stock	1,000	
Cash		1,000

The Treasury Stock account is a negative equity account. It is deducted from the other equity accounts to determine the amount of total stockholders' equity. Notice that the treasury stock is recorded at its cost ($1,000). The original issue price and the par value of the stock are not considered. The recording of treasury stock in this manner is called the **cost method of accounting for treasury stock** transactions. Although other methods could be used, the cost method is the most common and therefore is the approach used in this chapter. Assume that a few days later, Nelson resells 30 shares of treasury stock at a price of $25 per share. As with any other stock issue, the sale of treasury stock is an asset source transaction. In this case, it acts to increase assets and equity by $750 ($25 × 30 shares). The income statement is not affected. The cash inflow is shown in the financing activities section of the statement of cash flows. The effect of this event on the financial statements and the journal entry necessary to record it are as follows:

Assets	=	Liab.	+	Equity				Rev.	−	Exp.	=	Net Inc.	Cash Flow
Cash	=	Liab.	+	Other Equity Accounts	−	Treasury Stock	+	Paid in from Treasury Stk.					
750	=	n/a	+	n/a	−	(600)	+	150	n/a	−	n/a	=	n/a	750 FA

Account Title	Debit	Credit
Cash	750	
Treasury Stock		600
Paid-in Capital in Excess of Cost of Treasury Stock		150

Remember that the Treasury Stock account is a negative equity account. Accordingly, the decrease in the Treasury Stock account acts to increase stockholders' equity. Also, note that the $150 difference between the cost of the treasury stock (30 shares × $20 per share = $600) and the sales price ($750) is **not** reported as a gain. Stock transactions between a corporation and its shareholders represent one of two types of capital exchanges: transfers of capital to the business from the owners or transfers of invested capital from the company back to the owners. Corporations do not experience gains or losses on such capital exchanges.

After the sale of 30 shares of treasury stock, 20 shares remain in the account. Recall that these shares cost $20 each, so the balance in the Treasury Stock account is now $400 ($20 × 20 shares). The Treasury Stock account is a negative equity account. It is shown on the balance sheet directly below the Retained Earnings account and acts to reduce the total amount of equity shown on the balance sheet. Although this placement makes it appear that treasury stock reduces retained earnings, the reduction actually applies to the entire stockholders' equity section. Exhibit 11–5 shows the presentation of treasury stock in the balance sheet.

Cash Dividend

L.O. 6

Explain the effects of a declaration and payment of cash dividends on a company's financial statements.

A corporation generates net income for the benefit of its owners. If the company retains the income, then the price of the stock should increase to reflect the increase in the value of the firm. Alternatively, firms can distribute the income to their owners directly through the payment of cash dividends. Three important dates are associated with cash dividends: *declaration date, date of record,* and *payment date.* To illustrate the accounting treatment for a cash dividend, consider these circumstances. On November 1, 20X1, Nelson Incorporated declares a cash dividend on the 100 shares of its $10 stated value preferred stock. The dividend will be paid to the stockholders of record as of December 15, 20X1. The cash payment will be made on January 30, 20X2.

Declaration Date

November 1, 20X1, is the **declaration date.** On this day, the chairman of the board of Nelson Incorporated issued a press release to notify stockholders and other interested parties that a 7% cash dividend would be paid on the company's preferred stock. Although corporations are not required to declare dividends, they are legally obligated to pay those dividends that have been declared. Accordingly, a liability is recognized on the date of declaration. The increase in liabilities is offset by a decrease in retained earnings. The income statement and statement of cash flows are not affected. The effect of the *declaration* of the $70 ($10 × 7% × 100 shares) dividend on the financial statements and the journal entry necessary to record it are as follows:

Assets	=	Liab.	+	Equity			Rev.	−	Exp.	=	Net Inc.	Cash Flow
	=		+	Cont. Cap.	+	Ret. Earn.						
n/a	=	70	+	n/a	+	(70)	n/a	−	n/a	=	n/a	n/a

Account Title	Debit	Credit
Dividends	70	
Dividends Payable		70

The Dividends account is closed to retained earnings, thereby reducing stockholders' equity.

Date of Record

The cash dividend will be paid to the investors who own the preferred stock, as of the **date of record.** Any stock sold after the date of record but before the payment date is said to be traded **ex-dividend,** or sold without the benefit of the upcoming dividend. Since the date of record is merely a cutoff date, it does not affect the elements of the financial statements.

Payment Date

The corporation mails the dividend to the stockholders on the **payment date.** This event is treated the same as the payment of any other liability. The asset, *Cash,* and the liability, *Dividends Payable,* both decrease. The income statement is not affected. The cash outflow is shown in the financing activities section of the statement of cash flows. The effect of the cash payment on the financial statements and the journal entry necessary to record it are as follows:

Assets	=	Liab.	+	Equity			Rev.	−	Exp.	=	Net Inc.	Cash Flow
	=		+	Cont. Cap.	+	Ret. Earn						
(70)	=	(70)	+	n/a	+	n/a	n/a	−	n/a	=	n/a	(70) FA

Account Title	Debit	Credit
Dividends Payable	70	
Cash		70

Stock Dividend

Instead of distributing cash to stockholders, a company may choose to distribute shares of its stock. There are two primary reasons that a firm might decide to distribute a **stock dividend:**

1. There may not be enough funds available for a cash dividend, but the company wants to reward its stockholders in some way.
2. The price of the stock in the market may be getting so high that potential investors are discouraged from purchasing it.

To illustrate, assume that Nelson Incorporated decides to issue a 10% stock dividend on the 150 shares of its class B common stock that carry a $20 par value. Accordingly, Nelson issues 15 new shares of stock (150 shares × 10%). Assume that the distribution is made at a time when the market value of the stock is $30 per share. In this case, the stock dividend will act to transfer $450 ($30 × [150 shares × 0.10]) from the Retained Earnings account to the contributed capital section of the balance sheet.[1] Accordingly, it is an equity exchange transaction. The income statement and statement of cash flows are not affected. The effect of the stock dividend on the financial statements and the journal entry necessary to record it are as follows:

[1]The accounting treatment shown here is for a small stock dividend. The treatment for large dividends is left to more advanced courses.

Assets	=	Liab.	+	Equity					Rev.	−	Exp.	=	Net Inc.	Cash Flow
	=		+	C. Stk.	+	Paid-in Excess	+	Ret. Earn.						
n/a	=	n/a	+	300	+	150	+	(450)	n/a	−	n/a	=	n/a	n/a

Account Title	Debit	Credit
Retained Earnings	450	
Common Stock, Class B, $20 Par Value		300
Paid-in Capital in Excess of Par Value—Class B Common		150

The logic behind the accounting treatment for stock dividends may be clarified by observing the fact that the end result of issuing a stock dividend is the same as it would be if the company had issued the common stock for the market price and then used the funds to pay the cash dividends. This should be apparent from a review of the following journal entries. To make it easier to see, the offsetting entries to the Cash account are marked with strikethroughs to show that their elimination produces the same result as the issuance of a stock dividend.[2]

Account Title	Debit	Credit
~~Cash~~	~~450~~	
Common Stock, Class B, $20 Par Value		300
Paid-in Capital in Excess of Par Value—Class B Common		150
Retained Earnings	450	
~~Cash~~		~~450~~

Notice that assets are not affected by the stock dividend. However, the number of shares increases. Since there is a larger number of shares representing the ownership interest in the same amount of assets, the market value per share of the company's stock normally declines when a stock dividend is distributed. This result has the beneficial effect of making the stock more affordable and therefore may increase the demand for the stock. For this reason, a company's stock may not decline in exact proportion to the number of new shares issued.

Stock Split

A more dynamic way of lowering the market price of a corporation's stock is through a **stock split.** A stock split merely removes the old shares from the books and replaces them with new shares. For example, if Nelson Incorporated declares a 2-for-1 stock split on the 165 shares (i.e., 150 original issue plus 15 shares issued via stock dividend) of the class B common stock, a notation is made in the accounting records that the old $20 par value stock was replaced with 330 shares of $10 par value stock. Investors who owned the 165 shares of old common would now own 330 shares of the new preferred. Since the 330 shares represent the same ownership interst as the 165 shares previously represented, the market value (i.e., price) per share should be one-half as much as it was prior to the split. However,

---

[2]The authors express appreciation to Louis Dawkins of Henderson State University for the suggestion to include this illustration in the text material.

as with a stock dividend, the lower price will probably stimulate demand for the stock. Accordingly, the drop in market price is likely to be less dramatic than the increase in the number of shares. In other words, doubling the number of shares will cause the price to fall to a point that is slightly more than one-half of the value that existed before the split. If the stock was selling for $30 per share before the 2-for-1 split, it may sell for $15.50 after the split.

Appropriation of Retained Earnings

The retained earnings that is available for distribution as dividends may be restricted by the board of directors. This limitation may be required by restrictive covenants contained in credit agreements, or it may be completely discretionary. A retained earnings restriction, often called an *appropriation*, is an equity exchange transaction. It removes a portion of the general Retained Earnings account to the **Appropriated Retained Earnings** account. The amount of total retained earnings remains the same. To illustrate, assume that Nelson appropriates $1,000 of retained earnings for future expansion. The income statement and the statement of cash flows are not affected. The effect of appropriating the $1,000 of retained earnings on the financial statements and the journal entry necessary to record it are as follows:

L.O. 8

Understand how the appropriation of retained earnings affects financial statements.

Assets	=	Liab.	+			Equity				Rev.	−	Exp.	=	Net Inc.		Cash Flow
	=		+	Cont. Cap.	+	Ret. Earn.	+	App. Ret. Earn.								
n/a	=	n/a	+	n/a	+	(1,000)	+	1,000		n/a	−	n/a	=	n/a		n/a

Account Title	Debit	Credit
Retained Earnings	1,000	
Appropriated Retained Earnings		1,000

Financial Statement Presentation

Exhibit 11–5 contains the December 31, 20X1, balance sheet for Nelson Incorporated. The balance sheet reflects the 11 equity transactions that Nelson completed during 20X1. These events are summarized here for your convenience in analyzing the effect of each event on the balance sheet. (All transactions—except those affecting only equity accounts—are assumed to be cash transactions.)

1. Issued 100 shares of $10 par value common stock at a market price of $22 per share.
2. Issued 150 shares of class B $20 par value common stock at a market price of $25 per share.
3. Issued 100 shares of $10 stated value preferred stock at a market price of $22 per share.
4. Issued 100 shares of no-par common stock at a market price of $22 per share.
5. Earned and retained $5,000 cash from operations.
6. Purchased 50 shares of $10 par value common stock as treasury stock at a market price of $20 per share.

EXHIBIT 11–5

NELSON INCORPORATED
Balance Sheet
As of December 31, 20X1

Assets		
Cash		$15,030
Stockholders' Equity		
Preferred Stock, $10 Stated Value, 7% cumulative,		
300 shares authorized, 100 issued and outstanding	$1,000	
Common Stock, $10 Par Value, 250 shares authorized,		
100 issued, and 80 outstanding	1,000	
Common Stock, Class B, $10 Par, 800 shares authorized,		
330 issued and outstanding	3,300	
Common Stock, No Par, 150 shares authorized,		
100 issued and outstanding	2,200	
Paid-in Capital in Excess of Par—Preferred	1,200	
Paid-in Capital in Excess of Par—Common	1,200	
Paid-in Capital in Excess of Par—Class B Common	900	
Paid-in Capital in Excess of Cost of Treasury Stock	150	
Total Paid-in Capital		$10,950
Retained Earnings		
Appropriated	1,000	
Unappropriated	3,480	
Total Retained Earnings		4,480
Less: Treasury Stock, 20 shares @ $20 per share		(400)
Total Stockholders' Equity		$15,030

7. Sold 30 shares of treasury stock at a market price of $25 per share.

8. Declared and paid a $70 cash dividend on the preferred stock.

9. Issued a 10% stock dividend on the 150 shares of outstanding class B common stock that carried a $20 par value (15 additional shares). At the time of issue, the market price of the stock was $30 per share. There is a total of 165 (150 + 15) shares outstanding after the stock dividend.

10. Issued a 2-for-1 stock split on the 165 shares of class B common stock. After this transaction, there are 330 shares outstanding of the class B common stock with a $10 par value.

11. Appropriated $1,000 of retained earnings.

Assessment of Potential Investment Returns

L.O. 9

Understand how accounting information can be useful in making stock investment decisions.

Why does an investor acquire the stock of a particular company? Of course, the ultimate objective of any investment is to make money. However, money can be made in a variety of ways. Stockholders benefit when the companies they own generate profits. The profits may be distributed directly to the owners in the form of dividends. Alternatively, the business may choose to retain its earnings, whereupon the value of the stockholder's investment (i.e., market price of the stock) should increase. According to Financial Accounting Standards Board's *Concepts Statement No. 1,* "Financial reporting should provide information to help present and potential investors . . . in assessing the amounts, timing, and uncertainty of prospective cash receipts from dividends . . . and the proceeds from the sale, redemption, or maturity of securities . . . ."

Receiving Dividends

Will a company pay dividends in the future? Accounting information can help answer this question. First, the financial statements show whether dividends were paid in the past. Usually, a history of dividend payment is an indicator of future dividend payments. Also, to pay future dividends, the company must have cash. Although there is always uncertainty about the future, financial statements, especially the statement of cash flows, can help investors assess the probability of a company's future cash flows.

Note that very good reasons exist for a company not to pay dividends. A more thorough explanation of whether a company should pay dividends is a topic for finance courses, but do not assume that just because dividends were not paid, a company's stock is less desirable to investors. Businesses that are not paying dividends may be reinvesting the money in the company. If the company is earning a return on assets of 20%, it is wiser to reinvest available cash than to pay dividends to stockholders who would put the money in a bank account paying 6% interest.

Increasing the Price of Stock

Probably the most common reason that individual and institutional investors acquire stock is the hope that its value will increase over time. Why does the price of stock rise? The answer is very complex and certainly beyond the scope of this course. However, we can provide a partial explanation. Stock prices for the market as a whole tend to increase when the economy is good and when interest rates are low and/or falling. From this perspective, financial statements are of little benefit because they are not designed to provide information that is useful in predicting general economic conditions.

Beyond the assessment of general economic conditions, investors are interested in identifying particular companies whose stock price will increase more rapidly than the market as a whole. A particular company's stock price is likely to increase because investors believe the company will do well in the future. Financial statements do contain information that is useful in making predictions about future prospects for profitability. However, the limitations of accounting information must be recognized. Remember, accounting information is about the past. Investors want to know about the future. For this reason, stock prices are influenced more by "forecasted" net income than by last year's net income. Forecasted net income is definitely not in the financial statements. This does not mean that actual accounting results are not important but that forecasted accounting data are of equal or greater importance in explaining stock price behavior.

The following examples demonstrate this phenomenon:

- On July 12, 1996, Chrysler announced that its second-quarter profits were 700% higher than profits in the same quarter of 1995, but the stock market reacted by dropping the price of Chrysler's stock by 2%. Why did the market respond in this way? Because stock analysts who follow the company closely did not believe its revenues and net income for the second half of 1996 could keep up this pace.

- On July 16, 1996, General Motors announced that its second-quarter earnings were down 17% compared to the second quarter of 1995. The market's reaction to the news was to leave GM's stock at the same price that it had been the previous day because analysts had predicted the company's earnings would be even lower.

In each case, the investors reacted not only to the actual accounting information but to actual information compared with forecasted, or expected, information.

To illustrate another reason that financial statements cannot provide all the information relevant to the value of a company's stock, consider the following scenario. Assume that Exxon announced in the middle of its fiscal year that it had just discovered large oil reserves on property to which it held drilling rights. Based on this assumption, consider the following questions:

- What would happen to the price of its stock on that day?
- What would happen to its balance sheet on that day?
- What would happen to its income statement on that day?
- What would happen to its statement of cash flows on that day?

The price of Exxon's stock would almost certainly increase as soon as the discovery was made public. However, nothing would happen to its financial statements on that day. In fact, there would probably be very little effect on its financial statements for that year. Only after the company began to develop the oil field and sell the oil would its financial statements begin to change. Remember, accounting data are based primarily on past actions whereas the price of a company's stock is determined primarily by future expectations.

Understanding the Price-Earnings Ratio

There is a ratio that can provide some insight into how analysts view the future prospects of a company relative to its current net income. This ratio is called the **price-earnings ratio** and is defined as

$$\frac{\text{\underline{Selling Price of 1 Share of Stock}}}{\text{Earnings per Share}^\star}$$

This ratio, usually referred to as the **P/E ratio,** is one of only two ratios shown in stock price listings in newspapers such as *The Wall Street Journal*. As a general rule, the higher the P/E ratio, the more optimistic investors are about a company's future. In other words, investors are willing to pay higher prices for the stock of companies if the investors believe that the company will perform well (i.e., earnings will grow rapidly) in the future. If a company currently has negative earnings per share, its P/E ratio is not computed.

Exercising Control

Investors may also make money by influencing or controlling the operations of a business. There are several ways in which an investor can benefit by exercising some control over a company. As one example, consider a power company

---

**Earnings per share* (EPS) can be computed under a variety of assumptions. Indeed, the reporting of earnings per share in financial statements is a complicated task requiring the application of many technical accounting rules. However, for the purposes of this text, earnings per share is shown in its simplest form, which is net income divided by the number of shares of outstanding common stock.

that uses coal to produce electricity. The power company may purchase some of the common stock of a mining company to help ensure the stable supply of the coal it needs to operate its electric business. What percentage of the mining company's stock does the power company need to acquire in order to exercise significant control over the mining company? The answer depends on how many people own stock in the mining company and how the number of shares is distributed among the stockholders.

The more people who own a company's stock, the more *widely held* the company is said to be. If ownership is concentrated in the hands of a few persons, the company is said to be *closely held.* Generally, the more widely held the stock of a company, the smaller the percentage that must be acquired to exercise significant control. Accounting information can help determine how much stock is needed to exercise control. However, financial statements do not contain all the information needed. For example, the financial statements disclose the total number of shares of stock outstanding. However, the statements normally contain very little information about the number of shareholders and even less information regarding the nature of the relationships between shareholders. Information regarding such relationships is critically important because related shareholders, whether bound by family or business interests, might exercise control by voting as a block. (For "SEC companies," some information about the number of shareholders and the identity of some large shareholders can be found in reports filed with the SEC.)

A LOOK

BACK

If you wished to start a business, one of the first things you must do is to raise equity financing; you must have money to make money. Although you may wish to borrow money, lenders are unlikely to make loans to businesses without some degree of owner financing. Accordingly, equity financing is critical to virtually all profit-oriented businesses. The purpose of this chapter has been to examine some of the issues related to accounting for equity transactions.

The basic idea that a business must obtain financing from its owners was one of the very first events presented in this textbook. However, until this chapter, the organization of the business as a sole proprietorship, partnership, or a corporation has not been discussed. Some of the advantages and disadvantages associated with each type of ownership are discussed here:

1. *Double taxation*—Income of corporations is subject to double taxation, but that of proprietorships and partnerships is not.

2. *Regulation*—Corporations are subject to more regulation than are proprietorships and partnerships.

3. *Limited liability*—The concept that an investor's personal assets are not at risk as a result of an investment in corporate securities. The investor's liability is limited to the amount of the investment. In general proprietorships and partnerships do not offer limited liability. However, laws in some states permit the formation of limited liability companies that do limit the liabilities associated with ownership of proprietorships or partnerships.

4. *Continuity*—Proproietorships and partnerships dissolve when one of the owners leaves the business. Corporations are separate legal entities that continue to exist when the stockholders divest themselves of their ownership interest.

5. *Transferability*—Ownership interest in corporations is easier to transfer than ownership in proprietorships or partnerships.
6. *Management structure*—Corporations are more likely to have independent professional managers than are proprietorships or partnerships.
7. *Ability to raise capital*—Because they can be owned by millions of individuals, corporations have more opportunities to raise capital than do proprietorships or partnerships.

Ownership interest in corporations may be evidenced by a variety of financial instruments. A corporation can issue different classes of common stock and preferred stock. In general, *common stock* provides the widest range of privileges including the right to vote and participate in earnings. *Preferred stockholders* frequently give up the right to vote to receive other benefits such as the right to receive preference in the payment of dividends or the return of assets upon liquidation. Stock may be issued at *par value* or *stated value*, both of which are legal requirements that relate to the amount of capital that must be maintained in the corporation. Corporations may also issue *no-par stock* that avoids many of the legal requirements associated with par or stated value stock.

Stock that a company sells and then repurchases is called *treasury stock*. The purchase of treasury stock reduces the total amount of assets and equity. The sale of treasury stock does not lead to gains or losses. The difference between the issue price and the cost of the treasury stock is recorded directly in the equity accounts without appearing on the income statement as a gain or loss.

Companies may issue *stock splits* or *stock dividends*. The result of these transactions is to increase the number of shares of stock representing the same ownership interest in the net assets of a company. Accordingly, the per share market value usually drops when a company engages in stock splits or dividends. Beginning with Chapter 6, this course has been moving systematically down the balance sheet accounts. Along the way you have seen how each of these balance sheet accounts interacts with related accounts on the income statement. For example, when Chapter 8 examined the balance sheet effects of different methods of accounting for *inventory*, it also examined the related effects on *cost of goods sold*, which appears on the income statement. Owners' equity is the last section on the balance sheet.

A LOOK FORWARD

Chapter 12 presents a more detailed explanation of the statement of cash flows than has been presented in the past chapters. The format of the statement of cash flows that has been used to this point has been somewhat informal, although its informational content is very valid. Chapter 12 not only presents additional details about the statement of cash flows but also it examines the statement in the formal format used by most real-world companies.

APPENDIX

L.O. 10

Understand accounting for not-for-profit entities and governmental organizations.

Accounting for Not-for-Profit (NFP) Organizations

To this point, our primary focus has been on profit-oriented business organizations. We turn now to a group of organizations classified as *not-for-profit (NFP) entities*. These NFP organizations are distinguished from profit-oriented businesses by three characteristics: (1) the receipt of significant resources from contributors not expecting repayment or economic returns, (2) the operation for purposes other than profit, and (3) the absence of defined ownership interests. Types of organizations that clearly fall within the scope of the NFP classification include museums, churches, clubs, professional associations, and foundations. Organizations that clearly fall outside the scope of the NFP classification include investor-owned enterprises and mutual organizations that provide dividends, lower costs, or other economic benefits directly and proportionately to their owners, members, or participants. The line of demarcation between business and NFP organizations can be vague. Consider a nonprofit school that finances the majority of its capital needs from the proceeds of debt and operating activities. Should this organization be classified as a business or an NFP organization? The ultimate decision is left to the judgment of the interested parties.

Fortunately, much of the information about accounting for business organizations that you have learned is applicable to NFP organizations as well. For example, the financial statements of both profit and NFP organizations contain assets, liabilities, revenues, expenses, gains, and losses. However, investments by owners and distributions to them are not appropriate for NFP entities. Also, the composition of net assets for business and NFP organizations differs. Business organizations subdivide net assets into owner contributions and retained earnings. In contrast, NFP entities subdivide net assets into three classes based on the degree of donor-imposed restrictions: (1) permanently restricted, (2) temporarily restricted, or (3) unrestricted. The double-entry recording system, including debits and credits, journal entries, ledgers, T-accounts, trial balances, and so on, applies to organizations operating in an NFP context. Also, like business organizations, NFP entities are governed by a set of generally accepted accounting principles (GAAP) established by the Financial Accounting Standards Board (FASB).

The NFP organizations issue three general purpose external financial statements designed to help external users assess (1) the services an NFP organization provides, (2) the organization's ability to continue providing those services, and (3) the performance of the organization's management. The complete set of financial statements and accompanying notes includes a

1. Statement of financial position as of the end of the period;
2. Statement of activities for the period;
3. Statement of cash flows for the period.

The **statement of financial position** reports on the organization's assets, liabilities, and equity (i.e., net assets). This statement contains many common account titles, including Cash, Cash Equivalents, Accounts and Notes Receivable and Payable, Inventories, Marketable Securities, Long-Term Assets and Liabilities, Buildings, and Land. However, as indicated, the equity section of the statement of financial position is subdivided into three categories: permanently restricted net assets, temporarily restricted net assets, and unrestricted net assets.

The **statement of activities** reports on revenues, expenses, gains, and losses that increase or decrease net assets. Revenues and gains are increases in assets or decreases in liabilities generated by the organization's operating activities. Donor contributions are classified as revenues. Expenses and losses are decreases in assets or increases in liabilities incurred through operating activities. The statement is arranged in three sections: (1) changes in unrestricted net assets, (2) changes in temporarily restricted assets, and (3) changes in permanently restricted net assets. The bottom-line figure is computed by adding the net change in net assets to the beginning balance in net assets to arrive at the ending net asset balance.

The **statement of cash flows** reports the cash consequences of the organization's operating, investing, and financing activities. Unrestricted and temporarily restricted donor contributions are included in the operating activities section of the statement of cash flows. Permanently restricted donor contributions are considered financing activities. Other items are treated in a manner similar to the treatment used by profit-oriented businesses.

To illustrate financial reporting for NFP entities, assume that a private nonprofit school named Palmer Primary School of Excellence is established when it receives a $10 million cash contribution from Dana Palmer, a wealthy benefactor who wants to promote excellence in early childhood education for minority students. A total of $1 million was designated as unrestricted funds; $2 million was temporarily restricted for the purchase of land and construction of buildings. The remaining $7 million was permanently restricted for an endowed investment fund that will produce investment income to be used to supplement school operations. Parents are required to pay the school for educational services on a scale based on their level of income. During the first year of operation, $1,200,000 cash was spent to acquire land and buildings. The $7 million of cash was invested in the endowed fund. The endowment generated investment income amounting to $700,000 cash. Operating revenues amounted to $100,000 cash. Cash operating expenses amounted to $950,000, not including $50,000 of depreciation expense. The results of these events are reported in the set of financial statements in Exhibit 11–6. Study these statements carefully, noting the following differentiating features:

EXHIBIT 11-6

PALMER PRIMARY SCHOOL OF EXCELLENCE
Financial Statements
As of December 31, 20X1

Statement of Activities

Changes in Unrestricted Net Assets	
Donor Contributions	$1,000,000
Released from Temp. Building Restriction	1,200,000
Investment Revenue	700,000
Tuition	100,000
Expenses for Educational Programs	(950,000)
Depreciation Expense	(50,000)
Net Change in Unrestricted Net Assets	2,000,000
Changes in Temporarily Restricted Net Assets	
Temp. Restricted Contributions for Buildings	2,000,000
Released from Temp. Building Restriction	(1,200,000)
Changes in Permanently Restricted Net Assets	
Donor Contributions	7,000,000
Increase in Net Assets	9,800,000
Net Assets at Beginning of Period	0
Net Assets at End of Year	$9,800,000

Statement of Financial Position

Assets	
Cash	$1,650,000
Endowed Investment Fund	7,000,000
Buildings and Land	1,200,000
Less: Accumulated Depreciation	(50,000)
Total Assets	$9,800,000
Net Assets	
Permanently Restricted	$7,000,000
Temporarily Restricted	800,000
Unrestricted	2,000,000
Total Net Assets	$9,800,000

Statement of Cash Flows

Operating Activities	
Temp. Restricted Donor Contributions	$2,000,000
Unrestricted Donor Contributions	1,000,000
Investment Revenue	700,000
Tuition	100,000
Operating Expenses	(950,000)
Net Inflow from Operations	2,850,000
Investment Activities	
Endowed Investment Fund	(7,000,000)
Purchase Building and Land	(1,200,000)
Financing Activities	
Perm. Restricted Donor Contributions	7,000,000
Net Change in Cash	$1,650,000

1. That which is classified as equity in business statements is called *net asset* in the NFP statement. The net assets are subdivided into three components, depending on the nature of the donor restrictions originally placed on the use of the resources.

2. The statement of activities is divided into three categories, including activities that affect unrestricted, temporarily restricted, and permanently restricted assets. Notice that unrestricted contributions are treated in a manner similar to the way revenue is treated in profit-oriented businesses. Finally, observe the reconciliation between the beginning and ending balances in net assets shown at the bottom of the statement.

3. With respect to the statement of cash flows, unrestricted and temporarily restricted donor contributions are classified as operating activities. Only permanently restricted donor contributions are classified as financing activities. In contrast, all contributed capital of profit-oriented businesses is classified as a financing activity.

Governmental Accounting

Governmental entities have characteristics that require a unique accounting system in order to satisfy the needs of information users. These characteristics include (1) involuntary contributors of resources known as *taxpayers;* (2) monopoly supplier of goods and services; (3) resources heavily invested in nonrevenue-producing assets such as buildings, bridges, highways, schools, military and police forces; and (4) management by elected representation. The primary users of governmental financial reports include citizens, researchers, media agents, special interest groups, legislative and oversight bodies, and investors and creditors. The information contained in the financial reports is used to (1) compare actual results with budgeted estimates, (2) assess the entities' financial condition and operating results, (3) determine compliance with the laws and regulations, and (4) evaluate the effectiveness and efficiency of management.

> **L.O. 10**
>
> Understand accounting for not-for-profit entities and governmental organizations.

The GAAP for governmental accounting is set forth by the Governmental Accounting Standards Board (GASB); the GASB is a sister organization of the FASB. The presence of two separate standards-setting authorities can lead to confusion regarding which authoritative body has jurisdiction over certain types of organizations. For example, a hospital can be operated as a profit-oriented business enterprise, a private nonprofit entity, or a branch of a governmental entity. Often a single hospital will possess some mixture of the characteristics of the two or three forms of organization. Accordingly, the lines of distinction can be vague, and judgment may be required as to which GAAP applies.

The GASB has concluded that *the diversity of governmental activities and the need for legal compliance preclude the use of a single accounting entity approach* for governmental bodies. Instead, financial reporting is accomplished through distinct fiscal entities called *funds* or *account groups.* Accordingly, governmental accounting is frequently called **fund accounting.** A **fund** is an independent accounting entity with a self-balancing set of accounts segregated for the purpose of carrying on specific activities. For example, a local governmental municipality may maintain separate funds for schools, police, and parks and recreation. **Account groups** are self-balancing entities that account for the governmental unit's general fixed assets and the outstanding principal of its general long-term liabilities.

Because governmental entities are not subject to the constraints imposed by competition in the free markets, the GASB has taken a budgetary approach to accounting. Governmental entities frequently are required by law to establish budgets. When a governmental entity adopts a budget, GASB principles require that the budget be incorporated into the accounts, including the adoption of a report form that provides comparisons between budget and actual data in the financial statements. A formal budget is a critical component of accounting for government entities because it (1) provides an expression of public policy; (2) represents a statement of financial intent with regard to how funds raised through taxation will be spent; (3) acts as a legally enforceable instrument that limits spending by requiring financial managers to attain formally approved budgetary amendments prior to making expenditures that exceed the budgetary limits; (4) provides a standard to which actual results can be compared, thereby enabling the evaluation of performance; and (5) facilitates the planning process for the future needs of the governmental entity.

Governmental entities are required to issue a **comprehensive annual financial report (CAFR)** that covers all funds and account groups under their jurisdictions. The CAFR includes (1) the report of the independent auditor, (2) general-purpose financial statements, (3) combined statements organized by fund type when the primary entity has more than one fund of a given type, (4) individual fund statements when the primary governmental entity has only one fund of a given type, (5) schedules that provide detail sufficient to demonstrate compliance with specific regulations, and (6) appropriate statistical tables. Governmental reports are characterized by multiple columns that provide information on individual funds and account groups. No single summation is provided for the entity as a whole. Clearly, the appearance of financial statements prepared by governmental entities will differ significantly from that of those prepared by profit-oriented businesses.

The coverage of the details of accounting for governmental entities is beyond the scope of this book, but the preceding discussion should improve your understanding of the need for flexibility in financial reporting. Remember always that accounting should provide information that is useful to current and potential resource providers, consumers, and monitors of a variety of organizational entities. To preserve its relevance, accounting must maintain an appropriate level of versatility in reporting practices so as to meet the needs of its users.

KEY TERMS

Account Groups (appendix) Self-balancing entities that account for the governmental unit's general fixed assets and the outstanding principal of its general long-term liabilities. *(p. 543)*

Appropriated Retained Earnings Retained earnings restricted by the board of directors for a specific purpose (i.e., to repay debt or for future expansion). Although they are a part of total retained earnings, appropriated retained earnings are not available for distribution as dividends. *(p. 535)*

Articles of Incorporation Items on an application filed with a state agency for the formation of a corporation. This application often contains such information as the name of the corporation, the purpose of the corporation, the location of the business, its expected life, provisions for capital stock, and a list of the members of the board of directors. *(p. 518)*

Authorized Stock The number of shares that the corporation is approved by the state to issue. *(p. 525)*

Board of Directors A group of individuals elected by the stockholders of a corporation to oversee the operations of the corporation. *(p. 521)*

Book Value per Share Value of stock that is determined by dividing the total stockholders' equity by the number of shares of stock. *(p. 525)*

Closely Held Corporation Corporation whose stock is limited to exchanges between individuals. *(p. 519)*

Common Stock The basic class of corporate stock that carries no preferences as to assets or dividends. *(p. 526)*

Continuity A concept that describes the fact that a corporation's life may extend well beyond the time of which any particular shareholder decides to retire or to sell his or her stock. *(p. 521)*

Corporation A legal entity separate from its owners; it is formed when a group of individuals with a common purpose join together in an organization according to state laws. *(p. 517)*

Cost Method of Accounting for Treasury Stock The method of accounting for treasury stock in which the purchase of treasury stock is recorded at its cost to the firm. The original issue price or par value is not considered. *(p. 531)*

Cumulative Dividends Preferred dividends that accumulate from year to year until paid. *(p. 526)*

Date of Record The date that establishes who will receive the dividend payment. Shareholders who actually own the stock on the record date will be paid the dividend even if the stock is sold before the dividend is paid. *(p. 533)*

Declaration Date The date on which a dividend is actually declared by the board of directors. *(p. 532)*

Dividends Distribution of profits to stockholders. *(p. 526)*

Dividends in Arrears Cumulative dividends on preferred stock that have not been paid. These must be paid prior to paying dividends to common stockholders. *(p. 526)*

Double Taxation Situation in which corporate profits that are distributed to owners are taxed twice—once when the income appears on the corporation's income tax return and once when the distribution appears on the individual's return. *(p. 519)*

Entrenched Management Management that may have become ineffective but because of political implications may be hard to remove. *(p. 522)*

Ex-Dividend Stock that is traded after the date of record, but before the payment date. Stock traded ex-dividend does not receive the benefit of the upcoming dividend. *(p. 533)*

Fund (appendix) An independent accounting entity with a self-balancing set of accounts segregated for the purposes of carrying on specific activities. *(p. 543)*

Fund Accounting (appendix) Accounting for governmental entities. *(p. 543)*

Issued Stock Stock sold to the public. *(p. 525)*

Legal Capital Amount of assets that should be maintained as protection for creditors. Legal capital is the number of shares multiplied by the par value. *(p. 525)*

Limited Liability The concept that investors in a corporation may not be held personally liable for the actions of the corporation (i.e., the creditors cannot lay claim to the owners' personal assets as payment for the corporation's debts). *(p. 521)*

Limited Liability Company (LLC) An organizational form offering many of the best features of corporations and partnerships. The LLC has many of the legal benefits of a corporation (e.g., limited liability and centralized management), but the Internal Revenue Service has permitted it to be taxed as a partnership, thereby avoiding double taxation of profits. *(p. 520)*

Market Value The price that must be paid to purchase a share of stock. *(p. 525)*

Outstanding Stock Stock owned by outside parties. This is normally the amount of stock issued less the amount of treasury stock. *(p. 525)*

Paid-in Excess Account Account used to record any amount above the par or stated value of stock. *(p. 527)*

Par Value Arbitrary value assigned to stock by the board of directors. *(p. 525)*

Partnership Business entity consisting of at least two people who share talents, capital, and the risks of the business. *(p. 517)*

Partnership Agreement A legal document that defines the responsibilities of each partner and describes the division of income and losses. *(p. 518)*

Payment Date The date on which the dividend is actually paid. *(p. 533)*

Preferred Stock Stock that receives some form of preferential treatment (usually as to dividends) over common stock. Preferred stock normally carries no voting rights. *(p. 526)*

Price-Earnings Ratio (P/E Ratio) The ratio of the selling price per share to the earnings per share. Generally, a higher P/E ratio indicates that investors are optimistic about a company's future. *(p. 538)*

Securities Act of 1933 and **Securities Exchange Act of 1934** Acts passed after the stock market crash of 1929, designed to regulate the issuance of stock and govern the stock exchanges. The acts created the Securities and Exchange Commission (SEC), which has the authority to establish accounting policies for companies registered on the stock exchanges. *(p. 519)*

Sole Proprietorship A business (usually fairly small) that are owned by one person. *(p. 517)*

Stated Value Arbitrary value of stock assigned by the board of directors. *(p. 525)*

Statement of Activities (appendix) A statement that reports on the revenues, expenses, gains, and losses that increase or decrease the net assets of a not-for-profit organization. *(p. 541)*

Statement of Financial Position (appendix) A statement that reports on the assets, liabilities and equity of a not-for-profit organization. *(p. 541)*

Stock Certificate Evidence of ownership interest issued when an investor contributes assets to a corporation. The certificate describes the rights and privileges that accompany ownership. *(p. 518)*

Stock Dividend A proportionate distribution of additional shares of the declaring corporation's stock. *(p. 533)*

Stockholders Owners of a corporation. *(p. 519)*

Stock Split A proportionate increase in the number of outstanding shares, designed to reduce the market value of the stock and its par value. *(p. 534)*

Transferability A concept referring to the practice of dividing the ownership of corporations into small units that are represented by shares of stock, which permits the easy exchange of ownership interest. *(p. 521)*

Treasury Stock Stock that has been issued to the public and then bought back by the corporation. *(p. 525)*

Withdrawals Distributions to the owners of a proprietorship. *(p. 523)*

QUESTIONS

1. What are the three major forms of business organizations? Describe each.

2. How are sole proprietorships formed?

3. Discuss the function of a partnership agreement. Is such an agreement necessary for partnership formation?

4. What is meant by the phrase *separate legal entity*? To which type of business organization does it apply?

5. What is the purpose of the articles of incorporation? What information do they provide?

6. What is the function of the stock certificate?

7. What caused the passage of the Securities Act of 1933 and the Securities Exchange Act of 1934? What is their purpose?

8. What are the advantages and disadvantages of the corporate form of business operation?

9. What is a limited liability company? Discuss its advantages and disadvantages.

10. How does the term *double taxation* apply to corporations? Give an example of how the double tax is imposed.

11. What is the difference in contributed capital and retained earnings for a corporation?

12. What are the similarities and differences in the equity structure of a sole proprietorship, a partnership, and a corporation?

13. Why is it easier for a corporation to raise large amounts of capital than it is for a partnership?

14. What is the meaning of each of the following terms as it relates to the corporate form of organization?
    a. Legal capital
    b. Par value of stock
    c. Stated value of stock
    d. Market value of stock
    e. Book value of stock
    f. Authorized shares of stock
    g. Issued stock
    h. Outstanding stock
    i. Treasury stock
    j. Common stock
    k. Preferred stock
    l. Dividends

15. What is the difference between cumulative preferred stock and noncumulative preferred stock?

16. What is no-par stock? How is it recorded in the accounting records?

17. Assume that Best Co. has issued and outstanding 1,000 shares of $100 par value, 10%, cumulative preferred stock. What is the amount of the dividend per share? If the preferred dividend is 2 years in arrears, what total amount of dividends must be paid before the common shareholders can receive any dividend amount?

18. If Best Co. issued 10,000 shares of $20 par value common stock for $30 per share, what amount is credited to the Common Stock account? What amount of cash is received?

19. What is the difference between par value stock and stated value stock?

20. Why might a company repurchase its own stock?

21. What effect does the purchase of treasury stock have on the equity of a company?

22. Assume that Day Company repurchased 1,000 of its own shares for $30 per share and sold the shares 2 weeks later for $35 per share. What is the amount of gain on the sale? How is it reported on the balance sheet? What type of account is Treasury Stock?

23. What is the importance of the declaration date, record date, and payment date in conjunction with corporate dividends?

24. What is the difference between a stock dividend and a stock split?

25. What are the primary reasons that a company may choose to distribute a stock dividend instead of a cash dividend?

26. What is the primary reason that a company might declare a stock split?

27. If Best Co. had 10,000 shares of $20 par value common stock outstanding and declared a 5-for-1 stock split, how many new shares would then be outstanding and what would be the par value of the new stock?

28. When a company "appropriates retained earnings," does the company set aside cash for a specific use? Explain.

29. What is the largest source of financing for most U.S. businesses?

30. What is meant by *equity financing*? What is meant by *debt financing*?

31. What is a widely held corporation? What is a closely held corporation?

32. What are some reasons that a corporation may not pay dividends?

33. What does the price-earnings ratio generally indicate about a company?

EXERCISES

EXERCISE 11-1
L.O. 1, 2

Effect of Accounting Events on the Financial Statements of a Sole Proprietorship

A sole proprietorship was started on January 1, 20X9, when it received $20,000 cash from Kathy Jones, the owner. During 20X9, the company earned $14,500 in cash revenue and paid $9,300 in cash expenses. Jones withdrew $500 cash during 20X9 from the business.

Required

Prepare an income statement, capital statement, balance sheet, and statement of cash flows for Jones Company's 20X9 fiscal year.

Effect of Accounting Events on the Financial Statements of a Partnership

C. Hopkins and M. Miller started the CHMM partnership on January 1, 20X9. The business acquired $24,500 cash from Hopkins and $45,500 from Miller. During 20X9, the partnership earned $15,000 in cash revenues and paid $6,300 for cash expenses. Hopkins withdrew $600 cash from the business, and Miller withdrew $1,400 cash. The income retained in the business was allocated to the Capital accounts of the two partners in proportion to the amount of their original investment in the business.

Required

Prepare an income statement, capital statement, balance sheet, and statement of cash flows for CHMM's 20X9 fiscal year.

Effect of Accounting Events on the Financial Statements of a Corporation

Bell Corporation was started by the issue of 1,000 shares of $5 par value stock for cash on January 1, 20X9. The stock was issued at a market price of $18 per share. During 20X9, the company earned $23,000 in cash revenues and paid $17,000 for cash expenses. Also a $1,200 cash dividend was paid to the stockholders.

Required

Prepare an income statement, statement of changes in equity, balance sheet, and statement of cash flows for Bell Corporation's 20X9 fiscal year.

Effect of Issuing Common Stock on the Balance Sheet

Newly formed See-Max Corporation has 30,000 shares of $10 par value common stock authorized. On March 1, 20X9, See-Max issued 5,000 shares of the stock for $20 per share. On May 2 the company issued an additional 6,000 shares for $24 per share. See-Max was not affected by other events during 20X9.

Required

a. Record the transactions in a horizontal statements model like the following one. In the Cash Flow column, indicate whether the item is an operating activity (OA), investing activity (IA), or financing activity (FA). The letters (n/a) indicate that an element was not affected by the event.

Assets	=	Liab.	+	Equity		Rev.	−	Exp.	=	Net Inc.	Cash Flow
	=		+	C. Stk.	+ Paid-in Excess						

b. Determine the amount that would appear in the Common Stock account on the 20X9 balance sheet.
c. Determine the amount that would appear in the Additional Paid-in Capital in Excess of Par account.
d. What is the total amount of capital contributed by the owners?
e. What is the amount of total assets that would appear on the 20X9 balance sheet?
f. Prepare the journal entries to record the March 1 and May 2 transactions.

Recording and Reporting Common and Preferred Stock Transactions

Cane, Inc., was organized on June 5, 20X9. It was authorized to issue 200,000 shares of $5 par value common stock and 20,000 shares of 5% cumulative class A preferred stock. The class A stock had a stated value of $50 per share. The following stock transactions relate to Cane, Inc.:

1. Issued 10,000 shares of common stock for $8 per share.
2. Issued 3,000 shares of the class A preferred stock for $80 per share.
3. Issued 80,000 shares of common stock for $10 per share.

Required

a. Prepare the general journal entries for these transactions.

b. Prepare the stockholders' equity section of the balance sheet immediately after these transactions.

EXERCISE 11-6
L.O. 4

Effect of No-Par Value Common and Par Value Preferred Stock on the Horizontal Statements Model

Penny Corporation issued 4,000 shares of no-par value common stock for $30 per share. Penny also issued 1,000 shares of $50 par value, 6% noncumulative preferred stock at $80 per share.

Required

a. Record the events in a horizontal statements model like the following one. In the Cash Flow column, indicate whether the item is an operating activity (OA), investing activity (IA), or financing activity (FA). The letters (n/a) indicate that an element was not affected by the event.

Assets	=	Equity			Rev. — Exp. = Net Inc.	Cash Flow
Cash	=	C. Stk.	+ P. Stk.	+ Paid-in Excess		

b. Prepare the journal entries to record these transactions.

EXERCISE 11-7
L.O. 4

Issuing Stock for Assets other than Cash

Mike Abdullah, a wealthy investor, exchanged a plot of land that originally cost him $30,000 for 1,000 shares of $10 par value common stock of Junior Corp. On the same date, Junior Corp. issued an additional 400 shares of stock to Abdullah at a price of $31 per share.

Required

a. What is the value of the land at the date of the stock purchase?

b. Record the two stock issues on Junior's books in a horizontal statements model like the following one shown. In the Cash Flow column, indicate whether the item is an operating activity (OA), investing activity (IA), or financing activity (FA). The letters (n/a) indicate that an element was not affected by the event.

Assets		=	Equity		Rev. — Exp. = Net Inc.	Cash Flow
Cash	+ Land	=	C. Stk.	+ Paid-in Excess		

EXERCISE 11-8
L.O. 5

Treasury Stock Transactions

Tess Corporation repurchased 1,000 shares of its own stock for $38 per share. The stock has a par value of $10 per share. A month later Tess resold 500 shares of the treasury stock for $55 per share.

Required

a. Record the two events in general journal format.

b. What is the balance of the Treasury Stock account after these transactions?

Recording and Reporting Treasury Stock Transactions

The following information is available for Cohen Corp. at January 1, 20X9.

Retained Earnings	$75,000
Common Stock, $10 Par Value, 10,000 shares authorized,	
800 shares issued and outstanding	8,000
Paid-in Capital in Excess of Par, Common Stock	12,000

Cohen Corp. completed the following transactions during the period:

1. Issued 2,000 shares of $10 par value common stock for $43 per share.
2. Repurchased 300 shares of its own common stock for $38 per share.
3. Resold 100 shares of treasury stock for $40 per share.

Required

    a. How many shares of common stock were outstanding at the end of the period?

    b. How many shares of common stock were issued at the end of the period?

    c. Prepare the journal entries for these transactions.

    d. Prepare the stockholders' equity section of the balance sheet reflecting these transactions. Include the number of shares authorized, issued, and outstanding in the description of the common stock.

Effect of Cash Dividends on Financial Statements

On October 1, 20X9, Key Corporation declared a $120,000 cash dividend to be paid on December 30 to the shareholders of record on November 10.

Required

    a. Record the events occurring on October 1, November 10, and December 30 in a horizontal statements model like the following one. In the Cash Flow column, indicate whether the item is an operating activity (OA), investing activity (IA), or financing activity (FA).

Date	Assets	=	Liab.	+	Cont. Cap.	+	Ret. Earn		Rev.	−	Exp.	=	Net Inc.		Cash Flow

    b. Record the journal entries for all events associated with the dividend.

Accounting for Cumulative Preferred Dividends

When Mane Corporation was organized in January 20X7, it immediately issued 2,000 shares of $50 par value, 7%, cumulative preferred stock and 30,000 shares of $20 par value common stock. The corporation has never paid a dividend. The company's earnings history is as follows: 20X7, net loss of $25,000; 20X8, net income of $120,000; 20X9, net income of $250,000.

Required

    a. How much is the dividend arrearage as of January 1, 20X8?

    b. Assume that the board of directors declares a $30,000 cash dividend at the end of 20X8 (i.e., assume that the 20X7 and 20X8 preferred dividends are due). How will the dividend be divided between the preferred and common stockholders?

Cash Dividends for Preferred and Common Shareholders

Scene Corporation had the following stock issued and outstanding at January 1, 20X9:

1. 100,000 shares of $1 par value common stock.
2. 10,000 shares of $100 par value, 8%, noncumulative preferred stock.

On June 10, Scene Corporation declared a cash dividend on its 10,000 shares of preferred stock and a $1 per share dividend for the common shareholders. The dividend will be paid on July 1 to the shareholders of record on June 20.

Required

a. Determine the total amount of dividends to be paid to the preferred shareholders and common shareholders.

b. Prepare the general journal entries to record the declaration and payment of the cash dividend (be sure to date your entries).

EXERCISE 11-13   **Cash Dividends—Common and Preferred Stock**
L.O. 6   Appletree, Inc., had the following stock issued and outstanding at January 1, 20X9:

1. 200,000 shares of no-par common stock.
2. 10,000 shares of $100 par value, 8%, cumulative preferred stock. (Dividends are in arrears for 1 year, 20X8.)

On March 8, 20X9, Appletree declared a $200,000 cash dividend to be paid March 31 to shareholders of record on March 20.

Required

a. What amount of dividends will be paid to the preferred shareholders versus the common shareholders?

b. Prepare the journal entries required for these transactions. (Be sure to include the dates of the entries.)

EXERCISE 11-14   **Accounting for Stock Dividends**
L.O. 7   Fanfare Corporation issued a 5% stock dividend on 10,000 shares of its $10 par value common stock. At the time of the dividend, the market value of the stock was $14 per share.

Required

a. Compute the amount of the stock dividend.

b. Show the effects of the stock dividend on the financial statements using a horizontal statements model like the following one.

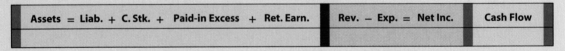

Assets	=	Liab.	+	C. Stk.	+	Paid-in Excess	+	Ret. Earn.		Rev.	−	Exp.	=	Net Inc.		Cash Flow

c. Prepare the journal entry to record the stock dividend.

EXERCISE 11-15   **Determining the Effects of Stock Splits on the Accounting Records**
L.O. 7   The market value of Noble Corporation's common stock had become excessively high. The stock was currently selling for $240 per share. To reduce the market price of the common stock, Noble declared a 4-for-1 stock split for the 100,000 outstanding shares of its $20 par value common stock.

Required

a. How will the books of Noble Corporation be affected by the stock split?

b. Determine the number of common shares outstanding and the par value after the split.

c. Explain how the market value of the stock will be affected by the stock split.

EXERCISE 11-16   **Using the P/E Ratio**
L.O. 9   During 20X7, Frontier Corporation and Companion Corporation reported net incomes of $80,000 and $55,000, respectively. Both companies had 15,000 shares of common stock issued and outstanding. The market price per share of Frontier's stock was $70 while Companion's sold for $90 per share.

Required

a. Determine the price-earning ratio for each company.

b. Based on the P/E ratios computed in part *a*, which company do investors believe has more potential for growth in income?

Not-for-Profit (Appendix)

Steve Thomas was arguing with his friend Suzy Key regarding contributions of financial resources that are acquired by an organization. Key contends that such events constitute revenue that should be reported in the operating activities section of the income statement and statement of cash flows. Thomas disagrees. He believes that acquisitions of capital should not be shown on the income statement and should be shown as a financing activity in the statement of cash flows.

Required

Write a brief memo explaining how both of the apparently contradictory arguments could be correct.

PROBLEMS—SERIES A

Effect of Business Structure on Financial Statements

Ramond Company was started on January 1, 20X9, when the company acquired $40,000 cash from the owners. During 20X9, the company earned cash revenues of $18,000 and incurred cash expenses of $12,500. Also, the company paid cash distributions amounting to $3,000.

Required

Prepare a 20X9 income statement, capital statement (i.e., statement of changes in equity), balance sheet, and statement of cash flows under each of the following assumptions. (Consider each assumption separately.)

a. Ramond was established as a sole proprietorship owned by Ramond Hazelwood.

b. Ramond was established as a partnership with two partners, Ramond Hazelwood and Buddy Veazey. Hazelwood invested $25,000 while Veazey invested the remaining $15,000 of the $40,000 cash that was used to start the business. Even though Veazey invested less, he was expected to assume the vast majority of the responsibility for operating the business. Accordingly, the partnership agreement called for Veazey to receive 60% of the profits and Hazelwood to get the remaining 40%. With regard to the $3,000 distribution, Veazey withdrew $1,200 from the business and Hazelwood withdrew $1,800.

c. Ramond was established as a corporation. It issued 5,000 shares of $5 par value stock for $40,000 cash to start the business.

Recording and Reporting Stock Transactions and Cash Dividends across Two Accounting Cycles

Pyramid Corporation received a charter that authorized the issuance of 100,000 shares of $10 par value common stock and 50,000 shares of $50 par value, 6% cumulative preferred stock. Pyramid Corporation completed the following transactions during its first year of operation.

20X8

Jan.	5	Sold 10,000 shares of the $10 par value common stock for $28 per share.
	12	Sold 1,000 shares of the 6% preferred stock for $70 per share.
Apr.	5	Sold 40,000 shares of the $10 par value common stock for $40 per share.
Dec. 31		During the year, earned $170,000 in cash revenue and paid $110,000 for cash expenses.
	31	Declared a cash dividend on the outstanding shares of preferred stock for 20X8. The dividend will be paid on February 15 to stockholders of record on January 10, 20X9. Closed the Revenue, Expense, and Dividend accounts to the Retained Earnings account.

20X9

Feb. 15   Paid the cash dividend declared on December 31, 20X8.

Mar. 3   Sold 10,000 shares of the $50 par value preferred stock for $78 per share.

May 5   Purchased 500 shares of the common stock as treasury stock at $43 per share.

Dec. 31   During the year, earned $210,000 in cash revenues and paid $140,000 for cash expenses.

      31   Declared a dividend for the preferred stock and a $.60 per share dividend for the common stock.

      31   Closed Revenue, Expense, and Dividend accounts to the Retained Earnings account.

Required

a. Prepare the journal entries for these transactions for 20X8 and 20X9.

b. Prepare the balance sheet for 20X8 and 20X9.

c. What is the number of common shares *outstanding* at the end of 20X8? At the end of 20X9? How many common shares had been *issued* at the end of 20X8? At the end of 20X9? Explain any differences in issued and outstanding common shares for 20X8 and for 20X9.

PROBLEM 11-3A
L.O. 4, 5

Recording and Reporting Treasury Stock Transactions

Rose Co. completed the following transactions for 20X9, the first year of operation:

1. Issued 20,000 shares of $5 par value common stock for $5 per share.
2. Issued 1,000 shares of $20 stated value preferred stock for $20 per share.
3. Purchased 1,000 shares of common stock as treasury stock for $7 per share.
4. Declared a $1,500 dividend on preferred stock.
5. Sold 500 shares of treasury stock for $10 per share.
6. Paid $1,500 cash for preferred dividend declared in Event No. 4.
7. Cash revenues were $54,000 and cash expenses were $32,000.
8. Closed Revenue, Expense, and Dividend accounts to the Retained Earnings account.
9. Appropriated $5,000 of the retained earnings.

Required

a. Prepare journal entries to record these transactions.

b. Prepare a balance sheet as of December 31, 20X9.

PROBLEM 11-4A
L.O. 4, 5

Analyzing Journal Entries for Treasury Stock Transactions

Assume that you find the following correctly prepared entries without explanations while you are examining the records of Premium Corporation.

	Account Title	Debit	Credit
1.	Cash	2,100,000	
	Common Stock		1,000,000
	Additional Paid-in Excess of Par Value		1,100,000
2.	Treasury Stock	22,500	
	Cash		22,500
3.	Cash	13,600	
	Treasury Stock		12,000
	Additional Paid-in Excess of Cost of Treasury Stock		1,600

The original sale (Entry No. 1) was for 200,000 shares, and the treasury stock was acquired for $15 per share (Entry No. 2).

Required

a. What was the sales price per share of the original stock issue?

b. How many shares of stock did the corporation acquire in Event No. 2?

c. How many shares were reissued in Event No. 3?

d. How many shares are outstanding immediately following Events No. 2 and 3, respectively?

Recording and Reporting Stock Dividends

Sand Pebbles Co. completed the following transactions in 20X9, the first year of its operation:

1. Issued 20,000 shares of no-par common stock for $10 per share.
2. Issued 5,000 shares of $20 par value, 6%, preferred stock for $20 per share (no shares were issued prior to this transaction).
3. Paid a cash dividend of $6,000 to preferred shareholders.
4. Issued a 10% stock dividend on no-par common stock. The market value at the dividend date was $15 per share.
5. Later that year, issued a 2-for-1 split on the shares of outstanding common stock. The market price of the stock at that time was $35 per share.
6. Produced $145,000 of cash revenues and incurred $97,000 of cash expenses.

PROBLEM 11-5A
L.O. 4, 6, 7

Required

a. Record each of the six events in a horizontal statements model like the following one. When you record amounts in the Cash Flow column, indicate whether the item is an operating activity (OA), investing activity (IA), or financing activity (FA). The letters (n/a) indicate that an element was not affected by the event.

Assets	=	Liab.	+	Equity			Rev.	−	Exp.	=	Net Inc.	Cash Flow
				C. Stk.	+ P. Stk.	+ Ret. Earn.						

b. Record the 20X9 transactions in general journal form.

c. Prepare the stockholders' equity section of the balance sheet at the end of 20X9. (Be sure to include all necessary information.)

d. Theoretically, what is the market value of the common stock after the stock split?

Analyzing the Stockholders' Equity Section of the Balance Sheet

The stockholders' equity section of the balance sheet for Liquid Real Estate at December 31, 20X9, is as follows:

PROBLEM 11-6A
L.O. 4, 7

Stockholders' Equity		
Paid-in Capital		
Preferred Stock, ? Par Value, 5% cumulative, 100,000 shares		
authorized, 5,000 shares issued and outstanding	$ 250,000	
Common Stock, $20 Stated Value, 200,000 shares		
authorized, 100,000 shares issued and outstanding	2,000,000	
Paid-in Capital in Excess of Par—Preferred	100,000	
Paid-in Capital in Excess of Par—Common	500,000	
Total Paid-in Capital		$2,850,000
Retained Earnings		500,000
Total Stockholders' Equity		$3,350,000

Note: The market value per share of the common stock is $36, and the market value per share of the preferred stock is $90.

Required

a. What is the par value per share of the preferred stock?

b. What is the dividend per share of the preferred stock?

c. What was the average issue price per share (i.e., price for which the stock was issued) of the common stock?

d. Provide a reasonable explanation for the difference between the issue price and the market price of the common stock.

e. If Liquid declares a 3-for-1 stock split of the common stock, how many shares will be outstanding after the split? What amount will be transferred from the Retained Earnings account because of the stock split? Theoretically, what will be the market price of the common stock immediately after the stock split?

PROBLEM 11-7A
L.O. 1

Different Forms of Business Organizations

Cook Hammer established a partnership with Karen Hills. The new company, HH Fuels, purchased coal directly from mining companies and contracted to ship the coal via waterways to a seaport, where it was delivered to ships that were owned and operated by international utilities companies. Hammer was primarily responsible for running the day-to-day operations of the business. Hills negotiated the buy-and-sell agreements. She recently signed a deal to purchase and deliver $2,000,000 of coal to Solar Utilities. HH Fuels purchased the coal on account from Miller Mining Company. After accepting title to the coal, HH Fuels agreed to deliver the coal under terms FOB destination, Port of Long Beach. Unfortunately, Hills failed to inform Hammer of the deal in time for Hammer to insure the shipment. While in transit, the vessel carrying the coal encountered storm damage that rendered the coal virtually worthless by the time it reached its destination. HH Fuels immediately declared bankruptcy. The company not only was responsible for the $2,000,000 due to Miller Mining Company but also was sued by Solar for breach of contract. Hills had a personal net worth of virtually zero, but Hammer was a wealthy individual with a net worth approaching $2,500,000. Accordingly, Miller Mining and Solar filed suit against Hammer's personal assets. Hammer claimed that he was not responsible for the problem because Hills had failed to inform him of the contracts in time to obtain insurance coverage. Hills admitted that she was personally responsible for the disaster.

Required

Write a memo describing Hammer's risk associated with his participation in the partnership. Comment on how other forms of ownership would have affected his level of risk.

PROBLEM 11-8A
L.O. 4–8

Effects of Equity Transactions on Financial Statements

The following events were experienced by If Apparel Inc.

1. Issued common stock for cash.

2. Paid cash to purchase treasury stock.

3. Declared a cash dividend.

4. Issued cumulative preferred stock.

5. Issued noncumulative preferred stock.

6. Appropriated retained earnings.

7. Sold treasury stock for an amount of cash that was more than the cost of the treasury stock.

8. Distributed a stock dividend.

9. Distributed a 2-for-1 stock split.

10. Paid a cash dividend that was previously declared.

Required

Show the effect of each event on the elements of the financial statements, using a horizontal statements model like the following one. Use the following coding scheme to record your answers: increase +, decrease −, and not affected n/a. In the Cash Flow column indicate whether the item is an operating activity (OA), investing activity (IA), or financing activity (FA). The first transaction is entered as an example.

Event No.	Assets	=	Liab.	+	Equity	Rev.	−	Exp.	=	Net Inc.	Cash Flow
1	+		n/a		+	n/a		n/a		n/a	+ FA

Not-for-Profit (Appendix)

PROBLEM 11-9A
L.O. 10

Sun County Public Library (SCPL) experienced the following accounting events during 20X9. Assume that all transactions are cash transactions unless otherwise stated.

1. Acquired $500,000 in contributions.
2. Paid $450,000 for facilities and equipment.
3. Earned $120,000 of revenue.
4. Incurred $80,000 in expenses.
5. Recognized an additional $25,000 of depreciation expense.

Required

a. Assume that SCPL is a profit-oriented corporation and that the first event results from the issue of no-par common stock. Prepare an income statement, balance sheet, and statement of cash flows.

b. Assume that SCPL is an not for profit organization and that the first event represents an unrestricted donor contribution. Prepare a statement of activities, statement of financial position, and statement of cash flows.

PROBLEMS—SERIES B

Effect of Business Structure on Financial Statements

PROBLEM 11-1B
L.O. 1, 2

Talcon Company was started on January 1, 20X9, when the owners invested $300,000 cash in the business. During 20X9, the company earned cash revenues of $80,000 and incurred cash expenses of $52,000. Also, the company paid cash distributions amounting to $10,000.

Required

Prepare a 20X9 income statement, capital statement (i.e., statement of changes in equity), balance sheet, and statement of cash flows under each of the following assumptions. (Consider each assumption separately.)

a. Talcon was established as a sole proprietorship owned by Justin Baker.

b. Talcon was established as a partnership with two partners, Justin Baker and Laura Parten. Baker invested $200,000 while Parten invested the remaining $100,000 of the $300,000 cash that was used to start the business. Even though Parten invested less, she was expected to assume the vast majority of the responsibility of operating the business. Accordingly, the partnership agreement called for Parten to receive 70% of the profits and Baker the remaining 30%. With regard to the $10,000 distribution, Parten withdrew $4,000 from the business and Baker withdrew $6,000.

c. Talcon was established as a corporation. The owners were issued 12,000 shares of $10 par value stock when they invested the $300,000 cash in the business.

PROBLEM 11-2B
L.O. 4–6

Recording and Reporting Stock Transactions and Cash Dividends across Two Accounting Cycles

Clean Water Corporation was authorized to issue 50,000 shares of $5 par value common stock and 10,000 shares of $100 par value, 8%, cumulative preferred stock. Clean Water Corporation completed the following transactions during its first year of operation:

20X8

Jan.   2   Issued 20,000 shares of $5 par value common stock for $8 per share.

15   Issued 4,000 shares of $100 par value preferred stock for $130 per share.

Feb. 14   Issued 10,000 shares of $5 par value common stock for $9 per share.

Dec. 31   During the year, earned $270,000 of cash revenues and paid $160,000 of cash expenses.

31   Declared a cash dividend on outstanding shares of preferred stock for 20X8. The dividend will be paid on January 31 to stockholders of record in January 15, 20X9.

31   Closed Revenue, Expense, and Dividend accounts to the Retained Earnings account.

20X9

Jan. 31   Paid the cash dividend declared on December 31, 20X8.

Mar.   1   Issued 2,000 shares of $100 par value preferred stock for $150 per share.

June   1   Purchased 400 shares of common stock as treasury stock at $11 per share.

Dec. 31   During the year, earned $250,000 of cash revenues and paid $175,000 of cash expenses.

31   Declared a dividend for the preferred stock and a $.20 per share dividend for the common stock.

31   Closed Revenue, Expense, and Dividend accounts to the Retained Earnings account.

Required

a. Prepare the journal entries for these transactions for 20X8 and 20X9.

b. Prepare the stockholders' equity section of the balance sheet for 20X8.

c. Prepare the balance sheet for 20X9.

PROBLEM 11-3B
L.O. 5, 6

Recording and Reporting Treasury Stock Transactions

Cluster Corp. completed the following transactions for 20X9, the first year of operation:

1. Issued 10,000 shares of $10 par value common stock at par.

2. Issued 2,000 shares of $30 stated value preferred stock at $30 per share.

3. Purchased 500 shares of common stock as treasury stock for $18 per share.

4. Declared a 6% dividend on preferred stock.

5. Sold 300 shares of treasury stock for $23 per share.

6. Paid the cash dividend on preferred stock that was declared in Event 4.

7. Revenue was $57,000 and expenses were $36,000.

8. Closed Revenue, Expense, and Dividend accounts to the Retained Earnings account.

9. Appropriated $6,000 of retained earnings.

Required

a. Prepare journal entries to record these transactions.

b. Prepare the stockholders' equity section of the balance sheet as of December 31, 20X9.

Recording and Reporting Treasury Stock Transactions

McCain Corporation reports the following information in its January 1, 20X9, balance sheet:

Contributed Capital	
Common Stock, $10 Par Value,	
50,000 shares authorized, 20,000 shares outstanding	$200,000
Paid-in Capital in Excess of Par Value	150,000
Retained Earnings	50,000
Total Stockholders' Equity	$400,000

During 20X9, McCain was affected by the following accounting events:

1. Purchased 1,000 shares of treasury stock at $16 per share.
2. Reissued 300 shares of treasury stock at $20 per share.
3. Earned $64,000 of cash revenues.
4. Paid $38,000 of cash expenses.

Required

    a. Provide the journal entries necessary to record these events in the accounting records.

    b. Prepare the equity section of the year-end balance sheet.

Recording and Reporting Stock Dividends

Champion Corp. completed the following transactions in 20X9, the first year of operation:

1. Issued 40,000 shares of no-par common stock for $10 per share.
2. Issued 1,000 shares of $50 par value, 5%, preferred stock at $50 per share.
3. Paid the required cash dividend to preferred shareholders.
4. Issued a 10% stock dividend on no-par common stock. The market value at the dividend date was $17 per share.
5. Later that year, issued a 2-for-1 split on 1,000 shares of outstanding preferred stock.
6. Earned $210,000 of cash revenues and paid $128,000 of cash expenses.

Required

    a. Record each of these events in a horizontal statements model like the following one. When you record amounts in the Cash Flow column, indicate whether the item is an operating activity (OA), investing activity (IA), or financing activity (FA). The letters (n/a) indicate that an element was not affected by the event.

Assets = Liab. +	Equity			Rev. − Exp. = Net Inc.	Cash Flow
	C. Stk. +	P. Stk. +	Ret. Earn.		

    b. Record the 20X9 transactions in general journal form.

    c. Prepare the stockholders' equity section of the balance sheet at the end of 20X9.

PROBLEM 11-6B   **Analyzing the Stockholders' Equity Section of the Balance Sheet**
L.O. 4, 7   The stockholders' equity section of the balance sheet for Faye Company at December 31, 20X7, is as follows:

Stockholders' Equity		
Paid-in Capital		
Preferred Stock, ? Par Value, 6% cumulative,		
50,000 shares authorized,		
20,000 shares issued and outstanding	$200,000	
Common Stock, $5 Stated Value,		
150,000 shares authorized,		
50,000 shares issued and outstanding	250,000	
Paid-in Capital in Excess of Par—Preferred	80,000	
Paid-in Capital in Excess of Par—Common	150,000	
Total Paid-in Capital		$680,000
Retained Earnings		125,000
Total Stockholders' Equity		$805,000

Note: The market value per share of the common stock is $15, and the market value per share of the preferred stock is $8.

Required

a. What is the par value per share of the preferred stock?

b. What is the dividend per share of the preferred stock?

c. What was the average issue price per share (i.e., price for which the stock was issued) of the common stock?

d. Provide a reasonable explanation for the difference between the issue price and the market price of the common stock.

e. If Faye declared a 2-for-1 stock split of the preferred stock, how many shares will be outstanding after the split? What amount will be transferred from the Retained Earnings account because of the stock split? Theoretically, what will be the market price of the preferred stock immediately after the stock split?

PROBLEM 11-7B   **Different Forms of Business Organizations**
L.O. 1   Michael Brice was working to establish a business enterprise with four of his wealthy

friends. Each of the five individuals would receive a 20% ownership interest in the company. One of the primary goals of establishing the enterprise was to minimize the amount of income taxes paid. Assume that the five business investors are in a 36% personal tax bracket and that the corporate tax rate is 25%. Also assume that the new company is expected to earn $100,000 of cash income before taxes during its first year of operation. All earnings are expected to be immediately distributed to the owners.

Required

Calculate the amount of after-tax cash flow available to each investor if the business is established as a partnership versus a corporation. Write a memo explaining the advantages and disadvantages of these two forms of business organization. Explain why a limited liability company may be a better choice than either a partnership or a corporation.

PROBLEM 11-8B   **Effects of Equity Transactions on Financial Statements**
L.O. 4–8   The following events were experienced by Monroes, Inc.:

1. Issued common stock for cash.

2. Issued noncumulative preferred stock.

3. Appropriated retained earnings.

4. Sold treasury stock for an amount of cash that was more than the cost of the treasury stock.
5. Distributed a stock dividend.
6. Paid cash to purchase treasury stock.
7. Declared a cash dividend.
8. Paid the cash dividend declared in Event No. 7.
9. Issued cumulative preferred stock.
10. Distributed a 2-for-1 stock split.

Required

Show the effect of each event on the elements of the financial statements, using a horizontal statements model like the following one. Use the following coding scheme to record your answers: increase +, decrease −, and not affected n/a. In the Cash Flow column, indicate whether the item is an operating activity (OA), investing activity (IA), or financing activity (FA). The first transaction is entered as an example.

Event No.	Assets	=	Liab.	+	Equity	Rev.	−	Exp.	=	Net Inc.	Cash Flow
1	+		n/a		+	n/a		n/a		n/a	+ FA

Not-for-Profit (Appendix)

The Playhouse is an NFP organization established to encourage the performing arts in Seattle, Washington. The Playhouse experienced the following accounting events during 20X9. Assume that all transactions are cash transactions unless otherwise stated.

1. Acquired cash contributions from donors, including $500,000 of permanently restricted, $300,000 of temporarily restricted, and $50,000 of unrestricted contributions.
2. The $500,000 of permanently restricted funds was invested in an endowed fund designed to provide investment income that will be made available for operating expenses.
3. The endowed investment fund produced $35,000 of cash revenue.
4. The $300,000 of temporarily restricted funds was used in accordance with the donor restrictions to purchase a theater in which plays will be presented. The theater had an expected useful life of 40 years and an anticipated salvage value of $20,000.
5. $30,000 of the unrestricted assets was spent to purchase theatrical equipment. The equipment was expected to have a 5-year useful life and zero salvage value.
6. Tickets sales produced $90,000 of revenue during the accounting period.
7. The company incurred $105,000 of operating expenses.
8. Recognized depreciation on theater and theatrical equipment.

PROBLEM 11-9B
L.O. 10

Required

Prepare a statement of activities, statement of financial position, and statement of cash flows.

analyze, communicate, think

BUSINESS APPLICATIONS CASE   **Gateway 2000 Annual Report**   **ACT 11-1**

Using the Gateway 2000 financial statements in Appendix B, answer the following questions:

Required

a. Does Gateway's common stock have a par value? If so, how much is it?

b. How many shares of Gateway's common stock were outstanding as of December 31, 1997?

     c. Did Gateway pay any cash dividends in 1997? If so, how much?

     d. Using the consolidated statement of stockholders' equity, determine why the number of shares of common stock outstanding increased from 1996 to 1997.

     e. On what stock exchange does Gateway's stock trade?

ACT 11-2

GROUP ASSIGNMENT **Missing Information**

Listed here are the stockholders' equity sections of three public companies for years ending 1997 and 1996:

	1997	1996
Wendy's (dollar amounts are presented in thousands)		
Stockholders' Equity		
Common stock, ?? Stated Value per share, authorized:		
200,000,000; 115,946,000 in 1997 and 113,148,000		
in 1996 shares, respectively	$ 11,595	$ 11,315
Capital in Excess of Stated Value	353,327	312,570
Retained Earnings	839,215	740,311
Other Adjustments (translation, etc.)	(18,191)	(5,712)
Treasury Stock, at cost: 129,000 shares	(1,712)	(1,712)
Coca-Cola (dollar amounts are presented in millions)		
Stockholders' Equity		
Common Stock, ?? Par Value per share, authorized:		
5,600,000,000; issued: 3,443,441,902 shares in 1997 and		
3,432,956,518 shares in 1996	861	858
Capital Surplus	1,527	1,058
Reinvested Earnings	17,869	15,127
Other Adjustments (translation, etc.)	(1,364)	(567)
Treasury Stock, at cost: (972,812,731 shares in 1997;		
951,963,574 shares in 1996)	(11,582)	(10,320)
Harley Davidson (dollar amounts are presented in thousands)		
Stockholders' Equity		
Common stock, ?? Par Value per share, authorized:		
200,000,000, issued: 157,241,441 in 1997		
and 156,252,182 shares in 1996	1,572	1,562
Additional Paid-in Capital	187,180	174,371
Retained Earnings	683,824	530,782
Other Adjustments (translation, etc.)	(3,949)	(2,062)
Treasury Stock, at cost: 4,916,488 for 1997 and 4,914,368 for		
1996	(1,114)	(1,496)

Required

     a. Divide the class in three sections and divide each section into groups of three to five students. Assign each section one of the companies.

     Group Tasks

Based on the company assigned to your group, answer the following questions.

     b. What is the per share par or stated value of the common stock in 1997?

     c. What was the average issue price of the common stock for each year?

     d. How many shares of stock are outstanding at the end of each year?

     e. What is the average cost per share of the treasury stock?

     f. Do the data suggest that your company was profitable for 1997?

     g. Can you determine the amount of net income from the information given? What is missing?

     h. What is the total stockholders' equity of your company for each year?

Class Discussion

i. Have each group select a representative to present the information about its company. Compare the share issue price and the par or stated value of the companies.

j. Compare the average issue price to the current market price for each of the companies. Speculate about what might cause the difference.

REAL-WORLD CASE **Computing P/E Ratios for Four Companies**   **ACT 11-3**

Many companies grant certain members of management stock options that allow them to purchase designated amounts of stock for less than its market price. These arrangements are referred to as *stock compensation plans* and are intended to help the company retain high-quality management and to encourage management to increase the market value of the company's stock.

Deciding on the appropriate way to account for these plans is complex and controversial. Therefore, companies are allowed to *exclude* the estimated costs of the options they grant their management from net earnings provided that they disclose the estimated costs in the footnotes to the financial statements. Listed here are data from four different companies that grant stock options to members of their management. The data are based on information provided in the companies' 10-K reports.

Federated Department Stores (owns Macy's and Bloomingdale's)

Basic EPS as reported in the January 31, 1998, income statement	$ 2.56
Basic EPS if stock compensation is deducted	2.49
Selling price of the company's stock on November 2, 1998	37.12

Sears

Basic EPS as reported in the December 31, 1997, income statement	$ 3.03
Basic EPS if stock compensation is deducted	3.00
Selling price of the company's stock on November 2, 1998	45.62

Microsoft

Basic EPS as reported in the June 30, 1998, income statement	$ 1.83
Basic EPS if stock compensation is deducted	1.60*
Selling price of the company's stock on November 2, 1998	105.81

Oracle (a large software company)

Basic EPS as reported in the May 31, 1998, income statement	$ .83
Basic EPS if stock compensation is deducted	.67
Selling price of the company's stock on November 2, 1998	29.94

*Estimated by the authors based on data in the company's 10-K.

Required

a. Compute each company's P/E ratio for November 2, 1998, based on EPS as reported and based on EPS with stock compensation deducted. You should have eight P/E ratios.

b. Assuming that the companies are representative of their respective industries (department stores and software companies), what conclusions can you draw from the data provided and from your P/E computations? Write a brief report presenting your conclusions and the reasons for them.

BUSINESS APPLICATIONS CASE **Finding Stock Market Information**   **ACT 11-4**

This problem requires stock price quotations for the New York Stock Exchange, the American Stock Exchange, and NASDAQ. These are available in *The Wall Street Journal* and in the business sections of many daily newspapers. Stock prices are also available on electronic data services such as CompuServe.

Required

For each company listed here, provide the requested information as of Thursday of last week. (*Hint:* Information about Thursday's stock market is in Friday's newspaper.)

Name of Company	Stock Exchange Where Listed	Closing Price	P/E Ratio
Berkshire Hathaway A			
Greyhound			
Intel			
Iomega			
Yahoo			
Xerox			

ACT 11-5

BUSINESS APPLICATIONS CASE   **Using the P/E Ratio**

During 20X7, Geolock Corporation and Minerals Corporation reported net incomes of $8,000 and $9,400, respectively. Both companies had 2,000 shares of common stock issued and outstanding. The market price per share of Geolock's stock was $48, while Minerals' stock sold for $94 per share.

Required

a. Determine the price-earning ratio for each company.

b. Based on the P/E ratios computed in part *a,* which company do investors believe has more potential for growth in income?

ACT 11-6

WRITING ASSIGNMENT   **Comparison of Organizational Forms**

Kim Talonga and Amy Keim are thinking about opening a new restaurant business. Keim has extensive marketing experience but does not know that much about food preparation. However, Talonga is an excellent chef. Both will work in the business, but Keim will provide most of the funds necessary to start the business. At this time, they cannot decide whether to operate the business as a partnership or a corporation.

Required

Prepare a written memo to Talonga and Keim describing the advantages and disadvantages of each organizational form. Also, from the limited information provided, recommend the organizational form you think they should use.

ACT 11-7

ETHICAL DILEMMA   **Bad News versus Very Bad News**

Louise Stinson, the chief financial officer of Bostonian Corporation, was on her way to the president's office. She was carrying the latest round of bad news. There would be no executive bonuses this year. Corporate profits were down. Indeed, if the latest projections held true, the company would report a small loss on the year-end income statement. Executive bonuses were tied to corporate profits. The executive compensation plan provided for 10% of net earnings to be set aside for bonuses. No profits meant no bonuses. While things looked bleak, Stinson had a plan that might help soften the blow.

After informing the company president of the earnings forecast, Stinson made the following suggestion: Since the company was going to report a loss anyway, why not report a big loss? She reasoned that the directors and stockholders would not be much more angry if the company reported a large loss than if it reported a small one. There were several questionable assets that could be written down in the current year. This would increase the current year's loss but would reduce expenses in subsequent accounting periods. For example, the company was carrying damaged inventory that was estimated to have a value of $2,500,000. If this estimate were revised to $500,000, the company would have to recognize a $2,000,000 loss in the current year. However, next year when the goods were sold, the expense for cost of goods sold would be $2,000,000 less and profits would be higher by that amount. Although the directors would be angry this year, they would certainly be happy next year. The strategy would also have the benefit of adding $200,000 to next year's executive bonus pool ($2,000,000 × 10%). Furthermore, it could not hurt this year's bonus pool because there would be no pool this year since the company is going to report a loss.

Some of the other items that Stinson is considering include (1) converting from straight-line to accelerated depreciation, (2) increasing the percentage of receivables estimated to be uncollectible in the current year and lowering the percentage in the following year, and (3) raising the percentage of estimated warranty claims in the current period and lowering it in the following period. Finally, Stinson notes that two of the company's department stores have been experiencing losses. The company could sell these stores this year and thereby improve earnings next year. Stinson admits that the sale would result in significant losses this year, but she smiles as she thinks of next year's bonus check.

Required

a. Explain how each of the three numbered strategies for increasing the amount of the current year's loss would affect the stockholders' equity section of the balance sheet in the current year. How would the other elements of the balance sheet be affected?

b. If Stinson's strategy were effectively implemented, how would it affect the stockholders' equity in subsequent accounting periods?

c. Comment on the ethical implications of running the company for the sake of management (i.e., maximization of bonuses) versus the maximization of return to stockholders.

d. Formulate a bonus plan that will motivate managers to maximize the value of the firm instead of motivating them to manipulate the reporting process.

e. How would Stinson's strategy of overstating the amount of the reported loss in the current year affect the company's current P/E ratio?

EDGAR DATABASE   **Analyzing PepsiCo's Equity Structure**   **ACT 11-8**

Required

Using the most current 10-K available on EDGAR, answer the following questions about PepsiCo for the most recent year reported. (PepsiCo is the company that produces Pepsi soft drinks, among other things.) Instructions for using EDGAR are in Appendix A.

a. What is the *book value* of PepsiCo's stockholders' equity that is shown on the company's balance sheet?

b. What is the par value of PepsiCo's common stock?

c. Does PepsiCo have any treasury stock? If so, how many shares of treasury stock does the company hold?

d. Why does the stock of a company like PepsiCo have a market value that is higher than its book value?

ACT 11-9

S P R E A D S H E E T   A N A L Y S I S   **Using Excel**

Annette's Accessories had the following stock issued and outstanding at January 1, 20X5.

> 150,000 Shares of $1 Par Value Common Stock
> 10,000 Shares of $50 Par Value, 8%, Cumulative Preferred Stock

On March 5, 20X5, Annette's declared a $100,000 cash dividend to be paid March 31 to shareholders of record on March 21.

Required

Set up a spreadsheet to calculate the total amount of dividends to be paid to preferred and common shareholders under the following alternative situations:

- *a.* No dividends are in arrears for preferred shareholders.
- *b.* One year's worth of dividends is in arrears for preferred shareholders.
- *c.* Two years' worth of dividends is in arrears for preferred shareholders.
- *d.* Instead of a $100,000 dividend, Annette's paid a $70,000 dividend and one year of dividends was in arrears.

Spreadsheet Tips

The following spreadsheet provides one method of setting up formulas for all possible alternatives. The spreadsheet also reflects the results of part *a.*

	Microsoft Excel - dch11-1.xls

C4   = =IF(B4<B3,B4,B3)

	A	B	C	D	E	F
1	**Alternative 1- Formulas**		Distribution to Shareholders			
2			Preferred	Common		
3	Total dividend declared	100000				
4	Preferred Arrearage	0	=IF(B4<B3,B4,B3)			
5	Current Preferred Dividend	=500000*8%	=IF(B5<B3-C4,B5,B3-C4)			
6	Available & Distributed to Common	=IF(B3-C4-C5>0,B3-C4-C5,0)		=B6		
7	Total	=B3-B4-B5-B6	=SUM(C4:C5)	=D6		
8						
9	Dividends in Arrears	=IF(B7<0,B7,0)				
10						
11	**Alternative 1- Actual Numbers**		Distribution to Shareholders			
12			Preferred	Common		
13	Total dividend declared	100000				
14	Preferred Arrearage	0	0			
15	Current Preferred Dividend	40000	40000			
16	Available & Distributed to Common	60000		60000		
17	Total	0	40000	60000		
18						
19	Dividends in Arrears	0				

Problem 11-1 Answer Key / **Problem** / Sheet2 / Sheet3 /

Notice the use of the IF function. The IF function looks like =IF(condition, true, false). To use the IF function, first describe a certain condition to Excel. Next indicate the desired result if that condition is found to be true. Finally, indicate the desired result if that condition is found to be false. Notice in cell C4 of the spreadsheet (dividends in arrears distributed to preferred shareholders) that the condition provided is B4<B3, which is asking whether the dividends in arrears are less than the total dividend. If this condition is true, the formula indicates to display B4, which is the amount of the dividends in arrears. If the condition is false, the formula indicates that B3 should be displayed, which is the total amount of the dividend.

The IF function can also be used to determine the amount of current dividend distributed to preferred shareholders, the amount available for common shareholders, and the dividends in arrears after the dividend.

SPREADSHEET ASSIGNMENT   **Mastering Excel**   **ACT 11-10**

Complete part *a* of Problem 11-5A using an Excel spreadsheet.

Statement of Cash Flows

1 Identify the types of business events that are reported in the three sections of the statement of cash flows.

2 Convert an accrual account balance to its cash equivalent.

3 Prepare a statement of cash flows using the T-account method.

4 Explain how cash flow from operating activity reported under the indirect method differs from that reported under the direct method.

5 Explain how the classifications used on the statement of cash flows could provide misleading information to decision makers.

The following information is available for Checkers Drive-In restaurants and Planet Hollywood, Inc. These data are for 1997; all numbers are in thousands.

	Checkers Drive-In	Planet Hollywood
Sales	$143,894	$475,125
Depreciation Expense	10,576	18,173
Net Cash Spent on Property, Plant, and Equipment	1,671	124,526

Notice that both of these companies are in the restaurant business. Why did Planet Hollywood spend 7 times more cash on property, plant, and equipment than it had in depreciation, whereas Checkers Drive-In spent only one-seventh as much cash on property, plant, and equipment as it recognized in depreciation?

Up to this point, the *statement of cash flows* was prepared by making reference to the Cash account. In practice, this approach may become impractical if cash transactions occur frequently. For example, think of the work required to prepare a statement of cash flows for Kmart by looking at the company's many Cash accounts. Fortunately, there are more efficient ways to obtain the information needed to prepare a statement of cash flows. Indeed, several alternative approaches can be used to prepare a statement of cash flows. This chapter focuses on the *T-account method*. However, before we introduce this approach, it is helpful to briefly review the fundamental features of the statement of cash flows.

Statement of Cash Flows

As discussed in Chapter 1, the *statement of cash flows* explains how a company obtained and used cash during some period. The sources of cash are known as **cash inflows,** and the uses are called **cash outflows.** The statement classifies cash receipts (i.e., inflows) and payments (i.e., outflows) into three categories: operating activities, investing activities, and financing activities. These activities were introduced in Chapter 1. The following sections review these activities and outline the types of cash flows that are normally classified under each category.

Operating Activities

Operating activities include cash inflows and outflows generated by running (i.e., operating) the business. Some of the specific items that are shown under this section are the following:

1. Cash receipts from sales, commissions, and fees, and receipts from interest and dividends.
2. Cash payments for inventories, salaries, operating expenses, interest, and taxes.

Note that gains and losses are not included in this section. The total cash collected from the sale of assets is included in the investing activities section.

Investing Activities

Investing activities include cash flows that are generated through a company's purchase or sale of long-term operational assets, investments in other companies, and lending activities. Some items included in this section are as follows:

1. Cash receipts from the sale of property, plant, equipment, marketable securities and from the collection of loans.
2. Cash payments used to purchase property, plant, equipment, marketable securities and loans made to others.

Financing Activities

Financing activities include cash inflows and outflows associated with the company's own equity transactions or its borrowing activities. Some items appearing under the financing activities section are as follows:

1. Cash receipts from the issue of stock and borrowed funds.
2. Cash payments for the purchase of treasury stock, repayment of debt, and payment of dividends.

When you are trying to classify transactions into one of the three categories, it is helpful to note that the identification of the proper category depends on the *company's perspective* rather than on the type of account being considered. For example, a transaction involving common stock is considered an investing activity if the company is purchasing or selling its investment in another company's common stock. In contrast, a common stock transaction is classified as a financing activity if the company is issuing its own stock or is buying back its own stock (i.e., treasury stock). Similarly, the receipt of dividends is classified as an operating activity, but the payment of dividends is classified as a financing activity. Furthermore, lending cash is considered to be an investing activity, and borrowing cash is a financing activity. Accordingly, proper classification centers on the behavior of the company involved rather than the type of instrument being used.

Noncash Investing and Financing Transactions

Occasionally, companies will engage in significant **noncash investing and financing activities.** For example, a company may issue some of its common stock in exchange for the title to a plot of land. Similarly, a company could accept a mortgage obligation in exchange for the title of ownership to a building (i.e., a 100% owner-financed exchange). Since these types of transactions do not involve the exchange of cash, they cannot be included as cash receipts or payments on the statement of cash flows. However, the Financial Accounting Standards Board (FASB) has concluded that full and fair reporting requires the disclosure of all material investing and financing activities regardless of whether they involve the exchange of cash. Accordingly, the FASB requires that the statement of cash flows include a separate schedule for the disclosure of noncash investing and financing activities.

Reporting Format for Statement of Cash Flows

The statement of cash flows is arranged with operating activities shown first, investing activities second, and financing activities last. Under each category, individual cash inflows are shown first, with cash outflows being subtracted and the net difference being carried forward. The schedule of noncash investing and financing activities is typically shown at the bottom of the statement. Exhibit 12–1 demonstrates this format of statement presentation.

With respect to the placement of the four primary financial statements, the statement of cash flows is usually presented last. However, a sizable number of companies show the statement of cash flows immediately after the income statement and balance sheet. These companies place the statement of cash flows before the other three statements. Exhibit 12–2 provides more details regarding the placement of the statement of cash flows relative to the other financial statements shown in annual reports.

Converting from Accrual to Cash-Basis Accounting

The operating activities section of the statement of cash flows is essentially a cash-basis income statement. Since accounting records are normally maintained on an accrual basis, it is necessary to convert data based on accruals and deferrals to cash equivalents to determine the amount of cash flow from operating activities. The following section discusses the conversion process.

L.O. 2

Convert an accrual account balance to its cash equivalent.

EXHIBIT 12–1

WESTERN COMPANY
Statement of Cash Flows
For the Year Ended 20X1

Cash Flows from Operating Activities		
Plus: List of Individual Inflows	$XXX	
Less: List of Individual Outflows	(XXX)	
Net Increase (Decrease) from Operating Activities		$XXX
Cash Flows from Investing Activities		
Plus: List of Individual Inflows	XXX	
Less: List of Individual Outflows	(XXX)	
Net Increase (Decrease) from Investing Activities		XXX
Cash Flows from Financing Activities		
Plus: List of Individual Inflows	XXX	
Less: List of Individual Outflows	(XXX)	
Net Increase (Decrease) from Financing Activities		XXX
Net Increase (Decrease) in Cash		XXX
Plus: Beginning Cash Balance		XXX
Ending Cash Balance		$XXX
Schedule of Noncash Investing and Financing Activities		
List of Noncash Transactions		$XXX

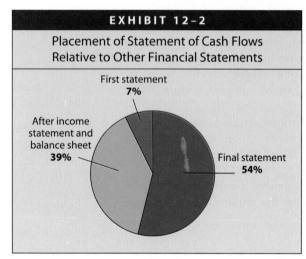

EXHIBIT 12–2

Placement of Statement of Cash Flows
Relative to Other Financial Statements

First statement
7%

After income
statement and
balance sheet
39%

Final statement
54%

Data source: AICPA, *Accounting Trends and Techniques*, 1998.

Operating Activities

Converting Accruals to Cash

Accrual accounting is the process through which revenues and expenses are recognized before cash is exchanged. When accrual accounting is applied, revenue and expense items recognized in the current period may have cash consequences in a later period. Furthermore, revenue and expense items recognized in a past period may result in cash receipts or payments that materialize in the current period. Accordingly, the amount of cash receipts and payments realized during any particular accounting period may be larger or smaller than the amount of revenue and expense recognized during that period. The following section discusses the adjustments needed to convert accrual accounting to cash-basis accounting.

Revenue Transactions   With regard to **revenue transactions,** the application of accrual accounting means that some revenue is likely to be reported on the income statement before the cash is received. Accordingly, the amount of revenue recognized is normally different from the amount of cash that the company realizes during any particular accounting period. Some customers purchase goods or services in the current accounting period but pay for them in a later period. Other customers may pay cash in the current period for goods or services purchased in

an **answer** for the curious accountant

Planet Hollywood operates and franchises a growing chain of restaurants. Of the 53 company-
owned restaurants operating at the end of 1997,
16 were opened in 1997. Thirteen of its 34 fran-
chised restaurants were also opened in 1997.

Checkers Drive-In restaurants, by contrast, was
not growing significantly in 1997. Only three of its
249 restaurants were added in 1997, and the number of its company-owned restaurants dropped
from 232 in 1996 to 230 in 1997.

a prior period. As a result, the cash received may be more or less than the amount
of revenue recognized.

To convert revenue recognized to the corresponding amount of cash collected, it is necessary to analyze both the amount of revenue appearing on the income statement and the change in the balance of the accounts receivable
account. For example, assume that a company reported $500 of revenue on its in-
come statement. Furthermore, assume that during the accounting period under
consideration, the beginning and ending balances in the company's Accounts Receivable account were $100 and $160, respectively. Accordingly, the balance in
the receivables account increased by $60 ($160 − $100). Taking this fact into con-
sideration, we can conclude that $60 of the $500 in sales was not collected in
cash. Therefore, the amount of cash collected must have been $440 ($500 − $60).

The conclusion that $440 of cash was collected from the revenue transactions
was derived through logic. This conclusion can be confirmed through a process
commonly called the **T-account method.** The T-account method begins with the
opening of the Accounts Receivable T-account with the appropriate beginning and
ending balances displayed. In this case, the beginning balance is $100, and the end-
ing balance is $160. Next a $500 debit is added to the account to record the recognition of the revenue. The resultant T-account appears as follows:

L.O. 3

Prepare a state-
ment of cash
flows using the
T-account
method.

	Accounts Receivable	
Beginning Balance	100	
Debit to Record Sales	500	?
Ending Balance	160	

Mathematically adding $500 to a beginning balance of $100 does not result
in an ending balance of $160. A $440 credit to the receivables account would be
required to arrive at the $160 ending balance. Since cash collections result in
credits to the Accounts Receivable account, it can be assumed that the Cash account was debited when the receivables account was credited. Accordingly, the
analysis of the T-account also leads to the conclusion that $440 of cash was col-
lected as a result of activities associated with the generation of revenue.

Expense Transactions   Accrual accounting results in the recognition of **expense
transactions** before the payment of cash occurs, which means that a liability is

normally recorded at the time the expense is recognized. The liability is later reduced as cash payments are made. Accordingly, the amount of accrued expense displayed on the income statement must be analyzed in conjunction with any change in the balance of the related liability account in order to determine the amount of cash outflow associated with the expense recognition. For example, assume that a company reports $200 of utilities expense on its income statement. Furthermore, assume that the beginning and ending balances in the Utilities Payable account are $70 and $40, respectively. This situation implies that the company not only made payments to cover the use of the utilities in the current period but also paid an additional $30 ($70 − $40) to reduce the obligations of prior periods. Accordingly, the amount of cash outflow associated with utility use is $230 ($200 + $30).

The T-account method can also be used to verify the $230 cash payment. A T-account for Utilities Payable is opened with beginning and ending balances placed into the account. Furthermore, a credit amounting to $200 is made to the account to reflect the recognition of the current period's utility expense. The resultant T-account appears as follows:

Utilities Payable

	70	Beginning Balance
?	200	Credit to Record Expense
	40	Ending Balance

Mathematical logic dictates that a $230 debit is required to arrive at the $40 ending balance ($70 + $200 − $230 = $40). Since debits to payable accounts are normally offset by credits to the Cash account, the T-account analysis indicates that cash outflows associated with utility expenses amounted to $230.

Converting Deferrals to Cash

Deferral transactions are events in which cash receipts or payments occur before the associated revenue or expense is recognized. Since revenue and expense recognition occurs in one accounting period and the associated cash receipts and payments occur in a different accounting period, differences arise between income reported in the financial statements and the cash-basis income. The following section discusses the procedures necessary to convert deferrals to their cash-basis equivalents.

Revenue Transactions   When cash is collected before the completion of the earnings process, a company incurs an obligation (i.e., liability) to provide goods or services at some future date. The revenue associated with the cash receipt is recognized in a later period when the work is accomplished. As a result, *the amount of revenue reported on the income statement and the amount of cash receipts normally differ.* The conversion of deferrals to cash requires an analysis of the amount of revenue reported and the change in the balance of the liability account, *Unearned Revenue.* For example, assume that the amount of revenue recognized was $400 and that the Unearned Revenue account increased from a beginning balance of $80 to an ending balance of $110. The increase in the liability account implies that the company received cash in excess of the amount of the revenue recognized. Not only did the company earn the $400 of revenue reported on the income statement, but also it received $30 ($110 − $80) for which it became obligated to provide goods and services in a future period. Accordingly, cash receipts associated with earnings activities amounted to $430 ($400 + $30).

An analysis of the T-account for unearned revenue confirms the receipt of $430 cash. The Unearned Revenue account is opened with the appropriate beginning and ending balances. A debit is made to the account to record the recognition of $400 of revenue. The resultant account appears as follows:

Unearned Revenue

		80	Beginning Balance
Debit to Recognize Revenue	400	?	
		110	Ending Balance

Clearly, $430 must have been added to the beginning balance of $80 so that when the $400 debit entry was subtracted, the resulting ending balance was $110. Since credit entries to the Unearned Revenue account are normally offset by corresponding debits to the Cash account, the analysis suggests that $430 of cash receipts was associated with revenue activities.

Expense Transactions   On many occasions, companies pay cash for goods or services that are not used immediately. The cost of the goods or services is normally capitalized in an asset account at the time the cash payment is made. The assets are then expensed in later periods when the goods or services are used in the process of earning revenue. Consequently, some items paid for in prior periods are expensed in the current period, while other items that are paid for in the current period are not expensed until later periods. *Accordingly, the amount of cash outflows normally differs from the amount of expense recognized for any given accounting period.*

To convert recognized expenses to cash flows, it is necessary to analyze the amount of change in the balance of certain asset accounts as well as the amount of corresponding expense that is recognized on the income statement. For example, assume that the beginning and ending balances in the Prepaid Rent account are $60 and $80, respectively, and that the amount of reported rent expense is $800. This situation suggests that the company not only paid enough cash to cover the $800 of recognized expense but also paid an additional $20 ($80 − $60). Therefore, the cash outflow associated with the rent payments amounted to $820 ($800 + $20).

The cash outflow of $820 for rent payments can be confirmed through T-account analysis. The beginning and ending balances are placed in a T-account for prepaid rent. The account is then credited to reflect the rent expense recognition of $800. The resultant T-account appears as follows:

Prepaid Rent

Beginning Balance	60		
	?	800	Credit to Recognize Expense
Ending Balance	80		

To have an ending balance of $80, there must have been an $820 debit to the account ($60 + $820 − $800 = $80). Since a debit to the Prepaid Rent account is normally offset by a credit to Cash, the analysis confirms that the cash outflow associated with rent payments is $820.

Investing Activities

Determining cash flow from investing activities may also require an analysis of changes in the beginning and ending account balances along with certain income statement data. For example, assume that the Land account had a beginning and ending balance of $900 and $300, respectively. Furthermore, assume that the income statement contained the recognition of a $200 gain on the sale of land. The $600 ($900 − $300) decline in the book value of the land suggests that the land was sold. The gain from the income statement implies that the land was sold for $200 more than its book value. Accordingly, the analysis suggests that the land was sold for $800 ($600 + $200) cash. Note that the amount of cash flow is different from the amount of gain appearing on the income statement. Indeed, the full $800 cash inflow appears in the investing activities section of the statement of cash flows. The operating activities section of the statement is not affected by the gain from the land sale.

The amount of cash inflow ($800) from investing activities can also be verified through the T-account method. An analysis of the beginning and ending balances in the Land account suggests that land costing $600 ($900 beginning balance − $300 ending balance) was sold. This amount, coupled with the $200 gain shown in the Retained Earnings account, suggests that $800 cash was collected from the sale. The appropriate T-accounts are as follows:

Cash	Land		Retained Earnings
?	900	600	200
	300		

It is possible that the company could have received some resource other than cash when the land was sold. However, other alternative explanations would be discovered when the other balance sheet accounts were analyzed.

Financing Activities

Cash flow from financing activities can frequently be determined by simply analyzing the change in the balances of liability and stockholders' equity accounts. For example, an increase in bond liabilities from $500 to $800 implies that the company issued new bonds that resulted in the receipt of $300 cash. This conclusion can be supported by an analysis using the T-account method. A T-account is opened with the beginning and ending balances shown here:

Bonds Payable	
	500	Beginning Balance
	?	
	800	Ending Balance

A $300 credit must be added to the $500 opening balance in order to arrive at the $800 ending balance. Since cash is normally increased when bond liabilities increase, the analysis supports the conclusion that $300 of cash inflow was derived from the incurrence of debt.

Other explanations are also possible. Perhaps some of the company's stockholders decided to exchange their equity securities for debt securities. Or the company may have been willing to incur the obligation in exchange for some asset (i.e., property, plant, or equipment) other than cash. Such transactions would be reported in the schedule of noncash investing and financing transactions.

Comprehensive Example Using the T-Account Approach

The preceding discussion emphasized the need to analyze financial statements and supporting data in the process of preparing a statement of cash flows. The beginning and ending balances in the accounts being analyzed can be drawn from two successive balance sheets. The revenues, expenses, gains, and losses can be found on the income statement. Also, notes to the financial statements may contain information needed to identify noncash transactions. Exhibits 12–3 and 12–4

L.O. 3

Prepare a statement of cash flows using the T-account method.

EXHIBIT 12–3		
THE NEW SOUTH CORPORATION **Comparative Balance Sheets** **As of December 31**		
	20X4	**20X5**
Current Assets		
Cash	$ 400	$ 900
Accounts Receivable	1,200	1,000
Interest Receivable	300	400
Inventory	8,200	8,900
Prepaid Insurance	1,400	1,100
Total Current Assets	11,500	12,300
Long-Term Assets		
Marketable Securities	3,500	5,100
Equipment	4,600	5,400
Less: Accumulated Depreciation	(1,200)	(900)
Land	6,000	8,500
Total Long-Term Assets	12,900	18,100
Total Assets	$24,400	$30,400
Current Liabilities		
Accounts Payable—Inventory Purchases	$ 1,100	$ 800
Salaries Payable	900	1,000
Other Operating Expenses Payable	1,300	1,500
Interest Payable	500	300
Unearned Rent Revenue	1,600	600
Total Current Liabilities	5,400	4,200
Long-Term Liabilities		
Mortgage Payable	0	2,500
Bonds Payable	4,000	1,000
Total Long-Term Liabilities	4,000	3,500
Stockholders' Equity		
Common Stock	8,000	10,000
Retained Earnings	7,000	12,700
Total Stockholders' Equity	15,000	22,700
Total Liabilities and Stockholders' Equity	$24,400	$30,400

EXHIBIT 12–4

THE NEW SOUTH CORPORATION
Income Statement
For the Period Ended December 31, 20X5

Sales		$20,600
Cost of Goods Sold		(10,500)
Gross Margin		10,100
Operating Expenses		
Depreciation Expense	$ 800	
Salaries Expense	2,700	
Insurance Expense	600	
Other Operating Expenses	1,400	
Total Operating Expenses		(5,500)
Operating Income		4,600
Other Operating Income—Rent Revenue		2,400
Total Operating Income		7,000
Nonoperating Revenue and Expenses		
Interest Revenue	700	
Interest Expense	(400)	
Loss on Sale of Equipment	(100)	
Total Nonoperating Items		200
Net Income		$ 7,200

Additional information:

1. The corporation sold equipment for $300 cash. This equipment had an original cost of $1,500 and accumulated depreciation of $1,100 at the time of the sale.

2. The corporation issued a $2,500 mortgage note in exchange for land.

3. There was a $1,500 cash dividend paid during the accounting period.

are the balance sheets, income statement, and additional information needed to prepare a statement of cash flows.

Preparation of Statement of Cash Flows

Begin the process of analyzing the financial statements by opening a T-account for each item on the balance sheets. Enter the beginning and ending balances for each item into the T-accounts. Use the 20X4 balance sheet (see Exhibit 12–3) to determine the beginning balance of each account and the 20X5 balance sheet to get the ending balances. The Cash account should be large enough to be divided into three components representing cash flows from operating, investing, and financing activities. Exhibit 12–5 contains a full set of T-accounts with all analytical transactions included. Each transaction is labeled with a lowercase letter. Since some analysis requires more than one entry, each letter is also followed by a number, which permits detailed labeling for each transaction. The following section explains each transaction in full detail.

Cash Flows from Operating Activities

Cash flow from operating activities is essentially a cash-basis income statement. Since accrual accounting is normally used in the preparation of formal financial

EXHIBIT 12–5

Balance Sheet T-Accounts

Assets	=	Liabilities	+	Stockholders' Equity

Cash

Bal.	400	

Operating Activities

(a2)	20,800	11,500	(b3)
(g2)	1,400	2,600	(d2)
(h2)	600	300	(e2)
		1,200	(f2)
		600	(i2)

Investing Activities

(k1)	300	1,600	(j1)
		2,300	(l1)

Financing Activities

(o1)	2,000	3,000	(n1)
		1,500	(p1)
Bal.	900		

Accounts Receivable

Bal.	1,200	20,800	(a2)
(a1)	20,600		
Bal.	1,000		

Interest Receivable

Bal.	300	600	(h2)
(h1)	700		
Bal.	400		

Inventory

Bal.	8,200	10,500	(b1)
(b2)	11,200		
Bal.	8,900		

Prepaid Insurance

Bal.	1,400	600	(e1)
(e2)	300		
Bal.	1,100		

Marketable Securities

Bal.	3,500	
(j1)	1,600	
Bal.	5,100	

Equipment

Bal.	4,600	1,500	(k1)
(l1)	2,300		
Bal.	5,400		

Accumulated Depreciation

(k1)	1,100	1,200	Bal.
		800	(c1)
		900	Bal.

Land

Bal.	6,000	
(m1)	2,500	
Bal.	8,500	

Accounts Payable—Inventory

(b3)	11,500	1,100	Bal.
		11,200	(b2)
		800	Bal.

Salaries Payable

(d2)	2,600	900	Bal.
		2,700	(d1)
		1,000	Bal.

Operating Exp. Payable

(f2)	1,200	1,300	Bal.
		1,400	(f1)
		1,500	Bal.

Interest Payable

(i2)	600	500	Bal.
		400	(i1)
		300	Bal.

Unearned Rent Revenue

(g1)	2,400	1,600	Bal.
		1,400	(g2)
		600	Bal.

Mortgage Payable

		0	Bal.
		2,500	(m1)
		2,500	Bal.

Bonds Payable

(n1)	3,000	4,000	Bal.
		1,000	Bal.

Common Stock

		8,000	Bal.
		2,000	(o1)
		10,000	Bal.

Retained Earnings

(b1)	10,500	7,000	Bal.
(c1)	800	20,600	(a1)
(d1)	2,700	2,400	(g1)
(e1)	600	700	(h1)
(f1)	1,400		
(i1)	400		
(k1)	100		
(p1)	1,500		
		12,700	Bal.

statements, it is necessary to convert the income statement data to cash equivalents. Accordingly, each item on the income statement should be analyzed separately to assess its cash flow consequences.

Cash Receipts from Sales

The first item appearing on the income statement is $20,600 of sales revenue. Assuming that all sales transactions were on account, the entry to record sales would have required a debit to Accounts Receivable and a credit to Sales Revenue. Because the T-account analysis includes only balance sheet accounts and sales revenue acts to increase Retained Earnings, the entry to record sales in the T-accounts is shown as a debit to Accounts Receivable and a credit to Retained Earnings. This entry is labeled (a1) in Exhibit 12–5. After the sales revenue transaction is recorded, the cash inflow from sales can be determined by analyzing the Accounts Receivable T-account. Notice that the beginning balance of $1,200 plus the debit to receivables of $20,600 resulting from sales transactions suggests that $21,800 of receivables was available for collection. Since the ending balance in the receivables account amounts to $1,000, there must have been $20,800 (i.e., $21,800 − $1,000) of receivables collected. This cash inflow is recognized with a debit to the Cash account under the operating activities section and a credit to the Accounts Receivable account. This entry is labeled (a2) in Exhibit 12–5.

The preceding discussion introduces several practices that apply to the analysis of all cash flows from operating activities. First, note that all revenue, expense, gain, and loss transactions ultimately affect the Retained Earnings account. Accordingly, to reconcile the beginning and ending balances in Retained Earnings, all income statement items are posted directly to the Retained Earnings account. Second, the determination of when to stop the analysis depends on the reconciliation between the beginning and ending account balances. In this case, the analysis of Accounts Receivable stopped with the $20,800 credit because the beginning balance plus the debit and minus the credit equaled the ending balance. Accordingly, the analysis of the account is completed because the beginning and ending balances have been reconciled (i.e., the change in the account has been fully explained). The analysis for the entire statement is completed when the beginning and ending balances in all the balance sheet accounts are reconciled. Since many of the balance sheet accounts remain to be reconciled, the cash flow analysis in this case will continue.

Cash Payments for Inventory Purchases

It is helpful to make two simplifying assumptions in analyzing cash payments for inventory purchases. First, assume that the company employs the perpetual inventory method; second, assume that all purchases are made on account. Based on these assumptions, the entry to record the cost of goods sold ($10,500, as shown on the income statement in Exhibit 12–4) would have required a credit to the Inventory account and a debit to Retained Earnings (i.e., cost of goods sold). This entry is labeled (b1) in the exhibit. This entry only partly explains the change in the beginning and ending balances of the Inventory account. A closer analysis of this account suggests that some inventory must have been purchased. Given that the beginning balance in the Inventory account was $8,200 and that $10,500 of inventory cost was transferred to cost of goods sold, it is logical to assume that $11,200 of inventory was purchased to arrive at the ending Inventory balance of $8,900. The entry to record the inventory purchase, labeled (b2), includes a debt to Inventory and a credit to Accounts Payable. This entry completes the explanation of the change in the beginning and ending balances but only partly explains the change in the beginning and ending balances in the Accounts Payable account. Given a beginning balance in Accounts Payable of $1,100 and additional purchases on account amounting to $11,200, there must have been $12,300 of accounts payable available for payment. Since the ending balance in the Accounts Payable account amounted to $800, there must have been cash payments of $11,500 ($12,300 − $800). The entry to record this cash outflow, labeled (b3), includes a credit to the operating activities section of the Cash account and a debit to the Accounts Payable account.

Noncash Effects of Depreciation

The next item on the income statement is depreciation expense. Depreciation expense is a noncash charge against revenues. In other words, no cash changes hands at the time the depreciation expense is recorded. Indeed, the entry to record depreciation expense (c1) includes a debit to Retained Earnings (i.e., depreciation expense) and a credit to Accumulated Depreciation. This entry only partly explains the change in accumulated depreciation, indicating that further analysis is required. However, cash flow consequences associated with long-term assets and their respective contra accounts affect the investing activities section of the statement of cash flows. Accordingly, further analysis is delayed until investing activities are considered. At this stage, the analysis of cash flows from operating activities continues.

Cash Payments for Salaries

The entry to record $2,700 of salary expense includes a debit to Retained Earnings (i.e., salary expense) and a credit to Salaries Payable. This entry, labeled (d1), partly explains the change in beginning and ending balances in the Salaries Payable account. The beginning balance of $900 plus the $2,700 increase for the current period's expense suggests that there were $3,600 of salaries available for payment during the period. Since the ending balance amounted to $1,000, there must have been a cash payment for salaries amounting to $2,600 ($3,600 − $1,000). The entry to record the cash payment for salaries includes a debit to the Salaries Payable account and a credit to the operating activities section of the Cash account. This entry is labeled (d2) in the exhibit.

Cash Payments for Insurance

The entry to record $600 of insurance expense requires a debit to Retained Earnings (i.e., insurance expense) and a credit to Prepaid Insurance. This entry, labeled (e1), partly explains the change in the beginning and ending balances in the Prepaid Insurance account. The beginning balance of $1,400 less the reduction of $600 associated with the recognition of insurance expense suggests an ending balance of $800. However, the balance sheet shows an actual ending balance of $1,100. Accordingly, a purchase of $300 ($1,100 − $800) of prepaid insurance must have been made during the accounting period. The cash outflow for the purchase of insurance is labeled (e2) and includes a debit to the Prepaid Insurance account and a credit to the operating activities section of the statement of cash flows.

Cash Payments for Other Operating Expenses

The $1,400 of other operating expenses appearing on the income statement is recorded in the T-accounts with a debit to Retained Earnings and a credit to the Operating Expenses Payable account. This entry, labeled (f1), partly explains the change in the beginning and ending balances in the Operating Expenses Payable account. Given a beginning balance of $1,300 and the $1,400 addition for current expenses, the total amount available for payment was $2,700 ($1,300 + $1,400). Since the ending balance amounted to $1,500, the cash payments must have amounted to $1,200 ($2,700 − $1,500). The entry to record the cash payment is labeled (f2) and includes a debit to the Operating Expenses Payable account and a credit to the operating activities section of the Cash account.

Cash Receipts for Rent

The entry to record $2,400 of rent revenue includes a debit to the Unearned Rent Revenue account and a credit to the Retained Earnings account. This entry, labeled (g1), partly explains the change in the beginning and ending balances in the Unearned Rent Revenue account. The beginning balance of $1,600 less the $2,400 reduction caused by the recognition of the rent revenue suggests that there must have been a credit (i.e., increase) in the account in order to arrive at an ending balance of $600. Since increases in the unearned account are offset by increases in cash, collections must have been equal to $1,400 ($1,600 + $1,400 − $2,400 = $600). The required entry for the cash receipt includes a credit to the Unearned Rent Revenue account and a debit to the operating activities section of the Cash account. This entry is labeled (g2) in Exhibit 12–5.

Cash Receipts from Interest

The entry to record $700 of interest revenue includes a debit to the Interest Receivable account and a credit to Retained Earnings (i.e., interest revenue). This entry, labeled (h1), partially explains the change in the beginning and ending balances in the Interest Receivable account. Given the beginning balance of $300 plus the $700 debit created through the recognition of interest revenue, the receivables account indicates that there was $1,000 ($300 + $700) of interest receivables available for collection. The ending balance of $400 implies that $600 ($1,000 − $400) of cash was collected. The entry to record this cash inflow is labeled (h2) and includes a credit to Interest Receivable and a debit to the operating activities section of the Cash account.

Cash Payments for Interest

The entry to record $400 of interest expense is labeled (i1) and includes a debit to Retained Earnings (i.e., interest expense) and a credit to Interest Payable. The entry partly explains the change in the beginning and ending balances in the Interest Payable account. The beginning balance of $500 plus the $400 that resulted from the recognition of interest expense suggests that there was $900 of interest obligations available for payment. The ending balance of $300 implies that $600 ($900 − $300) was paid in cash. The entry to recognize the cash outflow for this interest payment is labeled (i2) and includes a debit to the Interest Payable account and a credit to the operating activities section of the Cash account.

Noncash Effects of Loss

The loss on the sale of equipment does not affect cash flows from operating activities. The full proceeds from the sale constitute the amount of cash flow. The amount of any loss or gain is irrelevant. Indeed, the sale involves the disposal of an investment and therefore is shown under the investing activities section. Cash flow from operating activities is not affected by gains or losses on the disposal of long-term assets.

Completion of Analysis of Operating Activities

Since no other items appear on the income statement, the conversion process from accrual to cash is completed. The operating activities section of the Cash account contains all the cash receipts and payments necessary to determine the net cash flow from operations. This information is placed into the formal statement of cash flows (presented later in the chapter). With the completion of the assessment of cash flow from operating activities, the analysis proceeds to the cash flow effects associated with investing activities.

Cash Flows from Investing Activities

Investing activities generally involve the acquisition (i.e., purchase) or disposal (i.e., sale) of long-term assets. Accordingly, the analysis of cash flows from investing activities centers on changes in the beginning and ending balances in long-term assets.

Cash Payments to Purchase Marketable Securities

The first long-term asset shown on the balance sheets is Marketable Securities. An analysis of this asset account indicates that the balance in the account increased from $3,500 at the beginning of the period to $5,100 at the end of the period. The most reasonable explanation for this increase is that the corporation purchased additional securities in the amount of $1,600 ($5,100 − $3,500). In the absence of information to the contrary, it is assumed that the purchase was made with cash. The entry to record the purchase includes a debit to the Marketable Securities account and a credit to the investing activities section of the Cash account. This entry is coded (j1) in Exhibit 12–5.

Cash Receipts from Sale of Equipment

The next asset on the balance sheets is Equipment. Our earlier review of the income statement disclosed a loss on the sale of equipment, which suggests that some equipment was sold during the period. This sale is expected to result in a cash inflow in the amount of the sales price. The additional information at the bottom of the income statement discloses that equipment costing $1,500 with accumulated depreciation of $1,100 was sold for $300. The difference between the $400 ($1,500 − $1,100) book value and the $300 sales price explains the $100 loss on the income statement. The cash receipt from the sale is $300. The original cost, accumulated depreciation, and loss do not affect cash flow. The entry to recognize the cash receipt includes a debit to the investing section of the Cash account, a debit to Retained Earnings (i.e., loss), a debit to the Accumulated Depreciation account, and a credit to the Equipment account. The entry is labeled (k1) in the exhibit.

Cash Payments to Purchase Equipment

The sale of equipment partially explains the change in the beginning and ending balances in the Equipment account. However, further analysis suggests that some equipment must have been purchased. A beginning balance of $4,600 less $1,500 for the equipment that was sold suggests that $2,300 of equipment must have been purchased in order to arrive at the ending balance of $5,400 ($4,600 − $1,500 + $2,300 = $5,400). The cash payment necessary to purchase the equipment is labeled (l1) and includes a debit to the Equipment account and a credit to the investing activities section of the Cash account.

Noncash Transaction for Land Acquisition

The Land account increased from a beginning balance of $6,000 to an ending balance of $8,500, thereby suggesting that $2,500 ($8,500 − $6,000) of land was acquired during the accounting period. The additional information at the bottom of the income statement discloses the fact that the corporation acquired this land through the issuance of a mortgage. Accordingly, no cash consequences are associated with the transaction. The transaction recording this event is labeled (m1) in Exhibit 12–5. Since the transaction does not affect cash, it is shown in the separate schedule for noncash investing and financing transactions on the statement of cash flows.

Since all long-term asset accounts have been reconciled, the analysis of cash flows from investing activities is completed. The process continues with an assessment of cash flows associated with financing activities.

Cash Flows from Financing Activities

The long-term liability and stockholders' equity sections of the balance sheets are analyzed to assess the cash flows from financing activities. Note that the first long-term liability account on the balance sheet is Mortgage Payable. The change in this account was explained in the analysis of the land acquisition, discussed earlier in this chapter. As explained, this financing activity is shown along with the investing activity in the separate schedule for noncash transactions. Accordingly, the analysis of cash flows proceeds with the change in the Bond Liability account.

Cash Payment for Bonds

The balance in the Bonds Payable account decreased from $4,000 to $1,000. In the absence of information to the contrary, it is logical to assume that $3,000 ($4,000 − $1,000) was paid to reduce bond liabilities. The entry to record the cash outflow includes a debit to the Bonds Payable account and a credit to the financing activities section of the Cash account. This entry is coded (n1) in the exhibit.

Cash Receipt from Stock Issue

The balance in the Common Stock account increased from $8,000 to $10,000. In the absence of information to the contrary, it is logical to assume that $2,000 ($10,000 − $8,000) of cash was collected as proceeds from the issuance of common stock. The entry to record this cash inflow is labeled (o1) and includes a credit to Common Stock and a debit to the financing activities section of the Cash account.

reality bytes

How did Florida Power and Lighting (FPL) acquire $501 million of property and equipment without spending any cash? Oddly enough, the answer can be found in the company's statement of cash flows. The supplemental schedule of noncash investing and financing activities section of FPL's cash statement shows that it acquired $81 million of equipment by accepting lease obligations and that it acquired $420 million of property by assuming debt. In other words, FPL acquired $501 million (i.e., $81 million + $420 million) in property and equipment by agreeing to pay for it later.

Telegraph Colour Library/FPG

Cash Payments for Dividends

Finally, additional information at the bottom of the income statement discloses a cash dividend of $1,500. The transaction to record this cash outflow includes a debit to the Retained Earnings account and a credit to the financing activities section of the Cash account. It is labeled (p1) in Exhibit 12–5.

Presenting Information in the Statement of Cash Flows

Since all income statement items have been analyzed, changes in balance sheet accounts have been explained, and all additional information has been considered, the analytical process is completed. The data in the T-account for cash must now be organized in appropriate financial statement format. Recall that cash flow from operations is presented first, cash flow from investing activities second, and cash flow from financing activities third. Noncash investing and financing activities are shown in a separate schedule or in the footnotes. Exhibit 12–6 is a statement of cash flows and a separate schedule for noncash activities.

Statement of Cash Flows Presented under the Indirect Method

Up to now, the statement of cash flows has been presented in accordance with the **direct method.** The direct method is intuitively logical and is the method recommended by the Financial Accounting Standards Board. Even so, most companies use an alternative known as the **indirect method.** The difference between the two methods is in the presentation of the operating activities section. The indirect

> **L.O. 4**
>
> Explain how cash flow from operating activity reported under the indirect method differs from that reported under the direct method.

EXHIBIT 12-6

THE NEW SOUTH CORPORATION
Statement of Cash Flows
For the Period Ended December 31, 20X5

Cash Flows from Operating Activities

Cash Receipts from

Sales	$20,800		
Rent	1,400		
Interest	600		
Total Cash Inflows		$22,800	
Cash Payments for			
Inventory Purchases	11,500		
Salaries	2,600		
Insurance	300		
Other Operating Expenses	1,200		
Interest	600		
Total Cash Outflows		(16,200)	
Net Cash Flow from Operating Activities			$6,600
Cash Flows from Investing Activities			
Inflow from Sale of Equipment		300	
Outflow to Purchase Marketable Securities		(1,600)	
Outflow to Purchase Equipment		(2,300)	
Net Cash Flow from Investing Activities			(3,600)
Cash Flows from Financing Activities			
Inflow from Stock Issue		2,000	
Outflow to Repay Debt		(3,000)	
Outflow for Dividends		(1,500)	
Net Cash Flow from Financing Activities			(2,500)
Net Increase in Cash			500
Plus: Beginning Cash Balance			400
Ending Cash Balance			$ 900
Schedule of Noncash Investing and Financing Activities			
Issue of Mortgage for Land			$2,500

method uses net income as reported on the income statement as the starting point. The method proceeds by showing the adjustments necessary to convert the accrual-based net income figure to a cash-basis equivalent. The conversion process can be accomplished by the application of three basic rules, which are discussed next.

An increase in the balance of the Accounts Receivable account would suggest that not all sales were collected in cash. Accordingly, the amount of revenue shown on the income statement would overstate the amount of cash collections. Therefore, it is necessary to subtract the amount of the increase in the receivables account from the amount of net income to convert the income figure to a cash-equivalent basis. Similarly, a decrease in the receivables balance has to be added to the net income figure. Extending this logic to all current asset accounts results in the first general rule of the conversion process. **Rule 1: Increases in current** assets are deducted from net income, and decreases in current assets are added to net income.

The opposite logic applies to current liabilities. For example, an increase in accounts payable suggests that not all expenses were paid in cash. Accordingly, it is necessary to add the increase in the payables account to the amount of net income to convert the income figure to a cash-equivalent basis. Conversely, decreases in payable accounts are deducted from net income. Extending the logic to all the current liability accounts produces the second general rule of the conversion process. **Rule 2: Increases in current liabilities are added to net income, and decreases in current liabilities are deducted from net income.**

Finally, note that some expense and revenue transactions do not have cash consequences. For example, although depreciation is reported as an expense, it does not require the payment of cash. Similarly, losses and gains reported on the income statement do not have consequences that are reported in the operating activities section of the statement of cash flows. **Rule 3: All noncash expenses and losses are added to net income, and all noncash revenue and gains are subtracted from net income.**

These three general rules apply only to items affecting operating activities. For example, Rule 2 does not apply to an increase or decrease in the current liability account for dividends because dividend payments are considered to be financing activities rather than operating activities. Accordingly, some degree of judgment must be exercised in applying the three general rules of conversion.

Exhibit 12–7 shows the presentation of a statement of cash flows under the indirect method. The statement was constructed by applying the three general rules of conversion to the data for The New South Corporation shown in Exhibits 12–3 and 12–4. Notice that the only difference between the statement presented under the indirect method (Exhibit 12–7) and the statement shown under the direct method (Exhibit 12–6) is the Cash Flow from Operating Activities section. Cash flows from investing and financing activities and the schedule of noncash items are not affected by the alternative reporting format.

Consequences of Growth on Cash Flow

Why do decision makers in business need a statement of cash flows? Why is the information provided on the income statement not sufficient? Although it is true that the income statement shows how well a business is doing on an accrual basis, it does not show what is happening with cash. Understanding the cash flows of a business is extremely important because cash is used to pay the bills. A company, especially one that is growing rapidly, can have substantial earnings but be short of cash because it must buy goods before they are sold, and it may not receive cash payment until months after revenue is recognized on an accrual basis. To illustrate, assume that you want to go into the business of selling computers. You borrow $2,000 and use the money to purchase two computers that cost $1,000 each. Furthermore, assume that you sell one of the computers on account for $1,500. At this point, if you had a payment due on your loan, you would be unable to pay the amount due. Even though you had a net income of $500 (i.e., revenue of $1,500 − cost of goods sold of $1,000), you would have no cash until you collected the $1,500 cash due from the account receivable.

L.O. 5

Explain how the classifications used on the statement of cash flows could provide misleading information to decision makers.

EXHIBIT 12–7		
THE NEW SOUTH CORPORATION **Statement of Cash Flows (Indirect Method)** **For the Period Ended December 31, 20X5**		
Cash Flows from Operating Activities		
Net Income	$7,200	
Plus: Decreases in Current Assets and Increases in Current Liabilities		
Decrease in Accounts Receivable	200	
Decrease in Prepaid Insurance	300	
Increase in Salaries Payable	100	
Increase in Other Operating Expenses Payable	200	
Less: Increases in Current Assets and Decreases in Current Liabilities		
Increase in Interest Receivable	(100)	
Increase in Inventory	(700)	
Decrease in Accounts Payable for Inventory Purchases	(300)	
Decrease in Interest Payable	(200)	
Decrease in Unearned Revenue	(1,000)	
Plus: Noncash Charges		
Depreciation Expense	800	
Loss on Sale of Equipment	100	
Net Cash Flow from Operating Activities		$6,600
Cash Flows from Investing Activities		
Inflow from Sale of Equipment	300	
Outflow to Purchase Marketable Securities	(1,600)	
Outflow to Purchase Equipment	(2,300)	
Net Cash Flow from Investing Activities		(3,600)
Cash Flows from Financing Activities		
Inflow from Stock Issue	2,000	
Outflow to Repay Debt	(3,000)	
Outflow for Dividends	(1,500)	
Net Cash Flow from Financing Activities		(2,500)
Net Increase in Cash		500
Plus: Beginning Cash Balance		400
Ending Cash Balance		$ 900
Schedule of Noncash Investing and Financing Activities		
Issue of Mortgage for Land		$2,500

Real-World Data

The statement of cash flows frequently provides a picture of business activity that would otherwise be lost in the complexities of the application of accrual accounting. For example, consider the effects of restructuring charges on operating income versus cash flow experienced by IBM Corporation. For 1991, 1992, and 1993 combined, IBM reported operating *losses* (before taxes) of more than $17.9 *billion*. During this same period, it reported "restructuring charges" of more than $24 billion. Therefore, without the restructuring charges, IBM would have re-

EXHIBIT 12–8			
Operating Income versus Cash Flow from Operations (amounts in $000)			
Company		**1997**	**1996**	**1995**
Alaska Airlines	Income from Operations	$ 76,000	$ 45,600	$ 24,800
	Cash Flow from Operating Activities	323,200	203,000	104,400
Southwest Airlines	Income from Operations	37,772	207,337	182,626
	Cash Flow from Operating Activities	610,588	615,228	456,442
Boeing	Income from Operations	(178,000)	1,818,000	(36,000)
	Cash Flow from Operating Activities	2,100,000	3,611,000	2,135,000
Quaker Oats	Income from Operations	(930,900)	247,900	13,700
	Cash Flow from Operating Activities	490,000	410,400	84,300
Stanley Works	Income from Operations	(41,900)	96,900	59,100
	Cash Flow from Operating Activities	241,200	259,900	178,100
Office Max	Income from Operations	89,620	68,805	125,763
	Cash Flow from Operating Activities	(90,031)	(24,313)	(38,772)

ported operating *profits* of about $6 billion (before taxes). Are restructuring charges an indication of something bad or something good? Who knows? Different financial analysts have different opinions about this issue. There is something about IBM's performance during these years that can be more easily understood. The company produced over $21 billion in positive cash flow from operating activities. It had no trouble paying its bills.

Investors consider cash flow information so important that they are willing to pay for it, even when the FASB discourages its use. Consider the following situation. The FASB *prohibits* companies from disclosing *cash flow per share* in audited financial statements. However, one very prominent stock analysis service, *Value Line Investment Survey,* has a significant customer base that continues to purchase its stock charts, which are prepared on the basis of cash flow per share rather than earnings per share. These investors obviously value information regarding cash flows.

Exhibit 12–8 is a comparison of the income from operations and the cash flow from operating activities for six real-world companies from three different industries for the 1995, 1996, and 1997 fiscal years.

Several things can be observed from Exhibit 12–8. First, notice that in most cases, other than Office Max, cash flow from operating activities is higher than income from operations. This condition is true for many real-world companies because depreciation, a noncash expense, is usually significant. The most dramatic example of this is for Boeing in 1997. Even though Boeing reported a *net loss* from operations of $178 million, it generated *positive cash flow from operations* of more than $2 *billion.* This difference between cash flow from operations and operating income helps explain how some companies can have significant losses over a few years and continue to stay in business and pay their bills.

Next, the exhibit shows that the numbers for cash flow from operations are more stable than the amounts for operating income. Results for Boeing, Quaker, and Stanley demonstrate this clearly. Although all three companies fluctuated between net income and net losses from 1995 to 1997, their cash flows from operations were always positive. Therefore, some financial statement analysts might prefer cash flow from operations as a more useful number for trend analysis than accrual-based earnings.

Finally, what could explain why Office Max has *less* cash flow from operations than operating income? Does this mean that the company has a problem? Not necessarily. Office Max is simply experiencing the same kind of growing pains described earlier for your computer sales business. Its cash is being used to support growth in the level of inventory. Keep in mind that Office Max is a growing company; it opens new stores each year. However, it is not the new acquisitions of property, plant, and equipment that affect cash flow from operations because these purchases are included in the investing activities section of the statement of cash flows. The answer is that when a new Office Max opens, the company needs more inventory. Increases in inventory *do* affect cash flow from operations. Remember, increases in current assets decrease cash flow from operations. This fact alone might explain why the company has less cash flow from operations than operating income. Is this situation bad? Recall that in Chapter 8, the point was made that, *other things being equal*, it is better to have less inventory. At Office Max, however, other things are not equal; Office Max opened 253 new stores in 1997 alone.

The situation with Office Max highlights what some accountants think is a weakness in the format of the statement of cash flows. Some think it misleading simply to classify all increases in long-term assets as *investing activities* and all changes in inventory as an adjustment to operating income to arrive at cash flow from operations. They argue that the increase in inventory at Office Max that results from opening new stores should be classified as an investing activity, just as the cost of a new building is. Although it is true that inventory is classified as a current asset and buildings are classified as long-term assets, in reality there is a certain level of inventory that must be maintained permanently if the store is to remain in business. The GAAP format of the statement of cash flows penalizes cash flow from operations for increases in inventory that are really a permanent investment in assets.

Conversely, the same critics might argue that some purchases of long-term assets are not actually *investments* but merely replacements of old, existing property, plant, and equipment. In other words, the *investing activities* section of the statement of cash flows makes no distinction between expenditures that expand the business and those that simply replace old equipment (sometimes called *capital maintenance* expenditures).

Thus, the conclusion one must reach about using the statement of cash flows is the same as that for using the balance sheet or the earnings statement. Users cannot simply look at the numbers. They must analyze the numbers based on a knowledge of the particular business being examined.

Accounting alone cannot tell a businessperson how to make a decision. Making good business decisions requires an understanding of the business in question, the environmental and economic factors affecting the operation of that business, and the accounting concepts on which the financial statements of that business are based.

A LOOK BACK

Throughout this course, you have been asked to consider many different accounting events that occur in the business world. In many cases, you were asked to consider the effects that these events have on a company's balance sheet, income statement, and statement of cash flows. By now, you should be aware that each of the financial statements shows a different, but equally important, view of the financial situation of the company in question.

This chapter provided a more detailed examination of only one financial statement, the statement of cash flows. The chapter presented a more comprehensive review of how an accrual accounting system relates to a cash-based accounting system. It is important that you understand not only both systems but also how the two systems relate to each other. This is the reason that a formal statement of cash flows begins with a reconciliation of net income, an accrual measurement, to net cash flow from operating activities, a cash measurement. Finally, this chapter explained how the idiosyncrasies of classifying cash events as operating, investing, or financing activities may cause an inadequately educated user of financial information to reach incorrect conclusions.

A LOOK
FORWARD

This chapter probably completes your first course in accounting. We sincerely hope that this text has provided you a meaningful learning experience that will serve you well as you progress through your academic training and your ultimate career. Good luck and best wishes!

KEY TERMS

Accrual Accounting An accounting system that recognizes expenses or revenues before the associated cash payments or receipts occur. *(p. 570)*

Cash Inflows Sources of cash. *(p. 568)*

Cash Outflows Uses of cash. *(p. 568)*

Deferral Transactions Accounting transactions in which cash payments or receipts occur before the associated expense or revenue is recognized. *(p. 572)*

Direct Method The method of preparing the statement of cash flows that reports the total cash receipts and cash payments from each of the major categories of activities (i.e., collections from customers, payment to suppliers). *(p. 583)*

Expense Transactions Transactions completed in the process of operating a business that decrease assets or increase liabilities. *(p. 571)*

Financing Activities Business activities that generate cash inflows and cash outflows from transactions with a company's owners (i.e., stock or dividend transactions) or its creditors (i.e., borrowing or repayment transactions). *(p. 568)*

Indirect Method A method of preparing the statement of cash flows that uses the net income from the income statement as a starting point for the reporting of cash flow from operating

activities. The adjustments necessary to convert accrual-based net income to a cash-equivalent basis are shown in the operating activities section of the statement of cash flows. *(p. 583)*

Investing Activities Business activities that generate cash inflows and cash outflows through a company's purchase or sale of long-term operational assets, investments, and lending activities. *(p. 568)*

Noncash Investing and Financing Activities Business transactions that do not directly affect cash, such as exchanging stock for land or purchasing property by using a mortgage. These transactions are reported as both an inflow and outflow in a separate section of the statement of cash flows. *(p. 569)*

Operating Activities Business activities that generate cash inflows and cash outflows through the process of operating the business. *(p. 568)*

Revenue Transactions Transactions completed in the process of operating a business that increase assets or decrease liabilities. *(p. 570)*

T-Account Method A method of determining net cash flows by analyzing beginning and ending balances on the balance sheet and inferring the periods transactions from the income statement. *(p. 571)*

QUESTIONS

1. What is the purpose of the statement of cash flows?

2. What are the three categories of cash inflows and cash outflows shown on the cash flow statement? Discuss each and give an example of an inflow and outflow for each category.

3. What are noncash investing and financing activities? Give an example. How are these transactions shown on the statement of cash flows?

4. Best Company had a beginning balance in its Accounts Receivable account of $12,000 and ending Accounts Receivable of $14,000. If total sales were $110,000, what amount of cash was collected?

5. Best Company's Utilities Payable account had a beginning balance of $3,300 and an ending balance of $5,200. Utilities expense reported on the income statement amounted to $87,000. What was the amount of cash payment for utilities for the period?

6. Best Company had a balance in the Unearned Revenue account of $4,300 at the beginning of the period and an ending balance of $5,700. If the portion of unearned revenue that was recognized as being earned during the period amounted to $15,600, what amount of cash was collected?

7. Which of the following activities are financing activities?
   a. Payment of accounts payable.
   b. Payment of interest on bonds payable.
   c. Sale of common stock.
   d. Sale of preferred stock at a premium.
   e. Payment of a dividend on the stock.

8. Does depreciation expense affect net cash flow? Explain.

9. If Best Company sold land that cost $4,200 for a $500 gain, how much cash was collected from the sale of land?

10. If Best Company sold office equipment that originally cost $7,500 and had $7,200 of accumulated depreciation for a $100 loss, what was the selling price for the office equipment?

11. In which section of the statement of cash flows would the following transactions be reported?
    a. Cash receipt of interest income.
    b. Cash purchase of marketable securities.
    c. Cash purchase of equipment.
    d. Cash sale of merchandise.
    e. Cash sale of common stock.
    f. Payment of interest expense.
    g. Cash proceeds from loan.
    h. Cash payment on bonds payable.
    i. Cash receipt from sale of old equipment.
    j. Cash payment for operating expenses.

12. What is the difference between preparing the statement of cash flows using the direct approach and using the indirect approach?

13. Which method (i.e., direct or indirect) of preparing the statement of cash flows is more intuitively logical? Why?

14. What is the major advantage of using the indirect method in preparing the statement of cash flows?

15. What is the advantage of using the direct method of preparing the statement of cash flows?

16. How would the following transactions of Best Company be shown on the statement of cash flows?
    a. Purchased new equipment for $46,000 cash.
    b. Sold old equipment for $8,700 cash. The equipment had a book value of $4,900.

17. Can a company have a negative cash flow from operations for the year on the statement of cash flows but still have a net income on the income statement? Explain.

18. Why does the FASB prohibit disclosing cash flow per share in audited financial statements?

EXERCISES

EXERCISE 12-1 **Classifying Transactions into Categories of Cash Flows—Direct Method**
L.O. 1

Required

Identify each of the following activities as operating activities, investing activities, or financing activities for the statement of cash flows (assume that the direct method is used).
   a. Sale of merchandise for cash.
   b. Purchase of equipment for cash.

c. Payment of employee salary.

d. Interest income received on a certificate of deposit.

e. Sale of stock for cash.

f. Cash proceeds from bank loan.

g. Payment of interest on loan.

h. Payment of dividends.

i. Repayment of bank loan.

j. Sale of used equipment.

Identifying Operating Activities Cash Inflows—Direct Method

EXERCISE 12-2
L.O. 1

Required

Which of the following transactions produce cash inflow from operating activities (assume the direct method is used)?

a. Cash payment for salaries.

b. Cash payment for equipment.

c. Provision of services for cash.

d. Cash receipt from interest.

e. Cash payment for dividends.

f. Collection of cash from accounts receivable.

Using Account Balances to Determine Cash Flow from Operating Activities—Direct Method

EXERCISE 12-3
L.O. 2

The following account balances are available for Joy Gift Shop for 20X9.

Account Title	Beginning of Year	End of Year
Accounts Receivable	$19,000	$22,000
Interest Receivable	6,000	3,000
Accounts Payable	25,000	26,500
Salaries Payable	13,500	12,000

Other Information for 20X9

Sales on Account	$250,000
Interest Income	20,000
Operating Expenses	154,000
Salaries Expense for the Year	106,000

Required

a. Compute the amount of cash *inflow* from operating activities. (*Hint:* It may be helpful to assume that all revenues and expenses are on account.)

b. Compute the amount of cash *outflow* from operating activities.

Using Account Balances to Determine Cash Flow from Operating Activities—Direct Method

EXERCISE 12-4
L.O. 2

The following account balances were available for Dream Furniture Company for 20X9:

Account Title	Beginning of Year	End of Year
Unearned Revenue	$9,000	$4,000
Prepaid Rent	1,900	800

The portion of the unearned revenue that was recognized as having been earned during the period was $32,000. Rent expense for the period was $6,000. Dream Furniture Company maintained its books on the accrual basis.

Required

Using the T-account approach, determine the amount of cash inflow from revenue and cash outflow for rent based on the preceding information.

EXERCISE 12-5
L.O. 2

Using Account Balances to Determine Cash Flow from Investing Activities

The following account information is available for Action Construction Company for 20X9:

Land			Marketable Securities		
Bal.	10,000	25,000	Bal.	150,000	31,000
	50,000			60,000	
Bal.	35,000		Bal.	179,000	

The income statement contained a $9,000 gain on the sale of land and a $1,200 loss on the sale of marketable securities.

Required

Prepare the investing activities section of the statement of cash flows for 20X9.

EXERCISE 12-6
L.O. 2, 3

Using Account Balances to Determine Cash Flow from Financing Activities

The following account balances were available for Goldfish, Inc., for 20X7:

Mortgage Payable		Capital Stock		Paid-in Capital in Excess of Par	
	131,000 Bal.		100,000 Bal.		33,000 Bal.
55,000			30,000		56,000
	76,000 Bal.		130,000 Bal.		89,000 Bal.

Required

Prepare the financing activities section of the statement of cash flows for 20X7.

EXERCISE 12-7
L.O. 2, 3

Using Account Balances to Determine Cash Outflow for Inventory Purchases

The following account information is available for Filex Cruise Company. The company uses the perpetual inventory method.

Inventory			Accounts Payable		
Bal.	82,000			27,200 Bal.	
	?	149,000	?	152,000	
Bal.	85,000			40,500 Bal.	

Required

Compute the amount of cash paid for the purchase of inventory.

EXERCISE 12-8
L.O. 2, 4

Using Account Balances to Determine Cash Flow from Operating Activities—Indirect Method

Lemon Company uses the indirect method for preparing the statement of cash flows. The following accounts and corresponding balances were drawn from Lemon's accounting records.

Account Titles	Beginning Balances	Ending Balances
Accounts Receivable	$15,000	$17,200
Prepaid Rent	1,500	800
Interest Receivable	600	200
Accounts Payable	9,050	9,450
Salaries Payable	2,100	1,750
Unearned Revenue	1,000	1,850

Net income for the period was $35,000.

Required

Using the preceding information, compute the net cash flow from operating activities using the indirect method.

Using Account Balances to Determine Cash Flow from Operating Activities—Direct and Indirect Methods

The following information was drawn from the accounting records of Ming Company:

EXERCISE 12-9
L.O. 2–4

	20X8	20X9
Cash	$ 35,000	$ 84,700
Accounts Receivable	165,000	159,800
Prepaid Rent	4,200	5,600
Accounts Payable	124,000	125,000
Utilities Payable	13,200	8,400
Revenue		$240,000
Operating Expenses		(155,000)
Utilities Expense		(15,300)
Rent Expense		(20,000)
Net Income		$ 49,700

Required

a. Prepare the operating activities section of the statement of cash flows under the direct method for 20X9.

b. Prepare the operating activities section of the statement of cash flows under the indirect method for 20X9.

Explaining Information Contained in the Statement of Cash Flows

The following selected transactions are for Jackson Corp. for the 20X9 period.

EXERCISE 12-10
L.O. 3, 5

1. Purchased new office equipment for $4,500.
2. Sold old office equipment for $800 that originally cost $6,000 and had accumulated depreciation of $5,700.
3. Borrowed $10,000 cash from the bank for 6 months.
4. Purchased land for a cost of $115,000 by paying $30,000 in cash and issuing a note for the balance.
5. Exchanged no-par common stock for an automobile valued at $14,500.

Required

a. Prepare the appropriate sections of the statement of cash flows for the 20X9 period.

b. What information does the noncash investing and financing activities section of the statement provide? If this information were omitted, could it affect a decision to invest in a company?

PROBLEMS—SERIES A

PROBLEM 12-1A

L.O. 1

Classifying Transactions on the Statement of Cash Flows

Required

Identify each of the following transactions as an operating activity (OA), an investing activity (IA), a financing activity (FA), or a noncash transaction (NT).

  a. Declared a stock split.

  b. Provided services for cash.

  c. Bought land with cash.

  d. Issued common stock for cash.

  e. Issued a note payable in exchange for equipment.

  f. Recorded amortization of goodwill.

  g. Provided services on account.

  h. Paid cash for rent.

  i. Purchased office supplies on account.

  j. Paid cash for salaries.

  k. Collected cash from accounts receivable.

  l. Received interest on note receivable.

  m. Paid a cash dividend.

  n. Recorded depreciation expense.

  o. Received advance payment for services.

  p. Purchased marketable securities with cash.

  q. Paid insurance with cash.

  r. Purchased inventory with cash.

  s. Repaid principal and interest on a note payable.

PROBLEM 12-2A

L.O. 2, 3

Using Transaction Data to Prepare a Statement of Cash Flows

May & Company engaged in the following transactions during the 20X9 accounting period. The beginning cash balance was $24,400.

  1. Credit sales were $110,000. The beginning receivables balance was $86,000 and the ending balance was $92,000.

  2. Salaries expense for the period was $34,000. The beginning salaries payable balance was $2,500 and the ending balance was $1,300.

  3. Other operating expenses for the period were $32,000. The beginning Operating Expense Payable account was $3,100 and the ending balance was $7,200.

  4. Recorded $14,300 of depreciation expense. The beginning and ending balances in the Accumulated Depreciation account amounted to $12,000 and $26,300, respectively.

  5. The Equipment account had beginning and ending balances of $103,000 and $136,000, respectively. The increase was caused by the cash purchase of equipment.

  6. The beginning and ending balances in the Notes Payable account were $30,000 and $45,000, respectively. The increase was caused by additional borrowing for cash.

  7. There was $5,600 of interest expense reported on the income statement. The beginning and ending balances in the Interest Payable account were $2,500 and $2,000, respectively.

  8. The beginning and ending Merchandise Inventory account balances were $25,000 and $22,000, respectively. The company sold merchandise with a cost of $51,000 (cost of goods sold for the period was $51,000). The beginning and ending balances of Accounts Payable were $7,200 and $5,000, respectively.

9. The beginning and ending balances of Notes Receivable were $7,500 and $12,500, respectively. The increase resulted from a cash loan to one of the company's employees.

10. The beginning and ending balances of the Common Stock account were $50,000 and $75,000, respectively. The increase was caused by the issue of common stock for cash.

11. Land had beginning and ending balances of $22,500 and $16,500, respectively. Land that cost $6,000 was sold for $14,700, resulting in a gain of $8,700.

12. The tax expense for the period was $3,500. The Tax Payable account had a $320 beginning balance and a $220 ending balance.

13. The investments account had beginning and ending balances of $10,000 and $19,000, respectively. The company purchased investments for $17,000 cash during the period, and investments that cost $8,000 were sold for $6,000, resulting in a $2,000 loss.

Required

Convert the preceding information to cash-equivalent data, and prepare a statement of cash flows.

Using Financial Statement Data to Determine Cash Flow from Operating Activities

The following account information is available for Star Dust Company for 20X9.:

PROBLEM 12-3A
L.O. 2, 3

Account Title	Beginning of Year	End of Year
Accounts Receivable	$ 50,000	$ 42,500
Merchandise Inventory	190,000	174,600
Prepaid Insurance	4,500	4,000
Accounts Payable (Inventory)	72,500	87,500
Salaries Payable	8,800	7,250

Other Information

1. Sales for the period were $325,000.
2. Purchases of merchandise for the period were $243,000.
3. Insurance expense for the period was $6,000.
4. Other operating expenses (all cash) were $42,600.
5. Salary expense was $60,000.

Required

 a. Compute the net cash flow from operating activities.

 b. Prepare the cash flow from the operating activities section of the statement of cash flows.

Using Financial Statement Data to Determine Cash Flow from Investing Activities

The following information pertaining to investing activities is available for Turner Company for 20X9:

PROBLEM 12-4A
L.O. 2, 3

Account Title	Beginning of Year	End of Year
Machinery and Equipment	$310,000	$334,000
Marketable Securities	51,000	19,500
Land	67,000	94,000

Other Information for 20X9

1. Marketable securities were sold at book value. No gain or loss was recognized.
2. Machinery was purchased for $60,000. Old machinery with a book value of $8,000 (cost of $36,000, accumulated depreciation of $30,400) was sold for $8,500.

Required

a. Compute the net cash flow from investing activities.
b. Prepare the cash flow from the investing activities section of the statement of cash flows.

PROBLEM 12-5A

L.O. 2, 3

Using Financial Statement Data to Determine Cash Flow from Financing Activities

The following information pertaining to financing activities is available for V-Tech Company for 20X9:

Account Title	Beginning of Year	End of Year
Bonds Payable	$250,000	$180,000
Capital Stock	100,000	156,000
Paid-in Capital in Excess of Par	72,000	107,000

Other Information

1. Dividends paid during the period amounted to $31,000.
2. No new funds were borrowed during the period.

Required

a. Compute the net cash flow from financing activities for 20X9.
b. Prepare the cash flow from the financing activities section of the statement of cash flows.

PROBLEM 12-6A

L.O. 2, 3

Using Financial Statements to Prepare a Statement of Cash Flows—Direct Method

The following financial statements were drawn from the records of Blue Mountain, Incorporated.

Balance Sheets as of December 31		
	20X8	**20X9**
Assets		
Cash	$ 1,400	$24,200
Accounts Receivable	600	1,100
Inventory	3,000	2,800
Equipment	11,000	9,000
Accumulated Depreciation—Equipment	(8,700)	(9,000)
Land	5,200	8,600
Total Assets	$12,500	$36,700
Liabilities and Equity		
Accounts Payable	$ 2,100	$ 2,600
Long-Term Debt	3,200	2,800
Common Stock	5,000	9,700
Retained Earnings	2,200	21,600
Total Liabilities and Equity	$12,500	$36,700

(cont'd)

Income Statement for the Year Ended December 31, 20X9	
Revenue	$33,650
Cost of Goods Sold	(12,050)
Gross Margin	21,600
Depreciation Expense	(2,800)
Operating Income	18,800
Gain on Sale of Equipment	1,450
Loss on Disposal of Land	(50)
Net Income	$20,200

Additional Data

1. During 20X9, the company sold equipment for $4,450. The equipment originally cost $5,500. Accumulated depreciation on this equipment was $2,500 at the time of the sale. Also, the company purchased equipment for $3,500 cash.

2. The company sold land that cost $1,300. This land was sold for $1,250, resulting in the recognition of a $50 loss. Also, common stock was issued in exchange for title to land that was valued at $4,700 at the time of exchange.

3. Paid dividends of $800.

Required

Use the T-account method to analyze the data and prepare a statement of cash flows.

Using Financial Statements to Prepare a Statement of Cash Flows—Direct Method

The following financial statements were drawn from the records of Grace Corporation:

PROBLEM 12-7A
L.O. 2, 3

Balance Sheets as of December 31		
	20X5	20X6
Assets		
Cash	$ 14,100	$ 61,800
Accounts Receivable	33,000	28,500
Inventory	57,000	63,000
Notes Receivable	15,000	0
Equipment	127,500	73,500
Accumulated Depreciation—Equipment	(70,500)	(37,370)
Land	26,250	41,250
Total Assets	$202,350	$230,680
Liabilities and Equity		
Accounts Payable	$ 24,300	$ 21,000
Salaries Payable	12,000	15,000
Utilities Payable	600	300
Interest Payable	900	0
Note Payable	30,000	0
Common Stock	120,000	150,000
Ratained Earnings	14,550	44,380
Total Liabilities and Equity	$202,350	$230,680

(cont'd)

Income Statement for the Year Ended December 31, 20X6	
Revenue	$290,000
Cost of Goods Sold	(144,000)
Gross Margin	146,000
Operating Expenses	
Salary Expense	(92,000)
Depreciation Expense	(8,870)
Utilities Expense	(6,100)
Operating Income	39,030
Nonoperating Items	
Interest Expense	(1,500)
Gain or (Loss)	(900)
Net Income	$ 36,630

Additional Information

1. Sold equipment costing $54,000 with accumulated depreciation of $42,000 for $11,100 cash.
2. Paid a $6,800 cash distribution to owners.

Required

Use the T-account method to analyze the data and prepare a statement of cash flows.

PROBLEM 12-8A
L.O. 2, 4

Using Financial Statements to Prepare a Statement of Cash Flows—Indirect Method

The comparative balance sheet for Triumph Company for 20X8 and 20X9 is as follows:

Balance Sheets as of December 31		
	20X8	**20X9**
Assets		
Cash	$ 20, 300	$ 34,400
Accounts Receivable	11,000	15,000
Merchandise Inventory	88,000	80,000
Prepaid Rent	2,400	1,200
Equipment	144,000	128,000
Accumulated Depreciation	(118,000)	(73,400)
Land	40,000	96,000
Total Assets	$187,700	$281,200
Liabilities		
Accounts Payable (Inventory)	$ 38,000	$ 33,500
Salaries Payable	12,000	14,000
Stockholders' Equity:		
Common Stock, $25 Par Value	100,000	125,000
Retained Earnings	37,700	108,700
Total Liabilities and Equity	$187,700	$281,200

(cont'd)

Income Statement for the Year Ended December 31, 20X9	
Sales	$750,000
Cost of Goods Sold	(398,600)
Gross Profit	351,400
Operating Expenses	
Depreciation Expense	(11,400)
Rent Expense	(12,000)
Salaries Expense	(128,000)
Other Operating Expenses	(129,000)
Net Income	$ 71,000

Other Information

1. Purchased land for $56,000.
2. Purchased new equipment for $50,000.
3. Sold old equipment that cost $66,000 with accumulated depreciation of $56,000 for $10,000 cash.
4. Issued common stock for $25,000.

Required

Prepare the statement of cash flows for 20X9, using the indirect method.

PROBLEMS—SERIES B

Classifying Transactions on the Statement of Cash Flows

Required

Identify each of the following transactions as an operating activity (OA), an investing activity (IA), a financing activity (FA), or a noncash transaction (NT).

a. Purchased supplies on account.
b. Collected cash from accounts receivable.
c. Accrued warranty expense.
d. Borrowed cash by issuing a bond.
e. Loaned cash to a business associate.
f. Paid cash for interest expense.
g. Incurred a loss on the sale of equipment.
h. Wrote down inventory because the year-end physical count was lower than the balance in the Inventory account.
i. Paid cash to purchase inventory.
j. Paid cash for operating expenses.
k. Wrote off an uncollectible account receivable under the allowance method.
l. Wrote off an uncollectible account receivable under the direct write-off method.
m. Issued common stock for cash.
n. Declared a stock split.
o. Issued a mortgage to purchase a building
p. Purchased equipment with cash.
q. Repaid the principal balance on a note payable.
r Made a cash payment for the balance due in the Dividends Payable account.
s. Received cash dividend from investment in marketable securities.

PROBLEM 12-1B

L.O. 1

PROBLEM 12-2B

L.O. 2, 3

Using Transaction Data to Prepare a Statement of Cash Flows

Clair Cosmetics Co. engaged in the following transactions during the accounting period. The beginning cash balance was $43,000.

1. Credit sales were $24,000. The beginning receivables balance was $64,000 and the ending balance was $45,000.

2. Salaries expense for the period was $16,000. The beginning salaries payable balance was $8,000 and the ending balance was $4,000.

3. Other operating expenses for the period were $18,000. The beginning operating Expense Payable account was $8,000 and the ending balance was $5,000.

4. Recorded $15,000 of depreciation expense. The beginning and ending balances in the Accumulated Depreciation account amounted to $6,000 and $21,000, respectively.

5. The Equipment account had beginning and ending balances of $22,000 and $28,000, respectively. The increase was caused by the cash purchase of equipment.

6. The beginning and ending balances in the Notes Payable account were $22,000 and $18,000, respectively. The decrease was caused by the cash repayment of the debt.

7. There was $2,300 of interest expense reported on the income statement. The beginning and ending balances in the Interest Payable account were $4,200 and $3,750, respectively.

8. The beginning and ending Merchandise Inventory account balances were $11,000 and $14,700, respectively. The company sold merchandise with a cost of $41,800. The beginning and ending balances of Accounts Payable were $4,000 and $3,200, respectively.

9. The beginning and ending balances of Notes Receivable were $50,000 and $30,000, respectively. The decline resulted from the cash collection of a portion of the receivable.

10. The beginning and ending balances of the Common Stock account were $60,000 and $80,000, respectively. The increase was caused by the issue of common stock for cash.

11. Land had beginning and ending balances of $12,000 and $7,000, respectively. Land that cost $5,000 was sold for $3,000, resulting in a loss of $2,000.

12. The tax expense for the period was $3,300. The Tax Payable account had a $1,200 beginning balance and a $1,100 ending balance.

13. The Investments account had beginning and ending balances of $10,000 and $30,000, respectively. The company purchased investments for $25,000 cash during the period, and investments that cost $5,000 were sold for $11,000, resulting in a $6,000 gain.

Required

Convert the preceding information to cash-equivalent data, and prepare a statement of cash flows.

PROBLEM 12-3B

L.O. 2, 3

Using Financial Statement Data to Determine Cash Flow from Operating Activities

The following account information is available for Zoom-In Photo Shop for 20X9:

Account Title	Beginning of Year	End of Year
Accounts Receivable	$ 8,900	$10,500
Merchandise Inventory	68,000	71,400
Prepaid Insurance	800	600
Accounts Payable (Inventory)	9,400	9,800
Salaries Payable	3,200	2,900

Other Information

1. Sales for the period were $124,000.
2. Purchases of merchandise for the period were $93,000.
3. Insurance expense for the period was $4,000.
4. Other operating expenses (all cash) were $13,700.
5. Salary expense was $21,300.

Required

  a. Compute the net cash flow from operating activities.

  b. Prepare the cash flow from the operating activities section of the statement of cash flows.

Using Financial Statement Data to Determine Cash Flow from Investing Activities
The following information is available for Fresh Fish Mart Co. for 20X9 pertaining to investing activities:

PROBLEM 12-4B
L.O. 2, 3

Account Title	Beginning of Year	End of Year
Machinery and Equipment	$81,000	$85,000
Marketable Securities	33,000	25,600
Land	21,000	17,000

Other Information for 20X9

1. Marketable securities were sold at book value. No gain or loss was recognized.
2. Machinery was purchased for $20,000. Old machinery with a cost of $16,000 and accumulated depreciation of $12,000 was sold for $5,500.
3. Land that cost $4,000 was sold for $5,000.

Required

  a. Compute the net cash flow from investing activities.

  b. Prepare the cash flow from the investing activities section of the statement of cash flows.

Using Financial Statement Data to Determine Cash Flow from Financing Activities
The following information is available for Sturdy Marble Company for 20X9 pertaining to financing activities:

PROBLEM 12-5B
L.O. 2, 3

Account Title	Beginning of Year	End of Year
Bonds Payable	$ 85,000	$ 90,000
Capital Stock	105,000	140,000
Paid-in Capital in Excess of Par	42,000	58,000

Other Information

1. Dividends paid during the period amounted to $14,000.
2. Additional funds of $20,000 were borrowed during the period by issuing bonds.

Required

  a. Compute the net cash flow from financing activities for 20X9.

  b. Prepare the cash flow from the financing activities section of the statement of cash flows.

602

Chapter Twelve

PROBLEM 12-6B
L.O. 2, 3

Using Financial Statements to Prepare a Statement of Cash Flows—Direct Method
The following financial statements were drawn from the records of Slim Line Products Co.:

Balance Sheets as of December 31		
	20X8	**20X9**
Assets		
Cash	$ 970	$ 8,060
Accounts Receivable	1,000	1,200
Inventory	1,300	1,000
Equipment	8,550	6,850
Accumulated Depreciation—Equipment	(6,475)	(5,650)
Land	4,000	6,500
Total Assets	$9,345	$17,960
Liabilities and Equity		
Accounts Payable	$1,200	$ 1,800
Long-Term Debt	2,000	1,600
Common Stock	5,000	8,500
Retained Earnings	1,145	6,060
Total Liabilities and Stockholders' Equity	$9,345	$17,960

Income Statement for the Year Ended December 31, 20X9	
Revenue	$8,740
Cost of Goods Sold	(3,100)
Gross Margin	5,640
Depreciation Expense	(875)
Operating Income	4,765
Gain on Sale of Equipment	900
Loss on Disposal of Land	(300)
Net Income	$5,365

Additional Data

1. During 20X9, the company sold equipment for $3,400. The equipment originally cost $4,200. Accumulated depreciation on this equipment was $1,700 at the time of the sale. Also, the company purchased equipment for $2,500 cash.
2. The company sold land that cost $1,000. This land was sold for $700, resulting in the recognition of a $300 loss. Also, common stock was issued in exchange for title to land that was valued at $3,500 at the time of exchange.
3. Paid dividends of $450.

Required

Use the T-account method to analyze the data and prepare a statement of cash flows.

Using Financial Statements to Prepare a Statement of Cash Flows—Direct Method

The following financial statements were drawn from the records of Prestige Novelty Design Co.:

Balance Sheets as of December 31

	20X8	20X9
Assets		
Cash	$ 7,050	$ 47,150
Accounts Receivable	20,000	18,000
Inventory	32,000	36,000
Notes Receivable	8,000	0
Equipment	85,000	49,000
Accumulated Depreciation—Equipment	(47,000)	(23,900)
Land	15,000	23,000
Total Assets	$120,050	$149,250
Liabilities and Equity		
Accounts Payable	$ 13,200	$ 12,000
Salaries Payable	5,000	7,500
Utilities Payable	700	400
Interest Payable	500	0
Note Payable	12,000	0
Common Stock	55,000	75,000
Ratained Earnings	33,650	54,350
Total Liabilities and Equity	$120,050	$149,250

Income Statement for the Year Ended December 31, 20X9

Revenue	$150,000
Cost of Goods Sold	(72,000)
Gross Margin	78,000
Operating Expenses	
Salary Expense	(44,000)
Depreciation Expense	(4,900)
Utilities Expense	(3,200)
Operating Income	25,900
Nonoperating Items	
Interest Expense	(1,200)
Loss	(400)
Net Income	$ 24,300

Additional Information

1. Sold equipment costing $36,000 with accumulated depreciation of $28,000 for $7,600 cash.
2. Paid a $3,600 cash distribution to owners.

Required

Use the T-account method to analyze the data and prepare a statement of cash flows.

PROBLEM 12-8B **Using Financial Statements to Prepare a Statement of Cash Flows—Indirect Method**
L.O. 2, 4 The comparative balance sheet for Ajax Food Research Center for 20X8 and 20X9 is as follows:

Balance Sheets as of December 31		
	20X8	**20X9**
Assets		
Cash	$24,200	$ 3,150
Accounts Receivable	3,630	5,100
Merchandise Inventory	28,000	22,600
Prepaid Rent	1,070	350
Equipment	72,000	70,000
Accumulated Depreciation	(59,000)	(36,700)
Land	25,000	58,000
Total Assets	$94,900	$122,500
Liabilities and Equity		
Accounts Payable (Inventory)	$20,000	$ 18,600
Salaries Payable	5,300	6,100
Stockholders' Equity		
Common Stock, $50 Par Value	60,000	75,000
Retained Earnings	9,600	22,800
Total Liabilities and Equity	$94,900	$122,500

Income Statement for the Period Ended December 31, 20X9	
Sales	$240,000
Cost of Goods Sold	(132,000)
Gross Profit	108,000
Operating Expenses	
Depreciation Expense	(5,700)
Rent Expense	(3,500)
Salaries Expense	(47,600)
Other Operating Expenses	(38,000)
Net Income	$ 13,200

Other Information
1. Purchased land for $33,000.
2. Purchased new equipment for $31,000.
3. Sold old equipment that cost $33,000 with accumulated depreciation of $28,000 for $5,000 cash.
4. Issued common stock for $15,000.

Required
Prepare the statement of cash flows for 20X9 using the indirect method.

analyze, communicate, think

Using the Gateway 2000 financial statements in Appendix B, answer the following questions:

Required

a. Compare Gateway's 1997 *net income* to its *cash flow from operating activities.* Which is higher and by what amount?

b. What one item is most responsible for the difference between Gateway's *net income* and its *cash flow from operating activities* in 1997?

c. What one item is most responsible for the difference between Gateway's *net income* and its *cash flow from operating activities* in 1996?

d. In 1997, Gateway spent $360,665,000 of cash (net) on *investing activities.* Where did it obtain most of this cash?

The following financial statements and information are available for Bravo Ent.:

Balance Sheets as of December 31		
	20X8	**20X9**
Assets		
Cash	$ 60,300	$ 80,100
Accounts Receivable	42,500	51,600
Inventory	85,900	93,200
Marketable Securities (Held-to-Maturity)	110,000	142,000
Equipment	245,000	325,000
Accumulated Depreciation	(120,000)	(155,000)
Land	60,000	40,000
Total Assets	$483,700	$576,900
Liabilities and Equity		
Liabilities		
Accounts Payable (Inventory)	$ 33,100	$ 18,200
Notes Payable—Long-Term	125,000	115,000
Bonds Payable	50,000	100,000
Total Liabilities	208,100	233,200
Stockholders' Equity		
Common Stock, No Par	100,000	120,000
Preferred Stock, $50 Par	50,000	55,000
Paid-in Capital in Excess of Par—Preferred		
Stock	13,400	17,200
Total Paid-In Capital	163,400	192,200
Retained Earnings	132,200	166,500
Less: Treasury Stock	(20,000)	(15,000)
Total Stockholders' Equity	275,600	343,700
Total Liabilities and Stockholders' Equity	$483,700	$576,900

Income Statement 20X9		
Sales Revenue		$525,000
Cost of Goods Sold		(383,250)
Gross Profit		141,750
Operating Expenses		
Supplies Expense	$10,200	
Salaries Expense	46,000	
Depreciation Expense	45,000	
Total Operating Expense		101,200
Operating Income		40,550
Nonoperating Items		
Interest Expense		(8,000)
Gain from the Sale of Marketable Securities		15,000
Gain from the Sale of Land and Equipment		6,000
Net Income		$53,550

Additional Information

1. Sold land that cost $20,000 for $22,000.
2. Sold equipment that cost $15,000 and had accumulated depreciation of $10,000 for $9,000.
3. Purchased new equipment for $95,000.
4. Sold marketable securities that cost $20,000 for $35,000.
5. Purchased new marketable securities for $52,000.
6. Paid $10,000 on the principal of the long-term note.
7. Paid off a $50,000 bond issue and issued new bonds for $100,000.
8. Sold 50 shares of treasury stock at its cost.
9. Issued some new common stock.
10. Issued some new $50-par preferred stock.
11. Paid dividends. (*Note:* The only transactions to affect retained earnings were net income and dividends.)

Required

    a. Organize the class into three sections, and divide each section into groups of 3 to 5 students. Assign each section of groups an activity section of the statement of cash flows (i.e., operating activities, investing activities, and financing activities).

Group Task

Complete your assigned portion of the statement of cash flows. Have a representative of your section put your activity section of the statement of cash flows on the board. As each adds its information on the board, the full statement of cash flows will be presented.

Class Discussion

Have the class finish the statement of cash flows by computing the net change in cash. Also have the class answer the following questions:

    b. What was the issue price of the preferred stock?

    c. What is the cost per share of the treasury stock?

    d. What was the book value of the equipment sold?

R E A L - W O R L D   C A S E   **Following the Cash**

During 1997, as part of a major restructuring plan, Reynolds Metals Company sold at least nine plants that produced aluminum or aluminum products. It also sold coal properties and several distribution facilities. The statements of cash flows for Reynolds Metals for 1997, 1996, and 1995 are shown here.

REYNOLDS METALS COMPANY Consolidated Statement of Cash Flows (dollars in millions)			
	Years Ended December 31		
	1997	**1996**	**1995**
Operating Activities			
Net Income	$136	$ 89	$389
Adjustments to Reconcile to Net Cash Provided by Operating Activities			
Depreciation and Amortization	368	365	344
Operational Restructuring Effects	58	37	—
Cumulative Effect of Accounting Change	—	15	—
Other	28	26	18
Changes in Operating Assets and Liabilities Net of Effects from Acquisitions and Dispositions			
Accounts Payable, Accrued and Other Liabilities	74	(110)	(173)
Receivables	(194)	67	(59)
Inventories	(108)	93	17
Other	1	(62)	(47)
Net Cash Provided by Operating Activities	363	520	489
Investing Activities			
Capital Investments			
Operational	(152)	(195)	(219)
Strategic	(120)	(237)	(626)
Maturities of Investments in Debt Securities	—	—	125
Sales of Assets—Operational Restructuring	367	—	—
Other	(3)	(5)	(20)
Net Cash Provided by (used in) Investing Activities	92	(437)	(740)
Financing Activities			
Proceeds from Long-Term Debt	—	40	106
Reduction of Long-Term Debt and Other Financing Liabilities	(245)	(105)	(22)
Increase (decrease) in Short-Term Borrowings	(138)	111	(18)
Cash Dividends Paid	(99)	(135)	(106)
Stock Options Exercised	59	5	22
Net Cash Used in Financing Activities	(423)	(84)	(18)
Cash and Cash Equivalents			
Net Increase (decrease)	32	(1)	(269)
At Beginning of Year	38	39	308
At End of Year	$ 70	$ 38	$ 39
Supplemental Disclosure of Cash Flow Information			
Cash Paid during the Year for			
Interest	$164	$176	$179
Income Taxes	21	2	56
See Notes beginning on page 44. [Refers to the 10K report.]			

Required

a. During 1997, how much cash did Reynolds Metals receive from the sales of assets that resulted from its restructuring efforts?

b. What did Reynolds apparently do with the cash it received from the sales of the plants and other assets? The answer to this question requires the use of judgment. It might be helpful to rephrase the question as, What was Reynolds able to spend money on that would not have been possible had it not sold the assets? Write a brief explanation and justification of your conclusions.

ACT 12-4

BUSINESS APPLICATIONS CASE **Identifying Different Presentation Formats**

In *Statement of Financial Accounting Standards No. 95*, The Financial Accounting Standards Board (FASB) recommended but did not require that companies use the direct method. In Appendix B, Paragraphs 106–121, the FASB discussed its reasons for this recommendation.

Required

Obtain a copy of *Standard No. 95* and read Appendix B Paragraphs 106–121. Write a brief memo summarizing the issues that the FASB considered and its specific reaction to those issues. Your response should draw heavily on paragraphs 119–121.

ACT 12-5

WRITING ASSIGNMENT **Explaining Discrepancies between Cash Flow and Operating Income**

The following selected information was drawn from the records of Neon Company:

Assets	20X8	20X9
Accounts Receivable	$200,000	$420,100
Merchandise Inventory	360,000	740,000
Equipment	742,000	930,600
Accumulated Depreciation	(156,000)	(201,200)

Neon is experiencing cash flow problems. Despite the fact that the company reported significant increases in operating income, operating activities produced a net cash outflow. Indeed, recent financial forecasts indicate that Neon will have insufficient cash to pay its current liabilities within 3 months.

Required

Write a memo that provides a logical explanation for Neon's cash shortage. Include a recommendation for remedying the problem.

ACT 12-6

ETHICAL DILEMMA **Would I Lie to You, Baby?**

Bill and Sue Fullerton are involved in divorce proceedings. When discussing a property settlement, he told her that he should take over their investment in an apartment complex because she would be unable to absorb the loss that the apartments are generating. Mrs. Fullerton was somewhat distrustful and asked Mr. Fullerton to support his contention. He produced the following income statement, which was supported by a CPA's unqualified opinion that the statement was prepared in accordance with generally accepted accounting principles.

```
                    FULLERTON APARTMENTS
                      Income Statements
              For the Year Ended December 31, 20X3

  Rent Revenue                                      $290,000
  Less: Expenses
     Depreciation Expense          $140,000
     Interest Expense                92,000
     Operating Expense               44,000
     Management Fees                 28,000
     Total Expenses                                (304,000)
  Net Loss                                         ($ 14,000)
```

All revenue is earned on account. Interest and operating expenses are incurred on account. Management fees are paid in cash. The following accounts and balances were drawn from the 20X2 and 20X3 balance sheets:

Account Title	20X2	20X3
Rent Receivable	$20,000	$22,000
Interest Payable	6,000	9,000
Accounts Payable (Oper. Exp.)	3,000	2,000

Mrs. Fullerton is reluctant to give up the apartments but feels that she must because her present salary is only $25,000 per year. She says that if she takes the apartments, the $14,000 loss would absorb a significant portion of her salary, leaving her only $11,000 with which to support herself. She tells you that while the figures seem to support her husband's arguments, she feels that she is failing to see something. She knows that she and her husband collected a $10,000 distribution from the business on December 1, 20X3. Also, $75,000 cash was paid in 20X3 to reduce the principal balance on a mortgage that was taken out to finance the purchase of the apartments 2 years ago. Finally, $12,000 cash was paid during 20X3 to purchase a computer system used in the business. She wonders, "If the apartments are losing money, where is my husband getting all the cash to make these payments?"

Required

a. Prepare a statement of cash flows for the 20X3 accounting period.

b. Compare the cash statement prepared in part *a* with the income statement and provide Sue Fullerton with recommendations.

c. Comment on the value of an unqualified audit opinion when using financial statements for decision-making purposes.

ACT 12-7

EDGAR DATABASE   **How Much Cash Was Paid?**

Required

Using the most current 10-K available on EDGAR, answer the following questions about Home Depot for the most recent year reported. Instructions for using EDGAR are in Appendix A.

a. How many *new* stores did Home Depot open? (*Hint:* You will find this information in the MD&A section of the 10-K.)

b. How much *cash* did Home Depot spend on property, plant, and equipment (PP&E) during the most recent year? (See the statement of cash flows.)

c. Using your answers to parts *a* and *b*, what is a *rough estimate* of the average PP&E cost of opening a new store?

d. How much did Home Depot 's inventory increase during the most recent year? (*Hint:* Using the balance sheets, you need to compare last year's inventory balance to this year's balance.)

e. What is a *rough estimate* of the average inventory needed to open a new Home Depot?

f. When Home Depot opens a new store, which section of its statement of cash flows—operating activities or investing activities—is affected immediately the most? Explain your answer.

ACT 12-8

SPREADSHEET ANALYSIS   **Preparing a Statement of Cash Flows Using the Direct Method**

Refer to the information in Problem 12-8A. Solve for the statement of cash flows using the direct method. Instead of using the T-account method, set up the following spreadsheet to work through the analysis. The Debit/Credit entries are very similar to the T-account method except that they are entered onto a spreadsheet. Two distinct differences are as follows:

1. Instead of making entries on row 2 for Cash, cash entries are made beginning on row 24 under the heading Cash Transactions.

2. Entries for Retained Earnings are made on rows 15 through 20 since there are numerous revenue and expense entries to that account.

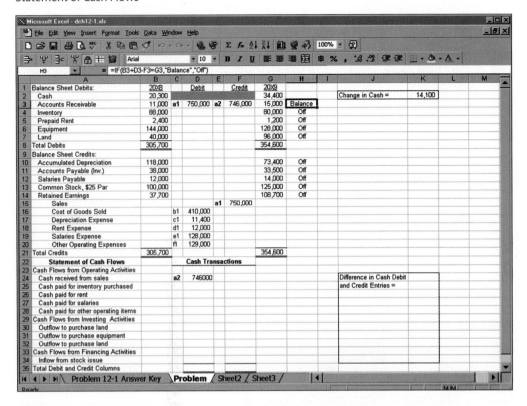

Required

- *a.* Enter information in column A.
- *b.* Enter the beginning balance sheet amounts in column B and ending balances in column G. Total the debits and credits for each column.
- *c.* To prevent erroneous entries to Cash in row 2, darken the area in columns C through F.
- *d.* In columns C through F, record entries for the revenue and expenses and then the related conversions to cash flow. The first entry (a1) and (a2) converting Sales to Cash Received from Sales has been provided for you. So has the labeling for the expense entries (b1 through f1).
- *e.* Record the four entries from the Other Information provided in Problem 12-8A. These are investing and financing activities.
- *f.* In column H, set up the IF function to determine whether the balance sheet accounts are in balance or not ("off"). Cell H3 for Accounts Receivable is provided for you. Cell H3 can be copied to all the balance sheet debit accounts. The balance sheet credit account formulas will differ given the different debit/credit rules for those accounts. The formula for Retained Earnings will need to include rows 14 through 20. *When the word "Balance" is reflected in every balance*

sheet cell in column H, the spreadsheet analysis is complete. For more information about the IF function, refer to Spreadsheet Tips in ACT 11-9 of Chapter 11.

g. Total the Debit and Credit columns to ensure that the two columns are equal.

h. As a final check, beginning in cell J2, compute the change in the Cash account by subtracting the beginning balance from the ending balance. The difference will equal $14,100. Also beginning in cell J24, compute the difference in the debit and credit cash entries in rows 24 through 34. The difference should also equal $14,100.

Spreadsheet Tip

1. Darken cells by highlighting the cells to be darkened. Select Format and then Cells. Click on the tab titled Patterns and choose a color.

ACT 12-9

SPREADSHEET ANALYSIS **Preparing a Statement of Cash Flows Using the Indirect Method**

(*Note:* If you completed ACT 12-8, that spreadsheet can be modified to complete this problem.)

Refer to the information in Problem 12-8A. Solve for the statement of cash flows using the indirect method. Instead of using the T-account method, set up the following spreadsheet to work through the analysis. The Debit/Credit entries are very similar to the T-account method except that they are entered onto a spreadsheet. Instead of making entries on row 3 for Cash, Cash Flow entries are made beginning on row 18.

	A	B	C	D	E	F	G	H	I	J	K	L	M
							H14	=IF(B14+F14-D14=G14,"Balance","Off")					
1	Balance Sheet Debits:	20X8		Debit		Credit	20X9						
2	Cash	20,300					34,400			Change in Cash =	14,100		
3	Accounts Receivable	11,000	(c)	4,000			15,000	Balance					
4	Inventory	88,000					80,000	Off					
5	Prepaid Rent	2,400					1,200	Off					
6	Equipment	144,000					128,000	Off					
7	Land	40,000					96,000	Off					
8	Total Debits	305,700					354,600						
9	Balance Sheet Credits:												
10	Accumulated Depreciation	118,000			(b)	11,400	73,400	Off					
11	Accounts Payable (Inv.)	38,000					33,500	Off					
12	Salaries Payable	12,000					14,000	Off					
13	Common Stock, $25 Par	100,000					125,000	Off					
14	Retained Earnings	37,700			(a)	71,000	108,700	Balance					
15	Total Credits	305,700					354,600						
16	**Statement of Cash Flows**												
17	Cash Flows from Operating Activities												
18	Net Income		(a)	71,000						Difference in Cash Debit			
19	Plus Noncash Charges									and Credit Entries =			
20	Depreciation Expense		(b)	11,400									
21	Changes in Current Assets & Liab.												
22	Increase in Accounts Receivable				(c)	4,000							
23	Decrease in Inventory												
24	Decrease in Prepaid Rent												
25	Decrease in Accounts Payable												
26	Increase in Salaries Payable												
27	Cash Flows from Investing Activities												
28	Outflow to purchase land												
29	Outflow to purchase equipment												
30	Inflow from sale of equipment												
31	Cash Flows from Financing Activities												
32	Inflow from stock issue												
33	Total Debit and Credit Columns				86,400		86,400						
34													
35													

Required

a. Enter information in column A.

b. Enter the beginning balance sheet amounts in column B and ending balances in column G. Total the debits and credits for each column.

c. To prevent erroneous entries to Cash in row 2, darken the area in columns C through F.

d. Record the entry for Net Income. This is entry (a) provided.

e. Record the entry for Depreciation expense. This is entry (b) provided.

f. Record the entries for the changes in current assets and liabilities. The entry for the change in Accounts Receivable has been provided and is referenced as entry (c).

g. Record the four entries from the Other Information provided in Problem 12-8A. These are the investing and financing activities.

h. In column H set up the IF function to determine whether the balance sheet accounts are in balance or not ("off"). Cell H3 for Accounts Receivable is provided for you. Cell H4 can be copied to all the balance sheet debit accounts. The balance sheet credit account formulas will differ given the different debit/credit rules for those accounts. *When the word "Balance" is reflected in every balance sheet cell in column H, the spreadsheet analysis is complete.* For more information on the IF function, refer to Spreadsheet Tips in ACT 11-9 of Chapter 11.

i. Total the Debit and Credit columns to ensure that the two columns are equal.

j. As a final check, beginning in cell J2, compute the change in the Cash account by subtracting the beginning balance from the ending balance. The difference will equal $14,100. Also beginning in cell J18, compute the difference in the debit and credit cash entries in rows 18 through 32. The difference should also equal $14,100.

Accessing the EDGAR Database through the Internet

uccessful business managers need many different skills, including communication, interpersonal, computer, and analytical skills. Most business students become very aware of the data analysis skills used in accounting, but they may not be as aware of the importance of "data finding" skills. There are many sources of accounting and financial data. The more sources you are able to use, the better.

One very important source of accounting information is the EDGAR database. Others are probably available at your school through the library or business school network. Your accounting instructor will be able to identify these for you and make suggestions regarding their use. By making the effort to learn to use electronic databases, you will enhance your abilities as a future manager and your marketability as a business graduate.

These instructions assume that you know how to access and use an Internet navigator, such as Netscape. After you activate the Navigator program on your computer, follow the instructions to retrieve data from the Securities and Exchange Commission's EDGAR database. Be aware that the SEC may have changed its interface since this appendix was written. Accordingly, be prepared for slight differences between the following instructions and what appears on your computer screen. Take comfort in the fact that changes are normally designed to simplify user access. If you encounter a conflict between the following instructions and the instructions provided in the SEC interface, remember that the SEC interface is more current and should take precedence over the following instructions.

1. To connect to EDGAR, type in the following address:
    http://www.sec.gov/edgarhp.htm
2. After the EDGAR home page screen appears, double-click on
    - Search the EDGAR Database
3. From the screen that appears, double-click on
    Quick Forms Lookup
4. On the screen that appears, scroll down to just below the heading
    Customized Forms Selection
    Below this heading is a small "window" with the word **ALL** in it and a downward-pointing scrolling arrow. Click and hold on the down arrow to activate the list of forms available through EDGAR. Scroll upward with the pointer to highlight **10-K,** and then release the mouse button.
5. Continue scrolling down the main screen to the small, blank window just below.
    Enter a company
    In the window, type the name of the company whose 10-K you wish to retrieve.
6. Continue scrolling down the main screen until you see a gray button labeled **Submit Choices.** Click this button. At this point, you probably

will get a **Waiting for reply** message. Depending on a number of factors, the wait can be very short or very long.

7. Next, you will get a screen listing companies with names exactly like or similar to the one you entered and the 10-Ks or related forms available for those companies. Choose the form you wish to retrieve, paying attention to the date of the accounting period to which the different forms relate. Usually, you will want the most recent form. (*Note:* The basic 10-K form has several variations, such as the 10-K/A. If there is more than one 10-K type of form for the accounting period in which you are interested, retrieve the form with the most recent *filing* date. If this form does not contain the data you want, go back and try another 10-K type of form.)

8. Once the 10-K has been retrieved, you can search it online or save it on your hard drive or diskette. If you want to save it, do so by using the **Save As** command from the pull-down menu at the top of the screen named **File.** The file will be saved as an ASCII text file that can be accessed using most word processing programs.

9. The financial statements are seldom located near the beginning of a company's 10-K, so it is necessary to scroll down the file until you find them. Typically, they are located about one-half to three-fourths of the way through the report.

10. Good luck! If you have never used the Internet before, you will find that it contains an incredible amount of stuff. Some of this stuff, such as the EDGAR database, actually contains useful information. However, you will also find that the Internet is often very slow and frustrating, especially during the middle of business days. Using EDGAR during off-hours is more enjoyable and efficient.

· 1 9 9 7 ·
Gateway Annual Report

Annual Report courtesy Gateway 2000, Inc. © 1997.

**November 6, 1997,
Aboard Space Station Mir**

Mir-24 commander Anatoly Solovyev and flight engineer Pavel Vinogradov used the Internet to order the first computers sold in space: two Gateway G6-233 multimedia PCs for $1999 each. (We threw in shipping – to Russia.)

E-mail order assisted by Virtual Emporium, Energia and Mission Control near Moscow. Photo courtesy RSC Energia Alexandria, VA.

Next

2   Gateway Chairman and CEO Ted Waitt

Level

Dear Fellow Stockholders:

Gateway did some great things in 1997, but overall it wasn't a great year for us.

The final stats were respectable, although they should have been even better. Our 1997 revenue increased 25% to $6.29 billion. Our earnings declined due to inventory issues and one-time charges in the middle of the year. However, we quickly sprang back to life and finished the year strong in the fourth quarter. In October, November and December we reduced SG&A, increased productivity, dramatically improved our capital management and rededicated ourselves to growing our business and building relationships with our customers. Q4 revenue hit a record $1.98 billion and we shipped 850,000 systems as Gateway sprinted hard through the December 31 finish line. Time to take a break? Not in this lifetime.

1997 Highlights

All was not bad in 1997. Actually, we did some amazing things. We increased our market share in the U.S. home market 67%, grew our education business by 178%, grew our mobile business by 73%, moved to the New York Stock Exchange, split our stock, increased brand awareness and spread a revolutionary concept in computer retailing: Gateway Country℠ stores.

We've learned from our mistakes. We're maturing at a rapid pace and are determined to take our business to the Next Level. The Next Level is more a quest than a specific destination. And the quest acknowledges something that success tempts us to forget: We're not on top yet and we've still got plenty of work to do to get there.

I hope you enjoy our 1997 Annual Report. Gateway is on its way to the Next Level. Come on along.

Ted Waitt
Chairman and CEO

· VISION ·

1997
$6.29 billion in revenue

2.58 million units shipped

Average Unit Price in 1997
was $2,434

Dataquest ranked Gateway 4th in U.S. shipments and 9th in global shipments in 1997

Stock listing (GTW) moved to NYSE on May 22, 1997

Ted Waitt ·
Chairman and CEO
"Our journey to the Next Level demands executing well on the basics of our direct model: forecasting, inventory management and cost controls. Beyond that, we need to cling to our corporate values, listen to our customers and work harder than everyone else."

3

Humanizing the

4   Sierra talks about her mom's job at Gateway during one of our fourth quarter TV ads.

TV   COMPUTER

Mixing Cow Spots and Computers

Drive down New York's Madison Avenue on any Tuesday during trash collection and you'll see empty cow-spotted boxes lining the street. Even half a block away, the black-and-white image says "GATEWAY" to a huge and growing number of people.

Selling computers direct means asking customers to charge $2,500 to their credit cards, over the phone or World Wide Web, for a system that doesn't actually exist when they order it. How we sustain that magical act of faith has a lot to do with spotted boxes.

Digital Revolution

Gateway Brand Promise

People love our computers and they love our spots. School children stack and cut our boxes into Holstein dinosaurs and send us photographs of their work. Customers send pictures of their spotted pets next to our boxes. Spotted mouse pads dot rows of office workers' desks.

What is it about our spots? They go beyond signifying a great computer at a great price. They symbolize Gateway's values. To customers they mark membership in a community we call the Gateway family.

Families operate on trust. Gateway customers trust us to deliver as promised, to be the kind of friendly, trustworthy people we claim to be and to help them harness technology to improve their lives. It really doesn't matter where customers live — Idaho or Iceland — they all expect Gateway to deliver on these core expectations.

Building Relationships – and Computers

By constantly affirming that customer trust, we develop friendly relationships. And in the edgy digital world, there's nothing like knowing someone you can trust.

Our "You've got a friend in the business"* slogan encourages relationships. The world of computers seems complex and confusing. Its history started with slick, high-margin sales. We changed all that. Now when customers want a fair deal and honest, respectful, caring treatment, they turn to Gateway.

Our spots symbolize what our slogan declares: trust. That promise, at home or office, means living up to some very high standards. That doesn't scare us. Sure, we face big risks if we don't deliver on that promise, but we also enjoy rewards when we do.

Only the Gateway brand claims the higher responsibility of being a friend. We embrace that commitment. We've staked our cow spots on it.

· CARING ·

Building the Brand

Gateway's unaided brand awareness has nearly doubled in the last two years.

80% of consumers and 95% of business customers in the U.S. are aware of Gateway.

Gateway started cow spotting its boxes in 1991.

The Gateway Foundation contributed to more than 280 U.S. charities in 1997.

Geraldine de Brit · (left)
German Portable Sales
European Headquarters
Dublin, Ireland

Francois Farge ·
French Sales Supervisor
European Headquarters
Dublin, Ireland

5

True

6   Telephone sales and support help keep Gateway in touch with customers.

A Future of Making History

Ever since Gateway came into the PC world in 1985, the vision hasn't wavered – deliver the highest value directly to customers.

It remains our company mission to this day. It also defines "the direct model," something held nearly sacred at Gateway. The direct model has repeatedly proven itself the most efficient way to deliver value to customers.

No Place Like Home and Small Business

A record number of PC buyers became members of the Gateway family in 1997. At the end of the year, Dataquest ranked us number three in the U.S. home market based on shipments. Our value focus also puts Gateway among the leaders in shipments to home offices and to small and medium businesses.

We credit those high marks to our devotion to the blend of price, performance, service and quality known as "value." Gateway only sells computers that we would (and do) proudly sell to members of our own families. Gateway will never skimp on performance, quality and service just to drop our prices through the floor. Instead, we give our customers the most for their money at prices within reach of most every budget.

to Our Roots

1-800-GATEWAY℠ or www.gateway.com

Gateway expanded into Vermillion, S.D., in 1997, opening a phone center we call the "Cow Palace."

The people who work in the Cow Palace are called "emissaries" and they answer calls to our sales numbers and 1-800-GATEWAY during regular business hours.

So while other companies wired in more answering machines to answer their calls, we've invested in building customer relationships by hiring people to answer the phones. Emissaries greet our customers, determine who can serve them best and transfer the call.

If you prefer to do business digitally, just point your modem at www.gateway.com. At its peak during the holidays, our Web site generated about $4 million in revenue a day.

We consider the Web yet another way to connect Gateway to its customers. But it's more than just a transactional tool. The Web lets us strengthen our customer relationship by sharing information, education and opinions.

Add in PC sales and technical support, and the Web equals a powerful tool for both companies and consumers.

· COMMON SENSE ·

Gateway Market Segments

Segments as percentage of Gateway's sales:

Home:	35%
Business:	30%
Education and Government:	20%
International:	15%

Dataquest reported Gateway's U.S. home market share grew by 66.9% between the end of 1996 and the end of 1997.

Europe and Asia Pacific

Gateway's operations in Europe shipped 261,000 systems in 1997, while our Asia Pacific region shipped 139,000 systems.

North Sioux City, S.D.
World Wide Web
Team Members

Lenny Jolin · (left)
Web Developer

Laurie Pick ·
Marketing Manager

Jon Lowy ·
Technical Director,
Global Marketing

7

A Place

Gateway Country stores like this one in South County, St. Louis, Missouri, give customers a chance to test drive our PCs.

Giving Gateway a Local Face

Customers have always had many choices of what to buy from Gateway. In 1997 we gave them more choices on *how* to buy from us. With the retail channel accounting for about one-third of all U.S. PC sales, many people obviously prefer to shop for computers in person. So while continuing to make it easy for customers to reach Gateway over the phone or World Wide Web, we also continued taking Gateway to the customers.

That's why Gateway formed a wholly owned subsidiary, Gateway 2000 Country Stores, Inc., which operates Gateway Country℠ stores. The stores bring the strengths and efficiencies of the direct model to a retail setting. At Gateway Country stores, customers can touch, test and custom configure a system to meet their needs with the help of highly trained sales representatives. Gateway then builds the systems at our factories and ships them directly to customers, just as we would for phone or World Wide Web orders.

Building Boom

Gateway Country had 37 stores open in the U.S. by the end of 1997. We expect our total number of stores to more than double during 1998. Our showrooms abroad inspired Gateway Country in the U.S. By the end of 1997 we had a total of 51 retail locations worldwide.

# of Our Own

Raising our Business, Consumer and Service Profile

When you have a small business with complex network or technology needs, sometimes you'd rather do things face to face. Business owners do just that by visiting Gateway Country. There they see for themselves how our systems can deliver reliability, manageability and scalability to their business. Gateway Country stores' sales representatives help small business owners choose the right technology to accomplish their business objectives.

Building stores around the country has also gotten us noticed. Each Gateway Country store raises brand awareness locally.

The stores also introduce thousands of PC shoppers to Gateway's culture and roots. The stores' Midwestern rural decor of silos, weather vanes, barns and tractor seats help customers discover that shopping for high tech can be low stress. Visit one and you'll know it's a better way to buy a better computer.

· FUN ·

Gateway Country
Built 22 new Gateway Country stores in Q4 1997, bringing our total to 37 in the U.S.

New Global Showrooms and Country Stores in 1997
Perth, Australia
Osaka, Japan
Kuala Lumpur, Malaysia
Auckland, New Zealand

Jesse Diehl ·
Sales Associate
Gateway Country
South County, St. Louis, Mo.

9

Cow Spots

⑩ President Gene Lu and his ALR team add server expertise to the Gateway family.

Built for Business: Quality, Stability, Compatibility

Do cow spots mix with power suits? Eighty percent of America's largest corporations think so.

To help spread the word that Gateway value isn't just for the home and small business, Gateway formed Gateway Major Accounts, Inc. A company within our company, Gateway Major Accounts focuses on the needs of our large corporate, government and education customers.

In 1997, 32% of Gateway's total U.S. shipments went to Gateway Major Accounts customers. Major Accounts' mission is to listen to its customers, understand their objectives and then deliver solutions and support that exceed their expectations. Last year we sent dozens of corporate account executives to work in major U.S. metro areas with that mission in mind.

and Wingtips

Different Customers, Different Products

Gateway Major Accounts armed its field and headquarters forces with the broadest product line in Gateway's history. Our E-Series line delivers everything from torture-tested network desktops to muscular workstations, all designed with the features corporate customers require. The Gateway Solo™ portable PC line keeps everyone productive and in touch at the office, across the hall or on the road. For group use in the classroom or board room, nothing beats the high value, power and big screen of the Destination Digital Media Computer.

Gateway's Major Accounts effort got a huge boost in 1997 with the acquisition of Advanced Logic Research, Inc. (ALR), known for innovation throughout the server industry. Based on ALR's server design, Gateway created its NS-Series servers to handle any business need.

Custom Integration Delivers

On top of our expanded product line, Gateway Major Accounts takes custom configuration to new levels with Custom Integration Services (CIS). For large orders, CIS builds Gateway PCs to customer specifications and even installs third-party hardware and software at the factory.

CIS helped Bull Information Systems, our government and education reseller in Alabama, rack up more than $18 million in Gateway sales in 1997.

Bull Information Systems Account Executive Alan Newman said his company "will use the CIS group more and more in 1998 to install school-wide and district-wide solutions throughout Alabama. We are moving fast to provide systems which include standard office and curriculum software pre-loaded on each unit. Only a capability such as CIS can provide this flexibility and competitive edge."

· AGGRESSIVENESS ·

Gateway Major Accounts
Australia's third-largest bank, Westpac Banking Corporation, is powered by Gateway E-Series PCs and our Custom Integration Services. Westpac has assets of more than AUS$121 billion and is the ninth largest business in Australia.

Education market growth
Computer Intelligence Projected Market Monitor in February 1998 ranked Gateway number 1 overall in sales to education. Dataquest reported Gateway's 1997 sales to education grew 178% compared to 1996.

Derek Schniedeman ·
President
Gateway 2000 Japan, Inc.
Yokohama, Japan

11

Gateway computer keyboards come in Japanese and many other languages.

Product

Gateway Solo™ Portable PCs

Gateway's portable business grew by 73% based on units sold, and by 56% in revenue compared to 1996. Overall, portables accounted for 11% of Gateway's total revenue. We've designed a Solo™ model for most everyone, starting with a system priced less than $2,000. Gateway also led the industry in developing "common modularity." That means using hard drives, memory, power supplies and docking station components that fit several Solo models.

In 1997, we introduced the Solo 2300 fleet machine, and the Solo 9100, which *Fortune* magazine called "the Rolls Royce of laptops."*

Value

Destination® Digital Media Computers

Gateway pioneered the category of TV, video and computer convergence in April 1996 with the Destination Big Screen PC/TV. That system has since evolved into the second-generation Destination Digital Media Computer. Gateway sees convergence products as a key component to the information age. The digital video marvel, DVD, looks breathtaking on our 35.5-inch Destination monitor. Destination system sales in 1997 soared by 50% compared to a year earlier.

Gateway™ G-Series and GP-Series Desktop Systems

Delivering the freshest desktop technology at unbeatable value made Gateway's desktop business into an industry force. When the Intel Pentium® II processor came out in 1997, some companies saw it as a high-end processor mainly for business. Gateway did what we've always done: discovered how to put the technology to work for our home *and* business customers. So we offered the Pentium II processor in configurations that fit customers' multimedia and business needs. During the last quarter of 1997, Pentium II processor-based desktop systems accounted for 43% of our shipments.

E-Series Desktops, Workstations and NS-Series Servers

In 1997, Gateway launched an entire line of PCs and servers built just for large businesses and institutions. Gateway E-Series desktops deliver stability and manageability to the network. Our workstations put brute power at your command without killing the bottom line. Based on our subsidiary ALR's award-winning systems, our NS-Series servers take good care of data for your small, medium or large group.

*August 4, 1997, page 217

· EFFICIENCY ·

gateway.net℠ ISP
Gateway was the first major computer company to also become an Internet service provider. Our gateway.net ISP is available exclusively to Gateway customers.

Pentium II processor does Japan
One hour after Intel announced its Pentium II processor on May 7, Gateway Japan shipped them to customers, selling more than 1,400 Pentium II processor-based Gateway systems on May 7 alone.

Karla Radle ·
Human Factors Engineer
Customer Experience
North Sioux City, S.D.

13

14   Testing and communication of customer concerns help
     maintain high product quality.

Showing

Backing Up the Brand

Our "You've got a friend in the business"® slogan is easy to say, but can we back it up? Price and performance help bring customers in the door, but service and support brings them, and their friends, back again and again. That's why Gateway sees service as a key part of being the industry's value leader.

Erasing Department Lines

Service and support starts with employees working together to create the highest quality products on the market. Gateway technical support technicians regularly spend time working in our manufacturing process. Then people in manufacturing spend time in technical support.

That dialogue, along with other enhanced communications processes, lets manufacturing and technical support share knowledge about and react to recurring technical issues and customer needs.

Gateway views its technical support and customer service departments as valuable assets for connecting our company with what customers like and dislike. By talking to customers every day, they get a great feel for the kinds of services and products customers want.

Our Support

First-Call Resolution

So how do you measure quality in technical support? One call at a time. During 1997, Gateway stressed the goal of solving customers' technical support concerns on the first call.

To help our technicians and customer service employees strive toward that goal, we continue to invest in tools and training and encourage employees to suggest ways to improve. And Gateway hasn't been afraid to scrap what doesn't work. In the third quarter of 1997, we wrote off part of a multi-year, multi-million dollar customer support information systems project because it wasn't working well enough to serve a new generation of customers. We've learned from that experience and are replacing the systems with more focused tools.

We also enhanced our technical support offering on our Web site, www.gateway.com, in 1997. Now customers can conveniently access help files, download software fixes, view the most frequently asked questions and even learn how computers work.

In the non-virtual world, Gateway added technical support centers in Rio Rancho, N.M., and Colorado Springs, Colo., in 1997. Both centers started taking calls in early 1998.

· RESPECT ·

Taking Calls

Gateway takes about 30,000 telephone calls a day for sales, technical support and corporate operations combined.

Brand Loyalty

In the summer and fall, IDC/LINK and AC Nielsen surveyed Gateway owners in the U.S. home market who had bought an additional PC. Some 77% of them chose Gateway again, the best repurchase rate of any PC maker in that market.

Gan Kok Ann · (left)
Software Engineer
Malacca, Malaysia

Eng Bak Kwang ·
Network Engineer
Malacca, Malaysia

15

Product &

16 Gateway employees build new systems in North Sioux City, S.D., Hampton, Va., Dublin, Ireland and Malacca, Malaysia.

Destination® Digital Media Computer

- 1997 MVP Award — *PC Computing*
- Best of the Year — *PC Magazine*
- Editor's Choice — *PC Gamer*
- Hot Stuff '97 Reviewer's Choice Award — *Home PC*
- Best of What Men Want in 1997 — *Men's Journal*
- Best 200 Products of the Year — *PC Computing*

GATEWAY™ GP-Series and 6-Series Desktop PCs

- Best Buy Award — *PC World* (P5-166)
- Best Buy Award — *PC World* (G6-233)
- Stellar Award — *Windows Sources* (G6-266)
- Best Place to Buy a Home and Office PC — *Computer Shopper*
- Best Value Desktop PC Line — *Computer Shopper*

Gateway Solo™ Portable PCs

- Editor's Choice (Solo 2200 and 9100) — *PC Magazine*
- Best Buy (Solo 2300) — *PC World*
- Portable of the Year (Solo 9100) — *PC Portables Magazine*
- First Class Award (Solo 9100) — *Mobile Computing and Communication*
- Stellar Award (Solo 2300 and 9100) — *Windows Sources*

Global Industry Publications

- France: Le Choix de la Redaction (G6-266XL) — *PC DIRECT*
- Germany: Technik Empfehlung, (Solo 9100) — *PC Direkt*

Service Awards

- Netherlands: Best in Test, Multimedia Group (P5-166M) — *Consumentengids*
- Sweden: Portable Machine of the Year (Solo 9100) — *Microdatorn*
- UK: Value Award (G6-266XL) — *PC Pro*
- Malaysia and Singapore: Top 5 High-End/Commercial Systems and Budget Systems — *PC World*
- Australia: 1997 Readers' Choice Awards, Best Business PC, Best Home PC, Best Notebook — Australian *PC World*
- Japan: Number 1 Performance Ranking, Portables (Solo 9100) — *Nikkei Personal Computing*

Servers

- Product of the Year, Server Hardware (ALR enterprise server) — *InfoWorld*

Service and Support

- Best Service and Support — *Computer Shopper*
- 5th Annual World Class Awards, Best Hardware Support — *PC World*
- #1 in service and support, third annual customer support survey — *Home PC*

17

On a

18   Leadership, teamwork and customer focus are the keys to 1998.

Gateway Family Members:

The lessons of our eventful 1997 are pretty clear: Build relationships, stay humble and hungry, and play like you're behind even when you are ahead.

Throughout 1998, we'll remember those lessons as we focus on what has brought us this far: delivering the best value to our customers.

Let Me Be Direct

The direct channel – delivering goods and services directly from manufacturer to customer – is simply the most efficient channel for business. Whether through the Web, over the phone, at Gateway Country℠ stores or while working with our partners, we're going to listen harder than ever to what customers say.

We entered 1998 with the most complete product line in Gateway's history – desktops, portables, servers and convergence systems for home and business. Our customer support won some impressive awards in 1997. We broadened our business with the purchase of ALR and Amiga Technologies.

The World Wide Web will continue to have a huge effect on Gateway in 1998. It will influence what products we sell, how we sell them, how we support our products and how we run our business. The Web also offers a dynamic way to interact with customers and develop that mutual trust and interdependence that builds truly great businesses.

Mission

Building the Team

Everything starts with leadership, and in January we hired Jeffrey Weitzen to be Gateway's President and COO. Jeff brings a well-earned reputation for building business by helping customers succeed. Jeff is also a genuinely great guy who does what he says he'll do, when he says he'll do it. He's a key part of taking this company to the Next Level.

Gateway's employees, customers and stockholders are also key parts of our future. In business, getting to the Next Level is always a group effort. Our team will remember the lessons of 1997 as we build a successful 1998.

Thanks for being part of the Gateway family.

Theodore W. Waitt
Chairman and CEO
Gateway 2000, Inc.
March 4, 1998

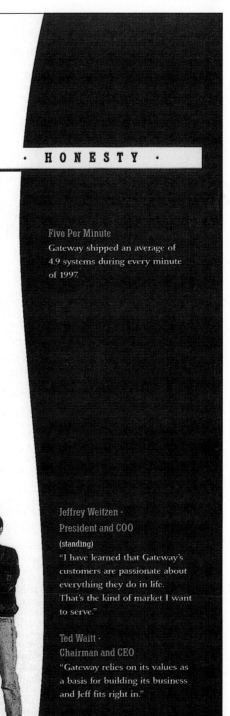

· **H O N E S T Y** ·

Five Per Minute
Gateway shipped an average of 4.9 systems during every minute of 1997.

Jeffrey Weitzen ·
President and COO
(standing)
"I have learned that Gateway's customers are passionate about everything they do in life. That's the kind of market I want to serve."

Ted Waitt ·
Chairman and CEO
"Gateway relies on its values as a basis for building its business and Jeff fits right in."

19

Management's Discussion and Analysis of Financial Condition and Results of Operations

This Report includes forward-looking statements made based on current management expectations pursuant to the safe harbor provisions of the Private Securities Litigation Reform Act of 1995. These statements are not guarantees of future performance and actual outcomes may differ materially from what is expressed or forecasted. There are many factors that affect the Company's business and its results of operations, including the factors discussed below.

Results of Operations

The following table sets forth, for the periods indicated, certain data derived from the Company's consolidated statements of operations, expressed as a percentage of net sales:

	1995	1996	1997
Net sales	100.0%	100.0%	100.0%
Cost of goods sold	83.5%	81.4%	82.9%
Gross profit	16.5%	18.6%	17.1%
Selling, general and administrative expenses	9.7%	11.5%	12.5%
Nonrecurring expenses	–	–	1.8%
Operating income	6.8%	7.1%	2.8%
Other income, net	0.3%	0.5%	0.4%
Income before income taxes	7.1%	7.6%	3.2%
Provision for income taxes	2.4%	2.6%	1.5%
Net income	4.7%	5.0%	1.7%

Sales. Sales in 1997 increased 25% to $6.29 billion from $5.04 billion in 1996. The increase in sales resulted from continued demand growth in the Americas and Asia Pacific markets, the acquisition of Advanced Logic Research, Inc. (ALR) on July 23, 1997, and the continued growth in sales of the Company's portable products.

Sales in the Americas region grew 25% over 1996 levels to $5.30 billion. International sales increased 25% to $989.8 million over the prior year. Sales in the Company's European region were $634.6 million, an increase of approximately 15% over the comparable period of 1996 despite a decrease in sales from the level in the second quarter of 1997. Sales for 1997 in the Company's Asia Pacific region totaled $355.2 million, an increase of 50% over 1996.

Unit shipments in 1997 increased 35% to approximately 2,580,000 from 1,909,000 in 1996. Unit shipments in the Company's Americas region grew 35% over 1996. In the Company's European region, unit shipments grew 20% over 1996, and unit shipments in the Company's Asia Pacific region grew 84% over 1996.

Sales from Pentium MMX-based and Pentium II-based desktop products accounted for approximately 32% and 24%, respectively, of the Company's total sales in 1997. Throughout 1997, sales from Pentium MMX-based and Pentium II-based products increased each quarter, to approximately 35% and 49%, respectively, in the fourth quarter. Portable products accounted for approximately 11% of total sales in 1997, versus approximately 9% in 1996. Portable products sales increased 56% and convergence product sales increased 55% over the prior year.

Weighted average unit prices (AUP) declined approximately 8% during 1997. Generally, unit prices for specific PC products have decreased over time, reflecting the effects of competition and reduced component costs associated with advances in technology. The Company has generally offset the impact of these declines in component costs by adding or improving product features and by introducing new products based on newer technology at higher unit prices, resulting in fairly stable unit prices over time. When the timing of component cost reductions and new technology introduction is different, AUPs can fluctuate. The reduction in 1997 AUPs from 1996 levels is partially due to abnormally high AUPs experienced in the first four months of 1996.

Beginning in the second quarter of 1996, in addition to normal component cost declines, the Company experienced significant declines in Dynamic Random Access Memory (DRAM) costs. AUPs throughout the second half of 1996 and the first half of 1997 were fairly stable, but began to decline in the third quarter of 1997 as component cost reductions again outpaced the introduction of new technology.

Sales in 1996 increased 37% to $5.04 billion from $3.68 billion in 1995. The increase resulted from continued demand growth in the Americas and European markets, expansion into the Asia Pacific region and accelerated growth in sales of the Company's portable products. Unit shipments in 1996 increased 43% to approximately 1,909,000 from 1,338,000 in 1995. Average unit prices declined approximately 4% during 1996, reflecting the normal rate of component cost declines, significant cost declines in DRAM and a slowing of new technology during 1996.

Gross Profit. Gross profit in 1997 increased approximately 15% to $1.076 billion from $936.2 million in 1996, but as a percentage of sales, gross profit decreased to 17.1% from 18.6% in 1996. The decline in gross profit as a percentage of sales was due to the effects of excess inventories during the third quarter of 1997. During this time period, there were significant declines in the market value of many inventory components. In order to promptly mitigate the impact of these excess inventories, the Company sold product with profit margins below targeted levels. In addition, reserves were recorded against excess and obsolete inventories still on hand at the end of the third quarter.

Gross profit in 1996 increased approximately 54% from $606.1 million in 1995. As a percentage of sales, gross profit increased to 18.6% from 16.5% in 1995. Gross profit improved during 1996 principally due to improvements in meeting product sales mix forecasts associated with the introduction of new products, a decrease in DRAM prices and decreases in aggregate royalty cost per unit. Gross margin as a percent of sales also increased due to the timing of component cost decreases being passed on to customers through price declines.

Selling, General and Administrative Expenses. Selling, general and administrative (SG&A) expenses in 1997 increased by approximately 36% to $786.2 million from $580.1 million in 1996. As a percentage of sales, these expenses increased to approximately 12.5% in 1997 from approximately 11.5% in 1996. The increase is primarily the result of increases in personnel, marketing, depreciation and amortization and the inclusion of the operating expenses of ALR. Beginning in 1997, certain expenses relating to the fulfillment of parts warranties have been reclassified from selling, general and administrative expenses to costs of goods sold.

Personnel-related costs increased approximately 33% in 1997 compared with 1996, as a result of the continued building of the Company's infrastructure and increased expenditures to expand the sales force and technical support. The Company expects to continue to make the necessary personnel-related expenditures and investments to manage the growth of the Company.

Marketing expenses increased approximately 52% in 1997 as compared to 1996. The increase represents the Company's continued efforts to target broader market bases, including the novice user. Also, marketing efforts were increased to support the expansion of the Gateway Country℠ Stores.

Depreciation and amortization expenses increased approximately 41% in 1997 compared to 1996, as a result of the Company's continued investments in facilities and software application. Amortization expense increased due to intangible assets obtained in the acquisition of ALR during 1997.

Selling, general and administrative expenses in 1996 increased 62% to $580.1 million from $357.1 million in 1995. As a percentage of sales, these expenses increased to 11.5% in 1996 from 9.7% in 1995. Significant factors contributing to this net increase included: higher personnel costs, additional marketing programs and overhead expenses associated with the Asia Pacific region.

Nonrecurring Expenses. The Company recorded several nonrecurring pretax charges totaling $113.8 million in the third quarter of 1997. Of the nonrecurring charges, $59.7 million was for the write-off of in-process research and development acquired with the purchase of ALR and certain assets of Amiga Technologies. Also included in the nonrecurring charges was a non-cash write-off of $45.2 million resulting from the abandonment of a capitalized internal-use software project and certain computer equipment. In addition, $8.6 million was recorded for severance of employees and the closing of a foreign office.

Operating Income. Due to the nonrecurring expenses incurred during the third quarter of 1997, a declining percentage of gross profit and the increase in operating expenses, operating income in 1997 decreased by 50% to $176.4 million from $356.1 million in 1996. Operating income, excluding nonrecurring items in 1997, decreased 18% from 1996 to $290.3 million. As a percentage of sales, operating income decreased to 2.8% in 1997 (4.6% excluding nonrecurring items) from 7.1% in 1996. In 1996, operating income increased 43% from $249.0 million in 1995, and remained relatively constant as a percentage of sales.

Other Income, Net. Other income, net includes other income net of expenses, such as interest income and expense, lease financing commissions, referral fees for on-line services and foreign exchange transaction gains and losses. Other income, net increased to $27.2 million in 1997 from $26.6 million in 1996. The principal cause of this increase was the generation of additional interest income as a result of the availability of additional cash and marketable securities in 1997 compared to 1996.

Other income, net in 1996 increased to $26.6 million from $13.1 million in 1995 primarily due to additional interest income generated as a result of the availability of additional cash and marketable securities as compared to 1995, and the generation of commissions from referrals for on-line services.

Income Taxes. The Company's effective tax rate was 46.1%, 34.5%, and 34.0% in 1997, 1996 and 1995, respectively. The increase in the 1997 effective tax rate was primarily due to the impact of nonrecurring expenses relating to the write-off of in-process research and development arising in connection with the acquisitions of ALR and certain assets of Amiga Technologies which were nondeductible for income tax purposes. The effective tax rate for 1997 excluding the nonrecurring items was approximately 35.5%. The change from 1996 is attributed to shifts in the geographic distribution of the Company's earnings, which also impacted the change in the 1996 rate versus the 1995 rate.

Liquidity and Capital Resources

The Company has financed its operating and capital expenditure requirements to date principally through cash flow from its operations. At December 31, 1997, the Company had cash and cash equivalents of $593.6 million, marketable securities of $38.6 million and an unsecured committed credit facility with certain banks of $225 million, consisting of a revolving line of credit facility and a sub-facility for letters of credit. At December 31, 1997, no amounts were outstanding under the revolving line of credit. Approximately $3.5 million was committed to support outstanding standby letters of credit. Management believes the Company's current sources of working capital, including amounts available under existing or future credit facilities, will provide adequate flexibility for the Company's financial needs for at least the next 12 months.

The Company generated approximately $442.8 million of cash from operations during 1997. Increases in accounts receivable and other current assets consumed approximately $96.5 million offset by decreases in inventory levels of $59.5 million. Also, increases in accounts payable, accrued liabilities and other liabilities contributed $156.9 million. The Company used approximately $360.7 million in cash for investing activities as a result of the Company's continued investment in facilities, a $38.6 million net investment in marketable securities, and a $142.3 million purchase of ALR, net of cash acquired. Of the purchase price, $58.6 million was allocated to in-process research and development projects. The Company expects ALR to continue

to develop these projects into commercially viable products in the normal course of business over the next 1 to 5 years.

At December 31, 1997, the Company had long-term indebtedness and capital lease obligations of approximately $21.2 million. These obligations relate primarily to the Company's expansion of international operations and its investments in equipment and facilities. Borrowings, exclusive of capital lease obligations, bear fixed and variable rates of interest currently ranging from interest free (for certain incentive funds from the Industrial Development Authority of the City of Hampton, Virginia) to 8.87% and have varying maturities through the year 2001. The Company's capital lease obligations relate principally to its computer and telephone system equipment.

The Company anticipates that it will retain all earnings in the foreseeable future for development of its business and will not distribute earnings to its stockholders as dividends.

New Accounting Pronouncements

In June 1997, the Financial Accounting Standards Board (FASB) issued Statement of Financial Accounting Standard (SFAS) No. 131 - Disclosures about Segments of an Enterprise and Related Information. SFAS 131 requires publicly-held companies to report financial and other information about key revenue-producing segments of the entity for which such information is available and is utilized by management. Specific information to be reported for individual segments includes profit or loss, certain revenue and expense items and total assets. A reconciliation of segment financial information to amounts reported in the financial statements is also to be provided. SFAS No. 131 is effective for the Company in 1998. Based on current internal reporting, the Company does not expect this new accounting pronouncement to have a significant impact on its segment reporting.

Year 2000

The Company recognizes the need to ensure that its operations will not be adversely impacted by Year 2000 software failures. Software failures due to processing errors potentially arising from calculations using the Year 2000 date are a known risk.

In 1997, the Company created a corporate-wide Year 2000 project team representing all business units of the Company. The Company's Year 2000 remediation efforts include the implementation of upgrades to existing system applications as well as the addition and implementation of new system applications.

The Company anticipates the implementation phase of this project to begin no later than the second quarter of 1998 and to be completed by the second quarter of 1999. If the necessary modifications and implementations are not made on a timely basis, the Year 2000 issue could have a material, adverse effect on the business, consolidated financial position, results of operations or cash flows of the Company.

In addition to internal Year 2000 software and equipment implementation activities, the Company is in contact with its suppliers to assess their compliance. There can be no absolute assurance that there will not be a material adverse effect on the Company if third parties do not convert their systems in a timely manner and in a way that is compatible with the Company's systems. The Company believes that its actions with suppliers will minimize these risks.

Through 1997, the Company had expensed incremental costs of approximately $350,000 related to the Year 2000 remediation efforts. The current total estimated cost to complete the Year 2000 remediation efforts is from $10 to $15 million, exclusive of upgrades to existing applications and implementation of new systems. Internal and external costs specifically associated with modifying internal-use software for the Year 2000 will be charged to expense as incurred. All of these costs are being funded through operating cash flows.

The Company's current estimates of the amount of time and costs necessary to implement and test its computer systems are based on the facts and circumstances existing at this time. The estimates were derived utilizing multiple assumptions of future events including the continued

21

availability of certain resources, implementation success and other factors. New developments may occur that could affect the Company's estimates for the Year 2000 compliance. These developments include, but are not limited to: (a) the availability and cost of personnel trained in this area, (b) the ability to locate and correct all relevant computer code and equipment, and (c) the planning and modification success needed to achieve full implementation. In addition, since there is no uniform definition of Year 2000 "compliance" and not all customer situations can be anticipated, the Company may experience an increase in warranty and other claims as a result of the Year 2000 transition.

Factors That May Affect Future Results

Factors that could cause future results to differ from these expectations include the following: growth in the personal computer industry; competitive factors and pricing pressures; component supply shortages; inventory risks due to shifts in market demand; changes in the product, customer or geographic sales mix in any particular period; the outcome of pending and future litigation; access to necessary intellectual property rights; changes in government regulation; foreign currency fluctuations; risks of acquired business; and general domestic and international economic conditions.

In addition to other information contained in this Report, the following factors, among others, sometimes have affected, and in the future could affect, the Company's actual results, and could cause future results to differ materially from those expressed in any forward-looking statement made by, or on behalf of, the Company.

The Company has experienced, and may continue to experience, problems with respect to the size of its work force and production facilities and the adequacy of its management information and other systems, purchasing and inventory controls, and the forecasting of component part needs. These problems can result in high backlog of product orders, delays in customer support response times and increased expense levels.

Short product life cycles characterize the PC industry, resulting from rapid changes in technology and consumer preferences and declining product prices. The Company's in-house engineering personnel work closely with PC component suppliers and other technology developers to evaluate the latest developments in PC-related technology. There can be no assurance that the Company will continue to have access to or the right to use new technology or will be successful in incorporating such new technology in its products or features in a timely manner.

Certain key management employees, particularly Ted Waitt, Chairman and Chief Executive Officer and a founder of the Company, have been instrumental in the success of the Company. The Company has not entered into an employment agreement with Ted Waitt. The loss of Ted Waitt's services could materially and adversely affect the Company.

Over the past several years, state tax authorities have made inquiries as to whether or not the Company's alleged contacts with those states might require the collection of sales and use taxes from customers and/or the payment of income tax in those states. The Company evaluates such inquiries on a case-by-case basis, and will vigorously contest any such claims for payment of taxes which it believes are without merit. The Company has favorably resolved these types of tax issues in the past without any material adverse consequences. However, there can be no assurance that the amount of any sales or use taxes the Company might ultimately be required to pay for prior periods would not materially affect the Company's results of operations or cash flows in any given reporting period.

The Company currently pays state income taxes in the states where it has a physical presence. The Company has not paid income taxes in other states, nor has it established significant reserves for the payment of such taxes. Management believes that the amount of any income tax the Company might ultimately be required to pay for prior periods would not materially and adversely affect the Company's business, consolidated financial position, results of operations or cash flows.

Quantitative and Qualitative Disclosures About Market Risk

The results of the Company's foreign operations are affected by changes in exchange rates between certain foreign currencies and the United States dollar. The functional currency for most of the Company's foreign operations is the U.S. dollar. The functional currency for the remaining operations is the local currency in which the subsidiaries operate. Sales made in foreign currencies translate into higher or lower sales in U.S. dollars as the U.S. dollar strengthens or weakens against other currencies. Therefore, changes in exchange rates may negatively affect the Company's consolidated net sales (as expressed in U.S. dollars) and gross margins from foreign operations. The majority of the Company's component purchases are denominated in U.S. dollars.

The Company uses foreign currency forward contracts to hedge foreign currency transactions and probable anticipated foreign currency transactions. These forward contracts are designated as a hedge of international sales by U.S. dollar functional currency entities and intercompany purchases by certain foreign subsidiaries. The principal currencies hedged are the British Pound, the Japanese Yen, the French Franc and the Deutsche Mark over periods ranging from one to six months. Forward contracts are accounted for on a mark-to-market basis, with realized and unrealized gains or losses recognized currently. Gains or losses arising from forward contracts which are effective as a hedge are included in the basis of the designated transactions. Fluctuations in U.S. dollar currency exchange rates did not have a significant impact on the Company's consolidated financial position, results of operations or cash flows in any given reporting period.

Foreign currency exchange contracts are sensitive to changes in foreign currency exchange rates. At December 31, 1997, a hypothetical 10% adverse change in foreign currency exchange rates underlying the Company's open forward contracts would result in an unrealized loss of approximately $27 million. Unrealized gains/losses in foreign currency exchange contracts represent the difference between the hypothetical rates and the current market exchange rates. Consistent with the nature of an economic hedge, such unrealized gains or losses would be offset by corresponding decreases or increases, respectively, of the underlying transaction being hedged.

Report of Independent Accountants

To the Stockholders and Board of Directors Gateway 2000, Inc.

We have audited the accompanying consolidated balance sheets of Gateway 2000, Inc., as of December 31, 1996 and 1997, and the related consolidated statements of operations, stockholders' equity and cash flows for each of the three years in the period ended December 31, 1997. These financial statements are the responsibility of the Company's management. Our responsibility is to express an opinion on these financial statements based on our audits.

We conducted our audits in accordance with generally accepted auditing standards. Those standards require that we plan and perform the audit to obtain reasonable assurance about whether the financial statements are free of material misstatement. An audit includes examining, on a test basis, evidence supporting the amounts and disclosures in the financial statements. An audit also includes assessing the accounting principles used and significant estimates made by management, as well as evaluating the overall financial statement presentation. We believe that our audits provide a reasonable basis for our opinion.

In our opinion, the consolidated financial statements referred to above present fairly, in all material respects, the consolidated financial position of Gateway 2000, Inc. as of December 31, 1996 and 1997, and the consolidated results of its operations and its cash flows for each of the three years in the period ended December 31, 1997 in conformity with generally accepted accounting principles.

Coopers & Lybrand L.L.P.

COOPERS & LYBRAND L.L.P.
Omaha, Nebraska
January 22, 1998

CONSOLIDATED STATEMENTS OF OPERATIONS

For the years ended December 31, 1995, 1996 and 1997
(in thousands, except per share amounts)

	1995	1996	1997
Net sales	$ 3,676,328	$ 5,035,228	$ 6,293,680
Cost of goods sold	3,070,234	4,099,073	5,217,239
Gross profit	606,094	936,155	1,076,441
Selling, general and administrative expenses	357,086	580,061	786,168
Nonrecurring expenses	-	-	113,842
Operating income	249,008	356,094	176,431
Other income, net	13,085	26,622	27,189
Income before income taxes	262,093	382,716	203,620
Provision for income taxes	89,112	132,037	93,823
Net income	$ 172,981	$ 250,679	$ 109,797
Net income per share:			
Basic	$ 1.19	$ 1.64	$ .71
Diluted	$ 1.09	$ 1.60	$ .70
Weighted average shares outstanding:			
Basic	145,256	152,745	153,840
Diluted	157,988	156,237	156,201

The accompanying notes are an integral part of the consolidated financial statements.

23

CONSOLIDATED BALANCE SHEETS

December 31, 1996 and 1997
(in thousands, except per share amounts)

	1996	1997
ASSETS		
Current assets:		
Cash and cash equivalents	$ 516,360	$ 593,601
Marketable securities	–	38,648
Accounts receivable, net	449,723	510,679
Inventory	278,043	249,224
Other	74,216	152,531
Total current assets	1,318,342	1,544,683
Property, plant and equipment, net	242,365	336,469
Internal use software costs, net	77,073	39,998
Intangibles, net	9,869	82,590
Other assets	25,762	35,531
	$ 1,673,411	$ 2,039,271
LIABILITIES AND STOCKHOLDERS' EQUITY		
Current liabilities:		
Notes payable and current maturities of long-term obligations	$ 15,041	$ 13,969
Accounts payable	411,788	488,717
Accrued liabilities	190,762	271,250
Accrued royalties	125,270	159,418
Income taxes payable	40,334	26,510
Other current liabilities	16,574	44,042
Total current liabilities	799,769	1,003,906
Long-term obligations, net of current maturities	7,244	7,240
Warranty and other liabilities	50,857	98,081
Total liabilities	857,870	1,109,227
Commitments and Contingencies (Notes 3 and 4)		
Stockholders' equity:		
Preferred stock, $.01 par value, 10,000 shares authorized; none issued and outstanding	–	–
Class A common stock, nonvoting, $.01 par value, 2,000 shares authorized; none issued and outstanding	–	–
Common stock, $.01 par value, 440,000 shares authorized; 153,512 shares and 154,128 shares issued and outstanding, respectively	1,536	1,541
Additional paid-in capital	288,744	299,483
Retained earnings	524,712	634,509
Other	549	(5,489)
Total stockholders' equity	815,541	930,044
	$ 1,673,411	$ 2,039,271

24 *The accompanying notes are an integral part of the consolidated financial statements.*

CONSOLIDATED STATEMENTS OF CASH FLOWS

For the years ended December 31, 1995, 1996 and 1997
(in thousands)

	1995	1996	1997
Cash flows from operating activities:			
Net income	$ 172,981	$ 250,679	$ 109,797
Adjustments to reconcile net income to net cash provided by operating activities:			
Depreciation and amortization	38,086	61,763	86,774
Provision for uncollectible accounts receivable	7,779	20,832	5,688
Deferred income taxes	(23,778)	(13,395)	(63,247)
Other, net	520	1,986	42
Nonrecurring expenses	–	–	113,842
Changes in operating assets and liabilities:			
Accounts receivable	(157,958)	(66,052)	(41,950)
Inventory	(103,202)	(54,261)	59,486
Other current assets	(10,847)	(13,311)	(54,513)
Accounts payable	51,765	176,724	66,253
Accrued liabilities	20,690	51,390	48,405
Accrued royalties	37,567	1,885	34,148
Income taxes payable	50,516	42,880	8,347
Other current liabilities	(7,252)	177	27,469
Other liabilities	12,890	22,699	42,256
Net cash provided by operating activities	89,757	483,996	442,797
Cash flows from investing activities:			
Capital expenditures	(95,817)	(112,187)	(162,010)
Internal use software costs	(39,040)	(31,559)	(13,646)
Purchases of available-for-sale securities	(10,679)	–	(49,619)
Purchases of held-to-maturity securities	(1,685)	–	–
Proceeds from maturities of held-to-maturity securities	5,000	–	–
Proceeds from maturities or sales of available-for-sale securities	33,023	3,030	10,985
Acquisitions, net of cash acquired	(3,620)	–	(142,320)
Other, net	(13,152)	2,667	(4,055)
Net cash used in investing activities	(125,970)	(138,049)	(360,665)
Cash flows from financing activities:			
Proceeds from issuance of notes payable	5,000	10,000	10,000
Principal payments on long-term obligations and notes payable	(24,600)	(14,047)	(15,588)
Stock options exercised	8,107	9,520	5,741
Net cash provided by (used in) financing activities	(11,493)	5,473	153
Foreign exchange effect on cash and cash equivalents	82	(1,457)	(5,044)
Net increase (decrease) in cash and cash equivalents	(47,624)	349,963	77,241
Cash and cash equivalents, beginning of year	214,021	166,397	516,360
Cash and cash equivalents, end of year	$ 166,397	$ 516,360	$ 593,601

The accompanying notes are an integral part of the consolidated financial statements.

25

CONSOLIDATED STATEMENTS OF STOCKHOLDERS' EQUITY

For the years ended December 31, 1995, 1996 and 1997
(in thousands)

| | Common Stock | | Additional Paid-in | Retained | | |
	Shares	Amount	Capital	Earnings	Other	Total
Balances at December 31, 1994	144,792	$ 1,448	$ 273,676	$ 101,052	$ (141)	$ 376,035
Net income	–	–	–	172,981	–	172,981
Stock issuances under employee plans, including tax benefit of $23,030	6,541	66	31,071	–	–	31,137
Stock retirement	(2,227)	(22)	(25,046)	–	–	(25,068)
Foreign currency translation	–	–	–	–	324	324
Other	–	–	–	–	110	110
Balances at December 31, 1995	149,106	1,492	279,701	274,033	293	555,519
Net income	–	–	–	250,679	–	250,679
Stock issuances under employee plans, including tax benefit of $ 30,451	6,545	66	39,905	–	–	39,971
Stock retirement	(2,139)	(22)	(30,862)	–	–	(30,884)
Foreign currency translation	–	–	–	–	225	225
Other	–	–	–	–	31	31
Balances at December 31, 1996	153,512	1,536	288,744	524,712	549	815,541
Net income	–	–	–	109,797	–	109,797
Stock issuances under employee plans, including tax benefit of $ 5,003	616	5	10,739	–	–	10,744
Foreign currency translation	–	–	–	–	(6,053)	(6,053)
Other	–	–	–	–	15	15
Balances at December 31, 1997	154,128	$ 1,541	$ 299,483	$ 634,509	$ (5,489)	$ 930,044

The accompanying notes are an integral part of the consolidated financial statements.

1. Summary of Significant Accounting Policies:

Gateway 2000, Inc. (the "Company") is a direct marketer of personal computers ("PCs") and PC-related products. The Company develops, manufactures, markets and supports a broad line of desktop and portable PCs, digital media (convergence) PCs, servers, workstations and PC-related products used by individuals, families, businesses, government agencies and educational institutions.

The significant accounting policies used in the preparation of the consolidated financial statements of Gateway 2000, Inc. are as follows:

(a) Principles of Consolidation:

The consolidated financial statements include the accounts of the Company and its wholly owned subsidiaries. All significant intercompany accounts and transactions have been eliminated.

(b) Cash and Cash Equivalents:

The Company considers all highly liquid debt instruments and money market funds with an original maturity of three months or less to be cash equivalents. The carrying amount approximates fair value because of the short maturities of these instruments.

(c) Marketable Securities:

The carrying amounts of the marketable securities used in computing unrealized and realized gains and losses are determined by specific identification. Fair values are determined using quoted market prices. For available-for-sale securities, net unrealized holding gains and losses are reported as a separate component of stockholders' equity, net of tax. Held-to-maturity securities are recorded at amortized cost. Amortization of related discounts or premiums is included in the determination of net income.

Marketable securities at December 31, 1997, consisted of available-for-sale mutual funds, commercial paper and debt securities, with a market value of $38,648,000 and an amortized cost of $38,636,000, with variable maturities through 1999. Realized and unrealized gains and losses are not material for any of the periods presented.

(d) Inventory:

Inventory, which is comprised of component parts, subassemblies and finished goods, is valued at the lower of first-in, first-out (FIFO) cost or market. On a quarterly basis, the Company compares on a part by part basis, the amount of the inventory on hand and under commitment with its latest forecasted requirements to determine whether write-downs for excess or obsolete inventory are required.

(e) Property, Plant and Equipment:

Property, plant and equipment are stated at cost. Depreciation is provided using straight-line and accelerated methods over the assets' estimated useful lives. Amortization of leasehold improvements is computed using the shorter of the lease term or the estimated useful life of the underlying asset. Upon sale or retirement of property, plant and equipment, the related costs and accumulated depreciation or amortization are removed from the accounts and any gain or loss is included in the determination of net income.

(f) Internal Use Software Costs:

The Company capitalizes costs of purchased software and, once technological feasibility has been established, costs incurred in developing software for internal use. Amortization of software costs begins when the software is placed in service and is computed on a straight-line basis over the estimated useful life of the software, generally from three to five years.

(g) Intangible Assets:

Intangible assets principally consist of technology, a customer base and distribution network, an assembled work force and trade name obtained through acquisition. The cost of intangible assets is amortized on a straight-line basis over the estimated periods benefited ranging from three to ten years. The realizability of intangibles is evaluated periodically as events or circumstances indicate a possible inability to recover their carrying amount.

(h) Royalties:

The Company has royalty-bearing license agreements that allow the Company to sell certain hardware and software which is protected by patent, copyright or license. Royalty costs are accrued and included in cost of goods sold when products are shipped or amortized over the period of benefit when the license terms are not specifically related to the units shipped.

(i) Warranty and Other Post-Sales Support Programs:

The Company provides currently for the estimated costs that may be incurred under its warranty and other post-sales support programs.

(j) Stock Split:

On May 15, 1997, the Board of Directors authorized a two-for-one stock split which was distributed on or about June 16, 1997, to shareholders of record on June 2, 1997. All references in the financial statements to number of shares and per share amounts of the Company's stock have been retroactively restated to reflect the increased number of common shares outstanding.

(k) Revenue Recognition:

Sales are recorded when products are shipped. A provision for estimated sales returns is recorded in the period in which related sales are recognized. Revenue from separately priced extended warranty programs is deferred and recognized over the extended warranty period on a straight-line basis.

(l) Net Income Per Share:

In 1997, the Financial Accounting Standards Board (FASB) issued Statement of Financial Accounting Standard No. 128 , "Earnings per Share" which replaced the calculation of primary and fully diluted earnings per share with basic and diluted earnings per share. Unlike primary earnings per share, basic earnings per share excludes any dilutive effect of options, warrants and convertible securities. Earnings per share amounts for all periods presented have been restated to SFAS 128 requirements.

The following table sets forth a reconciliation of shares used in the computation of basic and diluted earnings per share.

	1995	1996	1997
		(in thousands)	
Net income for basic and diluted earnings per share	$ 172,981	$ 250,679	$ 109,797
Weighted average shares for basic earnings per share	145,256	152,745	153,840
Dilutive effect of stock options	12,732	3,492	2,361
Weighted average shares for diluted earnings per share	157,988	156,237	156,201

(m) Foreign Currency:

The Company uses the U.S. dollar as its functional currency for the majority of its international operations. For subsidiaries where the local currency is the functional currency, the assets and liabilities are translated into U.S. dollars at exchange rates in effect at the balance sheet date. Income and expense items are translated at the average exchange rates prevailing during the period. Gains and losses from translation are included as a component of stockholders' equity. Gains and losses resulting from remeasuring monetary asset and liability accounts that are denominated in currencies other than a subsidiary's functional currency are included in "Other income, net".

The Company uses foreign currency forward contracts to hedge foreign currency transactions and probable anticipated foreign currency transactions. These forward contracts are designated as a hedge of international sales by U.S. dollar functional currency entities and intercompany purchases by certain foreign subsidiaries. The principal currencies hedged are the British Pound, the Japanese Yen, the French Franc, and the Deutsche Mark over periods ranging from one to six months. Forward contracts are accounted for on a mark-to-market basis, with realized and unrealized gains or losses recognized currently. Gains or losses arising from forward contracts which are effective as a hedge are included in the basis of the designated transactions. The related receivable or liability with counterparties to the forward contracts is recorded in the consolidated balance sheet. Cash flows from settlements of forward contracts are included in operating activities in the consolidated statements of cash flows. Aggregate transaction gains and losses included in the determination of net income are not material for any period presented. Forward contracts designated to hedge foreign currency transaction exposure of $132,930,000 and $257,051,000 were outstanding at December 31, 1996 and 1997, respectively. The estimated fair value of these forward contracts at December 31, 1996 and 1997, was $137,726,000 and $253,519,000, respectively based on quoted market prices.

The Company continually monitors its positions with, and the credit quality of, the major international financial institutions which are counterparties to its foreign currency forward contracts, and does not anticipate nonperformance by any of these counterparties.

(n) Use of Estimates and Certain Concentrations:

The preparation of financial statements in conformity with generally accepted accounting principles requires management to make estimates and assumptions that affect the reported amounts of assets and liabilities and disclosure of contingent assets and liabilities at the date of the financial statements and the reported amounts of revenues and expenses during the reporting period. Actual results could differ from those estimates.

Certain components used by the Company in manufacturing of PC systems are purchased from a limited number of suppliers. An industry shortage or other constraints of any key component could result in delayed shipments and a possible loss of sales, which could affect operating results adversely.

o) Reclassifications:

Certain reclassifications have been made to prior years' financial statements to conform to current year presentation. These reclassifications had no impact on previously reported net income or stockholders' equity.

2. Financing Arrangements:

(a) Credit Agreement:

The Company is party to an unsecured bank credit agreement (the "Agreement"), totaling $225 million. The Agreement consists of (1) a revolving line of credit facility for committed loans and bid loans; and (2) a sub-facility for letters of credit. Borrowings under the agreement bear interest at the banks' base rate or, at the Company's option, borrowing rates based on a fixed spread over the London Interbank Offered Rate (LIBOR). The Agreement requires the Company to maintain a minimum tangible net worth and maximum debt leverage ratio, as well as minimum fixed charge coverage. There were no borrowings outstanding at the end of 1996 and 1997.

At December 31, 1996 and 1997, approximately $4,360,000 and $3,515,000, respectively, was committed to support outstanding standby letters of credit.

(b) Long-term Obligations:

The carrying amount of the Company's long-term obligations approximates the fair value, which is estimated based on current rates offered to the Company for obligations of the same remaining maturities. Long-term obligations include notes and obligations under capital leases and consist of the following:

	December 31,	
	1996	**1997**
	(in thousands)	
Notes payable through 2001 with interest rates ranging from zero to 8.87%	$ 19,312	$ 20,568
Obligations under capital leases, payable in monthly installments at fixed rates ranging from 3.28% to 5.90% through 1999 (Note 3)	2,973	641
	22,285	21,209
Less current maturities	15,041	13,969
	$ 7,244	$ 7,240

The long-term obligations, excluding obligations under capital leases, have the following maturities as of December 31, 1997:

	(in thousands)
1998	$ 13,571
1999	4,928
2000	69
2001	2,000
2002	–
	$ 20,568

3. Commitments:

The Company leases certain operating facilities and equipment under noncancelable operating leases expiring at various dates through 2010. Rent expense was approximately $6,214,000, $11,873,000, and $16,105,000 for 1995, 1996 and 1997, respectively.

Future minimum lease payments under terms of these leases as of December 31, 1997 are as follows:

	Capital Leases	**Operating Leases**
	(in thousands)	
1998	$ 398	$ 15,336
1999	254	12,695
2000	3	9,250
2001	–	8,259
2002	–	6,360
Thereafter	–	3,625
Total minimum lease payments	$ 655	$ 55,525
Less amount representing interest	14	
Present value of net minimum lease payments	$ 641	

Appendix

645

The Company has entered into licensing and royalty agreements which allow it to use certain hardware and software intellectual properties in its products. Minimum royalty payments due under these agreements for the period 1998 through 2002 total approximately $346,600,000. Total royalty expense is expected to be greater than this minimum amount for these periods.

4. Contingencies:

The Company is a party to various lawsuits and administrative proceedings arising in the ordinary course of its business. The Company evaluates such lawsuits and proceedings on a case-by-case basis, and its policy is to vigorously contest any such claims which it believes are without merit. The Company's management believes that the ultimate resolution of such pending matters will not materially adversely affect the Company's business, financial position, results of operations or cash flows.

Over the past several years, state tax authorities have made inquiries as to whether or not the Company's alleged contacts with those states might require the collection of sales and use taxes from customers and/or the payment of income tax in those states. The Company evaluates such inquiries on a case-by-case basis, and will vigorously contest any such claims for payment of taxes which it believes are without merit. The Company has favorably resolved these types of tax issues in the past without any material adverse consequences. However, there can be no assurance that the amount of any sales or use taxes the Company might ultimately be required to pay for prior periods would not materially affect the Company's results of operations or cash flows in any given reporting period.

The Company currently pays state income taxes in the states where it has a physical presence. The Company has not paid income taxes in any other state, nor has it established significant reserves for the payment of such taxes. Management believes that the amount of any income tax the Company might ultimately be required to pay for prior periods would not materially and adversely affect the Company's business, consolidated financial position, results of operations or cash flows.

5. Income Taxes:

The components of the provisions for income taxes are as follows:

	For the year ended December 31,		
	1995	**1996**	**1997**
	(in thousands)		
Current:			
United States	$ 109,296	$ 140,451	$ 154,049
Foreign	3,594	4,981	3,021
Deferred:			
United States	(19,823)	(1,727)	(49,564)
Foreign	(3,955)	(11,668)	(13,683)
	$ 89,112	$ 132,037	$ 93,823

Income (loss) before income taxes included approximately $9,300,000, $2,400,000 and ($24,000,000) related to foreign operations for the years ended December 31, 1995, 1996 and 1997, respectively.

A reconciliation of the provision for income taxes and the amount computed by applying the federal statutory income tax rate to income before taxes is as follows:

	1995	**1996**	**1997**
		(in thousands)	
Federal income tax at statutory rate	$ 91,732	$ 133,951	$ 71,267
Nondeductible purchased research and development costs	–	–	20,704
Other, net	(2,620)	(1,914)	1,852
Provision for income taxes	$ 89,112	$ 132,037	$ 93,823

Deferred tax assets and deferred tax liabilities result from temporary differences in the following accounts:

	December 31,	
	1996	**1997**
	(in thousands)	
U.S. deferred tax assets:		
Inventory	$ 8,768	$ 20,572
Accounts receivable	4,955	6,775
Accrued liabilities	21,035	35,793
Other liabilities	16,101	36,912
Property, plant & equipment	539	–
Other	1,125	3,612
Total U.S.	52,523	103,664
Foreign deferred tax assets:		
Operating loss carryforward	12,619	17,832
Other	3,004	2,459
Total foreign	15,623	20,291
Total deferred tax assets	68,146	123,955
U.S. deferred tax liabilities:		
Intangible assets	20,126	34,006
Property, plant & equipment	–	2,668
Other	268	3,439
Total deferred tax liabilities	20,394	40,113
Net deferred tax assets	$ 47,752	$ 83,842

The Company has foreign net operating loss carryforwards of $49,000,000. Of this amount, $8,300,000 expires in the year 2000, $27,300,000 in the year 2002 and $13,400,000 in the year 2006. The Company has assessed its sales forecast and the expiration of carryforwards and has determined that it is more likely than not that the deferred tax asset relating to foreign net operating loss carryforwards will be realized.

29

6. Stock Option Plans:

In 1991, the Company entered into stock option agreements with certain officers providing for the purchase of 13,224,120 shares of the Company's Common Stock.

In December 1991, the Company and its stockholders adopted the Gateway 2000, Inc. 1992 Stock Option Plan ("the 1992 Option Plan") for the benefit of its officers and other managers. Under the 1992 Option Plan, options to purchase 1,105,104 shares of the Company's Class A Common Stock were granted. Shares of Class A Common Stock may be converted into an equal number of shares of Common Stock at any time after December 18, 1994. Options were first granted under the Plan in 1992 and generally vest over a four-year period, retroactive to an option holder's initial date of employment. These options expire, if not exercised, ten years from the date of grant.

In 1993, the Company and its stockholders adopted the Gateway 2000, Inc. 1993 Stock Option Plan (the "1993 Option Plan") which replaced the 1992 Option Plan. Under the 1993 Option Plan, options to purchase up to 3,874,416 shares of the Company's Common Stock or Class A Common Stock may be granted. Under the 1993 Option Plan, after December 14, 1993, only options for the purchase of Common Stock may be granted. These options generally vest over a four-year period beginning on either the grant date or the option holder's initial date of employment. These options expire, if not exercised, ten years from the date of grant.

In 1993, the Company and its stockholders also adopted the Gateway 2000, Inc. 1993 Non-Employee Directors Stock Option Plan (the "Director Option Plan"). The Director Option Plan authorized the issuance of up to 40,000 shares of Common Stock to non-employee directors. Options granted under this plan vest one year from the grant date and expire, if not exercised, ten years from the date of grant.

In 1996, the Company and its stockholders adopted the Gateway 2000, Inc. 1996 Long-Term Incentive Equity Plan (the "1996 Employee Plan"). Under the 1996 Employee Plan, participants may receive stock options, stock appreciation rights or stock awards as determined by the Compensation Committee of the Board of Directors. The aggregate number of shares of Common Stock which may be issued or transferred to participants under the 1996 Employee Plan is 12,800,000. Stock options granted under this plan vest over a four-year period beginning on the grant date and expire, if not exercised, ten years from the date of grant.

In addition, in 1996, the Company and its stockholders adopted the Gateway 2000, Inc. 1996 Non-Employee Directors Stock Option Plan (the "1996 Director Plan") which replaced the Director Option Plan. The 1996 Director Plan authorizes the issuance of up to 600,000 shares of Common Stock to non-employee directors. Options granted generally vest over a three-year time period beginning on the grant date and expire, if not exercised, ten years from the date of grant.

In 1997, the Company introduced the Gateway GoldShares stock option program and awarded stock options pursuant to the Company's 1996 Long-Term Incentive Equity Plan to eligible employees based on length of service and pay level. Under the GoldShares program, eligible employees were granted options to purchase approximately 1,300,000 shares of Common Stock at $32.63 per share in September 1997. Options granted under the plan vest at the rate of 25% per year from the grant date and expire, if not exercised, ten years from the date of grant.

The Company has adopted the disclosure-only provisions of Statement of Financial Accounting Standard No. 123 (SFAS No. 123), "Accounting for Stock-Based Compensation." Accordingly, no compensation cost has been recognized for the stock option plans. Had compensation cost for the Company's stock option plans been determined based on the estimated fair value at the grant date for awards in 1995, 1996 and 1997 consistent with the provisions of SFAS No. 123, net income and net income per share would have been reduced to the pro forma amounts indicated below:

	1995	1996	1997
	(in thousands, except per share amounts)		
Net income - as reported	$ 172,981	$ 250,679	$ 109,797
Net income - pro forma	$ 171,149	$ 241,729	$ 85,804
Net income per share - as reported			
Basic	$ 1.19	$ 1.64	$ .71
Diluted	$ 1.09	$ 1.60	$ .70
Net income per share - pro forma			
Basic	$ 1.18	$ 1.58	$ .56
Diluted	$ 1.08	$ 1.55	$ .55

The pro forma effect on net income for 1995, 1996 and 1997 is not fully representative of the pro forma effect on net income in future years because it does not take into consideration pro forma compensation expense related to the vesting of grants made prior to 1995.

The fair value of each option grant is estimated on the date of grant using the Black-Scholes option pricing model with the following weighted-average assumptions used for all grants in 1995, 1996 and 1997: dividend yield of zero percent; expected volatility of 60 percent; risk-free interest rates ranging from 5.2 to 7.2 percent; and expected lives of the options of three and one-half years from the date of vesting.

All options have exercise prices equal to the fair market value of the related stock on the date of grant. A summary of the status of the Company's stock option plans is presented below:

	Year Ended December 31, 1995			
	(in thousands, except per share amounts)			
	Common Stock	Weighted-Average Price	Class A Common Stock	Weighted-Average Price
Outstanding, beginning of period	13,650	$ 1.37	1,248	$ 2.10
Granted	1,384	12.14	–	–
Exercised and converted	(6,253)	1.21	(287)	1.97
Forfeited	(42)	6.82	–	–
Outstanding, end of period	8,739	$ 3.16	961	$ 2.14
Options available for grant, end of period	1,937		–	
Options exercisable, end of period	7,119	$ 1.30	810	$ 2.01
Weighted-average fair value of options granted during the year	$ 7.45		$ –	

| | Year Ended December 31, 1996 | | | |
| | (in thousands, except per share amounts) | | | |
	Common Stock	Weighted-Average Price	Class A Common Stock	Weighted-Average Price
Outstanding, beginning of period	8,739	$ 3.16	962	$ 2.14
Granted	3,260	15.75	–	–
Exercised and converted	(6,305)	1.43	(241)	2.13
Forfeited	(254)	14.15	(8)	3.25
Outstanding, end of period	5,440	$ 12.20	713	$ 2.12
Options available for grant, end of period	12,309		–	
Options exercisable, end of period	1,283	$ 4.28	672	$ 2.06
Weighted-average fair value of options granted during the year	$ 9.65		$ –	

| | Year Ended December 31, 1997 | | | |
| | (in thousands, except per share amounts) | | | |
	Common Stock	Weighted-Average Price	Class A Common Stock	Weighted-Average Price
Outstanding, beginning of period	5,440	$ 12.20	713	$ 2.12
Granted	5,253	36.08	–	–
Exercised and converted	(463)	11.56	(153)	2.50
Forfeited	(775)	23.69	–	–
Outstanding, end of period	9,455	$ 22.98	560	$ 2.02
Options available for grant, end of period	8,328		–	
Options exercisable, end of period	2,582	$ 9.86	556	$ 2.01
Weighted-average fair value of options granted during the year	$ 21.61		$ –	

The following table summarizes information about the Company's Common Stock options outstanding at December 31, 1997:

	Options Outstanding			Options Exercisable	
Range of Exercise Prices	Number Outstanding at 12/31/97	Weighted-Average Remaining Contractual Life	Weighted-Average Price	Number Exercisable at 12/31/97	Weighted-Average Price
$ 1.19 – 1.19	760	3.41 years	$ 1.19	760	$ 1.19
6.82 – 13.38	2,526	7.72 years	11.73	1,077	10.73
13.44 – 19.69	1,739	8.19 years	17.62	717	17.15
20.89 – 29.44	1,559	9.06 years	28.82	28	25.74
29.53 – 34.44	1,428	9.67 years	32.72	–	–
35.00 – 44.75	1,443	9.56 years	44.66	–	–

The following table summarizes information about the Company's Class A Common Stock options outstanding at December 31, 1997:

	Options Outstanding			Options Exercisable	
Range of Exercise Prices	Number Outstanding at 12/31/97	Weighted-Average Remaining Contractual Life	Weighted-Average Price	Number Exercisable at 12/31/97	Weighted-Average Price
$ 1.86 – 3.24	560	5.07 years	$ 2.02	556	$ 2.01

7. Retirement Savings Plan:

The Company has a 401(k) defined contribution plan which covers employees who have attained 18 years of age and have been employed by the Company for at least six months. Participants may contribute up to 20% of their compensation in any plan year and receive a 25% matching employer contribution of up to 1% of their annual eligible compensation for the first 12 months of participation, and a 50% matching employer contribution up to 2% of their annual eligible compensation for all subsequent months of participation. The Company contributed $640,000, $871,000, and $2,068,000 to the Plan during 1995, 1996 and 1997, respectively.

8. Acquisition:

During the third quarter of 1997, the Company acquired substantially all of the outstanding shares of common stock of Advanced Logic Research, Inc. (ALR), a manufacturer of network servers and personal computers, for a cash purchase price of approximately $196,400,000. Of the purchase price, approximately $58,600,000 was allocated to in-process research and development costs and expensed during the third quarter. These costs were expensed as the technological feasibility of the in-process research and development had not yet been established and the technology had no alternative use. In addition, $83,300,000 of the purchase price was allocated to certain identifiable intangibles (including intellectual property, work force and customer base) and the remaining to ALR's net tangible assets which included approximately $58,100,000 in cash. The acquisition was accounted for as a purchase business combination. Beginning July 23, 1997, the results of ALR have been included in the Company's consolidated financial statements. ALR's operating results for periods prior to the acquisition date were not material to the Company's consolidated results of operations.

9. Nonrecurring Expenses:

The Company recorded several nonrecurring pretax charges during the third quarter of 1997 totaling approximately $113,800,000. Of the nonrecurring charges, approximately $59,700,000 was for the write-off of in-process research and development acquired in the purchase of ALR and certain assets of Amiga Technologies. Also included in the nonrecurring charges was a non-cash write-off of approximately $45,200,000 resulting from the abandonment of a capitalized internal use software project and certain computer equipment. In addition, approximately $8,600,000 was recorded for severance of employees and the closing of a foreign office.

10. Selected Balance Sheet Information:

	December 31,	
	1996	1997
	(in thousands)	
Accounts receivable, net:		
Accounts receivable	$ 468,691	$ 530,743
Allowance for uncollectible accounts	(18,968)	(20,064)
	$ 449,723	$ 510,679
Inventory:		
Components and subassemblies	$ 269,959	$ 215,318
Finished goods	8,084	33,906
	$ 278,043	$ 249,224
Property, plant and equipment, net:		
Land	$ 14,888	$ 21,431
Leasehold improvements	5,096	21,666
Buildings, including construction in progress	131,180	177,766
Office and production equipment	144,477	186,281
Furniture and fixtures	25,084	42,055
Vehicles	3,754	4,105
	324,479	453,304
Accumulated depreciation and amortization	(82,114)	(116,835)
	$ 242,365	$ 336,469
Internal use software costs, net:		
Purchased software	$ 33,102	$ 42,926
Internally developed software	71,475	38,486
	104,577	81,412
Accumulated amortization	(27,504)	(41,414)
	$ 77,073	$ 39,998

Amortization expense of $7,674,000, $13,591,000, and $20,691,000 relating to software costs was included in the results of operations for the years ended December 31, 1995, 1996 and 1997, respectively.

11. Supplemental Statements of Cash Flows Information:

	Year ended December 31,		
	1995	1996	1997
		(in thousands)	
Supplemental disclosure of cash flow information:			
Cash paid during the year for interest	$ 2,119	$ 665	$ 716
Cash paid during the year for income taxes	$ 61,322	$ 101,774	$ 163,710
Supplemental schedule of noncash investing and financing activities:			
Capital lease obligation/long-term obligations incurred for the purchase of new equipment	$ 11,071	$ 3,126	$ 4,593
Acquisitions			
Fair value of assets acquired	$ 12,620		$ 271,189
Less: Liabilities assumed	9,000		70,773
Cash acquired	-		58,096
Acquisitions, net of cash acquired	$ 3,620		$ 142,320

12. Geographic Data:

The Company operates in one principal business segment across geographically diverse markets.

Transfers between geographic areas are recorded using internal transfer prices set by the Company. The Americas operating income is net of corporate expenses. 1995 geographic data have been restated to separately reflect the Europe geographic area.

Export sales from the Americas to unaffiliated customers are not material for any period presented.

The following table sets forth information about the Company's operations by geographic area.

	Americas	Europe	Asia Pacific	Eliminations	Consolidated
			(in thousands)		
1997:					
Net sales to					
unaffiliated customers	$ 5,303,828	$634,616	$ 355,236	$ –	$ 6,293,680
Transfers between					
geographic areas	56,922	16,163	21,071	(94,156)	–
Operating profit (loss)	198,638	(11,566)	(9,733)	(908)	176,431
Identifiable assets	1,701,654	187,215	150,402	–	2,039,271
1996:					
Net sales to					
unaffiliated customers	$ 4,246,047	$552,671	$ 236,510	$ –	$ 5,035,228
Transfers between					
geographic areas	30,208	23,538	4,087	(57,833)	–
Operating profit (loss)	347,348	19,930	(9,946)	(1,238)	356,094
Identifiable assets	1,349,781	178,988	144,642	–	1,673,411
1995:					
Net sales to					
unaffiliated customers	$ 3,210,658	$428,107	$ 37,563	$ –	$ 3,676,328
Transfers between					
geographic areas	250	40,062	–	(40,312)	–
Operating profit (loss)	235,259	27,195	(13,019)	(427)	249,008
Identifiable assets	967,682	124,796	31,533	–	1,124,011

13. Selected Quarterly Financial Data (Unaudited):

The following tables contain selected unaudited consolidated quarterly financial data for the Company:

	1st Quarter	2nd Quarter	3rd Quarter	4th Quarter
	(in thousands, except per share amounts)			
1997:				
Net sales	$ 1,419,336	$ 1,392,658	$ 1,504,851	$ 1,976,835
Gross profit	265,793	260,358	195,250	355,040
Operating income (loss)	94,878	79,851	(137,350)	139,551
Net income (loss)	67,516	56,483	(107,113)	92,910
Net income (loss) per share:				
Basic	$ .44	$ .37	$ (.70)	$ .60
Diluted	$ .43	$ .36	$ (.68)	$ .59
Weighted average shares outstanding:				
Basic	153,557	153,740	153,980	153,840
Diluted	157,291	156,231	156,875	156,526
Stock sales price per share:				
High	$ 32.63	$ 37.38	$ 44.75	$ 36.13
Low	$ 23.81	$ 26.19	$ 31.50	$ 25.13
1996:				
Net sales	$ 1,142,202	$ 1,137,262	$ 1,202,933	$ 1,552,831
Gross profit	212,331	206,171	223,378	294,276
Operating income	70,502	70,801	87,757	127,034
Net income	50,487	51,352	60,696	88,144
Net income per share:				
Basic	$ .33	$ .34	$ .40	$ .57
Diluted	$ .32	$ .33	$ .39	$ .56
Weighted average shares outstanding:				
Basic	151,192	153,126	153,257	153,394
Diluted	155,732	155,922	156,276	157,120
Stock sales price per share:				
High	$ 16.13	$ 20.75	$ 25.07	$ 33.13
Low	$ 9.00	$ 13.63	$ 13.88	$ 22.32

32

Corporate Headquarters

Gateway 2000, Inc.
610 Gateway Drive
North Sioux City
South Dakota 57049-2000
Telephone: 605-232-2000
Fax: 605-232-2023

European Headquarters

Gateway 2000 Ireland Limited
Clonshaugh Industrial Estate
Dublin 17, Ireland
Telephone: 353-1-797-2000
Fax: 353-1-797-2022

Asia Pacific Headquarters

Gateway 2000 (M) SDN BND
Letter Box No. 96, 14th Floor
UBN Tower - 10 Jalan P. Ramlee
50250 Kuala Lumpur, Malaysia
Telephone: 011-603-468-2000
Fax: 011-603-469-2040

Company Information

Copies of the Gateway 2000 Annual Report and Form 10-K for the fiscal year 1997 are available to shareholders without charge. If you wish to receive these reports or other company information, please contact:

Investor Relations
Gateway 2000, Inc.
610 Gateway Drive
North Sioux City
South Dakota 57049-2000
Telephone: 800-846-4508
Fax: 605-232-2465

Common Stock

The Company's Common Stock is traded on the New York Stock Exchange under the symbol GTW. For information on market prices of Gateway's Common Stock, please refer to page 32, note 13. There were 4,543 stockholders of record as of March 13, 1998.

Annual Meeting

The Annual Meeting of Stockholders of Gateway 2000, Inc. will be held at 9 a.m. on Thursday, May 21, 1998, at the Sioux City Convention Center, 801 Fourth Street, Sioux City, Iowa 51101.

Transfer Agent

If you have questions about stock certificates, change of address, consolidation of accounts, transfer of ownership or other stock matters, please contact Gateway's transfer agent:
UMB Bank, n.a.
Securities Transfer Division
P.O. Box 410064
Kansas City, MO 64141-0064
Telephone: 800-884-4225
Fax: 816-860-7761
E-mail: sec_xfer@umb.com

Independent Accountants

Coopers & Lybrand L.L.P.
Omaha, Nebraska

Gateway Board of Directors

Theodore W. Waitt
Chairman of the Board and
Chief Executive Officer
Gateway 2000, Inc.

Jeffrey Weitzen
President and
Chief Operating Officer
Gateway 2000, Inc.

Chase Carey
Chairman of the Board and
Chief Executive Officer
Fox Television Division
Fox Inc.
Los Angeles, California

James Cravens
Chairman of the Board
Sanborn Savings Bank,
Dickinson County Savings Bank,
Ocheyedan Savings Bank and
Dickinson County Memorial Hospital
Okoboji, Iowa

George H. Krauss
Partner
Kutak Rock Law Firm
Omaha, Nebraska

Douglas L. Lacey
Partner
Nichols, Rise & Company,
Certified Public Accountants
Sioux City, Iowa

James F. McCann
President and Chief Executive Officer
1-800-FLOWERS
Westbury, New York

Richard D. Snyder
President
Avalon Investments, Inc.
Ann Arbor, Michigan

Gateway Executive Officers

Theodore W. Waitt
Chairman of the Board and
Chief Executive Officer

Jeffrey Weitzen
President and Chief Operating Officer

David J. Robino
Executive Vice President, Chief Administrative Officer

Joseph J. Burke
Senior Vice President, Global Business Development

Robert J. Cheng
Senior Vice President, Gateway Direct

James P. Collas
Senior Vice President, Global Products

William M. Elliott
Senior Vice President, General Counsel and Corporate Secretary

Michael D. Hammond
Senior Vice President, Global Manufacturing

David J. McKittrick
Senior Vice President, Chief Financial Officer, Treasurer and Chief Information Officer

Robert M. Spears
Senior Vice President, Gateway Major Accounts

James A. Taylor
Senior Vice President, Global Marketing

"You've got a friend in the business."